THE LAW OF CRIMINAL AND CIVIL EVIDENCE

Principles and Practice

THE LAW OF CRIMINAL AND CIVIL EVIDENCE

PRINCIPLES AND PRACTICE

Martin Hannibal and Lisa Mountford

Senior Lecturers in Law,
University of Staffordshire

Longman

An imprint of Pearson Education

Harlow, England • London • New York • Reading, Massachusetts • San Francisco
Toronto • Don Mills, Ontario • Sydney • Tokyo • Singapore • Hong Kong • Seoul
Taipei • Cape Town • Madrid • Mexico City • Amsterdam • Munich • Paris • Milan

Pearson Education Limited
Edinburgh Gate
Harlow
Essex CM20 2JE
England

and Associated Companies around the world.

Visit us on the World Wide Web at:
www.pearsoneduc.com

First published 2002

© Pearson Education Limited 2002

ISBN-10: 0-582-43720-2
ISBN-13: 978-0-582-43720-3

British Library Cataloguing-in-Publication Data
A catalogue record for this book can be
obtained from the British Library

10 9 8 7 6 5 4 3
07 06 05

Typeset by 68
Printed in Great Britain
Printed in the UK by 4edge, Hockley, Essex

*Dedicated to the memory of our friend and colleague Joanne (Jo) Gater
1967–1999*

CONTENTS

section 78) · Obtaining admissions other than through a formal interview ·
Confessions by mentally handicapped persons · Statutory safeguards –
concluding comments · Human rights law · Procedure for dealing with the
admissibility of confession evidence · Editing confessions · Admissibility of
evidence found as a result of an inadmissible confession · Hearsay problems
occasioned by confessions · Mixed statements

PART 3 · CIVIL EVIDENCE

Dealing with witnesses who are 'absent' at the trial · Where 'new' evidence arises · Preparing documents for use at trial · Evidence in proceedings other than at trial · Evidence by affidavit

PREFACE

The law of evidence is becoming an increasingly complex subject. The introduction of the Civil Procedure Rules and the implementation of the Human Rights Act 1998, as well as ongoing political and public debate about the effectiveness of the criminal and civil justice systems ensures that the operation of the rules of evidence are topical, relevant and fast-developing.

Evidence is an area of the law that crosses the academic/practical divide. Whilst the rules of evidence provoke high-level and wide-ranging academic debate, it should not be forgotten that the rules are applied daily in the conduct of civil and criminal litigation throughout the land.

Our aim in writing this book, based on our experience of teaching the Law of Evidence on a wide range of academic and vocational courses, has been to present the law in a comprehensive but accessible and practical format. In this way, we have sought to meet the needs of undergraduates who study this subject at an academic level and those who are in or about to enter legal practice, including students taking the Legal Practice Course or the Bar Vocational Course and those students studying for the ILEX examinations. We hope the book will also be of interest to non-lawyers who are required to have an understanding of the operation of the rules of evidence because their professional duties bring them into contact with the criminal or civil justice systems.

The text is presented in a structured form, utilising leading authorities and illustrative case law. At the end of each chapter we have included a selection of further reading based on more authoritative works, legal journals and other sources of interest. Readers engaged in a scholastic approach to this subject are invited to pursue further reading in order to develop a deeper understanding and a critical appreciation of the wider issues surrounding this area of the law.

We have sought to place the rules of evidence in their procedural context and in the context of the overall process of proof. For those new to legal practice and the conduct of litigation the book contains a practical dimension and we have included a number of case scenarios to illustrate the operation of the rules of evidence. Our decision to accord a separate and detailed consideration of the rules of civil evidence is intended to facilitate an easier comprehension of the subject and reflects the fundamental distinction between the operation of the rules of evidence in the civil context from the criminal context.

There are a number of people we would like to thank for their assistance in the writing and publication of this book. We would like to thank our publishers Pearson Education for giving us the opportunity to put our ideas about the law of evidence into practice. In particular we thank Pat Bond for his unfailing support and encouragement, Mary Lince for her considerable help and patience, and Kathryn Swift for her tremendous hard work and helpful suggestions. We would also like to thank our friends and colleagues at Staffordshire University Law School for their advice, in particular, Denise O'Hara and Miceál Barden, Denis Lanser and Sue Whitfield.

Finally, we would like to thank our long-suffering families for their patience and help. Special thanks are due to Nick and Alexandra Mason, Laura Mason, Merryn, Matt, Nick and Charlie Hannibal.

The law is stated as at 1 March 2002.

Martin Hannibal
Lisa Mountford
Law School
Staffordshire University

TABLE OF CASES

TABLE OF STATUTES

TABLE OF STATUTORY INSTRUMENTS

TABLE OF CODES OF PRACTICE

TABLE OF TREATIES AND CONVENTIONS

Part 1

INTRODUCTION

Chapter 1

AN INTRODUCTION TO THE LAWS OF EVIDENCE

A NEW APPROACH

This book has been written to offer a new way of looking at the operation of the law of criminal and civil evidence. It aims to provide not only an academic perspective on the law of evidence but also to examine the operation of the evidential rules in their practical and procedural context. An important part of this innovative approach is to treat the operation of the principles of criminal evidence and civil evidence separately. Whilst many of the rules of civil and criminal evidence share a common heritage and some common principles in their application, since the introduction of the reformed system of civil litigation under the Civil Procedure Rules in April 1999, the philosophy and practice of the way in which civil cases are dealt with have taken the rules of civil evidence out of the adversarial context of fact adjudication into a judicially managed system of dealing with cases. As the adversarial tradition continues to be vigorously applied in criminal cases, it is no longer appropriate to deal with the rules of civil and criminal evidence side by side as they are traditionally treated.

To achieve this objective, the book is divided into three parts. Part 1 contains this introductory chapter providing an overview of some important core concepts of English evidence. In Chapter 2, we examine the European Convention for the Protection of Human Rights and Fundamental Freedoms 1950 as implemented by the Human Rights Act 1998. The importance of the Human Rights Act cannot be overstated and reflects our decision to include it as a chapter in its own right. Part 2 contains a detailed examination of the rules of criminal evidence, whilst the rules of civil evidence, often neglected to any significant degree in other works on this subject, are covered in Part 3. It will immediately be apparent that the rules of criminal evidence take up nearly two-thirds of the book reflecting the fact that they are more complex and far-reaching than the rules of civil evidence. The rules of civil evidence reflect the more flexible and less regulated science of proof that applies in civil cases, with the result that a civil court will hear virtually all relevant and admissible evidence.

This book is different to other law of evidence textbooks in a number of other ways. In particular we acknowledge the very close relationship between the rules of evidence and the procedural context in which the evidential rules operate. We have also highlighted for the reader the practical dimension that underpins the operation of the rules of evidence at all stages of the process of litigation. As you will see, an assessment of the evidence in the case is not something that can be solely confined to the trial. The operation of the evidential rules are relevant to all stages of the civil or criminal process from the time the lawyer initially advises his client, through to case preparation, pre-trial considerations, to the way in which a party presents its case to the court and finally, on appeal.

The practical dimension of this text is further illustrated by our identification of the tactical dilemmas that may confront the lawyer as to the advice he gives to his client. For example, should the lawyer acting for a client in a criminal case advise his client to remain silent to police questions put to him during interrogation? On the basis of the evidence in the case could the advice to give a 'no comment interview' be sustained at trial? If the advice to the client to remain silent could not be sustained, what are the evidential consequences for adverse inferences being drawn at trial against the client's silence? The point is that the lawyer's advice, which is based on his assessment of the evidence, may be vital to the eventual outcome of the case, and may have serious practical consequences for the client if the advice is wrong. In the modern era, these practical consequences may result in the defendant serving a long prison sentence or in a civil case being made bankrupt by having an award of damages and costs made against him that he cannot afford to pay.

The practical effect of the rules of evidence cannot be exaggerated: they have the potential to affect everyone's lives. In the case of R v *Mattan* (1998) *The Independent*, 4 March, the Court of Appeal quashed Mahmoud Hussein Mattan's conviction for murder 46 years after he was hanged because the Court of Appeal concluded that the identification evidence, which was the basis of the prosecution case against him, was demonstrably flawed. More recently, the Criminal Cases Review Commission referred the conviction of Stephen Downing for murder in 1973 back to the Court of Appeal. Downing had been convicted on the basis of his own confession. At the time he confessed he was 17 years old with the mental age of an 11-year-old. He was not represented by a solicitor and his confession came after nine hours of questioning by the police. As a result of the trial court accepting the admissibility of this flawed evidence, Downing spent nearly 27 years in prison before the Court of Appeal ordered his release on bail in 2000. His conviction was finally quashed by the Court of Appeal in January 2002. We assume the decision of the novelist and peer, Jeffrey Archer, not to give evidence at his recent trial for perjury for which he was convicted, was only taken after very careful consideration and having regard to the potential adverse evidential consequences that could follow.

The rules of evidence are not applied independently from other factors and do not exist solely as a matter of academic interest and debate. They are a dynamic set of principles which interact with other essential factors in a case including the rules of substantive law, the rules of procedure and the subjective characteristics of many of the participants in the trial. The latter includes the fact finder's prejudices, opinions and perceptions, the skill of the advocates, a party's or a witness's demeanour in court, his credibility, social class, criminal convictions and personality traits. All of these factors ultimately come together to provide the basis for the court's decision in the case.

The following chapters aim to present the rules of civil and criminal evidence in a readable and accessible form by setting out the general principles of the subject with reference to the leading cases and by the use of practical examples and case scenarios. Problem areas and other contentious aspects are also considered as a means of leading the reader into more specific reading. For this reason, at the end of each chapter, there is a selection of recommended further reading which takes the form of more authoritative texts and articles in legal journals, government reports and Law Commission reports.

THE PURPOSES OF THE LAW OF EVIDENCE

In both criminal and civil proceedings, the law of evidence has a number of purposes. In short, the law of evidence regulates the process of proof. At a fundamental level, the law of evidence prescribes the rules that allow a party in a case before a court or tribunal to put its version of the facts and interpretations of the law to the fact finder, ie to the person or persons deciding the factual issues in this case. The factual issue in a criminal case is whether the accused is guilty or innocent, whilst, in a civil case the factual issue relates to liability and/or the amount of damages the losing party will pay to the winning party, which is known as the quantum. The fact finder in the vast majority of civil cases will be a judge sitting alone, whilst in criminal cases the fact finder will usually be lay people, ie ordinary members of the public without any formal legal training who sit as jurors in the Crown Court and as lay magistrates in the magistrates' court. The rules of civil and criminal evidence, in conjunction with the rules of procedure, establish the framework for the process of proof and the conduct of litigation, so that a lawyer advising his client or preparing his case for trial or presenting it to the court or tribunal will know what issues his client must prove in order to succeed. He will also be aware of the issues that his opponent must prove to succeed, the ways in which the court or tribunal will receive the evidence from each party and the standard of proof that the party will have to reach in order to persuade the fact finder of the efficacy of his case. It would obviously be undesirable and chaotic if a judge had an unfettered discretion as to which evidence should be admitted in a case, and as such, there is clearly a need for there to be ground rules for the admission of evidence so that common standards are applied between all courts and tribunals dealing with the same type of case.

The law of evidence also has a moral purpose, by establishing and regulating the rules relating to the process of proof in proceedings in courts and tribunals. The operation of rules are meant to assist the court in establishing the truth (whatever the truth is!) between the party's conflicting versions of the facts in the case. In criminal proceedings, where the accused pleads not guilty, both the prosecution and the defence will submit to the court different versions of the events leading up to the commission of the alleged crime and the accused's involvement in the crime. The law of evidence prescribes the rules that will assist the members of the jury or the magistrates to decide where the truth lies between these apparently conflicting versions.

Whilst this moral dimension is important in civil proceedings, it has special currency in criminal cases as it reflects the powerful public interest in bringing the guilty to justice, whilst allowing the innocent to go free. In some cases the rules of evidence may actually prevent the truth from being discovered in the wider public interest. This observation lends itself to the well-known apocryphal story of the barrister being asked by the judge 'Am I not to hear the truth?' to which the barrister replies 'No, your honour is to hear the evidence'.

In criminal cases a further important purpose of the law of evidence is to protect the defendant from the State abusing its overwhelming superiority in terms of the resources that it has at its disposal to secure the defendant's conviction against the 'interests of justice'. The court's protectionist role applies to both the legal powers that are used during the investigation of the offence under, for example, the Police and Criminal Evidence Act 1984 (PACE) and also to the evidence that can be put to the court at trial by the prosecution as part of its case against the accused. An important aspect of the protection that is given to the accused is his right to a 'fair' trial, which since October 2000 has been further strengthened by the incorporation of Article 6 of the European Convention on Human Rights (the right to a fair trial) into English law by the Human Rights Act 1998. The protection of the accused against the case being proven against him by evidence which is prejudicial to his right to a fair trial is one of the main reasons why the law of criminal evidence contains so many rules which exclude potentially relevant evidence from the fact finder, including for example, the general rule that evidence of the defendant's character will not be admitted at trial. The court may also exercise its powers under section 78 or 82(3) of PACE to support the defendant's right to a fair trial by excluding evidence in the exercise of its discretion.

The fair trial provision is not as important in a civil case as there is greater equality in resources between the parties and under the overriding objectives of the Civil Procedure Rules 1998 (CPR), the court is required as far as is 'reasonably practicable' to ensure that the parties are on an 'equal footing'. Also, whilst losing a civil case may result in the claimant or the defendant suffering serious damage to his financial resources or property, he will not lose his liberty or suffer the same social stigma as a person who has been convicted of a criminal offence.

We now consider some of the key phrases and concepts in the law of evidence that you will encounter in the chapters which follow and which are relevant to the operation of both the rules of civil and criminal evidence. We begin by considering what needs to proved in a given case.

WHAT NEEDS TO BE PROVED?

Factual disputes giving rise to civil or criminal proceedings can only be proved through the admission of evidence. The actual process of proof in the context of criminal and civil cases is considered in Chapters 3 and 22. Common to all criminal and civil cases is the need to identify the facts requiring proof in a particular case to which evidence must be directed.

Facts in issue

In criminal cases, the substantive law determines what the prosecution must prove in order to establish an accused's guilt. In a trial for theft, the prosecution would have to prove all the elements that make up the offence of theft under section 1 of the Theft Act 1968 namely that:

> A person is guilty of theft if he dishonestly appropriates property belonging to another with the intention of permanently depriving the other of it.

All the essential elements of the crime are the facts in issue and evidence must be adduced in respect of each to the required standard of proof, beyond reasonable doubt, before the prosecution can succeed. As an exception to the general rule there are instances when the defendant is required to prove certain facts in order to achieve an acquittal. The circumstances in which this requirement arises are considered in Chapter 11.

In civil cases, the facts in issue are normally to be found in the pleadings: that is in the claimant's statement of claim and any defence put forward by the defendant. The pleadings identify the substantive law and the facts requiring proof. In a negligence action, the facts in issue which need to be proved by the claimant will be the assertions that: the defendant owed the claimant a duty of care; the duty of care was breached and, as a consequence, the claimant suffered loss. Where the defendant denies liability, he will have nothing to prove. Where the defendant asserts the claimant was responsible for the accident and counterclaims for his loss, this becomes a fact in issue, which the defendant must then prove. Whilst the pleadings in the case will largely determine what needs to be proved in a civil case, the parties may admit certain facts in issue with the result that no evidence need be adduced on that particular issue. In addition, under CPR rule 32.1, a judge can override the parties' view as to the issues on which it requires proof.

Collateral facts

A collateral or a subordinate fact, is one which is not of direct relevance to the outcome of the case, but which may nevertheless be raised at the trial. There are three types of collateral fact. First, those facts which affect the competence of a witness to give evidence. Evidence which proves a witness to be incompetent perhaps because the witness has a mental illness or evidence which proves that an expert witness lacks the necessary qualifications or degree of experience to be competent to give expert opinion evidence are common examples of collateral facts in a case.

Secondly, a fact which affects the credibility of a witness is a collateral fact. The weight to be attached to a witness's evidence depends, in part, on an assessment of the witness's credibility. Although it is a collateral matter, evidence may be adduced which is relevant to a witness's credibility such as exposing a motive for the witness to lie on oath.

Thirdly, collateral facts may have to be proved as a condition to the admissibility of certain types of evidence. For example, where a party submits that a document is original, the party may have to prove the document's authenticity to the court before it can be admitted in evidence. Another example is where, in a criminal case, it is represented that the accused's confession is unreliable or was obtained by oppression. Such a confession constitutes an evidential fact relevant to the facts in issue in the case. The prosecution would have to prove the conditions for the admissibility of the accused's confession before it could be admitted.

TYPES OF EVIDENCE

Evidence that is put to the court to prove the facts in issue may be presented in a number of forms. Whatever form evidence is presented in, it must be relevant and admissible and will either constitute direct or circumstantial evidence of a fact in issue or a fact relevant to a fact in issue. All of these terms are defined and considered below and are common to both criminal and civil cases.

Testimonial evidence

This comprises statements of a witness made orally on oath or affirmation in court. Witnesses can only give evidence of facts perceived with their own senses. The only exception to this is the expert witness who can give opinion evidence on matters outside the competency of the court. Oral testimony can sometimes be provided via a live television link or on a pre-recorded tape. Sometimes testimony is presented to the court in the form of a sworn written statement such as an affidavit or deposition.

Hearsay evidence

Hearsay is defined as a statement other than one made by a witness whilst giving evidence in the proceedings in question admitted to prove the truth of some fact asserted by the witness. Where a witness of fact (A) is unable to attend a trial a hearsay problem arises where a party seeks to call another person (B) to repeat in court what he heard A state. Similarly where either party seeks to place reliance on a document in which the absent witness has given an account of what they witnessed, at first hand, a hearsay problem arises. Hearsay evidence is felt to be inferior to first-hand oral testimony, chiefly because it is impossible to cross-examine the absent witness. Hearsay evidence is generally inadmissible in criminal cases because of the danger that lay fact finders might attribute too great a degree of weight to such inferior evidence than it truly deserves. In civil cases by contrast, hearsay evidence is generally admissible. This is primarily a reflection of the trust placed in legally qualified, experienced judges who try civil cases. Less importance is attached to the principle of orality (the preference for first-hand oral testimony in court) in civil proceedings, resulting in far greater reliance upon the admission of evidence in documentary form.

Opinion evidence

The general rule in all cases is that where a witness gives opinion evidence it will be inadmissible. A witness may only speak or depose of those facts that he has personally perceived, and not to any inference drawn from those facts. The major exception to this is that the court may receive the opinion of a suitably qualified expert witness on a matter which is outside the court's competency.

Documentary evidence

This can include photographs, plans, documentary hearsay, affidavits, videotaped evidence etc. A document may be adduced in evidence because its content, or merely its existence, is relevant. Documents must generally be proved by a witness who can verify the nature and authenticity of the document. The original document constitutes 'primary' evidence and a copy constitutes 'secondary' evidence. The law of evidence increasingly allows the admissibility of copies of documents. This is particularly true of criminal proceedings to which section 27 of the Criminal Justice Act 1988 applies. The section provides that where a statement in a document is admissible in criminal proceedings, it may be proved by the production of the document or a copy of the document authenticated in such manner as the court may approve. The equivalent provision applicable to civil cases is section 8 of the Civil Evidence Act 1995. A great number of public documents such as a birth certificate can be proved by a certified copy of the entry made in the register.

Real evidence

Real evidence comprises physical evidence produced in the form of exhibits before a court. Real evidence is sometimes referred to as being original evidence. It includes articles found in the defendant's possession pursuant to a search, the weapon used to commit a particular offence, photographs or video footage of the location of an accident or a claimant captured on video faking a personal injury, the print-out of a mechanical device or the demeanour of a witness whilst giving evidence on oath. In some cases, it may be necessary for the judge or the jury to make a site inspection for an out-of-court demonstration or in order to see that which has previously been represented in court.

Direct evidence

If believed, direct evidence establishes a fact in issue. Direct evidence is provided by witnesses giving oral testimony of something they perceived with their own senses. It is also afforded by the presentation of documents, photographs and the like which the fact finder is required to interpret with his or her senses and includes the physical presence of a witness in the witness box giving rise to an assessment by the fact finder of the witness's credibility. It can include any incriminating admissions by a party in the case. If the fact finder accepts the evidence it is directly relevant to the facts in issue in the case.

Circumstantial evidence

Circumstantial evidence is indirect evidence that tends to establish a conclusion by inference. It requires the fact finder first to accept the evidence as being true and accurate and then to draw a conclusion or inference from it. For this reason, criminal cases built entirely on circumstantial evidence are the most difficult to prove to the required standard of proof beyond reasonable doubt.

Circumstantial evidence requires the fact finder to draw generalisations from commonly held assumptions about human nature. In a murder case for example, evidence that a defendant lied to the police about his whereabouts at the relevant time and had a violent argument with the victim some days before the killing would constitute relevant circumstantial evidence of the accused's guilt. The inference is based on the common assumption that murderers normally have a motive for committing murder and will usually cover their tracks by lying.

The presence of a set of scales and a number of wrappers might constitute circumstantial evidence from which the fact finder might infer that a defendant had an intention to supply drugs. Of course the defendant may have an explanation for the presence of the scales and the wrappers inconsistent with an intention to supply drugs. It would be for the fact finder to weigh up the evidence in order to decide where the truth lay.

A very effective illustration of circumstantial evidence is provided by the much-publicised trial of Barry George in the summer of 2001 for the murder of Jill Dando, the well-known television personality. The facts of the case are set out in some detail since they help to illustrate a number of the key terms and core concepts covered in this chapter.

Ms Dando was shot dead on the doorstep to her home by a single bullet to her head. There were no witnesses to her murder and no murder weapon was ever recovered. There were many theories regarding the killing. They included the suggestion that she may have been the victim of a hired assassin either by someone in the criminal underworld or a Serbian extremist. Ms Dando had recorded an appeal on behalf of Kosovan refugees in the wake of the NATO bombing of Serbia shortly before her murder and she had been a co-presenter of the BBC's *Crimewatch* programme. Other theories included that she might have been the victim of an obsessed fan or a jealous former boyfriend.

The police sieved through thousands of pieces of information in the months following the murder. The arrest of Barry George came 395 days after the shooting. He had an interesting profile. He was a loner who had an acute obsession with celebrities. He had had a series of aliases and was known as Barry Bulsara (Freddie Mercury's real name) at the time of his arrest. He was a fantasist with numerous mental problems. He was also an epileptic.

In his flat the police found 736 newspapers, 54 of which contained features on Ms Dando. He had numerous magazines on guns and thousands of undeveloped photographs of women he had followed on the streets of London.

The police interviewed Barry George over the course of four days. The interviews concentrated on Barry George's movements on the day of the murder and his obsession with guns and yielded some highly relevant circumstantial evidence. He denied ever owning a gun. However, when he was shown a photograph of himself wearing a balaclava and carrying a handgun, he was forced to admit that he had lied. He denied knowing where Gowan Avenue (where Ms Dando's house was situated) was despite the fact that he had been a patient at a doctor's surgery in the road. He claimed to have an alibi for the time of the murder, which was around 11.30 am. He said he had been at a disability centre. Various staff at the centre put him as being there at times between 11 am and 2 pm on the day of the killing.

Barry George's actions in the days after the murder were interesting. Two days after the shooting he returned to the premises of a taxi company he had used on that day to ask the driver if he could remember him. The taxi company's records showed Barry George's request to be taken to the disability centre had been made at 1.15 pm. The police regarded Barry George's actions as an attempt by him to establish a firm alibi. One might reason why someone would need to establish an alibi if they were innocent of any involvement? Barry George had also been back to the disability centre to ask the staff what time he had turned up there. He had been agitated at the time. In the early days of the police investigation this information had been passed onto the police and logged into their computer. It was only when Barry George came under increasing suspicion much later during the investigation that the information assumed increasing relevance.

Mobile telephone records revealed Barry George could not have been at the disability centre at 12.32 pm. The prosecution contended the evidence pointed to Barry George having had the opportunity to commit the murder, return to his flat, get changed and go out in order to establish an alibi.

The only eyewitness to positively identify Barry George at an identification parade placed him in Gowan Avenue four and half hours before the murder. Another witness recalled having had a conversation with a man resembling Barry George at around 12.30 pm in the vicinity. Numerous other eyewitnesses failed to identify him.

Forensic scientists matched material on a pair of trousers taken from Barry George's flat to a single piece of fibre (real evidence) on the coat Ms Dando was wearing when she was shot. The defence undermined the weight of this evidence by adducing evidence to show the fibre was very common and could have come from any number of different sources.

Most significantly of all, forensic scientists discovered a minute particle of gun residue inside a pocket of one of Barry George's jackets. The particle was matched to gun residue found in Ms Dando's hair. Significantly the police had taken the jacket in which the particle of gun residue had been found to a photographic studio before being taken to the forensic laboratory. A week or so before the jacket was photographed the studio had been photographing guns and ammunition. It was possible that the particle could have come from one of these guns. In evidence, the forensic scientist for the defence doubted whether any residue from the original shooting would have remained after a year.

The evidence presented to the jury comprising the fibre, the gun residue, the testimony of eyewitnesses, Barry George's proven lies, his attempts to establish an alibi and his obsession with guns all comprised circumstantial evidence. There was no direct evidence to show Barry George had ever possessed the murder weapon used to kill Ms Dando. There were no eyewitnesses who could put him in Gowan Avenue at the relevant time and there was no direct evidence that he had any particular obsession with Ms Dando. Nevertheless, based on the cumulative circumstantial evidence presented, the jury found Barry George guilty of murder. Barry George's appeal against his conviction is due to be heard by the Court of Appeal in spring 2002.

It is important to be aware that evidence may fall into more than one category; for example, documentary evidence may constitute real evidence, circumstantial evidence, or hearsay evidence, in addition to its classification as documentary evidence. The category into which evidence falls depends very much on the purpose for which it is put before the court.

There are three core principles which underpin the rules of evidence in both criminal and civil cases. These core principles are: relevance, admissibility and weight, each of which is discussed below.

RELEVANCE

Relevance is the first principle of both civil and criminal evidence. The facts in issue in a case and any collateral facts can only be proved by adducing relevant evidence. Whatever the form of the evidence, whether testimonial, documentary, real, direct or circumstantial, to be admissible, evidence needs to be both logically and sufficiently relevant. Relevant evidence always has a bearing on the search for the true determination of a past event.

Evidence assumes logical relevance if it has a bearing on the facts in issue in a particular case or the facts relevant to a fact in issue.

The classic definition of relevance is provided by Lord Simon of Glaisdale in *DPP* v *Kilbourne* [1973] AC 729:

Evidence is relevant if it is logically probative of some matter which requires proof. I do not pause to analyse what is involved in 'logical probativeness' except to note that the term does not of itself express the element of experience which is so significant of its operation in law, and possibly elsewhere. It is sufficient to say, even at the risk of etymological tautology, that relevant (i.e. logically probative or disprobative) evidence is evidence which makes the matter which requires proof more or less probable.

A more simplistic definition is afforded by the Australian Evidence Act 1995 which defines relevant evidence as:

Evidence that is relevant in a proceeding is evidence that, if it were accepted, could rationally affect (directly or indirectly) the assessment of the probability of the existence of a fact in issue.

For evidence to be relevant a logical relationship needs to be established between the evidence tendered and the fact to be proved. All that is necessary to qualify evidence for admission at trial is that it should increase or diminish the probability of the existence of a fact in issue. It is for the trial judge to determine whether evidence is relevant. In a jury trial an argument as to the relevance of evidence is determined in the absence of the jury. Some judges speak of evidence requiring a sufficient degree of probative force for it to be relevant.

To be admissible, evidence must be sufficiently relevant. Evidence will possess a sufficient degree of relevance if the benefit of admitting it outweighs the 'cost' in terms of the risk that it might cause confusion, multiply the issues in the case, or lead to too many speculative inferences. In R v *Quinn and Bloom* [1962] 2 QB 245, as part of their defence to a charge of keeping a disorderly house, the defendants sought to have admitted into evidence a filmed reconstruction of a striptease show performed some weeks earlier which had led to the prosecution. The Court of Appeal (Criminal Division) deemed the evidence to be irrelevant. Such a reconstruction was not an acceptable method of proof. There were bound to be material differences between the original performance witnessed by the police officers and the one sought to be put before the jury which was likely to lead the jury astray. In *Agassiz* v *London Tramway Co* (1872) 21 WR 199, a passenger on a bus claimed damages for personal injury when the bus he was travelling on was in collision with another bus. The passenger blamed the driver of the bus he was travelling on and suggested to the conductor that the driver should be reported. The conductor replied that the driver had already been reported for steering off course five or six times that very day. This evidence was excluded at the trial as being irrelevant: it did not help explain how the accident had occurred and gave rise to a number of unhelpful side issues.

Since relevance has an infinitely variable quality, assessing whether evidence is relevant in a particular case is not always easy. Assessment of relevance is governed by the canons of logic, general experience and common sense. As logical reasoning is particular to the individual, differing conclusions as to the relevance of evidence are likely to arise. Two criminal cases provide a useful illustration.

R *v* Blastland [1986] AC 41

The defendant was charged with the sodomy and murder of a 12-year-old boy. He pleaded not guilty. He admitted to having buggered the boy but maintained he had panicked and ran off when he saw another man nearby. His defence at trial was that someone else had committed the murder, most probably the man he had observed. The defendant wanted to adduce evidence of the fact that a man, known only as Mark during the trial and who was a known homosexual, had told several people about the boy's murder before it had become public knowledge. In imparting this information, Mark was witnessed to have been in a highly excitable state. Mark was not called to give evidence at the trial. Counsel for the defendant sought to call the witnesses to whom Mark had imparted this information so that they could repeat on oath what Mark had said to them. The defence wanted the jury to infer that Mark could only have come by such knowledge if he had either witnessed the murder or committed it himself. Leave was refused on the basis that such evidence amounted to hearsay.

The House of Lords concluded the evidence of the witnesses would not amount to hearsay if the reason for seeking to have the evidence admitted was purely for the purpose of showing Mark's state of mind. Crucially however, the House of Lords did not regard Mark's state of mind as having any logical relevance to any fact in issue at the defendant's trial. It would require too much speculation on the part of the jury since Mark could have acquired such knowledge in a number of different ways and there was no admissible evidence available to show how he had acquired such knowledge. The decision has been much criticised as applying too strict a notion of relevance. The jury convicted the defendant in the ignorance of the statements Mark had made which may have been sufficient to raise a reasonable doubt.

R v Kearley [1992] 2 AC 228

The defendant was suspected of dealing in drugs. Drug squad officers raided his flat and were disappointed to find only a small quantity of drugs. Whilst they were at the defendant's flat a number of unidentified persons called at the flat asking to be supplied with drugs and officers took a number of telephone calls from individuals asking the defendant to supply them. The defendant was charged with possession of a controlled drug with intent to supply contrary to section 5(3) of the Misuse of Drugs Act 1971. He pleaded not guilty.

At the trial the prosecution sought to call the officers to give evidence of the conversations they had had with callers at the door and on the telephone. The evidence was highly useful to the prosecution. It constituted in its view, highly relevant and probative circumstantial evidence from which the jury might infer the defendant was dealing. The trial judge overruled the appellant's objections and allowed the police officers to give evidence recounting the callers' requests. The appellant was convicted and appealed. The Court of Appeal upheld the trial judge's decision. In a three to two majority decision however, the House of Lords overturned the defendant's conviction on the ground that the evidence in question was not relevant to the issues requiring proof.

The majority of their Lordships came to the conclusion that the repetition of what had been said on the doorstep and in the various telephone calls was relevant only to the state of mind of the callers, who might or might not have believed drugs to be available on the premises. However, the evidence of the callers' state of mind was irrelevant to prove that the defendant had been supplying drugs. The evidence did no more than show they believed drugs to have been available at the premises.

Objection to the admission of certain evidence may always be taken on the grounds of its relevance. Where a party does object, the burden of proving relevance rests on the party seeking to tender it. There have been numerous criminal cases requiring the prosecution to prove the possession of drugs with intent to supply which have given rise to some searching questions of relevance. What is relevant evidence when it comes to proving intent to supply? On the generalised assumption that drug dealers prefer to deal in cash, is evidence of loose cash and a lavish lifestyle relevant to proof that the defendant is currently dealing in drugs? The answer depends on the facts in each case.

In *R v Batt* [1994] Crim LR 592 a quantity of drugs were found in a rabbit hutch in the garden of the defendant's house. The defendant was charged with possession with intent to supply. She denied all knowledge of the drugs. At her trial the prosecution were allowed to adduce in evidence the discovery of £120 stuffed inside an ornamental kettle in the defendant's kitchen. Quashing the conviction, the Court of Appeal concluded the evidence of the cash had little relevance to proof of a future intention to supply since the amount was small and there might have been any number of innocent explanations for it.

By contrast in *R v Wright* [1994] Crim LR 55 the Court of Appeal held it had been right to admit into evidence £16,000 in cash and a gold necklace worth £9,000 found in the defendant's possession as being relevant to a charge of possession with intent to supply. It could generally be assumed that those who deal in drugs would be in possession of substantial quantities of cash because they had received the money from sales or because it was needed to purchase fresh supplies.

Is evidence of lifestyle and possession of drug paraphernalia relevant to proof of being knowingly in possession? Declining to follow a number of previous decisions on the point, the Court of Appeal in *R v Guney* [1998] 2 Cr App R 242 held there was no rule that such evidence could never assume relevance on a charge of being knowingly in possession. In this particular case the defendant maintained he had no knowledge of the drugs found in his possession. His defence was that the drugs had been planted on him. The presence of £25,000 in cash found in a wardrobe in the defendant's bedroom was rightly admitted as being relevant evidence capable of rebutting his defence.

ADMISSIBILITY

Inadmissible evidence may not be received before a court, no matter what its relevance might be. Admissibility is the second key principle of evidence law.

If relevancy is governed by the canons of logic and good sense, the separate issue of the admissibility of evidence proceeds from considerations other than relevance.

Relevant evidence is rendered inadmissible by the application of exclusionary rules of evidence. Some exclusionary rules of evidence are mandatory. In criminal cases this includes the rule against the admission of hearsay evidence and the exclusion of opinion evidence, evidence protected by a private privilege or public interest immunity, evidence of the defendant's past bad character and admission of a previous consistent statement by a witness. The rationales for excluding such evidence are various. Evidence of the defendant's past bad character is excluded because of the prejudice such information is likely to engender in the mind of the fact finder. Hearsay evidence is excluded because it is generally perceived to be inherently unreliable as the witness to the actual events is not available to give evidence on oath and to be cross-examined. Opinion evidence is excluded because it usurps the function of the fact finder and is of little probative value. Evidence of previous consistent statements are excluded because their evidential value is perceived to be minimal.

In other instances relevant evidence can be excluded in the exercise of the court's discretion. The exercise of judicial discretion to exclude evidence is most obviously associated with criminal trials where the need to ensure a fair trial is paramount. In criminal cases the discretion to exclude otherwise relevant evidence is available at common law and under section 78 of PACE. The former requires courts to exclude evidence where its probative value is outweighed by its prejudicial effect. The latter permits the court to exclude evidence the admission of which would adversely affect the fairness of the proceedings. The discretionary exclusion of evidence in an attempt to ensure a fair trial in criminal cases is considered at length in Chapter 5.

In civil proceedings, evidence which is relevant and probative of a fact which needs to be proved to the court will generally be admissible. There are no mandatory rules requiring the exclusion of evidence in civil cases. Under CPR rule 32.1 the trial judge has been given discretion to exclude otherwise relevant and admissible evidence as part of the court's control of civil cases to further the overriding objective of the Civil Procedure Rules contained within CPR rule 1.1. The exercise of discretion in civil cases is exercised comparatively rarely.

This state of affairs reflects the key difference between civil and criminal proceedings. In civil law virtually all cases are heard by a judge sitting alone. As a legally qualified individual it is generally felt that the judge can deal with and give appropriate weight to relevant but prejudicial evidence. In criminal cases however, where there is much greater involvement of lay people in the decision-making process (ie people without formal legal training, such as lay magistrates and jurors), potentially relevant and probative evidence is often excluded because of the danger that it might be accorded an inappropriate degree of weight.

Where one party raises an issue regarding the admissibility of a particular piece of evidence the decision whether or not to admit it is taken by a judge in a civil case. In criminal cases magistrates take the decision in summary cases. In the Crown Court admissibility of evidence is a question of law and is determined by the trial judge in the absence of the jury.

Evidence may be admissible for one purpose but not another. Where this is so it requires a very careful direction from the trial judge in a case tried before a jury. We shall see examples of this in relation to confession evidence where a confession by one defendant implicates another and in the context of the evidential uses that can be made of the defendant's past bad character evidence where rules of evidence allow for it to be admitted.

Having regard to the trial of Barry George above, several pieces of evidence were excluded from the jury's consideration by the trial judge. The jury was not told of the fact that Barry George had previous criminal convictions, including one for attempted rape, nor that he had a mental illness and a history of stalking women in his neighbourhood, nor that he had thousands of photographs of women in his flat. Such evidence was excluded on the basis that its prejudicial effect far outweighed its probative value.

WEIGHT

Where evidence has been admitted it is up to the fact finder (jury/magistrates in criminal cases and a judge in the vast majority of civil cases) to decide how much weight or probative value it wants to attribute to it. Whilst admissibility is a question of law, weight is a question of fact. Overall, in a criminal case the weight of the evidence must be sufficient to convince the fact finder that guilt is proved beyond reasonable doubt. In civil cases, issues are decided on the balance of probabilities.

How cogent a line of argument is, or whether a particular witness can be believed, depends on the fact finder's personal judgment. In many cases assessment of the weight of evidence is made on the basis of a wide range of factors. For example, in relation to assessing the cogency of a witness giving oral testimony to the court, the following factors will be significant:

- the fact finder's intuition based on his or her personal experiences,
- the type of case being tried,
- the age, demeanour, credibility of the witness, and
- the witness's involvement in the events about which he or she is testifying.

Less weight is likely to be attached to the evidence of a biased witness than to an independent witness. Similarly a jury is likely to be more wary of believing a witness who has previous convictions for dishonesty and may therefore not attribute as much weight to that witness's evidence as to a witness with an unimpeachable character. A confession which has been deemed admissible by a judge but which was obtained in dubious circumstances might be accorded less weight than a confession obtained in accordance with the rules. DNA evidence by contrast is capable of carrying significant weight.

The weight accorded to documentary evidence will also be determined by a number of factors including:

- whether the document is an original or a copy,
- the circumstances in which the document came into the possession of the party putting it in evidence, and
- whether the document is accompanied by a witness giving oral evidence to explain the significance of its contents.

There are very few rules prescribing how fact finders in criminal cases should evaluate the evidence they have heard. In some instances, as we shall see, the judge is required to leave the evidence to the jury accompanied by a warning. Sometimes the warning is mandatory; sometimes it is given in the exercise of the trial judge's discretion. In other instances the judge is required to explain to the jury precisely what it can do with a particular piece of evidence and, in some circumstances, what it needs to be satisfied of before it is able to make use of the evidence in the way prescribed. Section 4 of the Civil Evidence Act 1995 provides the judge with statutory guidance as to the assessment of weight to be accorded to hearsay evidence admissible in civil cases.

Although relevance, admissibility and weight are distinct they are inter-related. The relevance of a particular piece of evidence is often closely bound up with its weight. Similarly, the exercise of judicial discretion to admit or to exclude evidence is often based on an assessment of the true relevance of the evidence involving the trial judge weighing up the probative value of the evidence sought to be admitted as against its prejudicial effect. If the former exceeds the latter, the evidence may safely be admitted. In fact it is not entirely accurate to suggest that the weight of evidence is solely a matter for the fact finder. In criminal cases the trial judge has the power to withdraw a case from a jury where, in his view, the prosecution has failed to discharge its evidential burden of proof. In addition, in cases involving disputed identification the trial judge is required to make an initial assessment of the quality of the identification evidence before determining whether the matter should be left to the jury.

As you will come to see, the core concepts of relevance, admissibility and weight pervade the process of proof and fundamentally underpin the law of evidence.

Further reading

Choo, A., 'The Notion of Relevance and Defence Evidence' [1993] Crim LR 114.

Eggleston, Sir R. (1978) *Evidence, Proof and Probability,* Weidenfeld and Nicolson.

Woolf MR, Lord (1996) *Access to Justice, Final Report*, HMSO.

Zuckerman, A. (1989) *The Principles of Criminal Evidence*, Clarendon Press.

Chapter 2

HUMAN RIGHTS ACT 1998

INTRODUCTION

The Human Rights Act 1998 (HRA) came into force on 2 October 2000. The effect of the Act is to make a considerable number of the provisions of the European Convention for the Protection of Human Rights and Fundamental Freedoms 1950 enforceable in English law. Whilst almost every area of the English legal system will be affected by the passing of the HRA its provisions are especially significant to criminal and civil litigators. The purpose of this chapter is to explain the legal effect of the HRA, its operation in practice and to highlight those rights enshrined under the European Convention on Human Rights that are specifically relevant to the future application and development of criminal and civil evidence.

The European Convention on Human Rights is an international agreement between 41 European states which seeks to guarantee a number of fundamental social, political and civil rights in the legal systems of the member states. The United Kingdom is one of the original signatories to the treaty in 1950. It has long been a strange twist of constitutional fate that whilst the United Kingdom played an influential part in drafting the Convention, governments of all political persuasions have not required Parliament to pass legislation making the provisions of the Convention enforceable in English law.

Prior to the HRA coming into force, the Convention was used by English courts for the limited purpose of aiding statutory construction in cases where Parliament's legislative intention was ambiguous. For an individual who claimed his rights under the Convention had been infringed the only redress was to take the long and arduous route of petitioning the European Court of Human Rights in Strasbourg. This could only be undertaken by an applicant who had exhausted all available domestic routes by which redress could be sought. During this period the United Kingdom's record before the European Court of Human Rights was largely unimpressive. Indeed, it has been something of a serial offender where violation of the Convention is concerned, particularly in relation to Article 6, guaranteeing the right to a fair trial.

With the enactment of the HRA, Convention rights are now directly enforceable in domestic courts of the United Kingdom. Public authorities (including courts) have a duty not to act in a way that is incompatible with Convention rights. In taking a decision in a particular case which might involve construing a statutory provision, developing the common law, conducting a judicial review, or exercising judicial discretion, the court must ensure its decision is compliant with the rights defined under the Convention. The HRA has major implications for the doctrine of precedent as it is applied in the United Kingdom. Effectively, courts will be able to ignore legal precedents which cannot be applied in a manner compatible with Convention rights.

HOW DOES THE HUMAN RIGHTS ACT 1998 INCORPORATE THE EUROPEAN CONVENTION ON HUMAN RIGHTS?

Convention rights are enforceable in a number of different ways.

Duty to interpret statutes compatibly (section 3)

Section 3 of the HRA is hugely important. It imposes an interpretative obligation on courts. It provides that in so far as it is possible to do so, courts and tribunals must interpret existing and future primary and secondary legislation in a way that ensures compliance with Convention rights.

The wording in the section is very significant. There will be a positive duty on courts to take a broad and purposive approach to construing and interpreting legislation compatibly with Convention rights. This may require judges to adopt a construction which strains the literal meaning of the words used. It could also require judges to read words into a particular statutory section in order to give effect to Convention rights or, in some instances to adopt a narrow interpretation by reading down not only express words, but also the implication of provisions.

In adopting a particular method of construction Lord Hope has made it clear in the House of Lords decision in *R v Lambert* [2001] 3 All ER 577 that 'the interpretation of a statute by reading words in to give effect to the presumed intention must always be distinguished carefully from amendment. Amendment is a legislative act. It is an exercise which must be reserved to Parliament.'

The only instance in which a purposive approach to the construction of a statute will not be possible will be where the legislation is so clearly incompatible with the Convention in its wording that it is impossible to read the statute in a compliant way. In this way parliamentary sovereignty is maintained. Where this is the case, section 10 of the HRA stipulates that the superior courts (High Court, Court of Appeal and House of Lords) may make a declaration of incompatibility which can trigger a fast track legislative procedure for amending the legislation so as to ensure compliance with Convention obligations. Legislation promoted after the HRA will clearly state whether it is or is not intended to be compatible with the Convention. Where a statement of compatibility has been made it will lend great force to the argument that Parliament did not intend to infringe Convention rights thereby enabling a much more purposive interpretation of the particular statute.

The decision of the House of Lords in *R v A* [2001] 3 All ER 1 affords a good illustration of the intent behind section 3. The case concerned a challenge to section 41(3)(c) of the Youth Justice and Criminal Evidence Act 1999 which restricts a defendant's right to cross-examine a rape victim on her previous sexual relationship with the defendant. Lord Steyn observed:

> In accordance with the will of Parliament as reflected in section 3 it will sometimes be necessary to adopt an interpretation which linguistically may appear strained. The techniques

to be used will not only involve the reading down of express language in a statute but also the implication of provisions. A declaration of incompatibility is a measure of last resort. It must be avoided unless it is plainly impossible to do so.

Duty to take Strasbourg case law into account (section 2)

In determining a question concerning a Convention right, section 2 of the HRA requires courts to take Strasbourg jurisprudence into account. This includes considering not only judgments of the European Court of Human Rights, but also opinions as to the admissibility of a petition or the merits of a case taken by the European Commission on Human Rights or Committee of Ministers. As part of a re-structuring operation, the Commission ceased to exist in November 1998 and the Committee of Ministers no longer takes decisions on the merits of a case. The European Court of Human Rights in the form of a Chamber or Grand Chamber now makes all judgments and decisions as to the admissibility of a claim under the Convention.

Whilst section 2 of the HRA requires courts to take Strasbourg case law into account when determining Convention rights, it does not oblige domestic courts in the United Kingdom to follow it. Indeed, in some instances it may well be that existing domestic law confers a greater measure of protection than Convention jurisprudence. The margin of appreciation which is often applied by the European Court of Human Rights in its determination of cases also has a role to play in this regard (see below).

In addition, increasing use is likely to be made of human rights jurisprudence in other common law jurisdictions. The Privy Council regularly determines appeals from Commonwealth countries involving constitutional and human rights granted to citizens under Charter or Bill of Rights. In determining such appeals, the Privy Council has often found it both necessary and helpful to draw on the jurisprudence from countries such as Canada, Hong Kong and New Zealand. In interpreting rights under the European Convention on Human Rights it is confidently anticipated that common law decisions in these jurisdictions raising similar issues to those being considered will be cited in argument and in judgment. The available jurisprudence is therefore immense.

Public authorities must comply with Convention rights (section 6)

Section 6(1) of the HRA makes it unlawful for a public authority to act in a way that is incompatible with Convention rights, unless prevented from doing so by primary or secondary legislation which cannot be read compatibly with the Convention.

A public authority is any body that performs a public function including local authorities, courts, tribunals, the police, the Crown Prosecution Service and government ministers. It will include private bodies such as hospital trusts and public utilities whose functions are of a public nature.

The HRA does not directly apply to a dispute between private individuals. Where the matter proceeds to court however, the HRA may have an indirect effect. As the court is a public authority under section 6, it must ensure that a person's Convention rights are not breached. The court would therefore have to interpret the law in the private dispute to ensure compliance with Convention rights.

In practical terms section 6 of the HRA is of considerable importance. A defendant in a criminal trial will be able to rely on the Convention in the course of the trial itself as well as in any subsequent appeal. The HRA would, in appropriate circumstances, empower a court to stay a prosecution for an abuse of process. It could also be used by a court to exclude evidence which, for example, has been obtained unlawfully in excess of the coercive powers available to the police. It could also be used to prevent an adverse inference being drawn from a defendant's silence where the court considers this to be incompatible with the defendant's right to a fair trial. The Court of Appeal will have the power to quash a conviction based on a violation of the Convention where it concludes the violation rendered the trial unfair and the resulting conviction unsafe.

Section 7 of the HRA entitles a person who believes a public authority has acted in breach of section 6 to bring legal proceedings against the authority and to rely on Convention rights in so doing.

Under section 8 of the HRA a court finding that a public authority has acted unlawfully must grant a remedy that is 'just and appropriate'. The HRA creates a new cause of action for individuals against a public body that acts in an incompatible way with the victim's Convention rights. A remedy might include judicial review on the grounds of illegality; damages and/or injunctive relief for breach of statutory duty.

CONVENTION RIGHTS

Under the European Convention on Human Rights, the United Kingdom guarantees that its citizens and all others in its jurisdiction will enjoy a number of legal rights. Some of the rights such as that prohibiting the use of torture under Article 3 are absolute. Absolute rights do not permit member states to derogate from them even in times of national emergency. Other rights such as Article 8 (the right to individual privacy) guarantee a qualified right. A qualified right permits a state to interfere with the right provided:

- the interference is in accordance with law;
- it pursues a legitimate objective and;
- is no more than is necessary in a democratic society.

Convention rights most likely to be argued in the context of civil and criminal evidence include:

Article 3: Prohibition of torture

No one shall be subjected to torture or to inhuman or degrading treatment or punishment.

Article 3 is unlikely to be invoked on a regular basis. Section 76(2)(a) of the Police and Criminal Evidence Act 1984, which requires a court to exclude confession evidence obtained by oppression, partially adopts the substance of the wording in Article 3 in the definition of oppression in section 76(8). Article 3 might be utilised by a defendant as a means of excluding evidence in a criminal trial. A defendant might, for example, argue that the conditions of his detention at a police station or the manner in which an interrogation was conducted amounted to a violation of Article 3 and led him to make incriminating admissions.

Article 6: Right to a fair trial

1. In the determination of his civil rights and obligations or of any criminal charge against him, everyone is entitled to a fair and public hearing within a reasonable time by an independent and impartial tribunal established by law. Judgment shall be pronounced publicly but the press or public may be excluded from all or part of the trial in the interests of morals, public order or national security in a democratic society, where the interests of juveniles or the protection of the private life of the parties so require, or to the extent strictly necessary in the opinion of the court in special circumstances where publicity would prejudice the interests of justice.

2. Everyone charged with a criminal offence shall be presumed innocent until proved guilty according to law.

3. Everyone charged with a criminal offence has the following minimum rights:
   (a) to be informed promptly, in a language which he understands and in detail, of the nature and cause of the accusation against him;
   (b) to have adequate time and facilities for the preparation of his defence;
   (c) to defend himself in person or through legal assistance of his own choosing or, if he has not sufficient means to pay for legal assistance, to be given it free when the interests of justice so require;
   (d) to examine or have examined witnesses against him and to obtain the attendance and examination of witnesses on his behalf under the same conditions as witnesses against him; ...

Article 6(1) applies to both civil and criminal proceedings. Article 6(2) and (3) applies only in the context of criminal proceedings. The question of what amounts to a criminal charge is determined by criteria developed by the European Court of Human Rights and the now defunct Commission, based on an assessment of the true nature and possible outcome of the proceedings. The classification is important because of the more extensive rights available to those facing criminal proceedings under Article 6.

Article 6 is likely to prove the most widely used Convention right by defendants in criminal trials. Potentially it has many implications for rules of evidence and procedure. The right to a fair trial in Article 6(1) is drafted in absolute terms. The presumption of innocence in Article 6(2) however is, like the various specific rights contained in Article 6(3), a component of the general right to a fair trial under Article 6(1). In addition to the rights explicitly stated in Article 6, Strasbourg case law has developed a number of implied rights, including the privilege against self-incrimination, the right to be present at an adversarial hearing and the right to equality of arms. The latter requires neither party be placed at a procedural disadvantage and is enforceable in both civil and criminal proceedings.

In its assessment of the fairness of a trial, the European Court of Human Rights (the Court) has set certain parameters within which a state must operate. The Court is not concerned with the actual guilt or innocence of the applicant or whether a particular piece of evidence should have been deemed inadmissible. Its role under

Article 6 is restricted to an assessment of the overall fairness of the applicant's trial, making that assessment with the benefit of hindsight, based on an holistic overview of the entire proceedings, including any appeal process. In this way it gives member states a substantial degree of autonomy to devise rules of evidence and trial procedure. In *Schenk v Switzerland* (1988) 13 EHRR 242 the Court reiterated its position: 'While Article 6 of the Convention guarantees the right to a fair trial, it does not lay down any rules on the admissibility of evidence as such, which is primarily a matter for regulation under national law. The Court therefore cannot exclude as a matter of principle and in the abstract that unlawfully obtained evidence of the present kind, may be admissible. It has only to ascertain whether Mr Schenk's trial as a whole was fair.'

Given the enforceability of Convention rights in United Kingdom law with the implementation of the HRA, the argument that Convention rights have been violated may arise at any point in the proceedings. It is anticipated that Convention points will be taken in criminal trials at every level and that judges and magistrates will be called upon to rule on the issue of compatibility without the benefit of hindsight that has always been accorded to the Court. An incorrect ruling on a human rights point may have to be rectified on appeal, where the impact of the error on the fairness of the proceedings can more easily be ascertained. The relationship between a finding of unfairness by either the European Court of Human Rights or the Court of Appeal, and the safety of the resulting conviction (which is the sole criteria by which the Court of Appeal determines whether a conviction should stand or be quashed) is considered in Chapter 5.

In terms of criminal evidence, Article 6 may well be invoked to challenge such matters as the admissibility of confession evidence, hearsay, evidence of bad character, illegally obtained evidence, adverse inferences from the defendant's silence and the failure of the prosecution to provide evidential disclosure of its case. The list is by no means exhaustive.

In the civil context it could be argued that in appropriate cases the control exercised by the judge under the Civil Procedure Rules to restrict the issues on which he requires proof and the manner in which proof may be presented, violates a party's right to a fair trial.

Article 8: Right to respect for private and family life

1. Everyone has the right to respect for his private and family life, his home and his correspondence.

2. There shall be no interference by a public authority with the exercise of this right except such as is in accordance with the law and is necessary in a democratic society in the interests of national security, public safety or the economic well-being of the country, for the prevention of disorder or crime, ...

Article 8 seeks to protect the individual from arbitrary interference by the State. It is however a qualified right and permits interference with the right under established principles set out above. It may be used by defendants to challenge the admissibility of evidence obtained unlawfully in breach of the defendant's right to privacy. This is considered in more detail in Chapter 5. Article 8 may also be relied on by claimants in civil proceedings who maintain their substantive right to privacy has been violated by a public authority's actions.

The rights under the Convention represent the minimum rights available in English law. By virtue of section 11(4) of the HRA a person may rely on a Convention right without prejudice to any right conferred by domestic law. In some instances it is likely that existing domestic law goes further than the minimum rights guaranteed under the Convention.

STRASBOURG JURISPRUDENCE – HOW DOES IT WORK?

When applying the provisions of the HRA, courts, practitioners and students alike will be required to take into account a number of potentially difficult issues arising out of the European Convention on Human Rights' status as an international treaty.

The provisions of the Convention seek to balance the rights of individuals against other public interests and this is exemplified in the judgment of the European Court of Human Rights in *Soering v United Kingdom* (1989) 11 EHRR 439: 'Inherent in the whole of the Convention is a search for the fair balance between the demands of the general interest of the community and the requirement of the protection of the individual's human rights.' The principle of proportionality recurs time after time in the interpretation of Convention rights.

Section 2 of the HRA requires all courts and tribunals to take Strasbourg case law into account in interpreting Convention rights. Indeed, no attempt should be made to construe the Convention without reference to its jurisprudence. However, the Convention is interpreted in ways that are quite different from United Kingdom statutes. Decisions of the European Court of Human Rights and the Commission have always depended heavily on the facts of the particular case before them. Most strikingly Strasbourg jurisprudence is not restricted by the application of the *stare decisis* doctrine. In *Tyrer v United Kingdom* (1979–80) 2 EHRR 1, the Convention was described as a 'living instrument' which must be interpreted in the light of present day conditions. It is a body of law that changes with the times. Convention rights should therefore be interpreted by current standards of society which may require domestic courts to reconsider a particular decision of the European Court of Human Rights.

Key principles and doctrines

When called upon to determine whether interference with a human right is justified within the terms of the European Convention on Human Rights, the Court has developed a number of core concepts in its jurisprudence.

The concepts include:

1 the rule of law;
2 legitimacy of aims;
3 proportionality; and
4 margin of appreciation.

Rule of law

However justified an interference with a qualified right might be, it must be prescribed by law. In accordance with the decision in *Sunday Times* v *United Kingdom* (No. 1) (1979–80) 2 EHRR 245, for the interference to be in accordance with the law:

(a) there must be some legal regulation permitting the interference,
(b) the regulations must be readily accessible, and
(c) formulated with such precision as to enable an individual properly to regulate his conduct.

Legitimacy of aim

Where the Convention permits derogation from a right, any interference with the right must be directed towards an identified, legitimate aim. What constitutes a legitimate aim is defined within those articles granting qualified rights. In relation to Article 8, for example, an individual's right to privacy may be interfered with for the purpose of the prevention of disorder or crime.

Proportionality

Any interference with a Convention right must be a proportionate response when measured against the objective that the interference is intended to achieve. It must be no more than is necessary in a democratic society. If a less draconian measure would achieve the identified legitimate aim, the Court is likely to find the Convention right to have been violated. The principle of proportionality is the mechanism used to strike the balance between individual human rights and the protection of society as a whole, identified in the decision of *Soering* v *United Kingdom* above. Although the principle is invoked mostly in the context of qualified rights it can be applied to all Convention rights when determining their scope and substance.

The House of Lords confronted a problem of proportionality in the context of Article 6 in *R* v *A* [2001] 3 All ER 1. At a pre-trial preparatory hearing the defendant sought a ruling that his right to a fair trial under Article 6 was infringed by section 41(3)(c) of the Youth Justice and Criminal Evidence Act 1999 in that it prevented him from cross-examining the complainant about her previous sexual relationship with him. The defendant contended this line of questioning was relevant to his defence which was that the complainant had consented to sexual intercourse with him. The section in question replaced section 2(1) of the Sexual Offences (Amendment) Act 1976. Section 2(1) had been brought into considerable disrepute because it had consistently failed to limit the nature of questioning that could be put to a complainant of rape as regards her past sexual experiences with persons other than the accused. This had the effect of contributing to an absurdly low conviction rate for rape offences. Its replacement, section 41 of the 1999 Act, contains a blanket prohibition on questioning the complainant about a previous sexual relationship with the defendant where consent is in issue. The prohibition gives way to permitted questioning in very narrowly defined instances, which were inapplicable in *R* v *A*.

The House of Lords acknowledged that the restrictions imposed by section 41 of the 1999 Act were directed towards a legitimate aim. However, the right to a fair trial involved balancing a number of different competing interests, including those of the victim. In this particular case the court had to be satisfied that the limitation imposed by section 41 was a proportional response to the concerns it sought to address. In the view of the House of Lords, the blanket prohibition on cross-examination amounted to 'legislative overkill'. To rescue the situation, the House of Lords applied section 3 of the HRA, choosing to read into section 41 an implied provision to the effect that Parliament could not be said to have intended the section to be applied in a way that would impede the defendant's right to a fair trial. Consequently, if the questions to be put to the complainant were relevant to the accused's defence then, on basis of the construction adopted, section 41 did not prevent them from being asked.

Margin of appreciation

Related to the principle of proportionality is the margin of appreciation. The European Court of Human Rights confers on member states a significant degree of autonomy in the application of Convention principles in their domestic law by invoking a margin of appreciation. The rationale for the doctrine is best summed up in the words of the Court's judgment in *Handyside v United Kingdom* (1979–80) 1 EHRR 737:

> By reason of their direct and continuous contact with the vital forces of their countries, state authorities are in principle in a better position than the international judge to give an opinion on the exact content of those requirements as well as on the 'necessity' of a 'restriction' or 'penalty' intended to meet them...

The margin of appreciation is a tool of international law. It is applied by the Court as a means of enabling it to be sensitive to the diverse cultural values and traditions of the member states. It has been applied extensively in the Court's assessment of proportionality issues. After all, individual states are best placed to weigh the competing demands of the public interest on the one hand and individual rights on the other, which their domestic law seeks to accommodate. It has also been applied by the Court in the development of Article 6 rights. Provided the very essence of the right to a fair trial is observed the Court leaves it up to individual states to devise and apply rules of evidence.

As a tool of international law the doctrine should have no application in national law. In determining the actual scope and substance of rights under the Convention any constraint the Court felt in a particular case before it by the operation of the margin of appreciation ought to be ignored by domestic courts. Buxton LJ described the position in *R v Stratford Justices, ex parte Imbert* [1999] 2 Cr App R 276 as follows:

> The application of the doctrine of the margin of appreciation would appear to be solely a matter for the Strasbourg Court. By appealing to the doctrine that court recognises that the detailed content of at least some Convention obligations is more appropriately determined in the light of national conditions. In the hands of the Strasbourg Court, however, that approach is necessarily translated into a view of the meaning and reach of the detailed provisions of the Convention that is flexible or, according to the observer's point of view, relativist. ...

The English judge cannot therefore himself apply or have recourse to the doctrine of the margin of appreciation as implemented by the Strasbourg Court. He must, however, recognise the impact of that doctrine upon the Strasbourg Court's analysis of the meaning and implications of the broad terms of the Convention provisions: which is the obvious source of guidance as to those provisions, and a source that in any event the English court will be obliged, once section 2(1)(a) of the 1998 Act has come into force, to take into account.

Domestic courts should therefore feel free to develop human rights jurisprudence under the HRA unconstrained by the margin of appreciation applied in its international law sense in Convention jurisprudence. The signs are that the House of Lords is rising to the challenge particularly in the context of Article 6.

The right to a fair trial under Article 6(1) is absolute and is supplemented by specific safeguards guaranteed under Article 6(2) and (3). Fairness at trial is characterised in a number of different ways and, as we have already seen, in developing its jurisprudence on Article 6, a number of implied rights have been added by the European Court of Human Rights. As Lord Clyde in *Brown* v *Stott* [2001] 2 WLR 817 (Privy Council) correctly observes: 'while there can be no doubt that the right to a fair trial is an absolute right, precisely what is comprised in the concept of fairness may be open to varied analysis'.

Both the Privy Council and the House of Lords have invoked their own margin of appreciation in relation to proportionality issues arising in connection with Article 6. The House of Lords invoked it in the decision in *R* v *Lambert* [2001] 3 All ER 577, which raised an issue relating to the presumption of innocence guaranteed under Article 6(2) (considered at length in Chapter 11). In the Privy Council decision in *Brown* v *Stott* (a case alleging violation of the privilege against self-incrimination) Lord Bingham observed:

> The jurisprudence of the European Court very clearly establishes that while the overall fairness of a criminal trial cannot be compromised, the constituent rights comprised, whether expressly or implicitly, within article 6 are not themselves absolute. Limited qualification of these rights is acceptable if reasonably directed by national authorities towards a clear and proper public objective and if representing no greater qualification than the situation calls for. The general language of the Convention could have led to the formulation of hard-edged and inflexible statements of principle from which no departure could be sanctioned whatever the background or the circumstances. But this approach has been consistently eschewed by the court throughout its history.

Lord Hope concluded:

> I would hold therefore that the jurisprudence of the European Court tells us that the questions that should be addressed when issues are raised about an alleged incompatibility with a right under article 6 of the Convention are the following: (1) is the right which is in question an absolute right, or is it a right which is open to modification or restriction because it is not absolute? (2) if it is not absolute does the modification or restriction which is contended for have a legitimate aim in the public interest? (3) if so, is there a reasonable relationship of proportionality between the means employed and the aim sought to be realised? The answer to the question whether the right is or is not absolute is to be found by examining the terms of the article in the light of the judgments of the court. The question whether a legitimate aim is being pursued enables account to be taken of the public interest in the rule of law. The principle of proportionality directs attention to the question

whether a fair balance has been struck between the general interest of the community in the realisation of that aim and the protection of the fundamental rights of the individual.

A similar point is made by Lord Justice Auld in his Criminal Courts Review Report, published in October 2001 and considered further in Chapter 4. He regards the defendant's right to a fair trial is 'as near absolute as any notion can be'. However he observes: 'in its application to different circumstances and on a case by case basis, considerations of balance or proportionality inevitably intrude'.

CONCLUSION

The influence of the Human Rights Act 1998 is already being felt. Jurisprudence on human rights matters will continue to develop at a steady pace. The actual and anticipated impact of the HRA on various areas of criminal and civil evidence is addressed further in the chapters below.

Further reading

Ashworth, A., 'Criminal Proceedings After the Human Rights Act: The First Year' [2001] Crim LR 855.

Auld, Lord Justice (2001) *A Review of the Criminal Courts of England and Wales*, www.criminal-courts-review.org.uk.

Clayton, R. and Tomlinson, H. (2000) *The Law of Human Rights*, Oxford University Press.

Harris, D.J., O'Boyle, M. and Warbrick, C. (2001) *The Law of the European Convention on Human Rights*, Butterworths Law.

Wadham, J. and Mountfield, H. (2000) *Human Rights Act 1998*, Blackstone Press.

Part 2

CRIMINAL EVIDENCE

Chapter 3

THE PROCESS OF PROOF IN CRIMINAL TRIALS

INTRODUCTION

Whilst the principles of criminal evidence provide a fascinating forum for academic examination, they have a very real and practical application in the courts. As previously explained, this book seeks to steer a course between the analysis of the rules of evidence and their application in practice. In the following pages we explore the process of proof in the system of factual inquiry in England and Wales. The process will be familiar to those who apply the rules of evidence in criminal courts on a regular basis. For those interested in the academic study of this subject matter, the process of proof is explored with the intention of putting the rules of criminal evidence into their overall context. In this chapter we concentrate on the wider picture of what evidence is, how it is obtained, utilised and ultimately presented at trial.

PROOF

Whilst the rules of criminal evidence are of considerable importance, proving facts in a criminal case involves considerably more than their application.

Criminal trials are of course a feature of everyday life. Trials range from the mundane prosecutions of countless careless driving offences and petty thefts to infamous murder trials such as those of Rosemary West and Dr Harold Shipman, and trials involving celebrities such as that of the novelist and peer Jeffrey Archer, convicted of perjury and perverting the course of justice. Common to all criminal trials is the need to prove disputed versions of past factual events. Through the process of proof, the criminal trial aims to determine the guilt or innocence of the accused. Where an accused disputes the prosecution's version of the facts by pleading not guilty, the accused puts the prosecution to proof of its case.

Without evidence there can be no proof. Evidence provides the court with information. Proving facts through the presentation of evidence means convincing a court to accept a particular version of events. The vast majority of participants in the criminal justice process deploy the services of a trial advocate whose job it is to persuade the court that their client's version of events is truthful and accurate.

The search for the truth through the process of proof in a criminal trial is entirely dependent upon the involvement of a number of key participants. Human nature being what it is, such a system of inquiry can never be infallible. Witness testimony is based on the recollections of different people who witnessed the events with their own senses. Recollection is not always accurate, particularly if the witnessed event was over in a matter of seconds or was committed in circumstances of fear or excitement. Memory fades and is fashioned over time. A witness's evidence may not be received in court until many months after the incident. Not all witnesses give an account based on their honest recollection of events. Bias on the part of the witness or the will to perjure themselves may result in the court receiving evidence which is misleading and untrue. Magistrates and jurors are expected to see through the fallibility of witnesses but have in fact no training or special skills in fact finding. The fact finder is equipped only with his or her common sense. Trials may take days, even weeks. Evidence is extracted and presented in a protracted manner. Rather like the witness, the fact finder is expected to digest and recollect all the information which may be factually complex and is further expected to apply detailed legal directions to the information presented before reaching a verdict.

The decision as to whether a case has been proved to the requisite criminal standard is measured on the basis of what probably occurred as opposed to what certainly occurred. In reality a court can never know the true existence of a set of past facts. It cannot be transported back in time to view events as they happened. The best a court can do is to reach a decision based on what probably occurred. A not guilty verdict does not mean that a defendant is in fact innocent and a guilty verdict does not mean that a defendant is in fact guilty. A verdict is no more than the opinion of one or more fact finders (magistrates or jury) based on selective evidence presented to them by the prosecution and the defence. If the evidence presented to them was mistaken, fabricated or incomplete, or was ignored or not understood, then the verdict reached might well be erroneous.

Whilst all lawyers are taught to understand and apply the rules of evidence, very few are taught how to construct a logically sound argument based on evidential propositions, or how to spot a logical flaw in a case where the evidence seems convincing. For many advocates such skills are fashioned and honed through experience. The study of fact analysis is both rigorous and intellectually demanding.

Although the principles of logic can help the advocate to construct a plausible and coherent theory of a particular case based on the available and admissible evidence, the theory has to be presented and the fact finder must be persuaded of that party's version of the facts and the interpretation of the substantive law applied to those facts. Behavioural psychology and the art of communication have much to teach the aspiring advocate in this regard. Even when all the available evidence is ably presented to the fact finder in court, there is of course no guarantee that the jury or magistrates will find the facts proven.

The centrepiece of the process of proof in the adversarial system of justice is the trial itself, but the trial is the 'end game'. The process of proof begins with the commission of an offence and its consequent investigation. If the defendant maintains his innocence throughout, it ends with the verdict of a jury or magistrates. Concentrating purely on the application of the rules of evidence at trial ignores the fact that judgments about the state of the evidence and the likely application of the rules of evidence have to be made throughout the process.

Participants in the process of proof

Police

The criminal process is usually initiated by a police investigation. Sometimes it is preceded by an arrest; sometimes an arrest follows the process of investigation. As part of the process of gathering evidence, the police will talk to many different witnesses and take formal statements from some of them. Not every witness interviewed by the police will ultimately be called upon to give evidence if the case is prosecuted and goes to court. As part of the investigation, however, there is a statutory obligation upon the police to appoint a disclosure officer whose duty it is to record and retain all information and material gathered or generated during the investigation. The failure of the police to provide pre-trial disclosure of evidence damaging to its case has led to a number of well-publicised miscarriages of justice in the past. The obligation to disclose information and material recorded by the disclosure officer is now contained in the Criminal Procedure and Investigations Act 1996.

To assist the police in their task of unearthing evidence extensive investigative powers are available under various statutes, including the Misuse of Drugs Act 1971 and the Firearms Act 1980. The most important general investigative powers are those contained in the Police and Criminal Evidence Act 1984 (PACE). PACE gives the police extensive powers to search persons (sections 1 and 32) and their property and premises for evidence (sections 18 and 32). In addition PACE empowers the police to take fingerprints (section 61), non-intimate samples from a suspect without consent in certain circumstances (section 62) and the power to take intimate samples with the suspect's consent (section 63). Additionally the police have the power to seize evidence and powers to detain and interrogate the suspect (section 37).

General police powers under PACE are supplemented by five Codes of Practice, A–E. Various safeguards afforded to the suspect under PACE and the Codes of Practice circumscribe the investigative powers of the police. These include section 56 of PACE (the right of the suspect to have someone informed of his arrest) and section 58 of PACE (the right of the suspect to consult a solicitor in private at any time).

The Codes of Practice seek to regulate the proper conduct of criminal investigations. The safeguards detailed in the Codes of Practice are mainly designed to ensure the quality and reliability of evidence yielded as part of the investigative process. Code C is particularly important as it regulates the detention, treatment and questioning of suspects at the police station. It contains safeguards for suspects by making provision for the regular review of their detention, restricting the length of police interviews, prescribing hours of rest and breaks for refreshment. The Codes are not rules of law but, by virtue of section 67(11) of PACE, breach of them is admissible in evidence in criminal proceedings where their application appears relevant to any issue arising in the proceedings.

In conducting an investigation, the police will have in mind the rules relating to the admissibility of evidence at any subsequent trial. To some extent, the rules shape the manner in which crimes are investigated. This is particularly true of identification and confession evidence. A failure to collect or obtain evidence in accordance with the proper procedures set out in PACE and the Codes of Practice can lead to prosecution evidence, such as a confession, being excluded under sections 76 and 78 of PACE. The admissibility of illegally obtained evidence is considered in more detail in Chapter 5.

On arrest, the suspect is booked into custody by the custody sergeant. In evidential terms custody officers have a very important role in that they act as a buffer between the coercive powers available to the police and the rights of the suspect in custody. The custody sergeant, who is independent of the investigation, is responsible for compiling the custody record which may become a very important document in evidential terms at any later trial. The custody record is a complete record of all that occurs during a suspect's detention. It will include complaints made by the suspect in respect of treatment in custody, requests for medication or a solicitor. Also included in the custody record will be the decision to carry out various procedures such as an intimate search. One of the first things a defence representative will consult on being called to a police station to advise a suspect in custody is the custody record. In the event of proceedings being taken against the suspect, the defendant is entitled to a copy of the custody record which can be used for evidential purposes at a later criminal trial.

At the investigation stage the police are not constrained by the formal rules of evidence. The fact that someone has previous convictions for a similar offence may be used by the police to identify that person as a suspect and information on those convictions may well be crucial to the investigation. However, in taking the decision to charge the suspect, the police must bear in mind that such evidence may not be admissible when the matter comes to trial. Having sufficient evidence to charge an individual is not the same thing as having sufficient evidence to convict the defendant beyond reasonable doubt.

Investigations vary in length. Once the police have sufficient evidence to charge an individual, the formal commencement of the criminal litigation process begins. Of course the investigation does not end at this point, as the process of evidence gathering continues.

The formal commencement of the criminal process begins with a suspect being charged with a criminal offence or being summonsed to attend court to answer an allegation specified in the summons. The status of the individual changes from suspect to defendant.

All criminal offences are classified in one of three ways. Offences are either summary only, indictable only or either way. A summary offence must be tried summarily in the magistrates' court. Summary offences include the less serious offences of common assault, assaulting a police officer in the execution of his duty, taking a vehicle without the owner's consent and driving without due care and attention. An indictable offence must be tried on indictment in the Crown Court. Indictable offences are the more serious offences – rape, murder, manslaughter and causing death by dangerous driving are all examples. An either way offence may be tried on indictment in the Crown Court or summarily before a magistrates' court. Assuming the defendant is to plead not guilty to an either way offence, a mode of trial inquiry will be held to determine where the case should be tried. Either way offences include theft, obtaining property by deception and assault occasioning actual bodily harm. The classification of a criminal offence is important because it determines its procedural course.

Crown Prosecution Service

The Crown Prosecution Service (CPS) was created by section 1 of the Prosecution of Offences Act 1985. A major part of its function is to take over the conduct of all criminal proceedings commenced by the police and to prosecute the vast majority of criminal offences through the court.

Once the criminal litigation process has been formally invoked, the police file, containing copies of witness statements, record of searches and interviews with the suspect will be sent to the CPS. The file will comprise the evidence the police intend to use against the defendant in court. However, it will also contain a schedule of non-sensitive additional information which the police do not intend to use as evidence at trial. The evidence disclosed in the police file will be reviewed by a CPS lawyer who will decide whether the charges brought by the police are justified, both in terms of the evidence available and the public interest. If the CPS considers the charges are not justified it can discontinue the prosecution. It can also substitute different charges if it considers the evidence merits this. Such decisions are made without the opportunity of speaking with prosecution witnesses directly. In fact the CPS is unlikely to meet with prosecution witnesses until the day of trial.

The CPS is independent of the police. The decision to continue the prosecution is based on a two-stage test: the evidential test and the public interest test. The tests are explained in the Code for Crown Prosecutors (2000).

With regard to the evidential test, the CPS must first of all be satisfied that there is enough evidence for a 'realistic prospect of conviction in respect of each charge'. In ascertaining this, the CPS should consider amongst other things:

(a) The likelihood that evidence will be excluded by the court, for example because of an impropriety in the way that it was gathered, or because of the rule against hearsay.

(b) The reliability of the evidence, for example whether identification evidence is likely to be excluded on the basis of the guidelines in *R v Turnbull* [1977] QB 224.

Arguably the detachment of the CPS lawyer from the investigation process enables him to take a dispassionate and objective view of the evidence and is entirely consistent with his duty to assist the administration of justice in a fair, independent and objective manner. The CPS has significant obligations as regards the disclosure of evidence under the Criminal Procedure and Investigations Act 1996 and must keep the matter of disclosure of evidence under constant review.

The construction of the case for the Crown at trial is therefore the responsibility of the police and the CPS working in conjunction.

There are of course other prosecuting agencies, aside from the CPS, including the Inland Revenue, Customs and Excise, the Serious Fraud Office, local authority departments such as Trading Standards, the Health and Safety Executive and private organisations such as the RSPCA as well as private individuals. Whatever the prosecuting agency, they must all work within the recognised mechanisms in which proof is presented and ensure compliance with the rules of evidence.

The defendant

The defendant is not a voluntary or indeed willing participant in the criminal justice process. He may be charged with more than one offence or jointly charged with others.

For some repeat offenders the criminal justice system holds no fear and little mystery. For others however the experience may be bewildering and daunting. The extent of the defendant's involvement depends upon the course of events. At some stage he is likely to use the services of a defence solicitor. A significant number of defendants plead guilty to some or all of the offences with which they are charged. Considerable pressure is placed upon a defendant to plead guilty at an early stage in the process, as a timely guilty plea can result in a much reduced sentence by virtue of section 48 of the Criminal Justice and Public Order Act 1994. Where a defendant chooses to plead guilty the evidence against him is never tested in open court. The decision to plead guilty is often taken following consultation with a solicitor. Such a decision is usually based on the solicitor's view of the evidence as disclosed in written form by the CPS prior to trial.

The defendant who chooses to plead not guilty puts the prosecution to proof of its case. The defendant is not a competent witness for the prosecution in these circumstances but is a competent witness in his own defence and may therefore choose whether or not to give evidence on oath.

Defence advocate

The defence solicitor is immensely important in shaping the process of proof. The defendant is entitled to be represented by a solicitor of his choice or by a duty solicitor at either the police station or at court. The Duty Solicitor Scheme seeks to ensure that no suspect is without legal representation in the early stages of the criminal process. Access to legal advice helps protect the civil liberties of the suspect. It also helps to equalise the imbalance between the investigating authorities and the suspect, thereby ensuring greater reliability of any resulting evidence.

The defence solicitor is likely to be engaged in the evidence gathering process at an early stage. Having been arrested a suspect may well seek the advice of a solicitor. The instructed solicitor must make an assessment of the strength of the evidence against his client and be prepared to make appropriate representations. The solicitor may need to advise his client whether to answer police questions or to remain silent, whether to consent to giving a sample of body fluid such as semen for investigative purposes, or whether to participate in an identification procedure. His role extends to ensuring the police comply with PACE and the Codes of Practice in the conduct of their investigation. Every decision taken by a suspect based on his solicitor's advice including refusing to provide an intimate sample or to participate in an identification parade may have evidential repercussions at any subsequent trial. It can influence the decision to charge, the decision to plead guilty and may give rise to arguments about the admissibility of evidence at the trial itself. The evidential consequences of choosing a particular course of action at the police station whilst the suspect is under investigation must always be borne in mind.

After the defendant is charged or following the service of a summons upon him, he is likely to seek further help from a solicitor. The solicitor will want to hear his client's version of events. A detailed written statement will be taken from the defendant.

A solicitor will find it difficult to advise his client whether or not to plead guilty where little is known of the prosecution's case. Under the rules relating to pre-trial disclosure, which are considered in Chapter 9, the prosecution must disclose the nature of the evidence it intends to rely on at trial. This will take the form of written witness statements, records kept as part of the investigation into the offence and a copy of any tape-recorded interview. An important part of the solicitor's role will be to evaluate the strength or otherwise of the prosecution's case based on the written disclosure of its

evidence. This might well include consideration of possible challenges to the admissibility of prosecution evidence.

The process of gathering evidence on behalf of the defendant will begin as soon as
possible. This may involve tracing and interviewing potential defence witnesses. It can
include visiting the scene of an incident and obtaining an expert witness's opinion on
a particular matter.

The defence solicitor's primary obligation is to represent his client in court and to
put forward his client's version of the events. The solicitor is under no wider obligation to assist the court to reach a verdict based on the truth of what actually occurred.
Consequently, defence witnesses who are able to give relevant but unhelpful evidence
to the defendant's case may be ignored. There is no obligation on the defendant to give
the prosecution or the court notice of such individuals.

If the defendant is to plead not guilty, he will be subjected to a trial either in the magistrates' court or the Crown Court depending on the classification of the offence.
Sometimes magistrates will decline jurisdiction to try an either way offence summarily.
This is quite common where the case involves complex evidential or legal issues or the
magistrates consider that their powers of punishment will be insufficient in the event
of the defendant being convicted. If the magistrates are content to accept summary
jurisdiction of an either way offence, the defendant is given the choice as to where he
wishes to be tried. He can only be tried summarily with his consent and has the
absolute right to insist on a trial before a jury in the Crown Court. The decision as to
where to be tried is an important one and should only be made in consultation with a
solicitor. Pre-trial disclosure of prosecution evidence in either way cases has always
been mandatory for this reason. It helps the defendant to reach an informed decision
as to where his case is best tried. The dynamics of being tried summarily before magistrates are different from the dynamics of being tried before a jury. The solicitor's advice
as to where his client should be tried may well be based on a combination of evidential and extraneous evidential considerations.

Relevant evidential factors that favour a Crown Court trial in preference to a trial
before magistrates include:

1 The fact that there is a widely held perception that a defendant has a greater chance
   of being acquitted in the Crown Court where he is tried before a jury of his peers.
   This perception is based on the fact that magistrates try far more cases on a regular basis than jurors who try usually one or possibly two cases only. Magistrates are
   thereby perceived to be more 'case hardened' and less amenable to giving the defendant the benefit of the doubt. There is a further perception that magistrates are
   more inclined to believe the evidence of the police. It is said that juries are more
   mindful of the direction that they must only convict if they are satisfied beyond reasonable doubt.

2 The procedure for dealing with the admissibility of disputed evidence is more
   effective in the Crown Court because there is a separation of function between
   judge and jury. The jury is the sole arbiter of fact. The judge is the sole arbiter
   of law. The judge determines disputed evidence in the absence of the jury. In
   summary trials there is no separation of function. Magistrates must first hear the
   disputed evidence before ruling on its admissibility. If the evidence is deemed

inadmissible the magistrates are expected to put it out of their minds and to continue to try the defendant.

Whether the defendant is tried in the magistrates' court or in the Crown Court the preparation for the trial will involve both the prosecution and the defence advocates reviewing the evidence, engaging in legal research and making decisions as to how best to conduct the case. For the defence solicitor this might include pressing the prosecution to make further disclosure of its evidence and, if necessary, making an application to the court to force such disclosure.

Trial preparation requires advocates to think about the most logically persuasive way in which to present their case having regard to the rules of evidence. This will include critical judgments about which witnesses to call and in what order. Each side must ensure the attendance of its witnesses through the issuing of a witness summons, if necessary. Clearly the more detached and the more 'conventional' a witness appears to be, the greater his or her credibility is likely to be perceived. This exercise in critical judgment is much harder for the prosecution because the CPS will not have interviewed the witnesses who are likely to be called to give evidence for the prosecution at trial.

The decision as to whether the defendant should be called to give evidence in support of his own defence must be carefully considered. It has a number of important evidential consequences which are reviewed in Chapter 7.

An advocate's evaluation of the overall state of the evidence must include consideration of the rules relating to the admissibility of evidence. If a challenge to the admissibility of an item of evidence is anticipated the arguments for and against should have been thoroughly researched as part of the case preparation. Where a particular piece of evidence is disputed it is likely to be the subject of argument and a judicial ruling at the beginning of the trial or at a pre-trial hearing.

A solicitor usually provides representation at a summary trial. For trials on indictment, which tend to concern more serious criminal offences, representation is likely to be provided by a barrister or a solicitor-advocate with a higher right of audience qualification. In such a case, the defence solicitor will brief counsel to appear on behalf of the defendant. Most Crown Court barristers are experienced advocates who are well versed in the art of persuasion and are able to bring an air of detachment to the case. A barrister will usually review the evidence in the case in advance of the trial. As a result of the barrister's evaluation, further evidence or disclosure might be sought and in some cases the defendant may be persuaded to plead guilty based on counsel's view of the evidence.

As the burden of proving the defendant's guilt rests with the prosecution, the prosecutor begins the trial with an opening speech. In a summary trial the defence advocate may not give a closing speech if he chooses to make an opening speech. The intention behind the opening speech is to focus the minds of the fact finders. Such a speech should be delivered with convincing effect. The prosecutor will advance the prosecution's theory of the case based on the evidence and will explain what it must prove and how it intends to do so. This is followed by the prosecution's presentation of its evidence. Each prosecution witness will be examined in chief whereby the advocate elicits the witness's testimony through question and answer. In order to prepare for this stage of the trial, detailed consideration will have been given to the questions to be asked, based on witnesses' earlier written statements. Following examination-in-chief, the prosecution witnesses will be cross-examined by the defence. This again requires careful trial preparation as to the nature of the questions and the manner in which they are put to the opposing witnesses.

The party calling the witness then undertakes re-examination. Its purpose is strictly limited to repairing any damage occasioned by cross-examination. Any written evidence will be presented and the prosecuting advocate will close the case for the prosecution. The defence will then present its evidence, including that of the defendant if he chooses to give evidence. Witnesses for the defence will be subjected to an examination-in-chief followed by cross-examination and re-examination.

Once all the evidence has been presented each advocate will be called upon to make a closing speech. This is the final opportunity to appeal to the fact finders and as such it should be presented with full persuasive force. The closing speech gives each advocate the opportunity of putting their spin on the evidence presented by stressing the evidence in their favour, including any concessions gleaned in cross-examination and any weaknesses in their opponent's case. The defence advocate will usually take the opportunity of reminding the fact finders that if they are left in any doubt as regards the defendant's guilt, they must acquit.

Witnesses

Witnesses are indispensable to the process of proof in criminal proceedings. Lay witnesses are called for the purpose of giving evidence of facts witnessed by them which have relevance to the issues to be proved in a case. It should not be assumed however that all witnesses who give evidence on oath are likely to 'tell the truth, the whole truth and nothing but the truth'. In *Cross-Examination in Criminal Trials*, Marcus Stone concluded that lying witnesses are rife. Most witnesses are in a sense inherently biased in favour of the party calling them. The skill of the cross-examining advocate in exposing bias and lack of veracity in a witness is crucial, as the fact finder will inevitably assess a witness's credibility when deciding whether the witness is telling the truth. The contribution of the lay witness to the search for the truth is a most interesting one and has been the subject of numerous psychological studies (see Further reading below). The extent to which the adversarial trial enhances or detracts from this contribution is considered further in the following chapter.

In addition to lay witnesses, either side might instruct an expert witness to give evidence at the trial. The general rule is that opinion evidence is inadmissible. However, if the fact finder is required to reach a conclusion on a matter outside his or her general competency, expert opinion evidence may be admitted to assist in that task. Increasingly expert opinion evidence is becoming more and more important as regards the process of proof. In some trials guilt or innocence is determined by which of two competing expert opinions the fact finder believes. Expert opinion evidence is considered in detail in Chapter 17.

Fact finders

The trial is the culmination of the process of proof. The participants described above have been responsible for the collation, construction and presentation of the evidence.

The task of evaluating the evidence and deciding where the truth lies is ultimately that of the magistrates or a jury, depending on where the trial is conducted. In a jury trial, the jury is assisted in its task by the judge. In the magistrates' court, the justices' clerk provides assistance.

Magistrates

A summary trial is conducted before lay magistrates or occasionally before a district judge (magistrates' courts), formerly known as a stipendiary magistrate, who is legally qualified. A summary trial will be held whenever a defendant pleads not guilty to a summary only offence, or pleads not guilty to an either way offence in circumstances where the defendant has consented to have his case dealt with summarily.

Since magistrates summarily try 95% of all criminal cases their role in fact finding is vitally important. Their ranks are almost exclusively comprised of lay volunteers and as such they have no formal training in fact evaluation. A legally qualified justices' clerk (also known as the magistrates' adviser) advises them on matters of law, evidence and procedure. The justices' clerk is required to compile a verbatim record of the entire summary trial for the purposes of any subsequent appeal.

Magistrates are arbiters of both law and fact. This can create a problem in respect of the admissibility of disputed evidence. Where magistrates are invited to rule on the admissibility of evidence such as a disputed confession, they are required to hear argument about the circumstances in which the confession was obtained before applying the rules relating to the admissibility of confession evidence. If they decide to exclude the confession, they must put it out of their minds and go on hearing the case.

Magistrates have traditionally not given reasons for their decisions in court. As a consequence of the implementation of the Human Rights Act 1998 (see Chapter 2), magistrates must give reasons sufficient for the parties to understand the basis on which the court's decision has been reached. One further consequence of the 1998 Act has been to introduce an openness in the way in which justices' clerks advise magistrates. It has long been the practice that the clerk's advice to the magistrates is given in private, but the effect of the Act is that any advice given in private must now be regarded as provisional. It should be repeated in open court and the prosecution and defence should be invited to make representations on it. Depending on any representations made, the clerk's advice may need to be reformulated.

Jury

All indictable offences are dealt with in the Crown Court. Where a defendant pleads not guilty to an indictable only offence, or not guilty to an either way offence which has been committed to the Crown Court, the defendant will be tried on indictment by a jury of his peers. The choice of trial before a jury is regarded by many as a cherished fundamental right in a democratic society. The public participation of the jury lends credence and moral validity to verdicts in criminal trials. Cases are tried according to the evidence presented in court. Knowledge of the case or of any of the participants disqualifies a person from being a member of the jury for that particular case. The elimination of bias and possible prejudice is felt to be very important. Strict contempt laws apply in an attempt to immunise prospective jurors from prejudicial pre-trial publicity.

Most juries comprise 12 individuals selected at random from the electoral register in accordance with the Juries Act 1974. Each serving juror swears an oath by which they promise to faithfully try the defendant and give a true verdict according to the evidence. Jurors are the sole arbiters of fact. They must decide whether a particular witness can be believed and ultimately whether the prosecution has discharged its burden of proving the defendant's guilt beyond reasonable doubt. Decisions in relation to the law and the disputed admissibility of evidence remain the sole preserve of the trial judge. Jurors are instructed to apply the law and the rules of evidence as explained to them by the judge at the conclusion of the evidence in the case. If a dispute as regards the admissibility of evidence arises it is usually brought to the judge's attention before the jury is sworn in. Where an issue of law or disputed evidence arises during the trial, it is resolved in the absence of the jury. If the judge deems the disputed evidence to be inadmissible it is never referred to in the jury's hearing.

It is a serious and onerous task to sit as a juror. A finding of guilt in relation to a serious crime may well result in imprisonment for the convicted offender. The formality and solemnity of the trial is very visible.

Jurors are not trained to evaluate facts. Instead they are expected to apply their common sense in making decisions about the evidence in a case. They must sit passively and listen to evidence which may be technical and complex. As a result some trials can last for weeks, even months. Jurors are not allowed to discuss the evidence outside the jury room and they deliberate in secret and do not have to give reasons for the verdict they reach. The jury is required to concentrate over a long period of time and is expected to remember all of the evidence it hears. It cannot ask questions directly of the advocates or the witnesses and may be kept in ignorance of relevant evidence through the application of mandatory rules of evidence and the exercise of judicial discretion to exclude evidence. The current system does little to assist jurors in their task and is highlighted for specific criticism by Lord Justice Auld in his Criminal Courts Review Report, which is considered in Chapter 4. He observes:

> To anyone other than lawyers steeped in the procedural traditions of the criminal courts, this must seem a strange way to expect jurors, upon whose understanding and judgment so much depends, to do justice in the case. When they embark upon it they are given no objective or convenient outline in oral or written form of its essentials, the nature of the allegation, what facts have to be proved, what facts are in issue and what questions they are there to decide. And, mostly they have little in the way of a written aide-memoire to which they can have recourse as the case unfolds to relate the evidence to such questions. Any experienced court observer has only to note the exhaustion, and sometimes the distress, of jurors as a case of some length or complexity moves towards its end. ...
>
> Depending on the case, on the nature, volume and detail of the evidence and on the aptitude of individual jurors to absorb it, the repetitive nature of the process ... may become tedious in the extreme. (Chapter 11, at paragraphs 18 and 19; footnotes omitted)

There is little doubt that the presence of the jury is largely responsible for a number of the existing rules of evidence including hearsay and the rules restricting the admission of aspects of past bad character of the defendant. The formulation and application of many of the rules of evidence are based on assumptions about the way in which jurors reach decisions. Research cannot however verify these assumptions either way, as section 8 of the Contempt of Court Act 1981 forbids any empirical research into the way juries reach their decisions. The jury is expected to apply complex directions as to the use it can make of certain aspects of evidence in the case. To what extent the jury understands the instructions and abides by them is the subject of constant speculation by academics, practitioners and psychologists.

Judge

In the relatively small number of cases that are tried in the Crown Court, there is a strict division of responsibilities between judge and jury. The judge rules on all matters of law and procedure. He determines both the relevance and the admissibility of disputed evidence in the absence of the jury. Procedural matters which can have significant evidential repercussions for the defendant, such as the decision to sever an indictment and order separate trials for a person charged with more than one offence, are taken by the trial judge. The issue of how much weight to give to particular aspects of the evidence is the prerogative of the jury.

The trial judge keeps the worst excesses of the adversarial system of trial in check. He can for example limit the nature of questioning in cross-examination. He is impartial and completely independent of the parties and must always give the appearance of so being.

A judge has the power to withdraw a case from a jury and direct an acquittal. However, the judge has no power to direct the jury to convict, even though the evidence may be overwhelming. Fundamentally, it is the duty of the trial judge to ensure the defendant receives a fair trial. He discharges this duty in a number of different ways. He exercises control over the process of proof by ensuring the rules of evidence and procedure are complied with. Sometimes mandatory rules of evidence oblige the judge to render evidence inadmissible. In most other instances, however, the judge is imbued with discretion to exclude relevant evidence. A judge must exercise his discretion to exclude evidence if the fairness of the proceedings demands it. Fundamental to the right to a fair trial is the requirement that the trial judge exclude evidence the prejudicial effect of which exceeds its probative value. The right to a fair trial potentially encompasses many disparate aspects. The relationship between the right and the discretionary exclusion of evidence is considered fully in Chapter 5.

A very important part of the judge's function is to sum up the case and direct the jury. The judge directs the jury on what matters need to be proved by the prosecution and what matters, if any, need to be proved by the defendant. He will direct them as to the appropriate standard of proof. He must also direct them on specific aspects of evidence law, for example on the adverse inferences that can be drawn from a defendant's silence. If particular evidence needs supporting or corroborating in some way, it is the judge's duty to point this out. Similarly, in the context of identification evidence, the dangers of relying on such evidence need to be spelled out. If the jury has heard evidence of the defendant's good or bad character, the judge is required to explain what evidential use a jury can make of this. In the final part of his summing up the judge will remind the jury of the evidence it has heard. Providing the judge observes the fundamental requirement of fairness, he is entitled to give his opinion on the evidence, as a means of assisting the jury.

Incorrect verdicts

Evidence does not cease to be considered once a trial is over. Where a defendant has been convicted on indictment before a Crown Court the process of appeal is governed by section 2(1) of the Criminal Appeal Act 1968, as amended by the Criminal Appeal Act 1995. The section states quite simply that the Court of Appeal 'shall allow an appeal against conviction if the conviction is unsafe'. The test of what constitutes an 'unsafe' conviction is a subjective one. Lord Kilbrandon encapsulated its meaning in *Stafford* v *DPP* [1947] AC 878 by asking: 'Have I a reasonable doubt, or perhaps even a lurking doubt that this conviction is unsafe?'

Through the process of appeal the Court of Appeal hands down precedents and useful guidance on the application of rules of criminal evidence for use in future cases. The large number of miscarriages of justice that have come to light in recent years have highlighted serious flaws in the way in which evidence is gathered and disclosed and have led to a number of significant legislative changes affecting the rules governing the admissibility of evidence, including the Police and Criminal Evidence Act 1984 and the Criminal Procedure and Investigations Act 1996.

A fair trial process must be prepared to acknowledge its mistakes and change the outcome to avoid a miscarriage of justice. A miscarriage of justice has many causes: witness unreliability, witnesses providing fabricated evidence, errors of the trial judge in the way in which he conducts the trial, including admitting prejudicial evidence or preventing relevant defence evidence from being admitted. Most of the recent miscarriages of justice have stemmed from a failure by prosecuting authorities to disclose relevant evidence which either undermined the prosecution's case or which could have supported the defence case. The appeals of the Guildford Four and Judith Ward are examples of this. In other instances reliance on untrue confession evidence has resulted in a number of notorious miscarriages, including Judith Ward, the Birmingham Six and the Bridgewater Three. In some of these cases the confessions were obtained as a result of police mistreatment. In other instances they were obtained by a failure on the part of the police and prosecuting authorities to identify significant mental impairment of the suspect, rendering them particularly vulnerable to police pressure.

The Court of Appeal will hear argument on the points giving rise to the appeal and will decide whether the conviction can stand in accordance with the test in section 2(1) of the Criminal Appeal Act 1968, as amended. Section 23 of the Criminal Appeal Act 1968 gives the Court of Appeal discretionary power to receive fresh evidence on appeal. In deciding whether to receive such evidence, the Court of Appeal must have regard to whether the evidence:

(a) is capable of belief;
(b) appears to afford any ground for allowing the appeal;
(c) would have been admissible at trial; and
(d) there is a reasonable explanation for the failure to adduce the evidence at trial.

There is one further possible route which may lead to a successful appeal and that is through the Criminal Cases Review Commission (CCRC). This body was set up in 1997 as a response to the recommendations of the Royal Commission on Criminal Justice in 1993. It replaces the function once undertaken by the Home Secretary by which he had the power to refer a conviction back to the Court of Appeal. The CCRC is an independent body. It has considerable powers to investigate cases and to refer them back to the Court of Appeal if there is a real possibility that the conviction would not be upheld were such a reference made.

Appeals from magistrates' courts can either be made to the Crown Court by way of re-hearing, the Divisional Court by way of case stated or on application for judicial review to the High Court.

Given the importance attached to the search for the truth in cases based on disputed accounts of past events, it might be thought that the process of trial would continually seek to maximise the accuracy with which disputed facts are proved. To what extent the procedural context of proof and rules of evidence enhance the search for the truth at a contested trial is considered in the following chapter.

Further reading

Grove, T. (2000) *A Juryman's Tale*, Bloomsbury.

McBarnet, D. (1981) *Conviction*, Macmillan Press.

Sanders, A., 'Constructing the Case for the Prosecution' (1987) 14 Journal of Law and Society 229.

Stone, M. (1995) *Cross-examination in Criminal Trials*, Butterworths Law.

Chapter 4

CRIMINAL TRIALS AND THE AIMS
OF RULES OF EVIDENCE

INTRODUCTION

This chapter is intended primarily for the benefit of those interested in the academic study of this subject. The utilisation of an adversarial system of trial and the values it incorporates help explain the need for many of the rules of criminal evidence covered in this book. The characteristics of adversarialism are described below. This chapter also includes critical consideration of the aims of rules of criminal evidence. Why are they needed and how do they regulate the process of proof? Developing a critical understanding of the rules cannot begin without some consideration of the function of the criminal trial and its relationship to the rules of evidence. Is the function of a criminal trial limited simply to ascertaining the truth about a past event or is there a much wider context in which it must operate?

The process of proof is shaped as much by the functions of the various key participants outlined in the previous chapter, as it is by the procedural mechanisms used to conduct the process of inquiry. Historically the search for the true determination of facts based on disputed accounts in a criminal case has been and continues to be conducted through the medium of an adversarial trial. The Anglo-American trial is a prime example of this. The fact that we have an adversarial justice system has significant implications for the way in which evidence gets investigated, collected and ultimately presented at trial. Indeed, the development of certain rules of evidence can be traced back to the adoption of an adversarial system. The adversarial process of proof has a number of distinct characteristics. Its system of trial contrasts quite markedly with the inquisitorial system of justice adopted by a number of continental criminal justice systems including France. Which system of inquiry is best designed to discover the truth provokes a wide range of opinions.

CHARACTERISTICS OF ADVERSARIALISM

Adversarial trials provide a forum in which two parties present competing versions of the truth. The fact finders, comprising the jury in the Crown Court and lay justices in the magistrates' court, have no investigative role. Their function is to listen to the evidence presented and decide which version of the facts they feel is closest to the truth. The parties' advocates are not employed to assist the court in the search for an objective truth. Their function is to represent their client by putting forward that client's version of the facts. In short, the aim is to win. In the Crown Court the judge acts as an impartial umpire, policing the rules of the 'trial game', thereby ensuring fair play. Whilst a number of adversarial systems of inquiry use juries, the jury is not in fact a pre-requisite of such a system.

Control in the adversarial process rests with the parties. They have complete autonomy. For this reason the role of the advocate in the presentation of evidence cannot be underestimated. The court will learn of the facts in the case through the parties' advocates. The parties' legal representatives collect the evidence and decide what evidence should be presented and how it should be presented. There is no overall obligation on the part of the defence in an adversarial trial to assist the prosecution in any way. Evidence unhelpful to the defendant, which may nevertheless be relevant to the issues the fact finder is trying to determine, need not be disclosed.

The presentation of evidence in adversarial trials is tightly controlled and, as with the rest of the court proceedings, the principle of orality prevails. There is a clear preference for evidence to be tendered in oral form. Documentary evidence is generally regarded as being inferior to oral evidence. As already noted in the previous chapter, the trial begins with an opening speech and most of the evidence, particularly at criminal trials, is presented through the oral testimony of witnesses. Each party calls their own witnesses whose function is to give evidence favourable to the party calling them. The physical presence of the witness affords the fact finder the opportunity of observing the witness's demeanour. This is perceived as being a useful indication of a witness's truthfulness – although this perception is disputed by those who work in the courts and by academic and psychological studies. The principle of orality has been endorsed by Lord Justice Auld. In his view, the witness box provides the best place for critical evidence to be tested and challenged in that, aside from the witness's demeanour, it enables external and internal inconsistencies and matters going to the witness's credit to be tested (Criminal Courts Review Report, Chapter 11, paragraph 80; see further below). The physical presence of the witness also gives the accused the opportunity of confronting those who accuse him. This is widely felt to be a component of the right to a fair trial.

A great deal of expectation is placed on the shoulders of witnesses in the adversarial system of justice which, many would argue, is unrealistic. When giving evidence at trial, the event the witness has to recall may well have occurred many months previously. No witness has complete recall; nevertheless, the witness's inability to recall precise detail is likely to be used in cross-examination as a means of undermining their credibility. Under rules of evidence explained in Chapter 15, some latitude is accorded to witnesses in this regard in that they are allowed to refresh their memories from their earlier written statements before giving evidence and in the witness box whilst giving evidence.

The adversarial trial is not especially well designed to realise fully the potential of each witness and it is not clear to what extent this compromises the search for the truth. A witness who has never given evidence at a trial is likely to find the experience rather bewildering, frustrating and ultimately very nerve racking. Evidence must be given on oath or affirmation and testimony is extracted through a protracted process of question and answer. Testimony is given in public. When the witness enters the witness box, the stage is set. The anticipation may be very great, the witness will not have had any rehearsal and the sense of stage fright may be all too real.

Testimony is initially elicited through an examination-in-chief of the parties' own witnesses. To make certain that witnesses give their own, truthful account of events, rules of professional conduct prevent advocates from coaching witnesses in any way. An effective advocate will however phrase a question in such a way as to obtain the desired answer from his witness. Controlling the witness in this way prevents potentially damaging evidence coming to light. Rules of evidence prevent leading questions being asked in examination-in-chief and are intended to ensure that it is the witness who gives evidence and not the advocate. Where a particular party's witness fails to live up to expectation, there is little the trial advocate can do, since advocates are not allowed to cross-examine their own witnesses unless the witness develops a hostile intent. The rules relating to witness testimony are considered in Chapters 15, 16 and 17.

Having given evidence in examination-in-chief, the witness is then cross-examined by the opposing advocate.

There are several aims of cross-examination. The most readily identifiable aim is to cast doubt on the reliability of the witness's evidence and in some instances to attack his veracity. The defence will have been served with copies of the statement the witness originally made to the police and will therefore have some idea of what the witness is going to say in his evidence. The smallest departure by a witness from his earlier written statement is likely to be used by the cross-examining advocate as a weapon with which to attack the witness's credibility. A skilful cross-examiner can easily undermine a witness's account by probing and chipping away, thereby exposing weakness and inherent implausibility in the witness's account, mistakes, lack of detail, bias or a motive to lie. The emphasis is on the total control of the witness by the advocate.

Once cross-examination is concluded, there is a chance for the party calling the witness to engage in some damage limitation if necessary, in re-examination of his witness.

Supporters of adversarial trials maintain cross-examination is the most effective weapon in the armoury for discovering the truth. Detractors regard it in a more cynical vein, maintaining it can be used quite powerfully as a tool for obscuring and manipulating the truth. Some witnesses particularly children and victims of sexual offences have good reason to feel vulnerable in this respect.

The worst excesses of cross-examination have led some victims of crime (particularly rape victims) to feel as if it is they who are on trial and not the defendant. A series of measures designed to assist vulnerable witnesses to give evidence more easily was introduced by the Youth Justice and Criminal Evidence Act 1999. The measures are welcome and are considered in detail in Chapter 17. Overall however, evidence is presented in adversarial trials in a controlled and fragmented way.

A great deal of emphasis is placed on the trial itself in adversarial systems. The drama is played out for the most part to a public gallery and the tension in a courtroom waiting for a verdict to be delivered can be palpable.

In adversarial systems the first and only occasion on which the fact finder gets to consider the evidence is at the trial itself. There is limited pre-trial disclosure. The fact finder must listen to the evidence, absorb it and evaluate it with minimal assistance, other than common sense. The jury is forbidden to ask questions of witnesses or the parties and must reach its decision purely on the basis of the evidence provided. There is no power enabling it to call for additional information. Its deliberations are undertaken in secrecy and it does not have to account for its decision.

Along with the jury in Crown Court criminal trials, the judge is largely a passive recipient of the information presented. He acts as an impartial umpire. He takes no part in the investigation and rarely descends into the gladiatorial arena.

CHARACTERISTICS OF INQUISITORIAL SYSTEMS OF INQUIRY

The inquisitorial system of factual inquiry in the countries of Europe is said to be more akin to a scientific investigation of fact. The trial takes the form of an investigation as opposed to a contest or battle of wills. The court has the task of making inquiry. It questions witnesses, directs the police investigation, commissions the service of expert witnesses and examines all relevant evidence.

The trial judge plays a far more active role than his adversarial counterpart. Known as the *juge d'instruction* in France, he is actively involved in the investigation of the incident at a very early stage. He will decide how the search for evidence will be conducted. He will question witnesses and will determine what charges should be brought against the individual alleged to be involved. He will also question the suspect. On the completion of the investigation a dossier of information comprising witness statements will be handed to the court. To ensure objectivity and fairness the trial is not conducted by the *juge d'instruction* but by another judge. In contrast there is no supervision by the courts of the investigation into criminal offences in England and Wales.

The trial itself assumes less importance in the inquisitorial system of inquiry because a great deal of information is contained in the court dossier. All the groundwork is undertaken at this stage.

As the court is charged with the task of making inquiry, the role of the advocate is considerably less important and is largely confined to ensuring his client receives a fair trial by checking that correct law is applied and that procedural rights are respected. The judge obtains most of the evidence through the process of questioning witnesses. The advocates' questions are restricted to clarifying points and obtaining further information.

Evidence is generally extracted in a more humane and natural manner than that experienced by witnesses in the adversarial system of inquiry. Witnesses are allowed to give their evidence in an uninterrupted fashion although questions will be asked to obtain clarification and to prevent the witness from getting into irrelevancies. There will also be questions to the witness that seek to challenge his or her credibility. However it would be rare to see the type of rigorous, sometimes aggressive questioning associated with cross-examination in the adversarial system.

The adversarial and inquisitorial models of factual inquiry are commonly contrasted as being the truth versus fight methods of adjudication. Jerome Frank, an American jurist who describes himself, as a 'fact sceptic', powerfully argues that the axiom consistently applied to the adversarial trial that 'the truth will out' is a myth and that inquisitorial systems are far more conducive to facilitate the true determination of disputed facts.

Those who defend the adversarial system of justice do so passionately, arguing that it is in fact the most effective vehicle for ascertaining truth about past events. They do so in the belief that it minimises bias in the inquiry process and that it is likely to unearth more facts and greater information because there are two sides searching for an advantage, motivated by their own self-interest, which is to win.

As we shall see, law reform of the right to silence and to pre-trial disclosure of evidence has increasingly led to inquisitorial elements being incorporated within the adversarial system of inquiry. Greater emphasis on pre-trial disclosure has significantly reduced the risk of either side being taken by surprise on the day of trial. In truth no one system of justice is totally adversarial or totally inquisitorial. Many systems are a hybrid of each.

HOW DO THE RULES OF EVIDENCE SHAPE THE PROCESS OF PROOF?

The rules of criminal evidence covered in this book constrain what the fact finders hear and what use they can make of certain information received in determining whether the prosecution has proved the defendant's guilt beyond reasonable doubt.

A critical evaluation of the rules of criminal evidence requires consideration of their rationale and the policies and principles governing their operation in practice. Some of the rules are a product of the procedural context in which the process of proof is conducted. A critical evaluation of the rules cannot however be effectively undertaken without some consideration of what the function of a criminal trial in the adversarial system is perceived to be. Arguably, it is to reach a verdict that accords with the truth and therefore reaches a just result. If this is so then, we might plausibly expect the laws of evidence to be directed in the main to achieving this end.

THE AIM OF THE CRIMINAL TRIAL AND ITS RELATIONSHIP WITH RULES OF EVIDENCE

According to eminent legal thinkers like Jeremy Bentham and William Twining the overall aim of the process of adjudication is the 'rectitude of decision making'. This is achieved by the correct application of substantive law to the true facts in the particular case. In other words, the process of adjudication should strive to reach a factually accurate decision. In this way, the aims of justice are served.

Bentham long espoused a utilitarian theory that the best way to arrive at the truth was through an application of 'free proof'. He advocated abolition of all laws operating to exclude evidence. It was his considered opinion that a jury could be trusted to reach a factually correct verdict provided all relevant evidence was adduced. In his view, too many rules of evidence and procedure lead to the exclusion of too much relevant evidence, thereby diminishing the search for a factually correct truth. Recognising the need for some restrictions, Bentham felt laws of evidence were needed only to the extent of preventing 'vexation, expense or delay'.

As will become apparent, the rules of criminal evidence fundamentally operate to exclude relevant evidence from the fact finders' consideration. In some instances the rules provide for the mandatory exclusion of evidence. In other instances discretion is given to the judge or to magistrates to exclude relevant evidence in circumstances where fairness demands it. There is no judicial discretion to include relevant evidence, which might nonetheless have a bearing on the search for the truth, but which has to be deemed inadmissible by application of a rule of evidence. The relaxation of many of the technical rules of exclusion over the years has in fact meant greater evidence being placed before the jury, with judges pointing out what facts have a bearing and the weight the jury may wish to attach to them. The present status quo of evidential rules and procedures is however far from a system of free proof. Why is this so?

Few would dispute that the rectitude of decision making is an obvious objective of the criminal trial, but is it the only objective and even if it were, can such an objective be realistically attained via a process of free proof? On a pragmatic level, trials can last only a finite period of time and the resources available to the competing sides are not limitless. The search for an objective truth is thus immediately constrained in this way. Rules of criminal evidence assist in this regard by demanding only relevant evidence can be adduced at trial.

The search for the truth has to be conducted in a procedural context. The adoption of a sophisticated adversarial system of inquiry accounts in part for the rationale behind some of the rules of evidence. The system yields to the principle of party autonomy. It is the parties who search for, collect and present the evidence to the fact finder. Consequently rules exist to keep the protagonists in check. They limit the nature of questions that can be asked challenging the credibility of a witness in cross-examination, and in the admission of evidence that has little probative value such as the rules preventing the repetition of previous consistent statements made by witnesses. We have seen that the fact finder adopts an essentially passive and remote role. In a Crown Court trial the judge acts as umpire, deciding all issues of law. All games, including the adversarial trial game, must have rules. It is the function of the judge to ensure the rules are obeyed.

A number of the rules of evidence owe their *raison d'être* to the retention of juries in criminal trials, in particular the rule against the use of hearsay evidence and the rules restricting the use that can be made of the defendant's bad character. Created at a time when jurors were ill-educated, it was felt the rules would protect the defendant against erroneous reasoning on the part of those who could not be trusted to apportion an appropriate degree of weight to such evidence. Nowadays, jurors are mostly educated and literate. A major part of the rationale in support of a rule that excludes hearsay is no longer applicable. Indeed, relaxation of the rules against the admission of hearsay evidence in recent years bears witness to this. By way of contrast, in civil cases where the use of the jury is confined to a tiny minority of cases involving libel and malicious prosecution, hearsay evidence is admissible subject to considerations of weight.

As we have already seen, the adversarial trial embraces the principle of orality. The search for the truth is best conducted in the open. There is much emphasis on oral argument and persuasion. Cross-examination is regarded as an invaluable tool for laying bare the truth. The ability to observe a witness's demeanour is felt to be of considerable assistance in discerning whether or not the witness is speaking the truth. It is considered the right of the accused to confront his or her accusers. These perceived values provide additional rationales for the rule excluding reliance on hearsay evidence. Witnesses would be reluctant to come forward if advocates were entirely free to do as they please during cross-examination. Rules therefore have to exist to curb the worst excesses of cross-examination. In addition, as a concession to trying to ensure the truth is ascertained, there are rules regulating the conduct of the examination-in-chief so as to ensure the fact finder is not presented with a well rehearsed, scripted performance.

In reality, of course, a criminal trial can never reach an objective truth about the occurrence of past events. It can only reach an opinion as to the probable existence of disputed events. Such a system of justice must therefore seek to avoid errors in the adjudication process. In criminal cases the allocation of the burden of proof on the prosecution and the requirement that it proves the defendant's guilt to a very high standard, ie beyond any reasonable doubt, is intended to protect against such errors. As we shall see, a number of the rules relating to admissibility and use of evidence are directed towards minimising the risk of wrongful convictions. The main risks of error stem largely from the admission of unreliable or prejudicial evidence.

The concept of free proof also ignores the fundamental importance of procedural rights and the symbolic importance of trials. Trials must uphold basic human and constitutional rights if verdicts are to carry moral legitimacy. Justice must not only be done but be seen to be done. Most trials are held in public for this reason. The public nature of the proceedings has an instructive and educational effect giving verdicts, particularly criminal verdicts, moral validity. The public must have faith in its criminal justice system and the verdicts that are delivered by it and this can only be the case if the trial is perceived to be a fair one. The litany of miscarriages of justice, highlighted in the previous chapter, have done much to dent the public's confidence in the notion of a fair trial.

Respect for procedural rights is a key component of the right to a fair trial. Such rights include:

- The right to be presumed innocent.
- The right to a fair, open and impartial hearing.
- The right to affordable legal representation at trial.
- The right of the accused to know the charges and the nature of the evidence against him.
- The right of the accused to conduct a defence in an unfettered manner.
- The right of the accused to have mistaken verdicts corrected in a speedy manner on appeal.

The belief in the presumption of innocence lies firmly at the heart of the criminal justice process of inquiry. It finds expression in a number of different evidential rules, including the rules relating to the allocation of the burden of proof, the privilege against self-incrimination and the restricted use by the prosecution of evidence of the defendant's past bad character.

A rights-based approach to a system of judicial inquiry demands all necessary measures should be taken to protect the innocent. Many would say that the political desire to obtain convictions has led to the erosion of a number of fundamental rights and that the presumption of innocence is now more symbolic than real. The enactment of the Human Rights Act 1998 makes the question of what constitutes a fair trial and the role which the rules of evidence play in this regard a very pertinent one.

The notions of fair play and accountability are felt to be very important, but is it part of the function of the trial judge to discipline the police if they engage in unlawful or unfair means in order to secure evidence of guilt? Where evidence has been obtained from a suspect by unlawful means, should the decision of the judge to admit such evidence, if the evidence convicts the person responsible for the crime, concern us? Does the means not justify the end or does the verdict lack the necessary moral legitimacy?

Against this, of course, the defendant is not the only participant in the trial. The right to a fair trial must apply equally to the prosecution and to the victims of crime too. The Stephen Lawrence inquiry shows how wrongful acquittals rankle just as much as wrongful convictions. These competing rights give rise to an inevitable tension. A victim of crime might ask why should a defendant against whom there is a case to answer hide behind a right to silence? The defendant might answer: 'because I have the right to be presumed innocent'. Criminal trials have to try and strike a balance between all these competing demands. There is a need to recognise these competing demands if a critical understanding of the rules of evidence and their application is to be gained.

Is the right to a fair trial necessarily in conflict with the aim of reaching a factually correct verdict? Certain aspects of a fair trial positively assist the search for truth, but fundamentally they pull in different directions. The laws of evidence nevertheless have to accommodate the tensions between the competing aims of a criminal trial. This may explain why the policies behind recent legislative changes to the rules of evidence lack clarity and overall coherence and also why the application of judicial discretion, which creates a degree of uncertainty, is a necessary by-product of the flexibility it provides. This is most strikingly illustrated in Chapter 5 which analyses the law relating to the exclusion of unlawfully obtained evidence.

CRIMINAL EVIDENCE AND POLITICAL EXPEDIENCY

Law and order is always high on the political agenda. There have been a number of reforms to the criminal justice system in recent years. Indeed, the pace of legislative change in criminal proceedings has been nothing short of breathtaking. With the obvious exception of the Human Rights Act 1998 the perceived motivation behind many of the recent legislative changes has been the desire to ensure a greater conviction rate, coupled with the wish to speed up the criminal trial process and to make it more efficient and cheaper to administer. Many of the legislative changes have been criticised for being reactionary. In some instances, they have ignored the express recommendations of independent bodies such as the Law Commission and Royal Commission on Criminal Justice.

Some of the reforms have been aimed at the need to redress a perceived imbalance in favour of those accused of criminal offences. Concern was expressed some years ago by various police forces, for example, about the increasing instances of witness intimidation. The hearsay rule was consequently relaxed by the Criminal Justice Act 1988 to allow for the admission of the written statement of a witness too frightened to attend court.

With the enactment of the Criminal Justice and Public Order Act 1994 the cherished right to silence was curtailed, permitting the fact finder to draw an adverse evidential inference in certain circumstances from the defendant's decision to remain silent both at the police station and at trial. This was in fact against the findings of the Royal Commission on Criminal Justice 1993 which extensively examined the arguments on both sides and came to the conclusion that whilst some procedural amendments were needed to force the defendant to show his hand at an earlier stage, the right to silence should fundamentally remain intact. The Criminal Procedure and Investigations Act 1996 introduced a statutory framework regulating the disclosure of evidence prior to trial. Coming 'hot on the heels' of a number of miscarriages of justice based on failure by the prosecution to disclose relevant evidence that would have assisted the defence (including the cases of Judith Ward and the Guildford Four), it narrows the test of 'relevance to the defence' as established at common law and puts the onus on the police to decide what is in fact relevant to the accused's defence.

Legitimate concern for the victims of sexual offences recently led to the curtailing of the defendant's right to cross-examine the complainant in person and on her previous sexual relationship with the defendant, where the defendant claims such questioning is relevant to his defence (Youth Justice and Criminal Evidence Act 1999, sections 41–43).

Supporters of Jeremy Bentham's view of evidential rules would welcome such changes in that they represent a relaxation of many of the rules permitting more relevant evidence to be considered by the jury. They assist the search for the truth and also bring with them efficiencies. They also acknowledge the rights of victims of criminal offences. For others, the cherished cornerstones of the criminal justice system, such as the presumption of innocence and the right to a fair trial are being sacrificed in order to obtain results. The reforms epitomise the tension identified in the previous section as to the differing functions of the trial process itself. Some of the legislative changes have already been tested before the European Court of Human Rights and in the domestic courts under the Human Rights Act 1998.

CRIMINAL COURTS REVIEW REPORT

On 14 December 1999 the government appointed Sir Robin Auld to undertake an extensive review into the working of the criminal justice system. His terms of reference were to inquire:

> into the practices and procedures of, and the rules of evidence applied by, the criminal courts at every level, with a view to ensuring that they deliver justice fairly, by streamlining all their processes, increasing their efficiency and strengthening the effectiveness of their relationships with others across the whole of the criminal justice system, and having regard to the interests of all parties including victims and witnesses, thereby promoting public confidence in the rule of law.

The Criminal Courts Review Report was published in October 2001. It runs to several hundred pages and makes a number of radical recommendations. It is anticipated that the recommendations will form the basis of future legislative changes. The opportunity is taken here and in successive chapters that deal with the substantive rules of evidence, to highlight and consider some of Lord Justice Auld's proposals in the context of proof in criminal trials and in the shaping of future rules of evidence and procedure.

Rather pointedly, Lord Justice Auld comments in paragraph 34 of Chapter 1 that:

> It would be naïve to suggest that politics should be removed from the forces driving change in the criminal justice system. As for any other field of public concern, politicians have a legitimate interest in the formation of criminal justice policy and in legislative and other means of implementing it. However, the criminal justice system and the public's confidence in it are damaged if, as has happened all too often in recent years, insufficient

legislative reforms are hurried through in seeming response to political pressures or for quick political advantage. I take it as a legitimate starting point that there should be some mechanism of objective and informed assessment between the rawness of political enthusiasms of the moment and the transformation of their products into law. (footnotes omitted).

In Chapter 11, Lord Justice Auld mentions those who are 'impatient for principled reform of the trial process' and who 'complain of the piecemeal and muddled nature of our rules of procedure and evidence'. In paragraphs 76 and 77 he states:

> My terms of reference require me to examine the fairness and efficiency of the rules of evidence in the criminal justice process. That is an enormous subject in its own right, suffering, as Professor Colin Tapper has put it, from a 'blight' in the law of evidence as a whole. It is a blight that he and many distinguished academics have long attributed to incoherence, confusion and conflict in the aims and policy of the law of evidence. This is in large part due to our tradition of sporadic and piecemeal statutory reform and constantly evolving overlay of judge-made law softening its edges. It also suffers from a neglect of the needs of summary trial. Rules devised in the main for, or which have their origin in, jury trial are often too complex or artificial for application in the fast moving list of magistrates' courts. ...
>
> For these reasons there is an urgent need for a comprehensive review of the whole law of criminal evidence to make it a simple and efficient agent for ensuring that all criminal courts are told all and only what they need to know. (footnotes omitted).

Earlier, Lord Justice Auld recommends the establishment of a Criminal Justice Council and the creation of a Criminal Code. The review of the rules of evidence should, he says, be undertaken by the Criminal Justice Council in conjunction with the Law Commission and the result should be a comprehensive Code of Criminal Evidence. He urges that the reviewing body should take as its starting point and overriding objective 'an examination of the justice and feasibility of a general move away from rules of inadmissibility to trusting fact finders to give relevant evidence the weight it deserves'. With this in mind, he proposes that there should be reform of the hearsay rule, the rules relating to the admission of unfairly obtained evidence, the rules relating to the admission of a defendant's criminal record and changes in the manner in which the evidence of children and expert witnesses are presented at trial. In Lord Justice Auld's view any future reform of the rules of evidence must be undertaken in accordance with the following general principles:

- a continuation of a trial procedure that is in the main adversarial and that relies largely on oral evidence and argument;
- the involvement of juries and lay magistrates as the main fact finders on the issue of guilt;
- the criminal burden of proof and the defendant's right to silence in its present qualified form;
- relevance as a threshold of admissibility; and
- fairness as a criterion.

Within these constraints he concludes: 'rules of evidence should aid, not hinder, the search for truth; be such as to promote a fair trial for the defendant; be clear; be simple to apply; and so far as is consistent with those principles, secure an efficient trial process.'

The evidential implications of Lord Justice Auld's recommendations are discussed in the context of the specific chapters in which they arise. No repeal of section 8 of the Contempt of Court Act 1981 in order to facilitate research into the way in which juries reach their decisions is advocated.

Lord Justice Auld calls for the incorporation of more inquisitorial features within the existing adversarial structures, including earlier identification of issues and greater co-operation between the parties to enable a more efficient and effective disposal of cases.

If Lord Justice Auld's recommendations were to be implemented, they would change some of the less satisfactory aspects of the process of proof for the better. Jurors would, for example, be given far greater assistance than at present. At the start of the trial jurors would receive a copy of the charges. The judge would be required to address the members of the jury, introducing them to their task and the importance of taking notes, giving them an outline of the case and the questions that they must decide. Additionally, each juror would be provided with an agreed written summary of the case and the issues that need to be decided. At the close of evidence and before final speeches are given, there would be a period of reflection during which the judge and the advocates would be required to review the evidence and the issues in the absence of the jury. On the basis of this review a decision would be taken as to whether the case summary issued to the jury at the start of the trial needed to be amended. In the future juries would be required to deliver more reasoned verdicts by having to answer a series of structured questions which the judge would identify, replacing the existing summing up. The composition of the jury would be far more representative than it currently is in that no one in the future, except for the mentally ill and persons with criminal convictions, should be ineligible for or excusable as of right from serving on a jury. Greater use of information technology to assist jurors to follow the course of evidence is recommended.

The pace of legislative change shows no sign of slowing down. The government has indicated that it intends to act on the main recommendations in the Criminal Courts Review Report. There will be a short period of consultation until the end of January 2002, followed by a government White Paper and likely legislation in the parliamentary session 2002–03.

Further reading

Ashworth, A. (1998) *The Criminal Process*, Oxford University Press.

Ashworth, A., 'Article 6 and the Fairness of Trials' [1999] Crim LR 262.

Auld, Lord Justice (2001) *A Review of the Criminal Courts of England and Wales*, www.criminal-courts-review.org.uk.

Evans, K. (1993) *The Golden Rules of Advocacy*, Blackstone Press.

Frank, J. (1949) *Courts on Trial – Myth and Reality in American Justice*, Princeton University Press.

Jackson, J., 'Two Methods of Proof in Criminal Procedure' (1988) 51 MLR 549.

Macpherson of Cluny, Sir William (1999) *The Stephen Lawrence Inquiry*, Cm 4261-1, The Stationery Office.

McEwan, J. (1998) *Evidence and the Adversarial Process – The Modern Law*, Hart Publishing.

Twining, W. (1994) *Re-thinking Evidence: Exploratory Essays*, Northwestern University Press.

Twining, W. (1998) *Theories of Evidence*, Butterworths Law.

Zuckerman, A. (1989) *The Principles of Criminal Evidence*, Clarendon Press.

Chapter 5

THE EXCLUSION OF UNLAWFULLY OBTAINED EVIDENCE

INTRODUCTION

In this chapter, unlawfully obtained evidence refers to any evidence that has been obtained pre-trial in a 'questionable' manner. Such evidence could comprise prosecution evidence, such as a confession or evidence of identification obtained in violation of the safeguards under the Police and Criminal Evidence Act 1984 (PACE) and the Codes of Practice which accompany it. In relation to confession evidence the court has an additional and more specific statutory power of exclusion under section 76 of PACE. It can include evidence obtained as a result of an unlawful search of a person or his property as well as evidence obtained through the use of an agent provocateur or an undercover police officer and evidence of incriminating admissions obtained through unauthorised surveillance methods. It should be emphasised that this list is by no means exhaustive.

At the heart of the controversy surrounding the admissibility of unlawfully obtained evidence is the question of whether the means justify the ends. The police are motivated to ensure the conviction of those they believe to be guilty. If an unlawful method is used to gather evidence which is then used to convict those who are guilty of offences, should we care about the methods used or are there wider issues of the protection of civil liberties and the integrity of the criminal justice process at stake?

Illegally obtained evidence presents the court with a dilemma: to have a policy of excluding it every time would result in too many guilty defendants being acquitted, thereby diminishing law enforcement. However, to have a policy that continually condones police malpractice would damage the credibility of the criminal justice system in the eyes of the public. In an effort to resolve this dilemma, the criminal courts are given discretionary powers to exclude illegally and unfairly obtained evidence to be exercised in the particular circumstances of each case.

Both the common law and statute have afforded the courts clear and specific powers to exclude prosecution evidence that would have the effect of prejudicing a fair trial. The notion of what constitutes a fair trial is considerably less clear, as is the theoretical basis utilised by the courts to justify the exclusion of unlawfully obtained evidence in an attempt to ensure a fair trial. The concept of a fair trial has gained added importance in domestic law with the implementation of the Human Rights Act 1998. Article 6(1) of the European Convention on Human Rights guarantees an accused individual the right to a fair trial.

It is important to remember that the obligation of courts to ensure a fair trial does not arise exclusively in the context of the admissibility of unlawfully obtained

evidence. The right to a fair trial is all pervading and arises in many different evidential and procedural contexts. It might be argued, for example, in appropriate circumstances that to draw an adverse inference from a defendant's silence at the police
station would lead to unfairness. We will see the power of the court to exclude all manner of prosecution evidence in the interests of securing a fair trial, including hearsay
evidence and evidence of the defendant's bad character in subsequent chapters. This
chapter however focuses on the relationship between unlawfully obtained evidence
and the right to a fair trial.

The exclusion of unlawfully obtained evidence provokes a number of questions,
many of which are not answered by the current state of the law. What principles should
guide the court in the exercise of its discretion to exclude such evidence? If the method
used by the prosecuting authorities does not taint the reliability of the resulting evidence
in any way, can the evidence not safely be admitted, or does this condone the unlawful
activities of the prosecuting authorities? If the deception used to obtain the evidence is
relatively minor but the crime is grave, should this be a relevant factor for a court to
take into account in deciding whether to exercise judicial discretion to exclude the
evidence? Are the motives of the police relevant when they exercise their powers of
investigation unfairly or illegally? Is it part of the court's function to discipline the police
by depriving them, in evidential terms, of their ill-gotten gains, where they break the
rules? Does the fact that it would be exceedingly difficult to obtain evidence of guilt in
any other way make it easier to justify the admission of such evidence?

THE COMMON LAW

Courts have always retained the power at common law to exclude evidence capable of
prejudicing a fair trial. Such prejudicial evidence tends to be that which would unduly
sway the fact finder against the accused in that the jury gives the evidence more weight
than it deserves. In other words, the prejudice engendered by the particular piece of
evidence exceeds its probative value. Where a trial judge concludes that the prejudicial
effect of the evidence does in fact outweigh its probative value, the evidence must be
excluded in the interests of ensuring a fair trial. The position at common law is
summed up by Roskill J in *R* v *List* [1966] 1 WLR 9:

> A trial judge always has an overriding duty in every case to secure a fair trial, and if in any
> particular case he comes to the conclusion that, even though certain evidence is strictly
> admissible, yet its prejudicial effect once admitted is such as to make it virtually impossi-
> ble for a dispassionate view of the crucial facts of the case to be thereafter taken by the jury,
> then the trial judge, in my judgment, should exclude the evidence.

The common law has always adopted a narrow position with regard to the exclusion
of illegally obtained evidence. Provided the evidence is relevant and reliable, its admission is not generally regarded as prejudicing the defendant's right to a fair trial. The
following cases are illustrations of the exercise of the common law position.

Kuruma, Son of Kaniu v R [1955] AC 197

The accused was on trial for the unlawful possession of ammunition during a period of emergency
in Kenya. The police had found the ammunition during an unlawful search. The Privy Council was

quite adamant that such evidence remained admissible notwithstanding the manner in which it had been obtained. The rule has been reaffirmed on many occasions.

Jeffrey v Black [1978] 1 All ER 555

The accused had been arrested by officers on suspicion of having stolen a sandwich. Before being charged he was taken to his home by the officers who conducted an unlawful search of his property. A small quantity of cannabis was found. The defendant was further charged with possession of drugs. At his summary trial, the magistrates refused to admit the evidence yielded by the search. The prosecutor's appeal to the Divisional Court was upheld. Lord Widgery acknowledged the court always retained discretion to exclude prosecution evidence but that the discretion had been wrongly exercised in this instance as the evidence was clearly relevant and reliable and a fair trial had been possible.

The leading case illustrating the position at common law is *R* v *Sang* [1980] below.

R v Sang [1980] AC 402

Sang was a serving prisoner about to be released. He was known to deal in forged banknotes. Before his release he was approached by a fellow inmate, alleged by Sang to be a police informer. The inmate told Sang he knew a buyer on the outside and would put him in touch with Sang. Upon his release, Sang was contacted by an undercover police officer posing as the buyer. Sang agreed to supply him with forged currency. At the rendezvous to hand over the merchandise, Sang was arrested and charged with conspiracy to produce counterfeit banknotes. Sang's defence was one of entrapment. He maintained he had been induced to commit the offence by an informer who was acting on the instructions of the police. Entrapment does not provide a defence to a criminal charge in English criminal law. Sang therefore sought to persuade the trial judge to exclude the evidence in the exercise of his judicial discretion to ensure a fair trial. The arguments were addressed on the assumption that Sang's allegations were true. The trial judge felt he had no discretion to exclude the evidence because of the manner in which it had been obtained. The House of Lords upheld Sang's conviction.

The position at common law was summarised by Lord Diplock in *R* v *Sang*:

> (1) A trial judge in a criminal trial has always a discretion to refuse to admit evidence if in his opinion its prejudicial effect outweighs its probative value. (2) Save with regard to admissions and confessions and generally with regard to evidence obtained from the accused after commission of the offence, he has no discretion to refuse to admit relevant admissible evidence on the ground that it was obtained by improper or unfair means. The court isn't concerned with how it was obtained.

Earlier in his judgment Lord Diplock stated:

> the function of a judge at a criminal trial as respects the admission of evidence is to ensure the accused has a fair trial according to the law. It is no part of a judge's function to exercise disciplinary powers over the police or prosecution as respects the way in which the evidence to be used at the trial is obtained by them...

The application of common law principles seems clear: if the evidence is relevant it is admissible notwithstanding the manner in which the evidence was obtained.

Specific reference is made in *R* v *Sang* above to confession evidence and to evidence obtained from an accused of a self-incriminating nature after the commission of an offence. The common law is far more inclined to exclude evidence falling within these categories, particularly if trickery, threats or inducements have been used by prosecuting authorities to obtain them. As an illustration, consider the following case:

R v Payne [1963] 1 WLR 637

The defendant was convicted of a drink/driving offence. At the police station, before being charged, the defendant was asked to consent to a medical examination. The defendant only agreed to consent to such examination on the express understanding that the doctor who conducted it would not be called to give evidence against him as to his unfitness to drive. Despite this assurance by the police, the doctor who examined the defendant was called to give evidence for this very purpose. The Court of Appeal concluded that the evidence ought to have been excluded in the exercise of the judge's discretion to ensure a fair trial, as it had been obtained by trickery.

For a contrasting decision, see:

R v Apicella (1986) 82 Cr App R 295

The defendant was convicted on three counts of rape. He suffered from gonorrhoea. His victims had also contracted the disease. Whilst on remand in prison, the prison doctor had asked for a sample of his semen for diagnostic purposes. As a prisoner, the defendant had been under the impression that he could not refuse to give a sample. The sample was in fact later used in evidence against him. It was found that all his victims had an identical strain of gonorrhoea. The defendant argued he had been tricked into providing the specimen. Using the judgment in *R* v *Sang*, he argued that his semen sample was evidence of a self-incriminatory nature obtained after the commission of an offence. The Court of Appeal concluded there was no unfairness because in its view the defendant had not been tricked into providing a specimen and the evidence had been rightly admitted.

Physical evidence of the nature in *R* v *Apicella* often carries with it an inherent reliability and can provide conclusive evidence of guilt. Should it matter that it was obtained by trick or deception?

Although the common law has now been largely superseded by section 78 of PACE it is still used in legal argument. Section 82(3) of PACE preserves the common law discretion to exclude evidence where its prejudicial effect outweighs its probative value.

STATUTORY DISCRETION

The statutory power to render evidence inadmissible in the exercise of the court's discretion is contained in section 78 of PACE:

> (1) In any proceedings the court may refuse to allow evidence on which the prosecution proposes to rely to be given if it appears to the court that, having regard to all the circumstances, including the circumstances in which the evidence was obtained, the admission of the evidence would have such an adverse effect on the fairness of the proceedings that the court ought not to admit it.

On the face of it, section 78 as drafted gives the court a wider discretionary power than at common law. Specific mention in the section is made to 'the manner in which evidence is obtained' as being a relevant factor to be taken into account when assessing unfairness. Does the wording not then give courts a wider remit in determining what constitutes a fair trial? Why after all preserve the common law discretion, as section 82(3) does, if section 78 is merely to be regarded as a re-statement of the common law?

It was thought that by using section 78, judges might take advantage of the plain meaning of the words used in the section and use their discretion in a far more proactive way to exclude evidence as a means of promoting and protecting the rights of the accused and, where appropriate, as a means of punishing police malpractice. As we shall see however, whilst section 78 has been applied in far more varied circumstances than the discretion at common law, it is far from clear that the principles which govern the exercise of discretion under the section are as clearly discernible as those at common law. What is the rationale for the exclusion of evidence under this provision and what are the principles that shape the exercise of the discretion? In answering these questions, we need to consider some of the circumstances in which section 78 has been applied.

Entrapment

Entrapment is one area of potentially unfairly obtained evidence in which the application of discretion available under section 78 appears to go further than the common law as declared in *R v Sang*.

What is entrapment?

Example

It comes to the attention of the police that Angelina wishes to have her husband murdered. She has formed a new relationship and stands to inherit a large sum of money under her husband's will. She is unable to kill her husband herself and seeks the services of a contract killer. Officer X, an undercover police sergeant, is put in touch with her. Over a series of meetings she gives Officer X specific instructions of the date, time and place she wants the deed to be carried out. Angelina gives the family home as the place and instructs the 'hit man' to make it look like an armed robbery gone tragically wrong. Conveniently, Angelina has an alibi for the night of the killing. A sum of money is agreed for Officer X's services. The officer has a listening device hidden about his person. It records Angelina's instructions. Angelina is contacted by mobile telephone to confirm her husband is dead as per her instructions. She expresses her gratitude. She is charged with conspiracy to commit murder. In her defence, she claims she was befriended by a man she had never met before and that it was his suggestion that he do away with her husband for her. She claims she went along with his proposal at first not believing him to be serious. When she purported to call it off, she claims the man threatened her and that in the circumstances she felt she had to go along with the plan. She asserts she had a very happy marriage and denies any intent to commit murder.

The above example is intended to illustrate entrapment by prosecuting authorities. Has Angelina been enticed to commit an offence she would otherwise not have committed but for the activities of the undercover police officer?

A distinction is drawn here between the use of illicit tactics such as eavesdropping by the police in an attempt to obtain evidence of a crime that has already been committed and the tactics used to entrap those who have yet to commit an offence.

Law enforcement not infrequently requires the police to use the services of an agent provocateur such as an undercover police officer or an informer who infiltrates a criminal enterprise in an attempt to gather evidence. Evidence obtained in this way is susceptible to challenge both at common law and under section 78 of PACE as entrapment *per se* does not afford a defence in English law to a criminal charge. We have already considered the leading common law case of *R* v *Sang* where the House of Lords admitted the evidence gathered by means of entrapment.

The difficulty for the courts in choosing to exercise discretion under section 78 of PACE, is where to draw the line. At what point do the prosecuting authorities overstep the mark dividing the legitimate collection of evidence of a criminal enterprise and inciting someone to commit a crime they might not otherwise have committed? The difficulties associated with the admissibility of this type of evidence have exercised the courts on a number of occasions.

R v Christou [1992] 4 All ER 559

As part of an undercover operation to trace and recover stolen jewellery and to identify thieves and handlers, the police set up a shop to buy and sell jewellery. Cameras and recording equipment were placed in the shop. To attract the right sort of clientele, the undercover officers came across as shady dealers prepared to buy and sell stolen goods. Several individuals, including the defendant, came into the shop offering to sell stolen goods. He was subsequently arrested and charged with burglary and handling stolen goods. At his trial, he argued the admission of the evidence obtained in this underhand way would have an adverse effect on the fairness of the proceedings and should therefore be excluded.

Rejecting the argument, the Court of Appeal observed the defendant had not been forced, persuaded or encouraged to sell the goods. If he had not used the police officers' shop, he would have gone elsewhere.

Lord Taylor CJ explained the defendant's position in *R* v *Christou* as follows:

> Nobody was forcing the defendants to do what they did. They were not persuaded or encouraged to do what they did. They were doing in that shop exactly what they intended to do and, in all probability, what they intended to do from the moment they got up that morning. They were dishonestly disposing of dishonest goods. If the police had never set up the jeweller's shop, they would, in my judgment, have been doing the same thing though of course they would not be doing it in that shop, at that time. They were not tricked into doing what they would not otherwise have done ... I do not think that is unfair or leads to an unfairness in the trial.

R v Smurthwaite [1994] 1 All ER 898

The facts of *Smurthwaite* are similar to the example of Angelina above. It was alleged the defendant had solicited an undercover police officer to murder his wife. Two meetings in a hotel room had been secretly tape-recorded by the police. At his trial the defendant had argued that he had never wanted to have his wife killed and that he had not voluntarily or intentionally solicited the undercover officer to do so. He claimed to have acted under duress, believing the contract killer to have underworld connections. The defendant claimed a third party had gained the erroneous idea that he wanted to have his wife killed. It was the third party who had instigated matters and had given him the impression that the men he was dealing with were not to be messed with. Had the undercover officer not come upon the scene, he would never have sought to have his wife killed.

The Court of Appeal upheld his conviction on the ground that whilst section 78 had not altered the substantive law, namely that entrapment cannot constitute a defence to a criminal charge, the fact that evidence had been obtained in this way was relevant to the application of section 78. Setting out some guidance on the application of section 78 of PACE to entrapment cases, Lord Taylor CJ stated:

> In exercising his discretion whether to admit the evidence of an undercover officer, some, but not an exhaustive list, of the factors that a judge may take into account are as follows.
>
> Was the officer acting as an agent provocateur in the sense that he was enticing the defendant to commit an offence he would otherwise not have committed?
>
> What was the nature of any entrapment?
>
> Does the evidence consist of admissions to a completed offence, or does it consist of the actual commission of the offence itself?
>
> How active or passive was the officer's role in obtaining the evidence?
>
> Is there an unassailable record of what occurred, or is it strongly corroborated?

Lord Taylor CJ then went on to say:

> Beyond mentioning the considerations set out above, it is not possible to give more general guidance as to how a judge should exercise his discretion under section 78 in this field, since each case must be determined on its own facts...

On the facts, the Court of Appeal concluded the evidence was rightly admitted. Although there was an element of entrapment and trickery inherent in the use of an undercover police officer posing as a contract killer, the officer had played a minimal role and the defendant had not needed any persuasion. There was no dispute as to who said what and there was no dispute as to the authenticity of the tapes recording their conversations.

The decision in *R v Smurthwaite* represents a departure from the common law position espoused in *R v Sang*, in that the Court of Appeal recognises that there might be cases where the use of entrapment as a means of investigation, might lead to the exclusion of the evidence. Some of the factors identified by Lord Taylor CJ touch on the reliability of the evidence resulting from the method used, others however, such as the use of enticement, bring into question the integrity of the criminal justice process, as they touch on the moral acceptability of the methods used.

Does the use of an agent provocateur violate the right to a fair trial under Article 6(1) of the European Convention on Human Rights? The European Court of Human Rights has considered the matter most recently in the case of *Teixeira de Castro v Portugal*.

Teixeira de Castro v Portugal (1999) 28 EHRR 101

As part of a drugs operation, two Portuguese undercover police officers enlisted the help of a petty drug dealer in the hope that he would lead them to his supplier of hashish. When this proved futile, the officers asked to be supplied with heroin. At this request, the dealer suggested the name of Teixeira de Castro as a possible supplier. The officers met with him and told him they wished to buy a quantity of heroin. They named their price. Teixeira de Castro agreed to try and supply them. He obtained 20 grams of heroin from an undisclosed source and passed it on to the officers who then revealed their true identities. In his defence he claimed he had committed the offence solely at the behest of the officers. The Portuguese authorities maintained the officers were acting as legitimate agent provocateurs as part of an anti-drugs police operation. The defendant was found guilty and sentenced to six years' imprisonment.

Before the European Court of Human Rights, Teixeira de Castro complained he had not received a fair trial in violation of Article 6(1). The Court agreed with him. In its judgment, the Court observed that the Convention did not preclude reliance on the evidence of undercover agents but cautioned 'the use of undercover agents must be restricted and safeguards put in place even in cases concerning the fight against drug trafficking. The right to a fair administration of justice holds such a prominent place that it cannot be sacrificed for the sake of expedience.'

The Court went on to observe that a distinction had to be drawn between cases where the undercover agent's action created a criminal intent that had previously been absent and those in which the offender had already been predisposed to commit the offence. On the facts in this case, the Court concluded the officers had created a criminal intent where one had not been previously present.

Of significant relevance was the fact that the defendant had never been under suspicion of drug trafficking. Indeed, he was a man with no criminal record. He was not known to the police and had only come into contact with them through an intermediary. He had no drugs in his possession when he initially met with the undercover officers and had had to go through various sources in order to supply the officers. In no sense was he predisposed to commit the offence. It could not be said that the officers had confined themselves to investigating the defendant's criminal activity in an essentially passive manner. The use of entrapment in order to secure the evidence in this case had, in the opinion of the Court, made a fair trial impossible from the outset.

Extracting general principles from the decision in *Teixeira de Castro* v *Portugal* is not easy. In its judgment, the European Court of Human Rights observed:

> The general requirements of fairness embodied in Article 6 apply to proceedings concerning all types of criminal offence, from the most straightforward to the most complex. The public interest cannot justify the use of evidence obtained as a result of police incitement.

This particular statement of principle has caused the Court of Appeal some difficulty. The opportunity for an English court to consider and apply *Teixeira de Castro* has arisen in three subsequent cases.

Nottingham City Council *v* Amin [2000] 1 WLR 1071

The defendant was a taxi driver. Two officers posing as members of the public flagged his vehicle down. They asked him to take them to an area in which the defendant was not licensed to drive his taxi. The fare was paid. The defendant was summonsed for a licensing offence under the Town Police Clauses Act 1847. In his defence and relying on the judgment in *Teixeira de Castro*, he maintained the prosecuting authorities had enticed him to commit the offence and had not confined themselves to investigating his criminal activity in an entirely passive way.

In the Divisional Court, Lord Bingham took the view that the decision in *Teixeira de Castro* v *Portugal* could be distinguished as it was a decision made very much on the facts in that case. On the facts in *Amin*, the court concluded there had been no incitement and no pressure to commit the offence. The defendant had not needed any persuasion.

Summing up his view of the law in relation to entrapment, Lord Bingham stated:

> On the one hand it has been recognised as deeply offensive to the notion of fairness if a defendant were to be convicted and punished for committing a crime which he only com-

mitted because he had been incited, instigated, persuaded, pressurised or wheedled into committing by law enforcement officers.

However, Lord Bingham went on to add that it was the duty of the police to enforce the law. In his view objection could not be taken if:

a law enforcement officer gives a defendant an opportunity to break the law, of which the defendant freely takes advantage, in circumstances where it appears that the defendant would have behaved in the same way if the opportunity had been afforded by anyone else.

R v Shannon [2001] 1 WLR 51

In this case, the Court of Appeal was presented with its first opportunity to consider the application of section 78 of PACE in the context of entrapment and in the light of the Human Rights Act 1998. The entrapment however was not carried out by police officers but by an undercover journalist and his team from the *News of the World*.

The defendant was charged with possession of drugs with intent to supply. He was a star in a popular TV drama called *London's Burning*. It had come to the attention of the *News of the World* that the defendant had passed round cocaine at various celebratory parties. The source of the information was never disclosed at trial or on appeal despite the efforts of the defendant's legal team. Sensing it would make a big scoop, the *News of the World* decided to test their informant's information. In an elaborate and expensive charade, the *News of the World* journalist posed as a wealthy Arab sheikh.

The defendant was invited to the sheikh's apartment at the Savoy Hotel. A Rolls Royce was provided to get him there. The invitation had been issued on the basis of a fictitious offer for the defendant to go out to Dubai for the celebrity opening of a nightclub owned by the sheikh. There was little doubting the defendant was taken in by his surroundings. In the sheikh's apartment were his personal assistant and bodyguard, all *News of the World* employees. The conversation was secretly recorded by a private investigator in an adjoining room. It was evident from the initial conversations that the defendant was somewhat awestruck. The defendant was offered free flights to Dubai, free accommodation and women if he wanted them. In the course of the conversation, the sheikh made reference to some disappointing cocaine he had been supplied with the previous night. He intimated that it was difficult to find cocaine of quality in London. He was then recorded as saying: 'Why you can't get here? There must be some places?' The defendant was heard to reply: 'There is.' In response to a further question, 'So you know some places?', the defendant indicated that he did. The defendant then went on to say he used to have a cocaine habit and explained how to tell whether the cocaine is pure or not. Both the trial judge and the Court of Appeal felt the defendant's replies betrayed a degree of familiarity with the drug as to suggest he had the necessary predisposition to commit the offence.

During the course of the conversation, the sheikh made it known that he would shortly be hosting a party where it was expected that cocaine would be available. The defendant took the bait and offered to supply him with some cocaine. When the sheikh told him how much he wanted, the defendant was heard to express his uneasiness. As the evening wore on, arrangements were made for the defendant to obtain samples of the cocaine and cannabis he had agreed to supply for the sheikh's party. Given £300, the use of a car and a mobile telephone the defendant later returned and was captured on film handing over 2.037 grams of cocaine and 11.5 grams of cannabis. The 'sting' subsequently made the front pages of the *News of the World* and the tapes were passed to the police.

At his trial, the defendant contended the evidence of the investigative journalist should have been excluded under section 78 of PACE on the ground that it had been obtained through the use of entrapment and was contrary to the right to a fair trial under Article 6(1). Considerable reliance was placed on the decision in *Teixeira de Castro* v *Portugal*. The trial judge admitted the evidence and the defendant was convicted. His several grounds of appeal, including the use of section 78 of

PACE, were considered by the Court of Appeal. Its judgment is disappointing for those who might have thought the Human Rights Act 1998 would herald a change in approach towards the admission of this type of evidence.

As a starting point in *R v Shannon*, the Court of Appeal drew on the guidelines developed by Lord Taylor CJ in *R v Smurthwaite*. Although the Court of Appeal found the defendant had been enticed to commit the offence in this case (this being a key test under the guidelines in *R v Smurthwaite*), it reached the conclusion that notwithstanding this fact, the evidence could still be admitted providing other aspects of procedural fairness were met. In *R v Shannon*, this included consideration of the reliability of the evidence sought to be adduced and the fullness and fairness of the opportunity afforded to the defendant to effect a challenge. The defendant had challenged the evidence and there was little to doubt the credibility of the undercover reporter in this case or the quality of the evidence his investigation had yielded.

In its judgment, the Court of Appeal's major preoccupation was with procedural fairness. It was clearly of the opinion that there could be no objection in principle to the use of evidence obtained through means of entrapment.

The Court of Appeal distinguished *Teixeira de Castro v Portugal* on the basis that, whilst there was enticement in this case, there was no incitement of the defendant. This aspect of the Court of Appeal's decision is disappointing. Aside from the obvious difficulty of drawing the line that differentiates enticement from incitement, are the facts in this case so materially different from those in *Teixeira de Castro*? But for the activities of the *News of the World* reporter, would the defendant have committed this offence? There was no suggestion that the defendant had previous convictions. Much was made by both the Court of Appeal and the trial judge of the fact that the defendant displayed familiarity with the drug-dealing scene. In *Teixeira de Castro*, the defendant must have had some familiarity with his local drug scene, as how would he have known where to obtain the drugs? No explanation is offered as to why knowledge indicating a predisposition to commit an offence of this kind, which would normally be inadmissible at the defendant's trial to prove an intent to supply where such an intent is denied, can be used to justify the admission of evidence obtained by the use of entrapment.

Furthermore, no mention was made of the case of *Nottingham City Council v Amin* discussed above. Having regard to the words used by Lord Bingham in that case, might not the actions of the journalist in *R v Shannon* be described as having pressurised and instigated the defendant into committing the offence?

Citing *Teixeira de Castro* in support, it was argued in the Court of Appeal on behalf of the appellant that in cases where the prosecuting authority's conduct amounts to incitement, a court should not entertain a prosecution at all, since the defendant's trial would have to be regarded as being unfair from the outset. If such was the case, and there is a dictum in *Teixeira de Castro* to support this, might the defendant apply to have proceedings stayed for an abuse of process?

The Court of Appeal accepted that in cases where an abuse of process is argued the criteria for determining the fairness of admitting evidence differs from an application to have evidence excluded under section 78 of PACE. In abuse of process cases wider issues of policy can be addressed and the court can mark its disapproval of the way in which evidence is gathered by excluding it even if the way in which the trial was conducted was fair.

However, the Court of Appeal rejected the argument in this case, maintaining the judgment in *Teixeira de Castro* could not be read so widely. What this case leaves open for a future court to consider, is whether a defendant might apply for a stay of the criminal proceedings on the basis of an abuse of process where the undercover officer's conduct amounts to incitement. The answer has in fact been provided by the decision of the House of Lords in *R v Loosely* [2001]; *Attorney-General's Reference (No 3 of 2000)* [2001] 4 All ER 897. The whole issue of entrapment must now be reconsidered in the light of this decision which provides that entrapment should be dealt with on the basis of an abuse of process application as opposed to an application to have the evidence excluded under section 78 of PACE. According to the House of Lords, the relevant question in the context of entrapment is whether the proceedings should have been brought in the first place and not whether the accused can receive a fair trial. The decision in *R v Loosely* is further considered later in this chapter in the context of the abuse of process doctrine.

Trickery and the use of deceptive practices

As part of some police investigations, the use of trickery or deceptive practices may be part of the evidence gathering process. How do the courts approach the admissibility of evidence obtained in this way?

R *v* Mason [1988] 1 WLR 139

The defendant had been arrested in connection with a minor arson offence. He was represented at the police station by his solicitor. The police told both the defendant and his solicitor that his fingerprints had been found on a fragment of glass at the scene from a bottle used to contain an inflammable liquid. Perceiving his position to be hopeless, the defendant confessed. In fact the evidence did not exist.

The Court of Appeal held that the trial judge should have exercised his discretion to exclude the evidence. Lord Justice Watkins delivered the judgment stating:

> It is obvious ... that the police practised a deceit not only upon the appellant, which is bad enough, but also upon his solicitor whose duty it was to advise him. In effect they hoodwinked both solicitor and client. That was a most reprehensible thing to do. It is not because we regard as misbehaviour of a serious kind conduct of that nature that we have come to the decision soon to be made plain. This is not the place to discipline the police ... We are concerned with the proper application of law.

In considering whether the trial judge properly exercised his discretion to admit the evidence, the Court of Appeal concluded that he had not because he had failed to take sufficient account of the deceit practised on the accused's solicitor. Would the outcome have been different had the accused chosen not to be represented? This decision gave hope that section 78 of PACE would be used in a wider way than the narrow discretion exercised at common law. There was after all nothing inherently unreliable in Mason's confession. It may well have been true. The deceit practised on the solicitor, however, was too much for the Court of Appeal. It was injurious to the integrity of the criminal justice system.

Nevertheless, in the context of subsequent cases, the decision in *R v Mason* is something of an exception, as in the majority of cases where the police use deception and subterfuge, the court will turn a blind eye if relevant, reliable evidence results. As examples of the courts' normal practice, consider the following cases:

R v Bailey and Smith [1993] 3 All ER 513

The two accused were arrested in connection with an armed robbery. Both were legally represented and chose to exercise their right to remain silent. They were charged and brought before a magistrates' court where they were remanded into police custody for the purposes of organising an identification parade. The questioning of suspects after charge is prohibited under the Codes of Practice save in limited and defined circumstances. The investigating officers decided to put the accused in the same cell in an attempt to obtain further useful evidence. The officers had sought authorisation for their proposed course of action from a senior officer. They invented a charade, telling the accused it was not their choice to have them share but that they had been forced into it by an unco-operative custody sergeant. The two accused were taken in, notwithstanding the fact that their solicitor had warned them that the bugging of police cells was not uncommon. Whilst together in the cell, they made incriminating admissions. The police sought to use the tapes in evidence against them.

The Court of Appeal held the trial judge had rightly admitted the evidence. Lord Justice Simon Brown summed up his reasoning in the following way:

> Where, as here, very serious crimes have been committed ... by men who have not shrunk from using trickery and a good deal worse, and where there has never been the least suggestion that their covertly taped confessions were oppressively obtained or were other than wholly reliable it seems to be hardly surprising that the trial judge exercised his discretion in the way he did...

R v Chalkley and Jeffries [1998] 2 All ER 155

C and J were under suspicion of conspiracy to commit robbery. The investigating officers felt the only way they were going to obtain evidence against them was to install a listening device in the home of C without his knowledge. To do this the officers had to be sure of C and J's whereabouts. C had previously been under investigation for an unrelated offence of using a stolen credit card. The investigation into this offence had been stale for some time. The officers in charge of the conspiracy investigation asked colleagues to arrest C and J on suspicion of having used a stolen credit card. They were detained and searched at the police station. Whilst in detention, officers took C's keys and used them to gain access to his property in order to plant the listening device. A copy of C's keys was taken for later use and C and J were released. Evidence of a conspiracy to rob was recorded in conversations between C and J at C's home over a six-week period. On a further occasion when C and J came to the police station to answer police bail, officers used the duplicate key to regain entry to the property to re-charge the batteries in the listening device. C and J were convicted and a number of matters were raised on appeal. One of the matters was whether the trial judge had been right to admit the evidence obtained in this way under section 78.

Concluding that the trial judge had been right, Lord Justice Auld held that section 78 had not been intended to widen the common law rule as stated in R v Sang and that there was, as a consequence, no wider remit under section 78 for a court to mark its disapproval of the investigative methods used. The overriding consideration, so far as the application of section 78 is concerned, is the fairness of the proceedings.

> At first sight, the words in section 78 'the circumstances in which the evidence was obtained' might suggest that the means by which evidence was secured, even if they did not affect the fairness of admitting it, could entitle the court to exclude it as a result of a balancing exercise analogous to that when considering a stay for abuse of process. On that approach, the court could, even if it considered that the intrinsic nature of the evidence was not unfair to the accused, exclude it as a mark of disapproval of the way in which it had been obtained. That was certainly not the law before the 1984 Act. And we consider that the inclusion in section 78 of the words 'the circumstances in which the evidence was obtained' was not intended to widen the common law rule in this respect as stated by Lord Diplock in Sang.

Referring to the tape-recorded conversations in this case, the Court of Appeal concluded there had been no unfairness in admitting them because:

there was no dispute as to its authenticity, content or effect; it was relevant, highly probative of the appellants' involvement in the conspiracy and otherwise admissible; it did not result from incitement, entrapment
or inducement or any other conduct of that sort; and none of the unlawful conduct of the police or other of
their conduct of which complaint is made affects the quality of the evidence.

Chalkley and Jeffries is an important decision. The Court of Appeal is firmly of the
opinion that the resulting reliability of the evidence is the principal determining factor
in the exercise of judicial discretion under section 78 of PACE. If the reliability of the
evidence is unaffected by the way in which it has been obtained, according to this
authority, section 78 of PACE affords no discretion to exclude it. This is in spite of the
clear wording in the section, which specifically invites the court to consider the manner in which the evidence was obtained, and the endorsement by Lord Justice Auld of
the principles in R v *Smurthwaite* discussed above.

Breaching PACE and/or the Codes of Practice in order to obtain confession or identification evidence

Confession evidence and evidence of identification have generated most of the case law
on improperly obtained evidence. This is perhaps not too surprising as the specific
safeguards contained in PACE and the Codes of Practice are there to ensure not only
respect for the rights of suspects in custody but crucially to ensure the reliability of any
resulting evidence. Unreliable evidence should not be admitted precisely because of the
unfairness it may cause.

Evidence obtained in breach of the safeguards contained in PACE and the accompanying Codes of Practice is always vulnerable to challenge under section 78. It is nevertheless important to realise that simply because evidence has been obtained in breach
of PACE or the Codes, it does not automatically mean the evidence must be excluded.
The defendant must establish that the breach has resulted in unfairness to him, capable of prejudicing a fair trial.

Section 58 of PACE gives every suspect in custody the right to consult a solicitor in
private. Access to a solicitor can only be delayed in strictly defined circumstances. In
both the following cases, with contrasting outcomes, the decision to delay the suspect's
access to his solicitor was not warranted and a confession was duly obtained.

R *v* Alladice (1988) 87 Cr App R 380

Alladice was an experienced 'interviewee'. He accepted he had been properly cautioned and that
he understood he had the right to remain silent. At his trial, he claimed the officers had fabricated
incriminating admissions he had made in one of his interviews without the presence of his solicitor.
The interviews had been recorded by the police in the form of a contemporaneous note. The Court
of Appeal took the view that the presence of a solicitor would have added nothing to Alladice's existing knowledge at the time and that accordingly no unfairness resulted.

R *v* Walsh (1990) 91 Cr App R 161

Walsh was arrested in connection with robbery and possession of a firearm. Access to a solicitor
had been wrongfully denied. There were, in addition, breaches of Code C in that the police failed,
without good reason, to keep a contemporaneous note of what was said during the interview and
had denied the defendant the opportunity, required under Code C, to read and sign the record of

the interview. The Court of Appeal concluded in this case that the breaches had been 'significant and substantial'.

Saville J observed:

> To our minds it follows if there are significant and substantial breaches of section 58 or the provisions of the Code, then prima facie at least the standards of fairness set by Parliament have not been met. So far as this defendant is concerned ... to admit evidence against him which has been obtained in circumstances where these standards have not been met, cannot but have an adverse effect on the fairness of the proceedings. This does not mean of course that in every case of a significant or substantial breach of section 58 or the Code of Practice evidence will automatically be excluded. Section 78 does not so provide.

The court stated that the main objective of section 58 was to achieve fairness to both sides. Fairness to the suspect is provided in that a solicitor acts as an independent witness to what occurs and can protect the suspect against undue pressure to speak. Section 58 also shields the officers because they are protected against unfounded accusations of malpractice. The police had only themselves to blame.

R v Walsh confirms earlier authorities on the point that the absence of bad faith resulting in a breach of PACE or the Codes of Practice is largely irrelevant to the exercise of discretion under section 78, particularly in the context of confession evidence. This is made clear by Saville J, in stating:

> Although bad faith may make substantial or significant that which might otherwise not be so, the contrary does not follow. Breaches which are in themselves significant and substantial are not rendered otherwise by the good faith of the officers concerned.

R *v* Keenan [1990] 2 QB 54

The police failed to make a contemporaneous record of incriminating admissions that they alleged the defendant had made. The defendant denied ever making the admissions. He claimed the officer had 'verballed' him. No reason was given by the officers for their failure under Code C to record the admissions. The Court of Appeal concluded that the breaches had been 'serious and substantial'. To have admitted the statements would have put the defendant at a serious procedural disadvantage. Indeed, if he denied making the statements at all, he would effectively have to give evidence to this effect on oath, thereby depriving him of his right to silence. Furthermore, he would be accusing the officers of fabricating evidence. Having been forced to accuse the officers of fabricating evidence on oath, this would have serious implications for the conduct of his defence, as any of his previous convictions would have to be revealed under section 1(f)(ii) of the Criminal Evidence Act 1898. The Court of Appeal noted the provisions in the Code protected the police against unfounded allegations of 'verballing', as much as they protected the defendant.

A number of specific safeguards are contained in Code D of the Codes of Practice, which is designed to ensure the reliability of identification evidence obtained in advance of trial. The most important is the right of an accused to stand on an identification parade which is the procedure best felt to produce the most reliable evidence of identification. The specifics of Code D are examined in Chapter 8. Suffice to say, the admissibility of evidence of identification obtained in breach of Code D may be challenged under section 78. The trial judge will only exclude such evidence, however, if its admission would adversely affect the fairness of the proceedings. Relevant to this might be:

- what the reasons for the failure to observe the Code were;
- whether an accurate record of the identification procedure was compiled;
- whether the accused was represented by a solicitor;
- whether the judge specifically pointed out the weakness occasioned by the breach to the jury and the cogency of other evidence implicating the accused.

R v Nagah (1991) 92 Cr App R 344

The defendant had been arrested in connection with an offence of attempted rape. He had sought an identification parade to establish his innocence. His request was refused. In no sense had it been impractical for the police to convene one. Subsequently, the police convened a highly unsatisfactory street identification. The Court of Appeal concluded that the police had flouted Code D. The defendant had been prejudiced in that he had been denied a valuable opportunity to test the eyewitness's reliability. The prejudice was compounded by the material discrepancies between the description given by the eyewitness and the defendant's actual appearance.

Not every failure to convene an identification parade where one is requested will result in a conviction being quashed since a fair trial may still have been possible.

R v Rutherford (1994) 98 Cr App R 191

The defendant and another were convicted of robbery. It had been alleged that they had forced their way into the home of an elderly lady. They sprayed a liquid into her eyes, bound and gagged her. It was further alleged that £1,000, some Indian rupees and a scrap of paper with a telephone number written on it had been stolen. The defendant was arrested in the vicinity soon after. In his possession were a quantity of cash, some Indian rupees and a scrap of paper containing a telephone number. The defendant's appearance matched that of descriptions given by a couple of witnesses. Both the defendant and his companion were arrested. They both consented to an identification parade, but none was arranged. The police felt they had sufficient other evidence upon which to base a conviction. Notwithstanding this, the Court of Appeal held a suspect had a right to an identification parade under Code D 2.3 in circumstances where a witness indicates he would be able to identify the offender or there is a reasonable chance of him being able to do so. In this case however, the prejudice to the defendant had been dealt with in the judge's summing up and there had been ample circumstantial evidence upon which to convict the defendant.

Further case law examples of the use of section 78 of PACE in excluding both confession and identification evidence is considered in Chapters 6 and 8.

Unlawful seizure and use of real evidence

Three cases have provided further guidance on the operation of section 78.

R v Sanghera [2001] 1 Cr App R 299

Evidence was admitted following an unlawful search, contrary to Code B of the Codes of Practice. There had been a robbery reported at a post office of which the defendant was the owner. As part of the investigation into the crime, the police omitted to obtain the defendant's written consent to a search of his premises. In the course of their search, the police had found a hidden box containing a substantial quantity of cash, as a result of which their suspicion that the robbery was a sham was aroused. The money from the box was removed and a hidden camera installed. The defendant was arrested a few days later having been seen to look in the hidden box. The defendant did not contest the reliability of the evidence that the unlawful search had yielded. However, he maintained he would have wanted to be present at the time of the search, as this would have afforded him the opportunity of offering an immediate explanation of the presence of the money found in the box. In the circumstances, he argued the evidence should have been excluded under section 78 of PACE. This submission was rejected by the trial judge and the defendant was convicted. His appeal was dismissed by the Court of Appeal.

In its judgment in *R v Sanghera*, the Court of Appeal summarised the position as regards the relationship between breaches of the Codes of Practice and the exercise of discretion under section 78 as follows:

> In relation to section 78, it is of importance, in our judgment, that each particular case is considered on its facts and that no broad generalisation is made as to its application. However, there are clearly different situations with which the courts have to deal under section 78. There are situations where a serious breakdown in the proper procedures has taken place in the whole of the prosecution process. In such a situation, the courts may well take the view that the nature of the breakdown is so significant that it would not be appropriate to allow the evidence to be admitted. There are also situations lower down the scale where there has been a breach of the Code which can be regarded as being significant but not serious. That is not of the same gravity as indicated by the first category of situations. There may be cases where breaches of the Code can be said to be venial or technical. In the case of the latter category the court will almost inevitably come to the conclusion that there has been no injustice or unfairness involved and will exercise its discretion in favour of allowing the evidence to be given. There are difficulties with regard to the middle category, the category where it could be said the breach was significant but not serious. In that situation section 78 leaves the matter to be evaluated by the judge concerned, looking at all the circumstances.

On the facts, and given that the police had acted in good faith, it could not be said that the defendant had been prejudiced in any way. The evidence yielded was both relevant and reliable and the defendant had been afforded the opportunity of both explanation and challenge at his trial. The Court of Appeal went on to say that the process of ensuring fairness applied not only to the defence, but also to the prosecution. This point has recently been reiterated by the House of Lords.

Attorney-General's Reference (No 3 of 1999) [2001] 1 All ER 577

The defendant was acquitted of rape on the direction of the trial judge on the basis that a DNA sample taken from the rape victim had been found to match the defendant's DNA profile held on the national DNA database. This profile had been taken from the defendant in connection with an unrelated burglary offence for which he had been charged and subsequently acquitted. Section 64 of PACE clearly provides for the destruction of a DNA sample where an individual is cleared of the offence in relation to which the sample was taken. At the defendant's trial for rape the trial judge ruled that the DNA sample had been unlawfully retained and that the evidence of the match had to be deemed inadmissible. The Attorney-General referred the matter to the Court of Appeal, which in turn certified the matter for the consideration of the House of Lords.

The decision of the House of Lords is based upon the statutory interpretation of section 64(3B) of PACE and does not consider the application of section 78 of PACE directly. On the face of it, section 64(3B) clearly seems to prohibit the use of a sample that should have been destroyed, for the purposes of any investigation of an offence. Somewhat implausibly, the House of Lords came to the conclusion that the section can be interpreted in a way that did not render inadmissible, evidence obtained as a result of the prohibited investigation. Agreeing with the statutory interpretation of the other Law Lords, Lord Hutton took the opportunity to consider the exercise of discretion under section 78 of PACE in the context of the facts in this case. On an *obiter dicta* basis, he observed:

> In considering the interpretation of section 64(3B) my noble and learned friend Lord Steyn has stated in his speech that respect for the privacy of defendants is not the only value at stake, that the purpose of the criminal law is to protect citizens from harm and that there must be fairness to all, to the victim and to the public as well as to the defendant. I wish to express my concurrence with these observations, but in a case of this nature where very grave crimes were committed against an elderly woman in her own home, I consider that the observations of my noble and learned friend are also relevant to the exercise of the discretion under section 78. In the exercise of that discretion I consider that the interests of the victim and the public must be considered as well as the interests of the defendant.

Finally, in *R v Cooke* [1995] 1 Cr App R 318, the defendant claimed a non-intimate sample of his hair had been taken from him unlawfully. The sample yielded hugely compelling DNA evidence which convicted the defendant of rape and kidnap. The Court of Appeal held the evidence had not been obtained unlawfully and that, even if it had, section 78 would not require the court to exclude it, because such illegality would not have cast doubt on the reliability and probative strength of the resulting evidence. In this sense, the evidence could be distinguished from confession evidence obtained in breach of PACE and the Codes of Practice which tend to be of a more inherently unreliable nature.

Unauthorised surveillance methods

The increasing sophistication of technological surveillance devices allows the police to obtain evidence in many different covert ways. Where the use of such surveillance is unauthorised or involves the police acting in breach of the criminal and or the civil law should the evidence be admitted?

R v Khan [1996] 3 All ER 289

Khan was under suspicion of drug smuggling. In an attempt to obtain evidence against him, investigating officers attached a listening device to a property visited frequently by Khan of which neither Khan nor the property owner had any knowledge. There were Home Office guidelines in existence regarding the use of covert surveillance but there was no statutory authorisation for the use of such devices at the time, although the officers had sought and obtained permission for the surveillance from their Chief Constable. As a consequence of the operation, the police obtained a tape recording of Khan proving he was involved in the importation of heroin. They sought to use it in evidence against him at his trial.

At his trial the prosecution accepted that there was no statutory authorisation for the use of the device and that placing it on the property without the owner's permission constituted a civil trespass. Khan conceded that the tape was authentic and that it was his voice which could be heard. On appeal it was argued on his behalf that the evidence had been obtained in violation of Article 8 of the European Convention on Human Rights, guaranteeing a right of privacy, and that the trial judge should have excluded the tape-recorded conversations in the exercise of his discretion either at common law or under section 78 of PACE.

The arguments were firmly rejected by both the Court of Appeal ([1994] 4 All ER 426) and the House of Lords ([1996] 3 All ER 289). In the Court of Appeal, Lord Taylor, whilst accepting the importance of upholding rights of privacy, felt the right was subject to the wider public interest in law enforcement. In fact this was recognised in the wording of Article 8 itself.

The House of Lords held a right to privacy was not recognised in English law. (Note that the implementation of the Human Rights Act 1998 has since changed this.) Even if such a right had been recognised, the House of Lords went on to say that the authority of *R* v *Sang* had made it quite clear that such evidence, providing it is relevant, remains admissible subject to the discretion of the trial judge. Having regard to section 78, the House of Lords took the view that the wording of the section meant a breach of Article 8 was a relevant factor for a court to consider. According to Lord Nolan:

> If the behaviour of the police in a particular case amounts to an apparent or probable breach of some relevant law or convention, common sense dictates that this is a consideration which may be taken into account.

Notwithstanding there may have been a violation of Article 8, in the opinion of the House of Lords, the evidence was rightly admitted at common law and under section 78. The evidence was especially relevant and could not be said to have adversely affected the fairness of the proceedings. Expressing his relief at such an outcome, Lord Nolan continued:

> It would be a strange reflection on our law if a man who admitted his participation in the illegal importation of a large quantity of heroin should have his conviction set aside on the ground that his privacy has been invaded.

Whilst *R* v *Khan* afforded the House of Lords the first real opportunity to offer some concrete guidance on the principles governing the exercise of the discretion under section 78 of PACE, the decision is disappointing in that it adds little to the current debate surrounding the use that can be made of that discretion. *Khan*'s case has since been considered by the European Court of Human Rights in *Khan* v *United Kingdom* (2001) 31 EHRR 45.

The United Kingdom was found to be in violation of Article 8. It will be recalled from Chapter 2 that the right to privacy under Article 8 is not absolute and can be qualified, provided such qualification is:

- in accordance with law;
- pursues a legitimate objective; and
- is no more than is necessary in a democratic society, ie it is a proportional response to the objective identified.

The clear absence of any statutory authority for the surveillance used in *Khan*'s case, meant the interference could not be described as being in accordance with law. For this reason, the defendant's right to privacy had been violated.

Under Part III of the Police Act 1997, authority to carry out intrusive surveillance operations has now been placed on a statutory footing and, except in cases of an emergency, the prior authorisation of an independent commissioner must be obtained. Regulation of the interception of information and communication technologies such as e-mail and mobile telephones is now provided for by the Regulation of Investigatory Powers Act 2000.

Notwithstanding that the principal evidence against Khan had been obtained in violation of Article 8, the United Kingdom was not found to be in breach of Article 6, guaranteeing the right to a fair trial.

As regards Article 6(1), the European Court of Human Rights observed in *Khan* v *United Kingdom*:

> It is not the role of the Court to determine, as a matter of principle, whether particular types of evidence, for example, unlawfully obtained evidence may be admissible or, indeed,

whether the applicant was guilty or not. The question which must be answered is whether the proceedings as a whole, including the way in which the evidence was obtained, were fair. This involves an examination of the 'unlawfulness' in question and, where violation of another Convention right is concerned, the nature of the violation found.

The Court concluded the applicant had had a fair trial, notwithstanding the main evidence against him had been obtained in breach of a Convention right. In particular, the Court noted there had been no doubt as to the authenticity of the tape and the strength and reliability of the evidence it had yielded. There had been no inducement to confess or entrapment. Furthermore, section 78 of PACE had afforded Khan the opportunity to challenge the admissibility of the evidence. In these circumstances his trial had been fair.

Abuse of process

Given the restrictive nature of the way in which judicial discretion to exclude evidence is exercised at common law and under section 78 of PACE, can a defendant seek to have the proceedings stayed or a conviction quashed for an abuse of process where the case against him rests in the main on unlawfully obtained evidence? Are the principles governing the exercise of discretion under section 78 of PACE (in so far as they can be ascertained) the same as those governing the application of the abuse of process doctrine?

The abuse of process doctrine has both a procedural and an evidential context. In a procedural sense, a defendant might argue that although he has had a fair trial, his conviction should be quashed because a trial should never have taken place. In an evidential sense, the abuse of process doctrine clearly has the potential to overlap with section 78 in situations where the defendant claims the prosecution should never have been commenced in the first place because of the unlawful manner in which the principal evidence against the accused was obtained. In *R v Latif and Shahzad* [1996] 1 All ER 353, the defendant argued that he had been entrapped to commit an offence and that the resulting evidence should have been excluded under section 78 of PACE or the proceedings stayed for an abuse of process.

The defendant was charged in connection with drug trafficking. An undercover Customs and Excise officer arranged a meeting with the defendant during which the defendant expressed himself willing to arrange the exportation of drugs from Pakistan to England. It was in fact an undercover customs officer who brought the drugs into the country, thus himself committing an offence. In defining the test to establish whether the conduct of the prosecuting authorities amounts to an abuse of process, the House of Lords highlighted the dilemma of the courts and explained the approach to be taken:

> if the court always refuses to stay such proceedings, the perception will be that the court condones criminal conduct and malpractice by law enforcement agencies. That would undermine public confidence in the criminal justice system and bring it into disrepute. On the other hand, if the court were always to stay proceedings in such cases, it would incur the approach that it is failing to protect the public from serious crime. The weakness of both extreme positions leaves only one principled solution: it has to perform a balancing exercise. If the court considers that a fair trial is not possible it will stay the proceedings. That is not what the present case is concerned with. It is plain that a fair trial was possible and that such a trial took place. In this case the issue is whether, despite the fact that a fair

trial was possible, the judge ought to have stayed the criminal proceedings on broader considerations of the integrity of the criminal justice system. The law is settled. Weighing countervailing considerations of policy and justice, it is for the judge in the exercise of his discretion to decide whether there has been an abuse of process, which amounts to an affront to the public conscience and requires criminal proceedings to be stayed ... General guidance as to how the discretion should be exercised in particular circumstances will not be useful. But it is possible to say that in a case such as the present the judge must weigh in the balance the public interest in ensuring that those that are charged with grave crimes should be tried and the competing public interest in not conveying the impression that the court will adopt the approach that the end justified any means ... (*per* Lord Steyn)

On the facts of the case, the House of Lords rejected the argument based on abuse of process. The defendant was not a vulnerable or unwilling person. He was an organiser in the heroin trade, and crucially, he had taken the initiative in this case. Although the Customs and Excise officers had acted wrongly, the House of Lords concluded his conduct had not been 'so shameful and unworthy as to be an affront to the public conscience'.

As to the application of section 78 of PACE, the House of Lords confirmed that if the abuse of process argument failed, the argument on section 78 must also fail. The defendant had not been prejudiced in the presentation of his defence. He had been afforded a fair means of challenging the evidence.

Whilst the abuse of process doctrine clearly has a wider application than the discretion afforded to exclude prosecution evidence under section 78 of PACE, the rejection of it on the facts in R v *Latif and Shahzad* implies the conduct on the part of the police must be highly dubious.

The decision in R v *Latif and Shahzad* was applied in R v *Mullen* [1999] 3 WLR 777. Although the defendant accepted he had been properly convicted through the process of a fair trial and on very strong evidence, English and Zimbabwean authorities had conspired to deport him unlawfully from Zimbabwe. Although the offences the defendant had committed were very serious, the conduct of the authorities in this case had been so shameful and unworthy that it would have been, in the view of the Court of Appeal, an affront to public conscience to have allowed the prosecution to succeed.

A clarification of the differences between abuse of process and section 78 was provided by Lord Justice Auld in the Court of Appeal's decision in R v *Chalkley and Jeffries* [1998] 2 All ER 155, considered earlier:

The determination of the fairness or otherwise of admitting evidence under section 78 is distinct from the exercise of discretion in determining whether to stay criminal proceedings as an abuse of process. Depending on the circumstances, the latter may require consideration, not just of the potential fairness of a trial, but also of a balance of the possibly countervailing interests of prosecuting a criminal to conviction and discouraging abuse of power. However laudable the end, it may not justify any means to achieve it. ...

   At first sight, the words in section 78 'the circumstances in which the evidence was obtained' might suggest that the means by which evidence was secured, even if they did not affect the fairness of admitting it, could entitle the court to exclude it as a result of a balancing exercise analogous to that when considering a stay for abuse of process. On that approach, the court could, even if it considered that the intrinsic nature of the evidence was not unfair to the accused, exclude it as a mark of disapproval of the way in which it had been obtained. That was certainly not the law before the 1984 Act. And we consider that the inclusion in section 78 of the words 'the circumstances in which the evidence was obtained' was not intended to widen the common law rule in this respect as stated by Lord Diplock in *Sang*. That is that, save in the case of admissions and confessions and generally as to evidence obtained from the accused after the commission of the offence, there is no discretion to exclude evidence unless its quality was or might have been affected by the way in which it was obtained. ...

The exercise for the judge under section 78 is not the marking of his disapproval of the prosecution's breach, if any, of the law in the conduct of the investigation or the proceedings, by a discretionary decision to stay them, but an examination of the question whether it would be unfair to the defendant to admit that evidence.

Critical of the Court of Appeal's approach in *Chalkley and Jeffries*, Choo and Nash observe:

Whether one is considering the possibility of excluding evidence on account of pre-trial police impropriety, or the possibility of staying the proceedings as a whole on account of such impropriety, what is at stake is surely the same fundamental question: should the prosecution be deprived of the fruits of the pre-trial police impropriety. English law has already accepted that proceedings may be stayed on account of pre-trial impropriety even if there is no danger of the trial being 'unreliable' in terms of being unable to determine guilt or innocence accurately. Consistency dictates, therefore, that, by analogy, improperly obtained but reliable evidence should be capable of being excluded ... The peremptory dismissal in *Chalkley* of considerations drawn from the law of abuse of process is therefore particularly disappointing as it produces a glaring anomaly into the law.

Abuse of process and entrapment

As we have already seen, the admissibility of entrapment evidence under section 78 of PACE has taxed the Court of Appeal on a number of occasions resulting in few clear and comprehensive guidelines. The position has however changed in the light of the House of Lords' decision in R v *Loosely* which has taken the issue of entrapment out of the context of section 78 of PACE altogether and placed it firmly within the abuse of process doctrine.

R v Loosely [2001] 1 WLR 2060

The House of Lords considered two appeals, one arising out of a conviction (Loosely), the other arising from an acquittal following a referral by the Attorney-General to the Court of Appeal, whose decision is reported at [2001] Crim LR 645. In the case of the appellant, Loosely, an undercover officer posed as a prospective buyer of drugs. His actions were part of an authorised surveillance in the Guildford area which had seen a rise in the supply of heroin. The focus of suspicion fell on a particular public house in which the undercover officer had been given the defendant's contact number as a possible source of supply. On contacting the defendant, the officer asked if he could 'sort us a couple of bags'. The defendant responded willingly to the solicitation and immediately made arrangements to take the undercover officer to a place where he was able to obtain the drugs. In the other case, undercover officers offered the defendant contraband cigarettes. After a lengthy conversation about the cigarettes, one of the officers asked the defendant if he can 'sort him some brown'. It was only after numerous conversations, much persuasion and the offer of further contraband cigarettes, that the defendant eventually obtained a quantity of heroin for the officers. On handing the drug over to the undercover officers, the defendant was recorded as saying: 'I am not really into heroin myself'. In interview he maintained he had nothing to do with heroin and had only supplied the officers because of their requests and as a favour for the contraband cigarettes. The trial judge agreed to stay the prosecution on the ground of an abuse of process in the light of the decision in *Teixeira de Castro* v *Portugal* (1998) 28 EHRR 101, considered earlier in this chapter.

In formulating its decision, the House of Lords undertook an extensive review of the existing law relating to the use of evidence obtained through entrapment. The conclusion reached was that a clear distinction had to be drawn between an application to exclude evidence on the ground of its unreliability or procedural unfairness and an application to exclude the evidence on the ground that the defendant should not be tried at all or should never have been tried in the first place. The former falls within the ambit of section 78 of PACE whilst the latter falls within the abuse of process doctrine. In entrapment cases, the application to have the evidence excluded is in reality an application to stay the proceedings for an abuse of process since the evidence obtained through the use of entrapment usually forms the entire basis of the prosecution's case. If the evidence of entrapment were to be excluded the prosecution would collapse. For this reason, the abuse of process application was the appropriate remedy and, in this regard, the House of Lords drew support from a statement to this effect in the European Court of Human Rights' decision in *Teixeira de Castro* v *Portugal*. Accordingly the relevant test to be applied in English law was that set out in R v *Latif and Shahzad*, namely whether the prosecution amounts to an affront to the public conscience.

All of their Lordships in *Loosely* accepted the need for prosecuting authorities to use undercover officers in the detection and prosecution of crime. The use of entrapment however, or 'state-created crime', is an abuse of process. The difficulty remains as to what might be regarded as acceptable police conduct and what is not.

For Lord Nicholls, entrapment involves luring a citizen into committing a crime he would not otherwise have committed. Of particular importance in this regard is whether the police did no more than to present the defendant with what Lord Nicholls defined as being 'an unexceptional' opportunity to commit a crime. In other words, have the police done no more than might have been expected from others in the circumstances? Lord Nicholls identified the following factors as being relevant to an assessment of whether the actions of the police amount to entrapment:

> The nature of the offence. The use of pro-active techniques is more needed and, hence, more appropriate, in some circumstances than others. The secrecy and difficulty of detection, and the manner in which the particular criminal activity is carried on, are relevant considerations.
>
> The reason for the particular police operation. It goes without saying that the police must act in good faith and not, for example, as part of a malicious vendetta against an individual or group of individuals. Having reasonable grounds for suspicion is one way good faith may be established, but having grounds for suspicion of a particular individual is not always essential. Sometimes suspicion may be centred on a particular place, such as a particular public house. Sometimes random testing may be the only practicable way of policing a particular trading activity.
>
> The nature and extent of police participation in the crime. The greater the inducement held out by the police, and the more forceful or persistent the police overtures, the more readily may a court conclude that the police overstepped the boundary ...

The defendant's criminal record. The defendant's criminal record is unlikely to be relevant unless it can be linked to other factors grounding reasonable suspicion that the defendant is currently engaged in criminal activity...

Lord Hoffmann, citing with approval the dictum of Lord Bingham in *Nottingham City Council* v *Amin* [2000] 1 WLR 1071 (see above), identified the relevant factors of entrapment as follows:

1   Whether the police caused the defendant to commit the crime or merely provided him with the opportunity. Lord Hoffmann considered this factor to be the most important.
2   Whether the accused would have committed the offence with someone else.
3   Whether the police suspect an accused might commit an offence. In relation to this factor, Lord Hoffmann observed: 'The only proper purpose of police participation is to obtain evidence of criminal acts which they suspect someone is about to commit or in which he is already engaged. It is not to tempt people to commit crimes in order to expose their bad characters and punish them.' Relevant to this factor is the question of whether or not the particular police operation had been authorised.
4   The nature of the offence, ie whether the deployment of an undercover officer is the only way of achieving the desired result.

Interestingly, Lord Hoffmann concluded that a defendant's predisposition to commit crime did not make him fair game for the prosecuting authorities. Furthermore, the distinction made in *R* v *Smurthwaite* [1994] 1 All ER 898 (discussed above) between the active and passive involvement of an undercover officer was not felt to be helpful, since it had to be expected that in some instances an undercover officer would have to behave in an active manner in order to appear plausible.

In similar vein, Lord Hutton cited the factors identified by McHugh J in the Australian authority of *Ridgeway* v *The Queen* (1995) 184 CLR 19 with approval:

(1) Whether conduct of the law enforcement authorities induced the offence.

(2) Whether, in proffering the inducement, the authorities had reasonable grounds for suspecting that the accused was likely to commit the particular offence or one that was similar to that offence or were acting in the course of a bona fide investigation of offences of a kind similar to that with which the accused has been charged.

(3) Whether, prior to the inducement, the accused had the intention of committing the offence or a similar offence if an opportunity arose.

(4) Whether the offence was induced as the result of persistent importunity, threats, deceit, offers of rewards or other inducements that would not ordinarily be associated with the commission of the offence or a similar offence.

All of their Lordships concluded that the principles as stated above were entirely consistent with the decision of the European Court of Human Rights in *Teixeira de Castro* v *Portugal*.

Ultimately, each case has to depend on its own facts. Applying these guiding principles to the appeals before them, their Lordships concluded that Loosely's appeal should be dismissed. His arrest had come about as a result of legitimate concern in the rising supply of hard drugs in the Guildford area and from one public house in particular. As Loosely expressed himself keen to arrange a supply, the undercover officer had not needed to undertake any persuasion and therefore his actions clearly fell within the bounds of acceptable conduct. In relation to the Attorney-General's reference, the House of Lords concluded it would not interfere with the trial judge's exercise of discretion. The defendant in that case had come under considerable and sustained pressure by officers to supply them with a Class A drug and could be said to have been induced to commit the offence based on the continued supply of contraband cigarettes to him.

In the light of the decision in R v Loosely, it is submitted that previous cases like those of R v Smurthwaite, R v Christou and Nottingham City Council v Amin would not have been decided differently on their facts. It is interesting nevertheless to speculate whether R v Shannon would be decided differently. Had undercover police officers behaved in the same manner as the undercover journalist, their actions would, it is contended, have amounted to entrapment in accordance with the principles set out in R v Loosely.

In the Criminal Courts Review Report, Lord Justice Auld calls for consideration to be given to rationalising and simplifying the statutory and common law rules for the exclusion of evidence based on considerations of fairness together with the power to stay proceedings for an abuse of process. The decision in R v Loosely does however provide some simplification of the law and the relevant principles, at least in the context of entrapment.

FAIRNESS AND THE SAFETY OF A CONVICTION

A related but important procedural question is whether a trial can be unfair, but a conviction still safe within the meaning of section 2(1) of the Criminal Appeal Act 1968, as amended by the Criminal Appeal Act 1995. If the Court of Appeal, for example, were to conclude that a trial judge had been wrong to admit unlawfully obtained evidence, but it was satisfied that the defendant was guilty of the offence, would the conviction be unsafe within the meaning of the amended section 2(1)? The dicta in R v Chalkley and Jeffries [1998] 2 All ER 155 suggest a conviction could still be regarded as safe, even though aspects of the trial were unfair to the defendant. In R v Mullen [2000] 3 WLR 777, the Court of Appeal held it had always been the case, prior to the revised version of section 2(1) of the 1968 Act, that for a conviction to be regarded as safe, it had to be lawful. As the trial should never have taken place, Mullen's conviction had to be regarded as being 'unsafe'. The question posed at the outset of this section is a very pertinent one in the light of section 2 of the Human Rights Act 1998 (interpretation of Convention rights). Where the defendant's guilt seems beyond doubt, but there has, in the opinion of the European Court of Human Rights or the Court of Appeal been a violation of Article 6 of the European Convention on Human Rights, does this inevitably lead to a finding that the conviction must be regarded as unsafe?

In R v Davis, Johnson and Rowe [2001] 1 Cr App R 8 the Court of Appeal saw no difficulty in giving effect to the right to a fair trial when discharging its duty to consider the safety of the conviction. Although this case involved the quashing of convictions for non-disclosure of prosecution evidence, the Court of Appeal held there was no presumption that a finding by the European Court of Human Rights of a violation of Article 6 meant a conviction was unsafe within the meaning of the amended section 2(1). A finding of a breach under Article 6(1) may but will not necessarily lead to a finding that the conviction was unsafe. The effect of any breach on the safety of a conviction would depend on the nature and degree of the breach: 'A conviction can never be safe if there is doubt about guilt. However, the converse is not true. A conviction may be unsafe even where there is no doubt about guilt but the trial process has been vitiated by serious unfairness or significant legal misdirection.'

In *R v Togher, Doran and Parsons* [2001] 1 Cr App R 457 however, the Court of Appeal saw the matter of fairness and safety of a resulting conviction somewhat differently:

> As a matter of first principles, we do not consider that either the use of the word 'unsafe' in the legislation or the previous cases compel an approach which does not correspond with that of the ECHR. The requirement of fairness in the criminal process has always been a common law tenet of the greatest importance. The common law approach has been enhanced by legislation and in particular, the Police and Criminal Evidence Act 1984 and the codes of practice made thereunder (sections 66 and 67). Fairness in both jurisdictions is not an abstract concept. Fairness is not concerned with technicalities. If a defendant has not had a fair trial and as a result of that injustice has occurred, it would be extremely unsatisfactory if the powers of this Court were not wide enough to rectify that injustice. If, contrary to our expectations, that has not previously been the position, then it seems to us that this is a defect in our procedures which is now capable of rectification under section 3 of the Human Rights Act 1998 ('the 1998 Act'). The 1998 Act requires primary legislation and subordinate legislation to be read and given effect to in a way which is compatible with Convention rights. Section 6(1) of the 1998 Act makes it unlawful for a public authority to act in a way which is incompatible with a Convention right and a court is a public authority for the purposes of section 6 (section 6(3)). The 1998 Act emphasises the desirability of taking a broader rather than a narrower approach as to what constitutes an unsafe conviction. ...We would suggest that ... since the 1998 Act came into force, the circumstances in which there will be room for a different result before this Court and before the ECHR because of unfairness based on the respective tests we employ will be rare indeed. Applying the broader approach identified by Rose L.J. [in *R v Mullen*], we consider that if a defendant has been denied a fair trial it will almost be inevitable that the conviction will be regarded as unsafe. (*per* Lord Woolf CJ).

This statement of principle was further endorsed by the House of Lords in *R v Forbes* [2001] 1 AC 473 (a case involving disputed identification and considered in Chapter 8) and in the later Court of Appeal decision in *R v Craven* [2001] 2 Cr App R 181, where it was noted that any unfairness during the trial may be capable of being rectified on appeal by the Court of Appeal, which under section 3 of the Criminal Appeal Act 1968 has the power to receive fresh evidence.

In *R v Botmeh and Alami* (2001) *The Times*, 8 November (a case involving a failure by the prosecution to make pre-trial disclosure of evidence which was subject to a public interest immunity claim on appeal), the Court of Appeal endorsed the approach of its earlier decision in *R v Davis, Johnson and Rowe* to the effect that procedural unfairness in the conduct of the trial does not compel the Court of Appeal to quash a conviction where, having reviewed the evidence in the case, it concludes the defendant's conviction to be safe. Leave has been sought to take the decision to the House of Lords where it is hoped that the inter-relationship between the fairness of the trial and the safety of a resulting conviction will be considered and the law made clear.

HUMAN RIGHTS LAW

The use of unlawfully obtained evidence is bound to provoke considerable argument by lawyers based on the Human Rights Act 1998 and the jurisprudence of the European Court of Human Rights. Of particular relevance to this area of evidence are Articles 6(1) (guaranteeing the right to a fair trial) and 8 (guaranteeing the right of privacy) of the European Convention on Human Rights. The substance of each of these rights has been considered in greater detail in Chapter 2. The European Court of Human Rights has stated on many an occasion that the admissibility of evidence is a matter for regulation by national courts. Its task under the Convention is to consider whether the proceedings as a whole, including the way in which the evidence was used, was fair. The decisions of the European Court of Human Rights in relation to the use of an agent provocateur and its implications for a fair trial in *Teixeira de Castro* v *Portugal* (1998) 28 EHRR 101 and the lawfulness of unauthorised surveillance operations and its implications for both the right to privacy and a fair trial in *Khan* v *United Kingdom* (2001) 31 EHRR 45 have been considered above. However, as a result of the implementation of the Human Rights Act 1998, a number of new situations will arise where the lawfulness of the activities of the State's prosecuting authorities may be challenged under the Convention. The following cases highlight some of the new issues which have arisen.

R v P [2001] 2 WLR 463

The defendants were convicted of offences under the Misuse of Drugs Act 1971 for assisting in the United Kingdom the commission of drug offences in EU countries A and B, contrary to the laws of those countries. The evidence implicating them in the offences had been obtained by prosecuting authorities in EU country A. It consisted of intercepted telecommunications between the defendants and EU nationals in countries A and B. The prosecuting authorities in country A had gone through all the correct legal channels to obtain the evidence in this way and had accordingly acted in compliance with Article 8. In fact, the evidence had been used in the successful prosecution of EU nationals in country A.

Following the successful convictions in country A, the Crown Prosecution Service lawfully obtained the recordings implicating the defendants. It was intended that the CPS would also call one of the convicted nationals from country A to give evidence against the defendants based on what was contained in the intercepted recordings.

At their trial, an application was made under section 78 of PACE to prevent the CPS from using the recordings in evidence. Rejecting the defence arguments, the trial judge admitted the evidence. The defendants were convicted and appealed. Under English law the Interception of Communications Act 1985 (now largely supplanted by the Regulation of Investigatory Powers Act 2000) strictly limits the circumstances in which the prosecuting authorities may obtain evidence by interception of private mail and telephone calls. The Act, however, has no application to intercepts obtained outside the United Kingdom. On appeal, the defendants maintained that the use of the intercept evidence at their trial was without statutory authorisation and therefore could not be said to be 'in accordance with law' as required by Article 8. Consequently, the trial judge should have excluded the evidence as its admission violated their right to a fair trial under Article 6.

In rejecting the argument, the Court of Appeal approved the reasoning of the House of Lords in *R v Khan* [1996] 3 All ER 289 and, referring to the European Court of Human Rights later decision in that case, concluded the critical question in cases of this kind is whether 'fair use' is made of the resulting evidence. Lord Hobhouse observed:

> The critical question is the fairness of the trial. Questions of the admissibility of evidence are not governed by Article 8. The fair use of intercept evidence at a trial is not a breach of Article 6 even if the evidence was unlawfully obtained. It is a cogent factor in favour of the admission of intercept evidence that one of the parties to the relevant conversation is going to be a witness at the trial and give evidence of what was said during it.

The Court of Appeal granted leave to appeal to the House of Lords.

Is there any difference in essence between the right to a fair trial under Article 6(1) and the exercise of discretion to ensure a fair trial under section 78 of PACE? The decision in *Khan v United Kingdom* led the House of Lords in *R v P and others* to conclude that the right to a fair trial under Article 6 involves the same criterion as that applied under section 78.

> The importance of the ECHR decision is that it confirms that the direct operation of Articles 8 and 6 does not invalidate their Lordships' conclusion or alter the vital role of s.78 as the means by which questions of the use of evidence obtained in breach of Article 8 are to be resolved at a criminal trial. The criterion to be applied is the criterion of fairness in Article 6 which is likewise the criterion to be applied by the judge under s.78.

The approach in *R v P and others* is further endorsed by the decision in *R v Sanghera* [2001] 1 Cr App R 299 (above), where the Court of Appeal observed that if a defendant could not succeed by relying on section 78, he would not be able to succeed by relying on Article 6.

CONCLUSION

Consideration of the cases included in this chapter has shown there is little difference between the way in which judicial discretion is exercised at common law and under section 78 of PACE. Both are restrictive, although section 78 has the potential to be used to exclude evidence obtained by entrapment in certain circumstances. It is clear that evidence may be excluded to ensure the fairness of the trial process. Fairness, however, is a nebulous concept and necessarily involves subjective judgments. Whilst the wording of section 78 has given the courts the freedom to consider the notion of fairness in a context much wider than simply ensuring the quality of the evidence, it has not been used by the courts to promote a citizen's fundamental freedoms. Whether the Human Rights Act 1998 will change this remains to be seen. It is after all an area of evidence law ripe for imaginative argument and bold decision making, but recent case law is not encouraging.

Further reading

Akdeniz, Y., Taylor, N. and Walker, C., 'Regulation of Investigatory Powers Act 2000(1): BigBrother.gov.uk: State Surveillance in the Age of Information and Rights' [2001] Crim LR 73.

Ashworth, A., 'Excluding Evidence as Protecting Rights' [1977] Crim LR 929.

Ashworth, A., 'Should the Police be Allowed to Use Deceptive Practices? (1998) 114 LQR 108.

Ashworth, A., 'Article 6 and the Fairness of Trials' [1999] Crim LR 261.

Choo, A. and Nash, S., 'What's the Matter with Section 78?' [1999] Crim LR 929.

Dennis, I.H. (1999) *The Law of Evidence*, Sweet & Maxwell.

McEwan, J. (1998) *Evidence and the Adversarial Process – The Modern Law*, Hart Publishing.

Mirfield, P., 'Regulation of Investigatory Powers Act 2000(2): Evidential Aspects' [2001] Crim LR 91.

Uglow, S., 'Covert Surveillance and the European Convention on Human Rights' [1999] Crim LR 287.

Zuckerman, A. (1989) *The Principles of Criminal Evidence*, Clarendon Press.

Chapter 6

CONFESSIONS AND RELATED MATTERS

INTRODUCTION

The primary purpose of detaining and interrogating a suspect at a police station is to obtain information that is relevant to the crime under investigation. Notwithstanding the fact that a suspect enjoys a right to silence at the police station, the police hope that by persuading a suspect to talk they can encourage him to make incriminating admissions capable of being used in evidence against him. The interview with the suspect is seen as the centrepiece of the investigation. It is confrontational in nature and the normal rules of conversation are suspended and replaced in many cases by an intense exchange between the investigating officers and the suspect. As an investigative tool, interrogation is cheap and effective. Investigating officers are well versed in the cognitive techniques of persuasion designed to encourage the suspect to make incriminating admissions. Any admissions made by a suspect are likely to constitute highly persuasive evidence of guilt in the mind of the fact finder.

Where a suspect makes incriminating admissions which fall within the definition of a confession, his statement is admitted into evidence under an exception to the hearsay rule. The confession falls within the definition of a hearsay statement because it is an out-of-court statement made by the accused on an earlier occasion which is being relied on by the prosecution to prove the truth of facts asserted. The rationale behind the general rule excluding hearsay evidence is discussed in Chapter 12. Confession evidence is admitted as an exception to the hearsay rule because it is generally felt to be reliable: a confession is a statement against the maker's self-interest and why should such a statement be made unless it is true? In spite of this confident assertion the English criminal justice system is littered with a number of high profile miscarriages of justice which have been based on confession evidence. The cases of Judith Ward, Stefan Kiszko, the Guildford Four, the Birmingham Six, and the Bridgwater Three, Stephen Downing and many others are a testament to the dangers of a misplaced confidence in the reliability of confession evidence.

As a result of these miscarriages of justice attitudes have changed and a number of important safeguards have been introduced by the Police and Criminal Evidence Act 1984 and its accompanying Codes of Practice. The safeguards regulate the way in which a confession is obtained and the way in which its admissibility is determined at trial. It remains the case however that under English law it is quite possible for a defendant to be convicted on the strength of his confession alone. There is no requirement for confession evidence to be corroborated or supported by other independent evidence.

Even for the most experienced criminal, being detained by the police is a psychologically unpleasant experience. It can be even more alienating and daunting for the less experienced suspect. The investigating officers control all aspects of the suspect's detention and interrogation, including time, space and information. It is tempting for the police to feel the person they have in custody is guilty and therefore to regard the interview as a means of achieving a result which fits in with their initial impression of the suspect. The interview with the suspect serves to gather information and often represents a challenge to an investigating officer when faced with a suspect who is reluctant to talk. The police are trained in the techniques of interrogative suggestibility. Questioning often consists of repetitious allegations and the desire of the suspect to speak in order to alleviate the pressure may be intense. The risk of having an adverse inference drawn under section 34 of the Criminal Justice and Public Order Act 1994, where the defendant chooses to put forward a defence at trial which he failed to mention at the police station, does little to reduce the pressure to speak.

Experts in the field of psychology have conducted extensive research into confession evidence. Indeed, wide-ranging research was carried out as part of the Royal Commission on Criminal Justice (RCCJ) inquiry into the criminal justice system set up in response to a number of well-publicised miscarriages of justice in which confession evidence formed a major component of the prosecution's case. The inquiry found that 20% of suspects held in detention exhibited abnormal levels of stress and anxiety. Confession evidence lacks the objective reliability inherent in forensic evidence such as DNA. Experience has shown that suspects confess for all sorts of reasons even where they know that they are innocent of the allegations made against them. This may be due to the psychological make-up of a suspect, or may occur out of a desire to protect someone or to avoid embarrassment for themselves or others. Suspects also confess for reasons of short-term expediency, in the hope that matters will be satisfactorily resolved later. Psychologists claim there are two types of false confessions, the 'coerced compliant' confession and the 'coerced internalised' confession. The former comes about in order to escape persistent questioning and the oppressive surroundings of police detention, whilst the second category concerns suspects who come to believe they are guilty of the offence due to the psychological control engendered by the interrogation process. The more vulnerable the suspect, the more susceptible he is to making a false confession. In some situations, the police are not always able or willing to identify vulnerable suspects and see it as being in their interests to take advantage of their vulnerability.

The law relating to confession evidence has a well-developed case law. In this chapter, we examine the safeguards currently in place, which seek to ensure the reliability of a confession together with an examination of the role of the court in excluding such evidence.

Defining a confession

The definition of confession evidence is found in section 82(1) of the Police and Criminal Evidence Act 1984 (PACE). A confession is:

> Any statement wholly or partly adverse to the person who made it, whether made to a person in authority or not and whether made in words or otherwise.

Section 82(1) provides a wide definition of a confession, to include any incriminating admissions, whether made informally or not and made not only to police officers but to any other individual.

Statutory safeguards

The Police and Criminal Evidence Act 1984 contains a number of safeguards designed to ensure the reliability of confession evidence. The Act came into force on 1 January 1986 and introduced a new statutory regime for admitting confession evidence. There is therefore little to be gained by examining the former position at common law. The admissibility of a confession is now governed by sections 76, 78 and 82(3) of PACE and by the Codes of Practice issued under section 66 of PACE.

Section 76(2) provides two limbs under which a confession can be excluded:

(2) If, in any proceedings where the prosecution proposes to give in evidence a confession made by an accused person, it is represented to the court that the confession was or may have been obtained—
  (a) by oppression of the person who made it; or
  (b) in consequence of anything said or done which was likely, in the circumstances existing at the time, to render unreliable any confession which might be made by him in consequence thereof,
the court shall not allow the confession to be given in evidence against him except in so far as the prosecution proves to the court beyond reasonable doubt that the confession (notwithstanding that it may be true) was not obtained as aforesaid.

A confession must be excluded if it has been obtained oppressively under section 76(2)(a) or in circumstances rendering it unreliable under section 76(2)(b). Where the defence (or the court of its own volition under section 76(3)) raises the issue of the admissibility of a confession, it is for the prosecution to prove beyond reasonable doubt that the confession was not obtained by oppression and is not unreliable having regard to things said or done. It is important to note that section 76 does not give the court any discretion because where the grounds under section 76 are not disproved, the court has no choice but to exclude the confession.

A further ground for excluding a confession is provided by section 78 of PACE, which provides:

(1) In any proceedings the court may refuse to allow evidence on which the prosecution proposes to rely to be given if it appears to the court that, having regard to all the circumstances, including the circumstances in which the evidence was obtained, the admission of evidence would have such an adverse effect on the fairness of the proceedings that the court ought not to admit it.

The application of section 78 was extensively covered in Chapter 5. The section gives the court discretion to exclude prosecution evidence, which can of course include confession evidence, where the admission of the evidence would have an adverse effect on the fairness of the proceedings. The manner in which evidence is obtained is one of the factors the court can have regard to under section 78.

Section 76 can be used in conjunction with section 78. Whilst the case law confirms that there is considerable overlap between the two sections, it must not be forgotten that a confession may also be excluded under section 82(3) of PACE, which preserves the common law discretion to exclude evidence where the prejudicial effect outweighs its probative value. The principles governing the exercise of discretion at common law were also discussed in Chapter 5.

The suspect's rights under PACE and the Codes of Practice

The safeguards under the substantive provisions of PACE and in Code C of the Codes of Practice exist to try and ensure the quality and reliability of confession evidence yielded as part of the investigative process. Section 67(11) specifically provides:

> (11) In all criminal and civil proceedings any such code shall be admissible in evidence; and if any provision of such code appears to the court or tribunal conducting the proceedings to be relevant to any question arising in the proceedings it shall be taken into account in determining that question.

In determining the admissibility of a confession, the court will take account of any breaches of the safeguards under PACE in deciding whether the confession was obtained by oppression, or in circumstances that render it unreliable, or that it would be unfair to admit the confession in evidence.

The following provisions of PACE and the Codes of Practice are commonly the most important in assisting the court to decide whether a confession has been obtained lawfully.

Section 58 of PACE is a most important right. It guarantees every person arrested and held in custody the right to consult a solicitor in private at any time free of charge. If the suspect initially declines the services of a legal adviser he is at liberty to change his mind at any time. Access can be delayed for up to 36 hours in strictly defined circumstances laid down by section 58(8). They are that the suspect must have been arrested in connection with a serious arrestable offence, the delay must be authorised in writing by an officer of superintendent rank or above and the officer must have reasonable grounds for believing one or more of the following:

- if the suspect was allowed access to legal advice, it would either lead to interference with or harm to evidence connected with a serious arrestable offence or interference with or physical injury to another person; or
- it would lead to the alerting of other persons connected with the offence but not yet arrested for it; or
- it would hinder the recovery of any property obtained as a result of the offence.

After 36 hours, access to legal representation cannot be denied in any circumstances.

All police stations are covered by the Duty Solicitor Scheme. If the suspect is unable to contact his solicitor of choice he is entitled to see the duty solicitor.

Code C of the Codes of Practice supplements the safeguard guaranteed by section 58 of PACE.

No police officer is allowed to say anything with the intention of persuading a detained individual from obtaining legal advice (Code C 6.4).

The custody officer must ascertain the reasons as to why a detained individual wishes to waive his right to legal advice and to record the reasons in the custody record (Code C 6.5).

Section 56 of PACE gives a suspect the right not to be held incommunicado. It gives a suspect the right to have a friend, relative or other person likely to be concerned for his welfare informed of his arrest and the station at which he is being held. The right can be delayed for the same reasons and in the same circumstances as section 58 of PACE.

The importance of the rights guaranteed by sections 56 and 58 of PACE cannot be underestimated. For anyone detained at a police station, the knowledge that someone who cares about them has been informed will help to reduce feelings of alienation. Access to a solicitor also helps to redress the psychological imbalance often felt by suspects, particularly those who are vulnerable.

The longer a suspect is detained in custody, the greater the chance of them making admissions in order to escape their predicament. Safeguards are in place to keep detention times under strict review. Under section 37 of PACE, a suspect must be charged as soon as there is sufficient evidence against them. Also, detention can only be authorised by the custody sergeant provided it is necessary to secure or preserve evidence relating to an offence for which the suspect is under arrest or to obtain evidence by questioning. A suspect may only be detained for 24 hours unless the offence he has been arrested for is a serious arrestable offence and a number of conditions are met. Before charge, and in the investigation of only the most serious offences, the maximum period a suspect can be held in detention is 96 hours. Detention is subject to regular review in accordance with Code C 15. At the end of the 96 hours, the suspect must either be charged or released from custody.

Numerous other safeguards are contained in Code C including the following:

Code C 2 makes provision for the mandatory opening and compiling of a custody record for each detained individual. In evidential terms the custody record is a very important document as it records every aspect of a suspect's detention. It can be used by the prosecution to prove compliance with PACE and the Codes of Practice. Equally, it is a very important source of information to the defence and can be utilised by the defendant to prove relevant breaches of procedure.

There are significant safeguards as regards the conditions for detention. All cells must be adequately heated, cleaned and ventilated. Access to toilet and washing facilities must be provided as must two light meals and one substantial meal in any period of 24 hours (Code C 8).

Medical treatment must be provided for any suspect who requests it or who appears to be suffering from a physical illness or mental disability (Code C 9.2).

Provision for juveniles, the mentally disordered and mentally handicapped suspects is made in Code C 11. In short they should not be interviewed or asked to sign a written statement in the absence of an appropriate adult. An appropriate adult would include a parent, guardian or social worker. The right to have an appropriate adult present is in addition to the detained person's right to consult a solicitor. Code C 11.16 acknowledges a proactive role on the part of the appropriate adult which includes the right to advise the detained person during questioning and to facilitate communication.

Provision for the recording of non-taped interviews is also made in Code C 11. An accurate record must be made of each interview disclosing where and when it took place, all persons present etc. The record should be contemporaneous or written up as soon as is reasonably practicable thereafter. Written interviews must be signed by the maker.

The suspect must be cautioned *inter alia* upon arrest and prior to the start of an interview (Code C 10). The caution reads: 'You need not say anything. But it may harm your defence if you do not mention when questioned, something which you later rely on in court. Anything you do say may be given in evidence.'

The manner in which an interrogation is carried out is also safeguarded under Code C. A suspect has the right to a continuous period of rest of at least eight hours, free from questioning in any period of 24 hours, which should normally be taken at night. No person who is unfit through drink or drugs to the extent that they are unable to appreciate the significance of questions put should be questioned.

Suspects with hearing or language difficulties must not be interviewed without an interpreter (Code C 13).

A suspect who wants legal advice may not be interviewed or continue to be interviewed save in strictly defined circumstances until he has received it (Code C 6.6).

Code C 6D provides clarification of the solicitor's role at the police station. It specifically acknowledges that the duty of the solicitor may well extend to giving his client legal advice, which may result in the client withholding evidence which could have strengthened the prosecution's case, and that a solicitor may intervene in an interview situation to seek clarification or to challenge an improper question to his client. The solicitor may intervene to advise his client not to answer a particular question or to give his client further legal advice.

A legal adviser can only be asked to leave an interview where his conduct is such as to prevent the officer from properly putting questions to the suspect (Code C 6.9).

Section 60 of PACE makes provision for the tape recording of interviews. The specific detail is provided for in Code E. Code E 3 stipulates that tape recording is the norm for interviews conducted in relation to indictable and either way offences. Code E 2 contains details on the manner in which interviews should be conducted:

> The tape recording of interviews shall be carried out openly to install confidence in its reliability as an impartial and accurate record of the interview. (Code E 2.1)

EXCLUDING A CONFESSION ON THE GROUND OF OPPRESSION (PACE, SECTION 76(2)(A))

As already explained, under section 76(2)(a) a confession may be excluded if it is obtained by oppression of the person who made it. Oppression is partially defined in section 76(8) of PACE to include torture, inhuman or degrading treatment, and the use or threat of violence (whether or not amounting to torture).

The Court of Appeal has considered the meaning of oppression on a relatively small number of occasions.

R v Fulling [1987] QB 426

The defendant was arrested in connection with a false insurance claim. She was suspected of having acted in concert with her lover. She was questioned at the police station. At first she refused to answer questions put to her. One of the officers told her untruthfully that her boyfriend had been having an affair with a woman who was being held in an adjacent cell. In her emotionally distressed state she confessed to making the fraudulent claim. At her trial, denying her involvement in the offence, she insisted that her admission was made in order to get out of police custody. She argued her confession had been obtained through the use of oppression. Unreliability under section 76(2)(b) and unfairness under section 78 were not argued.

The Court of Appeal felt oppression should be given its ordinary dictionary meaning, which according to the *Oxford English Dictionary* is: 'the exercise of authority or power in a burdensome, harsh or wrongful manner; unjust or cruel treatment of subjects, inferiors, etc; the imposition of unreasonable or unjust burdens.'

Having regard to this definition and to the facts in the case, the Court of Appeal concluded that although the conduct of the police officers was 'unsporting', it was not oppressive in the context of admissibility of confessions. The court went on to observe that it would be 'hard to envisage any circumstances in which such oppression would not entail some impropriety on the part of the interrogator.' This statement clearly implies that breaches of PACE and Code C committed in good faith are unlikely to fall foul of section 76(2)(a). Oppression however is a question of degree and what is oppressive as regards one individual may not be oppressive to someone of a more phlegmatic disposition.

In determining whether oppressive conduct is apparent the individual characteristics of the accused are important.

R v Davison [1988] Crim LR 442

The defendant was arrested and taken to a police station where he remained for 13 hours. During that time he at first declined access to legal advice, after which he was interviewed for over an hour. The interview did nothing to associate him with the offence and, at the conclusion of the interview, there was no reason to detain him further. However, he was unlawfully kept in a police cell for several hours during which time evidence came to light that led the investigating officers to suspect the defendant might know something about another offence which had no connection with the original reason for his arrest. The defendant was interviewed again and was unlawfully denied access to legal advice. He confessed. It was held that the flouting of PACE and Code C by the investigating officers amounted to oppression in that this was an 'exercise of authority or power in a burdensome, harsh manner'. It was accepted that a hardened professional criminal who had often been interrogated in police custody could be subjected to more rigorous questioning than a first time offender, especially one that displayed timidity.

This case confirms the position in all cases contesting the admissibility of confession evidence, namely that there must be a causal link between the impropriety amounting to oppression or unreliability and the defendant's resulting confession.

R v Seelig [1992] 1 WLR 149

The defendant was arrested and subjected to interviews in which he was robustly interrogated and towards the end of which he eventually made a confession. The judge ruled that his confession was admissible because although there was, potentially, some oppressive conduct by the police, it had to be taken into account that the defendant was an experienced, sophisticated, and very intelligent man who had worked as a merchant banker. These qualities had to be weighed in the balance in deciding whether the interrogation he had undergone amounted to oppressive conduct towards him sufficient to cause him to confess.

R v Paris, Abdullahi and Miller (1993) 97 Cr App R 99

The defendants appealed against their conviction for murder. During the investigation, there were 19 interviews with the police which lasted for a total of 13 hours over five days. Solicitors were not present during the first two interviews and M consistently denied his involvement in the crime during the first seven interviews. During interviews eight and nine, M accepted that he was present at the crime scene. He was then pressed to say who had stabbed the victim. M finally confessed that he had. Having denied his involvement over 300 times on tape, he later agreed with the officer's suggestion that he may have been high on drugs and stabbed the victim without knowing what he was doing. He finally admitted: 'I just stabbed, not stabbed her ... just thumped her in the face I mean.' In allowing the appeal, the Court of Appeal held that short of physical violence, it was hard to conceive of a more hostile and intimidating environment. There was no doubt that the police conduct was 'oppressive' within the meaning of section 76(2)(a).

EXCLUDING A CONFESSION ON THE GROUND OF UNRELIABILITY (PACE, SECTION 76(2)(B))

A confession may be excluded under section 76(2)(b) if:

> ... in consequence of anything said or done which was likely, in the circumstances existing at the time, to render unreliable any confession which might be made by him in consequence thereof.

The second limb of section 76(2) is drafted in much wider terms than oppression in section 76(2)(a). In determining the admissibility of a confession under this limb much greater attention is paid to the defendant's subjective characteristics and state of mind. The section implicitly recognises that suspects do confess for reasons other than the truth. As the word 'unreliable' is not defined in the section, the judge or the magistrates must examine all the relevant circumstances of the accused's detention and interrogation, taking account of what was said or done and what effect the whole process of detention had on the suspect's state of mind. The decision as to whether a confession is unreliable has to be based on the facts as they existed at the time the confession was made. The test is not whether the actual confession was untruthful but whether what was said or done in the circumstances existing at the time was likely to have rendered unreliable the accused's actual confession or any such confession that he might have made. These principles were established in the Court of Appeal's decision in *R v Barry* (1991) 95 Cr App R 491 and were re-affirmed in the Divisional Court's decision in *Proulx v (1) The Governor of HM Brixton Prison (2) The Government of Canada* [2001] 1 All ER 57.

As well as the suspect's subjective characteristics, breaches of PACE and the Codes of Practice are also relevant to excluding a confession on the ground of unreliability. Although a breach will not render a confession automatically inadmissible the safeguards under PACE and the Codes are there to try and ensure reliability of confession evidence by protecting the suspect's basic rights. The presence or absence of bad faith on the part of the police is largely irrelevant. What is important is the effect any breach had on the suspect at the time. A failure by the police to spot a particular vulnerability, perhaps due to a medical condition or substance abuse, may provide grounds for seeking the exclusion of a confession under this section. Subtle or not so subtle inducements offered by the police to encourage the suspect to confess, such as a promise of bail or a lesser charge, are also relevant considerations. The following selection of cases illustrate the sort of factors courts have regard to when assessing admissibility under the second limb of section 76(2). Whilst it is possible to extract some general principles the outcome of each case is largely dependent on its facts. It will become evident that there is some overlap between the type of factors justifying exclusion under section 76(2)(b) and under section 78 of PACE.

R v Trussler [1988] Crim LR 446

The defendant was known to be a drug user. He was arrested on suspicion of burglary. He could not be interviewed for several hours due to the effect of drugs. He was interviewed twice, having declined the services of a solicitor. During the second interview however, he became agitated and asked to see a solicitor. He spoke with one on the telephone. Following a development with a co-accused in the case, one of the investigating officers took it upon himself to have a 'general chat' with the defendant. Conducted in the early hours the chat lasted an hour and a half. Following the chat a further formal interview was held by which time the defendant had been in custody for 18 hours with little rest. The Court of Appeal held there was no such thing as a general chat under Code C, only formal interviews. The defendant's confession could not be described as being reliable and should have been excluded.

R v Delaney (1989) 88 Cr App R 338

This case highlights the dangers of placing too much reliance on confession evidence. The defendant was convicted of the indecent assault of a three-year-old girl. The only evidence against him was his confession. He had been interviewed at length, having declined the services of a solicitor. Although he was 17, he had an IQ of only 80 and was educationally subnormal. The entire scenario was described by the Court of Appeal as being a set of circumstances 'in which, par excellence, any inter-rogation should have been conducted with meticulous care and with meticulous observance of the rules of fairness.' There was evidence from an educational psychologist, which if accepted, estab-lished the defendant to be a vulnerable suspect. The interview had been conducted on a sympathet-ic basis with the officers being at pains to minimise the seriousness of the defendant's position. On several occasions during the interview reference was made to the defendant's need for treatment rather than punishment. Given the nature of the questioning on such a vulnerable suspect, who was not legally represented, the risk of it producing a false confession was too high.

R v Howden-Simpson [1991] Crim LR 49

The appellant was an organist and choirmaster. His duties included paying junior choir members for their services at weddings. He failed to pay the money to the choristers and was charged with theft. The investigating officers indicated that they would proceed to charge only two of the non-payments if he admitted the theft. However, if he did not admit the two charges, they would interview every unpaid chorister and make a separate charge for each non-payment. In the circumstances the Court of Appeal had no hesitation in deciding the confession ought to have been excluded under section 76(2)(b). The predicament the appellant was placed in by the officers rendered his confession unreliable.

The physical condition and mental characteristics of the accused are part of the circumstances existing at the time for the purposes of section 76(2)(b).

R v McGovern (1991) 92 Cr App R 228

The defendant was arrested on suspicion of murder. She was 19 and six months pregnant. She had been sick in her cell shortly before the interview and according to a psychologist's evidence she had a mental age of a 10-year-old. The police were anxious to interview her because the victim in the investigation was still missing and it was not known whether she was alive or dead. The defendant was interviewed twice. She made damaging admissions in both interviews. As regards the first interview, she was wrongly denied access to a solicitor in breach of section 58 of PACE. There were further breaches in that there was a failure to keep a contemporaneous note of what was said. It was apparent from the beginning that the defendant had comprehension difficulties. She did not understand the caution which had to be explained to her several times. She was upset and her distress increased as further questions were put. Ultimately she confessed to stabbing the victim. There was no doubt that had a solicitor been present the outcome of the first interview would have been different. Indeed the interview would probably have been halted. During the second interview, this time in the presence of a solicitor the defendant gave a much more coherent account of her involvement in the killing.

Notwithstanding the confession in the first interview was true as the defendant herself had admitted in her second interview, the Court of Appeal concluded her admissions had been made in consequence of her being denied access to a solicitor. The second interview had been tarnished by the conduct of the officers in the first interview and consequently both interviews were inadmissible.

The decision in *R v McGovern* is a reminder that the court's role under section 76 is to consider the admissibility of the confession only and not its actual reliability. The focus of the court's attention is on the methods used by the police in order to obtain a confession. The fact that the confession may be true is irrelevant to the court's decision. The wording in parenthesis in section 76 'notwithstanding it might be true' makes this perfectly clear.

R v Walker [1998] Crim LR 211

The defendant, a prostitute, was convicted of robbery. She told the police doctor she was a heroin addict. She was prescribed methadone and valium. In interview she made a number of incriminating admissions. At her trial she maintained her victim had not been frightened and sought exclusion of the interview. At the inquiry into the admissibility of her confession, the defendant gave evidence that she had smuggled some crack cocaine into the police station. She had smoked the drug and was under its influence when interviewed. Psychiatric evidence was called to establish that she had a severe personality disorder, making her prone to provide inaccurate elaboration on events without appreciating the consequences. The defendant's mental state would have been made worse by the use of drugs. The trial judge rejected much of the evidence and allowed the confession into evidence. The Court of Appeal allowed her appeal. The wording in the section 'anything said or done', did not require any wrongdoing on the part of the police. The defendant's mental state was one of the circumstances to be taken into account and there was nothing in any of the earlier decided cases limiting mental conditions exclusively to intellectual impairment. Given the defendant's mental state, her confession could not be said to be reliable.

R v Walker re-affirms that police misconduct is not a pre-requisite for excluding a confession under section 76(2)(b) as the decision in the case indicates that unreliability can arise where the defendant himself is largely responsible for his vulnerable state of mind. This decision casts doubt on the earlier authority of *R v Goldberg* [1988] Crim LR 678 which held that self-induced vulnerability of itself did not fall to be dealt with under section 76(2)(b) if nothing could be said to have been said or done to the defendant. It was purely a matter of weight for the jury. It is submitted that to conduct an interrogation with a suspect who is high on drugs, even if this was not appreciated at the time, ought to fall within the meaning of unreliability under section 76(2)(b) since any confession obtained from an individual in such a vulnerable or suggestible state is likely to be unreliable.

The assessment of unreliability under section 76(2)(b) is based, for the most part, on a subjective assessment of the suspect's characteristics. What the above examples illustrate is that it is very much dependent on the personality of the defendant and the circumstances prevailing at the time. One important point to reiterate in relation to both limbs of section 76(2) is that the court must find a causal link between the act or omission of the police and the resulting confession. As the burden of proof rests with the prosecution, it is for the prosecution to prove the absence of a causal link.

PRACTICAL STEPS – POLICE INTERVIEW: ROLE OF THE LEGAL ADVISER

On a practical level, a solicitor needs to make a careful assessment of what is to be gained by his client making a full and frank confession or agreeing to answer police questions. A confession is defined in section 82(1) of PACE as 'any statement wholly or partly adverse to the person who made it'. The police will want to place considerable evidential reliance upon the record of the interview. The suspect needs to be carefully interviewed by his solicitor to enable the solicitor to evaluate the suspect's ability to handle the police interview. Furthermore, the solicitor should ensure full disclosure of the evidence held by the police to enable him to make a tactical decision as to the best course of action. Any advice he gives must also be made with section 34 of the Criminal Justice and Public Order Act 1994 in mind: an adverse inference may be drawn where a defendant puts forward facts at his trial which he could reasonably have been expected to mention at the police station. It is considered to be most unwise to advise a suspect to answer some questions but not others. If the case proceeds to trial, the legal adviser must consider how this will look before a jury. He should keep a careful note of all that is said in the interview. He should be proactive, stepping in where appropriate to advise his client not to answer a particular question, to request a break and to ensure the officers comply with the safeguards under PACE and the Codes of Practice. Where the adviser's representations are not recorded on tape, he should ensure they are recorded on any contemporaneous note and in the custody record.

The decision in *R v Dunn* (1990) 91 Cr App R 237 confirms that a legal adviser must be careful not to condone any malpractice by the police. An adviser's very presence during an interview can cure a breach of the Codes of Practice and tip the balance in favour of admitting the evidence.

EXCLUDING A CONFESSION ON THE GROUND OF UNFAIRNESS (PACE, SECTION 78)

In any proceedings the court may refuse to allow evidence on which the prosecution proposes to rely to be given if it appears to the court that, having regard to all the circumstances including the circumstances in which the evidence was obtained, the admission of evidence would have such an adverse effect on the fairness of the proceedings that the court ought not to admit it.

A confession may still be excluded on the grounds of unfairness even though it has not been obtained by oppression and may not be unreliable in the circumstances.

The power of the court to exclude confession evidence under section 78 where the admission of such evidence would have an 'adverse effect on the fairness of the proceedings' is illustrated by the cases of *R v Mason* [1988] 1 WLR 139, *R v Alladice* (1988) 87 Cr App R 380 and *R v Walsh* (1990) 91 Cr App R 161, which have been considered in Chapter 5 in the context of unlawfully and unfairly obtained evidence.

In seeking to exclude the confession, section 78 can be argued as an alternative to or in addition to section 76. The case law appears to indicate that confession evidence has proved to be most fertile ground for applying section 78.

Reasons for seeking exclusion of confession evidence under section 78 include:

* denying access to a solicitor;
* lying to the suspect or tricking him in some way;
* failing to protect a vulnerable suspect;
* deliberately flouting PACE or the Codes of Practice;
* failing to record the interview properly thereby rendering the police vulnerable to suggestions of 'verballing', ie disputing an oral admission was ever made.

As with excluding a confession under section 76(2)(b), breaches of PACE and the Codes of Practice are highly relevant to the exercise of judicial discretion under section 78 of PACE. The importance the appellate courts attach to the suspect's access to a solicitor whilst being detained at the police station (a right under section 58 of PACE) has been underlined in a number of cases including the Court of Appeal's decision in *R v Walsh* (1990) 91 Cr App R 161, where it was stated:

> To our minds it follows if there are significant and substantial breaches of section 58 or the provisions of the Code, then prima facie at least the standards of fairness set by Parliament have not been met. So far as this defendant is concerned ... to admit evidence against him which has been obtained in circumstances where these standards have not been met, cannot but have an adverse effect on the fairness of the proceedings. This does not mean of course that in every case of a significant or substantial breach of section 58 or the Code of Practice evidence will automatically be excluded. Section 78 does not so provide. (*per* Saville J)

The application of section 78 is further illustrated in the following cases:

R *v* Samuel [1988] 2 All ER 135

The defendant had been arrested on suspicion of burglary and robbery. He had asked for but had been denied access to a solicitor. After being detained for 24 hours he confessed to involvement in two burglaries for which he was charged. His solicitor and relatives were informed at this point. Questioning of the defendant continued however until he admitted to his involvement in the robbery. The Court of Appeal quashed his conviction for robbery. Whilst access to a solicitor had been legitimately denied prior to the first interview, there had been no justification for denial following the burglary charges. The decision to deny access and the resulting confession adversely affected the fairness of the proceedings. The Court of Appeal described access to a solicitor as being 'one of the most important and fundamental rights of the citizen'.

R *v* Canale [1990] 2 All ER 187

In this case the interviewing officers failed to make contemporaneous notes of two of the interviews they had with the defendant as required by Code C. The defendant alleged that he had been tricked and induced to confess. This was denied by the police. The Court of Appeal described the breaches of the Code of Practice as being 'flagrant, deliberate and cynical' and concluded the admissions were inadmissible in accordance with section 78. The absence of contemporaneous notes had deprived the trial judge of the very evidence that would have enabled him to resolve the conflicting version of events. The absence of the record severely prejudiced the defendant.

Since *R* v *Canale*, the requirement under Code E to tape record the vast majority of interviews in the investigation of all but the most minor offences has resolved some of the problems surrounding the use of contemporaneous records. However, as already noted, off the record remarks made in the back of the police car are still used by the police on occasion.

R *v* Aspinall [1999] Crim LR 741

This case has an important human rights dimension that was argued on appeal. The defendant, a schizophrenic, was arrested and ultimately convicted on drug charges. Two police surgeons pronounced him fit to be interviewed. During the inquiry into the admissibility of his confession, the defendant's consultant psychiatrist gave evidence to the effect that the defendant might well have been tired and stressed during his detention, contributing to a degree of passivity and lack of assertiveness on his part. When asked by the officers whether he wanted to see a solicitor, the defendant had replied: 'No I want to get home to my missus and kids.' The defendant was interviewed without the presence of a solicitor or appropriate adult. The trial judge rejected a section 78 submission, concluding the defendant had been lucid at the time of interview.

In allowing his appeal and quashing his conviction, the Court of Appeal held the defendant had been unable to judge what was in his best interests. The absence of an appropriate adult (a specific requirement under Code C 1.4 and 11.14 for vulnerable persons) rendered the confession unfair. The Court of Appeal concluded there had been a breach of Article 6 occasioned by the delay in access to legal advice; the duty solicitor had been otherwise engaged at the relevant time.

OBTAINING ADMISSIONS OTHER THAN THROUGH A FORMAL INTERVIEW

There are other ways of obtaining incriminating admissions other than through the process of formal interrogation. In *R* v *Khan* [1996] 3 All ER 289 (considered in Chapter 5), the unlawful installation of a covert listening device on the outside of a flat frequently visited by the defendant yielded highly reliable and incriminating evidence of drug trafficking. The House of Lords upheld the trial judge's refusal to exclude the evidence under section 78 of PACE. In *R* v *Bailey and Smith* [1993] 3 All ER 365 (also considered in Chapter 5), investigating officers staged a charade which led to two suspects, implicated in the same offence, being forced to share a cell. The defendants made incriminating statements to each other. They did not realise their conversation was being secretly recorded. The application of section 78 of PACE to get the evidence excluded was rejected. Code C has little, if any, application in such circumstances. The use of such methods, however, should not be adopted with the express intention of deliberately avoiding the Codes of Practice.

R *v* Christou [1992] 4 All ER 559

Undercover officers posed as 'shady jewellers', willing to receive stolen items of jewellery. The purpose of the operation had been to recover stolen goods and identify thieves and handlers. On the basis of information gathered the defendant and others were prosecuted. Refusing to exclude the evidence under section 78 of PACE, the Court of Appeal concluded the questions asked formed part of the officers' undercover pose. As receivers, they would be expected to ask questions about which areas the goods had been stolen from, to prevent their re-sale in the same area. As for the adoption of such methods for the purpose of circumventing Code C, the Court of Appeal observed:

> In our view, although Code C extends beyond the treatment of those in detention, what is clear is that it was intended to protect suspects who are vulnerable to abuse or pressure from police officers or who may believe themselves to be so. Frequently, the suspect will be a detainee. But the code will also apply where a suspect, not in detention, is being questioned about an offence by a police officer acting as a police officer for the purposes of obtaining evidence. In that situation, the officer and the suspect are not on equal terms.

With reference to the facts in this case, the Court of Appeal concluded that the appellants were not being questioned by police officers as such and that the conversation was on equal terms. Consequently, the Code was never intended to apply in such a context. The court went on to say that:

> It would be wrong for police officers to adopt or use an undercover pose or disguise to enable themselves to ask questions about an offence uninhibited by the requirement of the Code and with the effect of circumventing it. Were they t\o do so, it would be open to the judge to exclude the questioning and answers under section 78 of PACE.

R v Bryce [1992] 4 All ER 567

The defendant was suspected of handling stolen goods and theft. A police constable posing as a potential buyer agreed to buy a £23,000 car from the defendant for £2,800. In the course of the conversation, the constable asked the defendant how long the car had been stolen. It was contended that he replied two or three days earlier.

Quashing the conviction, the Court of Appeal held the question had not been necessary for the maintenance of the undercover pose. It had been directed to the critical issue in the case, that of the defendant's guilty knowledge. The defendant had not of course been cautioned before being asked to incriminate himself. Furthermore he denied he had spoken the words attributed to him. There was no contemporaneous record and no caution had been give. In R v Christou, the entire exchange had been taped and video recorded.

CONFESSIONS BY MENTALLY HANDICAPPED PERSONS

A common area of controversy before the passing of PACE were confessions made by the mentally disabled and suspects with a low IQ. The Police and Criminal Evidence Act 1984 and Code C provide procedural safeguards for the admission of confession evidence by mentally disabled suspects.

Code C, most importantly, specifically provides that the suspect must not be interviewed without the presence of an appropriate adult.

With regard to confessions made by mentally handicapped persons, section 77(1) of PACE provides:

where at such a trial—
(a) the case against the accused depends wholly or substantially on a confession by him; and
(b) the court is satisfied—
(i) that he is mentally handicapped; and
(ii) that the confession was not made in the presence of an independent person,

the court shall warn the jury that there is a special need for caution before convicting the accused in reliance on the confession, and shall explain that the need arises because of the circumstances mentioned in paragraphs (a) and (b) above.

Mentally handicapped is defined in section 77(3) as being 'in a state of arrested or incomplete development of mind which includes significant impairment of intelligence and social functioning'. The section has no application to the mentally ill or to juveniles.

Section 77 also applies in summary trials conducted in magistrates' courts and no doubt a defence advocate would want to remind the bench of its application where appropriate. It is for the judge or magistrates to decide whether a suspect is mentally handicapped. A failure to give a warning in an appropriate case can lead to a conviction being quashed as illustrated in *R v Lamont* [1989] Crim LR 813. There is little case law on section 77. This is largely due to the fact that any confession must first satisfy the admissibility tests under sections 76 and 78 of PACE. Indeed, where a confession has been obtained from a mentally handicapped suspect, in the absence of an independent person, the confession may well be excluded under section 76 or 78 of PACE (see *R v Aspinall* above). In a sense, section 77 provides additional protection for mentally handicapped suspects in the circumstances covered by the section.

Where the judge considers the confession to be wholly unconvincing, so that even with a section 77 of PACE warning there would still be a real danger of an unsafe conviction, the judge should withdraw the case from the jury, in accordance with the principles laid down in *R v McKenzie* [1993] 1 WLR 453.

In *R v McKenzie*, the Court of Appeal held that a judge should withdraw a case from the jury where the following three conditions apply at any stage of the case:

1   the prosecution case depends wholly upon a confession;
2   the defendant suffers from a significant degree of mental illness; and
3   the confession is unconvincing to the point where a jury, properly directed, could not properly convict on it.

In *R v Ward* [1993] 2 All ER 577, the Court of Appeal held that in certain cases the court may hear expert evidence of a psychiatric or psychological nature as to the reliability and likely truth of a confession but only in those cases where the defendant has a personality disorder, so severe as to be categorised as a mental disorder. The Court of Appeal cautioned that this was not an invitation to defendants who had made a confession, to adduce psychiatric evidence to challenge its truth. Where the admissibility of a confession is challenged during a trial at a *voire dire* (see below), similar principles relating to the admissibility of expert opinion evidence on the matter apply.

STATUTORY SAFEGUARDS – CONCLUDING COMMENTS

The provisions of section 76(2)(a) and (b) of PACE and the general discretion under section 78 of PACE give the defence advocate plenty of ammunition to seek the exclusion of a confession by the defendant. The inter-relationship between the three grounds for excluding a confession is complicated, as it is not altogether clear what the rationale is behind each provision. We saw in Chapter 5 the considerable reluctance of the courts to exclude evidence under section 78 merely because it was obtained in an unlawful manner. However, confession evidence, as exemplified in *R v Mason* [1988] 1 WLR 139, is singled out for different treatment under section 78, with the courts being much more prepared to deprive the police of confession evidence gained in inappropriate ways. The entire philosophy behind section 76(2)(b) is the reliability of the confession as opposed to its truth. Why is it necessary to have a second limb under section 76(2) of PACE on the ground of oppression, given that very few confessions obtained oppressively can be said to be reliable? The availability of the alternative ground for oppression says much about the philosophy behind the section. Such a ground enables the court to mark its disapproval clearly and to hold prosecuting authorities to account for the type of conduct that may get results, but which is injurious to the integrity of the criminal justice system.

HUMAN RIGHTS LAW

Confession evidence is an area of law that is likely to yield a number of arguments based on the violation of the defendant's Convention rights. The use of covert surveillance devices to record incriminating admissions has led to the United Kingdom being found to have violated Article 8 in *Khan v United Kingdom* (2001) 31 EHRR 45 (see Chapter 5). Despite this finding, the European Court of Human Rights held that Khan had not been deprived of his right to a fair trial under Article 6 given that *inter alia* he had been afforded the opportunity of challenge under section 78 of PACE. The types of safeguards contained in the Police and Criminal Evidence Act 1984 and under the Codes of Practice are at the heart of the fair trial provisions under the Convention. The European Court of Human Rights has stressed the paramount importance of a suspect's right to see a solicitor on numerous occasions. Courts will need to consider carefully whether confession evidence obtained in breach of the available safeguards is not only admissible within the meaning of section 76 of PACE but will also not lead to unfairness within the definition of Article 6.

PROCEDURE FOR DEALING WITH THE ADMISSIBILITY OF CONFESSION EVIDENCE

Questions relating to the admissibility of a confession or other disputed evidence are determined in the Crown Court by the judge in the absence of the jury. This requires a procedure known as the *voire dire* or trial within a trial.

In deciding the admissibility of a confession, it is only necessary to hold a *voire dire* where it is submitted that the confession was obtained by oppression or is unreliable or to admit it would be unfair. This will normally involve a mixed question of law and fact. In some cases however, where an accused simply denies making a confession at all (by maintaining that his signature has been forged or by denying words attributed to him which were never in fact recorded) a question of fact only arises. On a trial in the Crown Court, the issue of who is telling the truth will be decided by the jury without the need to hold a *voire dire* as in the case of *R v Flemming* (1988) 86 Cr App R 32.

When the trial reaches the stage for the confession to be put in evidence as part of the prosecution case, the procedure at the *voire dire* requires the jury be sent out of court without being told the reason why. The judge will then hold a *voire dire* at which he will hear evidence about how the confession was obtained. This is likely to involve the prosecution calling the interviewing officers, the custody sergeant and the police doctor if relevant. The prosecution witnesses will be subject to cross-examination in the normal way. The defendant may testify if he wishes, and if he does so, he is still entitled to remain silent in the main trial. The defence may call its own expert evidence in appropriate cases to explain how the defendant's physical or mental state contributed to his making a confession. In some instances the legal adviser who represented the defendant at the police station may be called to give evidence. The judge will decide whom he believes as to how the confession was obtained and will then decide the disputed issues of fact before applying the law and ruling on the question of admissibility. If the trial judge deems the confession inadmissible the jury are recalled and the case proceeds. No reference to the 'confession' by the prosecution is possible. If the judge deems the confession admissible the prosecution can use it in evidence against the defendant. However, the defendant is still entitled to repeat his allegations as to how it was obtained in the hope of persuading the jury that the confession is of little or no weight. This may lead to the word-for-word repetition of hours of evidence, once before the judge and then before the jury.

The procedure in summary trials differs from trials in the Crown Court, as the magistrates are required to be both arbiters of fact and law. Following the decision in *R v Liverpool Juvenile Court, ex parte R* [1988] QB 1, the magistrates trying the defendant will be in court during submissions about the legality of any confession but, procedurally, this should be conducted in a preliminary and separate investigation. If, as a result of this preliminary inquiry, the confession is deemed inadmissible, the magistrates are required to exclude from their minds the arguments about legality of the confession in deciding the issue of the defendant's guilt. This requires a great feat of mental ingenuity. For this very reason, the *voire dire* procedure works considerably less well in summary proceedings. This problem applies to all issues of admissibility in the magistrates' courts, not merely to confession evidence. In practice, where there is some question of admissibility, the prosecution and defence lawyers will normally meet before the case is heard and see whether they can resolve their differences, if necessary with advice from the justices' clerk.

Questions have been raised in the past about the purpose of the *voire dire* and its relationship to the full trial. In particular, if the defendant makes incriminating admissions in answers to questions put to him at the *voire dire*, can his answers be used in evidence against him at the full trial? In *Wong Kam Ming v R* [1980] AC 247 the following questions were posed for the Privy Council's consideration:

1   Can the prosecution ask the defendant during his cross-examination at the *voire dire*, whether his confession is in fact true?

The Privy Council answered in the negative. The whole purpose of the *voire dire* is to determine the admissibility of the confession. It is not an inquiry as to the truth of the confession.

2   Once the trial resumes, can the prosecution adduce evidence of any incriminating admissions made by the defendant during the *voire dire* as part of its case in chief?

The Privy Council was of the opinion that the prosecution would not be allowed to adduce evidence of what the defendant had said during the *voire dire*, as part of the prosecution's case in chief.

3   Can the prosecution use any incriminating responses made by the defendant at the
    voire dire in cross-examination of him at the full trial?

The view of the Privy Council was that where a confession had been excluded at the
voire dire, the prosecution would not be permitted to cross-examine the defendant at
the full trial with a view to exploring any inconsistencies in his evidence. However, the
Privy Council expressed *obiter* the view that it would be permissible for the prosecution to cross-examine where the trial judge had in fact deemed the confession admissible as a result of the *voire dire*.

The decision of the Privy Council was supported by the House of Lords in *R v
Brophy* [1981] 2 All ER 705. Any answers given by the accused that were relevant to
the issues at the *voire dire* should not be admissible at the main trial. In the view of the
House of Lords the due administration of justice demanded an accused should feel
completely free to give evidence at a *voire dire* on the matter of a confession, the
admissibility of which is disputed.

Both these cases pre-date the Police and Criminal Evidence Act 1984. Is the position
likely to be any different under section 76 of PACE? The point has never been decided.
Given the wording in section 76 however, it is not thought that the position would be
any different in relation to the first question posed in *Wong Kam Ming*. However, any
incriminating statements made by a defendant in answer to questions during the *voire
dire* would arguably fall within the definition of a confession under section 76. If the
point were to arise at some future date, it is thought the court could be persuaded to
exercise discretion under section 78 of PACE to exclude reference to the defendant's
answers on a *voire dire* as the inquiry at such a hearing should be unfettered.

EDITING CONFESSIONS

If an admissible confession contains material that is inadmissible under some other principle (for example, hearsay or a reference to the accused's previous convictions) the
accused is entitled to have the offending material edited out. The current rules are established by *Practice Direction (Crime: Evidence by Written Statements)* [1986] 1 WLR
805. The Practice Direction affords an opportunity for the prosecution and defence to
attempt to agree a transcript of any tape-recorded interview that may have occurred. The
defence is under an obligation to notify the prosecution within 21 days from the date of
committal whether or not a transcript of a tape-recorded interview is acceptable. In the
event that it is not, the Practice Direction encompasses various rules to promote the resolution of any difficulties. The practical effect is that the parties are under some pressure
to agree the edited transcript. Failing agreement, tapes must be played to the court. It is
however extremely difficult to play a tape to a jury in a constructive way when stopping
and starting a tape at every point where there are matters under dispute.

ADMISSIBILITY OF EVIDENCE FOUND AS A RESULT OF AN
INADMISSIBLE CONFESSION

Can the prosecution use evidence obtained pursuant to an inadmissible confession
against the accused? The finding of such evidence often proves the confession is true
and therefore reliable. The answer is to be found in section 76(4) of PACE:

(4) The fact that a confession is wholly or partly excluded in pursuance of this section shall not affect the admissibility in evidence—

    (a) of any facts discovered as a result of the confession; or

    (b) where the confession is relevant as showing that the accused speaks, writes or expresses himself in a particular way, of so much of the confession as is necessary to show that he does so.

However section 76(5) goes on to provide that where a confession has been excluded in whole or in part:

> Evidence that a fact ... was discovered as a result of a statement made by the accused person shall not be admissible unless evidence of how it was discovered is given by him or on his behalf.

Section 76 preserves the common law position which holds that the mere fact that a confession is inadmissible does not affect the admissibility of any incriminating facts discovered as a result of the confession. An important proviso to this, however, is that the prosecution will not be allowed to point to the inadmissible confession in order to explain how the incriminating evidence was found. Where incriminating facts cannot be adduced without the necessity of referring to the inadmissible confession, neither the confession, nor the facts discovered, will be admissible.

Example

Stuart is arrested on suspicion of kidnapping and sexually assaulting a four-year-old girl. He is educationally subnormal and chooses not to be represented by a solicitor at the police station. Under sustained pressure from investigating officers he confesses to the crime and tells them where the child's clothing can be found. Following a voire dire, *Stuart's confession is ruled inadmissible by the trial judge.*

If, as a result of what Stuart said in his interview, the child's clothing was found carefully hidden in Stuart's garage it would be admissible as part of the prosecution's case. It can be adduced without the necessity of referring to the confession, as the clothing would arguably have been found pursuant to the standard statutory power of search and seizure under PACE applicable in such a case. On the other hand, if Stuart were to tell the officer that the clothing could be found in a bag on a refuse tip in the area, it would be difficult for the prosecution to explain how the evidence came to light without linking it to the inadmissible confession. Indeed, the discovery would have little probative value, if it cannot be linked to the defendant. In these circumstances both the confession and the items discovered as a result of it would be inadmissible.

The fact that the discovery of articles as a result of an inadmissible confession helps legitimise that confession is immaterial and is entirely in line with the philosophy behind section 76, which is an unfettered inquiry into the admissibility of a confession and not its truth.

Case scenario

The police have long suspected Joanna and her boyfriend Felix of being animal rights activists.

Acting on the instructions of an informer, the police are notified of a plan to plant an explosive device outside the home of an eminent research scientist. An undercover officer stops Joanna and searches her. He finds a sketch map of the scientist's home and details of his daily movements tucked inside her training shoe. She is also in possession of a mobile telephone. Joanna is arrested and cautioned. She is taken to a local police station. She asks to see a solicitor but is told she is being held incommunicado as she is suspected of a serious arrestable offence involving others not yet arrested. Joanna is held for 28 hours before being charged. During this time she exhibits signs of anger and distress. She has a fear of enclosed spaces, which she does not disclose to the police. She admits to being somewhat infatuated with Felix. At first she refuses to answer the questions of investigating officers. In her third interview however, after having been falsely told by one of the officers that Felix has confessed and has implicated her in a conspiracy to cause an explosion and feeling claustrophobic, Joanna admits involvement and tells the police where they can find the explosive device. As a result of her remarks the police recover the device from a lock up garage registered to Felix. Felix is arrested. He refuses to answer questions. Joanna wishes to retract her confession. She denies any involvement in the conspiracy.

Joanna can challenge the admissibility of her confession under section 76(2) and section 78 of PACE. It is unlikely that she would succeed in establishing oppression within the meaning of section 76(2)(b), having regard to the decision in R v Fulling [1987] QB 426. However, she could argue her confession is unreliable and that it would be unfair to admit it. The trial judge would need to conduct a voire dire into the circumstances leading up to confession. This would involve the investigating officers and the custody sergeant giving evidence, which would be subject to cross-examination by Joanna's counsel. Questions in cross-examination would be directed at the collective failure of the officers to appreciate Joanna's vulnerability. One assumes there must have been some manifestation of this, which may be borne out in the custody record. The accusation that one of the officers lied to Joanna about Felix having confessed to the crime would be put to the officer. Joanna was arrested in connection with a serious arrestable offence. This would justify her being held incommunicado, providing the conditions set out in section 58 of PACE were met. Cross-examination would be centred upon these reasons and the justification for the length of her detention when the whereabouts of Felix was presumably known. For someone who is claustrophobic, 28 hours is a long time in which to be confined. Joanna should be called to give evidence at the voire dire in order to put her version of the facts in evidence and to give an account of her state of mind. If there is medical evidence that she suffers from claustrophobia, this ought to be tendered at the voire dire. It does not matter that Joanna hid her condition from the police. Her confession is still unreliable within the meaning of section 76(2)(b) of PACE. The failure to provide Joanna with access to a solicitor compounds the actions of the investigating officers. Had a solicitor been present, the outcome would probably have been different in that a solicitor might properly have advised Joanna to remain silent. To admit the confession in these circumstances would be unfair within the meaning of section 78 of PACE.

Joanna may not be asked at her voire dire whether her confession is true. However, as her confession led to the discovery of the explosive device, she would appear to have been complicit in the conspiracy. If the trial judge were to exclude Joanna's confession, under section 76(5) the prosecution would not be able to link the discovery of the device with Joanna's confession. This is important for Joanna. If she is successful in getting her confession excluded, then in the absence of any further compelling evidence linking her to the offence, her defence may well be able to press the trial judge to find that she has no case to answer. The submission of no case to answer is considered in Chapter 11.

HEARSAY PROBLEMS OCCASIONED BY CONFESSIONS

There are a number of complex hearsay issues relating to confession evidence. You are recommended to read Chapter 12, which explains the operation of the hearsay rule before reading this chapter further.

A hearsay statement comprises reliance by one of the parties at the trial on an earlier statement that was made out of court for the purpose of proving the truth of facts asserted in that earlier statement. A confession falls within this definition of hearsay precisely because it consists of a statement made on an earlier occasion, usually at a police station, being relied on by the prosecution in court, to prove the truth of facts asserted by the defendant in his statement.

The starting point when considering hearsay evidence in criminal proceedings is that such evidence is inadmissible unless the hearsay statement falls within a recognised common law or statutory exception. Confession evidence is admitted under a common law exception to the rule. Crucially however, a confession is only ever evidence against its maker.

Example

Suppose A and B are jointly charged with a crime. A confesses to the crime, implicating B. A's confession alone constitutes hearsay evidence. It comprises a statement made on an earlier, out-of-court occasion, being relied on in court by the prosecution as evidence of the truth of the contents to which it deposes. Although admissible, subject to sections 76 and 78 of PACE, A's confession may only be used in evidence against A. It cannot be used in evidence against B. As against B, it constitutes inadmissible hearsay evidence.

If, in the example given above, A were to plead guilty, becoming an accomplice and giving evidence for the prosecution against his co-accused B, no hearsay problems would arise. In such a case A would be giving a first-hand account of B's involvement.

R v Spinks [1982] 1 All ER 587

F had committed an arrestable offence of wounding. The defendant was arrested for trying to impede F's arrest. There was no proof at the defendant's trial that F had committed an actual offence, except for F's own confession. Although constituting evidence against F, the Court of Appeal held it was not evidence against the defendant that F had in fact committed an offence of wounding.

Where A and B are to be jointly tried, the knowledge that one of them has confessed implicating the other poses special dangers for the other co-defendant. Notwithstanding this, the decision in *R v Lake* (1977) 64 Cr App R 172 makes it clear that only in very exceptional cases will a separate trial be ordered in relation to each. Sometimes the confession of A can be edited to minimise the damage to B. The judge must direct the jury that the confession of A is evidence only against A and may not be used in evidence against B. The extent to which a jury can comply with such instructions is debatable.

Use of a confession by a co-accused to establish innocence

Suppose a co-accused A makes a confession, which in whole or in part exonerates B. Such a confession evidence would be extremely useful to B in B's defence. If the confession is made part of the prosecution's case, B will have no problem utilising it in support of his defence. Suppose however, the prosecution chooses not to rely on the evidence of A's confession or is prevented from doing so by a ruling from the court under section 76(2) or section 78 of PACE, can B still make use of A's confession if it assists his defence? This poses a complex problem of hearsay. The House of Lords grappled with this problem in *R v Myers* and its decision provides a substantial degree of clarification.

R v Myers [1998] AC 124

A and B were jointly charged with murder. A (the appellant) had made a number of admissions to the police in which she confessed to the crime, but also suggested B was not guilty of murder. The prosecution chose, of its own volition, not to rely on A's admissions because there had been breaches of Code C. It was nevertheless accepted that A's admissions had been freely made. At trial, A, asserting her innocence, indicated she would put forward a defence inconsistent with her earlier statements to the police, which would have the effect of implicating B. B was extremely anxious to place reliance on A's earlier statements as they greatly assisted his defence.

A sought to have a separate trial. This posed a significant conceptual problem for the judge. Were a joint trial to be ordered A would, to all intents and purposes, have to give evidence in support of her own defence. This would leave her vulnerable to cross-examination by B's counsel. If A gave evidence at a joint trial maintaining her complete innocence and placing the blame on B, B's counsel would have to cross-examine A. In an attempt to wholly undermine A's credibility B's counsel would have to prove A had made a previous inconsistent statement (her confession). A hearsay problem would not arise in this regard because cross-examination would be limited to proving A had made a previous inconsistent statement. The law in relation to the evidential use that can be made of a witness's previous inconsistent statement is covered in Chapter 15. The relevant law is contained within sections 4 and 5 of the Criminal Procedure Act 1865. In essence, where a previous inconsistent statement is admitted into evidence, it assumes relevance to its maker's credibility as a witness only and cannot be treated as evidence of the truth of any fact stated in it.

Were A to be granted a separate trial, B would be unable to cross-examine A. As a co-accused, A could not be compelled to give evidence at the trial of her co-defendant B. Counsel for B reasoned that if A did not give evidence, it would be necessary to call the officers who had heard A's admissions to repeat in court the substance of what she had said. This would raise a number of hearsay arguments.

The trial judge ruled in favour of a joint trial in the exercise of his discretion and the police officers were called to give evidence as part of the prosecution's case. A was convicted of murder, B of manslaughter. A appealed. A's conviction was upheld by the Court of Appeal. Leave to appeal to the House of Lords was granted on the following point:

> In a joint trial of two defendants A and B, is an out of court confession by A which exculpates B but which is ruled, or is conceded to be, inadmissible as evidence for the Crown nevertheless admissible at the instigation of B in support of B's defence, or does such a confession in all the circumstances offend the rule against hearsay?

The House of Lords upheld A's conviction. Analysing the law, the House of Lords considered two earlier inconsistent decisions. In *R v Campbell and Williams* [1993] Crim LR 448, three defendants, A, B and C were charged with robbery. The prosecution was unaware that B had in his possession a secretly taped conversation between himself and A in which A admitted the crime implicating C but exonerating B. The prosecution did not object to B making use of the recording and the Court of Appeal held that the evidence had rightly been admitted. In contrast, but raising the same issue, in *R v Beckford and Daley* [1991] Crim LR 833, three men were charged with murder. D1 admitted in interview with the police that it was he who had stabbed the victim. The prosecution was prevented from using D1's confession due to breaches of Code C – the trial judge having ruled against its admission under section 78 of PACE. The trial judge could see no exception to the hearsay rule which would have allowed D2 to call witnesses to repeat in court D1's confession. Nevertheless, the judge expressed concern about his decision observing that the hearsay rule can sometimes obstruct the search for the truth. The trial judge further ruled that the conditions of admissibility relating to confession evidence under section 76(2) of PACE applied only to the prosecution.

In R v *Myers*, the House of Lords concluded there was a material difference between the two decisions. In R v *Beckford and Daley*, there had been a finding of actual breaches of Code C, which was absent in R v *Campbell and Williams*. However, the crucial issue, as to whether one co-defendant can make use of another's confession when it is clearly relevant to the co-accused's defence, was the same. In upholding the conviction in R v *Myers*, the House of Lords overruled R v *Beckford and Daley*. The majority felt a co-accused should in principle be able to utilise his fellow co-accused's confession so long as it could not have been rendered inadmissible under section 76(2) of PACE, at the behest of the prosecution. Lord Slynn expressed the position thus:

> In my opinion a defendant should also be allowed to put a co-defendant's confession to witnesses to whom the confession was made so long as the confession is relevant to the defendant's defence and so long as it appears that the confession was not obtained in a manner which would have made it inadmissible at the instance of the Crown under section 76(2) of the Act of 1984. There may be doubt as to whether the co-defendant will be called (so that it may not be possible to put the confession to the co-defendant directly) and not to allow the defendant to introduce it by way of cross-examination of prosecution witnesses could lead to great unfairness.

Lord Slynn's observations are premised on the assumption that the trial judge has not in fact ruled against admission under section 76(2) of PACE. Were this to happen, Lord Slynn's *obiter* view was that the co-accused could be in no better position than the prosecution in this regard. Lord Hope took the view that such evidence would be worthless in any event.

The decision of the House of Lords in R v *Myers* is correct in terms of justice. It was extremely important for B to be able to present evidence relevant to proof of his innocence. However, rather like the decision in R v *Blastland* [1986] AC 41, which we consider below, the House of Lords does not really explain how the hearsay obstacle is to be overcome. In admitting the evidence it in effect creates a further exception to the hearsay rule, which is something many previously decided cases, including R v *Blastland*, have said is the prerogative of the legislature and not the judiciary.

If the Law Commission's proposals for the reform of the hearsay rule are implemented (Law Commission Report 245, *Evidence in Criminal Proceedings: Hearsay and Related Topics*), section 76(2) of PACE will be amended to extend the conditions for the admissibility of confessions to a co-defendant seeking to rely on a fellow co-accused's confession in his defence. The hearsay problem, which is not satisfactorily resolved by the House of Lords in R v *Myers*, would be removed as, under the Law Commission's proposals, courts would have an inclusionary discretion to admit hearsay evidence not falling within a recognised exception to the rule, where it would be in the interests of justice to admit it.

Confessions by third parties not charged in the proceedings

R v Blastland [1986] AC 41

The defendant was charged with the sodomy and murder of a 12-year-old boy. He pleaded not guilty. He admitted to having buggered the boy but maintained he had panicked and ran off when he saw another man nearby. His defence at trial was that someone else had committed the murder, probably the man he had observed. The defendant wanted to adduce evidence of the fact that a man, known only as Mark during the trial, who was a known homosexual, had told several people about the boy's murder before it had become public knowledge. In imparting this information, Mark was witnessed to have been in a highly excitable state. Mark had also made and retracted a series of confessions to the offences with which the defendant was charged. Such confessions were inadmissible hearsay as the trial judge had refused the defence leave to call Mark as a witness for the defence. Counsel for the defendant sought to call the witnesses to whom Mark had imparted certain information so that they could repeat on oath what Mark had said to them. The defence wanted the jury to infer that Mark could only have come by such knowledge if he had either witnessed the murder or committed it himself. Leave was refused on the basis that such evidence amounted to hearsay.

The defendant was convicted of murder and appealed. The Court of Appeal upheld his conviction but certified the following two questions of law for consideration by the House of Lords:

> (1) whether a confession by a person other than the defendant to the offence with which the defendant is charged is admissible in evidence where that person is not called as a witness and (2) whether evidence of words spoken by a third party who is not called as a witness is hearsay evidence if it is advanced as evidence of the fact that the words were spoken so as to indicate the state of knowledge of the person speaking the words, if the inference to be drawn from such words is that the person speaking them is or may be guilty of the offence with which the defendant is charged.

Unfortunately, the House of Lords would only give leave on the second question which meant the hearsay implications of a confession by a third party was never discussed. On this point however and on a purely *obiter* basis, Lord Bridge concluded that it was a well-established principle, 'never since challenged, that it was for the legislature, not the judiciary, to create new exceptions to the hearsay rule. To admit in criminal trials statements confessing to the crime for which the defendant is being tried, made by third parties not called as witnesses, would be to create a very significant and, many think, a dangerous new exception.'

The second question before the House of Lords touches on a common law exception to the hearsay rule which is dealt with more fully in Chapter 12. Words used by a witness on an earlier out-of-court occasion may be admitted under a common law exception to the hearsay rule where the intention is not to rely on the truth of facts asserted in the earlier statement but to prove the state of mind of the statement maker. The House of Lords concluded in *R v Blastland*, that Mark's state of mind, based on his knowledge at the time, was not logically relevant to proof of the issues in the defendant's case. It will be recalled from Chapter 1 that relevancy is a fundamental concept in evidence law. To be admissible, evidence must be logically relevant to an issue requiring proof. Lord Bridge reasoned that Mark could have acquired his knowledge in a number of different ways, some of them innocent. Whether the House of Lords was right to reject the evidence on the grounds of relevance has been the subject of much academic debate. Would the jury have reached a different conclusion had they been aware of the evidence?

Under the Law Commission's proposals for reform, the availability of an inclusionary discretion would permit the court to admit incriminating admissions made by third parties, notwithstanding their hearsay nature, where it was considered to be in the interests of justice.

MIXED STATEMENTS

It is not unusual for a defendant to give a mixed statement to investigating officers. Such a statement is partly incriminating and partly self-serving. A mixed statement would be something like: 'I murdered him but I acted in self-defence' or 'I admit I took the goods but I always intended to return them'. An admissible confession can be relied on as evidence of the truth because it is an admission against the maker's self-interest. A denial by the defendant generally carries little evidential weight because it is self-serving in its nature. Such self-serving statements constitute hearsay evidence where they are relied on as proof of the facts they state. As such they are inadmissible. Where however, the defendant gives evidence in support of his own defence at trial and puts forward a defence he mentioned at an earlier stage, the earlier statement may be admitted for the limited evidential purpose of showing the defendant's consistency as a witness. This principle is enshrined in R v *Storey* (1968) 52 Cr App R 334. This principle however has no application to a situation where the defendant chooses not to give evidence at his trial but simply wishes to rely on a self-serving statement made by him at the police station.

The evidential problem of the mixed statement only arises where the defendant chooses not to give evidence at his trial. The incriminating part of the statement is admissible as evidence of its truth under the established common law exception to the hearsay rule. What though of the self-serving portions of the statement? In fairness to the accused the entire statement must be put before the jury. The matter was considered by the Court of Appeal in R v *Duncan* (1981) 73 Cr App R 359 and by the House of Lords in R v *Sharp* [1988] 1 WLR 7. In short, the judge should direct the jury to consider the whole statement, in deciding where the truth might lie. The judge is entitled to point out that the incriminating aspects of the statement might carry more weight than the non-incriminating aspects, as these can be easily manufactured.

Further reading

Ashworth, A., 'Excluding Evidence as Protecting Rights' [1977] Crim LR 732.

Birch, D., 'The PACE Hots Up' [1989] Crim LR 95.

Choo, A., 'Confessions and Corroboration: A Comparative Perspective' [1991] Crim LR 867.

Gudjonsson, G. (1992) *The Psychology of Interrogation, Confession and Testimony*, Wiley.

Hirst, M., 'Confessions and Proof of Innocence' (1998) CLJ 146.

McEwan, J. (1998) *Evidence and the Adversarial Process – The Modern Law*, Hart Publishing.

Palmer, C., 'Still Vulnerable After All These Years' [1996] Crim LR 633.

Runciman of Doxford, Viscount (1993) *Report of the Royal Commission on Criminal Justice*, Cmnd 2263, HMSO.

Sanders, A., 'Constructing the Case for the Prosecution' (1987) 14 Journal of Law and Society 229.

Sanders, A. and Young, R. (2000) *Criminal Justice*, Butterworths Law.

Chapter 7

THE RIGHT TO REMAIN SILENT

INTRODUCTION

Considerable pressure may be placed on a suspect to answer questions during police interrogation. Sometimes this pressure may result in the suspect making incriminating admissions or a confession capable of being used in evidence against him. In spite of the extensive powers that are available to the police to detain and question the suspect and the psychological pressures that he may be placed under, a suspect cannot be compelled to answer questions at the police station. At common law the suspect has always enjoyed this right to silence. The caution a suspect is given on arrest and before interview reminds him of this right. The right extends to a refusal by a defendant to give evidence at trial.

In recent years, however, the right to silence has been substantially curtailed by statutory reforms, most notably under the Criminal Justice and Public Order Act 1994 and the Criminal Procedure and Investigations Act 1996.

This chapter will examine the evidential consequences that emanate from a defendant's decision to remain silent, both at the police station and at trial. It begins with a brief examination of the rules relating to the right of silence at common law. It goes on to consider the calls for a change in the law and concludes with an examination of the statutory changes and the implications these changes have had in the context of human rights.

RELATIONSHIP BETWEEN THE RIGHT TO SILENCE AND THE PRIVILEGE AGAINST SELF-INCRIMINATION

There is a close relationship between the right to silence and the well-established privilege against self-incrimination. To compel a suspect to disclose or to surrender information, which is then used in evidence against him in a subsequent prosecution, is *prima facie* a violation of the privilege against self-incrimination. The compulsion comes from the risk that by not providing the necessary information, the defendant will be subjected to a criminal charge or other penalty. This aspect of the privilege against self-incrimination and its compatibility with Article 6(2) of the European Convention on Human Rights, guaranteeing the right to be presumed innocent, is considered in detail in Chapter 10, which examines an individual's reluctance to disclose relevant evidence on the basis that such information is protected from disclosure by a private privilege. Under the provisions that permit an adverse inference to be drawn from a suspect's refusal to answer questions (discussed below), there is no direct compulsion on the suspect to answer questions in the sense that a failure to do so would result in contempt proceedings or the commission of another criminal offence.

THE RATIONALE BEHIND THE RIGHT TO SILENCE

The interrogation of the suspect is a vital and cost-effective tool in the armoury of the police. If a suspect cannot be pressurised into talking, the fight against crime would be substantially undermined as many successful prosecutions rely on incriminating admissions made in interview. On the other hand, the maxim *nemo debet prodere se ipsum* (no one should be forced to be his own betrayer) is felt to be a necessary and fundamental safeguard against the use of coercion on the part of prosecuting authorities and accounts, in part, for the suspect's long cherished enjoyment of the right to remain silent.

The right to silence has evolved over the centuries and has its origins in the ancient privilege against self-incrimination. The privilege against self-incrimination is closely associated with the presumption of innocence, a fundamental right which is enshrined in Article 6(2) of the European Convention on Human Rights and in the requirement of the prosecution to prove the guilt of the accused beyond reasonable doubt. Compelling the suspect to incriminate himself would appear to be contrary to the presumption of innocence. There is a perceived danger that by allowing the defendant's silence to form part of the prosecution's case, the privilege against self-incrimination is infringed and the requirement on the part of the prosecution to find evidence against the accused, sufficient to prove his guilt beyond reasonable doubt, is undermined.

It should be noted, however, that the privilege against self-incrimination is not an absolute right. If it were, the police would be unable to take forensic samples from a suspect even with his consent. Sections 61–63 of PACE (discussed in Chapter 8) give the police power to obtain samples of an intimate and non-intimate nature from a suspect. In the case of intimate samples, section 62 of PACE permits a court to draw an adverse inference from an unjustified refusal by the defendant to provide an intimate sample. Such evidence could not be of a more self-incriminating nature.

At the heart of the controversy surrounding the debate about silence is whether a court should in principle be permitted to use silence in evidence against an accused. What would be gained in evidential terms? What is the true evidential value of silence? Suspects remain silent for all sorts of reasons other than guilt. In contrast to an accused's silence, real evidence of a self-incriminating nature such as an intimate sample obtained from a suspect has an objective and inherently reliable quality about it that perhaps justifies the coercive powers available to the police in order to obtain it.

At common law the position is relatively straightforward: silence cannot be used in evidence against the defendant and the jury must be so instructed.

PRE-TRIAL SILENCE AT COMMON LAW

The defendant has always enjoyed a right to silence at common law. The leading case is *Hall* v *R* [1971] 1 WLR 298, in which Lord Diplock affirmed that:

> It is a clear and widely known principle of the common law...that a person is entitled to refrain from answering a question put to him for the purpose of discovering whether he has

committed a criminal offence.... It may be that in very exceptional circumstances an inference may be drawn from a failure to give an explanation or a disclaimer, but in their Lordships' view silence alone on being informed by a police officer that someone else has made an accusation against him cannot give rise to an inference that the person to whom this information is communicated accepts the truth of the accusation.

At common law therefore the trial judge must prevent the jury from speculating as to the reasons why the defendant may have decided to remain silent by directing the jury not to draw an adverse inference. Much has been made of the inclusion in Lord Diplock's statement of the words that '...in very exceptional circumstances an inference may be drawn from a failure to give an explanation'. It implies the right to silence at common law is not unfettered, although precisely what Lord Diplock intended is unclear. Later cases like *R v Chandler* [1976] 1 WLR 585 have used it to suggest that where a suspect is on 'even terms' with his accuser, in circumstances where it is reasonable to have expected the suspect to deny the allegation, this might be taken as an implicit acceptance on the part of the accused of the truth contained in the accusation. The reasoning in *R v Chandler* is based on the much earlier authority of *R v Mitchell* (1892) 17 Cox CC 508, in which Cave J explains how silence can be tantamount to a confession.

> Now the whole admissibility of statements of this kind rests upon the consideration that if a charge is made against a person in that person's presence it is reasonable to expect that he or she will immediately deny it, and in the absence of such a denial is some evidence of an admission on the part of the person charged, and of the truth of the charge. Undoubtedly, when persons are speaking on even terms, and a charge is made, and the person charged says nothing, and expresses no indignation, and does nothing to repel the charge, that is some evidence to show that he admits the charge to be true.

In *R v Chandler*, the Court of Appeal held no inference from silence could be drawn where the parties were not on 'even terms'. The Court of Appeal controversially suggested that a suspect might be said to be on 'even terms' with his accuser in the formal setting of a police interrogation providing the suspect's solicitor was in attendance. This aspect of the decision has been criticised. Whilst the 'even terms' aspect of *R v Chandler* remains good law, its effect in the context of police questioning is much diminished. The Court of Appeal acknowledged no inference could be drawn if the suspect had been cautioned and reminded of his right to remain silent, even though the parties could be said to be on 'equal terms'. Since the decision in *R v Chandler*, PACE Code C 10.1 makes it a mandatory requirement to caution an individual suspected of involvement in a criminal offence before any questions are put to him with a view to obtaining evidence against him.

The case of *R v Mitchell* was not cited in *Hall v R* above, which contains an unequivocal statement to the effect that 'silence alone on being informed by a police officer that someone else has made an accusation against him cannot give rise to an inference that the person to whom this information is communicated accepts the truth of the accusation'.

In *Parkes v R* [1976] 1 WLR 1251, the Privy Council allowed the suspect's silence to be used in evidence against him because his silence was part of an obviously guilty reaction. Unlike *Hall v R* and *R v Chandler* where the accusation was made in the presence of the police, in *Parkes* v *R*, the accusation had been made informally by the victim's mother. In response to the allegations the defendant made no comment but attempted to stab his accuser! It is perhaps in the context of the facts in *Parkes* v *R* that Lord Diplock's statement in *Hall* v *R* is best understood. Certainly, in such circumstances there is a clearer evidential rationale for using the accused's silence in evidence against him. The decisions in *Hall* v *R* and *R* v *Chandler* sit uneasily beside each other. *R* v *Chandler* was subsequently applied in *R* v *Horne* [1990] Crim LR 188. In this case police officers brought about a confrontation between the defendant and his victim. The victim, still bleeding from his wounds, accused the defendant who made no reply.

The common law remains good law except to the extent to which it has been subsequently modified by the Criminal Justice and Public Order Act 1994, which we consider in detail below.

SILENCE AT TRIAL – THE COMMON LAW POSITION

Section 1 of the Criminal Evidence Act 1898 clearly states that a defendant is not a compellable witness for the prosecution, although the defendant may be a competent witness in his own defence and in the defence of any co-accused. Whether a defendant should give evidence at his trial is a decision which defence advocates must give careful thought to. The jury may wonder why a defendant pleading not guilty has chosen not to have his version of events subjected to cross-examination like every other witness in the case. Does the defendant have something to hide? Are the jury permitted to speculate in this way at common law?

The position at common law is summed up in the leading case of *R* v *Bathurst* [1968] 2 QB 99:

> ... the accepted form of comment is to inform the jury that, of course he is not bound to give evidence, that he can sit back and see if the prosecution have proved their case, and that while the jury have been deprived of the opportunity of hearing his story tested in cross-examination, the one thing they must not do is to assume that he is guilty because he has not gone into the witness box. (*per* Lord Parker)

The decision in *R* v *Bathurst* confirms that even at common law a judge could make a thinly disguised attack on the defendant's decision not to give evidence by pointing out the absence of scrutiny that cross-examination affords. The principle in *R* v *Bathurst* was subsequently confirmed by the Court of Appeal in *R* v *Martinez-Tobon* (1994) 98 Cr App R 375.

(1) The judge should give the jury a direction along the lines of the Judicial Studies Board specimen direction based on *R. v. Bathurst*.
(2) The essentials of that direction are that the defendant is under no obligation to testify and the jury should not assume he is guilty because he has not given evidence.
(3) Provided those essentials are complied with, the judge may think it appropriate to make a stronger comment where the defence case involves alleged facts which (a) are at variance with prosecution evidence or additional to it and exculpatory, and (b) must, if true, be within the knowledge of the defendant.
(4) The nature and strength of such comment must be a matter for the discretion of the judge and will depend upon the circumstances of the individual case. However, it must not be such as to contradict or nullify the essentials of the conventional direction.

Whilst some comment was thus permitted in appropriate circumstances, the trial judge had to convey to the jury that the defendant was not under an obligation to testify and the jury should not assume his guilt simply because he had chosen not to give evidence.

A co-accused has always had an unfettered right to comment adversely on a failure of his fellow co-accused to testify.

In the light of the above, it could hardly be said that the common law right to silence at trial was totally unfettered. As we shall see, legislative changes brought about by the Criminal Justice and Public Order Act 1994 have put the matter beyond doubt in that an adverse inference can now be drawn in circumstances where the defendant chooses not to give evidence on oath at his trial.

IMPETUS FOR CHANGE TO THE RIGHT TO SILENCE

Concern amongst the judiciary as regards the use of ambush defences was first expressed in *R v Gilbert* (1978) 66 Cr App R 237. An ambush defence arises where a defendant fails to put forward his version of events at the police station but does so for the first time at trial. Effectively the defence springs a surprise by giving the prosecution precious little time to investigate the facts and to plan its strategy in response. In *R v Gilbert*, the defendant raised self-defence in relation to the killing of his victim for the first time at his trial. In the Court of Appeal, Viscount Dilhorne was of the view that the judge should be entitled to say something in these circumstances, stating:

> In our view it may not be a misdirection to say simply 'this defence was first put forward at this trial'…but if more is said, it may give rise to the inference that a jury is being invited to disregard the defence put forward because the accused exercised his right of silence…No accused can be compelled to speak before, or for that matter, at his trial…As the law now stands, although it may appear obvious to the jury in exercise of their common sense that an innocent man would speak and not be silent, they must be told that they must not draw the inference of guilt from his silence…

Therefore, even before the legislative changes brought about by the Criminal Justice and Public Order Act 1994, a certain amount of judicial comment on the failure by the accused to advance a defence until the day of his trial was permitted. A further, clear call for change came from the Lord Chief Justice in *R v Alladice* (1988) 87 Cr App R 380. Pointing to the rights and safeguards suspects enjoy under the Police and Criminal Evidence Act 1984, he intimated the quid pro quo for enforcing such rights, 'must be the right of the court to comment on failure by the defendant to reveal a defence which the defendant later springs on the prosecution …'.

Set against the background of increasing judicial unease about defendants abusing their right not to have to disclose the substance of their defence and the increasing public concerns about the apparent rising tide of crime, the Conservative government established the Royal Commission on Criminal Justice to investigate, amongst other issues, whether the right to silence should be modified. The Royal Commission reported in 1993.

ARGUMENTS FOR AND AGAINST REFORM

The Royal Commission on Criminal Justice heard a wide range of views both from those who advocated changing the right to silence and from those who supported the status quo.

Proponents in support of change argued that the existing law, far from protecting the innocent, was actually harmful to them and that it allowed experienced criminals to exploit the rules. Those who are innocent would want to proclaim their innocence just as those who are guilty would choose to hide behind the right to say nothing. According to the proponents for change, this accords entirely with common sense. Why not openly acknowledge what juries most probably do in any event behind the closed doors of the deliberation room, which is to reason that if the defendant has kept silent, he must have something to hide? The right to silence, it was argued, was more symbolic than real. This was supported by research studies whose findings suggested that only a small percentage of suspects actually chose to remain silent. Further, the availability of such a right has never prevented the police from using aggressive questioning techniques in order to get suspects to talk. Given the availability of legal assistance and the rights under PACE, the right to silence was unnecessary. The victim of a serious crime might well wonder, why, if a *prima facie* case has been made out against a defendant, he should not be made to answer the accusation levelled against him. Those supporting change persuasively argued that the interests of justice could not be served where the defendant was permitted to reserve his position until the day of the trial.

Those who opposed any changes to the common law vociferously argued to the contrary by maintaining that the absolute right to silence was a vital component within the criminal justice system. Far from seeking to diminish its worth, the right to silence needed to be strengthened in that it protected innocent people against the risk of being wrongly convicted. Abolishing the right to silence would be contrary to the long-established privilege against self-incrimination and would effectively reverse the burden of proof.

It was also strongly argued that the suspect's legal rights contained in PACE were more imaginary than real and that there was no empirical evidence to prove much would be gained in terms of law enforcement by diminishing the right to silence. Experienced criminals would devise their own strategy to avoid an adverse inference being drawn irrespective of any changes in the law. As for the argument that it was contrary to common sense not to want to protest one's innocence, those opposing change maintained common sense is not always a reliable indicator as suspects often behave in an irrational way when faced with accusations by the police and remain silent for all kinds of different reasons. There would be a real danger of fact finders attributing too much evidential significance to the defendant's decision to remain silent at the police station. Diminishing the right to silence would increase the risk of false confessions being made, particularly in the case of vulnerable suspects who might consider they would be damned if they do speak and damned if they said nothing.

The arguments and the evidence in support presented on both sides were taken on board. The Royal Commission recommended the right to silence be maintained in its current common law form, subject to some procedural changes requiring the defendant to make some pre-trial disclosure before trial. The government ignored the Commission's recommendations and went ahead with sweeping legislative changes.

CRIMINAL JUSTICE AND PUBLIC ORDER ACT 1994 – CHANGES TO THE RIGHT TO SILENCE

Failure to testify (section 35)

Section 35 of the 1994 Act provides that:

(1) At the trial of any person, subsections (2) and (3) below apply unless—
   (a) the accused's guilt is not in issue; or
   (b) it appears to the court that the physical or mental condition of the accused makes it undesirable for him to give evidence; ...

(2) Where this subsection applies, the court shall, at the conclusion of the evidence for the prosecution, satisfy itself ... that the accused is aware that the stage has been reached at which evidence can be given for the defence and that he can, if he wishes, give evidence and that, if he chooses not to give evidence, or having been sworn, without good cause refuses to answer any question, it will be permissible for the court ... to draw such inferences as appear proper from his failure to give evidence or his refusal, without good cause, to answer any questions.

(3) Where this subsection applies, the court or jury, in determining whether the accused is guilty of the offence charged, may draw such inferences as appear proper from the failure of the accused to give evidence or his refusal, without good cause, to answer any question.

(4) This section does not render the accused compellable to give evidence on his own behalf, and he shall accordingly not be guilty of contempt of court by reason of a failure to do so.

(5) For the purposes of this section a person who, having been sworn, refuses to answer any question shall be taken to do so without good cause unless—
   (a) he is entitled to refuse to answer the question by virtue of any enactment, whenever passed or made, or on the ground of privilege; or
   (b) the court in the exercise of its general discretion excuses him from answering it.

Section 35 must be read in conjunction with section 38(3) of the Act which reads:

A person shall not ... be convicted of an offence solely on an inference drawn from such a failure or refusal as is mentioned in section ... 35(3).

The provisions of section 38(3) constitute the very important safeguard that no decision to convict a defendant or to commit him for trial to the Crown Court may be made solely on an inference permitted under section 35.

Section 35 removes the defendant's 'unfettered' common law right not to give evidence in his own defence. It does not compel an accused to give evidence but it makes a decision by an accused not to do so subject to the risk of an adverse evidential inference being drawn. In this sense, it places an indirect pressure on an accused to give evidence. Where a defendant indicates he will not be giving evidence in support of his own defence, the judge, in the presence of the jury, or the justices' clerk, is required to ask of the defendant's advocate: 'Have you advised your client that the stage has been reached at which he may give evidence and that if he chooses not to do so, or having been sworn without good cause, refuses to answer any question, the jury magistrates may draw such inference as appear proper from his failure to do so?'

The application of section 35 is not confined to the defendant who decides not to give evidence at all.

R v Ackinclose [1996] Crim LR 747

The defendant was on trial for possession of a controlled drug with intent to supply. Shortly before his arrest he had been observed in the presence of another man. On being approached by the police, both men ran off. One of them was seen discarding a plastic bag containing drugs. At his trial the defendant gave evidence and denied drug dealing, alleging the other man he had been with was the dealer. Under pressure from the judge he refused to disclose the man's identity. The Court of Appeal held this was not a situation to which section 35(5) applied, and as such an inference was permissible under section 35(1).

Section 35(1)(b) provides that an adverse inference may not be drawn against an accused who does not have to give evidence on oath because he has a mental or physical condition making it undesirable for him to give evidence. What constitutes a mental or physical condition within the meaning of the section?

R v Friend [1997] 2 Cr App R 231

The defendant, who was 14 at the time of the offence, was convicted of murder. At trial, a *voire dire* was held in the absence of the jury to determine whether section 35 of the Criminal Justice and Public Order Act 1994 applied. At the inquiry a consultant clinical psychologist gave evidence that the defendant had a very low IQ, was educationally disadvantaged and had a mental age of a nine-year-old. The psychologist maintained the defendant could only give a coherent account if settled down and given plenty of time to answer. If put under pressure, he would find it hard to concentrate. Defence counsel asked the trial judge not to leave the issue of adverse inference to the jury. Given the defendant's mental state, he argued it would be undesirable for the defendant to give evidence and it would be wrong for the jury to be permitted to draw an inference. The trial judge rejected the submission and the Court of Appeal endorsed this rejection.

In the opinion of the Court of Appeal, section 35(1)(b) was intended to mitigate any injustice to a person who was physically or mentally handicapped. It was for the judge to determine whether or not it was undesirable for the accused to give evidence. Giving examples of the sort of medical conditions likely to come within section 35(1)(b) Otton LJ observed:

> A physical condition might include an epileptic attack, a mental condition, latent schizophrenia where the experience of giving evidence might trigger a florid state. If it appears to the judge on the *voire dire*, that such a physical or mental condition of the defendant makes it undesirable for him to give evidence he will so rule. The inference cannot thereafter be drawn and he will so direct the jury.

Where a defendant asserts he has a physical or mental condition within the meaning of section 35(1)(b) the decision in *R v A* [1997] Crim LR 883 confirms an evidential burden is cast upon the defendant to prove his assertion.

Prior to the operation of section 35, a defendant who was likely to become easily confused, excessively nervous or aggressive in the witness box, would have been advised, in no uncertain terms, not to give evidence on oath. Such advice could be given without the risk of an adverse inference being drawn against the accused. As a consequence of section 35, and in the light of the decision of the Court of Appeal in *R v Friend* above, such advice can no longer be given without risk.

Under section 35(2), a defendant who has been sworn to answer questions on oath may assert he has good cause not to answer a particular question. What constitutes good cause is restricted by section 35(5). The accused is entitled to refuse to answer a question on the ground of a recognised privilege or otherwise in the exercise of the court's discretion.

The first case to mount a substantive challenge to section 35 itself and hence the most significant authority on its provisions is considered below:

R v Cowan; R v Gayle; R v Ricciardi [1995] 3 WLR 818

Three appeals were heard before the Court of Appeal. All three defendants had chosen not to give evidence at their trials and all had been subject to a direction from the trial judge permitting the jury to draw an adverse inference from their failure to do so. It was contended on appeal that as a matter of principle, section 35 should be invoked only in exceptional circumstances as it infringed a defendant's unfettered right to silence and effectively watered down the burden of proof. In addition, all three argued that the judge's direction to the jury had been defective, albeit in different ways and that their resulting convictions should be set aside.

Both arguments were firmly rejected by the Court of Appeal.

In relation to the argument that section 35 was wrong in principle, the Court of Appeal in R v *Cowan* above commented that the right to silence had never been an unfettered right even at common law. Furthermore section 35(4) made it perfectly clear that a defendant still enjoyed a right to silence in that he could not be compelled to give evidence in support of his own defence. Rejecting the argument that the section watered down the burden of proof, the Court of Appeal made the following observations:

1 The prosecution must establish there is a *prima facie* case to answer before any question of the defendant testifying even arises.
2 Section 38(3) prevents a conviction being based solely on an inference from the failure to testify.
3 The burden of proving guilt continues to lie on the prosecution throughout.

In the judgment of Lord Taylor CJ, the Court of Appeal acknowledged that there is no mandatory requirement on the part of the fact finder to draw an adverse inference:

> We accept that apart from the mandatory exceptions in section 35(1), it will be open to a court to decline to draw an adverse inference from silence at trial and for a judge to direct or advise a jury against drawing such inference if the circumstances of the case justify such a course. But in our view there would need either to be some evidential basis for doing so or some exceptional factors in the case making that a fair course to take. It must be stressed that the inferences permitted by the section are only such 'as appear proper'. The use of that phrase was no doubt intended to leave a broad discretion to a trial judge to decide in all the circumstances whether any proper inference is capable of being drawn by the jury. If not he should tell them so; otherwise it is for the jury to decide whether in fact an inference should properly be drawn. ...
> Lord Taylor CJ added:
> ... It is not possible to anticipate all the circumstances in which a judge might think it right to direct or advise a jury against drawing an adverse inference.

The availability of such discretion affords an important safeguard.

As regards the direction to the jury, the Court of Appeal endorsed the specimen direction of the Judicial Studies Board but highlighted certain key essentials which include:

1   The judge will have told the jury that the burden of proof remains upon the prosecution throughout and what the required standard is.

2   It is necessary for the judge to make clear to the jury that the defendant is entitled to remain silent. That is his right and his choice. The right to silence remains.

3   An inference from failure to give evidence cannot on its own prove guilt. That is expressly stated in section 38(3) of the Act.

4   Therefore, the jury must be satisfied that the prosecution has established a case to answer before drawing any inferences from silence. Of course, the judge must have thought so or the question whether the defendant was to give evidence would not have arisen. But the jury may not believe the witnesses whose evidence the judge considered sufficient to raise a *prima facie* case. It must therefore be made clear to them that they must find there to be a case to answer on the prosecution evidence before drawing an adverse inference from the defendant's silence.

5   If, despite any evidence relied upon to explain his silence or in the absence of any such evidence, the jury concludes the silence can only sensibly be attributed to the defendant's having no answer or none that would stand up to cross-examination, it may draw an adverse inference.

In the Court of Appeal's view, the evidential impact of an adverse inference drawn under section 35 is limited in that it should be treated as but one further factor to be weighed up in the overall evidential equation.

A trial judge who confines his directions to the jury on section 35 to the specimen direction of the Judicial Studies Board will have little to fear on appeal.

R *v* Birchall [1999] Crim LR 311

The defendant had been arrested on suspicion of the murder of his former girlfriend's new lover. There were no eyewitnesses to the murder and there was no forensic evidence linking him to the vic-tim. The prosecution's case rested on motive, opportunity and the failure by the defendant to explain the disappearance of clothing he had been wearing on the day. There was further evidence from a remand prisoner who claimed the defendant had confessed to the murder. The defendant denied this. In his summing up, the trial judge omitted to remind the jurors that they had to find a *prima facie* case on presentation of the prosecution's case alone, before any account of the defendant's failure to tes-tify was considered by them. Quashing the conviction, the Court of Appeal concluded that the draw-ing of an adverse inference was a sensitive matter and that very careful directions to the jury were needed to ensure compliance with Article 6(1) and (2) of the European Convention on Human Rights.
In relation to the fourth key essential under *R* v *Cowan* (above), the Court of Appeal held:

> Inescapable logic demands that a jury should not start to consider whether they should draw inferences from a defendant's failure to give oral evidence at his trial until they have concluded that the Crown's case against him is sufficiently compelling to call for an answer by him. What was called the 'fourth essential' in *Cowan* was correctly described as such. There is a clear risk of injustice if the requirements of logic and fairness in this respect are not observed.

The requirement for the jury to find a *prima facie* case before any question of an adverse inference is even considered is confusing in the sense that the judge is required to dismiss the charges against the accused if he forms the opinion at the close of the prosecution's case that there is no case for the defendant to answer based on the prosecution's evi-dence. The decision in R v *Birchall* makes it clear that the jury is not being asked to find a *prima facie* case to answer in the same sense as the judge would be required to find in the event of a submission of no case to answer. Rather, it is a reminder to the jury that a conviction cannot be based wholly on the defendant's silence. In *R v Birchall*, the requirement of a *prima facie* case is described as the need to find a 'sufficiently compelling case'. This in turn is reinforced by dicta in *R v Cowan* to the effect that silence is but one further factor in the overall evidential equation. In essence, if there is any wavering doubt in the jury's mind as to the defendant's guilt, an adverse inference drawn under section 35 may tip the evidential scales to the point where guilt is proved beyond reasonable doubt. Citing *R v Birchall* with approval, the Court of Appeal in *R v Doldur* [2000] Crim LR 178, explained the requirement for the jury to find a *prima facie* case before drawing an adverse inference in the following way:

> Acceptance by a jury of the truth and accuracy of all or part of the prosecution evidence may or may not amount to sureness of guilt. Something more may be required, which may be provided by an adverse inference from silence if they think it proper to draw one. What is plain is that it is not for the jury to repeat the threshold test of the Judge in ruling whether there is a case to answer on the prosecution evidence, if accepted by them. The direction approved in *Cowan* has a different object. It is to remind the jury that they cannot convict on adverse inferences alone. It is to remind them that they must have evidence...which, when considered together with any such adverse inference as they think proper to draw, enables them to be sure of both the truth and accuracy of that evidence and, in consequence, of guilt.

The most recent version of the Judicial Studies Board specimen direction on section 35 reminds the jury that any adverse inference it draws under the section can only be regarded as providing additional support for the prosecution's case and that it may not convict the defendant wholly or mainly on the fact that he has not given evidence on oath. Furthermore, before the jury can draw an adverse inference, it must firstly conclude that the prosecution's case is so strong that it clearly calls for some comment from the defendant and secondly, that the defendant's failure to give evidence is explicable only on the basis that he has no case to answer, or one that would bear examination.

Where an accused has not given evidence at his trial and it is accepted that section 35 has no application in the particular case, the accused is entitled to a direction from the judge based on *R v Bathurst* and *R v Martinez-Tobon* above.

SECTION 35 AND THE HUMAN RIGHTS ACT 1998

Does the Human Rights Act 1998 have any implications for the future of section 35 and the subsequent decision of the Court of Appeal in *R v Cowan* above? Article 6(1) guarantees the right to a fair trial and a fundamental component of that right is the right to be presumed innocent under Article 6(2). There has been no decision by the European Court of Human Rights specifically on section 35. However, other aspects of the legislation governing silence at the police station have been challenged before the Court and a number of general principles have emerged. Strasbourg case law makes it clear that the right to remain silent is not an absolute right within the meaning of Article 6(1) and that providing certain pre-requisites are met and certain safeguards are observed, silence may be used in evidence against the accused (see further below). Although infringement of Article 6(1) is likely to be argued by defence advocates, provided the safeguards laid down in *R v Cowan* are complied with, it is generally felt that the operation of section 35 is broadly compatible with Convention rights.

PRACTICAL STEPS – GIVING EVIDENCE ON OATH

One of the most important decisions an accused must make in conjunction with his advocate is whether to give evidence on oath or not. The decision is often a tactically important one carrying with it evidential repercussions. A failure to give evidence may mean an adverse inference is drawn. Giving evidence, however, exposes the defendant to some searching questions in cross-examination, an assessment of his demeanour on oath and to the risk that he might 'throw away his shield' under section 1(f)(ii) of the Criminal Evidence Act 1898 which protects him against the revelation of any previous misconduct. In *R v Cowan* above, Lord Taylor CJ made it clear that the risk of a defendant having his previous convictions made known under section 1(f)(ii) of the Criminal Evidence Act 1898 was not a valid reason for directing a jury not to draw an adverse inference against the defendant for refusing to testify. Were the position otherwise, a defendant with a criminal record would be in a more advantageous position as regards section 35, than a defendant with no criminal record. The defence practitioner must carefully evaluate the risks and decide which course of action represents the lesser of two evils. The accused's dilemma is further considered in Chapter 21.

PRE-TRIAL SILENCE – STATUTORY CHANGES

Before considering sections 34, 36 and 37 of the Criminal Justice and Public Order Act 1994 (inferences from accused's silence), two points should be noted:

1   As a consequence of the decision in *Murray v United Kingdom* (1996) 22 EHRR 29, an amendment to sections 34, 36 and 37 of the Criminal Justice and Public Order Act 1994 was effected by section 58 of the Youth Justice and Criminal Evidence Act 1999. It provides that no adverse inference may be drawn from a defendant's silence under any of these sections during any period where access to legal advice was delayed in accordance with section 58 of PACE.
2   In accordance with the requirements of section 38(3) of the 1994 Act, no defendant will have a case to answer, be committed for trial or be convicted of an offence based solely on an inference drawn under the sections.

Criminal Justice and Public Order Act 1994, section 34

(1) Where, in any proceedings against a person for an offence, evidence is given that the accused—
   (a) at any time before he was charged with the offence, on being questioned under caution by a constable trying to discover whether or by whom the offence had been committed, failed to mention any fact relied on in his defence in those proceedings; or
   (b) on being charged with the offence or officially informed that he might be prosecuted for it, failed to mention any such fact,

being a fact which in the circumstances existing at the time the accused could reasonably have been expected to mention when so questioned, charged or informed, as the case may be, subsection (2) below applies.

(2) Where this subsection applies—

(a) ...

(b) ...

(c) the court, in determining whether there is a case to answer; and

(d) the court or jury, in determining whether the accused is guilty of the offence charged,

may draw such inferences from the failure as appear proper.

(3) Subject to any directions by the court, evidence tending to establish the failure may be given before or after evidence tending to establish the fact which the accused is alleged to have failed to mention.

(4) This section applies in relation to questioning by persons (other than constables) charged with the duty of investigating offences or charging offenders as it applies in relation to questioning by constables; and in subsection (1) above 'officially informed' means informed by a constable or any such person.

(5) This section does not—

(a) prejudice the admissibility in evidence of the silence or other reaction of the accused in the face of anything said in his presence relating to the conduct in respect of which he is charged, in so far as evidence thereof would be admissible apart from this section; or

(b) preclude the drawing of any inference from any such silence or other reaction of the accused which could properly be drawn apart from this section....

Section 34 does not abolish the defendant's right to silence. It merely provides for an adverse inference to be drawn in certain circumstances. An adverse inference may only be drawn under section 34 in circumstances where the defendant failed to mention a fact later relied on in his defence, being a fact which in the circumstances at the time was one the defendant could reasonably have been expected to mention. Not until the prosecution's case has closed will it be evident that the defendant has failed to mention a fact he is now relying on.

Section 34 is effectively aimed at curtailing the ambush defence. The evidential effect of section 34 is to weaken any defence put forward by the defendant. This is made clear in the words of the revised police caution, administered on arrest, before interview and on being charged: 'You do not have to say anything. But it may harm your defence if you do not mention when questioned something which you later rely on in court. Anything you do say may be given in evidence' (Code C 10.4).

Example 1

Howard is being questioned on suspicion of manslaughter. He refuses to answer questions put by the police. At his trial Howard gives evidence to the effect that he acted in self-defence.

Providing it was reasonable to have expected Howard to have mentioned his defence of self-defence whilst being questioned at the police station, he is at risk of an adverse inference being drawn under section 34 against him at his trial.

The operational effect of section 34 is not predicated on the strict assumption that the defendant remains completely silent. A defendant may not in fact have remained silent during interview. He may have put forward certain facts or an explanation. If, at trial, he puts forward a new or amended version of those facts he risks incurring an adverse inference under section 34.

Example 2

Sukindar is arrested on suspicion of murder. During his interview he puts forward a defence of provocation. At trial he gives evidence consistent both with provocation and self-defence.

Although Sukindar has put forward facts in support of a possible defence at trial, he failed to mention the possibility that he acted in self-defence. This is a fact he now relies on at court in his defence. If the jury finds he could reasonably have been expected to mention this fact, this could weaken his defence of self-defence.

Can a defendant put forward a fact in support of his defence without giving evidence? In *R* v *Bowers* [1998] Crim LR 817, the Court of Appeal held that a fact relied on by the defendant could be adduced in cross-examination of prosecution witnesses and is not confined to facts raised by the defendant whilst giving evidence.

Where the defendant does no more at his trial than to put the prosecution to proof of its case, the decision of the Court of Appeal in *R* v *Moshaid* [1998] Crim LR 420 makes it clear that section 34 has no application. Acting on legal advice, the defendant refused to answer any questions and did not give or call evidence at his trial. His defence was based purely on putting the prosecution to proof of its case.

Section 34 has generated considerable case law in its short history. The leading cases are considered below.

Section 34 case law

R v Condron [1997] 1 Cr App R 185

The defendants, William and Karen Condron, both drug addicts, were arrested on suspicion of the possession of heroin with intent to supply. Their premises had been under police surveillance and heroin had been found in their flat. There was strong evidence against them to suggest that they were dealing in drugs. They were both pronounced fit to be interviewed at the police station by a police doctor. However, their solicitor regarded them as being unfit for interview as he was of the opinion that they were both suffering drug withdrawal symptoms. In the circumstances he advised them not to answer any questions. The defendants acted on his advice. At trial they gave evidence denying an intention to supply. Their solicitor also gave evidence as to the reasons for his advice. It was submitted that no adverse inference should be drawn pursuant to section 34 of the Criminal Justice and Public Order Act 1994 as the defendants had acted on the advice of their solicitor and that the matter of an adverse inference should therefore have been withdrawn from the jury. The trial judge rejected the submission and the matter of silence was left to the jury with a direction from the judge as to the circumstances in which an adverse inference could be drawn. The defendants appealed to the Court of Appeal.

Although the Court of Appeal found the judge had misdirected the jury, it did not consider the defendants' convictions were unsafe, given the weight of evidence against them. Amongst the many points of argument on appeal was the central and important question of whether section 34 would permit an adverse inference to be drawn where the defendant had decided not to answer questions based on legal advice. In answering the question the Court of Appeal made some important observations of principle on the application of section 34.

The Court of Appeal was adamant that acceptance of the real reason for the defendant choosing not to put forward relevant facts in answer to police questions and hence, whether an adverse inference should as a consequence be drawn, was a matter for the jury and not the judge. If a defendant wanted the jury to consider his reasons for remaining silent, he had to ensure there was evidence before the jury on which it could act.

The operational effect of section 34 has clear implications for legal professional privilege. Communications between solicitor and client are, as we shall see in Chapter 10, protected from disclosure in evidence by legal professional privilege. The privilege belongs to the client and only the client may choose to waive it. However, as the Court of Appeal observed, for the defendant simply to assert, 'I chose not to answer questions on the advice of my solicitor' would be unlikely to impress the fact finder. If sufficient weight were to be given to the defendant's reasons for not mentioning relevant facts, more explanation would almost certainly have to be given. To achieve this the defendant would have to be prepared to waive his legal professional privilege in order to explain the basis on which his solicitor's advice had been given. Having waived his privilege, the defendant could expect to be subjected to cross-examination on precisely how much he told his solicitor at the relevant time. In some instances, it was likely that the defendant's solicitor might have to be called to give evidence, enabling the prosecution to explore whether there had been tactical reasons for the advice. The Court of Appeal explained the position as follows:

> Communications between an accused person and his solicitor prior to interviews by the police are subject to legal professional privilege. But the privilege can be waived by the client, though not the solicitor. If an accused person gives as a reason for not answering questions, that he has been advised by his solicitor not to do so, that advice, in our judgment, does not amount to a waiver of privilege. But, equally, for reasons which we have already given, that bare assertion is unlikely by itself [to] be regarded as a sufficient reason for not mentioning matters relevant to the defence. So it will be necessary, if the accused wishes to invite the court not to draw an adverse inference, to go further and state the basis or reason for the advice. Although the matter was not fully argued, it seems to us that once this is done that it may well amount to a waiver of privilege so that the accused, or if his solicitor is also called, the solicitor, can be asked whether there were any other reasons for the advice, and the nature of the advice given, so as to explore whether the advice may also have been given for tactical reasons.

As to the direction the judge should give to the jury on the effect of section 34, the Court of Appeal favoured the Judicial Studies Board specimen direction based on section 35 which it had previously endorsed in its decision in *R v Cowan; R v Gayle; R v Ricciardi* [1995] 3 WLR 818 (discussed above), suitably modified to take account of section 34. The sixth and most recent version of the Judicial Studies Board specimen direction, which takes account of a number of case law developments on section 34, is reproduced below. The specimen directions produced by the Judicial Studies Board provide all Crown Court judges with a starting point for correctly directing the jury on matters of law. The directions have to be adapted to the facts and circumstances of each particular case.

1. Before his interview(s) the defendant was cautioned ... He was first told that he need not say anything. It was therefore his right to remain silent. However, he was also told that it might harm his defence if he did not mention when questioned something which he later relied on in court; and that anything he did say might be given in evidence.

2. As part of his defence, the defendant has relied upon (*here specify the facts to which this direction applies...*). But [the prosecution say/he admits] that he failed to mention these

facts when he was interviewed about the offence(s). [If you are sure that is so, this/This] failure may count against him. This is because you may draw the conclusion ... from his failure that he [had no answer then/had no answer that he then believed would stand up to scrutiny/has since invented his account/has since tailored his account to fit the prosecution's case/(*here refer to any other reasonable inferences contended for*...]. If you do draw that conclusion, you must not convict him wholly or mainly on the strength of it...; but you may take it into account as some additional support for the prosecution's case ... and when deciding whether his [evidence/case] about these facts is true.

3. You may draw such a conclusion against him only if you think it is a fair and proper conclusion, and you are satisfied about three things: first, that when he was interviewed he could reasonably have been expected to mention the facts on which he now relies; second, that the only sensible explanation for his failure to do so is that he had no answer at the time or none that would stand up to scrutiny ...; third, that apart from his failure to mention those facts, the prosecution's case against him is so strong that it clearly calls for an answer by him....

4. *(Add, if appropriate:)* The defence invite you not to draw any conclusion from the defendant's silence, on the basis of the following evidence *(here set out the evidence...).* If you [accept this evidence and] think this amounts to a reason why you should not draw any conclusion from his silence, do not do so. Otherwise, subject to what I have said, you may do so.

5. *(Where legal advice to remain silent is relied upon, add the following instead of paragraph 4:)* The defendant has given evidence that he did not answer questions on the advice of his solicitor/legal representative. If you accept the evidence that he was so advised, this is obviously an important consideration: but it does not automatically prevent you from drawing any conclusion from his silence. Bear in mind that a person given legal advice has the choice whether to accept or reject it; and that the defendant was warned that any failure to mention facts which he relied on at his trial might harm his defence. Take into account also *(here set out the circumstances relevant to the particular case, which may include the age of the defendant, the nature of and/or reasons for the advice given, and the complexity or otherwise of the facts on which he relied at the trial).* Having done so, decide whether the defendant could reasonably have been expected to mention the facts on which he now relies. If, for example, you considered that he had or may have had an answer to give, but reasonably relied on the legal advice to remain silent, you should not draw any conclusion against him. But if, for example, you were sure that the defendant had no answer, and merely latched onto the legal advice as a convenient shield behind which to hide, you would be entitled to draw a conclusion against him, subject to the direction I have given you. ...

The specimen direction is largely self-explanatory. It reminds the jury of the fact that an accused person enjoys a right of silence at the police station. However, the jury is permitted to draw an adverse inference if it concludes the defendant's failure to answer questions was due to his having no answer to the allegations made against him, or none that would stand up to critical scrutiny. The direction warns the jury that it must not convict wholly or mainly on the strength of the defendant's failure to have put forward facts at the police station and that any adverse inference it draws can only constitute additional support for the prosecution's case where, aside from the issue of the defendant's silence, the prosecution's case was so strong as to call for an answer from the accused.

On the facts in *R v Condron* [1997] 1 Cr App R 185, the Court of Appeal concluded there had been a misdirection of the jury based on the trial judge's failure to properly direct the jury in strict accordance with the earlier version of the Judicial Studies Board specimen direction applicable at the time of this decision. However, having regard to the overall strength of other evidence in the case, it did not quash the convictions because they were not regarded as being unsafe in the light of the strength of the overall evidence.

The Court of Appeal did acknowledge in R v *Condron*, in very cautionary terms, that the trial judge retained discretion under section 34 to prevent an adverse inference from being drawn in appropriate circumstances, but felt that in most cases it was a matter to be left to the jury.

> If defence counsel wishes to object to prosecuting counsel cross-examining on the failure to mention the matters in interview, then it will be a matter for the judge to rule upon, if necessary after a *voire dire*. But, except in clear cases, where, in effect, it would be perverse for the jury to draw an adverse inference, we do not think this is an appropriate course, since the judge is likely to consider that the question why the accused did not answer is one for the jury. (*per* Lord Justice Stuart-Smith)

The defendants subsequently took their case to the European Court of Human Rights (*Condron* v *United Kingdom* (2001) 31 EHRR 1). The United Kingdom was found to have violated Article 6(1) (the right to a fair trial) for reasons we shall consider later in this chapter.

What inference may be drawn under section 34?

Section 34(2) permits the fact finder to draw such inferences as appear proper. Having regard to judgment in R v *Condron*, it was thought that the only inference that may be drawn was one to the effect that the defence now being put forward was made up after the interview. In fact, the fact finder is not so restricted. The later decision in R v *Randall* [1998] 6 Archbold News 1 provides that the fact finder may infer that his defence was in fact made up before the interview and that the defendant chose to remain silent because he did not want his defence exposed to the critical scrutiny of investigating officers at such an early stage. The effect of this judgment and the nature of the adverse inferences that may be drawn are reflected in the current version of the Judicial Studies Board specimen direction on section 34, reproduced earlier in this chapter.

The clearest guidelines on the operation of section 34 have been provided by the Court of Appeal in the decision of R v *Argent*.

R *v* Argent [1997] 2 Cr App R 27

The defendant was arrested in connection with a fatal stabbing. He had been arrested on the basis of an anonymous tip-off. As the police had very little evidence against him at the time of his arrest, the defendant was advised to remain silent. He was later identified at an identification parade and at a subsequent interview he again chose to remain silent on the basis of legal advice. In evidence, the defendant accepted that his solicitor had fully explained the implications of remaining silent and that his decision to remain silent had been his choice. At his trial, the defendant denied the assault and sought a ruling from the judge that no adverse inference should be drawn from either interview. The Court of Appeal rejected the argument, although it did acknowledge that there might be circumstances in which it was appropriate for the trial judge to direct the jury not to draw an adverse inference.

The judgment in R v *Argent* above sets out six formal preconditions which must be proved by the prosecution before an adverse inference may be drawn:

1 There must proceedings against a person for an offence.
2 The alleged failure to answer questions must occur before the defendant was charged.
3 The failure must occur during questioning under caution by a constable.
4 The questioning must be directed towards trying to discover whether, or by whom, the alleged offence had been committed.
5 The alleged failure by the defendant must be to mention any fact relied on in his defence in the proceedings. This raises two questions of fact: (a) is there some fact the defendant has relied on in his defence; and (b) did the defendant fail to mention it to the constable when questioned in accordance with the section?
6 The fact that the defendant failed to mention must be a fact, which, in the circumstances existing at the time, he could reasonably have been expected to mention when questioned.

In relation to the sixth condition, the Court of Appeal went on to identify what relevant matters might be taken into account:

> The courts should not construe the expression 'in the circumstances' restrictively: matters such as time of day, the defendant's age, experience, mental capacity, state of health, sobriety, tiredness, knowledge, personality and legal advice are all part of the relevant circumstances; and those are only examples of things which may be relevant. When reference is made to 'the accused' attention is directed not to some hypothetical, reasonable accused of ordinary phlegm and fortitude but to the actual accused with such qualities, apprehensions, knowledge and advice as he is shown to have had at the time. It is for the jury to decide whether the fact (or facts) which the defendant has relied on in his defence in the criminal trial, but which he had not mentioned when questioned under caution…is (or are) a fact (or facts) which in the circumstances as they actually existed the actual defendant could reasonably have been expected to mention.
> … Sometimes they may conclude that it was reasonable for the defendant to have held his peace for a host of reasons, such as that he was tired, ill, frightened, drunk, drugged, unable to understand what was going on, suspicious of the police, afraid that his answer would not be fairly recorded, worried at committing himself without legal advice, acting on legal advice, or some other reason accepted by the jury.
> In other cases the jury may conclude, after hearing all that the defendant and his witnesses may have to say about the reasons for failing to mention the fact or facts in issue, that he could reasonably have been expected to do so. This is an issue on which the judge may, and usually should, give appropriate directions. But he should ordinarily leave the issue to the jury to decide. Only rarely would it be right for the judge to direct the jury that they should, or should not, draw the appropriate inference.

The Court of Appeal concluded that on the facts in *R v Argent* only limited evidential disclosure had been forthcoming from the police in the first instance. However, by the time the defendant came to be interviewed a second time extensive disclosure had been made and there was little factual complexity in the case. The defendant either did or did not leave the nightclub before the trouble began and this was something which, in the circumstances, he could reasonably have been expected to know and therefore to mention.

What the Court of Appeal's decision in *R v Argent* makes abundantly clear is that it is for the jury to decide whether a defendant's failure to mention facts was reasonable, having listened to any explanation put forward by the defendant. A number of factors are likely to have a bearing on this.

It is perfectly proper for a solicitor or legal adviser at the police station to advise a suspect to remain silent where little or no evidential disclosure has been forthcoming from the police. This fact was recognised by the Court of Appeal in *R* v *Roble* [1997] Crim LR 449. In that case, the decision to remain silent had been based on legal advice. The solicitor in question had felt that inadequate disclosure had been provided by the police and therefore he had to advise his client to remain silent, since he was unable to make a proper evaluation of the evidence against him. The Court of Appeal held the lack of evidential disclosure was a relevant factor to be taken into account but, whilst it may well have been reasonable for the defendant to have remained silent in these circumstances, it was still a matter for the jury.

The correctness or otherwise of the legal advice given is irrelevant to the operation of section 34 – it is the effect the advice had on the mind of the suspect at the time that is the issue. There may be an argument under the Human Rights Act 1998 against drawing an adverse inference based on the equality of arms principle (discussed in Chapter 2) in circumstances where a defendant was advised to make no comment because of inadequate disclosure by the police. In terms of the investigative resources available, the police are at a considerable advantage when compared to those available to the suspect. Fairness demands the police should make disclosure of their case so that the suspect is in a position to know whether he has a defence to the allegation.

A failure by the judge to direct the jury in accordance with the six formal preconditions set out in *R* v *Argent* will invariably lead to an appeal against conviction and the possible quashing of the conviction. In *R* v *Gill* [2001] 1 Cr App R 11 the Court of Appeal observed:

> ...standard directions are devised to serve the ends of justice and the drawing of adverse inferences from silence is a particularly sensitive area with the potential for wrongful convictions in the absence of careful and full directions by the judge.

The Court of Appeal made it clear that the six preconditions in *R* v *Argent* are not the end of the matter and that the trial judge must go on to highlight the key essentials laid down in the judgment in *R* v *Cowan* (above).

What constitutes knowledge of facts for the purposes of section 34?

R v Nickolson [1999] Crim LR 61

The defendant had been arrested on suspicion of having raped his stepdaughter. In interview he denied the offence. He did say in interview that he was in the habit of masturbating in the bathroom. The girl's nightdress had been seized as part of the investigation. It was not appreciated at the time of the interview that traces of seminal fluid would subsequently be found on it. Asked at his trial to account for the seminal staining on the girl's nightdress, the defendant stated he had masturbated in the toilet on the evening of the alleged rape and that shortly after the girl had gone to the toilet. Any semen on the toilet seat could well have found its way onto the girl's nightdress. The prosecution maintained the defendant was offering this explanation as a fact. The trial judge agreed and directed the jury in accordance with the requirements of section 34. The Court of Appeal held the defendant's statement had been offered as a theory, a possible explanation and was therefore speculative in its nature.

If facts were not known at the time of the interview and the defendant subsequently offers an explanation for them at trial, section 34 has no application.

R v B (MT) [2000] Crim LR 181

The defendant was on trial for raping his stepdaughter. He had failed to mention in interview that his stepdaughter might have been motivated by jealousy which would explain why she had falsely accused him of raping her. In fact, whilst the defendant may have had suspicions as to his step-daughter's motives, he did not know this as a fact. He actually learned it was a fact when the victim herself gave evidence. The defendant pursued the victim's jealousy further in his evidence. The Court of Appeal concluded this was not a fact the defendant could reasonably have been expected to mention at the police station. He may have had his suspicions as to his stepdaughter's motives but this was not the same as knowing it as a fact.

What should the court do where a no comment interview has taken place but it is agreed that no section 34 inference arises?

R v McGarry [1999] 1 Cr App R 377

The defendant was arrested in connection with a serious assault outside a squash club. There was little evidence against him at the time of his arrest and at his initial interview. On the advice of his solicitor he remained silent during the initial interview. He was released on police bail. Several weeks later he was re-arrested; at which point there was much stronger evidence against him. Acting on the instructions of his solicitor he handed to the police a prepared written statement. The statement con-tained the bare bones of his defence, namely that he had punched the victim once in self-defence. This was of course a fact he could have put forward during his initial interview. The defendant refused to answer any further questions during interview, referring the police to his written statement. At trial, the prosecution did not ask the defendant about his initial no comment interview, nor did the prose-cution believe the defendant had relied on any new fact at his trial not covered by his written state-ment. The trial judge chose not to direct the jury in terms such that they were not permitted to draw an adverse inference. The defendant was convicted and successfully appealed to the Court of Appeal.

The Court of Appeal observed that section 34 had made a limited modification to the firmly estab-lished common law rule and where it was conceded or ruled that section 34 had no application in a particular case, the judge must direct the jury not to draw an adverse inference in accordance with the position at common law.

Despite the decision in *R v McGarry*, in *R v Francom* [2001] 1 Cr App R 237 the Court of Appeal somewhat surprisingly upheld a conviction in a case where the 'McGarry' direction should have been given but was not given. Notwithstanding the judgment of the European Court of Human Rights in *Condron v United Kingdom* (2001) 31 EHRR I (see below), the Court of Appeal concluded on the facts in *Francom* that no unfairness had resulted, having regard to the length of the trial and the rejection by the jury of the evidence of the defendant and his fellow co-accused in a case which was largely dependent upon which witnesses the jury believed. Notwithstanding the non-direction in this case, the Court of Appeal was satisfied that no reasonable jury could have come to a different conclusion had the direction been given. Consequently, the conviction could not be regarded as being unsafe.

Limitations of the application of section 34

Where an inference cannot logically be drawn without necessarily concluding that the defendant is guilty, does section 34 have any application? In R v *Mountford*, the Court of Appeal answered this question in the negative.

R v Mountford [1999] Crim LR 575

The defendant had been arrested on suspicion of the possession of heroin with intent to supply. He had been observed dropping a package, subsequently found to contain heroin, from the balcony of a flat into the street below. The flat's owner was also arrested and jointly charged with permitting premises to be used for the purpose of supplying drugs. He subsequently pleaded guilty and gave evidence against the defendant. In interview, acting on the advice of his solicitor, the defendant refused to make any comment. At his trial, accepting he had been in possession of the heroin, but denying any intent to supply, he maintained the flat's owner, his friend, had thrown him the package and instructed him to throw it over the balcony. Asked in cross-examination why he was raising these facts for the first time at his trial, the defendant explained he had not wished to incriminate his friend at the police station. The trial judge left the issue of drawing an adverse inference to the jury with the correct legal direction.

The problem in this case, however, was that the facts that the defendant had chosen not to put forward at the police station constituted a defence to the charge. If the jury concluded the facts had been ones which the defendant could reasonably have mentioned at the police station (effectively saying we believe the defendant has made up these facts in the light of what has occurred), then it would have to find the defendant guilty. Section 34 would have no independent operation in such circumstances. It could not provide additional support for the prosecution's case, as was the intention behind section 34. Consequently, the Court of Appeal quashed the conviction concluding that a section 34 direction was inapposite given the facts in this particular case. A similar outcome was reached in R v *Gill* [2000] Crim LR 921 on broadly similar facts.

In the later case of R v *Hearne* (below), the Court of Appeal concluded the decision in R v *Mountford* was confined to its own particular facts as the approach suggested in that case would have the effect of emasculating the operation of section 34.

R v Hearne [2000] 6 Archbold News 2

Co-accused (A) had been under surveillance by Customs and Excise. He was believed to be smuggling illegal tobacco. He was observed parking next to the appellant's car. The appellant was seen to hand over a sum of money. At this point officers intervened. In A's car, a quantity of cocaine was found. It was the officers' contention that A had been about to hand over the cocaine to the appellant in return for the payment. Both were arrested and charged with being knowingly concerned in the illegal importation of a controlled drug. The appellant exercised his right to remain silent. At his trial, he denied the offence. He admitted that he had imported illegal tobacco on a number of occasions and said the payment had been for a past transaction. He had not mentioned these facts at the police station because he had been afraid to. He did not want to get into any further trouble. The trial judge left the jury with the option of drawing an adverse inference. The appellant was convicted.

On appeal, the Court of Appeal distinguished R v *Mountford* on the basis that on the facts in *Hearne* the jury could still have drawn an adverse inference without necessarily finding the defendant guilty of the charge. The jury could, for example, have concluded that the defendant did not wish to offer an explanation because this might have implicated him in other shady conduct with which he was not charged.

Preferring the decision in *R v Hearne* to those in *R v Mountford* and *R v Gill*, the Court of Appeal held in *R v Gowland-Wynn* (2001) *The Times*, 7 December that the decisions in *Mountford* and *Gill* should be 'consigned to oblivion and not relied upon by the courts' in that section 34 had its most significant role to play precisely in those cases where a defendant had chosen not to comment on a matter going to the heart of his defence. Based on the Court of Appeal's decision in *R v Gowland-Wynn*, section 34 applies in cases where an adverse inference cannot in reality be drawn without necessarily concluding the defendant is guilty of the offence for which he is charged.

Adverse inference and judicial discretion

Where the prosecution seeks to place evidential reliance on silence, it is still subject to the court's discretion to exclude evidence both at common law and under section 78 of PACE, where its admission would have an adverse effect on the fairness of the proceedings. The discretion might be exercised in circumstances where the interview was not conducted in accordance with the safeguards contained in PACE and the Codes of Practice, or perhaps where the suspect did not understand the caution or its effect was misrepresented.

Failure to account for objects, substances or marks (section 36)

Section 36 of the Criminal Justice and Public Order Act 1994 states that:

(1) Where—
    (a) a person is arrested by a constable, and there is—
        (i) on his person; or
        (ii) in or on his clothing or footwear; or
        (iii) otherwise in his possession; or
        (iv) in any place in which he is at the time of his arrest, any object, substance or mark, or there is any mark on any such object; and
    (b) that or another constable investigating the case reasonably believes that the presence of the object, substance or mark may be attributable to the participation of the person arrested in the commission of an offence specified by the constable; and
    (c) the constable informs the person arrested that he so believes, and requests him to account for the presence of the object, substance or mark; and
    (d) the person fails or refuses to do so,
then if, in any proceedings against the person for the offence so specified, evidence of those matters is given, subsection (2) below applies.
(2) Where this subsection applies—
    (a) ...
    (b) ...
    (c) the court, in determining whether there is a case to answer; and
    (d) the court and the jury, in determining whether the accused is guilty of the offence charged,
may draw such inferences from the failure or refusal as appear proper.

(3) Subsections (1) and (2) above apply to the condition of clothing or footwear as they apply to a substance or mark thereon.

(4) Subsections (1) and (2) above do not apply unless the accused was told in ordinary language by the constable when making the request mentioned in subsection (1)(c) above what the effect of this section would be if he failed or refused to comply with the request. ...

Failure or refusal to account for presence at the scene (section 37)

Section 37 of the 1994 Act provides:

(1) Where—
 (a) a person arrested by a constable was found by him at a place at or about the time the offence for which he was arrested is alleged to have been committed; and
 (b) that or another constable investigating the offence reasonably believes that the presence of the person at that place and at that time may be attributable to his participation in the commission of the offence; and
 (c) the constable informs the person that he so believes, and requests him to account for that presence; and
 (d) the person fails or refuses to do so,
then if, in any proceedings against the person for the offence, evidence of those matters is given, subsection (2) below applies.

(2) Where this subsection applies—
 (a) ...
 (b) ...
 (c) the court, in determining whether there is a case to answer; and
 (d) the court or the jury, in determining whether the accused is guilty of the offence charged,
may draw such inferences from the failure or refusal as appear proper.

(3) Subsections (1) and (2) do not apply unless the accused was told in ordinary language by the constable when making the request mentioned in subsection (1)(c) above what the effect of this section would be if he failed or refused to comply with the request. ...

As with section 34, sections 36 and 37 do not remove the defendant's right to silence. An adverse inference may only be drawn under sections 36 and 37 in accordance with the strict wording of the sections. The evidential effect of an inference drawn under either section is to strengthen the prosecution's case, irrespective of any defence put forward by the defendant. Section 38(3) applies in that no one will have a case to answer, be committed for trial or be convicted of an offence, based solely on an inference drawn from a failure or refusal as prescribed in section 36(2) or 37(2).

Example 3

Jason is arrested on suspicion of attempted rape. The victim of the attack retaliated, scratching her assailant's face. In interview Jason is cautioned and asked to account for scratch marks that can be seen on his face. Jason chooses not to reply. In fact, he remains silent throughout the interview. Giving evidence at his trial, Jason's defence is one of mistaken identity.

Jason is at risk of a double adverse inference. Providing the circumstances set out in section 36 are met he risks an adverse inference in that he has failed to give an explanation for scratch marks visible on his face. The marks are on his person. The arresting constable or other investigating officer must reasonably have believed the presence of the marks might have been attributable to Jason's participation in a crime. The officer must have made Jason aware of his belief before requesting Jason to give an account, explaining in ordinary language the risk he faces from his failure to do so. In addition, Jason risks an adverse inference under section 34 as discussed above.

Example 4

Following a burglary, Andrew is arrested the following day. It is clear that the burglar exited the property along a mud track and over a wall topped with wire meshing. The police inform Andrew that he is under arrest on suspicion of burglary. In interview Andrew advances a defence of alibi. In the course of the interview he is cautioned and asked to account for a tear on the sleeve of his jacket and mud on his shoes. Andrew is unable to offer any explanation for either. At his trial Andrew gives evidence of alibi.

In this instance Andrew is at risk of an adverse inference under section 36. Section 36(3) makes it clear that the section applies to the condition of clothing as it does to footwear.

Example 5

Jane is arrested on a Sunday evening on suspicion of criminal damage. She is found by a police officer near to a field where genetically modified maize is under cultivation. Several crops have been uprooted. When questioned under caution about the alleged offence, Jane is asked to account for her presence near to the field. Jane refuses to reply. She also refuses to give evidence at her trial.

Providing the conditions set out in section 37 are met, Jane risks an adverse inference being drawn against her in that she has failed to give an explanation for her presence near the scene of a crime. The arresting constable or other investigating officer must reasonably have believed Jane's presence might have been attributable to her participation in a crime. The officer must have made Jane aware of her belief before requesting her to give an account, explaining in ordinary language the risk she faces from her failure to do so. Under the Criminal Justice and Public Order Act 1994 a 'place' is widely defined and includes buildings, vehicles and vessels. By refusing to give evidence at her trial, Jane also risks an adverse inference being drawn against her under section 35.

PRACTICAL STEPS – TO ANSWER POLICE QUESTIONS OR NOT?

In some circumstances there will be an advantage to the defendant in putting forward an explanation for certain facts at the earliest opportunity. Where the same explanation is offered at trial, the earlier statement provides useful evidence of consistency, capable of bolstering the defendant's credibility.

In other circumstances silence in the face of questioning by the police may be the defendant's best option. Where this is so, the legal adviser must always bear in mind the evidential consequences of his advice in the event of the matter going to trial. It is extremely important for the adviser to elicit full disclosure from investigating officers of the evidence they have against the suspect before an interview begins, particularly details of evidence which may form the basis of questioning under sections 36 and 37 of the 1994 Act. Where disclosure is not forthcoming, advisers can safely advise silence, although the evidential dangers of this must clearly be explained to the suspect. The adviser must make an assessment of his client's ability to deal with the interrogation. If the client is vulnerable in some way, the best advice may well be to remain silent. Similarly, if the suspect is not in a position at this early stage, to put forward a full defence to the charge, he may be best advised to remain silent for the time being. None of the above would guarantee a jury or magistrates not choosing to draw an adverse inference at trial, but they all provide a sound reason as to why a jury or magistrates should not.

In advising silence the legal adviser must take into account the very real risk that his client may have to waive his legal professional privilege in order to give an explanation of the reasons for the advice. It is quite common for legal advisers to explain their reasons for advising silence at the commencement of the tape-recorded interview. In *R v Fitzgerald* [1998] 4 Archbold News 2 and *R v Bowden* [1999] 2 Cr App R 176, the Court of Appeal held this practice amounted to a waiver of privilege entitling the prosecution to question the defendant about his discussions with his solicitor. The legal adviser is deemed to be acting within the scope of his authority as agent for the defendant in such circumstances. Alternatively, the defendant is taken to adopt what his solicitor has said, in that it is made in his hearing without objection being made. In the light of *Fitzgerald* and *Bowden*, the Law Society advises solicitors to state on tape: 'I am now advising my client to...' If any decision to offer an explanation for the advice is based on facts externally observed by the solicitor and not on any privileged conversation between himself and his client, the explanation will not amount to a waiver of privilege.

Where the advice is to remain silent, the suspect must be prepared for the interview experience. Is the suspect to say 'no comment' in response to every question asked or is he not to speak at all? The latter course is very hard to maintain.

If the adviser considers there is sufficient evidence to charge his client and that no interview is therefore necessary, he should make representations to this effect and ensure they are noted in the custody record and on tape if the officers insist on going ahead with an interview. In *R v Pointer* [1997] Crim LR 676 and *R v Gayle* [1999] Crim LR 502, the Court of Appeal held a section 34 inference could not arise where sufficient evidence existed to charge the suspect with the offence prior to an interview being commenced. In both cases it had been conceded that there had been sufficient evidence to charge the defendant with the offence he had been arrested for before the interview had taken place. Such an interview is contrary to the requirements of Code C 11.4 and 16.1, which provide that where an officer considers sufficient evidence exists for a prosecution to succeed and that person has said all that he wishes to say about the offence, he must bring the suspect before the custody officer without delay. Under section 37(7) of PACE, the custody officer must decide whether to charge or release the suspect forthwith. Interviewing the suspect, or continuing to interview the suspect in breach of Code C 11.4 and 16.1 cannot constitute questioning for the purpose of trying to discover whether or by whom the offence had been committed, within the meaning of section 34(1)(a) of the Criminal Justice and Public Order Act 1994.

The position is not however all that straightforward in that there would seem to be no reason why an adverse inference could not be drawn under section 34(1)(b) of the 1994 Act where the defendant remained silent on being charged, but later chose to put forward facts not mentioned at that stage. Upon being charged, the defendant is once more cautioned as to the effect of section 34 and is therefore given a further opportunity to put forward a denial, defence or explanation.

Further complications arise from the later cases of *R v McGuinness* [1999] Crim LR 318 and *R v Ioannou* [1999] Crim LR 586. In each case, the Court of Appeal chose not to feel constrained by the decisions in R v *Pointer* and R v *Gayle*. Investigating officers, it would seem, can easily overcome the restrictions recognised to apply in the decisions of *Pointer* and *Gayle*, if they indicate on oath that they were open minded enough to realise that the defendant might still be able to offer an explanation in interview even in the face of seemingly compelling evidence of guilt. Such explanation could then be taken into account by the police officer in determining whether there was sufficient evidence to charge. In *Ioannou*, the defendant had been witnessed supplying drugs to an undercover officer. His solicitor believed there was sufficient evidence to have charged him without the necessity of holding an interview. An interview had been held at which the defendant refused to make any comment. At his trial, he put forward the defence of duress, maintaining his supplier had threatened to harm him if he did not supply the undercover officer in question.

Where the suspect is seeking to put forward an explanation of events which will effectively form the basis of his defence at trial, the solicitor must interview his client carefully to ensure all the relevant facts are disclosed at this stage. If the defendant is putting forward an alibi, for example, the suspect should be warned that the police are likely to speak with any individuals who can confirm the alibi without delay. Once again, the suspect must be prepared for the interview experience. The solicitor should proactively look after his client's interests during the interview, objecting to such things as questioning based on evidence not previously disclosed and stopping the interview if further advice is needed.

Given the length and complexity of judicial direction on silence, a verbatim record of the judge's direction to the jury should always be taken. A misdirection affords clear grounds for an appeal in the event of a conviction.

Case scenario

Rachel is arrested on suspicion of possessing drugs. The police have had a particular flat under surveillance for the past week. Rachel is observed entering the property and emerging a few minutes later. She rounds the corner and is stopped by investigating officers. She is found in possession of a sealed envelope. When the envelope is opened, it is found to contain four wraps of a powdered substance. Rachel expresses her surprise and is arrested on suspicion of being in possession of a controlled drug. She requests access to a solicitor. The solicitor is satisfied with the disclosure provided by the police at this early stage. The police suspect the package contains heroin. Rachel's solicitor interviews her. Rachel tells the solicitor that her boyfriend sent her to collect the package and that she had no idea what was in the sealed envelope. She has only been seeing her new boyfriend for a matter of weeks and only moved in with him very recently. He did not tell her what the package would contain. Rachel has never previously been arrested. Should Rachel answer the officer's questions in interview?

The facts of this case scenario highlight the very real difficulties faced by some suspects in terms of whether to speak or to remain silent. Suppose the package does contain heroin? In the absence of any explanation by Rachel, she is likely to be found guilty of being in possession of a class A drug. Rachel could raise the defence of innocent belief at trial, namely she did not know nor had reason to suspect the package contained a controlled drug. Such a defence would have considerably less force if it is advanced for the first time at her trial. However, if she does not proffer an explanation, she cannot incriminate herself on the much more serious charge of possession with intent to supply, since it was clearly her intention to pass the package on to her boyfriend. What is more, by not putting forward her explanation, she would not implicate her boyfriend.

Should the substance prove to be heroin, the advantage of co-operating with the police by putting forward her defence of innocent belief as to the package's content is that it would greatly assist her credibility at trial. She is thus more likely to be believed when she states on oath she did not know what the packet contained. But what of the dangers of answering questions?

The knowledge the police would acquire would certainly mean trouble for Rachel's boyfriend. If Rachel's evidence as to the innocence of her belief is not believed, she may find herself convicted of possession with intent to supply. Suppliers of drugs do not take kindly to their customers implicating them and Rachel may have legitimate fears for her own safety in this regard. If Rachel has naively and unwittingly got herself involved in such a serious criminal enterprise, what should she be advised to do?

Arguably, silence is the best option, although this would almost certainly result in a conviction for possession, if the substance, when analysed, was found to be a controlled drug.

HUMAN RIGHTS LAW

The right to a fair trial under Article 6(1) of the European Convention on Human Rights includes the right to be presumed innocent under Article 6(2). Article 6(1) does not however specifically guarantee the right to remain silent, nor does it specifically guarantee the privilege against self-incrimination. Both rights are however implied into Article 6 and are regarded with some considerable importance by the European Court of Human Rights.

On a number of occasions, the Court has held that a statute making it a criminal offence for a person suspected of having committed a criminal offence, to refuse to answer questions, his answers to which can then be used in evidence against him in later criminal proceedings, will violate Article 6(2) (see, for example, *Funke* v *France* (1993) 16 EHRR 297). The United Kingdom was also found to have violated Article 6(2) in *Saunders* v *United Kingdom* (1997) 23 EHRR 313. The applicant, Saunders, had been under investigation by the Department of Trade and Industry. He was compelled to answer DTI inspectors' questions under statutory powers contained in the Companies Act 1985, section 436. A failure to answer would have resulted in contempt proceedings, a fine and possible imprisonment. The answers he gave were subsequently used in evidence against him at his later criminal trial. The European Court of Human Rights held that the manner in which the evidence had been obtained violated the applicant's privilege against self-incrimination and effectively abrogated the burden on the prosecution to prove his guilt. In effect the applicant had been compulsorily required to incriminate himself. This was a clear violation of the presumption of innocence under Article 6(2). The specific relationship between Article 6 and the privilege against self-incrimination is considered in Chapter 10. By contrast, there is no direct compulsion on a suspect to answer questions under sections 34, 36 and 37 of the Criminal Justice and Public Order Act 1994, in the sense that failure to answer questions would result in contempt proceedings or the commission of another criminal offence by the suspect.

Three decisions of the European Court of Human Rights have specific implications for the law in relation to section 34 of the Criminal Justice and Public Order Act 1994. They are *Murray* v *United Kingdom* (1996) 22 EHRR 29, *Averill* v *United Kingdom* (2001) 31 EHRR 36 and *Condron* v *United Kingdom* (2001) 31 EHRR 1.

Murray *v* United Kingdom (1996) 22 EHRR 29

This case concerned a challenge by a convicted terrorist to Northern Ireland legislation drafted in terms identical to section 34. The defendant had been denied access to a solicitor for the first 48 hours of his detention. Throughout the interview he refused to make any comment. At his trial, which was conducted before a single judge, he refused to give evidence. The trial judge chose to draw an adverse inference from the defendant's failure to account for his presence close to the scene and from his failure to give evidence in support of his defence at trial. Interestingly the European Court of Human Rights did not find the United Kingdom to be in breach of Article 6(1) having regard to the legislation permitting an adverse inference. It did however find the United Kingdom to be in violation of Article 6(3)(c) for reasons considered below.

In an important statement of principle the Court observed:

> Although not specifically mentioned in Article 6 of the Convention, there can be no doubt that the right to remain silent under police questioning and the privilege against self-incrimination are generally recognised international standards which lie at the heart of the notion of a fair procedure under Article 6. By providing the accused with protection against improper compulsion by the authorities, these immunities contribute to avoiding miscarriages of justice and to securing the aims of Article 6.

Significantly however, the Court declared the right to silence was not an absolute right within the meaning of Article 6:

> The Court does not consider that it is called upon to give an abstract analysis of the scope of these immunities and, in particular, of what constitutes in this context 'improper compulsion'. What is at stake in the present case is whether these immunities are absolute in the sense that the exercise by an accused of the right to silence cannot under any circumstances be used against him at trial or, alternatively, whether informing him in advance that, under certain conditions, his silence may be so used, is always to be regarded as 'improper compulsion'.
>
> On the one hand, it is self-evident that it is incompatible with the immunities under consideration to base a conviction solely or mainly on the accused's silence or on a refusal to answer questions or to give evidence himself. On the other hand, the Court deems it equally obvious that these immunities cannot and should not prevent that the accused's silence, in situations which clearly call for an explanation from him, be taken into account in assessing the persuasiveness of the evidence adduced by the prosecution.
>
> Wherever the line between these two extremes is to be drawn, it follows from this understanding of 'the right to silence' that the question whether the right is absolute must be answered in the negative.
>
> ...Whether the drawing of adverse inferences from an accused's silence infringes Article 6 is a matter to be determined in the light of all the circumstances of the case, having particular regard to the situations where inferences may be drawn, the weight attached to them by the national courts in their assessment of the evidence and the degree of compulsion inherent in the situation.

On the facts, the Court observed a number of safeguards enjoyed by the defendant which were felt to be significant:

1   The defendant had not been compelled to give evidence at the police station and had in fact remained silent.
2   He had been cautioned about the risks of remaining silent in terms that had been understood by him even though no solicitor had been present at the time.
3   His trial had been conducted by an experienced judge who had discretion as to whether to choose an adverse inference and who had given reasons for his decision to draw an adverse inference.

The legislation permitting an adverse inference to be drawn made it clear that a conviction could not be based on silence alone and that the prosecution had to establish a *prima facie* case before any question of using silence in evidence against the accused could arise. Indeed, the evidence against the defendant had been strong at an early stage and the circumstances in which he found himself had clearly called for an explanation on his part. The adverse inference drawn by the trial judge had formed only a small part of the overall evidence which clearly indicated the guilt of the accused. As a direct consequence of the judgment in this case, the current version of the Judicial Studies Board specimen direction on section 34 now directs the jury not to convict the defendant wholly or mainly on the fact of his failure to mention facts at the police station.

The denial of access to a solicitor was viewed differently and the United Kingdom was found to have violated Article 6(3)(c). The Court observed that the legislative scheme permitting an adverse inference to be drawn meant it was of 'paramount importance for the rights of the defence that an accused has access to a lawyer at the initial stages of the police investigation'. According to the Court, the matter of fairness arises as the suspect is faced with a dilemma. By choosing to remain silent he risks an adverse inference being drawn. By choosing to speak he runs the risk of prejudicing his defence. The decision as to which course of action to take is a difficult one and in all fairness it should not be taken without the benefit of legal advice. To deny access to legal advice in these circumstances is clearly wrong in principle.

The decision in *Murray v United Kingdom* was followed by a decision on similar facts in *Averill v United Kingdom*. Both decisions clearly provide that in certain circumstances, providing safeguards are in place, the drawing of an adverse inference will not prejudice the defendant's right to a fair trial. In *Averill*, the European Court of Human Rights accepted there were clear justifications for drawing an adverse inference enabling a more efficient prosecution of crimes, but cautioned:

> Notwithstanding these justifications, the Court considers that the extent to which adverse inferences can be drawn from the accused's failure to respond to police questioning must be necessarily limited. While it may no doubt be expected in most cases that innocent persons would be willing to co-operate with the police in explaining that they were not involved in any suspected crime, there may be reasons why in a specific case an innocent person would not be prepared to do so. In particular, an innocent person may not wish to make a statement before he has had the opportunity to consult a lawyer.

An opportunity for the European Court of Human Rights to consider the compatibility of section 34 of the Criminal Justice and Public Order Act 1994 with Article 6 in the context of a jury trial was afforded by the decision discussed below.

Condron *v* United Kingdom (2001) 31 EHRR 1

It will be recalled that the defendants chose not to answer questions at the police station on the advice of their solicitor. The facts in this case differ from those in *Murray v United Kingdom* in two significant respects. In this case the defendants did give evidence at their trial and explained the reasons for their silence. Furthermore their trial was conducted before a jury.

The Court of Appeal concluded that it had not been wrong for the judge to leave the matter of silence to the jury. Although there had been a misdirection to the jury, the evidence against the defendants had been overwhelming and it could not be said that their convictions were unsafe within the meaning of section 2(1) of the Criminal Appeal Act 1968. The misdirection had come about by the failure of the judge to direct the jury that an adverse inference could only be drawn if the jury concluded that the defendants' silence could only sensibly be attributed to their having no answer to the case against them or none that would stand up to cross-examination.

The European Court of Human Rights came to the conclusion that the United Kingdom had violated the applicants' right to a fair trial, specifically because of the misdirection. The misdirection meant the jury were left free to draw an adverse inference even though it may well have been satisfied that the defendants' reason for their silence was due to their drug withdrawal symptoms and that they were acting on the advice of their solicitor.

The European Court of Human Rights rejected the argument that the Court of Appeal's review of the case and its subsequent decision to uphold the convictions notwithstanding the misdirection had rectified any unfairness at the original trial. The Court of Appeal's inquiry had been limited to a review of the safety of the convictions in the light of other evidence and not to issues of fairness. In any event, it had been the jury's prerogative to draw an adverse inference. As a jury does not give reasons for its decision, it was impossible for the Court of Appeal to say whether or not silence had played an important part in the jury's decision. Given the nature of jury trials, it was imperative for the judge to direct the jury with the utmost caution.

Although in *Condron* v *United Kingdom* the European Court of Human Rights found against the United Kingdom on the narrow point of the misdirection, broader issues of policy in relation to section 34 were considered. In argument the applicants made much of the point that their decision to remain silent had been based on the advice of their solicitor and that it had been wrong in principle to allow the jury the option of holding their silence against them in these circumstances. This they felt was compounded by the fact that they had effectively been compelled to waive their right to legal professional privilege in disclosing to the jury the nature of the advice they had been given. In its consideration of the arguments, the Court observed the applicants had been under no compulsion to speak. They had been cautioned and the presence of their legal adviser throughout was felt to be a particularly important safeguard in this respect.

Reiterating the point made in *Murray* v *United Kingdom* about the importance of legal advice, the Court stated:

> ... particular caution is required when a domestic court seeks to attach weight to the fact that a person who is arrested in connection with a criminal offence and who has not given access to a lawyer does not provide detailed responses to questions the answers to which may be incriminating. At the same time, the very fact that an accused is advised by his lawyer to maintain his silence must also be given appropriate weight by the domestic court ... the question whether the trial judge gave sufficient weight to the applicants' reliance on legal advice to explain their silence at interview must equally be examined from the standpoint of his directions on this matter.

This important statement of principle was further underlined in the judgment of the European Court of Human Rights in *Averill* v *United Kingdom*:

> For the Court, considerable caution is required when attaching weight to the fact that a person arrested, as in this case, in connection with a serious criminal offence and having been denied access to a lawyer during the first 24 hours of his interrogation does not provide detailed responses when confronted with incriminating evidence against him. Nor is the need for caution removed simply because an accused is eventually allowed to see his solicitor but continues to refuse to answer questions. It cannot be excluded that the

accused's continued silence is based, on for example, bona fide advice received from his lawyer. Due regard must be given to such considerations by the fact-finding tribunal.

As a direct result of the decisions in *Condron* v *United Kingdom* and *Averill* v *United Kingdom*, the most recent version of the Judicial Studies Board specimen direction on section 34, reproduced earlier in this chapter, singles out the defendant's reliance on the advice of his solicitor as the reason for his silence, for special treatment by the jury. The direction now requires the jury not to draw an adverse inference if it concludes that the defendant reasonably relied on the legal advice he was given to remain silent.

In an aspect of the decision in *Condron* v *United Kingdom* which many will regard as disappointing, the Court concluded there was nothing in section 34 which had the effect of overriding the legal professional privilege which exists between solicitor and client. The decision to make the content of their solicitor's advice an issue at the trial had been the defendants' decision. Although this is strictly true, it ignores the fact that their decision was hardly an unfettered one. As the Court of Appeal itself said in *R* v *Condron* [1997] 1 Cr App R 185, a bare assertion by the defendant that he was acting on the advice of his solicitor is unlikely to be accorded much weight by the jury. If the defendant wants his reasons to be taken seriously he is effectively compelled to waive the privilege and in some instances to make his solicitor a witness in his defence. This can have the effect of exposing both the defendant and his solicitor to some searching questions in cross-examination.

DEFENCE STATEMENTS UNDER THE CRIMINAL PROCEDURE AND INVESTIGATIONS ACT 1996

In addition to the provisions under the Criminal Justice and Public Order Act 1994, the defendant remains at a procedural risk of an adverse inference being drawn under the Criminal Procedure and Investigations Act 1996. The disclosure regime under the 1996 Act is explained in Chapter 9. The requirement for the defendant to file a defence statement within the requisite time limit is mandatory in all cases to be tried on indictment. It is optional in the case of matters to be tried summarily. In drafting a defence statement, section 5 of the 1996 Act makes it clear that the defendant must set out in general terms the nature of his defence, indicating which matters he takes issue with the prosecution. In relation to the matters in dispute the statement should set out the reason why the defendant takes issue with the prosecution. If the defendant seeks to rely on the defence of alibi, he is required to give details of that person's name and address or such material information as would assist in the tracing of such a witness.

An adverse inference may be drawn under section 11 of the Criminal Procedure and Investigations Act 1996 in the following circumstances:

- late service of a defence statement;
- failure to disclose details of alibi;
- setting out inconsistent defences within the statement or putting forward a different defence at trial.

In *R* v *Wheeler* [2001] 1 Cr App R 10 the defendant gave evidence at his trial inconsistent with his defence statement. At his trial he explained there had been a mistake in his defence statement largely due to an error on the part of his solicitor. This was referred to in passing by the judge in his summing up. The Court of Appeal held the judge should have directed the jury to accept the mistake as a fact in this case. As the defendant's credibility had been at the centre of the case the conviction had to be quashed. The Court of Appeal strongly suggested it should be standard practice for defence statements to be signed by the defendant personally and should not be served on the prosecution until defence solicitors are sure as to their accuracy.

CONCLUSION

In contrast to the relatively straightforward position at common law, the drawing of an adverse inference under the provisions of the Criminal Justice and Public Order Act 1994 has become a complicated business. Case law has proliferated and the set directions to be given to the jury have become technical and lengthy. With further challenges likely to be made under the Human Rights Act 1998, it has prompted one distinguished academic commentator to conclude that the evidential benefits of the changes are far outweighed by the attendant costs incurred in terms of complexity and judicial time and that the time is ripe to consider reverting back to the common law position!

Further reading

Ashworth, A., 'Article 6 and the Fairness of Trials' [1999] Crim LR 261.

Birch, D., 'Suffering in Silence: A Cost-benefit Analysis of Section 34 of the Criminal Justice and Public Order Act 1994' [1999] Crim LR 769.

Dennis, I.H., 'The Criminal Justice and Public Order Act 1994: The Evidence Provisions' [1995] Crim LR 4.

Dennis, I.H. (1999) *The Law of Evidence*, Sweet & Maxwell.

Dennis, I.H., 'Silence in the Police Station: the Marginalisation of Section 34' [2002] Crim LR 25.

Easton, S., 'Bodily Samples and the Privilege Against Self-incrimination' [1997] Crim LR 18.

Easton, S. (1998) *The Case for the Right to Silence*, 2nd edn, Ashgate.

Easton, S. 'Legal Advice, Common Sense and the Right to Silence' (1998) 2(2) E & P 109.

Greer, S., 'A Review of the Current Debate' (1990) 53 MLR 709.

Mirfield, P. (1998) *Confessions and Improperly Obtained Evidence*, Clarendon Press.

Munday, R., 'Silence, Confessions and Improperly Obtained Evidence' [1996] Crim LR 370.

Pattenden, R., 'Inference from Silence' [1995] Crim LR 602.

Runciman of Doxford, Viscount (1993) *Report of the Royal Commission on Criminal Justice*, Cmnd 2263, HMSO.

Williams, C., 'Silence in Australia: Probative Force and Rights in the Law of Evidence' (1994) 110 LQR 629.

Zuckerman, A. (1989) *The Principles of Criminal Evidence*, Clarendon Press.

Chapter 8

IDENTIFICATION EVIDENCE

INTRODUCTION

Evidence of identification may sometimes be an integral part of the prosecution's case. If the defendant denies being at the scene of a crime or being involved in a particular incident, the prosecution bears the burden of proving the defendant was the person responsible for the alleged offence. That burden may well extend to refuting evidence of alibi tendered by the accused. Proof of the defendant's presence at the scene of a crime is presented at trial in a number of different ways. Perhaps the most common form of identification evidence is the visual identification of a suspect by an eye-witness. This evidence does however cause the most problems in practice. Juries in particular often find eyewitness identification hugely persuasive but this belies the fact that it is notoriously unreliable and has accounted for miscarriages of justice. The legal response to the problems associated with eyewitness evidence has been to provide pre-trial safeguards contained in Code D of the Codes of Practice and the application of mandatory guidelines at trials. We shall consider each of these in the course of this chapter.

The rapid advances in the use of technology in connection with crime control and crime detection is also now an important source of potentially probative identification evidence. The widespread use of closed circuit television surveillance has led to increasing use of videotape footage and photographic stills at trials. The admission of such real evidence can give the court a direct view of the incident enabling the fact finder to determine whether the defendant standing in the dock is the person seen participating in the criminal activity captured on film. Identification evidence may also be provided by the opinion evidence of forensic scientists establishing a connection between the defendant and the scene of the crime based on the scientific comparison of forensic samples found at the scene with evidence found on the defendant or otherwise in his possession.

EYEWITNESS IDENTIFICATION

Eyewitness identification has been the subject of extensive psychological research for many years which has consistently shown the errors that eyewitnesses are prone to make in terms of the way they observe, interpret and recall information. Identification evidence is often based on short periods of observation by the witness, sometimes in circumstances of surprise or fear, or where their view of the incident may have been less than perfect. It is compounded by the fallibility of witnesses' powers of recollection. Discussions with other potential witnesses can reinforce inaccuracies and research also shows that witnesses from one ethnic group have greater difficulty in accurately identifying suspects from other ethnic groups.

Where a witness has identified a suspect from a set of police photographs prior to a formal procedure taking place, any errors in the earlier process are likely to be compounded. If the witness was mistaken when making a selection from photographs the error might well be carried over into the formal identification procedure with the witness identifying the person selected from the photograph as opposed to the person who actually committed the crime. For many eyewitnesses their evidence is based on an honest recollection of what they observed at the time. Honest witnesses make very convincing witnesses and therein lies the danger associated with visual-based evidence of identification because honest witnesses can nevertheless be mistaken witnesses. We will examine the law's response to some of these problems later in this chapter.

Eyewitness identification may come about in many different ways. A witness to a crime will usually give an initial statement to the police which will include a description of those involved. The police may compile a photofit of a suspect they wish to interview. On occasions a witness may be taken on a tour of the area to see if he is able to spot the person or persons he considers to be involved. In some instances the police will show a witness 'mug shots' of convicted offenders to see if the witness is able to identify the culprit and in other instances the use of video footage or photographic stills can assist.

Once the police have a named suspect in mind and subsequently arrest that person the police will adopt more formal identification procedures. These formal procedures can comprise:

* an identification parade, or
* a group parade, or
* a video parade, or
* a confrontation.

Safeguards under Code D common to all identification procedures

Due to the highly persuasive nature of eyewitness identification and the inherent dangers associated with it, Code D of the Codes of Practice contains detailed rules designed to ensure the fairness and reliability of identification evidence obtained pursuant to whichever of the formal identification procedures are used.

All identification procedures must be conducted by an officer of at least the rank of inspector who is independent of the investigation. Under Code D 2.0, the police must record details of the original description given by witnesses to a crime. The suspect and his solicitor are entitled to see the records of description prior to any formal identification procedure taking place. The officer must compile a detailed record of the identification procedure carried out.

In cases where the identity of the suspect is not known at the start of the police investigation, Code D 2.17 permits a witness to be taken to a particular neighbourhood or place to see whether he can identify the person he believes was present at the scene of the crime.

Code D 2.18 prohibits the police from showing photographs to a witness if the identity of the suspect is known to the police and the suspect is available to stand on an identification parade. Showing photographs in advance of a formal identification procedure would seriously compromise the integrity of the identification process in that it would effectively render the procedure irrelevant.

If the suspect's identity is not known, the witness may be shown photographs subject to safeguards contained in Annex D of Code D. The safeguards include:

1 a requirement that witness be shown 12 photographs at a time which should be of a similar type;
2 a witness must not be prompted or guided in his or her choice in any way;
3 if a witness makes a positive identification from a set of photographs no other witness can be shown the set and each of the witnesses should be asked to attend a parade.

Where a witness attends a formal identification procedure having initially made a selection from photographs, this must be made known to the suspect and his solicitor before the procedure commences. Irrespective of whether an identification is made or not, none of the photographs used in the process may be destroyed since they may be required for evidential purposes at a subsequent trial.

The specific evidential safeguards relating to all the formal procedures can be found in Code D and its supporting Annexes A–E.

The identification parade

The identification parade generally provides the most reliable evidence of identification because it takes place in the most controlled conditions. As far as the suspect is concerned, the identification procedure affords him the greatest opportunity of not being picked out by the eyewitness. The disadvantage however is that where the witness confidently identifies the suspect in such controlled conditions the witness's evidence is likely to prove highly persuasive to the fact finder.

Code D 2.3 defines the circumstances in which a parade must be held.

> Whenever a suspect disputes an identification, an identification parade shall be held if the suspect consents unless paragraphs 2.4 or 2.7 or 2.10 apply. A parade may also be held if the officer in charge of the investigation considers it would be useful, and the suspect consents.

A parade need not be held where, by reason of the suspect's unusual appearance or for some other reason, the identification officer considers it would not be practicable to assemble sufficient people who resembled the suspect to make the parade fair.

The interpretation of Code D 2.3 has provided the appellate courts with a number of difficulties in recent years. Considerable problems have arisen where the victim or a witness has made a full and complete identification at or near the scene of the crime. Does the literal wording of Code D 2.3 give to the police a discretion as to whether to hold a parade or is it a mandatory requirement in all cases where identification of the suspect is disputed?

The first approach was developed in R v Popat (No 1) [1998] 2 Cr App R 208. The victim had been indecently assaulted. Some months later she saw her attacker again.

He made threatening remarks to her. A few weeks after this incident she saw him again. She was dragged into an alleyway, illuminated by a security light, where she was threatened and told to keep her mouth shut. She had a good look at her attacker. She reported the incident to the police and a surveillance operation was set up. On one occasion, whilst the police were present, she observed her attacker walking towards her house. She recognised him immediately and he was arrested. He denied any involvement. No identification parade was convened. The police saw little point in one being held as the witness had already clearly identified her attacker to the police. The Court of Appeal reviewed existing case law and came to the conclusion that there had been no breach of Code D 2.3 in this instance. Explaining what the Court of Appeal considered the position to be, Lord Justice Hobhouse stated:

> Therefore, in our judgment, the effect of the Code and the law is that when a suspect has become known and disputes his identification as the person who committed the crime alleged and the police wish to rely upon identification evidence provided by a witness, the question must be asked whether that witness has already made an actual and complete identification of that individual. If the answer to that question is yes then the mandatory requirement of the first sentence of paragraph 2.3 does not apply. If the answer is no paragraph 2.3 must be complied with and any failure to do so will amount to a breach of the Code. What is an actual and complete prior identification of the relevant individual by the relevant witness will depend upon the facts of each individual case...

Lord Justice Hobhouse went on to say that a complete identification meant a one-to-one identification carried out under good conditions where there was no risk of any corruption. In this case, the Court of Appeal took a pragmatic view of Code D 2.3, ignoring a literal approach to the wording, deeming an identification parade to be unnecessary where one would serve no useful purpose.

The decision in *Popat (No 1)* was followed in the later Court of Appeal decision in *R v Samir El-Hinnachi* [1998] 2 Cr App R 226. Lord Justice May regarded *Popat (No 1)* as 'a definitive analysis of the subject matter with which it deals'. *R v Samir El-Hinnachi* concerned an affray. The key eyewitness had been taken around the vicinity of the crime in a police car shortly after the incident. She spotted the appellants and identified them at the scene to the police. The Court of Appeal held a parade had been unnecessary.

It appeared that the matter was settled until a later decision of the Court of Appeal which took a different view.

R v Forbes [1999] 2 Cr App R 501

The victim was attacked and almost robbed at a cash-dispensing machine. He managed to get away and called the police. He was taken on a tour of the area and was able to point out the man who had robbed him. The appellant was arrested. He vigorously protested his innocence. No parade was held. The Court of Appeal disapproved of the decision in *Popat (No 1)*, maintaining too much of a qualitative assessment of the evidence had been placed in the hands of the trial judge. It took the view that Code D 2.3 was mandatory. Two separate questions had to be answered in cases of this kind:

1   Had there been a breach of Code D 2.3?
2   If so, should the other evidence of identification (ie that made in the street in this instance) be excluded under section 78 of PACE?

The Court of Appeal held that there had been a breach of the mandatory requirement to hold an identification parade, but the trial judge had been right to admit the evidence of identification in the exercise of his discretion under section 78 of PACE.

As a result of the Court of Appeal's decision in *Forbes*, the Criminal Cases Review Commission referred the case of *Popat* back to the Court of Appeal. In *Popat (No 2)* [2000] 1 Cr App R 387 the Court of Appeal overruled the decision in *Forbes* and declared the position to be as stated in *Popat (No 1)*.

The apparent conflicting decisions in *Popat (No 1)* and *Popat (No 2)* and *Forbes* about the interpretation and application of Code D 2.3 was finally resolved by the House of Lords' decision in *R v Forbes* below.

R *v* Forbes [2001] 1 AC 473

On appeal from the earlier Court of Appeal decision (see facts above), the House of Lords chose to overrule *R* v *Popat*. Code D 2.3 had to be read as meaning what it explicitly stated. It imposed a mandatory obligation on the police to hold a parade in the circumstances provided for in the wording of the paragraph. To read words into Code D 2.3 as the Court of Appeal had done in *R* v *Popat* (*No 1*) and (*No 2*) subverted its clear intention. The House of Lords held it was wrong in principle for police officers to take the decision on whether a parade should or should not be held. Their concern is to promote the investigation and prosecution of crime rather than to protect the interests of the suspect. The parade offers the defendant very real protection against the risk of a miscarriage of justice. Additionally, deciding whether an informal identification was satisfactory and complete, involved police officers in an exercise of their critical judgment which was bound to be challenged in the courts and on appeal. In conclusion the House of Lords held:

> ...the effect of D 2.3 is clear: if (a) the police have sufficient information to justify the arrest of a particular person for suspected involvement in an offence and (b) an eye-witness has identified or may be able to identify that person and (c) the suspect disputes his identification as a person involved in the commission of that an offence, an identification parade must be held if (d) the suspect consents and (e) paragraphs 2.4, 2.7 and 2.10 of Code D do not apply.

The decision of the House of Lords in *R v Forbes* provides much needed clarification as to when an identification parade must be held.

Circumstances where an identification parade need not be held

The Court of Appeal decision in *R v Montgomery* [1996] Crim LR 507 is authority for the proposition that an identification parade need not be held where a witness states he would be unable to pick the suspect out. The point is neatly illustrated in *R v Nicholson* below.

R *v* Nicholson [2000] 1 Cr App R 182

The victim was seriously assaulted from behind and beaten about the head. She was able to give a broad description of her assailant but did not think she would be able to identify him. The defendant was arrested. He denied any knowledge of the attack and declared himself willing to attend an identification parade. In the light of the victim's statement the police saw no point in convening one. There was other evidence against the accused including a purported confession to a friend and some weak forensic evidence linking him to the victim. The Court of

Appeal concluded that there must have been a visual identification before Code D 2.3 can come into play.

> A mere assertion by the defendant that he required an identification parade so as to rely on non-recognition by the witness simply for forensic purposes should not in our view be regarded as triggering an obligation on the police to indulge in the trouble and expense of organising an identification parade. (*per* Lord Justice Potter)

Application of Code D 2.3 where a witness can only describe the suspect but cannot identify him

R v Oscar [1991] Crim LR 778

The witness observed the suspect attempting to break into a neighbour's property from the window overlooking her garden. The man in question was wearing distinctive clothes. She could not observe his features but was able to give a description of his height and build. The police came round and arrested a man wearing clothing fitting the witness's description. No parade was necessary because there was no purported identification of the suspect. There was no unfairness in the way in which the evidence had come about.

All of the above decisions are supported by dicta in *R v Forbes* [2001] 1 AC 473.

It is not altogether clear whether Code D 2.3 applies to situations where an eyewitness purports to recognise the suspect. According to the decision in *Popat (No 1)* it has no application to a situation where the witness gives evidence of seeing the crime being committed and it is not disputed that the suspect was and is known to the witness. In such circumstances there would appear to be little to be gained by holding a parade, as the witness is virtually certain to choose the person known to them. This observation has been given some support by dicta in *R v Forbes* [2001] 1 AC 473 to the effect that: 'if a case is one of pure recognition of someone well-known to the eye-witness, it may again be futile to hold an identification parade'.

Admitting presence at the scene but denying participation

What if the defendant admits his presence at the scene but denies participation in the crime? Does a parade have to be held in these circumstances? Contrast the fortunes of H and L in the following case.

R v Hope, Limburne and Bleasdale [1994] Crim LR 118

H, L and B were all beggars. It was alleged that one, two or all of them had attacked D. D identified H early on in the investigation as being one of his attackers. H admitted being at the scene, but denied assault. L was not identified as an assailant until D was shown photographs of H, L, B and others in an attempt to figure out what role each had played. D identified L from the photograph. Both H and L sought exclusion of this evidence for breach of Code D 2.3 for failing to convene an identification parade. The Court of Appeal held Code D 2.3 had no application to H. In his case identification was not in dispute. H had admitted being at the scene and had been pointed out by D as being one of his attackers very early on. The issue in H's case was what he had or had not done. L's position was different. D had not described L as doing anything until he had been shown a photograph. There was a dispute as to L's involvement in the assault and as such, Code D called for the identification to be tested.

Further safeguards to ensure the fairness and reliability of evidence obtained by an identification parade

The specific conduct of identification parades is regulated by Annex A of Code D which contains detailed safeguards. The parade must consist of at least eight people in addition to the suspect. The participants should resemble the suspect in age, height, general appearance and position in life. This may require the identification officer to use a bit of ingenuity by, for example, disguising distinguishing features on a suspect's face. If the suspect has a blemish, say a facial scar or large mole that would make him stand out from the other participants in the parade he might be asked to conceal the blemish with a plaster. All the other participants on the parade would then be asked to wear a plaster in the same place.

Before witnesses attend the parade the identification officer must ensure they are unable to:

- communicate with each other,
- see any member of the parade,
- see the suspect either before or after the parade, or
- be reminded of any photographs or description of the suspect (Code D, Annex A, paragraph 12).

Witnesses must be brought into the room where the parade is being conducted one at a time. The officer in charge must explain that the person the witnesses saw may or may not be in the line-up and that if they cannot make a positive identification they should say so. If a witness wishes to hear a member of the parade speak or adopt a specified posture or to see him move, the identification officer must first ask the witness whether they can identify on the basis of appearance alone (Code D, Annex A, paragraph 17).

A colour photograph or video recording shall be taken of the parade (Code D 2.5).

Where a suspect refuses to participate in an identification parade or, having agreed to participate, fails to turn up, or the holding of a parade is impracticable, arrangements must be made for the adoption of an alternative identification procedure (Code D 2.6). A suspect must be warned that in refusing or failing to attend an identification parade his failure or refusal can be used in evidence against him.

The group parade

A group parade is considered the second best option when compared with an identification parade. A group parade can be held in the circumstances provided for in Code D 2.7.

> A group parade may take place with the consent and co-operation of a suspect or covertly where a suspect has refused to co-operate with an identification parade or group parade or has failed to attend. A group identification may also be arranged if the officer in charge of

the investigation considers, whether because of fear on the part of the witness or for some other reason, it is more satisfactory than a parade.

A group identification parade will be held in a place where the suspect can be viewed by a witness in an informal group setting. This might, for example, be at a shopping centre or on a railway platform.

The specific safeguards ensuring the proper conduct of a group parade are contained in Annex E of Code D. The choice of venue is a matter for the identification officer although he should listen to representations by the suspect, his solicitor or appropriate adult. In selecting the location the identification officer is required to consider the general appearance and numbers of people likely to be present. Thus, for example, a scruffy young man mingling with a group of church worshippers is likely to be all too noticeable. If the identification officer believes that by reason of the suspect's unusual appearance no location would be fair a group parade need not be held (Annex E, paragraph 6).

Annex E requires a colour photograph or a video to be taken of the general scene immediately after the procedure has taken place and anything a witness says during the group parade should be in the presence of the identification officer and, if present, the suspect's solicitor. Such safeguards help achieve a measure of objective fairness thereby minimising the probability of a dispute as to what actually occurred.

As with identification parades, the identification officer must ensure that before attending the group parade witnesses are unable to communicate with each other, see the suspect or be reminded of any photographs or description of the suspect. They should be reminded that the person they saw may or may not be in the group.

The video identification

Such a procedure may be adopted where an identification parade or group parade is not possible or the police consider this method to be the most satisfactory in the circumstances (Code D 2.10).

Annex B regulates the conduct of video identifications. The video film must include the suspect and eight other people who so far as possible resemble the suspect in age, height and general appearance and position in life. The suspect or his solicitor must be given the opportunity of seeing the complete film before it is shown to witnesses. Where objection is made the identification officer must record the objection and try to remove the grounds for it or explain why the objection cannot be met.

Where the suspect's solicitor is not present when the film is shown to a witness, the process must also be recorded on video.

Witnesses must not be allowed to communicate with each other or to overhear a witness who has seen the film. The witness should be requested to view the entire video twice before making a selection and must not be reminded of any earlier description he might have given or be prompted in any way.

The confrontation procedure

The least favoured method of identification is the confrontation as it is felt to produce the least reliable evidence of identification. At a confrontation the witness comes face to face with the suspect and is asked to confirm whether the suspect is the person

responsible. An accused faces the greatest risk of being identified through this procedure than with any of the other procedures highlighted above. The confrontation
procedure does not require the suspect's consent however and, in accordance with
Code D 2.13, it may only be utilised if none of the other identification procedures are
practicable.

The conduct of the confrontation procedure is regulated by Annex C of Code D. The
confrontation will usually be conducted at the police station and should take place in
a normal room there. The witness should be told that the person he is about to be confronted with may or may not be the person he saw. The suspect is confronted by the
witness who is asked: 'Is this the person?'

Dock identification

A dock identification occurs where the victim or another witness testifies on oath that
the accused standing in the dock is the person he saw at the scene of the crime. For a
number of reasons, dock identifications are very rarely used as they have little probative value because the identification of the accused in these circumstances is virtually
inevitable and therefore highly prejudicial. In exceptional circumstances, dock identification might be used where the defendant has resisted all other pre-trial methods of
identification. Even where it does occur, to ensure fairness, the defendant should be
asked to take a seat in the courtroom as opposed to standing alone in the dock to be
formally identified.

FAIRNESS OF ADMITTING IDENTIFICATION EVIDENCE AND THE APPLICATION OF SECTION 78 OF PACE

The safeguards under Code D are extensive. They exist to ensure identification procedures are carried out in a scrupulously fair manner having regard to the weight fact
finders attach to such evidence. Where identification evidence is obtained in breach of
Code D it is susceptible to exclusion under section 78 of PACE. The operation of section 78 of PACE was considered in Chapter 5. Section 78 gives the court discretion to
exclude prosecution evidence where the admission of such evidence would adversely
affect the fairness of the trial.

R v Finley [1993] Crim LR 50

Evidence of identification was excluded under section 78 of PACE for several breaches of Code D.
The defendant was implicated in a robbery at an insurance office. There were several eyewitnesses
who all worked together. One witness was shown a set of 12 police photographs from which she
selected the defendant. He was a blonde skinhead whilst most of the photographs were of dark-
haired men. The defendant was able to produce an alibi and nothing had been found to link him to
the robbery during a search of his flat. The composition of the parade was criticised in that most of
the volunteers were of heavier build than the defendant and had darker hair. Witnesses had been
kept together before the parade and the fact that one of their number had made a prior selection
from photographs and had probably discussed this with her colleagues was held to be very prejudicial by the Court of Appeal.

R v Gall (1990) 90 Cr App R 64

Identification evidence was excluded because of a breach of Code D 2.2 in that the chief identification witness had been brought to the parade by the investigating officer who came into the room whilst the parade was being conducted.

As with confession evidence the fact that identification evidence has been obtained in breach of Code D does not automatically mean the resulting evidence must be excluded. Decisions in relation to identification evidence largely turn on their own facts. Establishing a breach of Code D is helpful but not essential. Extracting general principles is difficult since the application of judicial discretion depends on the factors in each individual case. Regard will be had as to the reasons for the breach and all the other circumstances, including the strength of other evidence linking the defendant to the crime and the nature of the trial judge's summing up.

The following case (also considered in Chapter 5) further illustrates that even if Code D 2.3 is breached there is no obligation on the part of the court to exclude the evidence obtained in consequence. The decision is dependent on the court's assessment of whether the fairness of the proceedings is affected by the breach.

R v Rutherford (1994) 98 Cr App R 191

The police declined to convene an identification parade in spite of a request by the defendant because of what they perceived to be the strength of other evidence against the defendant. Although deemed to be a breach of Code D 2.3, the Court of Appeal refused to quash the conviction.

It had been alleged that the defendant and another had forced their way into the home of an elderly lady. They sprayed a liquid into her eyes, bound and gagged her. It was further alleged that 1,000, some Indian rupees and a scrap piece of paper with a telephone number written on it had been stolen. The defendant was arrested in the vicinity soon after. In his possession were a quantity of cash, some Indian rupees and a scrap piece of paper containing a telephone number. The defendant's appearance matched that of descriptions given by a couple of witnesses. The Court of Appeal concluded notwithstanding the breach of Code D 2.3 that the prejudice to the defendant had been dealt with in the judge's summing up and there had been ample circumstantial evidence upon which to convict.

By way of contrasting outcomes, the following cases are included:

R v Conway (1990) 91 Cr App R 143

Three persons were involved in a violent attack. The eyewitness claimed to know the suspects by sight, although she did not know their names. This information was obtained through others after the incident. The defendant was arrested. He requested an identification parade but none was held. In view of the fact that they had a named suspect, the investigating officers considered there was no point in convening a parade. The defendant denied knowing the female eyewitness. At an initial hearing before a magistrates' court permission was granted for a dock identification to take place. The defendant was picked out by the victim. The Court of Appeal quashed the defendant's conviction, concluding there had never been an acceptable pre-trial identification of the defendant. This was a clear violation of Code D 2.3. The circumstances of the dock identification were grossly unfair to the defendant.

R v Brown [1991] Crim LR 368

A young couple were robbed in the street. The female victim was able to identify the defendant as one of the robbers. Although the circumstances of the robbery would have made it difficult for her to identify the defendant she was taken round the neighbourhood in a police car and within a matter of minutes, picked out the defendant. He denied any involvement with the robbery and claimed to have just come from the pub. The defendant requested an identification parade but was refused. The police took the view that the street identification had rendered a parade otiose. Quashing the conviction the Court of Appeal highlighted the mandatory words of Code D 2.3: 'In a case which involves disputed identification evidence a parade must be held if the suspect asks for one ...' The rationale for holding a parade even in circumstances where it might be thought to be unnecessary was explained by Lord Justice Farquharson:

> It may in some circumstances be otiose where there has been a street identification but, as was pointed out in the course of argument in this case, there is always the possibility that the witness seeing the suspect ranged against a number of people of roughly similar appearance may have doubts...

R v Wait [1998] Crim LR 68

The defendant was convicted of attempted robbery and unlawful wounding. Three men had attacked the victim. All three perpetrators ran away. Two days later the victim saw all three of them and two days after this, the victim saw two of them again, including the appellant who was arrested in the victim's presence. No parade was held as the police did not consider anything could be gained from it. There were some discrepancies in the victim's description of his attackers. The Court of Appeal quashed the conviction maintaining the fact that the victim was present at the arrest was not a valid reason for declining to hold a parade. The judge was wrong to assume the victim was bound to identify his attacker from a line-up.

Directions to the jury where identification evidence is admitted in breach of Code D

The Court of Appeal's decision in *R v Allen* [1995] Crim LR 643 makes it clear that the judge must explain to the jury why he is admitting evidence of identification in breach of Code D. Furthermore, in accordance with several authorities including *R v Conway* (above) and *R v Quinn* [1995] 1 Cr App R 480, when summing up the judge should make reference to the specific breach or breaches of Code D leaving it up to the jury to decide how much weight it wants to place on the evidence of identification in the circumstances.

Further guidelines have been provided by the House of Lords in its decision in *R v Forbes* (above). In cases where there has been a specific breach of Code D 2.3, a trial judge must explain to a jury that the purpose of Code D 2.3 is to enable a suspect to test the reliability of a witness's identification. In cases where an identification parade has not been held contrary to the rules the suspect loses the benefit of the safeguard a parade affords him. The jury must be instructed to take account of this when assessing the case against the defendant. Additionally, even in a case where an informal identification is followed up by a properly conducted parade from which the defendant is chosen, a warning should still be issued to the jury. The judge must stipulate that although the prosecution's case is strengthened the jury should be aware of the possible risk that the witness might have identified not the culprit who committed the crime but the suspect identified by the witness on the earlier occasion.

LIMITATIONS OF CODE D

Code D is not all embracing and there are many instances in which identification is made which fall outside it. In circumstances where the Code has no application, there can be no breach of it. However, consideration of fairness remains paramount and evidence may still be excluded in the exercise of the court's discretion under section 78 of PACE.

R v Hickin [1996] Crim LR 585

A fight broke out between gangs of rival football supporters on Blackpool seafront resulting in a serious injury. Three eyewitnesses were taken round the area in a police car to see if they could identify the culprits. Having rounded up people the police considered to be involved, the witnesses were asked to identify those they considered responsible for the violent assault. Fourteen men were subsequently arrested and charged. No identification parades were held. There was little doubt that having arrived on the scene the police had to act fast and arrange for the available witnesses to confront the available suspects. In addition it was impracticable to convene 14 identification parades at short notice. The Court of Appeal felt the situation faced by the police was not specifically covered by the Codes and so there was not a breach of Code D. However, there were serious questions about the reliability of the evidence of identification having regard to the manner in which it had been obtained. In this regard the Court of Appeal noted the lack of any detailed descriptions taken from the eyewitnesses before seeing the suspects. This was coupled with the fact that the eyewitnesses travelled together in the police car and there was no record of what the witnesses had said when viewing the suspects. All in all, the evidence had to be excluded under section 78 of PACE in the interests of ensuring a fair trial.

R v Hersey [1998] Crim LR 281

This case involved identification based on hearing the suspect speak. This is a situation not currently covered by Code D. Two men wearing balaclavas robbed a shop. The raid lasted 15 minutes and some conversation was entered into during this time. The shop owner was convinced that he recognised the voice of one of the robbers as being that of the defendant, a long-standing customer. A voice identification was held. Eleven volunteers plus the defendant read a passage of text from an unrelated interview with the defendant. The shop owner identified one of the voices as being that of the defendant. Two other witnesses picked out a volunteer, with the other being unable to identify any of the voices.

During a *voire dire* the defence submitted that the evidence be excluded under section 78 of PACE. The defence called an expert witness who testified that 12 voices were too many and that all but one was of significantly higher pitch than the defendant. The trial judge allowed the evidence to go before the jury, a decision upheld by the Court of Appeal. The police had done the best they could do in the circumstances. This was not a case where expert evidence could assist the jury.

A contrasting decision is that of *R v Roberts* [2000] Crim LR 183. In this case, a Polish victim purported to identify her assailant through voice identification. Her recollection of her assailant's voice was based on a very short snippet of 'conversation' in circumstances of fear. The defendant was convicted but successfully appealed. Expert opinion evidence was relied on to establish the likelihood of error in such a case. Based on the expert's findings, the Court of Appeal quashed the conviction concluding voice identifications are fraught with even more dangers than visual identifications.

PRACTICAL STEPS – IDENTIFICATION EVIDENCE

Being mindful of the application of section 78 of PACE and the working of Code D, solicitors or legal representatives attending suspects at the police station have their part to play in the process by which identification evidence is obtained. A failure by a witness to select the person suspected of the crime from a properly convened parade can greatly increase that person's chance of not being charged with the offence and significantly decrease the risk of conviction. The solicitor should therefore ensure that the safeguards contained in Code D are complied with. On a practical level this would include:

- advising a suspect on whether or not to agree to attend an identification parade or to insist on a parade being convened where one has not been offered;
- keeping an independent record of all that goes on in relation to the identification procedures;
- checking the layout at the police station to ensure witnesses cannot communicate with each other or see members of the parade in advance;
- taking the opportunity to consider the original description of the perpetrator given by a witness and where there are varying descriptions of the suspect by different witnesses, making representations as to the composition of the parade;
- preparing the suspect for the experience and the need to behave normally;
- assessing and recording the degree of confidence with which an identification is made.

A decision by officers not to hold an identification parade should not be regarded as a fait accompli. The legal representative should be prepared to make such representations as might be appropriate and ensure that they are recorded for evidential purposes in the custody record. Such representations can enhance the advocate's chances of getting identification evidence excluded at trial under section 78 of PACE for a breach of Code D.

SAFEGUARDING IDENTIFICATION EVIDENCE AT TRIAL – THE *TURNBULL* GUIDELINES

Whilst Code D attempts to safeguard the manner in which evidence is obtained pre-trial, the Court of Appeal devised a set of guidelines to be followed in all cases involving disputed identification at trial. The guidelines were formulated in *R v Turnbull* [1977] QB 224 and aim to lessen the danger of a wrongful conviction based on identification evidence. The case followed hot on the heels of the Devlin Committee's *Report on Evidence of Identification in Criminal Cases* (1976). The Committee was set up in the light of miscarriages of justice based on identification evidence at the time. The *Turnbull* guidelines are reproduced below.

> First, whenever the case against an accused depends wholly or substantially on the correctness of one or more identifications of the accused which the defence alleges to be mistaken, the judge must warn the jury of the special need for caution before convicting the accused in reliance on the correctness of the identification ... In addition he should instruct them as to the reason for the need for such a warning and should make some reference to

the possibility that a mistaken witness can be a convincing one and that a number of such witnesses can all be mistaken.

Secondly, the judge should direct the jury to examine closely the circumstances in which the identification by each witness came to be made. How long did the witness have the accused under observation? At what distance? In what light? Was the observation impeded in any way, as for example by passing traffic or a press of people? Had the witness ever seen the accused before? How often? If only occasionally, had he any special reason for remembering the accused? How long elapsed between the original observation and the subsequent identification to the police. Was there any material discrepancy between the description of the accused given to the police by the witness when first seen by them and his actual appearance?... Finally, he should remind the jury of any specific weaknesses which had appeared in the identification evidence.

Recognition may be more reliable than identification of a stranger; but even when a witness is purporting to recognise someone whom he knows, the jury should be reminded that mistakes in recognition of close relatives and friends are sometimes made.

All these matters go to the quality of the identification. If the quality is good at the close of the accused's case, the danger of a mistaken identification is lessened; but the poorer the quality, the greater the danger.

...when the quality is good, as for example when the identification is made over a long period of observation, or in satisfactory conditions by a relative or neighbour, a close friend, a workmate and the like, the jury can safely be left to assess the value of the identifying evidence even where there is no other evidence to support it; provided always, however that an adequate warning has been given about the special need for caution.

When, in the judgment of the trial judge, the quality of the identifying evidence is poor, as for example a fleeting glimpse of a witness or a longer observation made in difficult conditions, the situation is very different. The judge should then withdraw the case from the jury and direct an acquittal unless there is other evidence which goes to support the correctness of the identification. This may be corroboration in the sense lawyers use that word; but it need not be so if its effect is to make the jury sure that there has been no mistaken identification...

The judge should identify to the jury the evidence capable of supporting the identification. If there is any evidence or circumstances which the jury might think was supporting when it did not have this quality, the judge should say so. ...

Care should be taken by the judge when directing the jury about the support for an identification which may be derived from the fact that they have rejected an alibi. False alibis may be put forward for many reasons: an accused, for example, who has only his own truthful evidence to rely on may stupidly fabricate an alibi and get lying witnesses to support it out of fear that his own evidence may not be enough. Further alibi witnesses can make genuine mistakes about dates and occasions like any other witnesses can. It is only when the jury is satisfied that the sole reason for the fabrication was to deceive them and there is no explanation for its being put forward can fabrication provide any sort for identification evidence. The jury should be reminded that proving the accused has told lies about where he was at the material time does not of itself prove that he was where the identifying witness says he was. (*per* Lord Widgery CJ)

The failure to give a *Turnbull* warning in cases of disputed identification will almost certainly lead to an appeal against conviction.

Under the guidelines the judge must make an initial qualitative assessment of the evidence. If he considers the evidence to be poor and unsupported by any other evidence, the judge must direct the jury to acquit. In those cases where supporting evidence is required, such evidence does not have to fulfil the formal requirements of corroboration. The types of evidence likely to benefit from corroborating evidence are examined in Chapter 18.

Supporting evidence of identification can come in a number of different forms. It can come from the defendant's incriminating admissions in a particular case or from his silence in appropriate situations. It can come from items found on the defendant or in his possession and from proven lies told by the defendant under the principles laid down in *R v Lucas* [1981] 2 All ER 1008. It can come from forensic evidence such as DNA linking the defendant to the crime scene or other circumstantial evidence and from the testimony of other witnesses in the case.

Where the evidence is left to the jury the judge must warn the jurors of the dangers of mistaken identity and the reasons for those dangers. The guidelines require the judge to make specific reference to the fact that honest witnesses are sometimes mistaken. He should invite them to examine closely all the circumstances in which the evidence of identification came about and he must deal with specific weaknesses in the evidence. Weaknesses could include a breach of Code D (see earlier), a failure by one or more witnesses to make a positive identification, discrepancies in the original description of the defendant given by different witnesses or the inability of the defence to cross-examine an eyewitness because their evidence is admitted in hearsay form. The guidelines themselves provide defence advocates with a useful aide-memoire for cross-examination purposes. Where the jury chooses not to believe alibi evidence advanced on behalf of the defendant, the trial judge must warn the jury, as detailed above, that rejection of such alibi evidence does not prove identification of the defendant.

The *Turnbull* guidelines apply with identical effect to trials in magistrates' courts. In a summary trial involving disputed identification of the accused, the clerk will remind the magistrates of the guidelines in open court.

When do the *Turnbull* guidelines apply?

Where the fact finder is given the task of attempting to identify the defendant from a photographic still or video, then although the full *Turnbull* direction is not required in such circumstances, the fact finder must still be warned of the dangers of mistaken identity. In some instances the defendant may well have changed his appearance since the film was recorded. Quite often the quality of video or photographic evidence is poor and evidence from an expert witness, using a technique known as facial mapping may be admitted to assist the jury in its task.

In *R v Bowden* [1993] Crim LR 379 the Court of Appeal reaffirmed its view that the guidelines do apply to cases of identification based on recognition. The rationale for its application is explained by the Lord Lane in *R v Bentley* [1991] Crim LR 620:

> Many people have experienced seeing someone in the street whom they know, only to discover that they were wrong. The expression, 'I could have sworn it was you' indicates the sort of warning which a judge should give, because that was exactly what a testifying witness did, he swore that it was the person he thought it was. But he may have been mistaken...

The guidelines do not apply to situations where police officers base identification on long periods of observation or surveillance. The chances of mistake are much diminished as the evidence can hardly be said to be based on a fleeting glimpse. The more difficult instance is where the defendant alleges the eyewitness is lying rather than mistaken. In *R* v *Courtnell* [1990] Crim LR 115 where the defence alleged a frame-up, the Court of Appeal took the view that the warning would only serve to confuse the jury. However in *Shand* v *R* [1996] Crim LR 422 the Privy Council held that even where the main issue was as to the eyewitness's credibility, only in exceptional cases, where the evidence of identification was very good, was a warning otiose.

In the two voice identification cases of *R* v *Hersey* and *R* v *Roberts* highlighted earlier, the Court of Appeal held that the trial judge must give a *Turnbull* warning in such cases suitably tailored to the specific dangers associated with voice identification or recognition. In *R* v *Roberts*, a case in which the victim purported to identify a stranger's voice, the Court of Appeal suggested that in the light of expert research on the particular dangers associated with such identification, the warning should be stronger than that given in relation to cases based on visual identification.

The *Turnbull* guidelines apply to cases of mistaken identity. But precisely what amounts to a mistake as to identity? If the defendant admits his presence at the scene but denies involvement in the crime would the situation call for a *Turnbull* warning? The answer depends on the circumstances of the case.

R v Thornton [1995] 1 Cr App R 578

An altercation developed between guests at a wedding reception. The appellant, a guest at the wedding and as such appropriately attired, had been identified by a neighbour and her son as being the assailant. He admitted being at the scene but said he had been trying to shield the victim. There were others in the vicinity all dressed the same. The Court of Appeal concluded it did not automatically follow that where the accused admitted his presence at or near the scene but denied involvement, the *Turnbull* direction had to be given. It would depend on all the circumstances. In this case, a direction was appropriate given the risk of error.

R v Slater [1995] Crim LR 244

The appellant, described as an unusually large man, admitted his presence at the scene of a fight but denied an assault on his part. There was no evidence to suggest anyone else at the scene, in this case a nightclub, was remotely of similar height to the appellant. There was no issue as to identity. The only issue was as to the appellant's conduct; hence the guidelines had no application.

Case scenario

Anthony is 17. He has been arrested on suspicion of burglary of commercial premises. The break-in of the premises occurred at around 2.15 am. A description of one of the youths involved has been provided by a security guard. He explained how he saw one of the youths running away from the factory and towards him when an alarm bell went off. He gave chase over a period of 30 or 40 seconds before the youth scaled a wall and disappeared. The factory yard was partially illuminated on the night in question. The youth was described by the security guard as being of average build and height, aged about 17. The youth was white and had very closely cropped hair, almost shaven. He was wearing white training shoes and a dark coloured jacket.

Police officers on patrol spotted Anthony at 2.40 am on the same night sauntering down a street in the vicinity. The police officers described Anthony as being, 5 feet 6 inches, white with close shaven hair. He was arrested. On his arrest Anthony was not wearing a jacket but was dressed in a dark coloured sweatshirt and was wearing white trainers. Anthony has one previous conviction for theft. He chose not to be represented by a solicitor at the police station and proceeded to deny any involvement in the burglary. He agreed to participate in an identification procedure. By reason of his unusual appearance, the identification officer decided to convene a group parade.

Four days later, Anthony answered his police bail and was taken to a railway station. He was asked to mingle with passengers leaving a busy commuter train. He did so and was picked out by the security guard. He was subsequently charged with burglary.

Anthony consults a solicitor. He maintains he was with his girlfriend until 2.30 am and was walking home when the patrol officers stopped him. The solicitor takes a statement from Anthony's 15-year-old girlfriend who states Anthony was with her until 2.30 a.m. Anthony tells his solicitor that the group parade was a farce and that he was bound to be picked out. What can the solicitor do about the evidence of identification?

Based on the pre-trial disclosure of evidence by the prosecution, the solicitor discovers there is no videotape footage of the group parade and the only set of photographs available were taken shortly after the parade when some members of the public had dispersed.

Burglary is an either way offence and as such Anthony may be tried before magistrates or before a jury in the Crown Court. Wherever the trial is held, the solicitor should apply for a voire dire and use section 78 of PACE to try and get the security officer's evidence of identification excluded on the basis that it would be unfair to admit it. The identification officer's decision to refuse an identification parade should be challenged. In what sense was Anthony's appearance deemed to be unusual? His decision to hold a group parade at a railway station should also be challenged. It could safely be anticipated that the majority of persons leaving the train would be older than Anthony, more smartly dressed and carrying luggage. In the absence of a contemporaneous photographic record of the group parade (a clear breach of Code D in any event), it would be difficult for the officer to deny this. It should be put to the officer that a fairer venue, such as a university campus, could easily have been chosen where there would have been large numbers of youths of comparable age and appearance.

If the trial judge or the magistrates admit the evidence of the security officer, notwithstanding proven breaches of Code D, the reason for doing so must be explained. A Turnbull direction would then need to be given at the end of the case. First, the judge or the magistrates would be required to assess the quality of identification evidence. If the evidence is of poor quality and is unsupported by other evidence, the case can proceed no further. If the evidence of identification is poor, but is supported by other evidence, it can be left to the fact finder with the necessary warnings. In Anthony's case, it would be the responsibility of the judge or the justices' clerk to remind the fact finders that evidence of identification is often unreliable and that an honest witness, like the security guard, can be mistaken. The circumstances in which the identification of the accused came about would need to be carefully examined by the fact finders. This incident occurred on poorly lit premises at night and was over in a matter of a few seconds. When arrested Anthony was not found to be wearing a dark jacket. Training shoes are commonly worn by youths of his age and he has given evidence of alibi which the fact finder would have to reject if they are to convict. The fact finder would also have to be reminded of any breaches of Code D and what the effect of those breaches has been in this case.

OTHER WAYS IN WHICH EVIDENCE OF IDENTIFICATION CAN BE DERIVED

The presence of forensic evidence found at the scene of a crime may provide compelling circumstantial evidence linking the defendant to the scene when compared with other forensic evidence found on the defendant or otherwise in his possession. Forensic evidence presents itself in many different forms. The person responsible for the crime may have left fingerprints, footprints, a dental impression or a sample of handwriting at the scene. Alternatively, specimens from the crime scene such as fragments of glass or foliage may be discovered on the defendant. DNA extracted from blood, semen stains or body hairs found at or near the crime scene or on the victim linking the surroundings or the victim to the defendant and vice versa may be available. The forensic science service has an important role to play in this regard. Such evidence is analysed by forensic scientists and an opinion is formulated. If the expert's opinion is accepted by the court it can provide strong circumstantial evidence of the defendant's presence at the scene and his consequent involvement in the crime. The role of expert opinion evidence in criminal cases is considered as part of Chapter 19.

The police are able to assist the process of forensic investigation in that they have powers under the Police and Criminal Evidence Act 1984 to obtain intimate and non-intimate body samples from suspects to enable forensic comparison with samples found at the crime scene. The powers of the police to obtain fingerprints and samples from the suspect are contained in sections 61–63 of PACE.

Sections 61 and 63 respectively authorise the taking of fingerprints and non-intimate samples without the suspect's consent. A non-intimate sample includes a sample of hair other than pubic hair, scraping from under a nail, a swab taken from the mouth, saliva and a footprint, or bodily impression. An intimate sample which includes a dental impression or a sample of blood, tissue fluid, urine, pubic hair or swabs taken from a body orifice other than the mouth may be taken from the suspect with his consent under section 62 of PACE. A failure to consent to providing an intimate sample, without good reason, can be used in evidence against the defendant (section 62(10)). Evidence from samples obtained unlawfully remain admissible, as we saw in Chapter 5, subject to the court's exclusionary discretion at common law and under section 78 of PACE.

The forensic techniques involved in extracting an individual DNA profile and comparing it with other DNA samples have attracted considerable attention from scientists, lawyers and the general public. The techniques are relatively new having been perfected in the late 1980s. Over the course of time however, the techniques have grown increasingly sophisticated so that DNA evidence can now yield very compelling evidence indeed. Every human being has a unique DNA make-up apart from an identical twin. DNA profiling enables a forensic scientist to compare two biological samples and to determine the likelihood that the two samples originated from the same individual. DNA evidence is perceived as being particularly cogent evidence of a defendant's presence at a crime scene because of the statistical improbabilities that profiling produces. The process of extraction and extrapolation of results is explained by Lord Justice Phillips in *R v Doheny* [1997] 1 Cr App R 369:

DNA Testing

Deoxyribonucleic acid, or DNA, consists of long ribbon-like molecules, the chromosomes, 46 of which lie tightly coiled in nearly every cell of the body. These chromosomes – 23 provided from the mother and 23 from the father at conception, form the genetic blueprint of the body. Different sections of DNA have different identifiable and discrete characteristics. When a criminal leaves a stain of blood or semen at the scene of the crime it may prove possible to extract from that crime stain sufficient sections of DNA to enable a comparison to be made with the same sections extracted from a sample of blood provided by the suspect. This process is complex and we could not hope to describe it more clearly or succinctly than did Lord Taylor CJ in the case of *Deen* (transcript: December 21, 1993), so we shall gratefully adopt his description.

'The process of DNA profiling starts with DNA being extracted from the crime stain and also from a sample taken from the suspect. In each case the DNA is cut into smaller lengths by specific enzymes. The fragments produced are sorted according to size by a process of electrophoresis. This involves placing the fragments in a gel and drawing them electromagnetically along a track through the gel. The fragments with smaller molecular weight travel further than the heavier ones. The pattern thus created is transferred from the gel onto a membrane. Radioactive DNA probes, taken from elsewhere, which bind with the sequences of most interest in the sample DNA are then applied. After the excess of the DNA probe is washed off, an X-ray film is placed over the membrane to record the band pattern. This produces an auto-radiograph which can be photographed. When the crime stain DNA and the sample DNA from the suspect have been run in separate tracks through the gel, the resultant auto-radiographs can be compared. The two DNA profiles can then be said either to match or not.'

Even if a number of bands correspond exactly, any discrepancy between the profiles, unless satisfactorily explained, will show a mis-match and will exclude the suspect from complicity. Thus the first stage in seeking to prove identity by DNA profiling is to achieve a match.

The characteristics of an individual band of DNA will not be unique. The fact that the identical characteristic of a single band are to be found in the crime stain and the sample from the suspect does not prove that both have originated from the same source. Other persons will also have that identical band as part of their genetic make-up. Empirical research enables the analyst to predict the statistical likelihood of an individual DNA band being found in the genetic make-up of persons of particular racial groups 'the random occurrence ratio'.

As one builds up a combination of bands, the random occurrence ratio becomes increasingly more remote, by geometric progression. Thus, if two bands, each of which appear in 1 in 4 of the population are combined, the combination will appear in 1 in 16 of the population, and if to these are added a further band that is found in 1 in 4 of the population, the resultant combination will appear in 1 in 64 of the population. This process of multiplication is valid on the premise that each band is statistically independent from the others. The frequency ratio of the blood group is a factor which is statistically independent and thus this can also validly be used as a multiplier. If the DNA obtainable from the crime stain permits, it may be possible to demonstrate that there is a combination of bands common to the crime stain and the suspect which is very rare. For instance, it may be that the match achieved with the crime stain is one which has a statistical probability of existing in the case of only one in a million of the populace. We shall take a match probability, or random occurrence ratio, of one in a million as an example to demonstrate the conclusions that can properly be drawn from such data and those which cannot. We shall start with the latter.

'The Prosecutor's Fallacy'

It is easy, if one eschews rigorous analysis, to draw the following conclusion:

1   Only one person in a million will have a DNA profile which matches that of the crime stain.
2   The defendant has a DNA profile which matches the crime stain.
3   Ergo there is a million to one probability that the defendant left the crime stain and is guilty of the crime.

Such reasoning has been commended to juries in a number of cases by prosecuting counsel, by judges and sometimes by expert witnesses. It is fallacious and it has earned the title of 'The Prosecutor's Fallacy'. The propounding of the Prosecutor's Fallacy in the course of the summing up was the reason, or at least one of the reasons, why the appeal against conviction was allowed in *Deen*. The nature of that fallacy was elegantly exposed by Balding and Donnelly in 'The Prosecutor's Fallacy and DNA Evidence' [1994] Crim LR 711. It should not, however, be thought that we endorse the calculations on pp. 715 and 716 of that article.

Taking our example, the Prosecutor's Fallacy can be simply demonstrated. If one person in a million has a DNA profile which matches that obtained from the crime stain, then the suspect will be one of perhaps 26 men in the United Kingdom who share that characteristic. If no fact is known about the Defendant, other than that he was in the United Kingdom at the time of the crime the DNA evidence tells us no more than that there is a statistical probability that he was the criminal of one in 26.

The significance of the DNA evidence will depend critically upon what else is known about the suspect. If he has a convincing alibi at the other end of England at the time of the crime, it will appear highly improbable that he can have been responsible for the crime, despite his matching DNA profile. If, however, he was near the scene of the crime when it was committed, or has been identified as a suspect because of other evidence which suggests that he may have been responsible for the crime, the DNA evidence becomes very significant. The possibility that two of the only 26 men in the United Kingdom with the matching DNA should have been in the vicinity of the crime will seem almost incredible and a comparatively slight nexus between the Defendant and the crime, independent of the DNA, is likely to suffice to present an overall picture to the jury that satisfies them of the Defendant's guilt.

The reality is that, provided there is no reason to doubt either the matching data or the statistical conclusion based upon it, the random occurrence ratio deduced from the DNA evidence, when combined with sufficient additional evidence to give it significance, is highly probative. As the art of analysis progresses, it is likely to become more so, and the stage may be reached when a match will be so comprehensive that it will be possible to construct a DNA profile that is unique and which proves the guilt of the Defendant without any other evidence. So far as we are aware that stage has not yet been reached.

The cogency of DNA evidence makes it particularly important that DNA testing is rigorously conducted so as to obviate the risk of error in the laboratory, that the method of DNA analysis and the basis of subsequent statistical calculation should – so far as possible – be transparent to the Defence and that the true import of the resultant conclusion is accurately and fairly explained to the jury.

R v Doheny establishes the procedure the prosecution should follow in respect of the disclosure and presentation of DNA evidence. The defence may call their own expert witness to challenge the validity of the opinion provided by the prosecution's expert witness. Issues of sample degeneration, cross-contamination and deliberate planting of samples by prosecuting authorities can significantly diminish the probative value of the DNA evidence. The ultimate evaluation of DNA evidence, as with other forensic opinion evidence, is a matter for the jury or magistrates.

A DNA database is presently maintained in England and Wales. Once a DNA profile has been developed it is put onto the database and checked against other profiles obtained from scenes of crime. Any matches between an arrested suspect and the crime scene or other crime scenes are communicated to the police. Currently, the database holds in excess of one million profiles and has been hugely successful. Before the enactment of section 82 of the Criminal Justice and Police Act 2001, a DNA profile had to be removed from the database where the suspect was not subsequently convicted of an offence in relation to which the sample was taken. As a result of section 82, a profile may now be retained even in cases where a defendant is subsequently acquitted of the offence for which he was charged. This change in the law, together with a broadening of the types of offence for which a sample may be taken is likely to see an increase in the samples currently held on the database. The techniques of analysing DNA have grown so sophisticated that it is now possible to extract a sample from a tiny droplet of blood and to yield a random occurrence ratio of a billion to one. In unsolved crimes dating back in some cases to 50 years where bloodstains and hair samples were retained in the hope of future technological advances, the technology of today has been used to provide a match with samples held on the database.

Addendum

Since writing this chapter, Paragraph 2 of Code D, regulating the conduct of identification procedures, has been revised with effect from 1 April 2002. As a result of its revision, video identification has been elevated to stand alongside the identification parade. Investigating officers now have a free choice as to which procedure to adopt in the first instance. The change is likely to result in far greater use of the video identification procedure, as it can often be undertaken sooner than an identification parade and is less intimidating for witnesses. The decision in *R* v *Forbes* [2001] AC 473 is fully embraced in revised Code D 2.15 which provides that a video identification or identification parade need not be held where it would serve no useful purpose. This would cover a case where the suspect is well known to the witness or where there is no reasonable possibility that a witness would be able to make identification. A group parade may now be offered in the first instance, where an investigating officer considers it more satisfactory than a video identification or identification parade (revised Code D 2.18).

Further reading

Alldridge, P., 'Forensic Science and Expert Evidence' (1994) 21 Journal of Law and Society 136.

Ashworth, P.B. (1998) *Psychology, Law and Eyewitness Testimony*, Wiley.

Balding, D.J. and Donnelly, P., 'The Prosecutor's Fallacy and DNA Evidence' [1994] Crim LR 711.

Cutler, B.L. and Penrod, S.D. (1995) *Mistaken Identification: The Eyewitness, Psychology and the Law*, Cambridge University Press.

Hain, P. (1976) *Mistaken Identity*, Quartet Books.

Loftus, E.F. (1979) *Eyewitness Testimony*, Harvard University Press.

O'Brien, D., 'When Is an Identification Parade Mandatory?' (2001) 5(2) E & P 127.

Ormerod, D., 'Sounds Familiar? Voice Identification' [2001] Crim LR 595.

Steventon, B. (1993) *The Ability to Challenge DNA Evidence*, Royal Commission on Criminal Justice Research Study No 9, HMSO.

Chapter 9

DISCLOSURE OF EVIDENCE

INTRODUCTION

Why, in an adversarial system of justice, where the ultimate aim is to win, is it necessary to have rules requiring the prosecution for the most part, and the defence to a lesser degree, to make pre-trial disclosure of evidence to each other? The answer, at least so far as prosecution disclosure is concerned, is succinctly expressed by Lord Justice Steyn in *R v Winston Brown* [1995] 1 Cr App R 191:

> The right of every accused to a fair trial is a basic and fundamental right. That means that under our unwritten constitution those rights are deserving of special protection by the courts. However, in our adversarial system, in which the police and prosecution control the investigatory process, an accused's right to fair disclosure is an inseparable part of his right to a fair trial...

The right of pre-trial disclosure of evidence is clearly enshrined in the European Convention on Human Rights as being a fundamental component of the right to a fair trial under Article 6(1). Article 6(3)(a) provides that everyone charged with a criminal offence has the right 'to be informed promptly, in a language which he understands and in detail, of the nature and cause of the accusation against him'. Article 6(3)(d) further provides the accused with a right to 'examine or have examined witnesses against him and to obtain the attendance and examination of witnesses on his behalf under the same conditions as witnesses against him'.

The failure of the prosecution to disclose evidence capable of assisting the defendant has been a striking feature in a series of miscarriages of justice, including the Guildford Four, Birmingham Six, the Bridgewater Three, Judith Ward (*R v Ward* [1993] 2 All ER 577) and Michelle and Lisa Taylor (*R v Taylor* (1998) 98 Cr App R 361). In the *Taylor* case, the defendants, who were sisters, were convicted of murder. One of the sisters had been having an affair with the deceased's husband. It was alleged that she had been consumed with jealousy and that the sisters, both white girls, had stabbed the victim to death. On appeal, it came to light that an investigative officer had failed to disclose to the prosecutor that an important eyewitness had initially given a statement in which he had said that one of the women he had seen was black. At trial, the witness gave evidence that he had observed two white women. Neither was it disclosed that this witness had received a reward for his information from the deceased's employers. This crucial omission, coupled with prejudicial pre-trial publicity, led to their convictions being quashed.

There are a number of justifications supporting the defendant's right of disclosure:

1 If the defendant is to answer the charges laid against him and mount an effective challenge to the prosecution's case, then in practical terms, knowledge of the strength or otherwise of the prosecution's case is essential.

2 Compared with the resources available to the defendant, the prosecution is in a far stronger position to unearth and investigate facts. Disclosure by the prosecution helps to reduce this imbalance. ·

3 Disclosure is a fundamental requirement of the proper administration of justice. If a court is to get at the truth then it must insist on the disclosure of all admissible evidence which is relevant to its inquiry.

4 The search for an objective truth within the adversarial system of factual inquiry is assisted by the imposition of positive obligations on the prosecution to make disclosure of its evidence which both assists and undermines its case. The Code for Crown Prosecutors requires CPS lawyers to 'always act in the interests of justice and not solely for the purposes of obtaining a conviction.' Disclosure of such evidence better assists the search for the truth and, at the same time, safeguards the integrity of the criminal trial. A recurrent concern on the part of senior police officers before the enactment of the Criminal Procedure and Investigations Act 1996 was that the interests of justice were not being served by the disclosure regime then in operation as the police were being expected to provide copious pre-trial disclosure of evidence of dubious relevance, with little or no reciprocation on the part of the defendant.

5 Expediency justifies the pre-trial disclosure of evidence. There are time-saving advantages in requiring pre-trial disclosure. On the basis of evidence disclosed, the defendant may be persuaded to plead guilty. Pre-trial disclosure enables more effective preparation for trial and greater clarification of the issues in contention. Consequently, it assists a more considered inquiry in that neither side is put on the spot by an unexpected turn of events.

The rules of evidence and procedure relating to disclosure temper some of the more unsatisfactory aspects of adversarialism, described in Chapter 4. They seek to ensure a measure of fairness between the trial protagonists. It is the duty of the court to ensure compliance with the rules relating to the pre-trial disclosure of evidence.

In criminal proceedings it is generally felt that fairness and the public interest in maintaining confidence in the administration of justice requires a jury or magistrates to hear and see all the relevant and admissible evidence in the case before them before determining an accused's guilt or innocence. Sometimes however, the prosecution or a third party in whose hands the information might lie will strenuously resist disclosing relevant material to the defendant because it is sensitive and would be damaging to the public interest were it released into the public domain. Where disclosure is opposed on this basis, the prosecution raises an issue of public interest immunity (PII). Whilst many aspects of disclosure are regulated by statute, the principles relating to PII remain governed by the common law.

PROCEDURAL CONTEXT OF DISCLOSURE

Disclosure is an area of law where rules of procedure have a direct evidential effect. To understand the evidential rules, it is necessary to consider the procedural context in which they are applied.

The entire process of disclosure has become unnecessarily complicated for a number of reasons:

1   The rules, some of which were created by statute, some of which were devised at common law, are not contained in one place.
2   Whilst some of the rules have the force of law, some do not and are more properly described as guidelines.
3   The application of the rules and guidelines differ depending on the classification of the offence being tried.

Critical to an understanding of the rules relating to disclosure is the differentiation that is made between 'used' and 'unused' material. These words are not defined in any statutory formulation of the rules but are convenient labels in what is a convoluted process.

'Used' material refers to evidence the prosecution intends to rely on at trial. 'Unused' material comprises evidence which the prosecution is aware of, but which will not form part of the prosecution's case against the accused at trial.

Depending on the classification of the offence to be tried (see Chapter 3), various rules require the prosecution to disclose its 'used' material at an early stage in the criminal litigation process.

Either way offences

The prosecution's responsibility to disclose 'used' material in offences triable either way is clear. Prior to the mode of trial hearing (the hearing which determines whether the case should be tried in the Crown Court or in the magistrates' court), the Magistrates' Court (Advance Information) Rules 1985 (SI 1985 No 601) require the CPS to have served on the defence either a summary of the prosecution case or copies of prosecution witness statements.

The rules on further disclosure of 'used' material will then depend on whether the case is to be tried summarily or on indictment at the Crown Court. Where the case is to be tried in the Crown Court, the prosecution is required to serve on the defendant a committal bundle prior to the case being committed to the Crown Court in accordance with rules laid down in the Magistrates' Courts Act 1980 and the Magistrates' Courts Rules 1981 (SI 1981 No 552). The committal bundle will comprise 'used' material, that is the substance of the evidence the prosecution intends to rely on at trial. It will be similar to advance information, but will be more detailed. Providing the examining justices conclude that the prosecution evidence discloses the defendant has a case to answer, the defendant will be committed to stand trial by jury in the Crown Court.

Where further evidence comes to light after committal to the Crown Court which the prosecution intends to place reliance on at trial, a notice of further evidence must be served on the defendant. This will usually take the form of service of a written statement under section 9 of the Criminal Justice Act 1967 (see Chapter 14). If the defendant objects to the admission of the written statement into evidence he must indicate his opposition to the prosecution.

Summary offences

In summary proceedings, the decision in *R v Stratford Justices, ex parte Imbert* [1999] 2 Cr App R 276 confirms there is no statutory requirement for the prosecution to disclose to the defence the evidence that it intends to use at the trial of a summary only offence. Somewhat controversially, the Divisional Court concluded that this state of affairs would not violate the defendant's right to a fair trial. Fairness had to be viewed in the context of the proceedings as a whole and, providing justices were mindful of this and granted adjournment time to enable instructions to be taken, the proceedings would be regarded as fair. The Divisional Court did however encourage the CPS as a matter of practice to make disclosure of the evidence it intended to rely on. Since this decision, paragraph 35 of the Attorney-General's guidelines on disclosure provide that it is good practice for the CPS to give disclosure of 'used' material to the defence in summary only cases.

Indictable only offences

In accordance with section 51 of the Crime and Disorder Act 1998, indictable only offences must be sent forthwith to the Crown Court for trial following the defendant's initial appearance before magistrates. The Crime and Disorder Act 1998 (Service of Prosecution Evidence) Regulations 2000 (SI 2000 No 3305) provide for the disclosure of 'used' material before the initial hearing in the Crown Court.

DISCLOSURE PROVISIONS RELATING TO 'UNUSED' MATERIAL

The disclosure of 'unused' material was regulated by the common law, but is now enacted in statutory form in the Criminal Procedure and Investigations Act 1996 (CPIA). The Attorney-General's guidelines on disclosure now supplement the provisions of the CPIA 1996.

The CPIA 1996 has gone some way to codifying certain aspects of the common law. To appreciate the full impact of the Act, it is necessary to consider the background relating to the disclosure of 'unused' material at common law, against which the CPIA 1996 was devised.

Disclosure of 'unused' material at common law

In the course of an investigation the police will often take a statement from a person who, if called as a witness, would assist the defence more than the prosecution. Whilst the prosecution will not want to undermine its case by calling that witness, the prosecution must not keep their existence a secret. This duty of disclosure in relation to 'unused' material at common law applied only to evidence that was deemed to be 'material'.

In the wake of high profile miscarriages of justice, the Court of Appeal in *R v Ward* [1993] 2 All ER 577, broadened the prosecution's obligation to make disclosure of 'unused' material. Lord Justice Glidewell stipulated that the defence should have the opportunity of considering all relevant evidence that the prosecution had gathered and from which it had made its own selection of evidence. The Court of Appeal determined the prosecution's disclosure obligations in relation to 'unused' material at common law as follows:

1 Where the prosecution has taken a statement from a person it knows can give material evidence, but who it decides not to call as a witness, the prosecution must make that person available as a witness to the defence. 'Material' means weakening the prosecution's case or strengthening the defence.
2 Copies of witness statements should be supplied or facilities made available for inspection and copy. If there are good reasons for not supplying copies, the witness's name and address must be supplied.
3 Subject to public interest immunity certificates, the defence must be supplied with copies of all statements made by the accused.
4 The Crown Court (Advance Notice of Expert Evidence) Rules 1987 (SI 1987 No 716) require disclosure of any finding or opinion on which the expert gives evidence and, if requested by the other party, copies of records, tests, etc on which the finding is based. This must include any tests tending to disprove an opinion of the expert.
5 If public interest immunity is claimed, notice of the assertion must be given so that the court can judge the issue. The prosecution cannot be a judge in its own cause on this matter.

In *R v Keane* [1994] 2 All ER 478, the Court of Appeal ultimately considered the test of materiality of evidence to be disclosed by the prosecution as being that which:

(a) was relevant or possibly relevant to an issue in the case; or
(b) raises or possibly raises a new issue whose existence is not apparent from the evidence the prosecution proposes to use; or
(c) holds out a real, as opposed to a fanciful, prospect of providing a lead on evidence which goes to (a) or (b).

Further, in *R v Brown* [1994] 1 WLR 1599 the Court of Appeal stated that the phrase, 'an issue in the case', must be interpreted broadly. It included material going beyond the actual issues in dispute and covered collateral matters such as the credibility of a prosecution witness.

Defence obligations to provide disclosure at common law

Prior to the CPIA 1996, the defendant had strictly limited pre-trial disclosure obligations. They consisted of giving notice of alibi in indictable cases (Criminal Justice Act 1967, section 11) and providing disclosure of expert evidence intended to be relied on at a trial on indictment (PACE, section 80). In addition, under section 9 of the Criminal Justice Act 1988, provision was made for a judge to direct disclosure of the substance of a defence in a serious fraud case.

Criticisms of the common law

A number of problems were identified in relation to disclosure of evidence at common law. Senior police officials openly criticised the disclosure obligation placed on the police as being too onerous. They were being deluged with requests for material and had no way of ascertaining its relevance in the absence of knowing what defence the accused might run at his trial. It was asserted that the greater willingness on the part of the courts to order disclosure of marginally relevant sensitive material was leading to the abandonment of many prosecutions including those for serious offences.

The troublesome issue of disclosure was examined by the Royal Commission on Criminal Justice 1993. Whilst supporting the continuance of the defendant's right to silence both at the police station and at trial, it recommended defendants should be made to disclose the substance of their defence prior to the trial. Such a change would ensure more effective preparation for trial, more efficient use of court time by clarifying and narrowing down the issues in dispute, and a reduction in the use of the ambush defence, whereby the defendant springs a defence on the prosecution at the last possible minute, giving the prosecution little time for a considered response.

The government's response was to enact the CPIA 1996. It codifies the law relating to the disclosure by the prosecution of 'unused' material and statutorily requires defendants in indictable cases to disclose the substance of their defence. The CPIA 1996 is said to adopt a stick and carrot approach to defence disclosure. The carrot is held out by limited 'primary prosecution disclosure' in the first instance. Further disclosure, 'secondary prosecution disclosure' is provided only where the nature of the accused's defence has been disclosed. The stick is provided in that an adverse evidential inference can be drawn against a defendant who fails to disclose the substance of his defence where this is a compulsory requirement, or raises a different defence at his trial.

The CPIA 1996 has no application to material obtained by the prosecution under the Regulation of Investigatory Powers Act 2000, which provides a separate statutory scheme regulating the admissibility of evidence obtained through the authorised interception of private mail and electronic-based communication systems, nor does it apply to information in the hands of third parties.

DISCLOSURE REGIME UNDER THE CRIMINAL PROCEDURE AND INVESTIGATIONS ACT 1996

The substantive provisions of the CPIA 1996 are supplemented by a detailed Code of Practice made under Part II of the Act. The Code recognises the fundamental importance of the role of the police in providing disclosure of evidence. It requires officers to behave with the utmost integrity.

The Code requires the recording and retention of all relevant information and material generated by an investigation. A disclosure officer has to be appointed to each investigation. It is the duty of the disclosure officer to examine material retained by the police during an investigation and to reveal it to the prosecutor. The disclosure officer may be a member of the investigative team. The requirement to record extends to all types of information, including evidence obtained during the investigation (searches of the person or his property), evidence generated by the investigation (incriminating admissions and no comment interviews, etc) and information received orally. The Code specifies the sort of relevant material which should be routinely retained in a criminal case. It includes:

- crime reports;
- custody records;
- records of telephone calls, ie 999 calls;
- final versions of witness statements (and draft versions where their content differs from the final version);
- interview records;
- forensic reports;
- any material casting doubt on the reliability of a confession;
- any material casting doubt on the reliability of a witness.

Disclosure schedules

Under the Code, material which is relevant to the investigation and which the disclosure officer thinks will not form part of the prosecution's case must be listed in a schedule of non-sensitive material. If the disclosure officer believes the material to be sensitive (see the discussion on public interest immunity below) it must be listed on a separate sensitive schedule. The schedules are then passed on to the Crown Prosecution Service. The schedules must be prepared in the following instances:

1 where the offence is indictable only,
2 it is an either way offence likely to be tried in the Crown Court, or
3 where the defendant is likely to plead not guilty to a matter which is to be tried summarily.

The material must be listed in the schedule with sufficient detail to enable the prosecutor to decide whether he needs to inspect it before a decision is made to disclose it to the defence. In addition to the listing of material, the disclosure officer must provide the prosecutor with a copy of any material which undermines the prosecution's case, including records of first description of a suspect and information relating to any explanation by the defendant for the offence charged. The schedules may need to be amended in the light of consideration of the evidence by a CPS lawyer.

The Code accompanying the CPIA 1996 is, by virtue of section 26, admissible in evidence where breach of its provisions is relevant to a question arising in the proceedings. The section further provides that a failure by the police to observe the Code will not however result in civil or criminal liability.

The prosecution's duties under the Act arise in two stages before the pre-trial stage. These are known as the prosecution's 'primary duty of disclosure' and the 'secondary duty of disclosure'. At the time when the prosecutor's duty to comply with its primary prosecution disclosure requirements arise under the Act, the defendant will already have received copies of 'used' material, comprising the evidence the prosecution intends to rely on at trial, be it a summary or indictable trial. The disclosure requirements for 'used' material were detailed earlier in this chapter.

PRIMARY PROSECUTION DISCLOSURE

Section 3(1) of the CPIA 1996 states:

(1) The prosecutor must—

(a) disclose to the accused any prosecution material which has not previously been disclosed to the accused and which in the prosecutor's opinion might undermine the case for the prosecution against the accused, or...

The test devised at common law requiring the disclosure of 'relevant' or 'possibly relevant' evidence is restricted under section 3 to a requirement that the prosecution disclose evidence that 'undermines' or 'might undermine' the prosecution's case. In the case of *R v Vasilou* [2000] Crim LR 845, the Court of Appeal felt this would include the disclosure of a prosecution witnesses' previous convictions.

The test the prosecutor must apply under section 3 is a subjective one. It is the responsibility of the prosecutor to decide what undermines the prosecution's case. In the Attorney-General's guidelines on disclosure, material which might potentially undermine the prosecution's case is defined as that which 'has an adverse effect on the strength of the prosecution's case'. The guidelines state that this will include:

36. ... anything that tends to show a fact inconsistent with the elements of the case that must be proved by the prosecution. Material can have an adverse effect on the strength of the prosecution case:
   (a) by the use made of it in cross-examination; and
   (b) by its capacity to suggest any potential submissions that could lead to:
      i. the exclusion of evidence;
      ii. a stay of proceedings;
      iii. a court or tribunal finding that any public authority had acted incompatibly with the defendant's rights under the ECHR.

37. In deciding what material might undermine the prosecution case, the prosecution should pay particular attention to material that has potential to weaken the prosecution case or is inconsistent with it. Examples are:
   i. Any material casting doubt upon the accuracy of any prosecution evidence.
   ii. Any material which may point to another person, whether charged or not (including a co-accused) having involvement in the commission of the offence.
   iii. Any material which may cast doubt upon the reliability of a confession.
   iv. Any material that might go to the credibility of a prosecution witness.
   v. Any material that might support a defence that is either raised by the defence or apparent from the prosecution papers. If the material might undermine the prosecution case it should be disclosed at this stage even though it suggests a defence inconsistent with or alternative to one already advanced by the accused or his solicitor.
   vi. Any material which may have a bearing on the admissibility of any prosecution evidence.

It should also be borne in mind that while items of material viewed in isolation may not be considered to potentially undermine the prosecution case, several items together can have that effect.

38. Experience suggests that any item which relates to the defendant' s mental or physical health, his intellectual capacity, or to any ill-treatment which the defendant may have suffered when in the investigator's custody is likely to have the potential for casting doubt on the reliability of an accused's purported confession, and prosecutors should pay particular attention to any such item in the possession of the prosecution.

Disclosure under section 3 of the CPIA 1996 is limited to information in the prosecutor's possession or which the prosecutor has inspected. The prosecutor's disclosure duty is thus entirely dependent on the efficiency and honesty of the disclosure officer who prepares the schedule provided to the prosecutor. Given the role of the police and the fact that the disclosure officer may be a member of the investigative team, it is questionable whether this individual can be regarded as being objective and independent. A number of criticisms of the current scheme were identified in the Criminal Courts Review Report. At paragraph 129 of Chapter 10 of the Report, Lord Justice Auld comments:

> All too often disclosure officers are late in providing schedules and material to prosecutors, leaving them little time for adequate review of the documents. Frequently the officers do not provide them with complete and accurate documentation to enable them adequately to review the schedules, or to make sound decisions as to disclosability. But even when the disclosure officer provides full, accurate and timely documentation, many prosecutors still do not have time to examine it properly to satisfy themselves of the officer's compliance and assessment as to disclosability. The seriousness of this inability is illustrated by the fact that when they do examine the material, they often disagree with the assessment of the disclosure officers.

The Criminal Courts Review Report identifies the onerous nature of the undertaking and the lack of adequate training of junior police officers as the principal cause of the failings under the current system.

If no primary prosecution disclosure is available, the CPS must provide a written statement to the defendant confirming this is the case. Along with primary prosecution disclosure, the CPS must also disclose a copy of the schedule of non-sensitive material prepared by the disclosure officer in the case.

Section 3(6) of the CPIA 1996 prevents the prosecution from disclosing information which the court, upon the prosecutor's application, concludes is not in the public interest to disclose.

Disclosure is made under the Act by providing the defendant with a copy of relevant material or by making arrangements for the material to be inspected.

DEFENCE DISCLOSURE

With regard to compulsory disclosure by the accused, section 5 of the CPIA 1996 provides:

(1) Subject to ... this section applies where—

    (a) ...
    (b) the prosecutor complies with section 3 or purports to comply with it.

    ...

(5) Where this section applies, the accused must give a defence statement to the court and the prosecutor.

(6) For the purposes of this section a defence statement is a written statement—

    (a) setting out in general terms the nature of the accused's defence,
    (b) indicating the matters on which he takes issue with the prosecution, and
    (c) setting out, in the case of each such matter, the reason why he takes issue with the
        prosecution.

(7) If the defence statement discloses an alibi the accused must give particulars of the alibi in the statement, including—

(a) the name and address of any witness the accused believes is able to give evidence
    in support of the alibi, if the name and address are known to the accused when the
    statement is given;
(b) any information in the accused's possession which might be of material assistance
    in finding any such witness, if his name or address is not known to the accused
    when the statement is given. ...

The defence has 14 days in which to file a defence statement, running from the date
on which the prosecution complies or purports to comply with its obligations under
section 3. The inclusion of the words 'purporting to comply' is worth highlighting. It
implies partial disclosure is enough to trigger the defence disclosure obligation under
section 5.

Submitting a defence statement is a compulsory requirement for all cases to be tried
on indictment. It is voluntary for cases to be tried in the magistrates' court (CPIA
1996, section 6). However, unless a defence statement is submitted in summary cases,
any available secondary prosecution disclosure will not be forthcoming, in accordance
with section 7 of the CPIA 1996.

Drafting a defence statement

Section 11 of the CPIA 1996 provides that where the accused:

- fails to give a defence statement (where this is compulsory),
- fails to serve a defence statement within the time limit,
- sets out inconsistent defences in the defence statement,
- puts forward at his trial a different defence than that set out in the statement,
- adduces evidence in support of alibi without having given particulars of the alibi, the
  court, or any other party (with the court's leave) may make such comment as appears
  appropriate and the court or jury may draw such inferences as appear proper in determining the defendant's guilt in connection with the offence for which he is being tried.

In practical terms, section 11 is very important. Whether a defence statement is
compulsory (indictable cases) or voluntary (summary cases), careful drafting is needed
to avoid comment and hence an adverse inference being drawn.

Under section 11(5), a person cannot be convicted on an adverse inference drawn
under section 11 alone. Section 11(3) gives the trial judge and magistrates discretion
as to whether comment is permissible and as a consequence whether an inference
might be drawn.

In choosing to permit comment, what must the court take into account? The defendant is entitled to put forward an explanation as to why an adverse inference should not
be drawn. Section 11(4) specifically requires a court to have regard to the defendant's justification where the defendant has set out inconsistent defences before making
or permitting comment. The nature of the inference drawn will therefore depend on
the nature of the omission under section 11 and the reasons for it. It may be that a different defence is put forward at trial because of a change in the prosecution's case from
that indicated in the service of committal papers. It must be assumed that in such an
instance no adverse comment would be made. There will thus be circumstances in
which comment and an adverse inference will not be drawn.

R v Wheeler [2001] 1 Cr App R 10

The defendant gave evidence at his trial inconsistent with his defence statement. At his trial he explained there had been a mistake in his defence statement. This was referred to in passing by the judge in his summing up. The Court of Appeal held the judge should have directed the jury to accept the mistake as a fact in this case. As the defendant' s credibility had been at the centre of the case the conviction had to be quashed. The Court of Appeal strongly suggested it should be standard practice for defence statements to be signed by the defendant personally and should not be served on the prosecution until defence solicitors are sure as to their accuracy.

The probable effect of an adverse inference drawn under section 11 will be to cast doubt on the defence an accused has raised. On its own, a section 11 inference cannot prove the defendant's guilt. Its evidential effect is similar to the adverse inference that may be drawn from a suspect's silence under the Criminal Justice and Public Order Act 1994, which is explained in some detail in Chapter 7.

Can the defence statement be put in evidence as part of the prosecution's case? The Attorney-General's guidelines on disclosure provide:

18. Prosecutors should not adduce evidence of the contents of a defence statement other than in the circumstances envisaged by section 11 of the Act or to rebut alibi evidence. Where evidence may be adduced in these circumstances, this can be done through cross-examination as well as through the introduction of evidence. There may be occasions when a defence statement points the prosecution to other lines of inquiry. Further investigation in these circumstances is possible and evidence obtained as a result of inquiring into a defence statement may be used as part of the prosecution case or to rebut the defence.

It would therefore seem that a defence statement can be put in evidence for the limited evidential purpose of proving inconsistencies in the nature of the defence or the particulars of an alibi and may be used for the purpose of pursuing further inquiries.

SECONDARY PROSECUTION DISCLOSURE

Section 7 of the CPIA 1996 provides:

(1) This section applies where the accused gives a defence statement under section 5 or 6.
(2) The prosecutor must—
    (a) disclose any prosecution material which has not previously been disclosed to the accused and which might be reasonably expected to assist the accused's defence as disclosed by the defence statement given under section 5 or 6...

After the accused has served the defence statement the prosecutor must make secondary disclosure of material that has not previously been disclosed and which might reasonably be expected to assist the accused's defence as disclosed in the defence statement. If there is no such material, the prosecution must provide written confirmation of this fact. The test in relation to secondary disclosure is objective when compared to the subjective test in support of primary prosecution disclosure.

Once a defence statement has been served the disclosure officer is required to look again at the retained 'unused' material to see what might assist the accused in putting forward the defence he has indicated in his defence statement. The prosecutor's judgment as to what amounts to material that might assist the accused's defence is largely determined by the police. Once again, it is highly questionable as to whether the police can be described as being best placed to decide what is of relevance to the accused's defence.

The accused is not entitled to inspect any of the items listed in the non-sensitive schedule that have not been disclosed as primary prosecution disclosure unless the defendant can show the material is likely to be of assistance to his defence, as articulated in his defence statement.

Paragraph 40 of the Attorney-General's guidelines on disclosure give examples of the sort of material that might reasonably be expected to be disclosed to the defence where it relates to the defence being put forward:

i. Those recorded scientific or scenes of crime findings retained by the investigator which:
   relate to the defendant; and
   are linked to the point at issue; and
   have not previously been disclosed.

ii. Where identification is or may be in issue, all previous descriptions of suspects, however recorded, together with all records of identification procedures in respect of the offence(s) and photographs of the accused taken by the investigator around the time of his arrest;

iii. Information that any prosecution witness has received, has been promised or has requested any payment or reward in connection with the case;

iv. Plans of crime scenes or video recordings made by investigators of crime scenes;

v. Names, within the knowledge of investigators, of individuals who may have relevant information and whom investigators do not intend to interview;

vi. Records which the investigator has made of information which may be relevant, provided by any individual (such information would include, but not be limited to, records of conversation and interviews with any such person).

Disclosure of video recordings or scientific findings by means of supplying copies may well involve delay or otherwise not be practicable or desirable, in which case the investigator should make reasonable arrangements for the video, recordings or scientific findings to be viewed by the defence.

Case scenario

Duncan's flat is raided by six police officers. At the time of the raid his flat is undergoing redecoration. In a wardrobe they find £25,000 in cash, a handgun, ammunition and a substantial quantity of heroin, all ill concealed. Duncan denies knowledge of the heroin, the gun or the ammunition. He admits the cash is his, but claims he secreted it away when facing bankruptcy proceedings. He is charged with several offences arising out of the search. Duncan claims two former business associates who have a grudge against him have set him up. He believes these two former associates have informed on him, and that the police knew full well what they would find at his flat and where they would find it. It transpires that three of the officers in the raid were formerly part of a disbanded Area Drugs Squad which had been subject to an extensive disciplinary investigation. No disciplinary proceedings were ever taken against the particular officers and they never faced any criminal charges arising out of the investigation. Duncan's solicitors seek disclosure of the inquiry's findings against the officers, statements making allegations against the officers collected as part of the inquiry and the transcripts of all trials in which the officers have given evidence where an acquittal resulted because their evidence was discredited.

Would the prosecution accede to such a request, and if not would a court order disclosure?

The facts in the above scenario are taken from the case of *R v Guney* [1998] 2 Cr App R 244. The trial judge refused the defendant's request for disclosure along the lines requested. The defendant was convicted and appealed to the Court of Appeal. The appeal was decided prior to the enactment of the Criminal Procedure and Investigations Act 1996. The relevant test for disclosure was therefore that devised in *R v Keane* (1994) 99 Cr App R 1, based on the materiality of the evidence. The Court of Appeal in *Guney* concluded that the defendant had tried to embark on a fishing expedition and that the trial judge had been right to refuse the request for such disclosure. The Court of Appeal observed:

> A justified claim that material in the possession of the prosecution is relevant in the sense explained in the authorities must be distinguished from a forensically manufactured opportunity for a general trawl through the prosecution papers, with the risk that the burden imposed on the prosecution will defeat the interest of justice by causing a discontinuance of the case where it otherwise should proceed. We anticipate that this risk will be significantly reduced in relation to those cases that are subject to the statutory regime established by the Criminal Procedure and Investigations Act 1996.

In terms of disclosure the Court of Appeal held that the defendant was entitled to be informed of any convictions and disciplinary findings against the police officers. Furthermore, the defendant was also entitled to the transcripts of any Court of Appeal decision involving them in which convictions had been quashed on the express basis of their misconduct or lack of veracity and also cases stopped or discontinued on the same basis. In the absence of any previous convictions or disciplinary finding against the officers, the disclosure sought in this case, against what the Court of Appeal described as a defence case 'involving veiled or implied allegations' against police officers which were to be 'explored', was not material in any way to the accused's defence. The outcome, it is contended, would have been no different under the provisions of the CPIA 1996.

PROSECUTOR'S CONTINUING DUTY

Section 9 of the CPIA 1996 provides that following primary disclosure, the prosecutor has a continuing duty to review whether any undisclosed material undermines the prosecution case, and following secondary disclosure, whether there is any undisclosed material which might reasonably be expected to assist the defence as disclosed in the accused's defence statement.

APPLYING FOR FURTHER DISCLOSURE

In accordance with section 8 of the CPIA 1996, the defendant may apply to the court for further disclosure where he is not satisfied that the prosecutor has complied with his obligations under section 7. The defendant can only make an application under section 8 where he has filed a defence statement in accordance with the requirements under section 5 or 6 of the Act. The defendant must prove to the court that he reasonably believes that there is prosecution material which may assist his defence. The defendant must be clear in his articulation and may not use a section 8 application as a 'fishing expedition'.

PRACTICAL STEPS – DISCLOSURE

The defence needs to be ever mindful of disclosure issues at all stages and should vigorously pursue legitimate requests for disclosure. A failure by the prosecution to disclose material falling within the definition of primary or secondary prosecution disclosure will give grounds for an appeal against conviction based on a material irregularity at trial although it does not guarantee a verdict being quashed. In *R v Craven* [2001] 2 Cr App R 181, the Court of Appeal held that, if on reviewing the withheld evidence it concluded that the defendant did not receive a fair trial, this will inevitably lead the Court of Appeal to the conclusion that the resulting conviction is unsafe and must therefore be quashed.

A failure by the police to seize or retain evidence which may be of relevance to the accused's defence can give rise to an application to have the proceedings stayed for an abuse of process. The availability of videotaped footage from CCTV has increased dramatically in recent years. In *R (Ebrahim) v Feltham Magistrates' Court, Mouat v Director of Public Prosecutions* [2001] 2 Cr App R 427, the Divisional Court heard two appeals. In the first appeal it was alleged that the police had failed to secure possibly relevant video footage of a particular incident captured on store security cameras, which might have been helpful to the accused. In the second appeal, it was contended that the police had wiped clear and subsequently re-used videotape of the defendant speeding having viewed the tape in the presence of the defendant. The Divisional Court held that a stay could only be ordered where the behaviour of the police had been so very bad that it would be unfair to try the accused. Relevant factors in assessing fairness would include: the extent to which the accused's defence was dependent on the existence or production of video evidence, whether the defendant chose to put forward his account of the incident, the ability to cross-examine the police officer who should have secured or preserved the evidence and the presence or otherwise of bad faith on the part of the police. The abuse of process doctrine is considered in more detail in Chapter 5.

In the light of the provisions in section 11 of the CPIA 1996, great care needs to be taken when drafting a defence statement if an adverse evidential inference is to be avoided. Solicitors must avoid putting forward inconsistent defences so there is a need to ensure the defendant's instructions will not change, or that the trial advocate will adopt a different approach. Disclosing an accused's defence has implications for lawyer–client confidentiality. Legal advisers should try to ensure their client's instructions are completely accurate, that full advice has been given to the defendant regarding the statement and that the defendant is asked to check and sign the statement.

A tactical judgment has to be made as to how much information the defence statement should contain. The more detail it contains the easier it is to facilitate more secondary disclosure and there will be less risk of an adverse inference being drawn from non-disclosure. Greater detailed disclosure does however undoubtedly assist the prosecution in that it discloses lines of intended cross-examination. It is doubtful that simply stating 'self-defence', 'no dishonest intent' or 'mistaken identity' would be sufficient to avoid an adverse inference under section 11.

Assistance is given to defence practitioners in the Attorney-General's guidelines on disclosure:

> 27. A defence statement should set out the nature of the defence, the matters on which issue is taken and the reasons for taking issue. A comprehensive defence statement assists

the participants in the trial to ensure that it is fair. It provides information that the prosecutor needs to identify any remaining material that falls to be disclosed at the secondary stage. The more detail a defence statement contains the more likely it is that the prosecutor will make a properly informed decision about whether any remaining material might assist the defence case, or whether to advise the investigator to undertake further inquiries. It also helps in the management of the trial by narrowing down and focussing the issues in dispute. It may result in the prosecution discontinuing the case. Defence practitioners should be aware of these considerations in advising their clients.

28. Defence solicitors should ensure that statements are agreed by the accused before being served. Wherever possible, the accused should sign the defence statement to evidence his or her agreement.

In the case of summary trials, the submission of a defence statement is entirely voluntary. Why then in an adversarial system would a defendant choose to reveal the substance of his defence? The answer comes down once again to tactics. The legal adviser knows secondary disclosure is not going to be made available if a defence statement is not served. The adviser therefore has to consider carefully the disclosure schedule when served with any primary prosecution evidence to ascertain whether it might contain material falling within the definition of secondary prosecution disclosure. If he thinks it a possibility, serving a defence statement is a pre-requisite to obtaining the information.

SEEKING DISCLOSURE OF INFORMATION HELD BY THIRD PARTIES

There is no duty on the prosecution either at common law or under the CPIA 1996 to obtain relevant material that may be in the hands of third parties. Sometimes the third party will provide information relevant to an investigation. When third party material comes into the possession of the police disclosure obligations under the CPIA 1996 will apply. The Attorney-General's guidelines on disclosure exhort the prosecution to seek access to information or material held by third parties (a local authority, a social services department, a hospital, a doctor, a school, providers of forensic services) which would be disclosable if held by the prosecution. If the third party refuses voluntarily to make disclosure of the information sought, the prosecution must pursue the matter and, if it is considered reasonable, a witness summons for disclosure should be sought. In the Crown Court application would be made under section 2 of the Criminal Procedure (Attendance of Witnesses) Act 1965, as amended by section 66 of the CPIA 1996, and in the magistrates' court under section 97 of the Magistrates' Courts Act 1980. The applicant must establish that the third party holds or can give evidence that is likely to be material. The wording is explicit in both sections.

Where the defendant seeks disclosure of information held by a third party, who refuses voluntary disclosure, the defendant must apply for a witness summons in the same way. The principles governing the court's decision in this regard were developed in R v Reading Justices, ex parte Berkshire County Council [1996] 1 Cr App R 239. This case concerned an application by a defendant for a witness summons under section 97 of the Magistrates' Courts Act 1980. The principles it establishes are equally applicable to applications heard before the Crown Court:

1   to be material evidence documents must be not only relevant to the issues arising
    in the criminal proceedings, but also documents admissible as such in evidence;
2   documents which are desired merely for the purpose of possible cross-examination are
    not admissible in evidence and, thus, are not material for the purposes of section 97;
3   whoever seeks production of documents must satisfy the justices with some mate-
    rial that the documents are 'likely to be material' in the sense indicated – 'likely' for
    this purpose involves a real possibility, although not necessarily a probability;
4   it is not sufficient that the applicant merely wants to find out whether or not the
    third party has such material documents. This procedure must not be used as a dis-
    guised attempt to obtain discovery.

Thus a defendant may not use an application under section 97 or section 2 in the speculative hope of it yielding useful material for use in cross-examination. Whether the
prosecution or the defence makes the request for disclosure, the third party may resist
the request on the basis of public interest immunity. The final decision in this regard
will be that of the relevant court. A recent illustration of a case involving a request for
disclosure in the hands of a third party, asserting a public interest immunity claim, is
R v Brushett [2001] Crim LR 471, considered later in this chapter.

CRIMINAL COURTS REVIEW REPORT – RECOMMENDATIONS

The Criminal Courts Review Report by Lord Justice Auld makes a number of sensible
proposals for reform of the law relating to the pre-trial disclosure in criminal cases. The
proposals are contained in Chapter 10 of the Report. Under them, the mutual disclosure
scheme established by the CPIA 1996 would remain but would be subject to a number
of reforms including a comprehensive single set of rules to ensure clarity and certainty in
the application of the law relating to the disclosure of evidence. The prosecution would
be obliged to provide disclosure in sufficient time to enable the defence adequately to
prepare for trial. The same test of 'disclosability' for both stages of prosecution disclosure is recommended which could include the disclosure of 'material which, in the
prosecutor's opinion, might reasonably affect the determination of any issue in the case
of which he knows or should reasonably expect'. Whilst the police would retain responsibility for collating and recording any material gathered or inspected in the course of the
investigation, one important change would be the removal of their responsibility for
identifying potentially disclosable material to the prosecution. The ultimate responsibility for complete disclosure would reside with the prosecutor. The requirement to provide
a defence statement would remain, with defence practitioners being exhorted to make
more effective use of them as part of the general aim to facilitate more efficient and effective preparation for trial. Finally, Lord Justice Auld recommends consideration is given
to the creation of a new statutory scheme for third party disclosure to operate alongside
and more consistently with the general provisions for disclosure of unused material.

The entire process of disclosure has recently been the subject of research commissioned by the Home Office. The Home Office's report, *A Fair Balance? Evaluation of
the Operation of Disclosure Law*, concludes that poor practice in relation to disclosure is widespread and that there is a systemic failure on the part of the police to
prepare disclosure schedules properly and to identify relevant material. Furthermore,

widespread dissatisfaction exists amongst the judiciary as regards the operation of the CPIA 1996, exemplified in the judiciary's considerable reluctance to deny the defence access to unused material. Overall, the report concludes that there is a crisis of trust in the system and an acute lack of consensus amongst all the key players on the principles that underpin the operation of the CPIA 1996. The recommendations in the report include better training and more resources, closer working practices between the police and the CPS and a judicial Practice Direction clarifying the scope of judicial case management in respect of disclosure. It is widely anticipated that the research and recommendations of the Home Office and the recommendations of Lord Justice Auld, who was made aware of the Home Office findings, will form the basis of future legislative reform in this area.

PUBLIC INTEREST IMMUNITY

Under section 21(2) of the CPIA 1996, the prosecution's duty of disclosure at both the primary and the secondary stage is subject to the rules of public interest immunity.

The CPIA 1996 does not change the common law rules which determine both the procedure by which public interest claims are conducted and the principles by which they are determined. At common law, where the prosecutor believes 'used' or 'unused' material should be withheld on the basis of public interest immunity, an application must be made to the court. Only a court can sanction the prosecutor's view that it would not be in the public interest for the material to be disclosed to the defendant. Where an accused applies for disclosure under section 8 of the CPIA 1996, section 8(5) provides the court with the power not to order disclosure where it would be contrary to the public interest.

Material which can be withheld in the public interest

The public interest in the proper administration of justice which demands the disclosure of all relevant information for a court's consideration sometimes conflicts with the need to withhold information in the public interest. Where disclosure would be damaging to the public interest, the issue of public interest immunity arises. Where a claim for public interest immunity is upheld, a witness may not be asked and the prosecution or possibly a third party will not be ordered to disclose the relevant information.

Evidence covered by the phrase 'public interest' will include: documents and other material relating to national security; confidential information; the identity of police informants and undercover police officers; details of premises used for police surveillance; and information pertaining to the welfare of children.

The Code of Practice issued under the CPIA 1996 requires the disclosure officer to list sensitive information on a separate 'sensitive schedule', which is disclosed to the prosecution only. 'Sensitive' material comprises any material which the disclosure officer believes it is not in the public interest to disclose.

The Code gives examples of 'sensitive' material such as:

* information relating to national security,
* information given in confidence,

- information relating to the identity of police informants,
- information revealing the location of property used by the police for surveillance,
- information relating to the welfare of young people used by a local authority social services department.

The CPIA 1996 creates procedures (section 14 in relation to indictable trials and section 15 in relation to summary trials) for reviewing court orders to withhold material in the public interest and provides a means by which a third party can intervene where there has been a request for material held by a third party that the third party considers it would not be in the public interest to disclose. In the Crown Court, the judge must keep his decision to withhold material from the defence under constant review.

Principles governing public interest immunity claims in criminal cases

Many of the key developments in the law relating to public interest immunity have been made in civil cases, and are considered in greater detail in Chapter 26.

There are, however, two fundamental points that should be made in relation to public interest immunity claims in criminal cases at the outset. First, it is for the court and not the prosecutor or a minister of the Crown to decide whether it is contrary to the public interest for relevant information to be disclosed. Secondly, contrary to the position in civil proceedings, in a criminal case the judge has a mandatory obligation to inspect the material over which immunity from disclosure is claimed.

A brief history – Crown privilege to public interest immunity

In the older and predominantly civil cases, the term public interest immunity is referred to as 'Crown privilege'. A number of these cases concerned requests for disclosure of material held by government departments. Such documents can of course have implications for national security and can disclose government policy on a particular matter. In such instances, the relevant minister would routinely sign a certificate objecting to disclosure on the ground of Crown privilege or public interest immunity, as it is now known. Such a certificate sets out the details of the documents in question; the reason for claiming public interest immunity and the damage disclosure is likely to cause. Objection to disclosure of information could then and can still be made on a class or contents basis. In relation to a claim for class immunity, the certificate will oppose the disclosure of documents on the basis that they belong to a class of documents, the disclosure of which would be damaging to the public interest. A contents claim is based on the information contained in an individual document whose disclosure is not in the public interest. An application under both grounds is possible, as they are not mutually exclusive.

In the leading civil authorities of *Conway v Rimmer* [1968] AC 910 and *Burmah Oil Co Ltd v Bank of England* [1979] 3 All ER 700, the House of Lords held it was for a court to decide whether the public interest in non-disclosure outweighed the public interest in the proper administration of justice. Furthermore, a court did not have to accept without question a minister's certificate and was entitled to look behind it, irrespective of whether objection was taken on a class or contents claim. If necessary a court could inspect the documents in question in order to conduct a balancing exercise. In the criminal case of *R v Ward* [1993] 1 WLR 619, the Court of Appeal concluded the principles developed in civil cases should apply equally to criminal cases. As a consequence, where the prosecution objects to the disclosure of relevant material, the actual decision to withhold the material can only be made by the court. If the court comes down in favour of disclosure (ie to disclose the identity of an informer), the prosecution is faced with a choice: either to make disclosure or to abandon the prosecution.

Ministerial certificates are relatively unusual in criminal cases. Most requests for disclosure relate to the identity of informants. Objections to such disclosure are often made by chief constables on the class/contents basis that to disclose such information would undermine the fight against crime and effective policing. It is argued that such information may not be forthcoming if informers thought their identities would be made public.

Although ministerial certificates are rare in criminal cases, a good example of a case involving their use which has had far-reaching consequences for public interest immunity claims by government ministers is provided by the Matrix Churchill affair. Matrix Churchill and Ordtec were manufacturing companies under investigation by HM Customs and Excise. In the case of the directors of Ordtec, it was alleged they had deceived the Department of Trade and Industry into granting them a licence to export components. The goods were exported to Iraq whilst the licence had in fact been applied for on the basis that the exports would be going to Jordan. The defendants pleaded guilty and were given custodial sentences. It had been contended that the government knew the real destination of the exports and were in effect turning a blind eye. The defendants were forced to plead guilty since they were prevented from gaining access to material held by government departments which they said would have substantiated their defence that the government was complicit. The requests for disclosure had been blocked by the issue of public interest immunity certificates. The defendants appealed against their convictions on the basis of non-disclosure of relevant evidence. Reviewing the material, the Court of Appeal concluded it should have been disclosed.

The impression given was that the government of the day had been prepared to see innocent men go to prison on the grounds of political expediency given the government's hostile relationship with Iraq at the time. In fact the advice not to disclose had been given by the Attorney-General, who felt it was the relevant minister's duty to assert public interest immunity, notwithstanding that the information might have proved the innocence of the defendants.

The political fallout from this case led to the setting up of the Scott Inquiry and the publication of the Scott Report (see Further reading below).

One of the recommendations in the Scott Report, which has since been adopted by the government, is that government ministers may no longer assert public interest immunity on a class basis regardless of the content of particular documents. Ministers are now required to take account of the administration of justice in reaching a decision to object to disclosure. If the minister concludes the administration of justice is outweighed by the damage disclosure would cause, only then may he sign a certificate withholding the material. The ultimate question of disclosure then becomes a matter for the court.

To all intents and purposes, the distinction between a class claim and a contents claim in criminal proceedings has become obsolete. The changes advocated in the Scott Report are in line with the general prosecution practice of claiming public interest immunity as laid down by the House of Lords' decision in R v *Chief Constable of the West Midlands Police, ex parte Wiley* [1994] 3 All ER 420. Contrary to the views expressed in *Makanjuola* v *Commissioner of Police of the Metropolis* [1992] 3 All ER 617, holders of sensitive information must no longer feel obligated to assert public interest immunity merely because documents happen to fall within a recognised class of documents which have traditionally been withheld. The House of Lords concluded that holders of the sensitive information must conduct an initial balancing exercise to consider whether voluntary disclosure should in fact be given. The test to be satisfied is whether the disclosure of the evidence would cause real harm to the public interest. Only where the prosecution concludes that the damage to the public interest would exceed the damage caused to the administration of justice would the matter need to be referred to the court for it to make the final decision. The Attorney-General's guide-lines on disclosure currently adopt this approach:

> 41. Before making an application to the court to withhold material which would other-wise fall to be disclosed, on the basis that to disclose would not be in the public interest, a prosecutor should aim to disclose as much of the material as he properly can (by giving the defence redacted or edited copies of summaries).

Principles by which prosecution public interest immunity claims are determined in criminal cases

Whilst the principles of public interest immunity are common to both civil and crimi-nal cases, their application differs in criminal cases. In civil cases, the judge must bal-ance the likely injury to the public interest occasioned by disclosure, as against the public interest in the proper administration of justice requiring disclosure of all relevant information. In a criminal case, the overriding principle which governs a judge's or mag-istrates' decision about whether to order disclosure, is based on ensuring an innocent defendant is not convicted. This principle is derived from the judgment of Lord Taylor CJ in R v *Keane* below (a case concerning the identity of a police informant):

> If the disputed material may prove the accused's innocence or avoid a miscarriage of jus-tice, then the balance comes down resoundingly in favour of disclosing it.

In essence, if disclosure would avoid a miscarriage of justice, there is no balancing act to be undertaken. Disclosure must be ordered. If the prosecution refuses to disclose, it must decide whether to abandon its prosecution.

R v Keane (1994) 99 Cr App R 1

The defendant was convicted of having counterfeit currency in his possession. He had been arrested in a car in which S, the car's owner, and D were both passengers. Counterfeit notes and materials for their manufacture were found inside the car. The prosecution alleged the accused had been seen handling an envelope in which there were a number of negatives. The accused admitted to having picked up the package but said he had not looked in it and denied any knowledge of the cur-rency. He claimed he had been 'fitted up'. His counsel asked the police in cross-examination from what source they had derived their information. The trial judge ruled they did not have to answer. The defendant was convicted and appealed. His conviction was upheld.

The Court of Appeal did not consider the disclosure sought in this case would prove the defendant's innocence or avoid a miscarriage of justice. Judges had to scrutinise applications for the disclosure of sensitive information with 'great care' and 'adopt a robust approach in declining to order disclosure'. Lord Taylor CJ went on to observe that the fuller and more specific the indications given by the defence of an issue likely to be raised, the more accurately the judge and the prosecution are able to assess the value of the material to the accused.

In *R v Keane* there was a clear public interest in favour of non-disclosure and the material, had it been disclosed, would not have assisted the defendant.

The principles governing disclosure of sensitive information in criminal cases were restated in *R v Brown (Winston)* [1994] 1 WLR 1599 by the Court of Appeal as follows:

1   It was for the court to rule on the question of exclusion on public policy grounds and that necessarily involved the judge studying the material for which non-disclosure was advocated.
2   A balancing exercise had to be performed by the judge, taking into account both the public interest and the interest of the accused.
3   'If the disputed material may prove the accused's innocence or avoid a miscarriage of justice', as stated by Lord Taylor CJ in *R v Keane*, 'then the balance comes down resoundingly in favour of disclosing it.'
4   Even if initially the trial judge decides against disclosure, he is under a continuous duty, in the light of the way in which the trial develops, to keep that original decision under review. Prosecuting counsel must be appraised of the contents of any disputed material, so that he may invite the judge to re-assess the situation if the previous exclusion of the material arguably becomes untenable in the light of developments in the criminal proceedings.

Whilst the categories of matters that may give rise to a claim of public interest immunity are never closed the following grounds are most commonly cited in applications not to disclose evidence in criminal cases:

Information relating to criminal investigations

The protection of information and evidence obtained by the police and other law enforcement agencies such as HM Customs and Excise is a growing area in the development of the law of public interest immunity. This is reflected in consistent judicial reasoning about the clear public interest in protecting the anonymity of police informers. In the civil case of *Marks v Breyfus* (1890) 25 QBD 494 the plaintiff in an action for malicious prosecution had called the Director of Public Prosecutions as a witness to ascertain the information on which the DPP had acted in ordering the criminal prosecution of the plaintiff. The Court of Appeal held that the trial judge had been correct in not allowing the disclosure of the informants' names and the nature of their information.

There are a number of circumstances where the courts are prepared to relax the strict application of these rules. The identity of an informer will be revealed where the accused has a defence that would be assisted by the disclosure of the informer's name, in accordance with the principles laid down in *R v Keane*.

Case scenario

Martin is arrested in connection with a robbery at a corner shop involving the use of a gun. There are several eyewitness descriptions of the robber but none are able to make a positive identification. As a result of a tip-off, the police recover clothing and a gun near to the scene of the crime. Martin is arrested a week later. He denies involvement in the robbery, putting forward an alibi in his defence. He accepts the clothes found near the scene belong to him but that they had been discarded and placed in a bag in his shed. During his interview with the police, Martin maintains he is the victim of a 'set-up' but chooses not to elaborate further. Martin explains to his solicitor in confidence that on the day of the robbery he met an old acquaintance Mitch who wanted to put the 'frighteners' on a man he believed was having an affair with his girlfriend. Martin agreed to purchase Mitch a second-hand gun. He also lent him the clothes discovered by the police, as he considered Mitch's attire would make him too conspicuous. Martin claims he was too scared to mention Mitch in his interview with the police.

On these facts would the defence seek disclosure of the informer's identity? If it did, the prosecution would most likely oppose the request on the ground of public interest immunity, that is the need to protect the identity of those who inform on criminals and their activities. Would the court order disclosure in accordance with the principles recounted above?

The above scenario is in fact taken from the Court of Appeal's decision in *R v Turner* [1995] 3 All ER 432. The trial judge refused to order disclosure and the defendant was convicted. On appeal the Court of Appeal endorsed the view expressed in *R v Keane* that applications for disclosure of details about informants should be scrutinised with great care, and observed:

> Since *R v Ward* there has been an increasing tendency for defendants to seek disclosure of informants' names and role, alleging that those details are essential to the defence. Defences that the accused has been set up and allegations of duress, which used to be rare, have multiplied. We wish to alert judges to the need to scrutinise applications for disclosure of details about informants with very great care. They will need to be astute to see that assertions of a need to know such details, because they are essential to the running of the defence, are justified. If they are not so justified, then the judge will need to adopt a robust approach in declining to order disclosure. Clearly there is a distinction between cases in which the circumstances raise no reasonable possibility that information about the informant will bear upon the issues and cases where it will. Again, there will be cases where the informant is an informant and no more; other cases where he may have participated in the events constituting, surrounding, or following the crime. Even when the informant has participated, the judge will need to consider whether his role so impinges on an issue to the defence, present or potential, as to make discovery necessary...

Applying the principles of *R v Keane* to the facts in the case, the Court of Appeal concluded disclosure should have been made. Lord Taylor CJ observed:

> It is sufficient for us to say that in this case, we are satisfied that the information concerning the informant showed a participation in the events concerning this crime, which coupled with the way in which the defence was raised from the very first moment by the defendant when he said that he was being set up, gave rise to the need for the defendant to be aware of the identity of the informant and his role in this matter.

A further illustration of the way in which the *Keane* principles are applied is provided in the following case:

R *v* Agar (1990) 90 Cr App R 318

The defendant had been convicted of the possession of drugs with intent to supply. At his trial he alleged he had been set up. The defendant had received a telephone call from X requesting him to come round to X's flat and to bring some videos with him. X paid the defendant's taxi fare. When the defendant arrived at X's flat, it was in the process of a drugs raid by the police. The police alleged the defendant ran away from X's flat when he saw the presence of police officers and was observed to discard a package containing drugs. The defendant denied this. He contended the police had already been at X's flat when X made the telephone call asking him to come round. When he turned up without any drugs, the police planted a quantity on him. X was already subject to a suspended prison sentence for drug dealing and had recently been re-arrested. X was therefore most keen to assist the police by naming his supplier. At his trial, the defendant's counsel asked a police officer in cross-examination whether X had been his informer. The trial judge ruled the officer did not have to answer the question and elicited an undertaking from defence counsel not to pursue such a line of inquiry with any other officer on the grounds of public interest immunity.

The defendant was convicted and subsequently appealed to the Court of Appeal. Quashing the conviction, the Court of Appeal concluded it was not wholly impossible that the jury might, by effective cross-examination of the police officers, be induced to feel some doubt about the defendant's guilt:

> The question as we see it is whether in the particular circumstances of this trial it would have been possible, with a reasonable degree of ingenuity, to have put the defendant's case to the officers without, as an integral part of the exercise, inquiring of the officers whether it was true that they had got their information from X. We do not see how this could be done. By adhering to the ruling counsel was forced to emasculate his client's attack upon the police. Now it is certainly not the case that a defendant can circumvent the rule of public policy so as to find out the name of the person who informed on him, for his own future reference and possible reprisal, simply by pretending that something is part of his case, when in truth it adds nothing to it. And it may be – and we emphasise 'may' – that if the defence is manifestly frivolous and doomed to failure the trial judge may conclude that it must be sacrificed to the general public interest in the protection of informers. We do not see the present case in this light. There was a strong ... overwhelming public interest in keeping secret the source of the information; but as the authorities now show, there is an even stronger public interest in allowing a defendant to put forward a tenable case in its best light. We venture to think that the learned judge lost sight of this countervailing factor. (*per* Lord Justice Mustill)

Public interest immunity will also be used to protect the identity of a person who has allowed his premises to be used for police observation.

R *v* Rankine (1986) 83 Cr App R 18

The accused was charged with supplying prohibited drugs. Crucial prosecution evidence related to observations made by two police officers who used a private house as a surveillance post and who saw the accused sell cannabis on ten occasions in one hour. The trial judge ruled that the precise location of the surveillance post should be withheld on the ground of public interest immunity. The defendant was convicted.

On appeal, the Court of Appeal upheld the trial judge's ruling, stating that to reveal the identity of the people who had allowed their premises to be used for the police surveillance would hinder their public duty of detecting crime as that property could not be used again for surveillance and the fear of vengeance being exacted by the offenders would deter members of the public from allowing such use to be made of their property.

Information relating to children

Documents and records containing confidential material and sensitive information relating to children's welfare held by social services departments and private organisations operating in the public sphere such as the NSPCC will be protected from disclosure by public interest immunity. However, if disclosure would help to avoid a miscarriage of justice, it will be ordered.

R v Brushett [2001] Crim LR 471

The defendant, a headmaster of a community school for children in care, was convicted of several offences of rape, buggery and indecent assault on children in his care between the years of 1974 and 1980. Protesting his innocence at his trial, the defendant sought disclosure of information held on social service files relating to a number of the complainants, most of whom had extensive criminal records. Social services opposed the summons for disclosure on the grounds of public interest immunity.

The trial judge faced a dilemma as to whether he should apply the principles in *R v Keane* given that the information lay in the hands of a third party, or the more restrictive principles laid down in the decision of *R v Reading Justices, ex parte Berkshire County Council* (see above). It will be recalled that the *Reading Justices* case seeks to prevent a defendant undertaking a fishing expedition in relation to third party material in the hope of finding information which can then be used to attack the credibility of prosecution witnesses.

The trial judge decided that he would apply the principles in the *Reading Justices* case, but would not be bound by them where to do so would contribute to a miscarriage of justice. Inspecting a substantial quantity of material held by social services, he ruled he would disclose any material which showed that any of the complainants or prosecution witnesses had made false accusations of sexual misconduct in the past, or that they might have engaged in sexual acts with other adults at the relevant time. In the trial judge's view, this resulted in the defendant being entitled to more disclosure than the principles of *Reading Justices* would permit.

Affirming the conviction, the Court of Appeal endorsed the balancing exercise undertaken by the trial judge, concluding that the judge had been correct in his ruling. A failure to make available material, which would have substantially undermined the credibility of prosecution witnesses, would have deprived the defendant of the opportunity to cross-examine effectively such witnesses on matters relevant to his innocence.

Procedure for asserting public interest immunity

The procedure governing the resolution of public interest immunity claims is contained in the Crown Court (Criminal Procedure and Investigations Act 1996) (Disclosure) Rules 1997 (SI 1997 No 698) and in the Magistrates' Courts (Criminal Procedure and Investigations Act 1996) (Disclosure) Rules 1997 (SI 1997 No 703). The statutory rules encompass the rules devised at common law, in the Court of Appeal's decision in *R v Davis, Johnson and Rowe* [1993] 1 WLR 613.

In most cases the prosecution is required to notify the defence that it is applying to the court for a ruling and to indicate the type of material over which the immunity is claimed. This is known as an *inter partes* application. The defence will be given an opportunity to make representations to the court that the material should be disclosed as it is relevant and important to the accused's defence. On the basis of each party's submissions, the nature of the case and the nature and significance of the evidence over which public interest immunity is being claimed, the judge will decide the issue.

In some cases it may not be in the public interest for the prosecution to reveal the category of the material to be disclosed. In these circumstances, the prosecution will notify the defence that an application has been made but will not reveal the category of the material that is the subject of the application. The application will then be made to the court and the initial hearing will be made on an *ex parte* basis without the defence attending. The judge will first consider whether the defence should be informed and have the opportunity of making representations. Where this decision is reached, an *inter partes* hearing will be held. Exceptionally, due to the highly sensitive nature of the material and the need to preserve secrecy, the prosecution will not inform the defence of its application at all. The judge may then order an *inter partes* hearing or take the decision on the evidence before him.

Two final points should be noted about the procedure at an *ex parte* application. First, there is a general presumption against the use of *ex parte* applications. In *R* v *Keane*, Lord Taylor CJ warned that *ex parte* applications were contrary to the general principles of open justice. As a result of the implementation of the Human Rights Act 1998 this principle has assumed greater force in protecting the accused's right to a fair trial under Article 6. Secondly, where an *ex parte* hearing is held, an *ad verbatim* record of the proceedings should be kept to enable the defence to appeal where it is considered appropriate.

HUMAN RIGHTS LAW

Article 6(3)(b) guarantees that everyone charged with a criminal offence has the right to be informed promptly, in a language which he understands and in detail, of the nature and cause of the accusation against him.

Article 6(3)(d) further guarantees an accused the right to examine or have examined witnesses against him and to obtain the attendance and examination of witnesses on his behalf under the same conditions as witnesses against him.

Both rights are important, specific aspects of the general right to a fair trial under Article 6. In *Edwards* v *United Kingdom* (1992) 15 EHRR 417, the European Court of Human Rights concluded that fairness necessitated disclosure to the defendant of all material evidence for or against the accused. However, on a number of occasions the Court has recognised that other competing public interests sometimes militate against the disclosure of evidence. Witnesses who wish to remain anonymous because they fear reprisals in the event of their identities being revealed have a right to life, liberty and security under Article 2 and a right to privacy under Article 8. The competing right of the defendant under Article 6 calls for a careful balancing exercise. In *Doorson* v *Netherlands* (1996) 22 EHRR 330, the Court observed:

> It is true that Article 6 does not explicitly require the interest of witnesses in general, and those of victims called upon to testify in particular, to be taken into consideration. However, their life, liberty or security of person may be at stake, as may interests coming generally within the ambit of Article 8 of the Convention. Such interests of witnesses and victims are in principle protected by other substantive provisions of the Convention, which imply that Contracting States should organise their criminal proceedings in such a way that

those interests are not unjustifiably imperilled. Against this background, principles of fair trial also require that in appropriate cases the interests of the defence are balanced against those of witnesses or victims called upon to testify.

Recognising the inevitable handicap the defence must labour under in these circumstances, the Court stressed the importance of providing counterbalancing measures, for example, prior judicial investigation of the whole matter.

The issue of disclosure was again raised before the European Court of Human Rights in *Rowe and Davis* v *United Kingdom* (2000) 30 EHRR 1. The applicants had been convicted of a brutal murder and a number of violent robberies in 1990, all of which occurred on the same night. The convictions occurred before the decisions in *R v Ward* and *R v Keane* and prior to the enactment of the CPIA 1996. The applicants and a third convicted perpetrator (Johnson) were all black. Three masked men had carried out the robberies. None of the victims had been able to identify the defendants but one did give evidence that he thought one of the men might have been white. Three white men (known as the 'Jobbins Group'), who all had criminal records, lived in flats very close to the applicants and were known to them. They admitted to having supplied a stolen vehicle used in one of the robberies.

Acting on information received, the police searched premises belonging to the applicants and found various items from the robberies in their possession. Considerable reliance had been placed by the police on the evidence of the 'Jobbins Group'. This evidence was never disclosed by the prosecution as it was protected by public interest immunity. This decision had been made by the prosecution without reference to the trial judge. The applicants denied the offences at their trial and relied on evidence of alibi.

On appeal to the Court of Appeal, counsel for the convicted men sought disclosure of the evidence withheld by the prosecution. The hearing in the Court of Appeal was conducted on an *ex parte* basis. The Court of Appeal's ruling in *R v Ward* had been made by this time, and, as a consequence of it, the Court of Appeal reviewed the sensitive material withheld by the prosecution at the trial. The Court of Appeal upheld the convictions of all three men. Their convictions were eventually referred to the Criminal Cases Review Commission (CCRC). The CCRC discovered that one of the 'Jobbins Group', who had implicated the defendants, was a known informer and that, as a result of the information he had given to the police, he had received a reward of over £10,000. The police records disclosed the fact that this individual had never informed the police that Johnson had been one of the gang. Despite the 'Jobbins Group' having admitted to being accessories to the offences, they had all been granted immunity from prosecution. All these facts had been unknown to the defence at the time of the trial. The defendants contended to the CCRC that it had been the 'Jobbins Group' who had in fact committed the robberies and the killing.

The CCRC concluded there was little evidence to implicate Johnson and as such the case against the other two defendants was substantially undermined. Had the jury been made aware of the nature of the evidence supplied by the 'Jobbins Group', it might well have taken a different view of the defendants' involvement. The CCRC referred the matter back to the Court of Appeal. In the meantime the applicants' case was heard before the European Court of Human Rights.

The Court concluded that the right to full disclosure was not an absolute right and was subject to limitations pursuing the legitimate aim of protecting national security, vulnerable witnesses and sources of information. Crucially however it held that any restriction to a defendant's rights had to be proportional and counterbalanced by procedural safeguards. The principal safeguard, the Court observed, was the adoption of an adversarial procedure by which the defence is given an equal opportunity to make representations as regards the withheld material as that afforded to the prosecution.

With this statement of principle in mind, the Court expressed reservations about the *ex parte* procedure which had denied the defence any opportunity, at either the trial stage or on appeal, to make representations. Whilst accepting the *ex parte* procedure might be needed in some cases, the Court favoured the appointment of a security cleared independent counsel, who would at least be allowed to review the documentation and make representations on a defendant's behalf. In the view of the Court, the Court of Appeal's review of the undisclosed material could not cure the breach which had occurred at the defendants' trial. The decision in this regard had to be made by the trial judge, as he had been the one individual best placed to assess its relevance throughout the course of the trial. As a result the United Kingdom was found to have violated the defendants' right to a fair trial and the applicants' convictions were subsequently quashed by the Court of Appeal. The European Court of Human Rights' decision in *Rowe and Davis* is supported by its later decision in *Atlan* v *United Kingdom* (2001) *The Times*, 3 July.

Since this decision by the European Court of Human Rights in *Rowe and Davis* the procedure for claiming public interest immunity has changed. The prosecution is no longer the advocate and judge in its own cause. Concern has been expressed regarding the future of the *ex parte* procedure used to resolve a number of such claims, but since the decision outlined above, the European Court of Human Rights has ruled that the *ex parte* procedure does not *per se* violate the right to a fair trial.

In *Jasper* v *United Kingdom*; *Fitt* v *United Kingdom* (2000) 30 EHRR 480 the withheld material had been scrutinised at an *ex parte* pre-trial hearing by a judge who subsequently conducted the trial. Defence counsel had been notified that a public interest immunity application was to be held on an *ex parte* basis and had been invited to outline the key points of the defence to the judge. Having regard to the procedural safeguards adopted in this case, the European Court of Human Rights (on a split decision of nine votes to eight) concluded the defendants' trial was fair.

Both the decisions of the European Court of Human Rights in *Rowe and Davis* and *Atlan* have implications for the Court of Appeal's function in reviewing the safety of a defendant's conviction where a public interest immunity claim is raised for the first time on appeal. In both cases, the conduct of an *ex parte* procedure before the Court of Appeal could not, in the opinion of the European Court of Human Rights, rectify the unfairness caused by having denied the trial judge the opportunity to consider the evidence now subject to a public interest immunity claim before the Court of Appeal.

In *R* v *Botmeh and Alami* (2001) *The Times*, 8 November, the Court of Appeal upheld the appellants' convictions having conducted an *ex parte* hearing into evidence which the prosecution had denied the existence of during the trial and which raised public interest immunity concerns. The Court of Appeal had invited the appellants' counsel to view the sensitive material provided he was prepared to give an undertaking to the court not to reveal the substance of it to his clients. Counsel for the appellants declined the invitation on the ground that it would professionally compromise him. The Court of Appeal reviewed the evidence with the benefit of written defence submissions and concluded the evidence was not of any material assistance to the appellants.

Having considered the decisions in *Rowe and Davis* and *Atlan*, the Court of Appeal rejected the argument that it would be contrary to Article 6 to have a public interest immunity claim conducted before it on an *ex parte* basis. It could find nothing in the judgments of the European Court of Human Rights to suggest that an *ex parte* examination of the material by the Court of Appeal, in the exercise of its function separate from that of the trial court, was of itself unfair. The Court of Appeal drew a distinction between the function of the European Court of Human Rights, which is to assess the fairness of the proceedings as a whole, and the function of the Court of Appeal, which is to assess the safety of the conviction. A finding of unfairness during the trial did not, in its view, necessarily mean that the conviction must be quashed, if, after having reviewed the evidence in the case, the Court of Appeal concluded the defendant's conviction was safe.

Leave has been sought to take the decision of the Court of Appeal to the House of Lords so that it can consider the legality of conducting an *ex parte* public interest immunity hearing before the Court of Appeal.

CONCLUSION

The procedures in relation to disclosure of evidence in general have been considerably tightened by the disclosure regime introduced by the Criminal Procedure and Investigations Act 1996. However the regime is still a cause for concern to defence practitioners. The prosecution is entitled to make the assessment of relevance to the defence and there is a widely held view that this infringes the principle of impartiality. Nevertheless, the current disclosure regime would seem to be in broad compliance with the European Convention on Human Rights. Suggestions that the requirement to file a defence statement is a violation of the defendant's privilege against self-incrimination must be considered doubtful in the light of the clear wording in the European Court of Human Rights' judgment in *Rowe and Davis* v *United Kingdom*:

> It is a fundamental aspect of the right to a fair trial that criminal proceedings, including the elements of such proceedings which relate to procedure, should be adversarial and that there should be equality of arms between the prosecution and defence. The right to an adversarial trial means, in a criminal case, that both prosecution and defence must be given the opportunity to have knowledge of and comment on the observations filed and the evidence adduced by the other party.

The entire process of disclosure has recently been the subject of a review commissioned by the Home Office. Its findings and the recommendations of Lord Justice Auld are likely to form the basis for future reform of the rules and procedures.

Further reading

Attorney-General's Guidelines on Disclosure: Disclosure of Information in Criminal Proceedings (November 2000) HMSO.

Niblett, J. (1997) *Disclosure in Criminal Proceedings*, Blackstone Press.

Plotnikoff, J. and Woolfson, R. (2001) *A Fair Balance? Evaluation of the Operation of Disclosure Law*, Home Office.

Pollard, C., 'A Case for Disclosure' [1994] Crim LR 42.

Runciman of Doxford, Viscount (1993) *Report of the Royal Commission on Criminal Justice*, Cmnd 2263, HMSO.

Scott, R. (1995–96) *Report of the Inquiry into the Export of Defence Equipment and Dual-use Goods to Iraq and Related Prosecutions*, House of Commons Paper 115.

Scott, R., 'The Accused and Unnaceptable Use of Public Interest Immunity' [1996] Public Law 427.

Sharp, S., 'Article 6 and the Disclosure of Evidence in Criminal Trials' [1999] Crim LR 273.

Smith, A.T.H., 'Public Interest Immunity and Sensitive Material' (1993) CLJ 357.

Tomkins, A., 'Public Interest Immunity and Sensitive Material' [1993] Public Law 650.

Zuckerman, A., 'Public Interest Immunity – A Matter of Prime Judicial Responsibility' (1994) 57 MLR 703.

Chapter 10

THE OPERATION OF PRIVATE PRIVILEGE

INTRODUCTION

The term 'private privilege' relates to a number of separate privileges that may be claimed by a person or any other legal entity such as a limited company or a local authority acting in its personal capacity. In criminal proceedings private privilege may be claimed in two situations. First, a client cannot lawfully be compelled to disclose any communication between himself and his lawyer and his lawyer and a third party where the communication has been given or created for the purpose of existing or contemplated legal proceedings. This branch of private privilege is known as legal professional privilege. Secondly, a witness may lawfully refuse to produce a document or to answer a question put to him whilst testifying where that answer might lead him to be later prosecuted for a criminal offence or to suffer a penalty or to forfeit property. This head of privilege is referred to as the privilege against self-incrimination. Where either privilege is successfully claimed, the evidential effect is the same as under the operation of the rules of public interest immunity – the court is denied the opportunity of hearing otherwise potentially relevant and admissible evidence.

The rationale for these heads of private privilege is that it is considered to be in the wider public interest in the administration of justice to maintain the confidentiality of communications between lawyers and their clients and to encourage witnesses when giving evidence to make a full and frank disclosure of the matters within their knowledge – even, where, as a consequence of the operation of the rules, the court is denied the benefit of the evidence covered by the privilege. As we noted above, whilst the evidential effect of claiming private privilege is the same as where public interest immunity is claimed, an important difference between them is that private privilege is a personal right that belongs to the client or to a witness and cannot be claimed by any other person, whereas public interest immunity seeks to protect the 'confidentiality' of the work of organisations that operate in the 'public' domain such as the police, the security forces, local authorities, government ministers and members of the diplomatic service. Finally, a related issue dealt with in this chapter is to what extent confidential communications are protected from being disclosed in criminal proceedings.

LEGAL PROFESSIONAL PRIVILEGE IN CRIMINAL PROCEEDINGS

At common law, in criminal proceedings legal professional privilege exempts from disclosure:

1 all written and/or oral communications between the legal adviser and the client; and

2 all written and/or oral communications between the professional legal adviser and the client and between the legal adviser, the client and a third party, where the sole or dominant purpose of the communication to the third party is to enable the legal adviser to act in contemplated or existing litigation.

Whilst the privilege has long been recognised at common law and continues to be governed by the common law in civil cases, in modern criminal proceedings, the operation of legal professional privilege has been placed on a statutory footing by section 10 of PACE. Section 10 provides:

(1) Subject to subsection (2) below, in this Act 'items subject to legal privilege' means—
  (a) communications between a professional legal adviser and his client or any person representing his client made in connection with the giving of legal advice to the client;
  (b) communications between a professional legal adviser and his client or any person representing his client or between such an adviser or his client or any such representative and any other person made in connection with or in contemplation of legal proceedings and for the purpose of such proceedings; and
  (c) items enclosed with or referred to in such communications and made—
    (i) in connection with the giving of legal advice; or
    (ii) in connection with or in the contemplation of legal proceedings and for the purposes of such proceedings;

when they are in the possession of a person who is entitled to possession of them.

Although, the effect of section 10 of PACE is to codify the two established heads of legal professional privilege, the courts will generally apply the statutory provisions according to the principles developed at common law. For example in *R v Inner London Crown Court, ex parte Baines & Baines (a firm)* [1988] 2 WLR 549, the police were trying to check where certain items had been disposed of following the Brinks-Mat bullion robbery at Heathrow Airport. A circuit judge granted the police a production order against a firm of solicitors requiring them to make available for inspection certain records in connection with the purchase of a number of properties. The Divisional Court quashed the order on the ground that the proper formalities had not been complied with and further decided that whilst the record of the conveyancing transactions were not privileged because they were not concerned with the giving of legal advice, all correspondence between the solicitor and the client were privileged and could not be seized.

LEGAL PROFESSIONAL PRIVILEGE AND THE COURTS

The rationale behind the operation of the rule is that it is considered to be in the public interest that, when seeking the advice of his lawyer, a client will feel able to discuss his case openly and to make a full disclosure of all relevant information in the knowledge that he will not be compelled to disclose the content of those discussions nor will he be compelled to give evidence about them in court. As the privilege underpins the administration of justice in both civil and criminal proceedings (although it assumes greater importance in civil cases, see Chapter 26), the courts adopt a strict approach to enforcing its application. This was illustrated in:

R v Derby Magistrates' Court, ex parte B [1996] AC 487

A sixteen-year-old girl was murdered. The appellant was arrested and made a statement to the police that he alone was responsible for the murder. He later retracted the statement and alleged that although he had been present at the scene of the crime, it was his stepfather who had killed the girl. Relying on this second statement, the appellant was acquitted in the Crown Court. Subsequently his stepfather was charged with the murder. At the stepfather's committal proceedings the appellant was called as a witness for the prosecution and repeated the statement that his stepfather had killed the girl. He was cross-examined by the defence about the instructions he had given to his solicitor concerning the murder. The appellant claimed legal professional privilege but the magistrate, on an application by the stepfather under section 97 of the Magistrates' Courts Act 1980, issued a summons directing the appellant and his solicitor to produce the relevant proofs of evidence on the ground that they would be 'likely to be material evidence' within the ambit of section 97 of the 1980 Act. In an application for judicial review, the Divisional Court upheld the magistrates' decision but certified that the case should be heard by the House of Lords.

The House of Lords held, in allowing the appeal, that a witness summons could not be issued under section 97 to compel the production of documents protected by legal professional privilege unless the privilege had been waived, which in the present case, it had not.

In reviewing the historical origins of the doctrine, Lord Taylor CJ explained the significance of the rule in modern law:

> The principle which runs through all these cases, and many other cases which were cited, is that a man must be able to consult his lawyer in confidence, since otherwise he might hold back on half the truth. The client must be sure that what he tells his lawyer in confidence will never be revealed without his consent. Legal professional privilege is thus much more than an ordinary rule of evidence, limited in its application to the facts of a particular case. It is a fundamental condition on which the administration of justice on a whole rests.

Therefore, according to Lord Taylor CJ, legal professional privilege was a fundamental condition on which the administration of justice rested and that given its absolute nature, no exception should be allowed to its application.

EXTENT OF THE PRIVILEGE

Under section 10 of PACE, legal professional privilege will apply in the following situations in criminal proceedings.

Communications between the lawyer and client (section 10(1)(a))

All communications passing between the lawyer and client in 'the giving or obtaining of legal advice' and within the proper scope of the lawyer's professional work will be privileged from disclosure. According to Lord Justice Taylor in *Balabel* v *Air India* [1988] Ch 317 the term 'the giving of legal advice' is not restricted to communications that specifically request or give legal advice but also includes communications and correspondence that are part of the ongoing relationship between the lawyer and the client. Therefore, in a criminal case, legal professional privilege will attach to all communications between a private practice solicitor and his client. The privilege will also attach to communications with counsel, to salaried legal advisers whether or not they hold a formal legal qualification and to foreign lawyers. The most obvious example is that an accused cannot be compelled to disclose any oral or written advice given to him by his solicitor or counsel in connection with the case.

Whilst the phrase 'the giving of legal advice' is broadly interpreted, it is not without boundaries and the courts are not prepared to extend the principles beyond these well-established boundaries. For example, in *R v Crown Court at Inner London Crown Court, ex parte Baines & Baines (a firm)* above, a record of a conveyancing transaction was held not to be privileged since its purpose was not the giving of legal advice. The privilege will not extend to a solicitor's documentary records of time spent with a client or to time sheets or to fee records or to the record of a client's appointment in a solicitor's appointment diary (see *R v Manchester Crown Court, ex parte R (Legal Professional Privilege)* [1999] 1 WLR 832). These documents are not covered by legal professional privilege as they are not concerned with the giving of legal advice. Consider the following example of the operation of the doctrine.

Example

George is charged with theft. In cross-examination the advocate asks him to tell the court about the advice given to him by his paralegal to plead not guilty. George is also asked about the contents of a letter that he had sent to his solicitor before he was charged with the theft.

George cannot be compelled to disclose the content of the advice he was given by his paralegal as the matter is covered by legal professional privilege. The advice is given by a lawyer to his client in connection with existing litigation. The contents of the letter will not be covered by legal professional privilege, as the letter came into existence before the litigation commenced. It is not sufficient to attract privilege that the letter was sent by George to his solicitor.

Communications with third parties (section 10(1)(b))

Legal professional privilege will attach to communications between the client, the legal adviser and a third party where the sole or dominant purpose of the communication was in connection with actual or pending litigation. In deciding the 'dominant purpose test', the court will take an objective view of all the evidence, taking into account the intention of the document's author and the purpose of preparing the document. The key requirement in maintaining the privileged status of communications with third parties is that the communication must relate to pending or contemplated litigation. This point is strictly observed by the courts. For example, in the civil case of *Wheeler v Le Marchant* (1881) 17 Ch D 675, it was held that communications between a solicitor and a surveyor were not privileged even though they were relevant to the matters being litigated because they were made when no litigation was contemplated by the client.

LEGAL PROFESSIONAL PRIVILEGE AND THE DISCLOSURE OF EXPERT EVIDENCE

The rules on legal professional privilege attaching to communications where the 'third party' is an expert witness should be read in conjunction with the obligation on both the prosecution and the defence to disclose the contents of their experts' reports as required by the Crown Court (Advance Notice of Expert Evidence) Rules 1987 (SI 1987 No 716) and the Magistrates' Courts (Advance Notice of Expert Evidence) Rules 1997 (SI 1997 No 705), which both state that where a party wishes to rely on expert evidence at trial, the expert's report should be disclosed to the other side before trial. The important point to note is that this requirement only applies where the party seeks to rely on the report at trial. As far as the defence is concerned, an expert's report will be covered by legal professional privilege and will not have to be disclosed where, for example, it is unhelpful to the defence case and the evidence will not be used at trial. The position in relation to the prosecution is not so clear, and should be considered in conjunction with the prosecution's general duty to disclose all scientific evidence as held in *R v Ward* [1993] 2 All ER 577. (Note that the wider issues of the law relating to the admission of expert evidence in criminal cases is dealt with in Chapter 19.) As an illustration of the operation of legal professional privilege applied to an expert's report, consider the following example.

Example

Andy is charged with burglary. The prosecution have obtained forensic evidence, which confirms that samples of glass shards discovered by the police in Andy's flat match with those discovered at the scene of the crime. The defence solicitor instructs an expert witness, Dr Lecter, to confirm that there is indeed a match between the samples. If, in his written report, Dr Lecter confirms the match, the report will be covered by legal professional privilege and will not have to be disclosed if the defence do not use the evidence at trial.

If Dr Lecter had been instructed by the prosecution and his findings undermined the prosecution case or assisted the defence case, under the prosecution's general duty of disclosure as outlined in R v Ward *above, the report would have to be given to the defence.*

WAIVING THE PRIVILEGE

Legal professional privilege vests in the client and may only be waived by the client either at the pre-trial stage or during the trial itself. If the client expressly or impliedly waives the privilege, the lawyer will be compelled to reveal the contents of the communications between himself and the client or between himself and a third party. The question of waiver commonly arises where the accused is required to explain his silence to questions at the police station under section 34 of the Criminal Justice and Public Order Act 1994 and where it is possible that adverse inferences may be drawn from his silence. The privilege will be waived where the accused discloses to the court that he was advised to remain silent by his legal adviser and explains the reasons that he was given by his lawyer for not answering police questions. In this situation both the accused and the legal adviser may be cross-examined about the content of the advice given at the police station. Guidance about the evidential effect of disclosing advice given at the police station was provided by the Court of Appeal in *R* v *Condron* [1997] 1 Cr App R 185. The implications of this important case and the operation of section 34 of the 1994 Act has been dealt with in Chapter 7.

LIFTING THE VEIL OF LEGAL PROFESSIONAL PRIVILEGE

Whilst the law will generally recognise and enforce the sanctity of legal professional privilege its application is not absolute and the veil of legal professional privilege will be lifted in the following situations.

Communication in the furtherance of a crime or fraud

Most significantly, the privilege may not be used as a vehicle for the furtherance of a criminal offence. It is immaterial whether the lawyer was aware of the illicit purpose of the communication or not and the 'crime' may relate to an offence under United Kingdom law or an offence in a foreign jurisdiction. According to the House of Lords in *O'Rourke* v *Derbyshire* [1920] AC 581, there should be *prima facie* evidence that it was the client's intention to use the advice in the furtherance of a criminal offence before the disclosure of the communication will be ordered. In deciding the issue, the court will be entitled to look at the communication itself as in *R* v *Governor of Pentonville Prison, ex parte Osman* (1990) 90 Cr App R 281. The well-known case on this point is described below.

R v Cox and Railton (1884) 14 QBD 153

The defendants had consulted a solicitor for advice on how a judgment against them in a civil action could be set aside without their having to comply with it. The solicitor advised them that it could not lawfully be done given the lapse of time. The defendants then executed a fraudulent document that they backdated to achieve their unlawful purpose. At the defendants' criminal trial, the solicitor was called as a prosecution witness and repeated in evidence his advice to the defendants.

The Court for Crown Cases Reserved held that if a client applies to a legal adviser for advice intending to facilitate a crime and the legal adviser is ignorant of the real purpose for seeking the advice, any communication between the parties will not be privileged.

The common law rule is now contained in section 10(2) of PACE which provides:

> (2) Items held with the intention of furthering a criminal purpose are not items subject to legal privilege.

The words 'furthering a criminal purpose' appears to include an illegal enterprise that does not necessarily amount to the commission of a specific crime but does include conduct that is broadly criminal in nature. In *R* v *Central Criminal Court, ex parte Francis & Francis* [1989] AC 346, the police obtained an *ex parte* order under section 27 of the Drug Trafficking Offences Act 1986 for the production within seven days of all files held by a firm of solicitors relating to the financial transactions of one of their clients who was known as G. The police believed that he had been given money to buy property by a person suspected of drug trafficking. The solicitors applied for a judicial review of the order on the ground that the material was covered by legal professional privilege as defined by section 10 of PACE. The application was dismissed by both the Divisional Court and by the House of Lords. By a majority, the House of Lords held that on a purposive construction of section 10(2) of PACE, the section was intended to reflect the position at common law and the items which would otherwise have come within the definition of items covered by legal privilege under section 10(1) of PACE were excluded from the definition if they were held with the intention of furthering the commission of a criminal offence.

Example

The police obtain a search warrant from a magistrate on the suspicion that certain documents held by a solicitor have been forged by her and her spouse as part of their fraudulent use of client's money. The solicitor claims that the documents cannot be seized as they are covered by legal privilege under section 10(1) of PACE. On the facts, the protection afforded by section 10(1) is unlikely to apply as the requirement that the documents should have been made in connection with legal proceedings meant that they had been created 'lawfully' and not for the intention of furthering a criminal offence. The court will order that the documents should be disclosed as the requirement of section 10(2) is satisfied.

Accidental loss of privilege

The veil of legal professional privilege may also be lifted accidentally. In *R v Tompkins* (1978) 67 Cr App R 181, the defendant was charged with handling stolen hi-fi equipment. The victim of the theft stated that he could identify his stolen equipment as it had a loose button. The defendant said in examination-in-chief that the button had never been loose and demonstrated this to the court. During an adjournment, an employee of the prosecution solicitor found a piece of paper on which the defendant had written to his barrister that the button had been loose but that he stuck it down with glue. Prosecution counsel then showed Tompkins the note and cross-examined him on it. As a result, Tompkins changed his answer and was convicted. On appeal, the Court of Appeal stated that there had not been a breach of legal professional privilege because the privileged document had been obtained independently of the privileged relationship and there had not been any improper conduct.

In applying *R v Tompkins*, the court reached a similar decision in *R v Cottrill* [1997] Crim LR 56, where a statement made by the accused to his solicitors was voluntarily disclosed to the prosecution without the accused's knowledge or consent. The court held that at the trial, the accused could be cross-examined on the contents of his statement subject to the court's powers to exclude the evidence under section 78 of PACE on the basis that the admission of the evidence would have an 'unfair effect on the fairness of the proceedings'.

Legal professional privilege and the secondary evidence rule

The veil of legal professional privilege may be lifted under the secondary evidence rule by a party producing the original or a copy of the document over which the other side claims privilege or by producing a witness who may have overheard a privileged conversation. Where the secondary evidence rule applies, the party can be compelled to produce the 'privileged' evidence. The cases of *R v Tompkins* and *R v Cottrill* discussed above are examples of where privileged documents came into the possession of the other party by inadvertent means. There is nothing to suggest that the principle will not also apply where the document was obtained by unfair or even illegal means. In all cases, the admission of a document under the secondary evidence rule is subject to the exercise of the court's exclusionary powers under section 78 of PACE, to ensure a 'fair' trial.

A leading authority on the point is the civil case of *Calcraft v Guest* (1898) 1 QB 759, where in 1887 certain documents came into existence over which the owner of a fishery in Dorset claimed legal professional privilege. In 1898 his successor in title to the fishery, Calcraft, brought an action for trespass to the fishery. Calcraft succeeded in his action at trial but one of the defendants appealed. Between the trial and the appeal the documents made in 1787 came to light and the appellant's solicitor took copies of the originals before the originals were handed back to the plaintiff in the main litigation. On the appeal from the action for trespass, the appellant sought to put in evidence copies of the original documents. This gave rise to two questions for the Court of Appeal to consider. First, were the original documents privileged from disclosure and, secondly, if they were privileged, could the copies be used as secondary evidence of their contents? The Court of Appeal held that the original documents were privileged in 1787 and had remained privileged ever since. In relation to the second question, the copies of the document were not privileged and were admissible in evidence at the trial as secondary evidence.

Cases involving the 'welfare' of children under the Children Act 1989

In a number of situations many of the normal rules of evidence and procedure are revised to deal with the overriding requirement of proceedings under section 1 of the Children Act 1989 to treat the welfare of the child as 'paramount'. In applying the 'welfare' principle, the courts have been required to consider the operation of legal professional privilege in proceedings under the 1989 Act. The present position is to be found in the House of Lords case of *Re L* below.

Re L (A Minor) (Police Investigation: Privilege) [1997] AC 16

A child whose parents were drug addicts were admitted to hospital after taking methadone. The mother's original explanation was that the child had ingested the substance accidentally and the police decided not to press charges. The local authority applied for a care order under Part IV of the Children Act 1989 and the court gave leave to the mother for the disclosure to a medical expert of court papers relating to the circumstances in which the child had swallowed the methadone. The expert prepared a report that contradicted the mother's account, and, on application of the police, the judge authorised the disclosure to them, with a view to possible prosecution. The mother appealed against the order on the ground that the disclosure offended her right to legal professional privilege.

In a majority decision, the House of Lords held that whilst legal professional privilege as applied to communications between the lawyer and client was absolute as stated in

R v Derby Magistrates' Court, ex parte B above, the application of the privilege to communications with a third party was not absolute and it was not appropriate to apply the doctrine strictly to proceedings under the Children Act and to any other proceedings involving the welfare of children.

DISCLOSURE OF CONFIDENTIAL INFORMATION IN CRIMINAL PROCEEDINGS

The principle of legal professional privilege is unique to the lawyer/client relationship. Whilst no other profession enjoys the same privilege as the lawyer enjoys with his client, in recent years the sanctity of this relationship has been extended by a limited number of statutes to cover, for example, communications between licensed conveyancers in the course of acting for clients under section 33 of the Administration of Justice Act 1985 and to communications with patent agents and registered trade mark agents under sections 280–284 of the Copyright, Designs and Patents Act 1988.

However, as a matter of public policy, the courts have generally refused to extend the operation of legal professional privilege at common law and claims for a similar privilege to apply to protect the following confidential relationships have failed:

- between a priest and a penitent (*Attorney-General* v *Clough* [1963] 1 QB 773); and
- between accountant and client (*Chantrey Martin & Co* v *Martin* [1953] 2QB 286); and
- between doctor and patient (*R* v *McDonald* [1991] Crim LR 122).

In each of the cases cited above, the courts have resisted extending the principle of legal professional privilege to other confidential relationships on the ground that it is clearly in the wider public interest that when testifying in court, there should be as few obstacles as possible to prevent a witness from giving a full and honest disclosure of his evidence. Therefore, provided the evidence is relevant and probative of a fact in issue, a witness will be required to answer a question put by an advocate or by the judge even though his answer may disclose information that had been given in confidence (see *Attorney-General* v *Mulholland* [1963] 2 QB 477).

In appropriate circumstances this position may be partially tempered by a number of possibilities. First, a witness may be able to rely on a head of private privilege or, where the issue is in the 'public domain', on the doctrine of public interest immunity. For example, a communication made in the course of seeking conciliation in matrimonial proceedings may attract both private and public privilege as explained in the speeches of Lords Hailsham and Simon in *D* v *NSPCC* [1978] AC 171. An interview with a child victim of a sexual offence may also be the subject of public interest immunity unless the disclosure of the information would tend to prove the accused's innocence, in which case, there would be a strong argument for disclosure as stated in *R* v *K (TD) (Evidence)* (1993) 97 Cr App R 342, whilst a similar immunity was claimed in respect of confidential documents relating to abortions carried out under the Abortion Act 1967 as held in *Morrow* v *DPP* [1994] Crim LR 58. Secondly, the material may not be admitted in evidence under the residual discretion enjoyed by the judge in a criminal trial to prevent the disclosure of confidential communications. In *British Steel Corporation* v *Granada Television Ltd* [1980] 3 WLR 774 Lord Wilberforce stated that:

> As to information obtained in confidence, and the legal duty, which may arise, to disclose it to the court of justice, the position is clear. Courts have an inherent wish to respect this confidence, whether it arises between doctor and patient, priest and penitent, banker and customer, persons giving testimonials to employees, or in other relationships. A relationship of confidence between a journalist and his source is in no different category; nothing in this case involves or will involve any principle that such confidence is not something to be respected. But in all these cases, the court may have to decide, in the particular circumstances, that the interest in preserving this confidence is outweighed by other interests to which the law attaches importance.

In a criminal trial therefore the judge will be required to consider two potentially competing interests in deciding whether a confidential communication should be disclosed to the court: the arguments in favour of preserving the confidentiality between the parties weighed against the wider public interest that wherever possible the decisions of the courts should be based on all relevant, admissible evidence.

As an illustration of some of the principles discussed above in relation to the operation of legal professional privilege and the status of confidential communications, consider the following example:

Example

Josie is a care worker who suffers very serious injuries whilst working in a complex for young offenders run by the local authority. David and Martin, who live at the complex, are arrested and jointly charged with causing grievous bodily harm with intent to Josie under s18 Offences Against the Person Act 1861. Whilst there is circumstantial evidence against each of them, it is not entirely clear whether the attack was carried out by one or both of them. David and Martin initially retain the same solicitor. David tells the solicitor that he carried out the attack with another whose identity he is not prepared to disclose and that Martin was not involved. David later retracts this statement and instructs a different solicitor. At trial, Martin will plead not guilty by putting responsibility on David for the offence in a so-called cut-throat defence.

In order to bolster his defence, Martin seeks disclosure of the interview between David and his solicitor. His application will be unsuccessful as the contents of the interview will be covered by legal professional privilege, which, as illustrated by the Derby Magistrates' Court *case, is strictly enforced by the courts.*

Martin also seeks the disclosure of the transcript of interviews that had been held before the attack between David and a psychiatrist, in which David suggested that on occasions he hears voices that tell him to behave violently. It is the psychiatrist's conclusion that David has psychopathic tendencies. The transcripts will not be covered by legal professional privilege as they were not prepared for the purpose of intended or contemplated litigation. David may also claim that the transcripts should not be disclosed as they are covered by confidentiality – but as we noted above, confidentiality per se *is not a ground that the court will recognise when deciding if evidence should be disclosed.*

It might be claimed that the interviews are protected by public interest immunity, where the diag-
nosis of David's psychopathic tendencies was part of the local authority's statutory duties in its
assessment of David's mental state. In spite of these possible reasons weighing against disclosing
the documents, the transcripts will probably be disclosed if Martin can show that they are relevant
to his defence and may prove his innocence of the crime charged.

PRIVILEGE AGAINST SELF-INCRIMINATION IN CRIMINAL PROCEEDINGS

The common law privilege against self-incrimination is an ancient, personal right that originated in the Star Chamber. It allows a witness to refuse to answer a question where his answer would expose him to the possibility of any criminal charge or forfeiture or a penalty. The privilege also applies where the witness refuses to produce documentary evidence or to give oral evidence about a document's contents. According to Lord Griffiths in *Lam Chi-ming* v *The Queen* [1991] 2 AC 212:

> The privilege against self-incrimination is deep rooted in English law ... It is better by far to allow a few guilty men to escape conviction than to compromise the standards of a free society.

The principle against self-incrimination is also recognised in many other jurisdictions. The Fifth Amendment to the Constitution of the United States provides that no person shall be compelled in any criminal case to be a witness against himself. Section 11(c) of the Canadian Charter of Rights and Freedoms provides that no person shall be a witness in proceedings against himself for that offence, whilst an equivalent provision is also found in a number of international treaties including the International Covenant on Civil and Political Rights 1966.

Whilst the privilege against self-incrimination in the context of the drawing of adverse inferences from an accused's silence under the Criminal Justice and Public Order Act 1994 has been discussed in Chapter 7, the privilege against self-incrimination is primarily a discrete topic within the general area of the law of private privilege. This position was confirmed in *R* v *Director of Serious Fraud Office, ex parte Smith* [1993] AC 1, where the House of Lords described the privilege as one of the 'disparate group of immunities known as the right to silence'.

The principle is based on the Latin maxim *nemo tenebatur prodere seipsum* that 'a man should not be his own accuser'. The modern rationale for the principle was identified by the Law Reform Committee, Sixteenth Report, at paragraph 8 that 'the coercive power of the state should not be used to compel a person to disclose information that would render him liable to punishment'.

An essential part of the operation of the privilege against self-incrimination is that for it to apply there must be a real danger of later criminal proceedings under United Kingdom law. The privilege does not extend to granting immunity from a charge being laid in a foreign jurisdiction. In terms of exposing the witness to the possibility of a future criminal prosecution, it will be sufficient for the witness's answer to disclose his guilt of an offence or that sufficient information is disclosed for the decision to be made to prosecute the witness. The possibility that the witness's answer may expose him to criminal proceedings is a matter for the judge to decide and, according to Lord Clauson in the civil case of *Blunt* v *Park Lane Hotel* [1942] 2 KB 253, must be 'reasonably likely'. In *R v Boyes* (1861) 1 B & S 311 it was suggested that the danger to be apprehended must be 'real and appreciable, with reference to the ordinary operation of law and in the ordinary course of things'.

If a witness wishes to raise the privilege against self-incrimination while giving evidence and the other party objects, the witness has the legal burden of proving that the privlege applies and some evidence will have to be adduced in support of the claim. The privilege may therefore not be invoked where the possibility of future criminal proceedings is merely fanciful or a remote possibility. A good illustration of this point is provided by the facts of *R v Boyes* above where a witness in a bribery trial was called to prove that he had received a bribe. He refused to answer questions put to him by the Solicitor-General, who was prosecuting. Even when the Solicitor-General then handed the witness a pardon under the Great Seal he still refused to answer the questions put to him by claiming the privilege. The trial judge ruled that the privilege did not apply and directed the witness to answer the questions. The Court of Queen's Bench upheld the judge's ruling as the pardon had removed the risk of the witness being prosecuted on the basis of his answers.

The privilege belongs to the witness

The privilege against self-incrimination belongs to the witness and must therefore be claimed by the witness during his testimony. Whilst according to *R v Coote* (1873) LR 4 PC 599, a witness is presumed to know the law sufficiently to appreciate that he is not compelled to answer a particular question or to produce a document, the preferred modern practice is for the judge or the magistrates' adviser to warn the witness that he does not have to answer the question. Once the court is satisfied that the privilege applies, the witness will not be compelled to answer even if his motive for remaining silent is based on bad faith or he has a motive of his own to serve. Consider the following example.

Example

Danny appears as a prosecution witness at Vinny's trial for robbery. In cross-examination he is asked to confirm whether he (Danny) was a member of the gang which raided the Stokeshire Bank in May of 2001. Danny was arrested by the police in connection with the robbery but was not charged. Under the operation of the privilege against self-incrimination there is nothing to prevent the advocate from asking the question. If however, by answering the question, Danny might expose himself to the possibility of a future criminal charge, he may invoke the privilege. If the cross-examiner disputes the issue, Danny has the burden of proving that the privilege against self-incrimination applies.

Waiving the privilege

As the privilege against self-incrimination attaches to the witness as a personal right, only the witness may waive the privilege. Where the witness does not waive the privilege and his answers incriminate him, they will be admissible as evidence in any proceedings against him (*R v Sloggett* [1856] Dears 656). If, however, the judge incorrectly compels the witness to answer the question, then according to *R v Garbett* (1847) 2 Car & Kir 474, the witness's answers are not admissible as evidence in any subsequent proceedings but remain admissible at the trial in which the answer was given as stated in *R v Kinglake* (1870) 11 Cox 499.

Application of the privilege

In considering the application of the privilege against self-incrimination in criminal cases, a distinction should be drawn between the position of the accused and other witnesses in the proceedings. In relation to the accused, the privilege may be relevant both during the investigation of the offence before the trial and at the trial itself. During a criminal investigation, a suspect's truthful answer to a question may incriminate him in respect of an offence for which he has not yet been charged. Whilst, in the majority of situations, the suspect cannot be compelled to answer the questions put to him, as explained in Chapter 7, where the suspect is later prosecuted for the offence, and it is relevant to do so, adverse inferences may be drawn from the accused's silence under section 34 of the Criminal Justice and Public Order Act 1994. As exceptions to this general rule, in a number of statutes that are considered later in this chapter, Parliament has either modified or abrogated the operation of the privilege.

With respect to the position of the accused at trial, the normal rules relating to cross-examination are amended to deal with the special position of the accused. The effect of section 1(e) of the Criminal Evidence Act 1898 abrogates the accused's privilege against self-incrimination by providing that the defendant may be asked any questions in cross-examination even though the answer may tend to incriminate him as to the offence charged. Whilst this provision is dealt with in more detail in Chapter 21 regarding the accused in a criminal trial, it is sufficient to make clear at this stage that if the accused could not be compelled to answer questions in respect to the offence charged, there would be little point in allowing the accused to testify as his evidence could not be tested by cross-examination.

The position of a witness other than the accused is much simpler. The privilege allows a witness to refuse to answer a question where his answer would expose him to the possibility of any criminal charge or forfeiture or a penalty.

Modifications by Parliament

Theft Act 1968, section 31(1)

A witness may not refuse to answer any questions in proceedings for the recovery or administration of property or the execution of a trust on the ground that to do so might incriminate him or his spouse in an offence under the Act. The section is subject to the important limitation that the witness's answers are not admissible against him or his spouse in subsequent proceedings under the Act.

Criminal Justice Act 1987, section 2

A similar provision is found in section 2(2) of the Criminal Justice Act 1987 where the Director of the Serious Fraud Office can compel a person to make a statement in a serious fraud investigation subject to section 2(8) which prevents the statement from being used in subsequent criminal proceedings. In *R v Director of the Serious Fraud Office, ex parte Smith* [1993] AC 1, the House of Lords held that the 1987 Act introduced an inquisitorial regime for the investigation of fraud, and the Director could compel a person to answer questions even after he had been charged with a criminal offence.

Parliamentary abrogation of the privilege

Whilst the provisions under the Theft Act 1968 and the Criminal Justice Act 1987 above make limited inroads into the traditional operation of the privilege against self-incrimination by allowing certain questions to be asked that are *prima facie* in breach of the privilege's traditional limits, nevertheless the witness's answers cannot be used in other proceedings. There is, however, a second group of statutes which permit not only potentially incriminating questions to be asked but also permit the witness's answers to be used against him in later proceedings. In the main, these statutes are part of the regulatory framework that give wide legal powers to the police and other law enforcement officers when investigating allegations of fraud and other malpractice in the running of companies. For example, in proceedings under section 236 of the Insolvency Act 1986, the House of Lords in *Re Arrows Ltd (No 4)* [1995] 2 AC 75 held that the Director of the Serious Fraud Squad could make full use in any prosecution of transcripts of examinations carried out under section 236 subject to the trial judge's discretion to exclude any evidence under section 78 of PACE where admitting it would have a sufficiently 'adverse effect on the fairness of the trial'.

However, the most controversial provision where Parliament has abrogated the operation of the privilege against self-incrimination has been in proceedings under sections 434–436 of the Companies Act 1985. The sections allow State officials to question witnesses and to seize documents and other 'relevant' material in the investigation of fraud in the running of companies. Section 434 permits inspectors appointed to investigate the affairs of a company to require a person to produce to the inspectors all documents of or relating to the company and to attend before the inspectors when required to do so and otherwise to give the inspectors all assistance in connection with the investigation which they are reasonably able to give. Answers given to an inspector by a person questioned under section 434 could be used in evidence against him as provided for by section 434(5), whilst a failure to answer would lead to a charge of contempt of court and the imposition of a fine or a committal to prison for up to two years.

The compatibility of the 1985 Act with the witness's privilege against self-incrimination has been challenged in both domestic law and at the European Court of Human Rights. In domestic law, the challenge arose in:

R *v* Saunders (Ernest) (No 2) [1996] 1 Cr App 463

The defendant was suspected of being connected with an unlawful share support operation in the shares of Guinness plc. This led to the appointment of government inspectors, who found evidence of criminal conduct and thereafter interviewed Mr Saunders, who was a director and the chief executive of Guinness, on nine occasions. Saunders was charged with a number of offences, and, at his trial, the prosecution sought to rely on the transcript of his interviews by the inspectors. The admissibility of such transcripts was challenged, but the judge ruled that under the relevant statute, the inspectors were entitled to ask witnesses questions and that the answers were admissible in criminal proceedings. The judge did, however, exclude the transcripts of the last two interviews which had been conducted after Saunders had been charged by applying section 78 of PACE. The defendants were convicted and the case went to the Court of Appeal.

On appeal, the defence submitted that the trial judge should have exercised his powers under section 78 of PACE to exclude all the transcripts of the interviews between the defendants and the DTI inspectors on the ground that the conduct of the interviews fell outside the protections afforded by the Police and Criminal Evidence Act 1984, the Codes of Practice and the privilege against self-incrimination. In rejecting this argument in the Court of Appeal, Lord Taylor CJ stated that Parliament's intention had been clear when passing the legislation in limiting the traditional protection afforded by the operation of the privilege against self-incrimination. Saunders petitioned the European Court of Human Rights in *Saunders* v *United Kingdom* (1997) 23 EHRR 313, which is considered in the next section.

HUMAN RIGHTS AND THE PRIVILEGE AGAINST SELF-INCRIMINATION

Whilst not specifically mentioned, the privilege against self-incrimination along with the right to silence are fundamental aspects of an accused's right to a fair trial under Article 6(1) of the European Convention on Human Rights. In *Funke* v *France* (1993) 16 EHRR 297, the European Court of Human Rights held that anyone charged with a criminal offence 'has the right to remain silent and not contribute to incriminating himself'. The rationale for the privilege, which is a common feature in the legal systems of all the Contracting Parties to the Convention, is to recognise the right of the accused to remain silent when questions are put to him and not to be compelled to break his silence. The privilege also embodies the principle that the prosecution in a criminal trial is required to prove its case without resorting to evidence that has been obtained through coercion or oppression in defiance of the will of the accused. In this sense the privilege operates in close conjunction with Article 6(2) of the Convention – the presumption of innocence.

As noted above, the important provisions of sections 434–436 of the Companies Act 1985 were challenged in the European Court of Human Rights in *Saunders* v *United Kingdom* (1997) 23 EHRR 313. The key issue before the Court was to decide whether the use by the prosecution of the statements obtained from Saunders, the applicant, by the DTI inspectors, amounted to an unjustifiable infringement of the applicant's right not to incriminate himself. The Court ruled that whilst the exercise of these powers are not in themselves in contravention of Convention rights, Saunders had been denied his right to a fair trial under Article 6 because that evidence obtained by those methods was used at trial. The Court did not accept the United Kingdom government's submission that as some of the applicant's answers contained admissions to knowledge of the offence, they therefore incriminated him as regards involvement in the offence. The Court also declined to accept that the complexities of corporate fraud, the vital public interest in the investigation of such fraud and the punishment of those responsible could justify such a marked departure from the traditional operation of the privilege against self-incrimination. In all the circumstances of the case, the use of the evidence obtained in this way at trial had deprived Saunders of his right to a fair trial under Article 6 of the Convention.

In response to the decision in *Saunders* v *United Kingdom*, section 59 of and Schedule 3 to the Youth Justice and Criminal Evidence Act 1999 amend section 434 of the Companies Act 1985. In criminal proceedings, the prosecution will now not be able to adduce evidence or put questions to the accused with regard to his answers to questions from inspectors conducting an investigation under the 1985 Act unless the question is asked or the issue is raised by or on behalf the accused.

Whilst in *Saunders*, the United Kingdom government's unsuccessful submission to the European Court of Human Rights was based on the 'public interest' argument, a similar argument was later successfully used in respect of a challenge under the Convention to the powers contained in section 172 of the Road Traffic Act 1988. Section 172 requires the keeper of a vehicle to answer questions as to the identity of the driver of the vehicle where the driver is suspected of being involved in a road traffic offence. Failure to provide such information is an offence under section 172(3) of the 1988 Act, which, it was suggested, was in breach of a driver's privilege not to incriminate himself (*Brown* v *Stott (Procurator Fiscal, Dunfermline)* [2001] 2 All ER 97, see below).

In *R* v *Chauhan and Hollingsworth* (unreported, 13 July 2000, Birmingham Crown Court) two defendants were charged with dangerous driving after the West Midlands police filmed them allegedly racing cars through Birmingham city centre. At the trial, the Recorder of Birmingham, Judge Peter Crawford, ruled that the notice sent to the defendants requiring them to confirm whether they were driving the vehicles at the time of the alleged offences was incompatible with the privilege against self-incrimination and therefore in breach of Article 6.

The court in *Chauhan and Hollingsworth* had followed the decision in *Brown* v *Procurator Fiscal, Dunfermline* (2000) *The Times*, 14 February. In *Brown*, the police were called to an all-night superstore where B was suspected of having stolen a bottle of gin. The officers thought that she had been drinking and asked her how she had got to the store. She replied that she had driven there and pointed to a car that she said was hers. At the police station a set of car keys was found in her handbag and pursuant to section 172(2) of the Road Traffic Act 1988, the police required her to say who had driven the car to the store. B replied that she had driven the car. A breath test was administered that proved positive. The High Court of Justiciary was required to give consideration to the compatibility of section 172(2)(a) of the Road Traffic Act 1988 with the appellant's right to silence and the common law privilege against self-incrimination that are embodied, it was submitted by the defence, in the appellant's right to a fair trial under Article 6 of the Convention. It was pointed out to the court that section 172 of the Road Traffic Act 1988 changes the common law privilege in two respects. First, the keeper of a vehicle has no right to remain silent in the face of questions put to her by a police officer and, secondly, the reply can be used in evidence against the keeper if it turns out that she was the driver. It follows therefore that the police do not caution the keeper when the statement as to the driver's identity is made. In upholding the appeal, the High Court of Justiciary decided that the provision infringed Article 6 and that the Crown could no longer lead with evidence of any reply made by a suspect to a question put to her under section 172, as a person suspected of a crime had the right not to incriminate herself.

The Procurator Fiscal appealed to the Privy Council against the High Court of Justiciary's decision. The appeal was reported as *Brown v Stott (Procurator Fiscal, Dunfermline)* [2001] 2 All ER 97, where it was unanimously held, in allowing the Procurator Fiscal's appeal, that the admission obtained under section 172 of the 1988 Act did not breach Article 6 and could be relied on at trial, since the privilege against self-incrimination was not an absolute right and had to be balanced against the clear public interest in the enforcement of road traffic legislation in order to address the high incidence of death and injury on the roads caused by the misuse of motor vehicles. The right to a fair trial could not be compromised, but the constituent rights within that overall right could be limited to the extent that it was necessary to fulfil a clear and proper public objective. Furthermore, the operation of section 172 did not sanction prolonged questioning but provided for the putting of a single question that could not, without other evidence, incriminate the suspect. Lord Bingham further argued that the provision was compatible because the penalty was moderate and non-custodial. The trial judge retained the right to exclude admissions where there was a suggestion of improper coercion or oppression as stated in *Saunders v United Kingdom* (1997) 23 EHRR 313. The regulatory scheme, of which section 172 was part, was therefore a proportionate response to the problem of maintaining road safety and anyone who owned or drove a car knowingly subjected themselves to that regime.

In light of the decision in *Brown v Stott*, consider the following example on the compatibility under the Convention of a statute that abrogates the traditional limits of the privilege against self-incrimination.

Example

Dermot has been arrested on suspicion of involvement in a terrorist bombing. He was informed of the terms of section 52 of the Offences Against the State Act 1939, which make it a criminal offence punishable with six months' imprisonment for a person detained on suspicion of a defined terrorist offence to refuse to give a full account to the police of his movements and actions during the specified period. Dermot refused to respond to police questioning and was convicted of an offence under section 52 of the 1939 Act.

Question: has his right to a fair trial under Article 6 of the Convention been violated by his conviction and imprisonment?

Answer: following the decision in Brown v Stott *above, it would appear that the 1939 Act does not violate the Convention. However, when the case went before the European Court of Human Rights as* Heaney and McGuinness v Ireland *[2001] Crim LR 481, it was held that the applicants' right to a fair trial under Article 6(1) and (2) had been infringed. The Court confirmed that whilst the right to silence and the privilege against self-incrimination are not absolute, the degree of compulsion created by the threat of a prison sentence under the 1939 Act, in effect destroyed the very essence of these rights in a manner incompatible with the Convention.*

The decision in *Heaney and McGuinness* came a few weeks after the decision in *Brown v Stott*. It has been suggested that it might be possible to distinguish the decisions on the basis that in *Heaney and McGuinness* the applicants were left with the choice of providing the information required by the statute or of facing six months' imprisonment. According to the European Court of Human Rights, it was this degree of compulsion that destroyed the applicants' privilege against self-incrimination and their right to silence. By comparison in *Brown v Stott*, Lord Bingham stated that the penalties available under section 172 of the Road Traffic Act 1988 were moderate and non-custodial. However, this comment appears to understate the serious penalties that may be imposed under the section, which can include a fine of up to £1,000, a mandatory endorsement of the defendant's driving licence and in some situations the defendant's disqualification from driving. Also, in a number of previous decisions including *Funke v France* (1993) 16 EHRR 297 and *Murray v United Kingdom* (1996) 22 EHRR 29 as well as in *Heaney and McGuinness*, the European Court of Human Rights has stated that the threat of accumulating a fine was sufficient to destroy the privilege against self-incrimination. On this point the Privy Council appears not to have applied the interpretative requirement under section 2 of the Human Rights Act 1998, which requires United Kingdom courts to take into account the decisions of the European Court of Human Rights when interpreting domestic legislation. It is therefore perverse that the Privy Council in *Brown v Stott* should have reached the conclusion it did on the compatibility of section 172 of the Road Traffic Act 1988 with the privilege against self-incrimination. The perversity of the decision is heightened by the unanimous ruling of the Privy Council and it remains to be seen whether the decision can be sustained as a proper interpretation of the privilege against self-incrimination under the obligations imposed by section 2 of the Human Rights Act 1998.

Further reading

Allan, T.R.S., 'Legal Privilege and the Principle of Fairness in the Criminal Trial' [1987] Crim LR 449.

Boniface, D.J., 'Legal Professional Privilege and Disclosure Powers of Investigative Agencies: Some Interesting and Troubling Issues Regarding Competing Public Policies' (1992) 16 Criminal Law Journal 320.

Murphy, G., 'The Innocence at Stake Test and Legal Professional Privilege: A Logical Progression for the Law ... But Not for England' [2001] Crim LR 728.

Newbold, A.L.E., 'The Crime/Fraud Exceptions to Legal Professional Privilege' (1990) 53 MLR 472.

Chapter 11

BURDENS AND STANDARDS OF PROOF

INTRODUCTION

In previous chapters we have largely been concerned with the pre-trial gathering of evidence. This and succeeding chapters focus on the conduct of the trial itself. The rules relating to burdens and standards of proof underpin the entire process of proof. Every step undertaken before the trial with a view to gathering evidence and every decision taken at trial is inevitably shaped by the participants' knowledge as to which party bears the burden of proof on a particular matter.

This chapter examines the rules relating to burdens and standards of proof in criminal cases. Fundamental to an understanding of this topic is the acknowledgement that two types of burden exist in any given case: the legal burden of proof and the evidential burden of proof.

The analogy of the criminal trial as being akin to a game or contest is often made. If the analogy is an accurate one, the rules relating to the allocation of the burden of proof effectively determine which of the two opposing sides lose the trial game. If the party, upon whom the burden of proof lies, fails to discharge that burden, that party loses the case.

The general rule in criminal cases is that the prosecution bears the burden of proving the defendant's guilt and the substantive law defines what the prosecution must prove in order to convict the defendant. This will usually comprise elements of the *mens rea* and *actus reus*: for example, when pursuing a conviction for theft, the prosecution must prove all the elements of the offence as laid down by section 1 of the Theft Act 1968 (namely a dishonest appropriation of property belonging to another with the intention to permanently deprive). Whilst the substantive law determines what needs to be proved, the rules relating to the burden of proof determine which side must prove the elements prescribed by the substantive law. The rules relating to the standard of proof determine how much proof is required for a party to persuade the fact finder.

THE LEGAL BURDEN OF PROOF

The legal burden is the requirement, most often on the part of the prosecution, to prove all the elements of the offence as prescribed by the substantive law beyond reasonable doubt. Terminology in this area can be confusing. The legal burden of proof is variously referred to as being the overall burden, the persuasive burden or the ultimate burden. Whenever a party bears a legal burden of proof in a particular case, then by necessary implication, it will also bear an evidential burden of proof, as the former cannot be discharged without the latter. The evidential burden expresses the requirement for a party to adduce sufficient, relevant and admissible evidence for the court to be in a position to consider that party's version of the facts in determining the overall legal burden of proof.

The prosecution's burden of proof

The classic authority as regards the allocation of the burden of proof in criminal cases is discussed below.

Woolmington v DPP [1935] AC 462

The defendant had shot his wife and was on trial for her murder. In his defence he asserted his gun had discharged itself accidentally. The trial judge directed the jury that once the prosecution had proved the defendant had killed the deceased, it was for him to show that the killing was not murder. This misapprehension was swiftly and firmly corrected in the House of Lords.

Woolmington v *DPP* gives rise to one of the most famous and memorable statements of principle in English evidence law as delivered by Viscount Sankey:

> Throughout the web of the English criminal law one golden thread is always to be seen, that is the duty of the prosecution to prove the prisoner's guilt ... No matter what the charge or where the trial the principle that the prosecution must prove the guilt of the prisoner is part of the common law of England and no attempt to whittle it down can be entertained.

This statement of principle sits squarely with Article 6(2) of the European Convention on Human Rights, namely that:

> Everyone charged with a criminal offence shall be presumed innocent until proved guilty according to law.

The allocation of the legal burden of proof on the prosecution is regarded as a fundamental expression of the presumption of innocence. It also reflects an aspect of procedural fairness in that the prosecution has considerably more resources at its disposal than the defendant and therefore it should bear the burden of proving the accused's guilt.

A practical consequence of the prosecution bearing the legal burden of proof is that the prosecutor always opens the case at trial and presents its evidence first. In discharging its burden the prosecution must disprove any defence or explanation raised by the accused. The legal burden of proof inevitably comes to the fore at the conclusion of the trial when the jury or magistrates retire to consider their verdict on the totality of the evidence presented, including any evidence presented by the defendant. Only if the accused is found guilty will the prosecution know it has discharged its legal burden of proof in the particular case to the required standard of proof.

THE EVIDENTIAL BURDEN OF PROOF

The evidential burden is inextricably linked with the legal burden of proof. The prosecution cannot discharge its legal burden of proof without adducing evidence. Such evidence may take the form of witnesses giving oral testimony, evidence admitted under the common law or statutory exceptions to the hearsay rule, documentary evidence and real evidence as exhibits before the court.

On occasion, the evidential burden of proof is independent of the legal burden of proof considered at the close of the prosecution's case, before the defence presents its evidence. This will be the case where the defence makes a submission that there is no case to answer. In the magistrates' court, the submission should be upheld where the circumstances outlined in the *Practice Direction (Submission of No Case)* [1962] 1 WLR 227 apply. The submission should succeed where:

1   there has been no evidence to prove an essential element of the offence charged; or
2   the prosecution evidence is so manifestly unreliable (or has been so discredited by cross-examination) that no reasonable tribunal could convict on it.

Whilst the procedure in the Crown Court is the same, the test applied is somewhat different and is to be found in Lord Lane's judgment in *R v Galbraith* [1981] 2 All ER 1060:

> How then should the judge approach a submission of 'no case'? (1) If there is no evidence that the crime alleged has been committed by the defendant, there is no difficulty. The judge of course will stop the case. (2) The difficulty arises where there is some evidence but it is of a tenuous character, for example because of the inherent weakness or vagueness or because it is inconsistent with other evidence. (a) Where the judge comes to the conclusion that the Crown's evidence, taken at its highest, is such that a jury properly directed could not properly convict upon it, it is his duty, on a submission being made, to stop the case. (b) Where however the Crown's evidence is such that its strength or weakness depends on the view to be taken of a witness's reliability, or other matters which are generally speaking within the province of the jury and where on one possible view of the facts there *is* evidence on which a jury could properly come to the conclusion that the defendant is guilty, then the judge should allow the matter to be tried by the jury.

In the Crown Court a submission of no case to answer is a matter for the judge to decide in the absence of the jury.

If, at the close of its case, the prosecution has discharged its evidential burden in the sense that a submission of no case to answer is not made or is unsuccessfully made, it must wait until the verdict is delivered to see if it has discharged its overall legal burden of proof. Avoiding or overcoming a submission of no case therefore represents the first evidential hurdle the prosecution is required to overcome.

Case scenario

X is charged with robbery. X denies the offence. To prove the allegation of robbery the prosecution will have to prove, in accordance with section 8(1) of the Theft Act 1968, that X dishonestly appropriated property belonging to another with the intention to permanently deprive (the mens rea *for theft) and that before or at the time of doing so and in order to do so, X used force on any person or put any person in fear of force being used.*

To discharge the legal burden of proof, the prosecution must adduce evidence (the evidential burden). This will involve calling witnesses such as the victim of the robbery, the investigating officers, and any other witnesses who can provide relevant evidence in support of the prosecution's case. The victim should be able to give evidence that items were stolen from her and that force was used in doing so. If X made incriminating admissions at the police station or if incriminating items were found in his possession linking him to the scene of the robbery, the investigating officers would be able to give evidence that this was the case. Other types of evidence may assist the prosecution, including real evidence such as video surveillance and the use of documentary evidence in appropriate cases. If any doubt existed as to X's presence at the scene of the robbery, forensic evidence in the form of expert opinion evidence might assist. The prosecution will adduce this evidence as part of its examination-in-chief of its own witnesses.

The defence is of course entitled to cross-examine the prosecution's witnesses with a view to exploring inconsistencies in the evidence or flaws in the prosecution's case. Equally the defence may choose to present its own evidence which, in turn, is tested by the prosecution in its cross-examination of defence witnesses.

In this case X might claim he had an alibi at the time of the robbery. If the prosecution is to discharge its overall legal burden of proof it must cast doubt on the alibi evidence. The defendant may choose to give evidence in support of his own defence, denying the allegation. In short, the evidential burden of proof is the practical way in which the prosecution discharges its legal burden and the way in which the defendant may raise a reasonable doubt as to the issue of his guilt.

In the above scenario, if the prosecution cannot adduce evidence to prove force was used against the victim or that the victim was put in fear of force being used against her, the judge either of his own volition or at the request of the defence, should direct the jury to acquit on the charge of robbery because the prosecution have failed to discharge the evidential burden of proving an essential element of the crime of robbery. The jury would still have the right to return a guilty verdict on the alternative lesser offence of theft, if satisfied of the defendant's guilt beyond reasonable doubt.

Similarly, if the issue were to revolve around disputed identification evidence and the prosecution's case in this regard is so inherently weak that no jury, properly directed could properly convict, the defence would be entitled to succeed on a submission of no case to answer'.

Is a legal burden of proof ever cast on the defendant?

According to Viscount Sankey in *Woolmington* v *DPP*, no attempt to whittle down the 'golden thread' principle that the burden of proving the defendant's guilt rests on the prosecution can be entertained. There are however three instances in which a legal burden of proof is cast upon the defendant to effectively establish his innocence: insanity, express statutory provisions and implied statutory provisions. We will consider each in turn.

Insanity

The rules relating to insanity, most commonly pleaded in murder cases, are contained in *M'Naghten's Case* (1843) 10 Cl & F 200. In short, where the defendant pleads not guilty by reason of insanity he has the legal burden of proving that at the time of the offence he was insane, ie he was suffering from a defect of reason caused by a disease of the mind so that he did not know the nature and quality of his act or, if he did know the nature and quality of his act, he did not know that what he was doing was wrong.

Example

A is charged with murder. He pleads insanity. The incidence of the legal and evidential burden of proof are as follows:

The prosecution has the legal and evidential burdens of proving the actus reus *and* mens rea *of murder beyond reasonable doubt. If these burdens are successfully discharged, the onus falls on the defendant to prove on the balance of probability that he was insane within the M'Naghten Rules at the time he committed the offence. Proof of insanity will be discharged on the evidence of expert psychiatric evidence which is likely to be challenged by the prosecution. If the jury believes the defence evidence, A will be entitled to a verdict of not guilty of murder by reason of insanity.*

Statutory provisions expressly imposing a legal burden of proof on the defendant

There are a number of statutes where Parliament has expressly imposed a legal burden on the defendant to prove one or more facts in issue, which in practice means that the defendant has to prove his innocence. The range of offences varies from minor offences to the more serious. Such provisions are sometimes referred to as 'reverse onus' or 'reverse burden clauses'. The statute sometimes gives rise to a presumption of guilt upon proof of certain facts, requiring the defendant to disprove his guilt. In some instances the burden relates to the proof of the mental element, of the offence which is often difficult for the prosecution to prove. Examples of statutes which by the words used expressly impose a legal burden of proof on the defendant include:

1 *Homicide Act 1957, section 2(2).* On a charge of murder, where the defendant seeks to rely on the defence of diminished responsibility, section 2(2) provides: 'it shall be for the defence to prove that the person charged is by virtue of this section not liable to be convicted of murder.' Where the accused proves his diminished responsibility, he will be convicted of voluntary manslaughter.

2 *Prevention of Crime Act 1953, section 1(1).* 'Any person who without lawful authority or reasonable excuse, the proof whereof shall lie on him, has with him in any public place any offensive weapon shall be guilty of an offence.'

3 *Sexual Offences Act 1956, section 30(1).* The subsection provides that it is an offence for a man knowingly to live wholly or in part on the earnings of a prostitute. Section 30(2) further states: 'for the purposes of this section a man who lives with or is habitually in the company of a prostitute, or who exercises control ... over a prostitute's movements in a way which shows that he is aiding, abetting or compelling her prostitution with others, shall be presumed to be knowingly living on the earnings of prostitution unless he proves to the contrary'.

4 *Prevention of Corruption Act 1906, section 2.* 'where in any proceedings against a person for an offence under the Act it is proved that any money, gift or other consideration has been paid or given to or received by a person holding a public office, the money, gift or consideration shall be deemed to have been paid or given and received corruptly ... unless the contrary is proved'.

Statutory provisions impliedly imposing a legal burden of proof on the defendant

The most controversial instance of a legal burden being cast on the defendant is in relation to those statutes which by implication cast a legal burden on the defendant to
establish his innocence. It is for the court to determine by interpretation whether a
statute imposes a burden by implication. A statutory section of some importance in
this respect is section 101 of the Magistrates' Courts Act 1980.

> Where the defendant to an information or complaint relies for his defence on any excep-
> tion, proviso, excuse or qualification, whether or not it accompanies the description of
> the offence or matter of complaint in the enactment creating the offence or on which the
> complaint is founded, the burden of proving the exception, exemption, proviso, excuse
> or qualification shall be on him; and this notwithstanding that the information or com-
> plaint contains an allegation negating the exception, exemption, proviso, excuse or
> qualification.

The wording of the section is clear enough! The difficulty however comes in trying to
differentiate between an element forming part of the definition of an offence, which
the prosecution must prove, and an element comprising an exemption, exception, or a
proviso which the defendant is required to prove.

Section 101 has its origins in cases like *R v Turner* (1861) 5 M & S 206. The defendant in this case was charged with poaching. There were ten exceptions to the offence
which legalised poaching. The court held it was for the defendant to prove which
exception his actions fell within. It would have been an onerous undertaking for the
prosecution to disprove all ten exceptions. For the defendant, however, it could more
easily be assumed that if one of the ten exceptions applied he would know which one
he fell within, as this was a matter 'peculiarly within his knowledge'. The rationale
behind the decision in *R v Turner* is therefore based on pragmatism and common
sense.

A more modern illustration of the above principle is illustrated below:

R v Edwards [1974] 2 All ER 1085

This case confirmed that the predecessor section to section 101 of the Magistrates' Courts Act 1980
applies to all statutory offences, including those tried on indictment. Edwards was prosecuted for selling alcohol without a licence. The prosecution proved he had sold alcohol, but it did not prove the
absence of a licence, contending the burden in this respect lay with the defendant. The court agreed.
The court adopted the following formulation of section 101:

> In our judgment this line of authority establishes that over the centuries the common law, as a result of
> experience and the need to ensure justice is done both to the community and the defendants, has
> evolved an exception to the fundamental rule of our common law that the prosecution must prove every
> element of the crime offence charged. The exception, like so much else in the common law, was ham-
> mered out on the anvil of pleading. It is limited to offences arising under enactment which prohibit the
> doing of an act save in specified circumstances or by persons of specified classes or with specialised
> qualifications or with the licence or permission of specified authorities. Whenever the prosecution seeks
> to rely on this exception, the court must construe the enactment....If the true construction is that the
> enactment prohibits the doing of acts, subject to proviso, exemptions and the like, then the prosecution
> can rely on the exception...
>
> In our judgment its application does not depend upon either the fact or the presumption that the defen-
> dant has peculiar knowledge enabling him to prove the positive of any negative averment.

The decision in *R* v *Edwards* widened the principle in *R* v *Turner*. It held that the issue of whether a legal burden of proof falls on the defendant is simply a question of construction of the relevant statutory section.

A number of offences likely to fall within the definition of section 101 will tend to be less serious, regulatory offences such as driving without a valid driving licence or policy of insurance. An example of a statutory section that would come within the meaning of section 101 is section 161 of the Highways Act 1980, which provides that:

> ... if a person without lawful authority, deposits anything whatsoever on the highway, in consequence of which a user of the highway is injured or endangered, that person shall be guilty of an offence.

Under section 161 of the Highways Act 1980 the prosecution would bear the legal burden of proving that on the date specified in the summons, the defendant deposited a substance on the highway which resulted in a user of the highway being injured or endangered. When the legal burden in this regard has been discharged, it passes to the defendant to prove, on the balance of probabilities, that he had a lawful excuse to deposit the material on the highway. A failure by the defendant to discharge that legal burden of proof will result in conviction for the offence.

Section 101 of the 1980 Act saves the prosecution time and the expense of proving something which the defendant is best placed to know or to which he can gain easy access. In this sense the application of the section is less controversial. In the following case however, an attempt was made to apply section 101 to an offence under the Misuse of Drugs Act 1971. Both the Court of Appeal and the House of Lords were given the opportunity to consider the reasoning in *R* v *Edwards*.

R *v* Hunt [1987] AC 352

The defendant was found in possession of morphine, a controlled drug. In accordance with section 5(2) of the Misuse of Drugs Act 1971 any preparation of morphine containing not more than 0.2% of morphine compound is exempt from prohibition. Somewhat unusually, the prosecution adduced no evidence to prove that the accused was in possession of more than 0.2% of morphine. The defendant contended that the prosecution had not discharged its legal burden of proof in accordance with the definition of the offence.

The Court of Appeal ([1986] QB 125) concluded that the defendant was trying to bring himself within an exception, as defined by section 101 of the Magistrates' Courts Act 1980 and therefore the legal burden of proving he was not in possession of a compound containing more than 0.2% morphine rested on him.

The House of Lords reversed the decision of the Court of Appeal.

In seeking to clarify the law, the House of Lords stated:

1 The suggestion in argument that any exceptions to the principle in *Woolmington* v *DPP* applied only to express statutory provisions was incorrect in that there were cases before the *Woolmington* decision which imposed a legal burden of proof on the defendant by implication.

2 Where a statute places a legal burden of proof on the defendant by implication, that burden is on the accused whether the case is tried summarily or on indictment.

3   Whether a statute places the burden of proof on the accused depends on the construction of the statute and the presence of words like 'exception, proviso, exemption' is not conclusive.

4   The formula expressed in R v *Edwards* should be used as an excellent but not conclusive guide to construction although occasions where a statute will be construed as imposing a burden of proof on the defendant which do not fall within the formulation will be rare.

In addition some useful guidelines can be distilled from the judgments in R v *Hunt* on the construction of statutory enactments in cases where the linguistic construction does not clearly indicate on whom the burden should lie:

(a)   as a starting point it should not be easily inferred that Parliament intended to transfer the burden of proof on the defendant;

(b)   the court should have regard to the intention of Parliament and to the mischief at which the statutory section is aimed;

(c)   the ease or difficulty a party would have in discharging the burden should be borne in mind;

(d)   the more serious the offence, the less it could be assumed that Parliament had intended to transfer a legal burden of proof onto the defendant;

(e)   if the statutory provision contains an ambiguity which cannot be resolved, the defendant should be given the benefit of the doubt.

Having construed the wording of the statute, the House of Lords concluded the strength of the morphine compound was an element of the offence and as such the burden of proving its strength lay with the prosecution. Applying its guidelines to the facts, the House of Lords observed that the offence with which the defendant was charged was a serious one and that the defendant would have very real practical difficulties in discharging a burden requiring him to prove the compound's strength. The defendant was not a qualified pharmacist and could not be described as being in a position analogous to that of the defendant in R v *Edwards* who could easily have produced his liquor licence or obtained a further copy of it. Additionally, a suspect substance in such a case is usually seized by the prosecution to enable analysis. There is no statutory provision entitling the defendant to a portion of it and indeed in the course of analysis the substance may well have been destroyed.

Whenever a legal burden is cast on the defendant, the standard of proof is always on the balance of probabilities (R v *Carr-Briant* [1943] KB 607). Here the defendant was charged with corruption under the Prevention of Corruption Act 1906. The prosecution had proved the defendant had made a gift to a government employee. Under the statute, corruption is presumed in such circumstances unless the defendant can prove otherwise. The trial judge directed the jury that they had to be satisfied that the defendant had established lack of corruption beyond reasonable doubt. Quashing the conviction, the Court of Appeal held the burden could be discharged on the balance of probabilities.

Wherever a secondary issue arises in a trial (for example, a dispute regarding the admissibility of a certain item of evidence) the burden of proof generally falls on the party who seeks to adduce the evidence. Where the prosecution wishes to adduce a confession the admissibility of which the defendant disputes, section 76 of the Police and Criminal Evidence Act 1984 makes it clear that the prosecution bears the burden of proving its admissibility beyond reasonable doubt. Similarly were the prosecution to seek to rely on a hearsay statement being admitted either at common law or under statute, it must prove the conditions for the admissibility of such hearsay evidence beyond reasonable doubt.

Is an evidential burden cast on the defendant?

In the exceptional circumstances where a legal burden of proof is cast on the defendant, the defendant can only discharge that burden by adducing sufficient evidence to convince the fact finder on the balance of probabilities. For example, where the defendant is pleading insanity, it will be necessary for the defendant to adduce evidence of a psychiatric nature. This will normally require the calling of an expert witness in the field to give evidence. The prosecution will be entitled to discredit this evidence through cross-examination and reliance upon its own expert witness. But what of those cases where no legal burden of proof is cast upon the defendant? Is there an obligation still for the defendant to adduce evidence?

The prosecution bears the overall burden of proof from first to last. By pleading not guilty to an offence the defendant does no more than put the prosecution to proof of its case. The defendant need do nothing to assist the prosecution, although recent statutory changes requiring the defendant to make pre-trial disclosure and modifying the right to silence put pressure on a defendant to offer an explanation. The defendant could choose to do nothing, leaving the matter to the jury. Simply because the prosecution has discharged its evidential burden of proof at the close of its case, does not mean it will convince the jury on the overall legal burden of proof.

However, a defendant choosing to do nothing takes a considerable risk. In this sense there is nearly always a tactical or evidential burden upon him. In short, all that the defendant has to do in any given case is to raise a reasonable doubt. The defendant may achieve this through the cross-examination of prosecution witnesses; choosing to call his own witnesses and/or giving evidence himself.

However, whenever the nature of the defence goes beyond a mere denial, the accused has an evidential burden of adducing sufficient evidence in support of that defence for the magistrates to consider or for the matter to be left to the jury. This is the case even though there is no legal burden on the defendant to prove his defence. Lord Morris in *Bratty* v *Attorney-General of Northern Ireland* [1963] AC 386 described the position as follows:

> ...where the accused bears the evidential burden alone, he must adduce sufficient evidence as would, if believed and left uncontradicted, induce a reasonable doubt in the mind of the jury as to whether his version might not be true.

Lord Hutton has recently explained the difference between the imposition of an evidential burden and a legal burden on the defendant in the decision of the House of Lords in *R* v *Lambert* [2001] 3 All ER 577 (a case we will return to later):

> A persuasive burden is one where the matter in question must be taken as proved against the defendant unless he satisfies the jury on the balance of probabilities to the contrary. An evidential burden is one where the matter must be taken as proved against the defendant

unless there is sufficient evidence to raise an issue on the matter but, if there is sufficient evidence, then the burden rests on the prosecution to satisfy the jury as to the matter beyond reasonable doubt.

In saying there is an evidential burden on the defendant it is not necessary for the defendant to adduce sufficient evidence to convince the fact finder on the balance of probabilities. It is simply the requirement to adduce some evidence in support which is sufficient to raise a reasonable doubt in the mind of the fact finder.

Case law has confirmed an accused bears an evidential burden of proof in relation to the following affirmative defences:

- provocation – *Mancini v DPP* [1942] AC 1;
- self-defence – *R v Lobell* [1957] 1 QB 547;
- drunkenness – *Kennedy v HM Advocate* 1945 SLT 11;
- duress – *R v Gill* [1963] 1 WLR 841;
- non-insane automatism – *Bratty v Attorney-General of Northern Ireland* [1961] 3 WLR 965;
- intoxication – *Majewski v DPP* [1977] AC 443.

Where the defendant is merely denying he had the necessary *mens rea* for an offence (for example, in a rape case he asserts the victim consented or in a murder case that the killing was accidental) it is the duty of the prosecution to prove the necessary *mens rea* and not for the defendant to prove lack of it.

Where the accused discharges the evidential burden in the above situations, it is up to the prosecution to challenge the evidence in an attempt to convince the jury or magistrates that the defence cannot be sustained in the light of the prosecution evidence in the case.

PRACTICAL STEPS – ESTABLISHING A LEGAL OR EVIDENTIAL BURDEN

On a practical level it is important for the practitioner, as part of the case preparation, to undertake legal research into the offence with which his client is charged in order to ascertain whether a legal or evidential burden falls on the defendant. This is of fundamental importance in evaluating the overall strength of the prosecution's case before advising the defendant on the appropriate plea.

Where a client's case is being tried in the Crown Court, a careful note should always be taken of the judge's direction to the jury on the allocation of the burden of proof. A failure to direct or an incorrect direction that results in a conviction will almost certainly provide grounds for appeal and could lead to a conviction being quashed. For trials before magistrates, the defence advocate should take the opportunity in his closing speech to remind the bench upon which party the legal burden rests in order to prove its case successfully.

HUMAN RIGHTS LAW

The area of the law relating to the legal burden of proof which is most vulnerable to challenge under the Human Rights Act 1998 relates to where Parliament has expressly or impliedly placed a legal burden of proof on the defendant. On the face of it such a requirement is a violation of the right to a fair trial under Article 6 of the European Convention on Human Rights in that it clearly runs contrary to the presumption of innocence as declared in Article 6(2). Research conducted by Andrew Ashworth and Meredith Blake (see Further reading below) established that some 40% of offences tried in the Crown Court imposed a legal burden of proof on the defendant in potential violation of the presumption of innocence. Such a finding led the authors to conclude that Parliament has made inroads into the presumption of innocence all too frequently and in an arbitrary and indiscriminate manner.

As we saw in Chapter 2, the Human Rights Act 1998 requires courts to interpret primary legislation in a way that is compatible with Convention rights unless the wording of the statute clearly prevents them from doing so. The question therefore arises as to the status of those provisions that place a legal burden of proof on the defence.

The European Court of Human Rights has in fact already considered the compatibility of reverse onus clauses (imposing a legal burden of proof on the defendant to establish his innocence) in the case of *Salabiaku* v *France* (1991) 13 EHRR 379. Giving its judgment, the Court provided the following guidance:

> Presumptions of fact or of law operate in every legal system. Clearly, the Convention does not prohibit such presumptions in principle. It does however require the Contracting States to remain within certain limits in this respect as regards criminal law ... Article 6(2) does not therefore regard presumptions of fact or of law provided for in criminal law with indifference. It requires States to confine them within reasonable limits which take into account the importance of what is at stake and maintain the rights of the defence.

Such clauses do not therefore violate Article 6(2) *per se*, provided that such an imposition falls within 'reasonable limits' having regard to what is the overriding purpose of the enactment. The House of Lords chose to consider the compatibility of a reverse onus clause with the rights guaranteed under Article 6 in *R* v *Lambert* below. This important case requires careful consideration since the ramifications of the decision raise questions about the general validity of reverse onus clauses in English law.

The appeal in *R* v *Lambert* was dismissed by the majority in the House of Lords on the ground that the Human Rights Act 1998 had no application as it had not been fully implemented at the time the case was tried and could not be applied retrospectively. Thus, although the observations made by their Lordships in relation to reverse onus clauses were purely *obiter*, their judgments have significant implications for the way in which courts might in the future choose to interpret those statutes in which Parliament has expressly or impliedly placed a legal burden of proof on the accused.

R v Lambert [2001] 3 All ER 577

The defendant was convicted of an offence of possession of a controlled drug with intent to supply contrary to section 5(3) of the Misuse of Drugs Act 1971. Two police officers gave evidence that they had witnessed the defendant get off a train in Liverpool, meet with two men at the station and then proceed with the men to two cars parked outside the station. When the defendant returned to the station he was in possession of a duffel bag and was on his own. He was stopped by the two officers who asked him what he had got in the bag. The defendant stated he did not know and that he had simply been paid to pick the bag up and to deliver it. The bag was found to contain two kilogrammes of cocaine.

In his defence the defendant maintained he had no knowledge of the contents of the bag. He had received a telephone call the previous evening from a man he knew by the name of John who was in the business of printing tee shirts. He had met with John and had been given an envelope containing money and had been asked by John to make a collection on Liverpool train station. The defendant maintained he had made trips on John's behalf before in order to pay his supplier. He would normally be given packages of tee shirts in return for the money. In evidence the defendant stated that on this particular occasion he had asked the two men at the station what the bag contained. They had told him it was scrap gold. When he tried to look in the bag the two men had threatened him. At no stage did he know or suspect the bag contained controlled drugs. At trial the defendant maintained he had acted under duress and that he had not known or suspected or had reason to suspect that he was in possession of a controlled drug.

Section 5(3) of the Misuse of Drugs Act 1971 has to be read in conjunction with section 28 of the Act. Section 5(3) provides:

> (3) Subject to section 28 of this Act, it is an offence for a person to have a controlled drug in his possession, whether lawfully or not, with intent to supply it to another...

Section 28 provides:

> (2) Subject to subsection (3) below, in any proceedings for an offence to which this section applies it shall be a defence for the accused to prove that he neither knew of nor suspected nor had reason to suspect the existence of some fact alleged by the prosecution which it is necessary for the prosecution to prove if he is to be convicted of the offence charged.
>
> (3) Where in any proceedings for an offence to which this section applies it is necessary, if the accused is to be convicted of the offence charged, for the prosecution to prove that some substance or product involved in the alleged offence was the controlled drug which the prosecution alleges it to have been, and it is proved that the substance or product in question was that controlled drug, the accused—
> > (a) shall not be acquitted of the offence charged by reason only of providing that he neither knew nor suspected nor had reason to suspect that the substance or product in question was the particular controlled drug alleged; but
> > (b) shall be acquitted thereof—
> > > (i) if he proves that he neither believed nor suspected nor had reason to suspect that the substance or product in question was a controlled drug; or
> > > (ii) if he proves that he believed the substance or product in question to be a controlled drug, or a controlled drug of a description, such that, if it had in fact been that controlled drug or a controlled drug of that description, he would not at the material time have been committing any offence to which this section applies.

The trial judge directed the jury that it was for the prosecution to prove the defendant was in possession of a controlled drug and then for him to prove on the balance of probabilities that he neither knew nor suspected nor had reason to suspect that the substance in his possession was a controlled drug. In relation to the defence of duress, the trial judge explained to the jury that it was for the prosecution to prove beyond reasonable doubt that the defendant had not acted under duress. The jury convicted the defendant and he subsequently appealed.

The Court of Appeal delivered its judgment on the assumption that the Human Rights Act 1998 was applicable even though the Act was not in force at the time of the appeal. It concluded that section 5(3) read in conjunction with section 28 of the Misuse of Drugs Act 1971 was compliant with the presumption of innocence in accordance with the European Court of Human Rights' decision in *Salabiaku* v *France*. The imposition on the defendant was within reasonable limits taking into account the importance of what was at stake and the defendant's rights had been maintained throughout.

Analysing the statutory provisions, the Court of Appeal held that in enacting section 5(3) of the Misuse of Drugs Act 1971, Parliament had deliberately chosen to simplify the prosecution's task. The prosecution was merely required to prove that the defendant was in fact in possession of a controlled drug. Proof of possession requires the prosecution to show that the defendant had knowledge of the presence of the object found to contain the drugs. In this case the defendant had been found in possession of the duffel bag. The prosecution did not have to prove the defendant knew the nature of the contents of the bag, which happened to be a controlled drug.

In the Court of Appeal's view, Parliament had made a deliberate choice to restrict the extent of the defendant's knowledge required for the commission of the offence and due deference ought to be given to Parliament's intentions in this matter. Parliament had mitigated the defendant's position by making it a defence for him to prove he had no knowledge or suspicion that the contents of the bag were in fact a controlled drug. The approach adopted by the legislature was a proportional response. To require the prosecution to prove guilty knowledge on the defendant's part would undermine the fight against the trade in drugs, in that a defence of 'I didn't know what was in the box' would be a very easy assertion for a defendant to make and one that would be difficult for the prosecution to refute.

Although upholding the conviction, the majority in the House of Lords took a different view from the Court of Appeal. Lords Steyn, Slynn, Hope and Clyde all came to the conclusion that the legislative interference with the presumption of innocence by the imposition of a legal burden of proof on the defendant was not a proportional response having regard to what was at stake. Accordingly, unless section 3 of the Human Rights Act 1998 could be applied in order to read the section in a compliant way with Convention rights, the House of Lords would be forced to make a declaration of incompatibility. In fact, each Law Lord came to the conclusion that section 5(3) of the Misuse of Drugs Act 1971 read in conjunction with section 28 could be 'read down' as imposing an evidential burden of proof only on the defendant. Therefore the wording in the statute 'to prove' could be read as saying 'to give sufficient evidence'. (For further explanation of the operation of the Human Rights Act 1998 and the application of section 3 in particular, see Chapter 2. Chapter 2 also explains the principle of proportionality, a core concept in Strasbourg jurisprudence, which is considered and applied at length in R v *Lambert*.)

Of concern to the majority in the House of Lords in R v *Lambert* was the fact that the defence contained within section 28 of the Misuse of Drugs Act 1971 was very closely linked to the *mens rea* element of the crime, ie the need to establish the defendant's knowledge of what he was carrying. It was proof of this element of the offence that could justify a substantial term of imprisonment in the event of the defendant being convicted. What then was the legislature's justification for imposing the legal burden of proving the absence of knowledge or belief on the defendant in this particular instance? Lord Clyde articulated the reasons as follows:

> Reasons can readily be adduced to support the imposition of the burden of proof on the accused in the present context. Firstly, the question whether the accused was ignorant or had no reason to suspect that what he possessed was a controlled drug is a matter very much within his own knowledge. There are sound practical reasons for imposing the burden on him to prove his ignorance. Secondly, the proof may be relatively easy for him, as I

have already noted. Thirdly, there is a serious consideration of the public interest in the discouragement of what is well recognised as a grave social evil, the unlawful distribution of controlled drugs. Fourthly, the knowledge of the defendant of the nature of what he possessed is brought in as a defence, not as an ingredient of the offence. In some cases it may never arise. It can be strongly argued that a transfer of a persuasive burden of proof onto the defendant under section 28 could be compatible with Article 6(2).

In short, the legitimate aim behind the legislation had been to facilitate the easier conviction of individuals who pick up sealed containers that happen to contain drugs and for whom it would be all too easy to assert that they were unaware of their contents. The prosecution would face considerable practical difficulties in proving the defendant's actual knowledge. Overall, the section had a legitimate aim, but was the response by imposing a legal burden of proof on the defendant no more than was necessary in a democratic society? Lord Steyn reasoned:

> A transfer of a legal burden amounts to a far more drastic interference with the presumption of innocence than the creation of an evidential burden on the accused. The former requires the accused to establish his innocence. It necessarily involves the risk that, if the jury are faithful to the judge's direction, they may convict where the accused has not discharged the legal burden resting on him but left them unsure on the point. This risk is not present if only an evidential burden is created.
>
> The principle of proportionality requires the House to consider whether there was a pressing necessity to impose a legal rather than evidential burden on the accused. The effect of section 28 is that in a prosecution for possession of controlled drugs with intent to supply, although the prosecution must establish that prohibited drugs were in the possession of the defendant, and that he or she knew that the package contained something, the accused must prove on a balance of probabilities that he did not know that the package contained controlled drugs. If the jury is in doubt on this issue, they must convict him. This may occur when an accused adduces sufficient evidence to raise a doubt about his guilt but the jury is not convinced on a balance of probabilities that his account is true. Indeed it obliges the court to convict if the version of the accused is as likely to be true as not. This is a far reaching consequence: a guilty verdict may be returned in respect of an offence punishable by life imprisonment even though the jury may consider that it is reasonably possible that the accused had been duped. It would be unprincipled to brush aside such possibilities as unlikely to happen in practice. Moreover, as Justice has pointed out in its valuable intervention, there may be real difficulties in determining the real facts upon which the sentencer must act in such cases. In any event, the burden of showing that only a reverse legal burden can overcome the difficulties of the prosecution in drugs cases is a heavy one.

The majority took the view that the difficulties faced by the prosecution if it were required to prove the defendant's knowledge were far from insurmountable. The fact that an individual is found to be in possession of a sealed container which happens to contain drugs effectively compels him to offer an explanation if he wishes to avoid conviction. In addition the provisions under sections 34 and 35 of the Criminal Justice and Public Order Act 1994 permitting an adverse evidential inference to be drawn in certain circumstances greatly assist the prosecution in this regard. In the majority view of the Law Lords it was unnecessary to impose a legal burden of proof on the defendant, as the imposition of an evidential burden would suffice.

Lord Hope further highlighted the conceptual difficulties faced by the jury in cases where the defendant bears a legal burden of proof:

The lack of clarity and the inconvenience of applying a different rule to defences created by statute is obvious in the present case. Section 28(4) of the 1971 Act provides that nothing in that section shall prejudice any defence which it is open to a person when charged with an offence to which that section applies to raise apart from that section. In this case the appellant did raise such a defence. It was his defence of duress. That defence was intimately bound up with his defence under the statute, as it depended entirely upon what the jury made of his evidence. But the trial judge had to direct the jury that the onus as regards the defence of duress rested on the prosecution. The jury were not told why there was a difference as to where the onus lay. There was no need for this information to be given to them. But it would not be surprising if they found it hard to maintain a clear distinction between the two positions as to onus when they examined the evidence...

Supporting the view that section 28 could be read as imposing an evidential as opposed to a legal burden of proof on the defendant, Lord Hope saw the following benefits.

The change in the nature of the burden is best understood by looking not at the accused and what he must do, but rather at the state of mind of the judge or jury when they are evaluating the evidence. That is why, in the interests of clarity and convenience as well as on grounds of principle, a fair balance will be struck by reading and giving effect to these subsections as imposing an evidential burden only on the accused.

Refuting the belief that the imposition of such a burden would be no more than illusionary, Lord Hope added that it would require the defendant to put evidence before the court which if believed by the jury would help establish a defence to the charge. Both Lords Hope and Steyn drew support for their position from the enactment of the Terrorism Act 2000. Responding to observations made on an *obiter* basis in the House of Lords earlier decision in *R v DPP, ex parte Kebilene* [1999] 3 WLR 972, the Terrorism Act 2000 contains several provisions which explicitly place an evidential as opposed to a legal burden of proof on the defendant to help establish various defences to different charges capable of being brought under the Act.

In what he hoped would be regarded as an opinion on the imposition of reverse onus clauses in general, Lord Clyde strongly observed:

The advent of the Human Rights Act 1998 has certainly sharpened a consciousness of the human right which is embodied in the presumption of innocence and invites a closer scrutiny of what Ashworth and Blake ('The Presumption of Innocence in English Criminal Law' [1996] Crim LR 314) have described as a large-scale derogation from basic principle. They quote the advice of the Eleventh Report of the Criminal Law Revision Committee that 'both on principle and for the sake of clarity and convenience in practice, burdens on the defence should be evidential only'. The 1998 Act should encourage a reconsideration of a trend which has for over a decade been exposed to powerful criticism.

   While it may be that offences under section 5 of the Misuse of Drugs Act may be described as regulatory they can lead to the most serious of consequences for the accused. Of course trafficking in controlled drugs is a notorious social evil, but if any error is to be made in the weighing of the scales of justice it should be to the effect that the guilty should go free rather than that an innocent person should be wrongly convicted. By imposing a persuasive burden on the accused it would be possible for an accused person to be convicted where the jury believed he might well be innocent but have not been persuaded that he probably did not know the nature of what he possessed. The jury may have a reasonable doubt as to his guilt in respect of his knowledge of the nature of what he possessed but still be required to convict. Looking to the potentially serious consequences of a conviction at least in respect of class A drugs it does not seem to me that such a burden is acceptable.

But I have no difficulty in finding the solution by an application of section 3 of the Human Rights Act 1998. It requires no straining of the language of section 28 to construe the references to proof as intending an evidential burden and not a persuasive one. Indeed, as I have already stated, it would be a construction to which I would in any event have inclined, even without the added compulsion of the Human Rights Act. The construction seems to me to be something which is well within the scope of what is 'possible' for the purposes of section 3 ... It seems to me that the proper way by which that harshness should be alleviated is to recognise that the accused should have the opportunity to raise the issue of his knowledge but to leave the persuasive burden of proof throughout on the prosecution. Respect for the 'golden thread' of the presumption of innocence deserves no less.

The one dissenting opinion came from Lord Hutton who was of the view that the imposition of an evidential burden on a defendant would serve no practical purpose. It would require nothing more than an assertion outside the witness box or through a third party that the defendant lacked the necessary knowledge and belief thereby making the prosecution's task of proving guilt an evidentially difficult one. The suggestion made by the majority of their Lordships that juries must find it difficult to differentiate between the various standards of proof dependent upon the defence raised by the accused is dismissed by Lord Hutton who cited the observations of Lord Pearce in the case of *Sweet* v *Parsley* [1970] AC 132:

Parliament might, of course, have taken what was conceded in argument to be a fair and sensible course. It could have said, in appropriate words, that a person is to be liable unless he proves that he had no knowledge or guilty mind. Admittedly, if the prosecution have to prove a defendant's knowledge beyond reasonable doubt, it may be easy for the guilty to escape. But it would be very much harder for the guilty to escape if the burden of disproving *mens rea* or knowledge is thrown on the defendant. And if that were done, innocent people could satisfy a jury of their innocence on a balance of probabilities. It has been said that a jury might be confused by the different nature of the onus of satisfying 'beyond reasonable doubt' which the prosecution have to discharge and the onus 'on a balance of probabilities' which lies on a defendant in proving that he had no knowledge or guilt. I do not believe that this would be so in this kind of case. Most people can easily understand rules that express in greater detail that which their own hearts and minds already feel to be fair and sensible.

Overall, Lord Hutton felt that Parliament's choice in framing the statutory sections in the way it had was a balanced and proportional response when directed towards the need to convict those guilty of supplying drugs. The corollary of requiring innocent individuals to prove their innocence is that fewer guilty individuals go free.

Despite the *obiter* nature of the observations made in *R* v *Lambert* the decision is one of constitutional significance which highlights the practical importance of the Human Rights Act 1998. The judgments draw attention to some fundamental concerns with reverse onus clauses and their compatibility with the presumption of innocence.

As evidenced by the Terrorism Act 2000, Parliament will in future have to give some searching thought as to whether it wants to impose a legal, as opposed to an evidential, burden of proof on a defendant regarding some aspect of an offence. The indiscriminate and unthinking manner in which Parliament has placed such a burden on the defendant in numerous statutory offences must now be regarded as a thing of the past.

What is unclear is how far the observations of the House of Lords in R v *Lambert* go. Is it a decision based purely on the Misuse of Drugs Act 1971? If an offence of greater social evil than the supply of drugs were to be considered by a later court would the public interest more easily justify the imposition of a legal burden of proof on the defendant? Given the strength of feeling expressed in some of the judgments it would seem not. Whether the lower courts will follow the House of Lords and apply section 3 of the Human Rights Act 1998 so as to impose an evidential burden in the context of other statutory offences remains to be seen.

THE STANDARD OF PROOF

The rules relating to the standard of proof determine the degree of proof required of the party bearing a legal burden of proof. There is a keen public interest in ensuring an accused is protected against the risk of a mistaken conviction. It stems in part from the philosophy that it is better ten guilty men go free than one innocent man be convicted. Of course, mistaken convictions cannot be prevented since no system of justice is infallible but the desire to guard against the risk of a mistaken conviction finds expression in the presumption of innocence and in the requirement that the prosecution prove the accused's guilt beyond reasonable doubt.

But what does 'proof beyond reasonable doubt' mean and how do judges convey the meaning of this venerable phrase to juries?

It is notoriously difficult to define proof beyond reasonable doubt, especially in the abstract. One juror's definition is likely to be different from another. When confronted with a set of conflicting facts each juror must reach a decision on the basis of what they understand its meaning to be. It is not an expression that is capable of being articulated in numerical terms. For example, if a juror were to state he was 95% sure of the defendant's guilt, would the remaining 5% constitute a reasonable doubt? In some instances a single piece of evidence such as DNA might be so cogent and compelling that by itself it proves the defendant's guilt to the required standard of proof. In cases which depend substantially or wholly on circumstantial evidence it may take the jury substantially longer to reach a conclusion because each piece of evidence requires careful consideration before it is placed in the overall evidential picture. Taken as a whole, circumstantial evidence is also capable of yielding proof beyond reasonable doubt.

In *Miller* v *Minister of Pensions* [1947] 2 All ER 372 in an often cited dictum Denning J described proof beyond reasonable doubt in the following terms.

> It need not reach certainty, but it must carry a high degree of probability. Proof beyond reasonable doubt does not mean proof beyond a shadow of a doubt. The law would fail to protect the community if it admitted fanciful possibilities to deflect the course of justice. If the evidence is so strong against a man as to leave only a remote possibility in his favour which can be dismissed with the sentence 'of course it is possible, but not the least probable', the case is proved beyond reasonable doubt, but nothing short of that will suffice.

The dictum was felt to be unsatisfactory and in R v *Summers* [1952] 1 All ER 1059, Lord Goddard suggested the phrase meant, 'satisfied so that you feel sure'.

Arguably the definitive view of the law in this regard is contained in *Walters* v R [1969] 2 AC 26. The Privy Council concluded definitions were unhelpful to the jury and should for the most part be avoided. Attempts in the past to define the standard of proof have led to confusion and numerous appeals. Precise wording is unnecessary as long as the substance is conveyed namely that it is a high standard of proof. The Privy Council went on to say that in exceptional circumstances where a jury needs help, a judge might say 'a reasonable doubt is one which you can assign a reason to, the sort of doubt which may affect the conduct of important affairs'.

Observing trials in real life will give a clearer picture of the personal preferences of judges. In truth, it does not really matter what particular form of words are used as long as the judge makes it clear that the burden rests on the prosecution, that it is an onerous one and that the jury must not convict if they entertain a reasonable doubt in their minds as to the defendant's guilt.

In those circumstances in which the defendant bears the burden of proving a particular defence, the burden is discharged on a balance of probabilities. This was defined by Denning J in *Miller* v *Minister of Pensions* as being: 'If the evidence is such that the tribunal can say: "We think it more probable than not", the burden is discharged, but, if the probabilities are equal, it is not.'

A failure to instruct the jury correctly on the standard of proof will almost certainly give grounds for an appeal which could result in a conviction being quashed on the basis of it being unsafe.

PROOF WITHOUT EVIDENCE?

As a general rule all facts in issue have to be proved in a case by relevant, admissible evidence. There are exceptions to this principle. Facts can be proved by the court taking judicial notice of them. They can be proved through the medium of presumptions and by the parties agreeing to formal admissions of facts. We shall consider each exception briefly.

Judicial notice and use of personal knowledge in place of proof or as an alternative to it

As a general rule a judge, juror or magistrate may not rely on his personal knowledge in a case as a form of proof. However, it is very difficult for a fact finder simply to put aside personal knowledge or expertise where it may have some value in assessing the evidence. In reality fact finders make use of their general knowledge and common assumptions in evaluating evidence all the time, mostly by a product of unconscious thought. If the case involves driving and the fact finder drives a car, such a person will make judgments based on his experience as to what can occur on the highway. The leading case on the prohibition of specialised personal knowledge is discussed below.

Wetherall *v* Harrison [1976] QB 773

The defendant was charged with failing to provide a specimen of blood in a drink/driving case. His defence was one of reasonable excuse; he had a phobia of needles. He contended the sight of a needle was likely to provoke a hysterical reaction. He adduced no medical evidence to substantiate his phobia. One of the justices in the case was a doctor. He discussed the matter with his fellow justices and stated that in his professional opinion the defendant's reaction was genuine. The other justices had wartime experience of inoculations and had come across cases of men refusing to be inoculated. The defendant was acquitted. The prosecution appealed on the basis that the justices had used their personal knowledge. The appeal was rejected with the Divisional Court making it clear that whilst personal knowledge could be used to interpret evidence presented, it should not be used extraneously to contradict evidence or as a substitution for evidence not actually presented.

The distinction between use of personal knowledge to interpret evidence but not to contradict is difficult to maintain in practice. In *Ingram v Percival* [1969] 1 QB 548, the defendant was charged with fishing in tidal waters which was unlawful. The prosecution did not adduce evidence to prove the waters were in fact tidal. The justices stated that they knew the waters to be tidal and convicted the defendant. In a decision which must be considered doubtful, the Divisional Court upheld the conviction concluding the justices were entitled to use their local knowledge. It is difficult to see how the justices were not supplying evidence omitted by the prosecution. At its best, this might be considered a case in which judicial notice of the fact that the fished waters were tidal was taken.

Where a court takes judicial notice of a fact, it declares itself satisfied of a particular fact without the need to call evidence to prove it. The need for proof on the particular point is thus obviated. Some notorious facts are judicially noticed without the need to make inquiry. In other instances judicial notice may be taken having consulted appropriate sources of information.

In theory a notorious fact is one so well known in the community at large that it would be a complete waste of time and expense to call evidence to prove it. Examples of notorious facts would include the acceptance of the unique nature of human fingerprints, the common knowledge that Christmas Day fell on 25 December and that in Great Britain motorists drive on the left. Once the judge has taken judicial notice of a fact it may not be contradicted and may be used as a precedent in future cases. His decision is final and in a case being tried on indictment the jury will be instructed to accept as fact the matter of which judicial notice has been taken.

Past cases include *R v Vice Chancellor of Oxford University* (1857) 21 JP 644 in which judicial notice was taken of the fact that Oxford University is a place for the advancement of learning and *Nye v Niblett* [1918] 1 KB 23 where judicial notice was taken of the fact that cats are kept for domestic purposes.

Previous case law has confirmed that a notorious fact does not need to be known amongst the entire population. Where a matter is common knowledge within a locality or profession or trade, judicial notice may be taken of such matters. This extension of common knowledge does however have a bearing on the use by the fact finder of his or her own specialised knowledge in a case, which is itself prohibited, as discussed above. The distinction between the use of personal knowledge and knowledge generally known within the community is arguably a fine one. In *Ingram v Percival* above it is not clear that the justices' knowledge of the tidal waters could be said to have been generally known in the locality. In light of the Human Rights Act 1998 and the right to a fair trial, this decision must be considered doubtful since no opportunity was afforded to the defendant to contradict or challenge the fact of which judicial notice was taken.

Judicial notice can be taken of facts following an inquiry by a judge or magistrates. In this instance the fact is not a notorious one but can readily be ascertained by consulting learned sources or hearing from appropriate witnesses. Judicial notice is often taken of political matters such as the extent of territorial waters or the sovereign status of a particular country. Inquiry in these instances would be made of the relevant government Minister or his agent. Reference is sometimes made to dictionaries as a means of clarifying the meaning of words or to historical works to establish ancient facts. A further illustration is afforded by the civil case of *McQuaker v Goddard* [1940] 1 KB 687. The claimant had been bitten by a camel in a zoo. For the purposes of the personal injury action it was necessary for the judge to determine whether a camel was a wild or tame animal. Having questioned a number of witnesses from each side on the nature and habits of camels and having consulted a number of published works on camels, the judge took judicial notice of the fact that a camel is a tame animal.

Formal admissions

In criminal proceedings both the defence and the prosecution can formally admit facts under section 10 of the Criminal Justice Act 1967. The use of formal admissions helps narrow down the issues in a trial, saving time and expense. On a charge of rape, for example, where the defence is to be one of mistaken identity, there is little point in putting the prosecution to proof of the rape itself. The precise means by which formal admissions can be made before trial are set out in section 10. Admissions must be made in writing and approved by the defendant's legal representatives. Formal admissions must be distinguished from informal admissions such as a confession, which must be proved by the prosecution.

Presumptions

There are different types of presumptions. Presumptions of fact do not compel the court to draw a conclusion. In other words when certain facts are presumed the court may choose to draw a particular inference unless the contrary is proved. The doctrine of recent possession, which applies in the context of stolen goods, illustrates the point. Where such goods are found in the presence of the defendant, then in the absence of a credible explanation from the defendant as to how they came to be in his possession, the jury may infer he is the thief or a handler of stolen goods. The jury is not compelled to draw such an inference but as a matter of common sense in the absence of an explanation, it might.

In addition there are irrebuttable presumptions of law. Where such presumptions apply an inference must be drawn and no evidence to the contrary can be entertained. Such presumptions form part of the substantive law; an example is the presumption that children under the age of ten cannot be guilty of a crime.

Finally there are rebuttable presumptions of law. They are defined such that, upon proof of certain facts, a conclusion must be drawn unless there is proof to the contrary. The death of a person is presumed at common law if he has been absent for a continuous period of seven years and during this time there has been no acceptable evidence that the person is alive. Furthermore, if there are people who would have been likely to hear from the absent person but they have not and all due inquiries have been made of his whereabouts without success, a rebuttable presumption of death arises. Evidence from a person claiming to have met or corresponded with the absent person within the last seven years would, if believed, rebut the presumption of death.

Further consideration of proof without evidence can be found in Chapter 23, which considers the burden of proof in civil cases.

Further reading

Ashworth, A. and Blake, M., 'The Presumption of Innocence in English Criminal Law' [1996] Crim LR 306.

Birch, D.J., 'Hunting the Snark: The Elusive Statutory Exception' [1998] Crim LR 221.

Healey, P., 'Proof and Policy: No Golden Threads' [1987] Crim LR 361.

Redmayne, R., 'Doubts and Burdens: DNA Evidence, Probability and the Courts' [1995] Crim LR 464.

Roberts, P., 'Taking the Burden of Proof Seriously' [1995] Crim LR 783.

Smith, J.C., 'The Presumption of Innocence' (1987) 38 NILQ 223.

Williams, G., 'Evidential Burdens on the Defence' (1977) 127 NLJ 182.

Zuckerman, A. (1989) *The Principles of Criminal Evidence*, Clarendon Press.

Chapter 12

THE HEARSAY RULE

INTRODUCTION

The hearsay rule has long had a reputation for its difficult and complex nature, causing students, legal practitioners and judges alike to approach it with a degree of apprehension.

The starting point when considering the rule in criminal cases is straightforward enough: evidence which satisfies the definition of hearsay is generally inadmissible. The rule applies to both the prosecution and the defence. The complexity associated with hearsay evidence arises, for the most part, from problems associated with its definition and the huge number of exceptions to the rule. The hearsay rule has a mandatory application in criminal cases and as such it can have the effect of excluding relevant evidence from the fact finders' consideration. In an attempt to overcome the rigid application of the rule, fine distinctions have been made by the judiciary to enable what, on the face of it, looks like hearsay evidence to be admitted at trial as non-hearsay evidence. The complexity associated with the rule's definition is further compounded by the fact that, notwithstanding the general rule of exclusion, a considerable patchwork of common law and statutory exceptions exist to admit hearsay evidence. The current status of the hearsay rule in criminal cases has developed over many years. It has generated a wealth of material and a plethora of case law. As a consequence, hearsay is discussed in this and the following two chapters of this book.

We begin this chapter by defining hearsay evidence and examining the rationale behind the general rule which excludes its use in criminal trials. We then go on to consider some conceptually difficult case law illustrations of hearsay. In Chapter 13 we consider the large number of common law exceptions which admit hearsay in defiance of the general exclusionary rule. Finally, Chapter 14 deals with the statutory exceptions to the hearsay rule.

The Law Commission extensively reviewed the hearsay rule in Consultation Paper No 138, *Evidence in Criminal Proceedings: Hearsay and Related Topics*. The Law Commission issued Report No 245, similarly entitled, in 1997. The report contains a number of recommendations for reform of hearsay evidence in criminal cases and is accompanied by a draft Criminal Evidence Bill. Consideration will be given to the Law Commission's criticisms of the current law and its proposals for reform in Chapter 14.

DEFINING HEARSAY

Hearsay has been variously defined. In the important case of *R v Kearley* [1992] 2 AC 228, it was described as 'an assertion other than one made by a person while giving oral evidence in the proceedings and tendered as evidence of the matters stated'.

Whenever a witness who perceives an event and subsequently gives an account of the event (perhaps by giving a statement to the police) or records certain information (perhaps by documenting it in a record of some description), later becomes unavailable to give a first-hand account in court of what he saw or did, a hearsay problem is likely to arise where an attempt is made to get the absent witness's evidence heard in court in some other form. This might include relying on a document in which the absent witness has given an account of the events he witnessed (ie the statement given to the police or the record). It can also include calling another witness to give an account in court of what the absent witness was heard to say or do.

Hearsay evidence therefore comprises the repetition in court of a statement or assertion made on an earlier out-of-court occasion for the purpose of proving the truth of some fact or facts asserted on the earlier occasion.

The following considerations apply in determining whether evidence falls within the hearsay rule:

1   The word 'assertion' covers all forms of communication, including written statements, oral statements and gestures, together with facts asserted in documents and records of all description, including in many instances computer records and tape-recorded interviews.
2   An assertion will have been made on a prior occasion if it was made other than in the course of the present proceedings before the court, for example, at a police station.
3   The rule on hearsay evidence only applies where the purpose of putting the earlier out-of-court assertion in evidence is to prove the truth of some fact asserted in the earlier statement. Where the earlier statement is being adduced for some purpose other than proving the truth of some fact asserted it will lack a hearsay quality. Making this distinction is not always straightforward and this is why some conceptually difficult illustrations of hearsay arise.
4   The ambit of the rule not only relates to one witness testifying in court about what he was told by another person but also extends to the witness repeating to the court what he himself has said on a previous occasion, so-called self-serving statements. As a general rule such self-serving statements are objectionable on the ground that they possess a hearsay quality and are to all intents and purposes evidentially irrelevant in that they add little, if anything, to what has already been said on oath. The general exclusionary rule is subject to exceptions. The rule and its exceptions are specifically dealt with in Chapter 15 as an aspect of examination-in-chief.

IDENTIFYING HEARSAY EVIDENCE

Consider the following examples:

Example 1

X witnesses a bank robbery. He memorises the registration number of the get-away car. It is FGH 465. X repeats this statement of fact in court, inviting the jury to accept the truth of what he is say-

ing, namely that the get-away car (containing four masked men) bore the registration number above. There is no hearsay problem with X's evidence since it is a first-hand account of what the witness perceived with his own senses.

Example 2

Suppose X told Y the registration number was FGH 465 and that for some reason X is unable to attend trial. For Y to repeat what X told him is hearsay and is prima facie inadmissible. The prosecution would be trying to prove facts through the mouth of Y when it is X who should be giving evidence in court. Unless an exception to the rule against hearsay can be found Y's evidence would be inadmissible.

Example 3

Varying Example 2, let us suppose X makes a statement to the police containing the registration number of the vehicle. Let us further suppose that X cannot attend the trial of the robbers. To admit the written statement would be an infringement of the rule against hearsay because it consists of a statement other than one made by a person whilst giving oral evidence in the proceedings (that person being X in this case), for the purpose of proving the truth of facts asserted by X on an earlier occasion. The written statement would constitute first-hand hearsay.

Example 4

Suppose A and B are jointly charged with a crime. A confesses to the crime, implicating B. A's confession constitutes hearsay evidence. It comprises a statement made on an earlier, out-of-court occasion, being relied on in court, most often by the prosecution, as evidence of the truth of the contents to which it deposes. Confessions are, as we saw in Chapter 6, an established common law exception to the rule against the admission of hearsay evidence. However, a confession in itself is only ever evidence against its maker. As against any other person implicated it constitutes inadmissible hearsay evidence. Were the prosecution to rely on A's confession in this instance, a jury would have to be directed not to use it in evidence against B.

Example 5

C, an employee, deposits a sum of money in the firm's accounts. C tells D, the firm's cashier, of this fact and D records it in the firm's ledger. Adducing the ledger as proof of the money deposited would constitute hearsay evidence.

In essence hearsay is second-hand evidence. The repetition of what another person said can amount to first-hand or multiple hearsay. Examples 2 and 3 are examples of first-hand hearsay. In Example 2, Y is one step removed from X. The written statement in Example 3 is one step removed from X.

Suppose Example 2 is varied in that what X said to Y, Y then repeats to Z. If Z were now to get into the witness box and repeat what Y told him X had said, this would amount to second-hand or multiple hearsay. Witness Z is two steps removed from the original maker of the statement.

Also, in Example 2, if Y had reduced into writing the substance of what X had told him, Y's written statement would be multiple hearsay because X's evidence has gone through two stages of reporting. The ledger in Example 5 is also an illustration of second-hand hearsay. The original information has gone through two stages of reporting. The theory is that the more stages of reporting an original statement goes through, the less reliable it is likely to be.

The following cases provide classic illustrations of hearsay evidence.

Sparks *v* R [1964] 1 All ER 727

The defendant was charged with having indecently assaulted a young girl. The child was too young to give evidence at the trial. The defendant sought to call the mother of the girl to explain to the court that soon after the incident her daughter had told her that her assailant was a black boy. The defendant was a white man. The Privy Council held the mother's evidence constituted hearsay because the purpose of adducing it would have been to invite the court to accept the truth of her daughter's earlier out-of-court assertion. As there was no recognised exception to the hearsay rule which applied in this instance, the evidence was inadmissible. This classic illustration of hearsay highlights the danger of a rigid rule. The excluded evidence was highly relevant to the defendant's case and to proof of his innocence. Once evidence satisfies the definition of hearsay, in the absence of a recognised exception, the rule deems the evidence to be inadmissible.

Patel *v* Comptroller of Customs [1965] 3 All ER 593

A dispute arose over the question of payment of duty on imported goods. The goods were in sacks which had stamped on them 'Produce of Morocco', and it was crucial that the country of origin of the goods be decided by the court. On appeal from the Supreme Court of Fiji to the Privy Council, it was held that the phrase on the sacks was inadmissible as evidence of the origin of the goods, because it was an assertion of a fact in a manner which amounted to hearsay.

All forms of communication come within the hearsay rule. A gesture such as an affirmative nod or negative shake of the head may be implied hearsay.

R *v* Gibson (1887) LR 18 QBD 537

The accused was charged with wounding the victim by striking him on the head with a heavy stone. The victim testified that an unidentified woman had said to him shortly after the incident: 'The man who threw the stone went in there', pointing to the house in which the defendant was found. On appeal it was held that for the victim to repeat what the unidentified source had said was hearsay. The woman could herself have given direct oral evidence as to what she saw, but she could not be found. The victim's purpose in relating to the court what the woman had said was to invite the court to accept it as true. This rendered it hearsay and inadmissible.

The decision of the House of Lords in *Myers v DPP* below may also be usefully referred to in the context of identifying hearsay evidence.

Myers *v* DPP [1965] AC 1001

The defendant was charged with receiving stolen goods and conspiracy to defraud. It was alleged he was a 'ringer' of cars. He purported to sell to the public renovated wrecks of cars that had been involved in an accident. He was however selling stolen cars made to look like renovated wrecks. Each stolen car had a unique number stamped on its cylinder block which could not be removed or disguised. The prosecution called an employee from the car production company whose job it was to keep and compile manufacturer's records. The employee explained how production line workers completed the cards. Each card included a record of the cylinder number stamped on the vehicle.

cards were subsequently microfilmed and filed away. The evidence went to show that the cylin-
numbers on the so-called wrecked cars were identical to those on the records produced by the
ompany, effectively proving the wrecked cars were in fact new vehicles. In the light of what was after
ll highly reliable evidence, the defendant was convicted.

The House of Lords allowed the defendant's appeal, although his conviction was not quashed.
Their Lordships held that the evidence of the manufacturer's records was inadmissible hearsay. The
records constituted evidence of assertions made on an earlier out-of-court occasion by unidentified
persons being adduced as evidence of the truth of what they asserted.

At the time of this decision, there were no common law or statutory exceptions which would have
permitted such records to be admitted notwithstanding their hearsay quality. The House of Lords
refused to create a new exception, deeming it a matter for Parliament. Extremely useful and cogent
evidence was thus denied the prosecution. The law has moved on since this case was decided –
ndeed it was the catalyst for subsequent statutory changes. Such evidence would be admissible
er current law.

have included the above cases as unproblematic illustrations of hearsay. Before
oking at more complex definitional examples of hearsay evidence, we consider
low the rationale behind the general rule which excludes hearsay evidence in
riminal trials.

REASONS FOR EXCLUDING HEARSAY EVIDENCE

In short, hearsay evidence is not considered to be the best evidence chiefly because the
accuracy of the evidence cannot be tested in cross-examination. There is therefore a
danger that untrained fact finders, in particular the jury, might give such evidence
undue weight.

In *R v Blastland* [1986] AC 41, Lord Bridge explained the reasons for excluding
hearsay evidence:

> The rationale of excluding as inadmissible, rooted as it is in a system of trial by jury, is a
> recognition of the great difficulty, even more acute for a trained juror than for a trained
> judicial mind, of assessing what, if any weight can properly be given to a statement by a
> person whom the jury have not seen or heard and which has not been subject to any test
> of reliability by cross-examination.

The importance that the adversarial system of adjudication attaches to the principle
of orality was explained in Chapter 4. The Anglo-American adversarial tradition
favours first-hand oral testimony in preference to all other forms of evidence. As
such, cross-examination assumes considerable importance. A skilful advocate can
cast considerable doubt on the accuracy and veracity of a witness's account. Hearsay
evidence is frequently not the best evidence available since it invariably involves a
second-hand account of what another witness saw or heard. With hearsay evidence,
the fact finder is denied the opportunity of observing three key features which he
would be able to observe were a first-hand account being given on oath by a witness:

1   The accuracy of the witness's account cannot be tested by cross-examination.
2   The lack of cross-examination means the truthfulness of the witness's account
    cannot be scrutinised. The absence of cross-examination leads to the fear that

juries, in particular, will attribute far more weight to the untested hearsay evide
than it truly deserves in the circumstances.   ⅃6

3 The fact finder cannot assess the witness's demeanour whilst giving evidence.
   Assessment of demeanour is felt to assist the fact finder in determining whether a
   witness is being truthful.

Additionally, given the absence of a first-hand account, there is the increased danger
that such evidence can more easily be manufactured or misrepresented than other
forms of evidence. Finally, the defendant is denied the opportunity of confronting those
who purport to give evidence against him in court. The right of confrontation is an
aspect of the right to a fair trial.

   The application of the hearsay rule in criminal cases is in stark contrast to its appi-
cation in civil cases where, by virtue of the Civil Evidence Act 1995, all hearsay e-
dence is admissible subject to considerations of weight and safeguards in the form
certain procedural requirements. The vast majority of civil trials are of course co
ducted before a legally qualified fact finder in the shape and form of the judge. As
consequence of the recommendations contained in the Woolf Report and sea-chang
in culture brought about by the Civil Procedure Rules 1998, civil proceedings nov
have considerably more inquisitorial characteristics than criminal proceedings, with
the result that the principle of orality assumes less importance.

   The Law Commission subjected the justifications for the hearsay rule as it applies to
criminal cases to particular critical scrutiny (Report No 245):

1 *Hearsay does not constitute the best evidence.* The Law Commission concluded
   that this stated the position far too simplistically. For example, where a witness is
   dead, hearsay evidence may constitute the best, or indeed, the only evidence available and as *Myers v DPP* illustrates, hearsay evidence is sometimes superior to oral
   testimony.
2 *There are inherent dangers of concoction, particularly where information is passed
   from one witness to another before being repeated in court.* On this point the Law
   Commission felt such dangers were most acute in situations where the oral evidence
   sought to be adduced comprised multiple hearsay or was from an unidentified
   source. It recommended that any reform of the rule should contain a safeguard of
   excluding multiple hearsay and hearsay from an unidentified source.
3 *Juries attribute too great a probative value to such evidence.* The Law
   Commission's view was that this particular problem could be overcome with an
   appropriate direction from the judge.
4 *To admit hearsay evidence is to deny the defendant the right to confront his accusers.*
   The Law Commission noted that substantial inroads had already been made to the
   right of confrontation, including the use of screens and video links to shield
   vulnerable witnesses from defendants. Whilst the right contributed very little in
   terms of evidential value, the Law Commission acknowledged the importance of
   justice not only being done but also being seen to be done. In this sense, a defendant
   who is not given the right to see evidence against him tested in court may feel he
   has been treated unfairly. The right of confrontation finds expression in Article

6(3)(d) of the European Convention on Human Rights and is a component of the right to a fair trial under Article 6(1). (The implications of hearsay in the context of human rights are discussed more fully in Chapter 14.)

5 *Admitting hearsay evidence deprives the fact finder of the opportunity to observe the demeanour of the witness.* Placing reliance on the work of psychologists in this field who concluded that witness demeanour does little to assist fact finders in reaching an accurate assessment, the Law Commission felt this rationale was ill founded. In so far as the right was perceived to be important by participants in the criminal justice system, it could be mitigated by a warning from the judge to the effect that the jury has not had the advantage of seeing the witness give evidence on oath.

6 *Hearsay evidence cannot be subjected to cross-examination.* For the Law Commission, the most significant and valid justification for the exclusionary rule of hearsay was the inability to cross-examine the absent witness, thus depriving the court of the ability to see the evidence tested and to attribute to it an appropriate degree of weight.

HEARSAY AS AN EXCLUSIONARY RULE

However plausible the justifications might be, a rigid exclusion-based rule can have the effect of withholding relevant evidence from the court's consideration leading to a possible miscarriage of justice. In *Sparks* v R above the jury convicted the accused in ignorance of what the victim had said about her attacker to her mother because the evidence amounted to hearsay. *Myers* v *DPP* above illustrates much the same point. Highly relevant prosecution evidence was withheld because the documentary records constituted hearsay evidence and, in the absence of a recognised exception, could not be admitted. *Myers* also illustrates how the rationales in support of the rule have considerably less application to documentary records and to business records in particular. Records of the type sought to be admitted in *Myers* are not prone to the same types of error or risk associated with oral testimony.

The straightjacket effect of the rule has led to the development of a large number of common law and statutory exceptions in order to allow hearsay evidence to be admitted. Much of the statutory reforms have been piecemeal. The judiciary have also been complicit by choosing, in a number of cases, to classify what on the face of it looks like hearsay evidence as non-hearsay in order to ensure relevant evidence is admitted. These 'judicial fudges' and the patchwork of exceptions to the rule create the complexity associated with this area of criminal evidence law.

DEFINITIONAL DIFFICULTIES WITH HEARSAY

The definition of hearsay becomes problematic as regards the following:

* Statements admitted for purposes other than proving truth.
* Statements admitted as circumstantial evidence of their maker's state of mind or of a state of affairs.

- Statements containing implied assertions.
- Statements admitted to prove the non-existence of an alleged fact (negative assertions).
- Real evidence as distinct from hearsay evidence.
- Miscellaneous examples of hearsay treated as non-hearsay by the courts.

Statements admitted for purposes other than proving truth

A hearsay statement was defined earlier as 'a statement of fact (an assertion) made out of court, being adduced in court to prove the truth of the fact or facts asserted on the earlier out of court occasion'. A statement's hearsay quality depends on the purpose for which it is tendered in evidence. Where it is tendered simply to show that the statement was made, or that it was made on a particular occasion or has a certain legal effect, it will lack a hearsay quality. This is because it is not being adduced to prove the truth of some fact asserted on the earlier out-of-court occasion on which it was made.

In *R v Davis* [1998] Crim LR 659, the defendant sought to prevent the jury from drawing an adverse inference under section 34 of the Criminal Justice and Public Order Act 1994. He had remained silent at the police station based on advice given to him by his solicitor. On oath, he sought to repeat the advice his solicitor had given him, but was prevented from doing so by the trial judge who ruled it would infringe the hearsay rule. The Court of Appeal held that this was not always the case. Where a defendant simply wants to give an account of his solicitor's advice to show the jury the effect it had on him and hence his reasons for remaining silent, the evidence lacks a hearsay quality since the defendant is not seeking to demonstrate the truth of anything his solicitor said to him.

Statements admitted as circumstantial evidence of their maker's state of mind or of a state of affairs

Similarly, where a party seeks to rely in court on a statement made on an earlier occasion for the purpose of proving simply that the statement made had some effect on a relevant party's state of mind or on a state of affairs, it will lack a hearsay quality. Such a statement is being relied upon for a purpose other than to prove the truth of facts stated in the earlier out-of-court statement. The earlier statement assumes relevant circumstantial evidence of either its maker's state of mind or of the existence of a certain state of affairs.

A number of cases provide illustrations of out-of-court statements adduced as relevant circumstantial evidence:

Subramaniam v Public Prosecutor of Malaya [1956] 1 WLR 965

During a state of emergency in Malaya, the defendant was convicted of unlawful possession of ammunition. His defence was that he had been captured by terrorists, who had forced him to carry ammunition, threatening him with torture and eventually death, if he refused. He wished to repeat to the court the content of his conversations with the terrorists, including the specific nature of the threats they had made. The trial judge refused to allow the defendant to repeat the substance of the conversations because it would amount to the admission of hearsay evidence. For the content of the conversations to be admitted in evidence, the terrorists themselves would have to testify as to what they had said.

On his appeal against conviction, the Privy Council held that the trial judge had made a fundamental error. The purpose of the defendant relating the conversations was not to persuade the court of their truth, but to show that he had acted under duress in possessing the ammunition. In other words, the conversations provided useful circumstantial evidence of the defendant's state of mind, which were clearly relevant to the facts in issue in the case.

Ratten *v* R [1972] AC 378

The defendant was alleged to have shot and killed his wife. He maintained his gun had gone off accidentally whilst he was cleaning it. In his evidence, the defendant denied any telephone call had been made from the house until he called the ambulance. The shooting occurred between 1.12 pm and 1.20 pm. The prosecution wanted to call a telephonist who had taken a call from a distressed woman at the property at 1.15 pm. The woman could be heard sobbing, shouting, 'Get me the police, please.' Counsel for the defendant opposed its admission, maintaining it amounted to a hearsay assertion, albeit an implicit one, that the defendant had an intention to kill. The Privy Council held that the evidence of what the wife had said to the telephone operator was admissible as circumstantial evidence of her state of mind at the time. The wife's state of mind was clearly relevant to the issues in the case, as it went a considerable way to refuting the defence of accident. If the gun had discharged itself accidentally why had she made the call in such a state of fear and distress? Lord Wilberforce justified the repetition of the words used as:

> relevant and necessary evidence in order to explain the fact of the call being made. A telephone call is a composite act, made up of manual operations together with the utterance of words ... To confine the evidence (to the fact that a call was made) would be to deprive the act of most of its significance. The act had content when it was known that the call was made in a state of emotion. The knowledge that the caller desired the police to be called helped to indicate the nature of the emotion, anxiety or fear at an existing or impending emergency. It was a matter for the jury to decide what light (if any), this evidence, in the absence of an explanation from the appellant who was in the house, threw on what situation was developing at the time...

In the alternative, the Privy Council held that if the evidence amounted to hearsay, it would still have been admissible under the common law exception of *res gestae*, considered later in Chapter 13.

R v *Blastland* below has been considered in the context of confession evidence as it concerned the admissibility of incriminating admissions of a third party who was not charged in connection with the offence. It is included here as confirmation of the point that had the evidence been regarded as relevant, it would have been admitted as circumstantial evidence of its maker's state of mind, thereby avoiding the hearsay rule.

R *v* Blastland [1986] AC 41

The defendant was charged with the sodomy and murder of a 12-year-old boy. The defendant wanted to adduce evidence of the fact that a man, known only during the trial as Mark, who was a known homosexual, had told several people about the boy's murder before it had become public knowledge. In imparting this information, Mark was witnessed to have been in a highly excitable state. Mark was not called as a witness at the trial. The trial judge refused a request by the defendant to call witnesses to whom Mark had given this information, for them to repeat on oath what Mark had said to them. In his view the evidence provided by such witnesses would amount to hearsay. The defendant would be asking the jury to infer Mark could only have acquired such information because he was in fact the murderer. In this way, the defendant was seeking to rely on the truth of facts implicitly stated in the words Mark had used.

The defendant's appeal against conviction was eventually heard by the House of Lords. It was accepted that the evidence of the various witnesses would not amount to hearsay if the reason for calling them and getting them to repeat what Mark had said to them had been purely to show Mark's state of mind. In this way, the court would not have been invited to accept the truth of facts impliedly stated by Mark. What the witnesses were able to recount did therefore yield circumstantial evidence of Mark's state of mind. Crucially however, the House of Lords did not regard Mark's state of mind as having any logical relevance to any fact in issue at the defendant's trial. As the evidence was irrelevant, it could not be admitted and it was therefore legally correct for the jury to have convicted in ignorance of Mark's statements. The decision of the House of Lords on the point of relevance has been extensively criticised (see Chapter 1).

R v Lydon (1987) 85 Cr App R 221

The accused, Sean Lydon, was charged with armed robbery of a post office. Near to the site where the gun used in the robbery was found, there were two pieces of paper on which had been written in ink 'Sean Rules 85' and 'Sean Rules'. There was ink of a similar colour and appearance on the barrel of the gun. At his trial, the defendant maintained he had an alibi. On appeal, the Court of Appeal ruled that the pieces of paper did not constitute hearsay, as there was nothing written on them which amounted to an assertion of truth. They constituted real items of evidence from which circumstantial inferences might be drawn connecting the defendant with the robbery by refuting his alibi. Had the prosecution sought to rely on the statement as proof that 'Sean Rules', then it would have assumed a hearsay quality.

It is difficult to contradict the conclusion of the Court of Appeal that no written assertion had been made on the pieces of paper found near the crime scene. However, it might be said that the words used were making an implicit assertion that Sean had been present. In the end, the Court of Appeal admitted the evidence by classifying it as relevant circumstantial evidence of a state of affairs helping to place the defendant at the scene of the crime at the relevant time.

The observation that the hearsay rule is capable of excluding relevant and cogent evidence has already been made. Where judges have been unable to find an established exception in which to place the disputed evidence, refuge has been sought in classifying the evidence as relevant circumstantial evidence of a certain state of affairs. Zuckerman has explained this form of judicial convenience in the following terms: 'A certain type of statement is taken to be reliable. To avoid exclusion the court searches for a convenient tag which may be given to this type of evidence so that it may pass for something other than hearsay. To fulfil its function the tag or label must be associated with admissible evidence. Hence the usefulness of notions such as "operative words" and "circumstantial evidence directly relevant to the issue". Once the label is attached to a piece of evidence, the inhibiting effect of the hearsay disappears.' (See Further reading below.)

One final illustration of the 'circumstantial evidence' exception is provided by the problematic case of *R v Rice* [1963] 1 QB 857. It involved an allegation of conspiracy and part of the prosecution's case rested on proving Rice had taken a flight to Manchester on a certain date, in the company of the co-accused, Hoather. The prosecution produced an airline ticket which was in the name of Rice and Moore, another co-accused. The ticket was dated. It was alleged that Hoather had flown in place of Moore. The defendant Rice denied any knowledge of the offence on the flight. On appeal he argued the ticket constituted hearsay evidence as it had been admitted for no other purpose than to lead the jury to conclude that Rice had in fact flown to Manchester on the day in question. The Court of Appeal, upholding his conviction, held the ticket constituted circumstantial evidence from which the jury might choose to infer Rice had made the journey.

There has been much academic comment on whether this case was correctly decided. Arguably it was. In similar vein to *R* v *Lydon* above, it is not easy to see what explicit assertion the ticket could be said to be making. The lack of an intention to assert arguably justifies the admission of such evidence as non-hearsay, since it is less likely to be manufactured and hence is more reliable.

All the above cases overlap with an aspect of hearsay evidence that has vexed many a judicial mind, that of the implied assertion. In *R* v *Rice* was the ticket not being relied on by the prosecution as an implicit assertion that Rice had in fact flown to Manchester on the relevant day?

Statements containing implied assertions – hearsay or not hearsay?

An implied assertion is a statement or gesture which is not intended by its maker to explicitly assert a fact but which does assert a fact by necessary implication. In *Ratten* v *R* above, the wife did not actually say 'Help, my husband is trying to kill me!' However, it could be argued that, in allowing the telephonist to repeat the words, 'Get me the police please', an assertion to this effect could be implied. The Privy Council, it will be recalled, chose to classify the statement as relevant circumstantial evidence of the maker's (the victim's) state of mind. If it did impliedly assert an intention to kill on the defendant's part, thus amounting to hearsay, the Privy Council would, in the alternative, have admitted the statement under the common law *res gestae* exception to the rule.

Do implied assertions fall within the definition of hearsay? The leading earlier authorities on implied assertion are the cases of *Wright* v *Doe d Tatham* (1837) 7 Ad & El 313 and *Teper* v *R* [1952] AC 480. The former case concerns a disputed will. Tatham, the testator's heir at law in the event of intestacy, challenged the deceased's mental capacity to make a will, in which he had left his estate to his steward. In seeking to uphold the will, Wright sought to adduce in evidence various letters written to the deceased not long before his death. Had the authors of the letters been called to give evidence, they would have opined to the view that the deceased had been sane. The letters did not expressly assert that opinion, but did so implicitly. Why write them, if the recipient was not of sound mind? The court concluded the letters amounted to an assertion of fact, albeit implied, and as such constituted hearsay evidence.

In *Teper* v *R* [1952] AC 480, the defendant had been convicted of arson. The defendant had denied the allegation claiming to have an alibi for the relevant time. At his trial the prosecution had been allowed to adduce evidence that an unidentified woman had been heard to shout to a passing motorist, who resembled the defendant, 'your place burning down and you going away from the fire'. The words used had not been intended as a formal identification of the defendant on an earlier occasion; however, they were being relied on as such by the prosecution. The words had been adduced for the purpose of leading the court to conclude that the person seen driving away at the time was the defendant. In these circumstances, the evidence amounted to hearsay.

The fact that the communication was not intended to make an explicit assertion makes the likelihood that the evidence was manufactured less likely. As such the evidence assumes greater reliability than is usually the case with hearsay evidence. Nonetheless, implied assertions are treated as hearsay. The only way to avoid this is, as illustrated above, to treat the evidence as relevant circumstantial evidence of a particular state of affairs from which the jury might choose to draw an inference.

Woodhouse v Hall (1981) 72 Cr App R 39

Two plain clothes police officers visited a massage parlour where, according to the prosecution, they were offered sexual services by women working there, who gave details of the services they would give, which included 'hand relief', and the cost. The officers were called to repeat in court the content of these conversations. Were the words used by the women not being repeated precisely because they contained the implicit assertion that the premises were being used as a brothel? The Divisional Court concluded they were not and that the conversations could be admitted as relevant, circumstantial evidence that the owner was acting in the management of a brothel. There was no question at all of the court being invited to believe the truth of the women's statements. What the women may or may not have intended to assert was irrelevant. If the court accepted the officer's evidence as a truthful and accurate account of what the women had said, it could draw the inference that the massage parlour was being used as a brothel.

Had the police sought to repeat on oath a statement from a customer to the effect that 'you know this place is a brothel don't you?', this would have been a clear infringement of the hearsay rule.

The prosecution had to prove the premises were being used as a brothel. Sexual services are usually on offer in a brothel. The offer of 'hand relief' constituted a sexual service. Although the words clearly implied the premises were being used as a brothel, their admission was justified on the basis that the evidence was relevant and provided useful circumstantial evidence from which it could be inferred that the premises were being used for such a purpose.

R v Harry (1988) 86 Cr App R 105

The defendant was jointly charged with his co-accused P with possession of drugs with intent to supply. The defendant denied the charge. He sought to have evidence adduced of various telephone calls from unidentified callers made to the premises where the drugs were found. The callers asked his co-defendant P to supply them with drugs.

The Court of Appeal held that the evidence amounted to inadmissible hearsay: it was being put to the court to prove the implicit assertion in the calls that it was co-defendant P and not the defendant who was the drug dealer. The defendant was thus denied the benefit of evidence relevant to his defence because no exception to the hearsay rule could be found to admit it.

The definitive statement of the law on implied admissions in relation to hearsay is provided by the House of Lords in *R* v *Kearley* below. The importance of this case is indicated by the fact that the court heard five days of legal argument and its judgment runs to 52 pages in the report.

R v Kearley [1992] 2 AC 228

The defendant was charged with possession of a controlled drug with intent to supply contrary to section 5(3) of the Misuse of Drugs Act 1971. He pleaded not guilty. At the trial the prosecution sought to adduce evidence of a number of telephone calls that had been made to the defendant's house in which the callers requested to speak to him by his nickname of 'Chippie' and were heard asking for drugs to be supplied. The prosecution also wished to adduce evidence of the fact that a number of people had called at the house asking to be supplied with drugs. The evidence was highly useful to the prosecution. However, all of it had been obtained following the accused's arrest, and not in his presence or hearing. None of those who called at the house were asked to give evidence. The trial judge overruled the defendant's objections and allowed the police officers to give evidence recounting the callers' requests. The defendant was convicted and appealed.

The Court of Appeal followed the decision in *Woodhouse* v *Hall* above. It concluded the evidence amounted to relevant circumstantial evidence of a state of affairs from which the inference that the defendant was dealing drugs could be inferred.

On appeal to the House of Lords, the decision of the Court of Appeal was overruled by a majority of three to two.

Lord Oliver succinctly summed up the issue to be decided in *R* v *Kearley*: 'the question which presents itself in the instant appeal can be expressed thus: was the evidence of the police officers being tendered simply as evidence of the fact of the conversation or was it introduced "testimonially" in order to demonstrate the truth either of something that was said or of something that was implicit in or to be inferred from something that was said?'

The majority, comprising Lords Bridge, Ackner and Oliver came to the conclusion that the repetition of what had been said in the various telephone calls was relevant only to the state of mind of the callers, who might or might not have believed drugs to be available on the premises. However, the evidence of the callers' state of mind was irrelevant to proof that the defendant had been supplying drugs. The evidence did no more than show that they believed drugs to have been available at the premises. In the alternative, the majority concluded that even if the evidence was relevant it could not be admitted as it would offend the rule against the admission of implied hearsay assertions clearly laid down in *Wright* v *Doe d Tatham*.

Lord Ackner analysed the position as follows:

Each of those requests was, of course, evidence of the state of mind of the person making the request. He wished to be supplied with drugs and thought that the appellant would so supply him. It was not evidence of the fact that the appellant had supplied or could or would supply the person making the request. But the state of mind of the person making the request was not an issue at the trial; accordingly evidence of his request was irrelevant and therefore inadmissible. If the prosecution had sought to call any of the persons who had made such requests, merely to give evidence of the making of the request, in order to establish their appetite for drugs and their belief that such appetite would be satisfied by the appellant, such evidence could not have been properly admitted...

It will be apparent from what I have already stated that the application of the hearsay rule does not, on the facts so far recited, fall for consideration. The evidence is not admissible because it is irrelevant. It is as simple as that. But in case I have been guilty of over-simplification, let me consider the position upon the assumption that the very nature of the request or requests carries with it a permissible implication that the appellant was a supplier of drugs. It is only in such a situation that the request, spoken not in the appellant's presence or hearing and by a person not called as a witness, that the rule against the admission of hearsay evidence falls to be considered. As was made abundantly clear by the judge in his summing up, there was no impediment to the prosecution calling the persons who made the inquiries. The prosecution had decided to rely not on their direct evidence but upon recollection of the police officers to whom they allegedly spoke ... the precise scope of the rule against hearsay is in some respects a matter of controversy, there are a variety of formulations of the rule...

In deciding whether the rule is being breached, it is essential to examine the purpose for which the evidence is tendered. In the opinion of the Privy Council in *Subramaniam v Public Prosecutor* [1956] 1 WLR 970, it was said:

> 'Evidence of a statement made to a witness by a person who is not himself called as witness may or may not be hearsay. It is hearsay and inadmissible when the object of the evidence is to establish the truth of what is contained in the statement. It is not hearsay and is admissible when it is proposed to establish by the evidence, not the truth of the statement, but the fact that it was made.'

Such being the law, Miss Goddard [for the Crown] frankly concedes that if the inquirer had said in the course of making his request 'I would like my usual supply of amphetamine at the price which I paid you last week' or words to that effect, then although the inquirer could have been called to give evidence of the fact that he had in the past purchased from the appellant his requirements of amphetamine and had made his call at the appellant's house for a further supply on the occasion when he met and spoke to the police, the hearsay rule prevents the prosecution from calling police officers to recount the conversation which I have described. This is for the simple reason that the request made in the form set out above contains an express assertion that the premises at which the request was being made were being used as a source of supply of drugs and the supplier was the appellant.

If, contrary to the view which I have expressed above, the simple request or requests for drugs to be supplied by the appellant, as recounted by the police, contains in substance, but only by implication, the same assertion, then I can find neither authority nor principle to suggest that the hearsay rule should not be equally applicable and exclude such evidence. What is sought to be done is to use the oral assertion, even though it may be an implied assertion, as evidence of the truth of the proposition asserted. That the proposition is asserted by way of necessary implication rather than expressly cannot, to my mind, make any difference.

The object of tendering the evidence would be to establish the truth of what is contained in the statement. That is precisely what the rule prohibits...

The Court of Appeal's decision in *R v Kearley* had relied on the earlier case of *Woodhouse v Hall* (1980) 72 Cr App R 39. The House of Lords, however, distinguished that case, saying:

> In the Court of Appeal (Criminal Division), 93 Cr. App. R. 22 the problem was approached by treating the evidence tendered as raising two separate, though possibly interrelated, questions. First, it was asked, was it admissible solely for the purpose of proving that amphetamines either had been or were being supplied from the premises where the appellant lived? That was answered in the affirmative simply by reference to *Woodhouse v. Hall*, 72 Cr. App. R. 39. Lloyd L.J., in the course of his judgment at p. 224, postulated the question, 'What difference could there be between offers to sell sexual services and offers to buy drugs?' and observed at pp. 224–225:
>
> > 'If the police officers could give original evidence, without infringing the hearsay rule, that offers were made in the one case in order to establish that the premises were a brothel, then they could give original evidence to the like effect in the other case to establish that the premises were being used for the supply of drugs.'
>
> Such analogical reasoning, however, does not, with respect, stand up to analysis. There is a world of difference between evidence by a witness of his own observation of disorderly

conduct by persons employed at the premises tendered to prove their use as a disorderly house and evidence of what a witness has heard from an unconnected caller regarding his belief as to what goes on at the premises. Whilst it is no doubt true that the mere supplying of drugs from premises necessarily implies the existence of customers anxious to acquire them, that is not a proposition which can legitimately be used to demonstrate the converse, i.e. that the existence of such customers implies the supply of drugs. That can be demonstrated only by establishing the truth of the customer's belief that they will be supplied. That belief cannot by itself be prayed in aid to substantiate its own veracity. (*per* Lord Oliver)

In his dissenting opinion, Lord Browne-Wilkinson's analysis of the evidence and the use for which it was tendered differed from the majority, but is equally acceptable:

I accept that the opinions or beliefs of the callers were irrelevant and as such inadmissible. But in my judgment the calls prove more than the opinions or beliefs of the callers.

The evidence was, in my judgment, relevant because it showed that there were people resorting to the premises for the purpose of obtaining drugs from Chippie (the defendant's pet name). Although evidence of the existence of such would-be buyers is not, by itself, conclusive, the existence of a substantial body of potential customers provides some evidence which a jury could take into account in deciding whether the accused had an intent to supply. The existence of a contemporaneous potential market to buy drugs from Chippie, by itself, shows that there was an opportunity for the accused to supply drugs...

The reasons for a third party doing an act will, normally, be irrelevant and inadmissible. Any action involving human activity necessarily implies that the human being had reasons and beliefs on which his action was based. But the fact that his action (viz. asking for drugs or queuing for coffee) is capable of raising an inadmissible inference of irrelevant fact does not mean that evidence of that action cannot be admitted with a view to proving a relevant fact.

In my view therefore the fact that there were a number of people seeking to buy drugs was legally relevant and admissible as showing that there was a market to which the appellant could sell, even though such evidence was also capable of giving rise to an impermissible secondary inference, viz. that the callers believed Chippie supplied drugs.

On the hearsay point, Lord Browne-Wilkinson distinguished *Wright v Doe d Tatham*:

If ... I am correct in thinking that the calls show an admissible fact, i.e. the existence of a potential market, the case is not in point. The letters in *Wright v. Doe d. Tatham* were being tendered testimonially to prove the belief of the writers: the calls in this case are being tendered to prove a relevant fact (the existence of a market for the purchase of drugs) and not the belief of the callers. Accordingly the hearsay rule does not apply.

Calling for the reform of the hearsay rule, Lord Browne-Wilkinson commented further:

I can only express the view that there may well be a good case for the legislature to review the hearsay rule in criminal law. In cases such as the present it hampers effective prosecution by excluding evidence which your Lordships all agree is highly probative and, since it comes from the unprompted actions of the callers, is very creditworthy. The hearsay rule can also operate to the detriment of the accused, as the decisions in *Reg. v. Harry*, 86 Cr. App. R. 105 and *Reg. v. Blastland* [1986] AC 41 both show. A review of the operation of the hearsay rule in criminal cases is long overdue.

Notwithstanding the lengthy analysis of matters in *R v Kearley*, the rules on implied assertions remain clear. They fall squarely within the hearsay rule. In the view of the

House of Lords this is entirely logical. If an assertion would be inadmissible hearsay because it was made expressly, why should it make any difference that it was made impliedly? The effect is the same. The real difficulty lies in ascertaining whether the words used constitute an implied assertion at all. This in turn depends on the court's view of what the relevance of the words might be, having regard to their intended use by the party seeking to place reliance on them.

Statements admitted to prove the non-existence of an alleged fact (negative assertions)

The conceptual problem of a negative assertion is not dissimilar to that of the implied assertion. A negative assertion is made by using the absence of recorded information as proof that a certain matter or state of affairs did not come about. It is based on the premise that had the event or matter occurred there would have been recorded proof of it. Hence, in the absence of a record, the implication has to be that the event did not occur. The problem is best illustrated with an example taken from the case discussed below.

R v Shone (1983) 76 Cr App R 72

The defendant was charged with handling stolen goods. The prosecution needed to prove the goods were in fact stolen. The goods were identified as having come from a particular shop. The prosecution called the stock clerk of the company and the sales manager. The shop recorded the receipt, sale and use of all its items in its ledgers. There was no record of the goods in the defendant's possession having been sold or used by the shop. The evidence was left to the jury for it to infer that the goods had left the shop without payment. On appeal, the defendant maintained the use of the records in evidence offended the rule against hearsay, in that they were being adduced to prove the truth of non-payment, a fact asserted by the prosecution.

The Court of Appeal rejected the defendant's analysis of the matter. It concluded the records themselves, and the very absence of the goods having been recorded for sale or use in them, was direct evidence from which the jury were entitled to infer the goods had been stolen. In other words, the absence of a record constituted circumstantial evidence of the fact that the goods had been stolen. The justification for admitting the evidence in this way stems from the fact that the dangers traditionally associated with hearsay are significantly reduced. Such records are normally compiled in an honest manner by persons with first-hand knowledge of what they are dealing with.

The decision in *R* v *Shone* draws on an earlier decision.

R v Patel [1981] 3 All ER 94

The defendant was charged with assisting in the illegal importation of a foreign national. The Home Office holds records on all lawful immigrants. In this case, the prosecution called a senior immigration officer who had examined Home Office records to give evidence of the fact that he could find no mention of the foreign national in question. The prosecution sought to rely on the absence of a documented entry as proof that the immigrant in question had entered the United Kingdom unlawfully.

The Court of Appeal quashed the conviction because the immigration officer's evidence amounted to inadmissible hearsay, as he was not responsible for compiling the actual record. Invariably, his evidence would have to rely on the assertions of others who had compiled the records. At the time of this decision there was no recognised common law or statutory exception which would have enabled the records to be adduced as an exception to the hearsay rule. The Court of Appeal did however observe that had the officer responsible for the compilation and safekeeping of the records been called, the absence of a record could have been utilised as proof of the immigrant's status. The Court of Appeal did not go on to explain why the hearsay status of the evidence is altered in this way and in effect ignored the hearsay implications of the evidence.

Both cases stress the importance of calling witnesses who can testify to the way in which the records are compiled and kept. The probative value of the evidence derived from an absent record can only truly be assessed where evidence of method of compilation is available. Where a company adopts lax procedures in the way in which its transactions are recorded, the evidential significance of the absence of a record is much diminished and open to challenge.

The Law Commission addressed the problem of implied and negative assertions in Consultation Paper No 138 and in its report No 245. The Law Commission's proposals for reform in this regard are considered later in this chapter.

Real evidence as distinct from hearsay evidence

As we saw in Chapter 1, facts in issue in a case can be proved by evidence received in different forms, including oral testimony and documentary evidence. Real evidence is a term used to refer to evidence directly observed by the court. It includes physical objects brought into court, the use of photographs, videotaped recordings, the demeanour of a witness and evidence produced by a mechanical device. Items of real evidence may be used by the jury as direct or circumstantial evidence of a fact in issue. Is there an inter-relationship between evidence produced by a mechanical device and hearsay?

Incriminating admissions recorded on tape constitute hearsay evidence. The words recorded on tape are being utilised as proof of the truth of certain facts asserted. The evidence is admitted as confession evidence under an established common law exception to the hearsay rule. Where video footage is played to a court, it is usually played for the purpose of showing a crime was committed and who the participants in the crime were. No hearsay problem arises – the court will make of the video recording what it will according to what it sees and hears.

The difficulty arises from the use of computer printouts and information provided by other mechanical devices. If the computer's output is based on information inputted by a human, the printout will amount to hearsay if it is relied on to prove the truth of some fact asserted in the computer record. Such evidence may in fact be admissible under section 23 or 24 of the Criminal Justice Act 1988. However, if the computer is acting as an automated device (in other words, there is no human input), the information it produces will be classed as real evidence. In *Castle v Cross* [1984] 1 WLR 1372, evidence yielded from the printout of an Intoximeter machine was deemed not to be hearsay. The machine analyses a specimen of breath and produces an automated reading based on the sample provided. Similarly in *R v Spiby* (1990) 91 Cr App R 186, the Court of Appeal concluded that a printout from an exchange device in a hotel which automatically recorded the numbers to which telephone calls were made did not amount to hearsay because nothing in the operation of the mechanical device depended on human intervention.

The party seeking to rely on evidence produced by an automated mechanical device is aided by an evidential presumption of fact. If the party can show the device is usually in order and functioning correctly, it will be presumed that it was working correctly when it yielded the evidence sought to be relied on. It used to be the case that the presumption of regularity did not apply to evidence yielded by computer. Section 69 of the Police and Criminal Evidence Act 1984 (PACE) provided that where a statement in a document produced by a computer was being relied on as evidence of facts stated, such a document could not be received into evidence unless there were no reasonable grounds for believing that the statement was inaccurate because of improper use of the computer and that at all material times the computer had been working properly. Provision was made under PACE for a certificate to be adduced to this effect, signed by 'a person occupying a responsible position in relation to the operation of the computer'. The decision of the House of Lords in R v *Shephard* [1993] AC 380 held that section 69 of PACE applied to all computer records whether adduced as admissible hearsay or as real evidence. In its report, the Law Commission recommended the abolition of section 69 of PACE as serving no useful purpose. The section has now been abolished without replacement by section 60 of the Youth Justice and Criminal Evidence Act 1999.

Miscellaneous examples of hearsay treated as non-hearsay by the courts

There are a number of instances in which the courts have sought to avoid the inconvenient effects of the hearsay rule in order to admit relevant evidence. In some of these instances the rule has simply been ignored; in other instances the problematic nature of the evidence has been redefined to take it out of a hearsay context.

Most of the examples of hearsay statements being treated as non-hearsay come within the heading of self-serving statements. These are statements a witness made on an earlier out-of-court occasion, which are subsequently repeated by the witness in court. Where the earlier statement is being relied on as proof of the facts stated, it assumes a hearsay quality. Examples of such self-serving statements include:

- evidence of previous identification;
- prompt complaints by victims of sexual offences;
- exculpatory statements on arrest;
- statements rebutting suggestions of recent fabrication.

The admissibility of self-serving statements and the Law Commission's proposal for their reform are considered at some length in Chapter 15. The hearsay nature of such evidence is basically overcome by a direction to the fact finder that the evidence must be treated as evidence of a witness's consistency which has a bearing on a witness's credibility and not as evidence of the truth of any fact asserted.

Mixed statements made on arrest

A mixed statement is one in which a suspect makes both incriminating admissions and exculpatory statements and therefore gives rise to a hearsay problem in both contexts. An example might be: 'Yes I admit I took the goods but I did not steal them.' The rules relating to the admissibility and evidential effect of mixed statements are explained in Chapters 6 and 15.

Memory refreshing rule

It is not uncommon for a witness to refresh his memory of events shortly before giving evidence or even in the witness box by reading a statement he made earlier when the events were much fresher in his mind. Where the view is taken that by refreshing his memory from an earlier statement, the witness is simply confirming on oath what he said in his earlier statement, a hearsay connotation arises. The rules relating to memory refreshing and the Law Commission's proposals for reform of them are considered in Chapter 15.

Expert opinion

The use of expert evidence in criminal trials is extensive. In formulating an opinion, however, the expert often has to draw on the research findings of others in his field. By adopting the opinion of others, the expert is making an assertion that the statements and conclusions made in the earlier researched findings are true. This potentially offends the rule against the admission of hearsay evidence. The courts have been prepared to turn a blind eye to the potential hearsay problem, otherwise expert evidence would become impossible to tender due to the fact that a party would need to call anyone whose research has formed the basis of the expert evidence. This would pose immense practical difficulties, not to mention considerable expense.

In *R v Abadom* [1983] 1 WLR 126, the defendant was charged with robbery. It was the opinion of the expert witness for the Crown that fragments of glass found in the defendant's shoes matched glass from the broken window at the crime scene. According to the Crown's expert, the refractive index in the glass taken from the crime scene matched the refractive index in the glass found under the defendant's shoes. The expert gave evidence that he had consulted Home Office statistics and had found that the index occurred in only 4% of all glass samples. The defendant appealed on the basis that the expert's evidence was hearsay as he had no personal knowledge of the statistics. The Court of Appeal confirmed that an expert's opinion must always be based on primary facts, in this case the refractive indices of the glass samples. Consequentially, the person with personal knowledge of the primary facts must be called to give evidence of those facts. However once the primary facts upon which an opinion is based have been proved by admissible evidence, the expert is entitled to draw on works of others as part of the process of arriving at his conclusion.

In its proposals for reform, the Law Commission would put the decision in *R v Abadom* on a statutory footing subject to some procedural safeguards. The admissibility of expert evidence in criminal trials is more fully discussed in Chapter 19.

REDEFINING HEARSAY

In order to solve some of the problems associated with the definition of hearsay in its current form, the Law Commission has recommended that hearsay be redefined. In deciding the crucial question of whether an assertion has been made at all, the Law Commission adopts the following form of words in clause 2(3) of the draft Criminal Evidence Bill (Law Commission Report No 245, Appendix A):

> (3) A matter stated is one to which this Act applies if (and only if) the purpose or one of the purposes of the person making the statement appears to the court to have been—
> (a) to cause another person to believe the matter, or
> (b) to cause another person to act or a machine to operate on the basis that the matter is as stated.

In the view of the Law Commission:

> the crucial question is whether the person whose words or conduct are in question intended to convey the impression that the fact which it is now sought to infer from those words or that conduct was true. Only if that person did not intend to convey that impression could it safely be assumed that he or she was not deliberately seeking to mislead. It follows that what is crucial is not the way in which that person happened to express himself or herself, but the impression that his or her words or conduct were intended to convey.

The Law Commission concluded that had this form of words been operative at the time of cases like *R v Kearley* and *R v Harry*, the courts would have had little difficulty in concluding that it had not been the callers' intention to cause anyone to believe that an individual person at the particular premises was (or was not) selling drugs. As such the evidence would have been admissible as it would not have fallen within the Law Commission's definition of an implied assertion. As regards negative assertions, the same result would follow, as the failure to record is not normally intended to give the impression that the particular event had not occurred.

Further reading

Allen, T., 'Implied Assertions as Hearsay' (1992) 142 NLJ 1194.

Carter, P.B., 'Whether and Whither?' (1993) 109 LQR 573.

Guest, S., 'Hearsay Revisited' (1988) 41 Current Legal Problems 33.

Law Commission Consultation Paper No 138 (1995) *Evidence in Criminal Proceedings: Hearsay and Related Topics*, HMSO.

Law Commission Report No 245 (1997) *Evidence in Criminal Proceedings: Hearsay and Related Topics*, HMSO.

Pattenden, R., 'Conceptual Versus Pragmatic Approaches to Hearsay' (1993) 56 MLR 138.

Zuckerman, A. (1989) *The Principles of Criminal Evidence*, Clarendon Press.

Chapter 13

COMMON LAW EXCEPTIONS PERMITTING THE USE OF HEARSAY EVIDENCE

INTRODUCTION

The exceptions to the hearsay rule covered in this chapter exist by virtue of the common law and have been developed on a piecemeal basis over many years and, as such, lack an overall coherence. The common law exceptions have developed to admit hearsay evidence in circumstances where it was generally felt to be reliable and in instances where it would be pragmatic to do so. In some situations the common law rules have been circumvented by statute, most notably the Criminal Justice Act 1988, which is considered in detail in Chapter 14.

The following categories of statements are admissible at common law as exceptions to the hearsay rule:

- admissions and confessions;
- statements by persons since deceased;
- statements forming part of the *res gestae*;
- statements in public documents.

ADMISSIONS AND CONFESSIONS

A confession comprises any statement made by a defendant in which he makes an incriminating admission as to the offence for which he is under suspicion. The majority of confessions are extracted by the police in interview with the defendant at the police station. A confession satisfies the definition of hearsay evidence because it comprises a statement made on an earlier out-of-court occasion, relied on in court, most often by the prosecution, for the purpose of proving the truth of facts asserted by the defendant on the earlier occasion. Confessions are admitted as a common law exception to the hearsay rule because they are statements made against the defendant's self-interest. Why make such a statement unless it is true? Sections 76 and 78 of the Police and Criminal Evidence Act 1984 govern the actual admissibility of confession evidence. There are a number of interesting, albeit conceptually difficult, hearsay problems associated with confession evidence. In particular, can a defendant rely on a confession to the crime of which he is charged by a third party who has not been charged in connection with the offence and therefore has no connection with the proceedings? Can co-accused A rely, as proof of his innocence, on a confession made by co-accused B, in circumstances where the prosecution is not relying on B's confession and B maintains it is untrue in any event? The admissibility of confession evidence and the special problems of hearsay associated with them were considered in Chapter 6.

STATEMENTS BY PERSONS SINCE DECEASED

Without a common law exception permitting hearsay evidence of statements where the maker had died before the start of the trial, it would have been impossible to prove many facts that were crucial to the administration of justice. Most of these statements may now in fact be admitted under the Criminal Justice Act 1988 providing they are in written form. The common law exceptions still have a function where a witness wishes to adduce in evidence oral statements made by a person who has later died. There are three categories of such statements:

Dying declarations

Dying declarations are admissible only at the trial for the murder or manslaughter of the declarant. Logically there would seem to be no reason why they may not also be admitted at a trial for causing death by dangerous driving or aiding and abetting a suicide. The statement of the victim, whether written or oral, as to the cause of his injuries, usually naming or identifying the assailant must have been made when he was under a 'settled, hopeless expectation of death'. It is this 'settled, hopeless expectation of death' that constitutes the main reason for this exception. It is assumed that someone who knows he is about to die and is resigned to that fate would not wish to die with a lie on his conscience. Therefore it was considered safe for his statement to be adduced in evidence by someone to whom it was addressed or who heard or read it. The rationale was stated by Eyre CB in *R v Woodcock* (1789) 1 Leach 500:

> the general principle on which the species of evidence is admitted is that they are declarations made in extremity, when the party is at the point of death, and when every hope of this world is gone, when every motive to falsehood is silenced, and the mind is induced by the most powerful considerations to speak the truth.

In effect, it was considered that if the necessary conditions for a dying declaration were fulfilled, the statement was akin to someone testifying on oath in court.

The prosecution must prove the 'settled, hopeless expectation of death' for the declaration to be admissible, in addition to which the declarant must have been a competent witness at the time of making the declaration. Hence, in *R v Pike* (1829) 3 C & P 598, a declaration made by a four-year-old child was held to be inadmissible.

The reference by Eyre CB in *R v Woodcock* above to the victim being 'at the point of death' does not mean that death must occur immediately. In the case of *R v Mosley* (1825) 1 Mood CC 97 a dying declaration was admitted where the victim survived for 11 days, during which time he was constantly told that he was going to recover. In the case of *R v Bernadotti* (1869) 11 Cox CC 316, the declarant lingered for three weeks before dying.

Provided that the prosecution satisfies the court that the hearsay evidence fulfils the requisite criteria for admission, the dying declaration will be admitted even if it provides the only relevant evidence as to the cause of the victim's death. There can still be a conviction, and there is no need for the judge to warn the jury that the evidence is not corroborated or supported in some way. This was confirmed in *Nembhard* v *R* [1982] 1 All ER 183.

The witness testifying as to the declaration must be able to swear that what he recalls of an oral declaration is either the declaration verbatim, or that what he recalls and repeats is substantially the whole statement. Thus, where the victim dies before completing his statement it will be inadmissible even though the witness can recall every word the victim uttered. For instance, in *Waugh* v *R* [1950] AC 203, where the victim in referring to the defendant, Waugh, said: 'The man has an old grudge against me simply because ...', but then died before completing his sentence, it was held that the evidence should not have been admitted as a dying declaration at the defendant's trial for murder. Where the declaration is oral and does not qualify as a dying declaration, it may be admissible in a homicide trial if it is accepted as a *res gestae* statement. The *res gestae* exception to the hearsay rule will be considered shortly.

Similarly, where the declaration is written and is not admissible as a dying declaration, it may well be admissible under the provisions of sections 23–26 of the Criminal Justice Act 1988, subject to the exclusionary discretion given to the judge by the Act.

As with all prosecution evidence in criminal proceedings, the court has a residual discretion to exclude it in the interests of a fair trial.

Under the legislative scheme proposed by the Law Commission, which is considered in Chapter 14, the dying declaration exception need not be retained.

Declarations against interest

The attitude of the common law was in general that if a person made a statement against his own interest, it was more likely to be true than a self-serving statement where the maker could have a multitude of reasons for lying. The statements which are admissible at common law in this regard are declarations against a pecuniary or proprietary interest of the maker. A person may, for instance, have acknowledged that he owed money to another, or that he is not the owner of certain property but merely the trustee on behalf of another.

However, one interest, which does not appear to be included under this head, is penal interest, that is, a declaration which could have resulted in a prosecution if the maker had survived. The only English authority is the *Sussex Peerage Case* (1844) 11 Cl & F 85 where the issue in dispute was the validity of a marriage conducted by a member of the clergy who had died before the proceedings came to court. Evidence that the vicar had stated that he officiated at the ceremony, which was contrary to the Royal Marriages Act 1772 and thus would have rendered him liable to a prosecution, was held to be inadmissible as it did not fall into any recognised category of admissible declarations against interest. It was neither against his pecuniary, nor proprietary, interest. The omission is somewhat illogical.

A much more recent illustration of the exception is provided by *R* v *Rogers* [1995] 1 Cr App R 374. The Court of Appeal held that an oral or written statement by the deceased of a fact that he knew was against his pecuniary or proprietary interest when the declaration was made was admissible evidence of that fact in both criminal and civil proceedings.

Declarations in the course of duty

This exception to the hearsay rule has long been recognised because such evidence is generally considered to be reliable. Statements are admissible, whether made orally or in writing, if made in pursuance of a duty on the maker to report or record his activities, made roughly contemporaneously with the performance of the activity, and without any motive on the part of the maker to distort or misrepresent the facts in the statement. It appears that the 'duty' must be a legal or professional one, although there is no case where a moral duty has been specifically excluded.

The requirement of approximate contemporaneity means that there is some flexibility. Provided the record is made while the person can be expected to have a clear recollection, it is more likely to be accurate. However, in the case of *The Henry Coxon* (1878) 3 PD 156 a delay of two days in recording in the ship's log details of a collision in which the ship was involved was deemed too long. In addition, the first mate who made the entry in the log and had died by the time of the hearing had a motive to distort the facts because he was at the wheel at the time of the collision.

The common law exception is limited to factual matters, rather than statements of opinion. This is illustrated in *R v McGuire* (1985) 81 Cr App R 323. The defendant was charged with arson. It was alleged that he had set his own hotel on fire in order to obtain cash from an insurance company. A scientific officer from the Home Office had inspected the hotel soon after the fire and had recorded factual matters regarding *inter alia* the size of the fire. His recorded opinion was that the fire probably started in a certain room of the hotel. This opinion was favourable to the defendant's self-exculpatory explanation and, as the officer had died by the time of trial, the defendant wished to adduce the entire report, including the scientific officer's opinion in evidence. It was held that only the factual part of the declaration could be adduced under this exception.

Finally under this heading, any declaration contained in a document may well now be admissible in criminal proceedings under section 24 of the Criminal Justice Act 1988. A declaration made orally however can only be admitted under the common law exception.

Declarations as to public or general rights

An oral or written statement by a deceased person concerning the reputed existence of a public right of way or a right generally enjoyed by a section of the public is admissible as evidence of the existence of such a right. However, as a condition for admissibility it must be proved that the declarant had sufficient knowledge of the right and that the declaration was made before a dispute as regards its existence arose. Such evidence is admitted because it is generally felt to be reliable and because other available evidence may not be in existence.

Declarations as to pedigree

Examples of declarations as to pedigree include statements relating to date of birth, next of kin, legitimacy of children and the existence of marriage. At common law an oral or written statement by a deceased person concerning a matter of pedigree is admissible as evidence of the truth of the facts stated where a person's pedigree is directly in issue. As a condition of its admissibility the deceased declarant must have been a blood relation or spouse of a blood relation of the person concerned and the declaration must have been sometime before a dispute arose. The rationale for admitting such evidence stems from the fact that there may be no other evidence in existence to prove the fact and its reliability may be assumed.

RES GESTAE STATEMENTS

The actual meaning of the words *res gestae* ('things done') is of little importance but the words do serve a purpose in the law of evidence in that they bring together situations where hearsay evidence is admissible at common law to explain some contemporaneous act or state of affairs in cases where the act and the statement taken individually would not be completely self-explanatory. In fact the act and the statement are so intertwined that the statement, albeit hearsay, has to be admitted in evidence to complete the unfinished picture portrayed by the act or circumstance.

The rationale of the *res gestae* exception to the hearsay rule was given succinctly by Grove J in *Howe* v *Malkin* (1878) 40 LT 196:

> Though you cannot give in evidence a declaration per se, yet when there is an act accompanied by a statement which is so mixed up with it as to become part of the res gestae, evidence of such a statement may be given.

To some extent the words 'so mixed up with it ...' beg the question of what exactly a *res gestae* statement is, but the following four types of statement nevertheless exemplify the *res gestae* exception.

Spontaneous statements by actors or observers

This first common law exception to the hearsay rule is of substantial antiquity, and for a considerable time was strictly interpreted as regards contemporaneity, until decisions of appellate courts in the 1970s and 1980s rationalised the relevant factors for admissibility of such hearsay evidence.

In *Thompson* v *Trevanion* (1693) Holt KB 286 the claimant (Thompson) sued the defendant (Trevanion) for damages for a battery on the claimant's wife. The court allowed a witness to state what the wife had said about the attack and her assailant almost immediately after the battery. Holt CJ held that the witness could relate what the wife had said because she said it 'immediately upon the hurt received, and before she had time to devise or contrive anything for her own advantage'. This indicates the need for spontaneity and contemporaneity which motivates against concoction or distortion and renders the statement more reliable than it would otherwise be. This requirement however gradually became more rigid, until the extreme rigidity and incongruity seen in *R* v *Bedingfield* (1879) 14 Cox CC 341.

The defendant, Harry Bedingfield, was charged with the murder of a young woman who, stumbling from the room where she had been alone with him, her throat fatally slashed, uttered: 'Look what Harry's done!' and shortly thereafter died. Her aunt, to whom her exclamation was addressed, was not allowed to testify as to what the victim had said, because the court decided it was not contemporaneous with the fatal act! The statement was not, and still would not be, admissible as a dying declaration, because the victim had not had sufficient time to be under a 'settled, hopeless, expectation of death' at the time she uttered her statement.

A modern restatement of the rule is contained in *Ratten* v R [1972] AC 378, a case reviewed in Chapter 12 in the context of implied assertions. It will be recalled that the defendant was convicted of the murder of his wife. His appeal against conviction eventually reached the Privy Council where it failed. The contested evidence was that of a telephone switchboard operator, who testified that on the day in question, and at about the time that Mrs Ratten was shot and killed, she took a call from the defendant's house from a female who was hysterical and sobbed 'Get me the police, please'. It was not in dispute that only Mr and Mrs Ratten were home at this time. This evidence was highly relevant to rebut the defendant's contention that he was cleaning his gun when it went off accidentally and just happened to kill his wife. The defendant appealed on the basis that the trial judge had allowed inadmissible hearsay evidence to be admitted in order to refute his defence of accident.

The Privy Council found against the defendant on two alternative bases. On one basis, the Privy Council held it was legitimate to conclude that the evidence of the telephonist lacked a hearsay quality because it was circumstantial evidence of the state of affairs which were prevailing in the house and strongly contradicted the defence of accident. This aspect of the case is discussed more fully in Chapter 12. As an alternative reason for upholding the trial judge's ruling, the Privy Council held that even if there were elements of hearsay (the words she used implied she was in fear and had good reason to be fearful) in the evidence, her words were still admissible under the *res gestae* exception, being words which were spoken spontaneously while the speaker's mind was dramatically involved with a contemporaneous event.

Whatever the argument as to the hearsay element in the woman's words, the decision in *Ratten* v R dragged the *res gestae* exception into the twentieth century and moved the emphasis from strict contemporaneity to spontaneity evinced by the dramatic event which controlled the mind of the speaker.

The admission of 'spontaneous statements' under the *res gestae* rule came before the House of Lords in *R* v *Andrews* [1987] AC 281. This case contains the modern-day statement of the rule and the criteria by which it operates. The case overrules *R* v *Bedingfield* and approves *Ratten* v R. The facts of *Andrews* were that a fatally stabbed victim named his two assailants a few minutes after the injuries had been sustained. The victim had been drinking heavily, and there had been a vendetta between the assailants and himself as he believed that they had on one occasion burgled his flat. The House of Lords, upholding the conviction for murder, held that the trial judge was right to admit the evidence of the victim's statements. In upholding the conviction the House of Lords set out the criteria for admissibility of *res gestae*:

> My Lords, may I therefore summarise the position which confronts the trial judge when faced in a criminal case with an application under the res gestae doctrine to admit evidence of statements, with a view to establishing the truth of some fact thus narrated, such evidence being truly categorised as 'hearsay evidence':
>
>   1. The primary question, which the judge must ask himself – is can the possibility of concoction or distortion be disregarded?

2. To answer that question the judge must first consider the circumstances in which the particular statement was made, in order to satisfy himself that the event was so unusual or startling or dramatic as to dominate the thoughts of the victim, so that his utterance was an instinctive reaction to that event, thus giving no real opportunity for reasoned reflection. In such a situation the judge would be entitled to conclude that the involvement or the pressure of the event would exclude the possibility of concoction or distortion, providing that the statement was made in conditions of approximate but not exact contemporaneity.

3. In order for the statement to be sufficiently 'spontaneous' it must be so closely associated with the event which has excited the statement, that it can be fairly stated that the mind of the declarant was still dominated by the event. Thus the judge must be satisfied that the event, which provided the trigger mechanism for the statement, was still operative. The fact that the statement was made in answer to a question is but one factor to consider under this heading.

4. Quite apart from the time factor, there may be special features in the case, which relate to the possibility of concoction or distortion.... The judge must be satisfied that the circumstances were such that having regard to the special feature of malice, there was no possibility of any concoction or distortion to the advantage of the maker or the disadvantage of the accused.

5. As to the possibility of error in the facts narrated in the statement, if only the ordinary fallibility of human recollection is relied upon, this goes to the weight to be attached to and not to the admissibility of the statement. ... However, here again there may be special features that may give rise to the possibility of error. In the instant case there was evidence that the deceased had drunk to excess, well over double the permitted limit for driving a motor car. Another example would be where the identification was made in circumstances of particular difficulty or where the declarant suffered from defective eyesight. In such circumstances the trial judge must consider whether he can exclude the possibility of error. (*per* Lord Ackner)

The issue of the spontaneity of the victim's statement continues to cause problems for the courts and is the key element in deciding whether a statement can be admitted under the *res gestae* rule. This is evident from a number of cases decided since *R* v *Andrews*.

R v Carnall [1995] Crim LR 944

The victim, who was badly beaten and stabbed, took an hour to crawl for help before naming the defendant as his assailant, first to two witnesses in the street who saw him bleeding and asking for help and later to a police officer in an ambulance. The Court of Appeal held that the evidence had been properly admitted despite the time lapse and despite the fact that the victim had only named his assailant in response to questions.

The approach taken in *R* v *Carnall* may be contrasted with that taken in *Tobi* v *Nicholas* [1987] Crim LR 774, where the trial judge admitted as a *res gestae* statement an assertion made by a car driver some 20 minutes after a minor traffic accident in which there was only minimal damage. The Court of Appeal ruled that the judge had erred in allowing the witness to testify as to what the driver had said. In addition to the lapse of time, there was no evidence of any event of sufficient drama to control or affect his mind even for a much shorter time; the hearsay evidence was unreliable and an unsafe basis for a conviction.

Similarly in *R* v *Newport* [1988] Crim LR 581 a friend of the victim of an alleged murder received a telephone call from the deceased 20 minutes before the killing in which she sounded agitated and frightened and asked if she could come to the friend's house. The Court of Appeal held that this evidence was inadmissible as part of the *res gestae* as it was not part of the immediate incident and was not a spontaneous and unconsidered reaction to an immediately impending emergency.

One final point in relation to spontaneous utterances needs to be made clear. The rule is not confined to statements made in these circumstances by deceased persons as it can apply to a case where the maker of the statement is alive but is unable to attend court for some reason. It can even be admitted where the maker is available to give evidence (see *R* v *Nye and Loan* (1978) 66 Cr App R 252).

Statements explaining actions

The statement of the actor can quite often be the best means of explaining the significance of the act which is relevant to some issue before the court.

For such a statement to be admissible hearsay it must be shown that it relates directly to the act; that it was made contemporaneously with the act; and that the actor made it. For example, if, in the middle of a heated dispute as to the boundary line between two properties, one of the arguing occupiers were to draw a line on a plan of the area, then in some litigation many years later it could be that a person who witnessed the incident could give evidence not just of the marks on the plan but also of what the maker of the marks had said at the time.

Statements as to physical or mental condition

Statements about the contemporaneous physical or mental condition of the speaker, including his emotions, are admissible under the *res gestae* exception where a person's state of mind is a fact in issue or is relevant to a fact in issue. Who else is best placed to prove a person's past state of mind than the person himself? Statements as to sensations and symptoms may be admitted under the exception, but not the reasons for, or causes of, the sensation or condition of the speaker. The cause or causes might be admissible under another exception, for example as a dying declaration, in which case the whole statement would be admitted in evidence under that exception.

R v Conde (1867) 10 Cox CC 547

A person caring for a young child was charged with neglect, in that the baby had not been properly fed. Evidence was admitted of a witness who testified that she had heard the child complaining of hunger pains. Were it not for this exception to the hearsay rule, the witness's evidence would have been excluded on the grounds that it impliedly asserted want of care and neglect on the part of the carer.

R v Gilfoyle [1996] 3 All ER 883

The defendant had been convicted of the murder of his wife. She had been found hanging from a beam in the garage of the marital home. It was initially thought that the wife had committed suicide since a suicide note in her handwriting had been found. As a result of further police inquiries, colleagues of the dead woman came forward to say that a few weeks before her death her husband's behaviour had been concerning her. He had asked her to write a suicide note for a project he was undertaking on suicide and he had apparently shown her how to put a rope up in the garage, again as part of his student research. At trial, the defendant maintained his wife had committed suicide and notwithstanding a ruling by the trial judge which excluded the evidence of the work colleagues the defendant was still convicted of his wife's murder. On appeal, the Court of Appeal held it was at liberty to reconsider decisions as to admissibility as part of its duty to receive fresh evidence. In the Court of Appeal's view the evidence was admissible to prove that when she had written the notes she was not then in a suicidal frame of mind. It was admissible under the *res gestae* principle as a contemporaneous statement as to the victim's state of mind.

Statements of intention

A statement of what the speaker intended to do is admissible as evidence of that intention. Such evidence is capable of affording useful circumstantial evidence of the existence of an intention which may be highly relevant to proof, for example of motive in a murder case. Whether it is in addition admissible evidence of his acting in accordance with his intention is less certain. Evidence that a person had an intention to do something may give rise to a presumption of fact that he had that intention for some time afterwards; but as the presumption of continuance, even without any rebutting evidence, will not necessarily lead to the court's coming to the conclusion indicated, it is not incumbent on the court to conclude that the person did the act intended. In fact, it does not follow that the court will decide anything other than that the person evinced an intention and another heard what he said. There is some conflict in the authorities on whether the doing of an act can be inferred from a statement of intent. The following cases highlight that conflict:

R v Wainwright (1875) 13 Cox CC 171

The defendant was prosecuted for the murder of a woman who, on the afternoon of her death as she left her lodgings, told her friend that she was going to the defendant's house. The friend was not permitted to testify to this effect. The court concluded that the victim's statement did not form 'part of the act of leaving but was an incidental remark. It was a statement of intention which might, or might not, have been carried out'.

R v Buckley (1873) 13 Cox CC 293

The defendant was charged with the murder of a police constable. On the night the constable met his death, he told his superior officer that he was going to keep observation on the defendant's movements. The officer was allowed to testify as to what the constable had said to him, the court holding that this evidence was admissible to show what the constable was doing when he was killed, and thus effectively to reveal the identity of his killer.

The difference between these two cases could be the fact that a constable has a duty not merely to inform a superior what he intends to do, but actually to act accordingly. Though the evidence of the superior officer was admitted apparently as part of the *res gestae*, it could be that the court also considered the exception of declarations made in the course of duty.

However, in *R v Thomson* [1912] 3 KB 19 the defendant was charged with using an instrument on a pregnant woman with intent to procure her miscarriage. The woman later died. The trial judge refused leave to allow the defendant's counsel to cross-examine a prosecution witness as to whether the deceased woman had told her that she intended to use an instrument on herself to procure her own miscarriage, and whether she some time later told her that she had operated on herself. The Court of Criminal Appeal upheld the trial judge's ruling, stating that the witness's evidence would have been hearsay, whether given in examination-in-chief or in answer to questions put to her in cross-examination. The second statement by the deceased woman amounted to a freely made confession and therefore could have been admissible if declarations against penal interest were recognised under English laws of evidence.

STATEMENTS IN PUBLIC DOCUMENTS

Statements in public documents or certified true copies of them are admissible at common law as evidence of the truth of their contents. This exception to the hearsay rule has long been recognised because such evidence was considered to be reliable and very often the public official who compiled the document would have no recollection of the facts, or be dead, or be unfit to testify. The safeguard at common law comprised the circumstances in which the document came into being. For the document to be admissible, four conditions must be satisfied:

1 the document must have been compiled for public use, and therefore the public must have access to it;
2 the person making the record had a public duty to make the entry and compile the document from his personal knowledge;
3 the record or document must have been made by the public official at a time when he could reasonably be expected to have recollection of the events recorded; and
4 the document must have been intended to form a permanent record.

Many statutes now make provision for the admissibility of certain specific classes of documents, such as certified true copies of entries in a register of deaths compiled by the Registrar of Births, Deaths and Marriages, as evidence of the date of a person's death where this is a relevant fact in issue in any proceedings.

In addition to such specific provisions, most statements in public documents will be admissible in criminal cases by virtue of section 24 of the Criminal Justice Act 1988.

The Law Commission's proposals for reform preserve the vast majority of the common law exceptions permitting the use of hearsay at trials and are considered in greater detail in Chapter 14.

Further reading

Law Commission Consultation Paper No 138 (1995) *Evidence in Criminal Proceedings: Hearsay and Related Topics*, HMSO.

Law Commission Report No 245 (1997) *Evidence in Criminal Proceedings: Hearsay and Related Topics*, HMSO.

Zuckerman, A. (1989) *The Principles of Criminal Evidence*, Clarendon Press.

Chapter 14

STATUTORY EXCEPTIONS PERMITTING THE USE OF HEARSAY EVIDENCE

INTRODUCTION

The common law's historical distrust of hearsay evidence was made abundantly clear by the House of Lords' decision in *Myers v DPP* [1965] AC 1001 (see Chapter 12). *Myers v DPP* was overturned when Parliament passed the Criminal Evidence Act 1965, permitting documentary evidence to be admitted at criminal trials in certain instances. Whilst the 1965 Act marked a significant step forward in extending the categories of admissible hearsay evidence, it proved to be too restrictive. For example, computer records were not covered by the legislation. The categories of admissible evidence were further extended with the enactment of sections 68–72 of the Police and Criminal Evidence Act 1984. However, despite these provisions, it became obvious that widespread reform was needed to ensure adequate safeguards were put in place and to prevent unfairness.

The main statutory provisions permitting the use of hearsay evidence at criminal trials are contained in sections 23–26 of the Criminal Justice Act 1988 and it is to these that we now turn our attention. The 1988 Act has no impact on confession evidence, the admissibility of which continues to be governed by section 76 of the Police and Criminal Evidence Act 1984.

CRIMINAL JUSTICE ACT 1988, SECTION 23

Section 23 of the 1988 Act provides:

(1) ... a statement made by a person in a document shall be admissible in criminal proceedings as evidence of any fact of which direct oral evidence by him would have been admissible if—

    (i) the requirements of one of the paragraphs of subsection (2) below are satisfied; or

    (ii) the requirements of subsection (3) below are satisfied.

(2) ...

    (a) that the person who made the statement is dead or by reason of his bodily or mental condition unfit to attend as a witness;

    (b) that—

        (i) the person who made the statement is outside the United Kingdom; and

        (ii) it is not reasonably practicable to secure his attendance; or

    (c) that all reasonable steps have been taken to find the person who made the statement, but that he cannot be found.

(3) The requirements mentioned in subsection (1)(ii) above are—
    (a) that the statement was made to a police officer or some other person charged
        with the duty of investigating offences or charging offenders; and
    (b) that the person who made it does not give oral evidence through fear or because
        he is kept out of the way.
(4) Subsection (1) above does not render admissible a confession made by an accused
person under section 76 of the Police and Criminal Evidence Act 1984.

The effect of section 23(1) is to make first-hand documentary hearsay, of which direct
oral evidence would have been admissible itself, admissible in criminal trials. In
Example 2 given at the beginning of Chapter 12, section 23 would have no application because the information provided to Y is in oral form and the section only applies
to first-hand hearsay evidence contained in a document. However, in Example 3,
section 23 would allow X's written statement to be admitted, provided that a specified
reason for X's non-attendance can be established. Section 23 would, however, have no
application if, in Example 2, Y had reduced into writing what X had told him. Y's
written statement would constitute multiple hearsay and section 23 is confined to first-
hand documentary hearsay.

    A 'document' for the purpose of section 23 is defined widely as 'anything in which
any information of any description is recorded'. It therefore includes correspondence,
memoranda, reports, files, diaries, entries in account books, audiotapes, videotapes,
films, photographs and computer files. It would also extend to a situation where the
witness dictated his statement to another and in some way, for example by signing,
acknowledged the statement's contents.

    In order to be admissible under section 23, the statement must be made by a per-
son in a document. In effect, where a party wishes to put evidence before the court
it must be in either written or documentary form. This latter point is illustrated by
R v McGillivray (1993) 97 Cr App R 232. The victim, who was critically injured,
dictated a statement to a police officer, who then read it back to him. Due to his
injuries the victim was unable to sign the statement but agreed that it was accurate.
The Court of Appeal confirmed the victim's statement was admissible under section
23 as being a statement contained in a document. In R v Nazeer [1998] Crim LR 750,
the Court of Appeal concluded that where a computer was incapable of producing a
printout which would have been admissible under section 24 of the Criminal Justice
Act 1988 in conjunction with section 69 of PACE and it was physically impossible to
produce the computer in court, the statements could be proved by a witness giving
oral evidence of what he had read on screen. The computer itself was a 'document'
within the meaning of section 24 and, as the original could not be produced,
secondary evidence was admissible under section 27 of the Criminal Justice Act 1988.

    The party seeking to rely on hearsay evidence being admitted under section 23 must
prove the non-availability of a witness for one of the specified reasons set out in section
23. In R v Ashford Justices, ex parte Hilden [1993] QB 555, the non-availability of a
witness was held to include a witness who is called to give evidence and who starts to
do so, but then feels unable to continue whether due to illness or fear.

    Whilst proof of the non-availability of a witness for one of the specified reasons in
section 23 is a condition of the admissibility of the absent witness's statement, it is not
the only condition. Notwithstanding that a specified reason is proved to the court's

satisfaction, the court must go on to apply its discretion under either section 25 or 26 before finally deciding whether to admit the evidence in hearsay form.

Case law on section 23

Witness cannot attend because he is dead or unfit (section 23(2)(a))

The decision in *R v Setz-Dempsey* (1994) 98 Cr App R 23 recognises that 'unfitness to attend' includes the witness's mental capacity and not just physical infirmity. This ground is easily proved by the prosecution tendering a certified copy of a death certificate or obtaining appropriate medical evidence.

Witness cannot attend because he is outside the United Kingdom and it is not reasonably practicable to secure his attendance (section 23(2)(b))

This particular provision has generated a number of appeals against conviction.

R v Case [1991] Crim LR 192 confirms that where the prosecution wishes to rely on this ground, both reasons (the fact that the witness is outside the United Kingdom and that it is not reasonable to secure his attendance) must be proved. In this case, Portuguese tourists were the victims of theft. In their statements to the police the address they had given was that of a London hotel together with an indication that their stay in England was of a temporary nature. The statements did not include the date on which were expected to return to Portugal, nor how long they were expected to remain in England. The Court of Appeal concluded that the prosecution was unable to prove that it had not been reasonably practicable to secure the witnesses' attendance.

In *R v Castillo* [1996] 1 Cr App R 438, the inability of one witness to attend the trial was proved by the admission of another witness in his statement admitted under section 23. The case is important as the Court of Appeal usefully reviews what a court should bear in mind in deciding whether it was reasonably practicable to secure the absent witness's attendance. Relevant factors include:

- the importance of the witness;
- the extent of the prejudice it would cause to the defendant were the absent witness's statement read out, affording no opportunity to cross-examine;
- the expense and inconvenience of securing the witness's attendance;
- the seriousness of the offence itself.

As regards the seriousness of the offence, where, for instance, the charge is one of smuggling Class A drugs, and the witness's evidence is important to the prosecution, the court may well require greater efforts to be made to try to ensure the attendance of a witness from outside the United Kingdom than perhaps would be the case were the charge less serious and the defendant's liberty was not at stake.

R *v* Gonzales de Orango [1992] Crim LR 180

Two crucial prosecution witnesses failed to appear. The prosecution sought to adduce documentary evidence and dispense with the oral testimony of the witnesses. Both were travel agents' booking clerks who were based in Bogota, Colombia, and it was asserted that it was impracticable to call them. They had been spoken to by telephone but refused to come to England for the trial. Three months later, they were called on the telephone and again refused. At no time were they asked for a reason for their unwillingness. The trial judge allowed the documentary evidence and the accused and co-accused were convicted of smuggling cocaine. The defendants appealed to the Court of Appeal.

The Court of Appeal found more could have been done by the prosecution to secure the attendance of the witnesses. The reasons for their unwillingness should have been ascertained and an offer made to pay their fare in case they were refusing on financial grounds. Letters rather than telephone calls could have been more effective; an approach could have been made by letter to the manager of the travel agency, and if necessary the assistance requested of the British Embassy or Colombian Customs. The conviction of one of the co-accused, which depended largely on the documentary evidence, was quashed; in the case of the others, there was overwhelming evidence of their guilt without the documentary evidence.

Where the absent witness is a prosecution witness, the court must be satisfied beyond reasonable doubt that all reasonable efforts have been made. If the defence allege that the attendance of a witness is impracticable, or he is untraceable, then the civil standard of proof on balance of probabilities will suffice.

Witness cannot attend to give evidence because he cannot be found and all reasonable steps have been taken to find him (section 23(2)(c))

Where a witness is in the United Kingdom the question of impracticability of his attendance does not arise. However, it may be shown that he is untraceable despite all reasonable steps having been taken to trace him. Once again, the party seeking to rely on this ground would have to tender admissible evidence of the steps taken to trace the witness.

Witness has made a statement to a police officer but does not give oral evidence through fear or because he is kept out of the way (section 23(3))

The refusal of witnesses to come to court to give evidence is obviously detrimental to the criminal justice process and the search for the truth. Section 23(3) aims to remedy the situation by ensuring that the written statement of a frightened or intimidated witness can still be put before the court even though the witness refuses to come to court.

As a condition of admissibility the statement must have been made to a police officer or some other person charged with the investigation of a crime and the maker of the statement must then fail to give oral evidence 'through fear or because he is kept out of the way'. The subsection is almost always relied upon by the prosecution. It will have the burden of proving that the conditions for admissibility are made out. But, in what form can such evidence of fear be presented? Can the witness confirm in a written statement that he refuses to attend the trial to give evidence because he is in fear? Can a police officer give evidence to the effect that he has spoken to the witness who told him he is not giving evidence through fear? What has emerged from the case law in answering these questions is that proof of fear cannot be provided in hearsay form unless the hearsay evidence falls within an established exception.

Neill v North Antrim Magistrates' Court [1992] 4 All ER 846

A police officer gave evidence of a conversation he had had with the frightened witness. The House of Lords felt the evidence was admissible under the common law exception to the rule prohibiting reliance on hearsay evidence as a contemporaneous declaration as to state of mind. Presumably the common law exception can apply to words spoken orally or contained in a statement by the frightened witness.

R v Acton Justices, ex parte McMullen (1991) 92 Cr App R 98

The Divisional Court concluded 'fear' and 'is kept out of the way' were disjunctive and therefore alternative grounds. Fear would be made out where the court was 'sure the witness was in fear as a consequence of the commission of the offence or something said or done subsequently in relation to that offence and the possibility of the witness testifying to it'. The Divisional Court rejected the argument that the witness's fear should be based on rational grounds. Therefore it is not essential that the fear be rational. If the person is exceptionally timid, his fear of some consequence of testifying need not be fear that the reasonable man would have, but the reason given for the fear must be credible.

The decision in *R v Martin* [1997] Crim LR 589 broadens the ground still further. The Court of Appeal concluded that the fear of the witness does not have to be reasonable. So long as the witness is in fear, the source of that fear would appear to be irrelevant. In other words, it need not arise from the crime itself or the consequences of testifying thereto. The simple fact that the witness is in fear and that such fear is credible would appear to be enough.

In *R v Ashford Justices, ex parte Hilden* [1993] QB 555, the witness began to give his evidence but was unable to continue through fear. His demeanour was sufficient to satisfy the court of his fear, and so his earlier witness statement was admitted. Therefore 'does not give oral evidence' is not restricted to situations where the witness does not begin to testify at all.

If the reason for the non-attendance of a witness is that he 'is kept out of the way', this does not of course mean that the side who would have called the witness can rely on section 23(3) simply by keeping him away from the court. What is envisaged is a person or group of people preventing the witness from attending court.

CRIMINAL JUSTICE ACT 1988, SECTION 24

Section 24 of the Criminal Justice Act 1988 makes provision for the admissibility of hearsay evidence contained in a document of any fact of which direct oral testimony would be admissible provided that certain specified conditions are fulfilled. These conditions are:

(i) the document was created or received by a person in the course of a trade, business, profession or other occupation, or as the holder of a paid or unpaid office; and

(ii) the information contained in the document was supplied by a person (whether or not the maker of the statement) who had, or may reasonably be supposed to have had, personal knowledge of the matters dealt with;

(iii) if the information was supplied indirectly, each person through whom it was supplied must have received it in the course of a trade, business, profession or other occupation, or as the holder (of a paid or unpaid office).

Section 24 is poorly drafted and has generated considerable case law. Unlike section 23, it is not confined to first-hand documentary hearsay. The wording of the section provides that the person who supplied the information and the maker of the statement need not be the same person and, indeed, the information comprised in the document may have been provided through intermediaries.

Unlike section 23, section 24 does not require that the statement should be made in a document, only that it is contained in a document. In common however with section 23, section 24 applies widely to include, for example, a report from a bank, computer printout of stock records, a transcript of evidence and a letter written or received in the course of a business.

Reliability is safeguarded by the fact that the original supplier of the information must have had or might reasonably be supposed to have had personal knowledge of the matters dealt with. The document containing the information must have been created or received in the course of a trade, business, profession or other occupation etc. Where the information reaches the compiler through more than one source each intermediary must also have received the information in the course of a business, trade, profession etc.

The following points may be made in relation to section 24:

1 It is not strictly necessary for the party tendering evidence under section 24 to call witnesses to give oral testimony that the supplier of the information had personal knowledge of the facts or that the compiler of the document was acting in the course of a trade or business etc. In some cases this will be inferred by the court. In R v *Foxley* [1995] 2 Cr App R 523, the Court of Appeal indicated that 'The courts can draw inferences from the documents themselves and from the method or route by which the documents have been produced before the court'.
2 It is not necessary for the eyewitness to be acting in the course of a trade but it is necessary for the compiler of the document and any intermediary.
3 The party seeking to tender evidence under section 24(1) does not have to specify the reason for the original supplier of the information or the compiler of the document not being able to attend the court to give oral testimony.

Admissibility of statements prepared for criminal proceedings or investigations (section 24(4))

Section 24(4) of the 1988 Act is most important. In short, it specifically governs the admissibility of a statement in a document prepared for the purposes of pending or contemplated criminal proceedings, or of a criminal investigation. This is apt to cover a large number of written statements which are ultimately admitted most often under section 23 and sometimes under section 24. Section 24(4) provides that where a statement has been prepared for the purposes of pending or contemplated criminal proceedings or for a criminal investigation such a statement will not be admissible unless the requirements of section 23(2) or (3) are made out. It will be recalled that the requirements of section 23 include the fact that:

• the witness might be dead or by reason of his bodily or mental condition unfit to attend; or

- the person who made the statement is outside the United Kingdom and it is not reasonably practicable to secure his attendance; or
- all reasonable steps have been taken to find the person who made the statement, but he cannot be found; or
- the statement was made to a police officer or some other person charged with the duty of investigating offences or charging offenders and the person who made it does not give oral evidence through fear or because he is kept out of the way.

Section 24(4) does however provide an additional reason for the admission of a statement made in contemplation of criminal proceedings in hearsay form. Section 24(4)(iii) states: 'the person who made the statement cannot reasonably be expected (having regard to the time which has elapsed since he made the statement and to all the circumstance) to have any recollection of the matters dealt with in the statement.'

A problem does however arise as to the identity of maker of the statement for the purposes of section 24(4). Is it the person who supplied the information or the person who compiled the document on the basis of it? Under section 24 the maker of the statement can be attributed to different people. The issue arose in the case of R v *Derodra* [2001] 1 Cr App R 41.The defendant was implicated in a fraudulent insurance claim. He had sought to claim on a policy of insurance for a burglary which the prosecution contended had occurred before the policy was in fact taken out. The prosecution was permitted to adduce in evidence a record of a telephone call made to a police incident room by a lodger at the defendant's address informing the police of a burglary at the premises. The date of the report was logged into the police incident computer by a police officer. The lodger could not be traced and the prosecution did not call the police officer who had received the original information to give oral testimony. The defendant contended the police officer had been the maker of the statement and that there had been no specified reason to explain his absence. The Court of Appeal however read into the section a requirement that the 'maker of the statement' was the person who had supplied the information sought to be relied on and not the person who had actually made a note or record of it. As a consequence, the evidence was rightly admitted.

Having regard to the examples of hearsay given at the beginning of Chapter 12, section 24 allows the ledger referred to in Example 5 to be admitted as a business record notwithstanding the presence of multiple hearsay. In Example 3, providing a section 23 reason can be made out to explain why X cannot attend trial, X's statement may be admitted only with leave of the court, since X's statement would have been prepared for the purposes of a criminal investigation within the meaning of section 24(4).

Where the conditions for admissibility of a statement tendered under section 24(4) are made out, the court is prevented from actually admitting the statement into evidence unless, having applied its discretion under section 26, it gives leave to admit the statement because it deems it to be in the interests of justice to do so. The factors the court can have regard to in exercising its discretion under section 26 are considered below.

CRIMINAL JUSTICE ACT 1988, SECTIONS 25 AND 26 – REQUIREMENT TO EXERCISE JUDICIAL DISCRETION BEFORE ADMITTING HEARSAY EVIDENCE

In all criminal trials the court has an inherent power at common law to exclude otherwise admissible prosecution evidence where the admission of the evidence would prejudice a fair trial. In addition, there is a general discretion under section 78 of the Police and Criminal Evidence Act 1984 (PACE) to exclude prosecution evidence which would, in the opinion of the court, have an adverse effect on the fairness of the proceedings. The principles governing the exercise of discretion in these two instances are discussed in Chapter 5. Whilst section 78 and the common law discretion which is preserved by section 82(3) of PACE can apply to documentary hearsay evidence tendered under sections 23 and 24 of the Criminal Justice Act 1988, the court is more likely to consider the admissibility of such evidence under sections 25 and 26 of the 1988 Act.

Section 25

If having regard to all the circumstances ... [a court of trial or an appeal court] ... is of the opinion that in the interests of justice a statement which is admissible by virtue of section 23 or 24. ... nevertheless ought not to be admitted, it may direct that the statement shall not be admitted.

Section 25 establishes a general exclusionary discretion. Where the conditions for the admissibility of hearsay evidence under either section 23 or 24 are made out, there is a presumption that such evidence will be admitted, unless the court is of the opinion that it would not be in the interests of justice to do so. The factors, which shape the exercise of discretion under section 25, are spelled out in subsection (2):

(2) Without prejudice to the generality of subsection (1) above, it shall be the duty of the court to have regard —
    (a) to the nature and source of the document containing the statement and to whether or not, having regard to its nature and source and to any other circumstances that appear to the court to be relevant, it is likely that the document is authentic;
    (b) to the extent to which the statement appears to supply evidence which would otherwise not be readily available;
    (c) to the relevance of the evidence that it appears to supply to any issue which is likely to have to be determined in the proceedings; and
    (d) to any risk, having regard in particular to whether it is likely to be possible to controvert the statement if the person making it does not attend to give oral evidence in the proceedings, that its admission or exclusion will result in unfairness to the accused or, if there is more than one, to any of them.

Section 26

Where a statement which is admissible in criminal proceedings by virtue of section 23 or 24 above appears to the court to have been prepared ... for the purposes—
    (a) of pending or contemplated criminal proceedings; or
    (b) of a criminal investigation,

the statement shall not be adduced in evidence without the leave of the court, and the court shall not give leave unless it is of the opinion that the statement ought to be admitted in the interests of justice; and in considering whether its admission would be in the interests of justice, it is the duty of the court to have regard—

(i) to the contents of the statement;

(ii) to any risk, having regard in particular to whether it is likely to be possible to controvert the statement if the person making it does not attend to give oral evidence, that its admission or exclusion will result in unfairness to the accused or, if there is more than one, to any of them; and

(iii) to any other circumstances that appear to the court to be relevant.

Where a document prepared in contemplation of criminal proceedings satisfies the condition for its admissibility as laid down by either section 23 or 24, there is a presumption under section 26 against the admission of such evidence unless the court is of the opinion that it is in the interests of justice to admit it. This contrasts with the position under section 25. The factors which shape the exercise of discretion under section 26 are contained within the section. The inter-relationship between the factors listed in support of section 25 and those listed in support of section 26 is unclear.

DEVELOPING JUDICIAL DISCRETION

In the leading case of *R v Cole* [1990] 1 WLR 865, Lord Justice Ralph Gibson explained the rationale behind sections 25 and 26 as follows:

> The nature of the discretion to be exercised by the court under sections 25 and 26 of the Act of 1988, and the matters to which in exercising that discretion the court is required to have regard, have been laid down by Parliament and, in the view of this court, are clearly expressed. There will be difficulty in applying those provisions to the facts of particular cases.
>
> The overall purpose of the provisions was to widen the power of the court to admit documentary hearsay evidence, while ensuring that the accused receives a fair trial. In judging how to achieve the fairness of a trial a balance must on occasion be struck between the interests of the public in enabling the prosecution case to be properly presented and the interest of a particular defendant in not being put in a disadvantageous position, for example by the death or illness of a witness. The public also has a direct interest in the proper protection of the individual accused. The point of balance, as directed by Parliament, is set out in the sections 25 and 26.

Section 25 is largely self-explanatory. It seeks to strike a balance between the court being appraised of all relevant evidence on the one hand and safeguarding the interests of the accused by restricting as necessary the admissibility of hearsay evidence on the other.

One important difference is that under section 26 the burden of persuading the court that it is in the interests of justice to admit the statement rests with the party tendering the evidence. Under section 25, the party objecting to the evidence has to put forward the argument that it is in the interests of justice to exclude the statement.

Where computer records are sought to be admitted as hearsay evidence under section 23 or 24, it might be supposed, given the abolition of section 69 of PACE, that a court would also now need to consider under sections 25 and 26 whether there was anything in the computer's operation or the way in which the information was fed into the machine that could affect the accuracy or reliability of the information it subsequently yields.

There has been little case law on the application of section 25. An exception is *R v Foxley* [1995] 2 Cr App R 523 which concerned the admission of certain records under section 24. The records had not been prepared for use in criminal proceedings, hence the application of section 25 as opposed to section 26. The Court of Appeal made reference to the importance of the documents to the prosecution's case and their reliability as important factors to bear in mind when exercising the discretion to refuse to admit them. In addition, it was held to be of some significance that the defendant could have given evidence in his own defence, contradicting the content of the records.

In *R v Cole*, applying section 26, the Court of Appeal held that a careful balancing act of the factors listed in that section was required and in addition to those factors the courts should also have regard to:

- the quality of the evidence sought to be relied on;
- the importance of the evidence to the side seeking to use it; and
- the unfairness occasioned to the other side by the inability to cross-examine the absent witness and to have the witness's demeanour assessed.

Arguably, the less reliable the evidence, the more important cross-examination becomes. In *R v Setz-Dempsey* (1993) 98 Cr App R 23, Lord Justice Beldam concluded:

> The mere fact that the statements sought to be given in evidence go to prove matters which are vital or of great significance in the case is not, in our judgment, a ground for exclusion. The interests of justice are not generally served by refusing to admit admissible evidence which is of importance to the issues a jury have to consider any more than they are served by admitting evidence of poor quality or evidence which could substantially be weakened by cross-examination.

Both section 25 and 26 are based on the exercise of judicial discretion. As such, provided that the judge did not err or act unreasonably, the Court of Appeal will often be reluctant to interfere and overturn the conclusion reached by the judge. Three cases provide illustrations of the careful balancing exercise undertaken by the court when exercising its inclusionary discretion under section 26.

R v Dragic [1996] 2 Cr App R 232

The sole identification witness was too ill to give evidence at the trial. The prosecution sought leave to admit the statement the witness had made to the police under section 23. Leave was granted. The defendant appealed pointing out the importance of this witness to the prosecution and the inability of the defence to conduct a cross-examination. The Court of Appeal rejected the argument pointing out the alibi notice had been served and it had been possible for the appellant to controvert the section 23 statement with his evidence of alibi. The Court of Appeal refused to interfere with the judge's exercise of discretion.

R v Gokal [1997] 2 Cr App R 266

The defendant controlled companies which as a result of false documents were lent far greater sums by a bank than the regulatory authorities would have permitted. The defendant was charged with conspiracy to account falsely and conspiracy to defraud. He denied the charges. At a preparatory hearing the prosecution sought to adduce evidence pursuant to sections 23 and 26 of the Criminal Justice Act 1988. This comprised the statement of the defendant's brother-in-law, C, who claimed to have acted as the defendant's general assistant, but who was outside the United Kingdom and was unwilling to return. The defence argued that C was an accomplice and that his evidence was unreliable. The judge concluded that the admission of C's statement would not result in unfairness to the accused and ruled it admissible. The defendant sought a ruling, that the evidence should not be included because of its effect on the privilege against self-incrimination. Effectively, he would be compelled to give evidence in order to contradict C's statement. In refusing the application the Court of Appeal concluded the language of section 26(ii) of the 1988 Act was plain and its purpose clear. When considering the interests of justice regard must be had to the fact that the defendant could contradict the evidence of an absent witness by giving evidence himself. In the court's view the defendant's right to silence was not abrogated and there was no breach of Article 6(3)(d) of the European Convention on Human Rights.

R v W [1997] Crim LR 678

The defendant was convicted of indecent assault, rape and attempted buggery against his children and his wife in relation to a series of offences which occurred over a period of 20 years. The defendant's wife made a written statement and an application was made by the defence, under sections 23 and 26 of the Criminal Justice Act 1988, for her statement to be read to the jury. The trial judge concluded that the defendant's wife could not give evidence because she was unfit and that her statement had been prepared for use in criminal proceedings. The judge ruled further that it was not in the interests of justice to admit the evidence for three reasons:

1   The wife had originally been a co-accused, and having received all the depositions was in a position to anticipate most of the prosecution case.
2   If the statement were admitted, the prosecution would have no opportunity to ask the defendant's wife about other events and would not be able to assess her as a witness.
3   There was a risk of hearsay evidence being admitted through the statement.

The defendant was convicted and was granted leave to appeal. In dismissing the appeal, the Court of Appeal found that the 'interests of justice' ground in section 26 applied to both prosecution and defence. The judge had correctly weighed up the prejudice to the prosecution to admit the document against the unfairness to the accused not to admit it, and had come to the conclusion that it was in the interests of justice not to admit the document.

One further important safeguard against the use of hearsay evidence is contained in paragraph 1 of Schedule 2 to the Criminal Justice Act 1988. Where a statement is admitted under the Act, the party against whom the document is admitted may still attack the weight to be attached to the evidence and can otherwise discredit the evidence contained in the document by putting forward evidence that casts doubt on the credibility of its maker. Thus, although it is not possible to cross-examine the witness in person, if, for example, evidence of bias exists on the part of the absent witness or the witness previously made a statement inconsistent with the one being adduced in evidence, it would still be possible to attack the credibility of the maker of the statement along the same lines.

HUMAN RIGHTS LAW

Article 6(3)(d) of the European Convention on Human Rights provides that everyone charged with a criminal offence has the right 'to examine or have examined witnesses against him and to obtain the attendance and examination of witnesses on his behalf under the same conditions as witnesses against him'.

Article 6(3)(d) is a specific component of the general right to a fair trial guaranteed under Article 6(1). Does hearsay admitted under the common law or statutory exceptions breach the defendant's right to a fair trial? In *Blastland* v *United Kingdom* (1998) 10 EHRR 528, the European Commission of Human Rights found that the rationale behind the rule, which is to ensure only the best evidence is put before a jury, was legitimate and not contrary to Article 6(1). The Commission ultimately found the applicant's claim to be inadmissible.

The use of hearsay evidence in the context of the right to a fair trial has been considered by the Strasbourg authorities on a number of occasions – see *Unterpertinger* v *Austria* (1991) 13 EHRR 175; *Kostovski* v *The Netherlands* (1990) 12 EHRR 434; *Windisch* v *Austria* (1991) 13 EHRR 281; *Isgro* v *Italy* (1990) Series A No 194; *Asch* v *Austria* (1993) 15 EHRR 597; and *Saidi* v *France* (1994) 17 EHRR 251. Any attempt to deduce clear guidance from these decisions is problematic as they are far from consistent. This is largely due to the fact that the European Court of Human Rights does not see its role as being to regulate the domestic laws of individual states but to ensure the applicant's trial was fair overall. In *Kostovski* v *The Netherlands*, the European Court of Human Rights unanimously held:

> In principle, all the evidence must be produced in the presence of the accused at a public hearing with a view to adversarial argument ... This does not mean, however, that in order to be used as evidence, statements of witnesses should always be made at a public hearing in court: to use as evidence such statements obtained at a pre-trial stage is not of itself inconsistent with paragraph 3(d) and 1 of Article 6 (art. 6-3-d, art. 6.1), provided the rights of the defence have been respected. As a rule, these rights require that an accused should be given an adequate and proper opportunity to challenge and question a witness against him, either at the time the witness was making his statement or at some later stage of the proceedings ...

Having regard to the above statement, documentary evidence admitted under section 23 of the Criminal Justice Act 1988 would on the face of it not comply with Convention requirements because no provision is made at any stage for the defendant or his counsel to cross-examine the witness whose written statement is ultimately to be relied on. Several of the cases cited above subscribe to the point of view expressed in *Kostovski* v *The Netherlands*. In almost all of them, however, the out-of-court statement the prosecution wished to rely on constituted a vital part of the prosecution's case and in *Windisch* v *Austria*, the unfairness arose from the fact that the two principal prosecution witnesses remained anonymous throughout the trial process.

Complicating the picture somewhat, later cases have cast doubt on the requirement that the defendant must be permitted to confront the absent witness at some stage. In *Asch* v *Austria*, the Court held that the inability of the prosecution to arrange a means by which an accused can confront a witness as required under Article 6(3)(d) does not necessarily violate the right to a fair trial under Article 6(1) providing there is a legitimate reason for the witness's absence and that person's evidence does not consti-tute the main evidence against the defendant. In *Isgro v Italy* the Court seemed to accept some derogation from a strict interpretation of Article 6(3)(d) is permitted where there is other evidence in the case, although in this case a confrontation had been arranged before an investigating judge at an early stage in the proceedings. The witness subsequently became untraceable by the date of trial, necessitating that the witness's earlier statement be read out to the court.

What of the use of written statements under sections 23 and 24 of the Criminal Justice Act 1988? Provision is made in the 1988 Act to enable the opposing party to call evidence challenging the credibility of the author of the statement. Furthermore there is the separate question of judicial discretion under sections 25 and 26 and section 78 of PACE. These were felt to be significant safeguards in the following cases:

Trivedi *v* United Kingdom [1997] 89 A DR 136, ECHR

At his trial, statements against the defendant, a British citizen, had been admitted under section 23 due to illness of the witness. In declaring his application inadmissible, the Commission noted the trial judge had made inquiry into the witness's condition and had directed the jury to attach less weight to the evidence because of the absence of challenge. Furthermore, there was other evidence against the defendant and his counsel had been afforded the opportunity of comment. These were viewed as important safeguards. It is not clear what the position might have been had the prosecu-tion's case rested in the main on the evidence of an absent witness. The prevailing view is that a conviction based solely or mainly on hearsay evidence is likely to violate Article 6(3)(d).

R *v* Thomas and Flannagan [1998] Crim LR 887

This case afforded the Court of Appeal the opportunity of directly considering whether the admis-sion of hearsay evidence in accordance with section 23 of the Criminal Justice Act 1988 was com-patible with the Convention. The hearsay evidence of an accomplice was admitted under section 23, the trial judge having concluded it was in the interests of justice to admit it under section 26. The Court of Appeal was of the view that the admission of the evidence in this case did not infringe Article 6(3)(d), given the numerous safeguards available. Those safeguards included the fact that the trial judge had carefully weighed up the argument for its admission under section 26 and that he had warned the jury about the dangers of relying too heavily on the statement. Furthermore, coun-sel for the appellants had been afforded the opportunity of attacking the credibility of the absent witness.

R *v* Radak [1999] Crim LR 223

The witness was in the United States. He refused to attend trial. The witness's evidence was of some importance to the prosecution. Had the prosecution chosen to do so, it could have taken advantage of section 3 of the Criminal Justice (International Co-operation) Act 1990. Under this Act, testimony under cross-examination could have been elicited in the United States. Given the impor-tance of the evidence and the inability to cross-examine or contradict the absent witness's evidence with other evidence, the Court of Appeal concluded that the trial judge had been wrong to admit the evidence in the exercise of his discretion. Article 6(3)(d) had been infringed.

In its analysis of the current law with regard to hearsay evidence, the Law Commission concluded that at present it is compliant with Convention rights and that if the

Commission's proposals for reform were implemented, they too would be considered compliant having regard to the number of recommended safeguards. A summary of the Law Commission's overall proposals is given below.

MISCELLANEOUS STATUTORY PROVISIONS PERMITTING THE ADMISSION OF HEARSAY EVIDENCE

Criminal Justice Act 1967, section 9

Section 9 of the Criminal Justice Act 1967 is a most important statutory provision relating to hearsay evidence and is subject to daily use in criminal proceedings. Statements admitted under this section obviate the need for the witness to attend and give oral evidence. Consequently the matters such statements deal with tend to be uncontroversial. Where one party is served with a request to admit a written statement under section 9, they need to consider what, if anything can be gained from insisting that the witness attend court for the purposes of cross-examination. The Court of Appeal's decision in *Lister* v *Quaife* [1983] 1 WLR 48 is authority for the proposition that where the evidence in question is crucial to a party's case, section 9 should not be used. The witness should be called to give oral evidence.

Section 9 makes admissible written, signed statements which contain a declaration by the maker that the statement's contents are true and that he knows he is liable to prosecution if he states anything untruthfully. The statement must be served on the opposing party who may object to its admission. Where any objection is made, which can be for any reason and does not have to be justified, the court has no power to over-rule the party objecting and the statement cannot be admitted. The courts follow a strict approach to ensure that the procedural requirements for section 9 statements are complied with. In *Paterson* v *DPP* [1990] RTR 329, the accused was convicted of driving with excess alcohol and as part of the case against him a seven-page statement by a police officer was tendered as evidence under section 9. The statutory declaration required by the Act was at page 7 and referred to '6 pages signed' by the officer. The officer had also not signed one of the pages. The court excluded the evidence, holding that the requirements of section 9 must be strictly complied with.

Criminal Procedure and Investigations Act 1996, section 68 and Schedule 2, paragraphs 1 and 2

The above provisions of the 1996 Act concern the use of written statements and depositions in committal hearings in magistrates' courts. The committal hearing is now used only in conjunction with either way offences that are to proceed to the Crown Court and is basically a screening process, designed to weed out evidentially weak cases at an early stage. All the prosecution need do to ensure that the case is committed to the Crown Court is to establish that there is a case to answer. At the committal hearing, the prosecution's evidence must be presented in forms prescribed by sections 5B–5E of the Magistrates' Courts Act 1980. It will comprise written statements signed and declared as true by the witness who makes the statement. It will also include sworn depositions (which are exceedingly rare) and any statements which the prosecutor believes will be admissible under section 23 or 24 of the Criminal Justice Act 1988.

Section 68 and Schedule 2, paragraphs 1 and 2 provide that written statements presented at committal proceedings under section 5B of the Magistrates' Courts Act 1980 and depositions admitted under section 5E may be put in evidence at the trial of the accused and, without further proof, shall be read as evidence to the trial court. The court has a discretion to order that the deposition or statement should not be read and must listen to any objections raised about the evidence being given in this form. The court can override any objections where it considers that it is 'in the interests of justice' to allow the statement to be read. The court may therefore hear the evidence of witnesses without the requirement that they shall be called for cross-examination. The provision relates to prosecution evidence only as, following the implementation of the 1996 Act, only prosecution evidence can be presented at the committal stage. In theory, a court can consider the evidence of a witness in written form in the absence of cross-examination and without the prosecution being required to prove a reason as to why the witness is not being called. In practical terms, it is important for the defence to notify the Crown Prosecution Service of its objection to the use of such statements at trial within 14 days of a committal taking place.

These provisions are generally regarded as controversial and the Law Commission has recommended their repeal.

Criminal Justice Act 1988, sections 30 and 32A

Section 30 of the Criminal Justice Act 1988, relating to the use of expert reports at criminal trials, and section 32A of the same Act, relating to the use of video-recorded testimony of child witnesses, also create statutory exceptions to the rule against hearsay. Section 32A will be replaced by the comprehensive provisions of the Youth Justice and Criminal Evidence Act 1999, which are dealt with in Chapter 18. When the relevant provisions of the 1999 Act come fully into force, they will facilitate the availability of special measures to a wide range of vulnerable witnesses. Where those special measures include the use of pre-recorded video evidence, such evidence will be admitted as a statutory exception to the rule against hearsay.

LAW COMMISSION PROPOSALS FOR REFORM

A wide-ranging review of the current operation of the hearsay rule was undertaken by the Law Commission in 1995 (Consultation Paper No 138, *Evidence in Criminal Proceedings: Hearsay and Related Topics*). A number of defects in the operation of the rule were identified. Fundamentally, it was felt that the rule operated in a haphazard and erratic way and was capable of frustrating the ends of justice by excluding relevant and cogent evidence. Numerous conceptual problems associated with the definition of hearsay had given rise to unnecessary complexity resulting in the wasting of too much court time. Some of the common law exceptions, the dying declaration in particular, were felt to be based on dubious psychological premises. Section 23 of the Criminal Justice Act 1988 was criticised for its failure to allow the admission of high quality first-hand oral hearsay. Section 24 of the 1988 Act was also criticised for its numerous anomalies occasioned by its poor drafting. Overall, the availability of judicial discretion under sections 25 and 26 was extensively criticised as leading to uncertainty as regards the admission of evidence.

The criticisms of the hearsay rule in criminal cases identified in the Law Commission's Report No 245 (1997) are endorsed in the Criminal Courts Review Report by Lord Justice Auld. He states at Chapter 11, paragraph 96:

> It is common ground that the present law is unsatisfactory and needs reform. It is complicated, unprincipled and arbitrary in the application of a number of the many exceptions. It can exclude cogent and let in weak evidence. It wastes court time in requiring it to receive oral evidence when written evidence would do so. And it confuses witnesses and prevents them from giving their own accounts in their own way.

In its review, the Law Commission canvassed several options for reform ranging from retaining the law in its present form to complete abolition of the rule and various shades of reform in between. Despite an extensive review of the operation of the hearsay, the opportunity to undertake radical reform similar to that implemented in the civil context with the Civil Evidence Act 1995 was not favoured by the Law Commission. Its final proposals recommended that the exclusionary hearsay rule should continue with specified exceptions. The Law Commission found that the most convincing reason for retaining the rule in its present exclusionary form was the lack of opportunity to cross-examine the witness and to observe his or her demeanour whilst giving evidence. This could not be ignored particularly when a person's liberty was at stake.

In an attempt to simplify the ambit of the rule, hearsay would be redefined to avoid the problems associated with its current definition. (An account of the Law Commission's redefinition of hearsay is given in Chapter 12.) Hearsay falling within the suggested definition would be admitted with the agreement of the parties.

The Law Commission proposed there should be three categories of automatically admissible hearsay and two categories of hearsay admissible at the court's discretion. The automatic categories would allow the admission of confession evidence, reliable hearsay (similar to section 24 of the Criminal Justice Act 1988) and the evidence of a witness who is unavailable (similar to section 23 of the Criminal Justice Act 1988).

Section 23 of the Criminal Justice Act 1988 would be reformed to permit first-hand hearsay evidence to be automatically admitted provided the absent witness could be identified and would have been competent to testify. An explanation for the witness's absence would have to be given which could include the fact that he was dead, ill, or outside the jurisdiction and it had not been reasonably practicable to secure attendance, or the witness could not be found despite all reasonable steps having been taken. This automatic exception category would apply to oral as well as written statements. The evidence of frightened witnesses would still be admitted in hearsay form but only with the leave of the court where it was in the interests of justice to do so having regard to a list of statutory factors.

Section 24 of the Criminal Justice Act 1988 would also be amended. Under the new provisions business documents would continue to be automatically admitted providing the document or part of it was created by a person in the course of a trade, business, profession or other occupation or as the holder of a paid or unpaid office. However, the person who supplied the information, referred to as the 'relevant person', would have had or might be reasonably supposed to have had personal knowledge of the matters dealt with. Where the information is passed from the 'relevant person' through intermediaries, the intermediaries must have received the information in the course of a business, profession or trade etc.

Statements prepared in contemplation of criminal proceedings would automatically be admitted on the ground of the unavailability of a witness, with an additional ground for admission; namely that the 'relevant person' could not reasonably be expected to have any recollection of the matters dealt with in the statement, having regard to the length of time since he supplied the information. Where there was reason to doubt the reliability of the statement, the court would have the power to prevent its admission.

The advantage of having categories of hearsay automatically admitted would mean that the current requirement for the court in addition to apply judicial discretion under sections 25 and 26 would be ameliorated. This would have the effect of simplifying matters and removing the uncertainty currently created by the exercise of judicial discretion. The discretion to exclude prosecution evidence under section 78 of the Police and Criminal Evidence Act 1984 would continue to apply. The need for discretion in relation to the admission of the hearsay evidence of a frightened witness would be retained as a safeguard against dishonest witnesses who might be tempted to give a written statement and then claim to be frightened in order to avoid being cross-examined.

One important novel and welcome feature of the Law Commission's draft Criminal Evidence Bill (published with Report No 245) would be the availability of a safety valve in the form of an inclusionary discretion, which would enable the court to admit hearsay not covered by the legislation's proposed exceptions, where it is deemed in the interests of justice to do so. Such a safety valve might have avoided the problems associated with *Sparks v R* [1964] 1 All ER 727 and *R v Blastland* [1986] AC 41 by allowing the admission of relevant evidence of the defendant's innocence which did not happen to fall within a recognised exception. The inclusionary discretion would be available to both the prosecution and defence alike.

The Law Commission expressed itself keen to ensure safeguards should be in place as regard the admission of all types of hearsay. It proposed that rules of court should be introduced requiring either side to give notice of its intention to adduce hearsay evidence and the preservation of the current rules allowing evidence to challenge the competence and credibility of the absent witness whose evidence is to be relied on. The Law Commission also proposed that there should be the power on the part of the court to refuse to admit a statement where, notwithstanding that the conditions for admissibility are made out, the statement's probative value is outweighed by the prejudicial effect of admitting it. One further important safeguard, which must be regarded as an attempt to ensure compliance with Article 6 of the European Convention on Human Rights, would give the court the power to direct an acquittal or dismiss the charge in a case where the prosecution's case is based wholly or mainly on hearsay evidence where such evidence is unconvincing.

The majority of the common law *res gestae* exceptions covered in Chapter 13 would be preserved under the new statutory scheme. The dying declaration exception would however be rendered otiose. Changes would be made to the evidential uses that can currently be made of self-serving statements admitted as an exception to the rule against narrative and statements used to refresh a witness's memory before or whilst giving evidence. An account of the changes is provided in Chapter 15.

It remains to be seen whether the government will adopt the Law Commission's proposals and convert them into legislation. Various academic commentators have expressed disappointment with the proposals contained in Report No 245 considering that they do not go far enough. It is a view shared by Lord Justice Auld who suggests that the subject should be looked at again as part of a comprehensive review of all the rules of evidence (Criminal Courts Review Report). In his view the implementation of the Law Commission's recommendations would not significantly change the landscape, nor remove the scope for dispute. In advocating a general move away from the technical rules of inadmissibility in favour of trusting the fact finder to evaluate the evidence, Lord Justice Auld favours reform of the hearsay rule in criminal cases along similar lines to that undertaken in civil cases. Such a reform would lead to the admission of all relevant hearsay evidence, subject to the best evidence rule (an obligation on each side to produce the original source of the information if available), leaving the question of how much weight to attach to it to the fact finders' judgment.

Further reading

Auld, Lord Justice (2001) *A Review of the Criminal Courts of England and Wales*, www. criminal-courts-review.org.uk.

Birch, D.J., 'The Criminal Justice Act 1988: (2) Documentary Evidence' [1989] Crim LR 15.

Law Commission Consultation Paper No 138 (1995) *Evidence in Criminal Proceedings: Hearsay and Related Topics*, HMSO.

Law Commission Report No 245 (1997) *Evidence in Criminal Proceedings: Hearsay and Related Topics*, HMSO.

Ormerod, D.C., 'The Law Commission Consultation Paper No 138 on Hearsay: (2) The Hearsay Exceptions' [1996] Crim LR 16.

Osbourne, C. 'Hearsay and the Court of Human Rights' [1993] Crim LR 255.

Smith, J.C., 'Sections 23 and 24 of the Criminal Justice Act 1988: (1) Some Problems' [1994] Crim LR 426.

Spencer, J.R., 'Law Commission Consultation Paper No 138 on Hearsay: (3) Hearsay Reform: A Bridge Not Far Enough?' [1996] Crim LR 29.

Tapper, C., 'Hearsay in Criminal Cases: An Overview of the Law Commission Report 245' [1997] Crim LR 771.

Zuckerman, A., 'Law Commission Consultation Paper No 138 on Hearsay: (1) The Futility of Hearsay' [1996] Crim LR 4.

Chapter 15

EXAMINATION-IN-CHIEF OF A WITNESS

INTRODUCTION

As we noted in Chapter 3, the English criminal trial is based on the adversarial system of fact adjudication as opposed to the inquisitorial model that is the feature in most Continental jurisdictions. The modern rules of evidence have been developed to meet the demands of the procedural context in which the English criminal trial operates. A major characteristic of the adversarial system is the primacy of the trial in deciding the defendant's guilt or innocence as opposed to the important pre-trial procedures that are a feature of the inquisitorial system of fact adjudication. As a consequence, the preferred way in which evidence is received in the adversarial system is from a witness attending court to give oral testimony 'live' before the jury or the magistrates through the rigorous process of examination-in-chief, cross-examination and re-examination. This is often referred to as the 'best evidence' rule. A second important facet of the adversarial system is the autonomy enjoyed by each party as to how it presents its case to the court. This autonomy is exercised subject to the relevant rules of evidence, procedure and the prosecutor's responsibilities as the 'minister of justice'. Whilst the judge has a residual power at common law to call witnesses up to any time before the jury retires (a power that is rarely exercised), his primary role is that of the 'neutral' umpire in deciding issues of law and evidence and ensuring that the defendant receives a 'fair' trial.

These fundamental characteristics of the adversarial system have profoundly influenced the modern rules of evidence which govern the conduct of the English criminal trial. Some of these important rules such as the law relating to the admission of hearsay evidence and the disclosure of the defendant's character and convictions are dealt with in other chapters. The purpose of this chapter is to concentrate on the procedural aspects of the English criminal trial and to examine the evidential issues that arise as both the prosecution and the defence call witnesses to give oral evidence and to present its case to the tribunal of fact in examination-in-chief.

THE ORDER OF CALLING WITNESSES

Both the prosecution and the defence advocate have a discretion in which order to call their witnesses, although it is common practice for the accused to be called first as part of the defence case. Generally, the parties must ensure that all their witnesses have been called before the close of their case (*R v Day* [1940] 1 All ER 402), although the judge has the discretion to allow a witness to testify after a party's case has closed if the need for the witness could not have been foreseen or anticipated earlier (*R v Scott* (1984) 79 Cr App R 49).

Before each witness begins to testify, two preliminary issues will be dealt with. First, either the prosecution or the defence or the court may raise an issue about the witness's competence to give evidence, and secondly, the witness will be required to swear an oath or to affirm.

THE COMPETENCE AND COMPELLABILITY OF A WITNESS

A witness is said to be competent if, as a matter of law, the court can receive his evidence. A witness is compellable if, as a matter of law, he can be made to give evidence and a failure to give evidence may result in that person being committed to prison for contempt of court.

A witness's competence to give evidence is a matter of law to be decided by the court in a *voire dire*. In most cases, where the objection to a witness's competence is taken, the issue should be raised before the witness begins to testify according to the decision in *Bartlett v Smith* (1843) 11 M & W 483. In the case of a prosecution witness, the issue may even be raised before the trial commences or before he begins to testify. Where it does not become apparent until the witness has begun his examination-in-chief that he might be incompetent, his testimony will be halted until the issue has been decided.

The law dealing with the competence of a witness to give evidence in criminal proceedings is being reformed by sections 53–57 of the Youth Justice and Criminal Evidence Act 1999, which is expected to be implemented during 2002. However, at the time of writing the statutory provisions under the Criminal Justice Act 1988 and the common law remain in force and therefore both the present law and the proposals for reform are considered in this chapter.

The general rule in criminal proceedings is that all witnesses are competent and compellable to give evidence. This presumption will be given statutory effect by section 53 of the Youth Justice and Criminal Evidence Act 1999. Section 53(1) states:

> At every stage in criminal proceedings all persons are (whatever their age) competent to give evidence.

There are several categories of witnesses against whom the presumption of competence and compellability may be rebutted either by the operation of public policy or due to the witness's relevant subjective characteristics such as their age or arrested intellectual development. Witnesses falling into the first category of exceptions include the Sovereign, diplomats and bankers, the accused and the accused's spouse. Witnesses falling into the second category include children, young people and persons of unsound mind. The position with respect to each of these witnesses is considered below.

Public policy considerations

The competence and compellability of the following categories of witnesses are determined by wider considerations of public policy such as maintaining the privileged status of diplomatic personnel, the sanctity of marriage and the accused's right to a fair trial.

The Sovereign

The Sovereign is a competent but not a compellable witness. The same principle applies to the heads of other sovereign states.

Diplomats

A member of the diplomatic service will be a competent witness, but the extent of the witness's compellability is subject to the requirements of a number of statutes including the:

- Diplomatic Privileges Act 1964;
- Consular Relations Act 1968; and
- State Immunity Act 1978.

Bankers

Where the bank is a party to the proceedings, the normal rules of competence and compellability will apply to its servants or agents. Where the bank is not a party to the proceedings, the position is dealt with by section 6 of the Bankers' Books Evidence Act 1879, which provides:

> A banker or official of a bank shall not, in any legal proceedings to which the bank is not a party, be compellable to produce any banker's book the content of which can be proved under this Act, or to appear as a witness to prove the matters, transactions and accounts therein recorded, unless by order of a judge made for special cause.

The effect of section 6 is that in any proceedings to which the bank is not a party, bank personnel cannot be compelled to produce the originals of the bank's books or records or to give evidence about any matters recorded in them unless the judge makes a special order.

The accused

The rules relating to the competence and compellability of the accused are governed by the wider public policy considerations, which ensure that the accused has the right to a fair trial both under domestic law and under Article 6 of the European Convention on Human Rights. The statutory considerations are set out below.

The accused as a competent witness for the defence

Under section 53(1) of the Youth Justice and Criminal Evidence Act 1999, the accused is a competent witness for the defence at every stage of the criminal proceedings, including at a *voire dire* or in mitigation after pleading guilty. The defendant's right to give evidence in his own defence is a fundamental principle of fairness in the criminal justice system and is strictly enforced by the courts. In *R v Cunningham* [1988] Crim LR 543, the Court of Appeal quashed the defendant's conviction where the trial judge had prevented him from testifying in his own defence because he was wearing a dress!

A number of other points about the position of the accused should be noted. First, where the accused gives evidence he must do so on oath or after affirming. Secondly, where the accused testifies he will give evidence from the witness box, unless the judge otherwise directs, for example where the accused is too old or infirm to walk to the witness box (*R v Symonds* (1924) 18 Cr App R 100). This requirement ensures that the accused's evidence will be received in the same way as the evidence of other witnesses, therefore ensuring, as far as possible, that the accused will not prejudiced in the eyes of the fact finders by having to give evidence from the dock.

Whilst the accused is a competent witness at all stages of the proceedings, he is not a compellable witness for the defence under section 1 of the Criminal Evidence Act 1898, as amended by the Police and Criminal Evidence Act 1984 (PACE). It is important to remember that the implementation of section 35 of the Criminal Justice and Public Order Act 1994 has not made the accused a compellable witness. Section 35(4) of the 1994 Act confirms that the accused is not a compellable witness to give evidence on his own behalf and shall not be guilty of contempt where he exercises his right to silence. The main effect of section 35 is to permit the magistrates or the jury in deciding whether the accused is guilty of the offence charged, to draw such inferences as appear proper from the failure of the defendant to give evidence or having been sworn, by his failure to answer questions. The full evidential implications of the accused's silence has been considered in Chapter 7.

The issue of the accused's competence is less clear-cut where he is jointly charged with others. A defendant is a competent but not a compellable witness for any co-accused charged in the same proceedings. Of course, there is nothing to prevent a co-accused from giving evidence on his own behalf which has the effect of strengthening the prosecution case against another co-accused, ie a so-called cut-throat defence. Where in giving evidence, one co-accused undermines the defence of another co-accused or strengthens the prosecution case against that co-accused, the person giving evidence may lose his shield under section 1(f)(iii) of the Criminal Evidence Act 1898 and, where the ground applies, will be cross-examined about his previous conviction(s) by the other co-accused, and, with the leave of the judge, also by the prosecution. (The law relating to the cross-examination of the accused about his character is considered in Chapter 21.)

The accused as a competent witness for the prosecution

Section 53(4) of the Youth Justice and Criminal Evidence Act 1999 provides that the accused, whether charged solely or jointly, is an incompetent witness for the prosecution. Section 53(4) and (5) states:

> (4) A person charged in criminal proceedings is not competent to give evidence in the proceedings for the prosecution (whether he is the only person, or is one of two or more persons, charged in the proceedings).
> (5) In subsection (4) the reference to a person charged in criminal proceedings does not include a person who is not, or is no longer, liable to be convicted of any offence in the proceedings (whether as a result of pleading guilty or for any other reason).

Under section 53(5), where there are two or more defendants charged in the same indictment, one co-accused may become a competent and a compellable witness for the prosecution where he has ceased to be a co-accused and therefore becomes a competent prosecution witness. A party will cease to be a co-accused where one of the following situations apply:

1   the Attorney-General discontinues the proceedings against one co-accused by entering the plea of *nolle prosequi*;
2   he has been acquitted;
3   the prosecution has successfully applied for the co-accused to be tried separately;
4   at the joint trial of the co-accused the prosecution offers no evidence against one co-accused who is then formally acquitted of the charges against him;
5   at the trial of the co-accused, one co-accused pleads guilty to one or more of the charges against him, and where the party pleading guilty has been sentenced before being called to give evidence for the prosecution.

The most common situation is where one co-accused has pleaded guilty and, preferably, has been sentenced before he gives evidence for the prosecution. Where the co-accused has not been sentenced, his evidence needs to be approached with a degree of caution. He may be simply motivated out of spite or he may be seeking to gain an advantage as regards his sentence by appearing as a Crown witness, see *R v Moran* (1985) 81 Cr App R 51. In directing the jury the judge may exercise his discretion under the decision *R v Makanjuola* [1995] 3 All ER 730 in giving a corroboration warning about an accomplice's evidence. The law relating to corroboration is dealt with in Chapter 18.

The accused's spouse

The accused's spouse as a witness for the defence

The accused's spouse is a competent witness for the defence under section 80(1)(b) of PACE. This position applies even where the spouse is jointly charged. The spouse is a compellable witness for the defence, section 80(2) of PACE, unless jointly charged under section 80(4) of PACE.

The accused's spouse as a witness for the prosecution

Before the coming into force of section 80 of PACE, one spouse was competent to testify against the other spouse only in certain limited classes of case and was never a compellable witness for the prosecution as the common law sought to protect the sanctity of marriage and recognised the difficulties that would be caused if one spouse was compelled to give evidence against another spouse.

The basis for the present statutory position, which was enacted largely on the recommendations of the Criminal Law Revision Committee in the Eleventh Report (1972), attempts to establish a compromise by recognising the importance of the sanctity of marriage whilst at the same time, acknowledging that it is in the wider public interest that in the prosecution of a small range of offences involving threats of violence or acts of violence by the accused or allegations of sexual misconduct, many cases may only be taken to court if one spouse can be compelled to testify against the other spouse.

The competence of the accused's spouse for the prosecution is determined by section 53(1) and Schedule 4, paragraph 13(2) of the Youth Justice and Criminal Evidence Act 1999, which, when in force, will repeal section 80(1) of PACE. Section 53(1) provides that the accused's spouse is competent to give evidence for the prosecution, unless, as in the case of other witnesses, she is jointly charged with the same offence or with different offences (section 53(4)). Section 53(5) indicates that she will only become a competent witness for the prosecution if she ceases to be a co-accused by, for example, pleading guilty or being acquitted.

The general rule is that the accused's spouse is not a compellable witness for the prosecution subject to the exceptions provided by section 80(2A)–(4A) of PACE set out below:

> (2A) In any proceedings the wife or husband of a person charged in the proceedings, shall, subject to subsection (4) below, be compellable—
>
> (a) to give evidence on behalf of any other person charged in the proceedings but only in respect of any specified offence with which that other person is charged; or
>
> (b) to give evidence for the prosecution but only in respect of any specified offence with which any person is charged in the proceedings.
>
> (3) In relation to the wife or husband of a person charged in any proceedings, an offence is a specified offence for the purposes of subsection (2A) above if—
>
> (a) it involves an assault on, or injury or a threat of injury to, the wife or husband or a person who was at the material time under the age of 16;
>
> (b) it is a sexual offence alleged to have been committed in respect of a person who was at the material time under that age; or
>
> (c) it consists of attempting or conspiring to commit, or of aiding, abetting, counselling, procuring or inciting the commission of, an offence falling within paragraph (a) or (b) above.
>
> (4) No person who is charged in any proceedings shall be compellable by virtue of subsection (2) or (2A) above to give evidence in the proceedings.
>
> (4A) References in this section to a person charged in any proceedings do not include a person who is not, or is no longer, liable to be convicted of any offence in the proceedings (whether as a result of pleading guilty or for any other reason).

Whilst the general rule is that spouses are competent but not compellable witnesses for the prosecution against their wife or husband, section 80(3) of PACE provides a limited range of cases where spouses are both competent and compellable prosecution witnesses. This special category of 'serious' cases includes where the spouse is charged with an offence of personal violence against his or her spouse or against a child under 16; or the spouse is charged with a sexual offence against a child under the age of 16 or where the spouse is charged with an inchoate offence that falls within the same category. Whilst the precise ambit of the offences to which section 80(3)(a) applies provides the courts with a discretion, it will most commonly cover the broad range of non-fatal offences comprising the infliction of an injury or a threat of injury to the victim. Section 80(3)(b) covers offences under the Sexual Offences Act 1956, the Indecency with Children Act 1960 and the Sexual Offences Act 1967. Consider the operation of the law relating to the competence and compellability of the spouse of the accused in the situations given in the example below.

Example

Terry has been charged with raping Rose, aged 14, and with perverting the course of justice. What are the rules relating to the competence and compellability of Diane, who is Terry's wife?

For both offences, Diane is a competent and a compellable witness for the defence.

In respect of the offence of perverting the course of justice, Diane is a competent but not a compellable witness for the prosecution as the offence does not come within one of the exceptions in section 80(3) of PACE.

In respect of the rape offence only, Diane is a competent and a compellable witness for the prosecution because the offence comes within section 80(3)(b) of PACE.

If Diane is jointly charged with Terry in connection with both offences, Diane would not be a competent witness to give evidence for the prosecution under section 80(4) of PACE unless she ceased to be a co-accused under section 80(4A) of PACE by, for example, pleading guilty.

The meaning of 'spouse'

The ambit of section 80 of PACE appears to extend to spouses in a polygamous marriage. In *R v Khan* (1987) 84 Cr App R 44, a case decided before the implementation of PACE, the Court of Appeal held that a Muslim woman who had undergone a Muslim marriage ceremony with a man who was already married under English law was a competent witness for the prosecution against the defendant and his co-defendant. There appears to be nothing that suggests that the grounds of section 80(3) would not apply to a spouse in a polygamous marriage.

Former spouses

Where the parties are no longer married at the time of the trial, former spouses are competent and compellable for the prosecution, a co-accused or the defence as if the marriage had never existed, regardless of whether or not the evidence concerns events which occurred whilst the marriage subsisted as under section 80(5) of PACE.

Comment on the failure of a spouse to give evidence

Section 80(A) of PACE prohibits the prosecution from commenting on the failure of the accused's spouse to give evidence for the defence. In *R v Naudeer* [1984] 3 All ER 1036, the Court of Appeal quashed the defendant's conviction for shoplifting because prosecution counsel told the jury that they had been deprived of material evidence as the defendant had not called his wife who had been at the scene of the offence at the time it had been allegedly committed. The prohibition on the prosecution commenting on the accused's failure to call his spouse does not extend to the judge. In appropriate circumstances, as in relation to any witness, the judge may comment on the failure of the spouse to give evidence.

The competence of a witness as determined by his personal characteristics

The presumption in favour of all witnesses being competent to give evidence under section 53(1) of the Youth Justice and Criminal Evidence Act 1999 may be rebutted by the witness's relevant personal characteristics which may bring him within the operation of section 53(3). Section 53(3) provides that:

> (3) A person is not competent to give evidence in criminal proceedings if it appears to the court that he is not a person who is able to—
> > (a) understand the questions put to him as a witness, and
> > (b) give answers to them which can be understood.

The categories of witnesses whose competence has traditionally been questioned on the basis of their personal characteristics are children, young people and people suffering from a mental incapacity. Depending on the facts of the particular case, it may be appropriate for the judge to give a warning to the jury about the dangers of convicting the accused on the unsupported evidence of these witnesses in a corroboration warning. The law relating to corroboration is considered in Chapter 18.

Children

Historically, a witness who testified to a criminal court was required to give evidence on oath by swearing on the Bible as decided in *R v Brasier* (1779) 1 Leach 199. A person was considered to be competent where he understood the significance of taking the oath, and the importance of not lying to the court. In a more religious and God-fearing age this requirement influenced the court's view of the suitability of children and young people to give evidence. The consequence was that for many years the law treated the evidence of children and young people with scepticism believing that a child witness was not generally capable of being aware of the moral significance of testifying in court. A typical view was propounded by Lord Justice Goddard in *R v Wallwork* (1958) 42 Cr App R 153 who stated that children as young as five or six should not be called as witnesses and indicated that the minimum age of competency should be eight. This view went unchallenged in judicial circles for 30 years and even found support in the Court of Appeal as late as 1987 in *R v Wright and Ormerod* (1990) 90 Cr App R 91. A consequence of the law taking a restrictive view of the value of child testimony resulted in the failure of many criminal prosecutions for offences of sexual or physical abuse of children, as often the child was the only witness the prosecution could call in order to prove its case. This was the position in the infamous case of *Wallwork* above, where a five-year-old girl was regarded as to being too young to give evidence against her father on a charge of incest.

In addition to the limitations placed on the proper administration of justice in securing convictions for serious offences against children, the traditionally restrictive and ill-informed view of the value of children's evidence failed to take account of changing social attitudes and scientific opinion. It had come to be generally recognised that even young children were capable of giving reliable evidence and were not particularly prone to giving untrue or unreliable evidence.

The first tentative step towards a more inclusive approach to children's evidence was provided by Parliament in passing section 38 of the Children and Young Persons Act 1933, which permitted a child to give unsworn evidence in criminal proceedings provided two conditions were satisfied. First, the court had to be satisfied that the child understood the duty of speaking the truth, and secondly, that the child was possessed of sufficient intelligence to justify the reception of the truth. This became the standard test for determining a child's competence to give unsworn evidence.

The courts also made a significant contribution to relaxing the rules about children giving sworn evidence. In *R v Hayes* (1977) 64 Cr App R 194, the Court of Appeal recognised that the secular nature of life in the late twentieth century made the devoutly religious test of competence of an earlier time inappropriate to modern social conditions. In *Hayes*, two boys, aged 11 and 13 were questioned by the trial judge about their knowledge of God and the religious instruction they received at school. Both boys claimed to be unaware of the existence of God and to have received no religious instruction at school. Whilst upholding the trial judge's decision to allow the boys to give sworn evidence, the Court of Appeal adopted a secular test to decide the competence of a witness to give sworn evidence. According to Lord Bridge, a child would be competent to give evidence where he had a sufficient appreciation of the solemnity of the occasion and understood the duty of speaking the truth. If the child was aware of these points, it was not necessary for him to also be aware of the religious implications of lying on oath. This became known as the 'Hayes' test and until the reforms under the Youth Justice and Criminal Evidence Act 1999 are introduced, remains the test to decide whether the witness is capable of giving sworn evidence.

The climate for change was also shared by the Advisory Group on Video Evidence (the Pigot Report) (1989), which concluded the existing unsatisfactory state of the law was based on the archaic belief about the inability of children to give reliable evidence. The Pigot Report recommended that the general requirement to formally prove a child's competence to give evidence should be abolished and that young people aged between 14 and 17 years should be allowed to give sworn evidence and that children aged below 14 years should always give unsworn evidence. The recommendation formed the basis of the reforms introduced by the Criminal Justice Act 1991, which amended the Criminal Justice Act 1988 to provide the test of competence of children and young people to give evidence in criminal proceedings.

The competence of children and young people under the Criminal Justice Act 1988

In following the recommendations of the Pigot Report, the Criminal Justice Act 1988, as amended by the 1991 Act, drew a distinction between the rules relating to a witness who was aged below 14 years and a witness who was 14 years and above. A witness aged under 14 years was classified as a child and could only give unsworn evidence as provided by section 33A of the Criminal Justice Act 1988 where the child was capable of giving 'intelligible testimony'. In R v D (1995) *The Times*, 15 November, the Court of Appeal provided guidance as to how the courts approached the meaning of 'intelligible testimony'. It appeared to include such factors as whether the child understood the questions put to him; his ability to communicate and to give a coherent and comprehensive account of his evidence; and his maturity to distinguish between fact and fantasy. Generally, the courts would presume that the child would be competent to give evidence within the limitations allowed by law. Where a child was to be called, the Court of Appeal in R v Hampshire [1995] 3 WLR 260 stated *obiter* that the judge was not required to investigate the competency of the child and could regard the child as competent unless one of the parties or the court raised the issue.

The case of R v *Hampshire* involved an alleged indecent assault on a five-year-old girl. The Court of Appeal held that the inquiry about the child's competence need only be made where it appeared to the prosecution, the defence or the judge that the child was incapable of giving evidence because of his age or where he had difficulty in expressing himself. Where the competency of the child witness called by the prosecution was questioned, the prosecution had the legal burden of proving the child's competence beyond reasonable doubt as in R v *Yacoob* (1981) 72 Cr App R 313. Whilst there was no direct authority on the issue, where a child's competence called by the defence was questioned, the defence had the legal burden of proving the witness's competence to the civil standard of proof on the balance of probabilities. Where the child was regarded as competent to give evidence he was also compellable.

If the witness was aged between 14 and 17 years, the young person was presumed to be competent to give sworn evidence, ie evidence taken on oath or affirmation. Where the young person's competence was questioned, the test in *R v Hayes* above applied. The witness would be asked whether he understood the nature of the oath, the importance of telling the truth and had sufficient understanding of the solemnity of the occasion in giving sworn evidence. Where the young person failed the Hayes test he was considered to be incompetent to give evidence. It was not possible for him to give unsworn evidence, which proved a major loophole under the 'old' law. This unsatisfactory position has been remedied under new provisions introduced by section 56 of the Youth Justice and Criminal Evidence Act 1999, which provide that where a witness who is aged 14 years or over fails the test to give sworn evidence, his oral testimony may now be received unsworn.

The reforming provisions inserted into the Criminal Justice Act 1988 by the Criminal Justice Act 1991 and their interpretation and application by the courts resulted in the adoption of a more realistic attitude to the reception of the evidence of children and young people. However, in order to give full force to the developing provisions, it was considered necessary for further legislation to be passed. The necessary statutory authority is provided by the Youth Justice and Criminal Evidence Act 1999, which introduces a number of new provisions to deal with the competence of all witnesses in criminal proceedings including children and young people, which are considered below.

Persons suffering from a mental incapacity

Traditionally, the courts have used the phrase a 'person of unsound mind' to describe a person who is suffering from a mental handicap, incapacity or a mental illness. Prior to the enactment of the Youth Justice and Criminal Evidence Act 1999 (see below), the general rule was that where a witness was not capable of understanding the nature of the oath and giving coherent evidence, he would be incompetent to give evidence. Where either the prosecution or the defence or the court raised a doubt about the mental capacity of a witness to give evidence, it was for the judge to decide the issue in the absence of the jury, after having heard expert evidence, where appropriate. The test to be applied was laid down in *R v Hill* (1851) 2 Den 254. In this case a witness called to give evidence was an inmate in a mental hospital who claimed that he had been the subject of numerous spirits who talked to him. Medical evidence was called to prove that he was capable of testifying about any incident to which he had been an eyewitness. The judge ruled that the witness was competent to give evidence.

Where a witness was competent it would be up to the jury or the magistrates to decide what degree of weight should be attached to the testimony. In *R v Bellamy* (1985) 82 Cr App R 223, the witness was a 33-year-old woman with a mental age of ten. The Court of Appeal decided that the woman's competence should be decided on the application of the Hayes test, namely did the witness have a sufficient appreciation of the seriousness of the occasion and a realisation that taking the oath involved something more than the duty to tell the truth in everyday life.

The present position is that in common with all other witnesses, a person of unsound mind is presumed to be competent to give evidence in criminal proceedings under section 53(1) of the Youth Justice and Criminal Evidence Act 1999. Also, where the presumption applies, the witness may get the benefit of a 'special measures' direction that will assist the quality of his testimony. The law relating to the making of a 'special measures' direction under section 19 of the 1999 Act is considered in Chapter 18 below.

COMPETENCE OF A WITNESS UNDER THE YOUTH JUSTICE AND CRIMINAL EVIDENCE ACT 1999

When in force, the Youth Justice and Criminal Evidence Act 1999 will reform the law relating to the competence of all witnesses in criminal proceedings. The Act's provisions are based on the recommendations contained in *Speaking Up for Justice*, which is the report of the Interdepartmental Working Group on the Treatment of Vulnerable and Intimidated Witnesses in the Criminal Justice System (June 1998). The proposals contained in *Speaking Up for Justice* confirmed the general view that it is in the public interest that, whenever possible, the evidence of all witnesses, regardless of age or physical or mental incapacity, should be heard. The 1999 Act introduces a range of measures that gives the court much greater discretion to allow witnesses to give evidence in criminal cases. The main provisions are as follows.

Presumption that all witnesses are competent to give evidence (section 53)

Section 53(1) provides:

> (1) At every stage in criminal proceedings all persons are (whatever their age) competent to give evidence.

Section 53(1) creates the presumption that all witnesses shall be competent to give evidence. This may be regarded as the codification of the Court of Appeal's decision in *R v Hampshire* [1995] 3 WLR 260, discussed above. The presumption of competence may be rebutted if, under section 53(3):

> it appears to the court that he is not a person who is able to—
> > (a) understand questions put to him as a witness, and
> > (b) give answers to them which can be understood.

Under section 53(3) a witness shall be treated as being unable to answer questions put to him or to give answers which can be understood, where for example the witness is unable to distinguish between truth and fiction or fact and fantasy.

Procedure for deciding the witness's competence (section 54)

Section 54(1) provides that where the issue of the witness's competence is raised, it shall be determined by the court in accordance with the conditions laid down in the section. Under section 54(2) the legal burden of proving the witness's competence lies with the party calling the witness on the 'balance of probabilities'. The court will take into account whether the witness will be the subject of any 'special measures' direction under section

19 of the Act. The availability of the court's power to grant a special measures direction represents a positive step forward in assisting vulnerable witnesses to give evidence and, in certain situations, will enable a non-competent witness to be regarded as competent.

Section 54(4) requires that the determination of the witness's competence will be made in the absence of the jury. In deciding the issue the court may have the benefit of expert evidence under section 54(5). Any questions put to the witness whose competence is being determined by the court shall be in the presence of the parties (section 54(6)). It is likely that where the witness is a child, the practice and procedure developed under the 'old' law in R v *Hampshire* above will continue to apply in that it should be the judge's perception of the child's understanding of the ordinary course of proceedings that will form the basis of his decision.

Test for deciding whether the witness may give sworn evidence (section 55)

Section 55(1)–(4) of the 1999 Act states:

(1) Any question whether a witness in criminal proceedings may be sworn for the purpose of giving evidence on oath, whether raised—
(a) by a party to the proceedings, or
(b) by the court of its own motion,
shall be determined by the court in accordance with this section.
(2) The witness may not be sworn for that purpose unless—
(a) he has attained the age of 14, and
(b) he has sufficient appreciation of the solemnity of the occasion and of the particular responsibility to tell the truth which is involved in taking an oath.
(3) The witness shall, if he is able to give intelligible testimony, be presumed to have a sufficient appreciation of those matters if no evidence tending to show the contrary is adduced (by any party).
(4) If any such evidence is adduced, it is for the party seeking to have the witness sworn to satisfy the court that, on a balance of probabilities, the witness has attained the age of 14 and has a sufficient appreciation of the matters mentioned in subsection (2)(b).

Under section 55, a competent witness may give sworn evidence provided the two-stage test in section 55(2) is met. First, the witness should be aged 14 years or over (this requirement preserves the former position under the Criminal Justice Act 1988) and, secondly, the witness must have sufficient appreciation of the solemnity of the occasion and the responsibility of telling the truth as in the Hayes test.

There is a presumption in section 55(3) that a witness who is aged 14 years or more is competent to give sworn evidence where he satisfies the test of 'intelligible testimony' within the meaning of section 53(3) in that he is able to understand the questions put to him as a witness and to give answers to them which can be understood.

Test for deciding whether the witness may give unsworn evidence (section 56)

Section 56 introduces a number of important changes to the law of witness testimony. It provides:

(1) Subsections 2 and (3) apply to a person (of any age) who—
    (a) is competent to give evidence in criminal proceedings, but
    (b) (by virtue of section 55(2)) is not permitted to be sworn for the purpose of giv-
       ing evidence on oath in such proceedings.
(2) The evidence in criminal proceedings of a person to whom this subsection applies shall be given unsworn.
(3) A deposition of unsworn evidence given by a person to whom this subsection applies may be taken for the purposes of criminal proceedings as if that evidence had been given on oath.
(4) A court in criminal proceedings shall accordingly receive in evidence any evidence given unsworn in pursuance of subsection (2) or (3).

An important change to the previous law is provided by section 56(1) and (2), to the effect that where a witness of any age is incompetent to give sworn evidence, the witness may still give unsworn evidence. As well as imposing a mandatory requirement that a child under the age of 14 shall give only unsworn evidence, section 56 permits a person over 14 to give unsworn evidence where he is competent to testify notwithstanding that evidence is adduced that he does not have a sufficient appreciation of the solemnity of the occasion and of the particular responsibility to tell the truth under oath and the party seeking to have him give sworn evidence has failed to persuade the court that on the balance of probabilities, that he has such an appreciation. Consider the circumstances in the example below, which illustrate the law relating to the competence of a witness to give evidence in criminal proceedings.

Example

Alex is eight years old. She understands questions and can give coherent answers but she has no understanding of God or the solemnity of the occasion. Alex is competent to give unsworn evidence.

Bernie is aged 36. He is mentally retarded. He is unable to give intelligible answers and he does not appreciate the solemnity of the occasion or the importance of telling the truth. Therefore he is not competent to give sworn or unsworn evidence. The availability of a special measures direction may assist him to give unsworn evidence.

Carol is 12 years old. She is very distressed about giving evidence. She understands the importance of telling the truth and can give intelligible answers with the benefit of a special measures direction. She will be competent to give unsworn evidence.

David is 14 years old. He has speech problems and is mentally retarded. He does not understand the importance of telling the truth but with the benefit of a special measures direction, he is able to understand questions put to him and will be able to give answers that can be understood. David will be competent to give unsworn evidence.

Erin is 15 years old. She is bright and intelligent. She does not believe in God but does understand the concept of perjury. Erin is competent to give sworn evidence.

TAKING THE OATH OR AFFIRMING

The common law requires that a witness may not give oral evidence in court unless he has been sworn to speak the truth. Where the witness is a religious observer, section 1 of the Oaths Act 1978 allows the oath to be taken on the New Testament or, in the case of a Jewish witness on the Old Testament. The witness will be required to state: 'I swear by Almighty God...' and then the appropriate form of words as prescribed by law. Where the witness follows another faith an appropriate form of oath will be taken. For example, a Muslim witness is sworn on the Koran 'I swear by Allah ...', whilst a Sikh will swear on the Sunder Gutka 'I swear by Waheguru ...'. If the witness refuses to take an oath or the oath is contrary to his religion, section 5 of the Oaths Act 1978 allows the witness to make a solemn affirmation in the following form: 'I [*name*] do solemnly, sincerely and truly declare and affirm ...'

EXAMINATION-IN-CHIEF

Where the preliminary formalities have been dealt with, the advocate will call his first witness and the examination-in-chief will begin.

Leading questions

The general rule is that questions put in examination-in-chief should be 'relevant' either to a fact in issue in the case or directed to a collateral issue. In raising these issues a party may not ask its witness leading questions. A leading question either suggests to the witness the desired answer or assumes the existence of disputed facts that have not yet been satisfactorily proven. Consider the following example.

Example

The advocate puts to the witness the following question: 'The car you saw the defendant drive away from the crime was red, wasn't it?'

This question clearly offends against the rule prohibiting leading questions as it suggests to the witness the answer the advocate is expecting and wants. It is also a good illustration of why leading questions are not allowed during evidence-in-chief as such questions either prompt the witness into giving the answer the advocate requires or they may mislead the jury into thinking that the disputed fact has been established.

Where the rule against asking leading questions is broken the judge or the magistrates' adviser will suggest to the advocate that the question should be put differently. Whilst an answer given to a leading question is not inadmissible, the normal practice is for the court to give such an answer little weight as in *R v Wilson* (1913) 9 Cr App R 124.

As an exception to the general rule, leading questions are permitted at the start of a witness's testimony with regard to purely formal or introductory matters, or where the evidence is not in dispute between the parties such as confirmation of the witness's name, address and occupation. The prohibition on leading questions applies only to examination-in-chief and re-examination. In cross-examination, leading questions are permissible and, indeed, essential since the purpose of cross-examination is, in part, to try to persuade the witness to agree to the truth of an alternative version of the facts.

Calling own witnesses

On the day of the trial, it is the responsibility of a member of the prosecution and the defence team to ensure that all their witnesses are present in the precincts of the court. A witness will remain out of court until he is called to give evidence because if the witness was present in court his evidence may be influenced by the testimony of previous witnesses. There are two exceptions to this general rule. First, an expert witness will usually be permitted to sit in court before giving evidence and, secondly, the police officer in charge of the case will also be present providing the defence gives its consent. The concession to the investigating officer's presence in court is out of respect to his position as, in effect, being the prosecution's client. The officer will therefore be available to advise the prosecutor on any issues that will inevitably arise during the course of the trial. If the officer is not in court, the trial will have to be halted whilst the officer's instructions are obtained – such delays result in a lot of wasted time and additional expense and therefore the investigating officer's presence in court is a necessity.

The use of memory refreshing documents during examination-in-chief

The defendant's trial may be a number of months after the incident giving rise to the prosecution and therefore to assist witnesses to give reliable evidence, they are permitted to refresh their memories out of court before examination-in-chief and whilst they are testifying.

Out of court before giving evidence

Whilst waiting out of court to give evidence, it is common for a witness to read over his statement to remind himself of the matters about which he is going to testify in court. The prosecution witnesses are normally entitled to look over a copy of the statement that was taken from them by one of the investigating police officers. The defence witnesses will refresh their memories from the proof of evidence taken by a member of the defence team. It is not necessary for the statement to have been made contemporaneously or verified by the witness when the events were still fresh in the witness's memory.

The practice of allowing a witness to refresh his memory before giving evidence was approved by the Court of Appeal in *R v Richardson* [1971] 2 QB 484.

In *Richardson*, the accused was convicted of burglary offences committed 18 months earlier. Before the trial, four prosecution witnesses were shown their police statements, which they had made some weeks after the alleged offences. On appeal, the appellant argued that the evidence of the witnesses was, in the circumstances, inadmissible. The appeal was dismissed on the ground that there could be no general rule that a witness was not able to see before the trial the statement he had made at some period reasonably close to the events which are the subject of the trial. Lord Justice Sachs in giving the judgment of the Court of Appeal noted that whilst a rule preventing a witness from refreshing his memory out of court before testifying would be unenforceable, it was also in the interests of justice to allow a witness to refresh his memory, otherwise his evidence would be a test of memory rather than an exercise in seeking the truth.

Lord Justice Sachs noted with approval the observations of the Hong Kong Supreme Court in *Lau Pak Ngam v R* [1966] Crim LR 443. In *Lau*, the day before the trial the police officer in charge of the case read over to the principal witnesses in the presence of all of them the statements that had been taken by the police. The Supreme Court of Hong Kong, in dismissing the defendant's appeal against conviction, commented that the statements should not be read in the presence of all of the witnesses but that each witness should be given a copy of his statement. The Supreme Court commented that:

...testimony in the witness box becomes more a test of memory than truthfulness if witnesses were deprived of the opportunity of checking their recollection beforehand by reference to statements or notes made at the time closer to the events in question.

Whilst a witness may refer to a memory refreshing document when waiting to give evidence, a practice that was the subject of adverse comment in *Lau* is where several witnesses 'pool' their resources and compare with another witness what each had said. Generally, therefore, discussions between witnesses about their evidence should not take place – especially just before going into the witness box to testify. In the case of *R v Skinner* (1994) 99 Cr App R 212, the Court of Appeal held that it is also bad practice for one witness to read another witness's statement or to have the other witness's statement read in his presence.

In court whilst giving evidence

A witness may also refresh his memory whilst giving evidence by referring to a written record of the events about which he is testifying. Examples of such memory refreshing documents include a police officer's notebook or where, at the scene of a crime, a witness notes the registration number of a car on a piece of paper. The witness may refer to the paper to remind him of the registration number that he wrote down at the time of the incident. Before a witness can refer to his written statement a number of conditions have to be satisfied.

First, the memory refreshing document must have been written by the witness or must have been verified by him. Where the statement has been written by someone other than the witness, the contents must either have been read by the witness or read to him whilst the events were fresh in the witness's memory and he knows the statement's contents to be correct.

R v Kelsey (1982) 74 Cr App R 213

A witness saw a car at the scene of a burglary. Twenty minutes later he recounted the car's registration number to a police officer, who wrote it down. The witness did not read what the officer had written but the officer read the registration number back to the witness. The Court of Appeal held that the witness was entitled to refresh his memory from the note made by the police officer.

The decision in *R v Kelsey* may be contrasted with the decision of *R v Eleftheriou* below.

R v Eleftheriou [1993] Crim LR 947

The appellants were charged with being knowingly concerned with the fraudulent evasion of VAT. They ran a fish and chip restaurant and take-away shop and it was alleged that they failed to disclose all of their takings in their VAT returns. Customs officers concealed opposite the restaurant counted out their observations in pairs, one officer calling out what he saw, the other officer writing it down. Neither observed what the other officer saw or wrote. There was no contemporaneous cross-checking of the other's records and no independent verification. At the trial, the judge allowed the officers to refresh their memories from the records, on the basis that, in the opinion of the judge, the documents had been verified by each officer looking up from time to time and seeing that his colleague was making entries in the record. A submission of no case to answer was made by the defence which was rejected by the trial judge. The defendants were convicted and appealed. In allowing the appeal, the Court of Appeal decided that no verification of the document had taken place since the writer had not read back to the observer what he had written and because of the pace at which the entries had been made, no verification had occurred. The observer could not give evidence on behalf of the other observer or vice versa.

Secondly, there is a general requirement that the document from which the witness refreshes his memory must have been made at substantially the same time as the occurrence of the events about which the witness is testifying – the issue of contemporaneity. The issue is decided on the particular facts and circumstances of each case. Normally, a gap of several hours between the events taking place and the making of the written record will not be fatal. This often occurs where a police officer writes up his notebook after coming off a shift. A common interpretation of the rule was applied in R v Simmonds (1967) 51 Cr App Rep 316 where notes made by customs officers at the first convenient opportunity after returning to their office from conducting lengthy interviews were held to comply with the requirement of contemporaneity. In Anderson v Whalley (1852) 3 Car & Ker 54, it was held that entries in a ship's logbook made by the mate and verified by the captain one week later could be used to refresh the captain's memory.

The leading authorities in modern law have developed the use of memory refreshing documents even further by placing less emphasis on the requirement of contemporaneity.

In R v Da Silva [1990] 1 WLR 31, the Court of Appeal held that it was a matter of the trial judge's discretion to be exercised in the interests of justice to permit a witness who had begun to give evidence to refresh his memory from a statement made near to the time of the events. This may be allowed even if the time lapse between the events and the writing of the statement did not fall within the natural meaning of 'contemporaneous' providing the judge was satisfied of the following factors:

- the witness indicates that he cannot now recall the details of events because of the lapse of time since they took place;
- the witness made a statement much nearer the time of the events and that the contents of the statement represented his recollection at the time he made it;
- the witness had not read the statement before he continued to give evidence; and
- the witness wished to read the statement before he continued giving evidence. It did not matter whether the witness withdrew from the witness box to read the statement or whether he read it in the witness box.

The key difference between a statement used under the 'Da Silva principle' and a document that had been compiled when the events were fresh in the witness's mind is that under Da Silva the memory refreshing document should be taken away from the witness when he resumes his evidence but where the document satisfies the 'contemporaneous test' the witness can refresh his memory from the statement whilst he was giving evidence.

The law relating to memory refreshing documents was further developed by the Divisional Court in R v South Ribble Stipendiary Magistrate, ex parte Cochrane [1996] 2 Cr App R 544. Under the ruling in Da Silva it appears acceptable to allow the witness to refer to his statement whilst giving evidence even though the statement was not compiled contemporaneously. In giving the judgment of the court in *Ex parte Cochrane*, Lord Justice Henry stated that the use of memory refreshing documents during the trial should be decided by the overriding principles of fairness and justice. His Lordship identified two situations where the interests of justice test would be satisfied to allow a witness to refresh his memory from a non-contemporaneous document. The first situation related to the position of an elderly witness who might be nervous and confused when giving evidence, whilst the second situation covered the position of a witness in a fraud trial whose statement might run to many hundreds of pages.

The Criminal Courts Review Report recommends extending the principles developed in *R v Da Silva*. These and other proposals for reforming the law and practice of witness testimony are considered below.

Admissibility and value of a witness's previous consistent statement

One of the characteristics of the adversarial trial is the reliance placed on the oral testimony of a witness giving evidence 'live' in court. Therefore, as a general rule, a party cannot during examination-in-chief or during cross-examination adduce evidence of his witness's prior statement to support his case at trial. The rule also prohibits the witness from referring to his written statement to prove the consistency of his evidence. This principle is known as the rule against previous consistent statements and may also be referred to as 'the rule against narrative' or 'the rule against self-serving statements'. The rationale for this general proposition is clearly shown in the case considered below.

R v Roberts [1942] 1 All ER 187

The accused shot his girlfriend whilst attempting to persuade her to return to him. Several hours after his arrest, he told his father who visited him in the police cell that his defence to the charge would be accident. At the trial he wished to call his father to give evidence of this conversation. It was held that the father could not give evidence of this conversation because it added nothing to the testimony that was being given in the court. The reasons for excluding such evidence are that (1) it can be easily fabricated and (2) it has little or no evidential value. How could it assist the jury to know that some hours after his arrest the defendant had already thought of a line of defence? Anyone who had been arrested would clearly be applying his mind to what lines of defence were open to him and therefore it was of no evidential value.

There are a number of important exceptions to this general rule where an advocate may put to the court evidence of his client's previous statement in examination-in-chief.

A 'recent' complaint by the victim of a sexual offence

The male or female victim of a sexual offence may be allowed to give evidence that he or she made a complaint to another person 'spontaneously' and as soon as 'reasonably practicable' after the incident. Where the statement is admissible, the person to whom the complaint was made may also give evidence about what the victim had told him. A classic illustration of where a witness's previous consistent statement was admitted under the 'recent' complaint rule is provided by the case of *R v Osborne* [1905] 1 KB

551. The defendant, who was the owner of a fried-fish shop, was alleged to have indecently assaulted a girl under 13. The assault had occurred whilst the complainant had been left alone with the defendant whilst her two friends had gone to fetch some chip fat, which they intended to sell to the defendant. On her way home the complainant met her two friends who were returning to the shop. The complainant was asked by her friends why was she going home. The complainant replied that she did not like the defendant as he had 'unbuttoned her drawers'. At the trial the defence counsel submitted that the complainant's statement was inadmissible as hearsay. The prosecution stated that the statement was admissible to prove the consistency of the complainant's conduct. The court ruled that the evidence of the complainant could be put before the jury accompanied by a careful direction that the statement is not evidence of the truth of the allegations and can only be regarded as supporting the witness's credibility.

Generally, the requirements that the statement should be made by the victim spontaneously and as soon as reasonably practicable are a matter of fact and degree in each case taking into account the victim's age and emotional distress and whether there was anybody else to whom the victim could have spoken. In *R v Rush* (1860) 60 JP 777 a complaint that was made a day following the attack was held not to be sufficiently recent, whilst in *R v Hedges* (1910) 3 Cr App R 262 the complaint, which was made one week after the attack, was admitted.

A good example of the modern judicial approach is provided by *R v Valentine* [1996] 2 Cr App R 213. The victim alleged that the defendant had raped her as he walked her home at night, using a knife to threaten her. After the rape she returned home where her parents and brother were asleep. The next morning she told her brother that she had been attacked with a knife but she added that she did not want to tell her parents, and then she went to work. It was only that evening that she told a friend about the rape. The trial judge assessed the victim as a tense person who would bottle up the matter until she could find a friend to trust and allowed the complaint to be put in evidence. The defendant was convicted and appealed. In dismissing the appeal and finding that the statement had been properly admitted, Lord Justice Roche stated:

> We now have a greater understanding that those who are the victims of sexual offences ... often need to bring themselves to tell what has been done to them; that some victims will find it impossible to complain to anyone other than a parent or a member of their family, whereas others will find it impossible to tell their family.

Where the court accepts the victim's statement to be spontaneous and made as soon as reasonably practicable, the prosecution may call the person to whom the complaint was made to give evidence. It is important to note that the rule only applies where the victim is considered to be competent to give evidence. In *R v Wallwork* (1958) 42 Cr App R 153, where the defendant was charged with several counts of incest against his five-year-old daughter, the court held that as the victim was incompetent to give evidence due to her age, the prosecution could not call another witness to whom the child had complained about her father's behaviour. As a result the defendant's conviction was overturned on appeal.

Two points need to be made about the evidential effect of the rule's operation. First, the evidence of the complaint is only admissible to show the witness's consistency. It cannot prove the truth of the complainant's testimony, because it would offend the hearsay rule, as it is a statement made on a prior occasion other than whilst giving evidence.

Secondly, it is important to note that the evidence of the recent complaint does not amount to corroboration of the prosecution case against the defendant as the evidence is not independent of the witness (ie the victim) to be corroborated as required by the conditions laid down for corroborative evidence in *R v Baskerville* [1916] 2 KB 658. For example, in *R v Islam* [1999] 1 Cr App R 22, the defendant was convicted of three counts of indecent assault. At the trial, the Crown presented evidence of complaints made by two of the victims to the police or friends or relatives shortly after each incident had occurred in order to show both the basis of the complaint and the distress exhibited by the complainant. The defendant appealed against his conviction on the ground that the jury had not been properly directed that the evidence of the complaints could not amount to corroborative evidence as it did not come from a source that was independent of the victim. The jury should be directed that the probative effect of the complaint is to assist them to decide whether or not the complainant is telling the truth.

Statements forming part of the res gestae

The law relating to the admission of statements under the principle of *res gestae* has been dealt with in detail in Chapter 13, as an exception to the hearsay rule at common law. However, the *res gestae* principle also applies as an exception to the rule against admitting a witness's previous consistent statement. Where a witness's previous statement is so closely associated in the time or place or in the circumstances of an event, it may be admitted as evidence of the witness's consistency. As an illustration of the rule consider *R v Fowkes* (1856) *The Times*, 8 March. The accused, who was commonly referred to as 'the Butcher', was charged with murder. The victim's son gave evidence that he and a police officer were in a room with his father when a face appeared at the window, through which the fatal shot was then fired. The son stated that the face he saw at the window belonged to the accused and that he had shouted, 'There's the Butcher'. The police officer was allowed to give evidence in support of the son's evidence.

Evidence of previous identification

Whilst evidence of the witness's previous identification of the defendant offends the general rule against the admission of a previous consistent statement, it is considered to be in the interests of justice to admit such evidence because in many cases as there may be a considerable time lapse between the offence and the trial the cogency of the witness's identification may be diminished by the time of the trial. In the House of Lords' case of *R v Christie* (1914) 10 Cr App R 141, a small boy, who was the victim of an indecent assault, gave unsworn evidence of the assault and identified the accused but was not questioned about his previous identification. The boy's mother and a police constable were allowed to testify that, shortly after the alleged offence, they saw the boy approaching the accused saying 'That is the man'. The evidential effect of the statement was explained by Viscount Haldane as showing that the boy was able to identify the accused at the time and to exclude the idea that the identification of the accused in the dock was an afterthought or a mistake. The rule admitting evidence of earlier identification was also applied in the case of *R v Fowkes* above.

Statements made on accusation

Where a defendant is accused of a crime, his reaction to the accusation may be 'relevant' at trial to show the consistency of his evidence. The evidential effect of the accused's response depends on the nature of his response to the accusation.

An exculpatory statement

Where the accused makes a totally exculpatory response, ie he denies his involvement in the crime, his response is admissible to show his reaction – but because of its self-serving nature, it is not admissible to prove the truth of its contents. A good example of the operation of this rule is provided by *R v Storey* (1968) 52 Cr App R 334. The police found a large quantity of cannabis in the accused's flat. She explained that it belonged to a man who had brought it to her flat against her will. The Court of Appeal approved of the admission of the statement in evidence because, according to Lord Justice Widgery, of 'its vital relevance as showing the reaction of the accused when first taxed with incriminating facts'.

An exculpatory statement made on accusation is only admissible to show the consistency of the accused's evidence where he elects to give evidence. Where the accused exercises his right to silence, the judge does not appear to be under a duty to remind the jury of a statement made voluntarily to the police proclaiming his innocence.

In accordance with the decision in *R v Pearce* (1979) 69 Cr App R 365, it is not necessarily fatal to the admissibility of an exculpatory statement where there has been a lapse of time between the allegations being put by the police and the accused making a statement denying wrongdoing. In *R v Pearce*, on 6 March, the appellant, the manager of a betting shop, was faced by a number of incriminating facts relating to the handling of stolen goods put to him by his employer's security officer. The appellant denied knowing anything of the allegations. Two days later he was arrested by the police and made a voluntary statement in the presence of his solicitor. In an interview with the police, the appellant gave certain answers that were relied on by the prosecution. The next day he made a voluntary self-serving statement. The trial judge excluded evidence of all the statements made to the police, except those parts of the interview on which the prosecution relied, on the ground that the statements were self-serving and therefore inadmissible. On appeal, it was submitted that the statements had been properly excluded on the basis that they had not been made when the incriminating accusations had been put to the appellant.

In rejecting this argument and quashing the appellant's conviction, the Court of Appeal summarised the principles:

> (1) A statement which contains an admission is always admissible as a declaration against interest and is evidence of the facts admitted. With this exception, a statement made by an accused person is never evidence of the facts in the statement.

(2)(a) A statement that is not an admission is admissible to show the attitude of the accused at the time when he made it. This however, is not to be limited to a statement made on a first encounter with the police. The reference in *Storey* to the reaction of the accused 'when first taxed' should not be read as circumscribing the limits of admissibility. The longer the time that has elapsed after the first encounter, the less the weight which will be attached to the denial. The judge is able to direct the jury about the value of such statements.

In deciding whether to admit the exculpatory statement where a long time has elapsed between the accused facing the allegations and making the statement, the decision in *R v Pearce* confirms that the judge must exercise his discretion on the particular facts of the case. It is suggested, however, that even where a statement is admitted, the longer the time that elapses, the less weight the court will give to the evidence.

There are several limitations to the rule that prevent the accused's exculpatory statement being admitted at trial. First, the rule will not apply where evidence of the accused's reaction has already been admitted in other evidence.

R v Tooke (1990) 90 Cr App R 417

The accused made an exculpatory statement shortly after the offence of unlawful wounding had occurred at 9 pm. Some 40 minutes later he went to the police station and made a witness statement that set out his version of the events. At trial, the judge admitted the statement made at the crime scene but ruled that he would not permit the defence to cross-examine a police officer to prove that the accused had made the later exculpatory statement at the police station. The Court of Appeal held that the judge had been correct not to admit the statement since it added nothing to the evidence already before the jury.

Secondly, the accused will not be allowed to take unfair advantage of the rule by seeking to admit in evidence a carefully constructed and premeditated statement designed to persuade the fact finders of the accused's innocence. In *R v Pearce* above, it was suggested that:

> (3) Although in practice most statements are given in evidence even where they are largely self-serving, there may be a rare occasion when an accused produces a carefully prepared written statement to the police, with a view to it being made a part of the prosecution evidence. The trial judge would probably exclude such a statement as inadmissible.

In *R v Newsome* (1980) 71 Cr App R 325, the defendant was charged with rape. It was held that a self-serving statement dictated by the accused to the police after consultation with, and in the presence of his solicitor, some 13 hours after the alleged offence and subsequent to a number of interviews with the police, was inadmissible under the ground outlined in the extract (3) above from *R v Pearce*, as the statement was a contrived attempt to persuade the court of the accused's denial of the charge against him.

An inculpatory statement

Where the accused makes an inculpatory statement, ie he admits his guilt and the statement is adverse to his interests, it may be admitted as evidence of the truth of the facts contained in it as an admission or a confession under section 76 of PACE. The law relating to the admissibility of confession evidence has been dealt with in Chapter 6.

A 'mixed' statement

Whilst some defendants deny their involvement in a criminal offence, others may make a 'mixed' statement, ie a statement that is partly exculpatory and partly inculpatory, as illustrated by the following example.

Example

The witness states to the police: 'Yes, I hit the victim but I was only defending myself'.

The general rule is that the whole statement is admissible. In *R v Pearce* (1979) 69 Cr App R 365, the Court of Appeal gave the following guidance about the position of a mixed statement:

> (2)(b) A statement that is not in itself an admission is admissible if it is made in the same context as an admission, whether in the course of an interview, or in the form of a voluntary statement. It would be unfair to admit only the statements against interest while excluding part of the same interview or set of interviews. It is the duty of the prosecution to present the case fairly to the jury; to exclude answers which are favourable to the accused while admitting those unfavourable would be misleading.

It would appear therefore that in the case of a 'mixed' statement, where the prosecution relies on those parts of the witness's statement that are unfavourable to the accused, as a matter of fairness, those parts of the statement that are favourable to the accused should also be put in evidence. The rule will apply even where the accused has elected not to testify. In *R v Duncan* (1981) 73 Cr App R 359, the appellant, who was charged with murder, elected not to testify and was convicted. The trial judge had refused to admit in evidence on the basis that it was self-serving, a statement made by the appellant in which he admitted that he killed the victim but suggested that he must have lost his temper when she teased him. The Court of Appeal decided that in refusing to admit the statement the judge had erred in law. Lord Lane CJ stated:

> Where a 'mixed' statement is under consideration by the jury in a case where the defendant has not given evidence, it seems to us that the simplest, and therefore, the method most likely to produce a just result, is for the jury to be told that the whole statement, both the incriminating parts and the excuses and explanations, must be considered by them in deciding where the truth lies. It is, to say the least, not helpful to try to explain to the jury that the exculpatory parts of the statement are something less than evidence of the facts they state. Equally, where appropriate, as it usually will be, the judge may, and should, point out that the incriminatory parts are likely to be true (otherwise why say them?) whereas the excuses do not have the same weight.

R v Duncan was approved by the House of Lords in *R v Sharp* [1988] 1 All ER 65, which confirmed that the whole statement was evidence in the case, although it might be appropriate for the jury to be directed that the exculpatory parts may carry less weight than the inculpatory parts.

Unfavourable and hostile witnesses

The final evidential issue arising out of examination-in-chief relates to the practice and procedure where the party's witness appears to be either 'unfavourable' or 'hostile'. At an early stage in the proceedings a party's solicitor will have taken a proof of evidence from each witness that will form the basis of the evidence that the witness will give to the court if the case proceeds to trial. In examination-in-chief where the witness's oral evidence in court largely reflects the content of his proof, the witness is regarded as 'coming up to proof'. However, it is quite common for a witness during examination-in-chief not to give the answers expected of him by his examiner or to give evidence unfavourable to the party calling him. A witness who displays these tendencies is known as an 'unfavourable' witness. If the witness cannot recollect some fact even after having refreshed his memory, the advocate cannot assist him by putting leading questions, and will be frustrated that his witness's answers are unhelpful. It is not permissible for the witness's written statement to be put to him, nor can his examiner attack the credibility of his witness's evidence. At common law all that can be done is for the advocate to engage in a damage limitation exercise by calling other witnesses to give evidence of those matters that the unfavourable witness was expected to testify about. This principle is illustrated by the civil case of *Ewer* v *Ambrose* (1825) 3 B & C 746, in which a witness called by the defendant to prove a certain partnership, gave evidence to the contrary. The judge ruled that all that the party could do was to call other witnesses to contradict the unfavourable witness's evidence.

The second explanation as to why a witness does not come up to proof is that the witness is hostile to the party calling him. A hostile witness is a witness who is 'not desirous of telling the truth at the instance of the party calling him' or the witness shows animosity to the party calling him. The clearest example is where a witness has deliberately changed his evidence since his previous statement, whether from a desire not to be involved in the case or through fear or through malice, or as a result of some other motive, such as where for example he has been bribed. Where an advocate is examining-in-chief his own witnesses and considers the witness to be hostile, the advocate must ask the judge to send the jury out of court and in their absence will apply to the judge for leave to treat the witness as hostile. The judge will be shown the witness's previous written statement as evidence in support of the application and will decide whether the witness is hostile or merely unfavourable by considering the witness's demeanour, attitude and any other relevant factor. In summary proceedings the issue is a matter for the magistrates to decide in consultation with their clerk.

The courts approach this issue with caution. In *R* v *Maw* [1994] Crim LR 841, the Court of Appeal said that in many cases where the witness has departed from his proof of evidence, it is undesirable for the court to proceed immediately to treat the witness as hostile. A better approach is to invite the witness to refresh his memory from the proof. Then, if the witness did not allow his memory to be refreshed or does not give an explanation as to why his oral evidence is different from his proof, the court could then consider treating the witness as hostile.

Where the issue has been decided, the jury is recalled and, if the judge has ruled the witness only unfavourable, as noted above, there is nothing much that the advocate can do. Where the judge rules the witness as hostile, however, the advocate can do a little more by undermining the witness's credibility in a number of ways. First, at common law, the advocate calling the witness may ask the witness leading questions and cross-examine him by putting the client's version of events to the witness as in *Rice v Howard* (1886) 16 QBD 681 and *Price v Manning* (1889) 42 Ch D 372.

Secondly, section 3 of the Criminal Procedure Act 1865 states:

> A party producing a witness shall not be allowed to impeach his credit by general evidence of bad character; but he may, in case the witness shall, in the opinion of the judge prove adverse, contradict him by other evidence, or by leave of the judge, prove that he has made at other times a statement inconsistent with his present testimony, but before such proof can be given the circumstances of the supposed statement must be mentioned, and he must be asked whether or not he has made the statement.

Under section 3 the advocate can ask the witness whether or not he has made an earlier statement which is inconsistent with his present oral testimony. Where the witness agrees his earlier written statement or parts of it as the truth, then, in effect, he is adopting that version as being his evidence, subject to an assessment of his credibility by the court. The oral evidence he has given earlier has no evidential value.

Where the witness admits making the statement but continues to give evidence that is inconsistent with the statement, the jury must be directed to try the case on the witness's oral testimony and cannot rely on the witness's earlier statement as fact. This point was made in *R v Nelson* [1992] Crim LR 653, where the judge directed the jury that testimony at trial is the only evidence on which the jury may act. Previous witness statements help only in assessing the reliability of the oral evidence in court. As an illustration of the way in which the law relating to unfavourable and hostile witnesses operates, consider the following example.

Example

Brian is being prosecuted for assault occasioning actual bodily harm against the victim, David. In her statement to the police, Sandra, Brian's estranged wife, states that on the night of the assault she saw Brian go up to David and punch him three times in the stomach. At trial, in examination-in-chief, Sandra, who is called by the prosecution, testifies that Brian did not hit David and after the attack the real assailant ran away into the night.

By taking the incremental approach adopted in R v Maw*, the advocate may ask Sandra to refresh her memory from her statement. If the statement was made contemporaneously with the events, Sandra may continue to refer to the document whilst testifying. If the statement was not contemporaneous it will be taken from Sandra after she has refreshed her memory. The prosecutor may put the question again to Sandra. If Sandra continues to state that she did not see Brian assaulting David the prosecutor may conclude that she shows no desire to tell the truth. The advocate will apply to the judge to have Sandra ruled as hostile. If the judge rules Sandra as hostile, the prosecutor may ask Sandra leading questions and/or ask her whether or not she has made the previous written statement which is inconsistent with her present oral testimony. If Sandra adopts her written statement, it becomes her evidence at trial, subject to the judge's*

*direction about her credibility. If Sandra adopts her later oral testimony as her evidence, the jury
must be directed that the accused must be tried on Sandra's oral evidence.*

Reforming the law of witness testimony in examination-in-chief

The Criminal Courts Review Report made a number of recommendations about
reforming the practice and procedure of witness testimony. First, in respect to the use
by a witness of a memory refreshing document, Lord Justice Auld acknowledged that
the operation of the present law is unsatisfactory. In many cases the witness, when
referring to a 'contemporaneous' document, is not refreshing his memory but is in fact
reading a note of matters about which he has little or no recollection. In practice, due
to the witness being unable to remember in sufficient detail the events about which he
is testifying, the memory refreshing document becomes his evidence-in-chief. This is an
inevitable consequence of the complexity of many of the issues involved in the witness's evidence and the time lapse between the commission of the alleged offence and
the defendant's trial. To illustrate the point, Auld uses the example of a police officer
who is expected to go through the charade of seemingly not reading his notebook but
only glancing at it when his memory needs prompting. The absurdity of the present
position is further exacerbated by the fact that the witness will have refreshed his memory from a written statement immediately before entering the witness box, yet when
testifying he will be expected to give evidence from memory. The relaxation of the rules
contained in the decisions of *R* v *Da Silva* and *R* v *South Ribble Magistrates', ex parte
Cochrane* (above), which place less emphasis on the requirement for contemporaneity,
are cited with approval and should provide the basis for reforming the law. Auld
recommends that a witness should be allowed to use a memory refreshing document
where there is good reason to believe that the witness would have been significantly
better able to recall the events in question when he made or verified his statement than
at the time of giving evidence. This would recognise a basic principle of the criminal
justice system that witness testimony should be an exercise in truthfulness rather than
a test of long or short-term memory. Similar criticisms of the unsatisfactory operation
of the present law in the use of memory refreshing documents was identified by the
Law Commission in its report *Evidence in Criminal Proceedings: Hearsay and Related
Topics* (1997). The Law Commission pointed out that potentially valuable evidence
may be lost where the witness's statement was written down by someone other than
the witness and not checked by the 'percipient' witness, as is well illustrated by the case
of *R* v *Eleftheriou and Eleftheriou* above. To remedy the problems the Law
Commission proposed that a witness's previous statement should be admitted as evidence of its truth where the witness is unable to remember details contained in a statement which he had adopted when the events were fresh in his memory and it is
unreasonable at the date of the trial to expect the witness to be able to recall the facts.

A related issue to the use of a memory refreshing document is the use of a witness's
previous statement. As we noted above, the rule against narrative, as it is also sometimes referred to, excludes evidence of a witness's previous statement except where it
contradicts his oral testimony, when it can be used to challenge his reliability or his
truthfulness. Auld considers that if a witness is going to be able to refer to a broader
range of memory refreshing documents and read them whilst giving evidence, it would

be sensible and expeditious for the document to stand as the witness's evidence-in-chief provided the witness authenticates the statement. This is based on the well-established practice in civil and family cases and in other jurisdictions, including Scotland and some Commonwealth countries. The witness would be able to add to his statement by giving oral evidence to the court and could also be cross-examined on the contents of his statement. The proposals to reform the rules enhancing the use of a witness's previous consistent statement are not new. The issue was raised by the Law Commission in its 1997 report above, which recommended that a previous statement made by the witness should not only be admissible to support the witness's credibility but also as evidence of the truth of its contents where the statement is used to rebut an allegation of recent fabrication or to support a prior identification or the description of a person or of an object or of a place. According to the Law Commission, the third situation where a witness's previous consistent statement could be admitted as evidence of the truth is where a witness has made a recent complaint in a sexual offence.

Finally, as a long term aim, Auld also recommends extending the present provisions for the use of video-recorded evidence to the evidence of all critical witnesses in cases of serious crime, coupled with the provision, where required of a record and/or transcripts or summaries of such evidence and also of that in cross-examination and re-examination. It remains to be seen which, if any of these proposals, will be given legislative effect.

Further reading

Auld, Lord Justice (2001) *A Review of the Criminal Courts of England and Wales*, www.criminal-courts-review.org.uk.

Law Commission Final Report No 245 (1997) *Evidence in Criminal Proceedings: Hearsay and Related Topics*, HMSO.

Gooderson, R.N., 'Previous Consistent Statements' [1968] Camb LJ 64.

Home Office (1998) *Speaking Up for Justice*, Report of the Interdepartmental Working Group on the Treatment of Vulnerable or Intimidated Witnesses in the Criminal Justice System.

Jerrard, R.R., 'The Police Officer's Notebook' (1993) 157 Justice of the Peace 5.

Newark, M., 'The Hostile Witness and the Adversary System' [1986] Crim LR 441.

Watson, A., 'Witness Preparation in the United States and England and Wales' (2000) Justice of the Peace and Local Government Law 816.

Chapter 16

EVIDENTIAL ISSUES ARISING OUT OF CROSS-EXAMINATION AND RE-EXAMINATION

INTRODUCTION

The right of a party to cross-examine the other party's witness lies at the very heart of the adversarial system of fact adjudication. Many of the most dramatic and decisive moments in the great English criminal trials have occurred during cross-examination as it is the point in the trial when the forensic skills of the advocate are most apparent. According to Lord Sankey in *Mechanical and General Inventions Co and Lehwess v Austin and Austin Motor Co* [1935] AC 346, cross-examination is 'a powerful and valuable weapon for the purpose of testing the veracity of a witness and the accuracy and completeness of his story'. In practice not only is the accuracy of the witness's recollection of his factual evidence tested, but also the witness's demeanour and credibility as a person may come under the careful scrutiny of the court.

In most criminal cases, at the conclusion of the examination-in-chief, the witness will be cross-examined by the other side. Where a witness is sworn he is liable to be cross-examined whether or not he has given evidence-in-chief. In a case involving two or more co-accused, a defendant has the right to cross-examine a co-defendant whether or not the co-defendant has given evidence against him or not. The same rule applies to a witness called by a co-defendant. On the rare occasion when a witness is called by the judge, the witness may only be cross-examined by the parties with the leave of the judge.

Cross-examination has two purposes. First, to obtain information about the facts in issue favourable to the cross-examining party's case and, secondly, to test the truthfulness of the evidence the witness has given in examination-in-chief or to cast doubt on the witness's evidence. This may be done by challenging the factual evidence given by the witness in examination-in-chief and/or by challenging or impeaching the witness's personal credibility by suggesting, for example, that the witness is biased in favour of the party calling him or by proving that he has criminal convictions.

The purpose of this chapter is to examine the evidential issues arising out of the cross-examination of a witness and to consider the third stage of witness testimony – re-examination.

THE ADVOCATE'S ROLE IN CROSS-EXAMINATION

When conducting cross-examination, it is the advocate's duty:

- to challenge every part of a witness's evidence that is in conflict with his own case;
- to put his own case to the witness in so far as the witness is able to say anything relevant about it; and
- to put any allegation that may be put about the witness's credibility.

Where it is intended to contradict the witness on his factual evidence, the advocate should put his party's version of the facts so as to give the witness an opportunity to explain the contradiction. A failure to cross-examine a witness on his factual evidence will be taken as an acceptance of the witness's evidence-in-chief on that particular issue and in his closing speech the advocate will not be allowed to attack that part of the witness's evidence, which he did not attempt to contradict in cross-examination – see *R v Wood Green Crown Court, ex parte Taylor* [1995] Crim LR 879. Consider the example below.

Example

Trevor is a prosecution witness and, during cross-examination, the defence advocate fails to put to him that he was the one who in fact committed the offence, not the accused. It will not therefore be possible for the defence advocate to refer to this fact in his closing speech as it was not raised in cross-examination of the witness.

In challenging the other side's witnesses, questions asked in cross-examination are not restricted to the issues raised during examination-in-chief but may be directed to any fact in issue or to an issue relating to the witness's credibility, and, unlike during examination-in-chief, leading questions are allowed. In spite of operating under a wide discretion, the advocate's conduct in cross-examination is constrained by a number of evidential, procedural and ethical considerations. First, questions should be put in such a way as to encourage the witness to state facts and not to engage in an argument with the advocate, nor should the questions be used as a vehicle for the advocate to make comments on the evidence in the case or about the witness. The appropriate time for commenting on the issues in the case will be during the advocate's closing speech. Secondly, the issues that may be raised in cross-examination are subject to the normal rules of relevance and admissibility. Questions therefore cannot be put which are inadmissible in their own right, for example, where they offend the hearsay rule or are protected by legal professional privilege. In *R v Treacy* [1944] 2 All ER 229, the Court of Criminal Appeal held that the accused, who was charged with murder, had been improperly cross-examined upon certain inadmissible confessions. Thirdly, to ensure that the accused receives a fair trial, the judge has an inherent power to restrain unnecessary, improper or oppressive questions. Finally, the advocate is required to comply with the rules of professional conduct. Where the advocate is a barrister, his conduct in cross-examination will be subject to the Code of Conduct of the Bar for England and Wales, which requires that it is the duty of the barrister to guard against asking questions that are intended to insult or annoy the witness and that questions should be avoided that are unnecessarily or gratuitously offensive or will waste the court's time.

Also, there are a number of other restrictions which apply to the cross-examination of the complainant in proceedings for a sexual offence (see Chapter 17).

ISSUES THAT MAY BE RAISED IN CROSS-EXAMINATION

Questions that may be asked in cross-examination may be directed to two issues:

- a fact in issue in the case; or
- to undermine the witness's credibility in the opinion of the fact finder.

Facts in issue

As we noted above, the advocate is under a duty to challenge in cross-examination those parts of the witness's factual evidence that contradict his party's case. Therefore, a witness's answer in cross-examination about a fact in issue may be contradicted by the advocate questioning the witness or by calling further evidence. Consider the following example.

Example

The accused's identity is an issue between the parties and in examination-in-chief the prosecution witness testifies that the person she saw 'spoke and looked very much like the accused'. The defence advocate is consequently under a duty in cross-examination to seek to contradict the prosecution witness's evidence of identification by suggesting that the person the witness identified was not the accused.

Issues that go to the witness's credit and collateral issues

As well as attempting to undermine the factual evidence given by the witness during examination-in-chief, the cross-examiner may also seek to undermine the witness's personal credibility to persuade the fact finder that the witness ought not to be believed on oath. This may be achieved by highlighting any inconsistencies between the witness's oral testimony at trial and a previous written or oral statement or by cross-examining the witness on a range of collateral issues. Each of these provisions will now be considered.

Where the witness has made a previous inconsistent statement

An issue that may be raised in cross-examination to undermine the witness's credibility is to show the court that the witness has made a previous written or oral statement that is inconsistent with his present oral testimony. This provision is especially important to a defence advocate who, when cross-examining a prosecution witness, will be in possession of a copy of the witness's written statement that has been disclosed under the pre-trial disclosure provisions and therefore expects the witness to give an answer consistent with his written statement. What action may the advocate take when the witness gives contradictory evidence? The answer depends on whether the question relates to a fact in issue or to a collateral issue. Where the question relates to a collateral issue, the general rule is that the witness's answer is final. However, where the question relates to a fact in issue, the advocate may put to the witness evidence of his own previous inconsistent statement. The procedure for dealing with previous inconsistent statements is dealt with by sections 4 and 5 of the Criminal Procedure Act 1865. Section 4 provides:

> (4) If a witness upon cross-examination as to a former statement made by him relative to the subject-matter of the indictment or proceeding and inconsistent with his present testimony does not directly admit that he has made such a statement, proof may be given that he did in fact make it; but, before such proof can be given the circumstances of the supposed statement, sufficient to designate the particular occasion, must be mentioned to the witness, and he must be asked whether or not he has made such statement.

The effect of section 4 is that where the witness denies having made a previous oral or written statement (or a statement contained in a video or audiotape) which is inconsistent with his present testimony, the advocate must put to the witness the circumstances in which the alleged statement was made and then ask the witness whether he ever made such a statement. Where the witness denies that he has made the earlier statement that is inconsistent with his present testimony, the cross-examining party may prove that the previous statement was made, by calling a witness or witnesses who heard the oral statement or by producing the written statement. It does not matter whether the previous inconsistent statement was made on oath or not. Whilst the House of Lords in *R v Derby Magistrates' Court, ex parte B* [1996] 1 AC 487 stated that section 4 applied to both oral and written statements, there is some logic to the proposition that section 4 will be applied to previous inconsistent oral statements made by the witness as section 5 applies to written statements only. Consider the following example of the operation of section 4.

Example

Harry became involved in an argument with Duncan at a party. Harry claims that as Duncan attacked him with a bottle, Harry picked up a knife and inadvertently wounded Duncan. Harry is charged with wounding. Robert and Jim witnessed the incident. Robert tells the police that he did not see Duncan holding a bottle. Jim claims that whilst he did not see Duncan holding the bottle, he heard the sound of a bottle breaking. Robert is called to give evidence for the prosecution and testifies Duncan did not have a bottle. In cross-examination, Harry's advocate asks Robert whether, shortly after the attack, he (Robert) had told Jim that Duncan was holding a bottle. Robert denies having the conversation with Jim.

As Robert denies making a previous statement that is inconsistent with his present oral testimony, section 4 of the Criminal Procedure Act 1865 permits the defence advocate to call Jim to give evidence that on the previous occasion Robert had made an oral statement that is contrary to his evidence at trial.

It is a matter for the jury to decide whether it believes Robert's evidence or Jim's evidence.

Where the witness gives oral evidence that is inconsistent with his earlier written statement the position is governed by section 5 of the 1865 Act, which states:

> A witness may be cross-examined as to previous statements made by him in writing, or reduced in writing, relative to the subject-matter of the indictment or proceeding, without such writing being shown to him; but if it is intended to contradict such witness by the writ-

ing, his attention must, before such contradictory proof can be given, be called to those parts of the writing which are used for the purpose of so contradicting him: Provided always, that it shall be competent for the judge, at any time during the trial, to require the production of the writing for his inspection, and he may thereupon make such use of it for the purposes of the trial as he thinks fit.

Section 5 covers 'previous statements made ... in writing or reduced in writing' to include not only the witness's written proof of evidence but also where the statement is contained, for example, in an accident report book in a prosecution under the Health and Safety at Work etc Act 1974. Section 5 gives the cross-examiner an element of surprise because the witness can be asked about those parts of his written statement that are inconsistent with his oral evidence without being shown his statement. If the witness continues to deny his previous statement and the advocate wishes to contradict the witness by using it, he must draw the witness's attention to those parts of his statement that are inconsistent with his oral testimony. This is usually done by the witness reading the relevant parts of the statement himself. The witness will then be asked which version of his evidence he wishes to be put before the court. The operation of section 5 is illustrated by the following example.

Example

David and Sheila are jointly charged with three counts of theft and false accounting. David pleaded guilty to the first two counts in the indictment to which Sheila pleaded not guilty. In cross-examination David denies that in an earlier written statement given to the police he had suggested that Sheila had committed with him the offences detailed in counts 1 and 2 of the indictment.

In order to cross-examine the witness about his previous inconsistent written statement, the cross-examining advocate must have David's written statement available, as under section 5, the judge may require the statement's production for inspection. The cross-examination may occur in two stages. First, David may be asked about his statement without it being shown to him. If he denies having made the statement, the advocate may give David a copy. If David accepts the truth of the statement, it becomes part of his evidence. If David still refuses to acknowledge the statement, the advocate has two choices. The matter may be left at this point where the advocate is satisfied that the witness's credibility has been sufficiently damaged. This approach is appropriate where the inconsistency relates to an unimportant part of the witness's evidence. If the advocate, however, wishes to contradict the witness, the document will be put in evidence by the advocate reading the contradictory statement out aloud to the court. The statement may then be inspected to see the extent of the contradiction with the witness's oral testimony and to consider, whether taken as a whole, the statement confirms or contradicts the evidence the witness has given in court. It is then a matter for the judge to decide whether the statement or a part of it should be put before the jury, as section 5 prescribes that the judge may 'make such use of it for the purposes of the trial as he may think fit'.

Evidential effect of a previous inconsistent statement

The evidential effect of proving a witness's previous inconsistent statement under section 4 or section 5 goes to the issue of the witness's consistency and credibility as stated in *R v O'Neill* [1969] Crim LR 260. The evidence cannot be treated as the truth of the facts asserted apart from those parts which the witness accepts as the truth and, according to *R v Jarvis* [1991] Crim LR 374, the judge is required to warn the jury of the limited evidential effect of the witness's evidence.

Cross-examination on the witness's credibility

The witness may be asked questions in cross-examination to undermine his general credibility in the eyes of the jury or the magistrates, although the questions that may be asked are closely controlled by a number of factors. First, cross-examination on the witness's general credibility is subject to the general judicial discretion to ensure that the accused enjoys a fair trial. Secondly, it should be remembered that the witness's credibility is a collateral issue that runs alongside the main issue at trial, which is the determination of the accused's guilt or innocence. The general rule at common law is that the answers a witness gives to collateral issues should be final to prevent the cross-examining party from adducing evidence to contradict the answer the witness gives. This is referred to as the 'finality' rule. If the finality rule did not apply, a lot of valuable time would be taken up at the trial in considering issues that were not strictly relevant to deciding the case. Thirdly, the advocate is not permitted to go on a 'fishing expedition' where the sole purpose is to denigrate gratuitously the witness's character. A good illustration of how the court approaches these issues is provided by the case of R v *Sweet-Escott* below.

R v Sweet-Escott (1971) 55 Cr App R 316

The accused was charged with perjury relating to evidence given by him for the prosecution in committal proceedings in 1970. Under cross-examination he was asked about his convictions between 1947–50, which he initially denied but subsequently admitted. From 1950 he had no convictions at all. The jury were directed to acquit on the ground that the prosecution had failed to establish that the false statements were 'material' in the committal proceedings. Lawton LJ posed the question: 'How far back is it permissible for advocates when cross-examining as to credit to delve into a man's past and to drag up such dirt as they can find there?' The Court of Appeal held that:

> Since the purpose of cross-examination as to credit is to show that the witness ought not to be believed on oath, the matters about which he is questioned must relate to his likely standing after cross-examination with the tribunal which is trying him or listening to his evidence.

The decision in R v *Sweet-Escott* was applied by the House of Lords in the case described below.

R v Funderburk [1990] 1 WLR 587

The defendant was charged with three specimen counts of unlawful sexual intercourse with a girl of 13. In examination-in-chief she described a number of acts of intercourse with the defendant and stated that before the first act of intercourse she was a virgin. The defence submitted that she was lying and that the detailed description that she had given about the acts of intercourse could only have been made from a person with sexual experience. In support of this contention the defence wished to call a witness, P, to give evidence of a conversation that he had with the girl during which she intimated that before the first incident with the accused she had sexual intercourse with two men and wanted to undergo a pregnancy test, or, alternatively, if the girl denied ever having the conversation with P, he could be called to rebut her denial. The judge ruled that in each case the evidence was inadmissible as it was irrelevant to establishing or refuting the charge that this defendant had sexual intercourse with the complainant and that section 4 of the Criminal Procedure Act 1865, which deals with admissibility of the witness's previous inconsistent statement, did not apply on the facts. The defendant was convicted and appealed.

On appeal, the House of Lords held that the appropriate test in deciding whether the witness should be cross-examined as to her credit was not found in section 4 of the 1865 Act but in Lord Justice Lawton's judgment in *R v Sweet-Escott* (1971) 55 Cr App R 316. On the facts, their Lordships decided that cross-examination should have been allowed as the jury, on hearing the complainant's evidence, might have wished to re-appraise her evidence about the loss of her virginity. The House of Lords further decided that the conversation between P and the girl should have been heard by the jury as the conversation did not merely go to the issue of the witness's credit but was relevant to the subject matter of the indictment and therefore should have been admitted under section 4 of the 1865 Act.

A good illustration of the issues that may be raised as to a witness's credibility is provided by *R v Edwards* [1991] 2 All ER 266, which concerned the extent to which a police officer could be asked questions about his behaviour in previous cases to show the reliability of his evidence in the present case. The prosecution alleged that the defendant, who was charged with robbery, had made certain oral admissions to police officers, which, at trial, the officers confirmed in their evidence. The defendant had refused to sign the notes of the interview saying that they were fabrications.

On appeal, the issue was raised whether it could have been possible for the defence to question the officers about the evidence they had given in other trials, where it had been similarly suggested by the defendants that the officers had fabricated their statements. It was held that generally a witness could be asked about any improper conduct of which he had been found guilty for the purposes of testing his credit. On the facts of *R v Edwards*, the officers could have been cross-examined about any criminal charges or disciplinary proceedings that had been proved against them. Cross-examination on a number of other issues would not be allowed. These issues included charges of perjury made against the officers but not yet proven and complaints by members of the public but not yet investigated by the Police Complaints Authority. The issue that proved most problematic concerned those previous cases in which the witnesses had given evidence but where the accused had not been convicted or the conviction had been overturned on appeal. On this issue, Lord Lane CJ recommended the following approach:

> This is an area where it is impossible and would be unwise to lay down hard and fast rules as to how the court should exercise its discretion. The objective must be to present to the jury as far as possible a fair, balanced picture of the witness's reliability, bearing in mind on the one hand the importance of eliciting facts which may show, if it be the case, that the police officer is not the truthful person he represents himself to be, but bearing in mind on the other hand the fact that the multiplicity of complaints may indicate no more than what was described as the 'band-wagon' effect.

Cross-examination on the witness's credibility – exceptions to the finality rule

As we noted above, the general rule is that questions directed in cross-examination to undermine the witness's general credibility are subject to the finality rule in that no evidence may be called to rebut the witness's answer. There are however a number of important exceptions to this general rule where the cross-examiner may put evidence before the court to contradict the witness's answer. The exceptions to the finality rule relate to:

- where it is alleged that a witness is biased; or
- a witness's previous convictions; or
- where the witness has a reputation for untruthfulness; or
- where medical evidence may be introduced to undermine the witness's reliability.

Each of these exceptions is considered below.

Where it is alleged that the witness is biased

Whilst very few witnesses are truly independent and will favour and support the side calling them, where a witness purports to be independent but in practice is biased or shows a particular partiality to the party calling him, the allegation of his biased evidence may be put to him in cross-examination. Where the witness denies the allegation, his denial may be rebutted by evidence and independently proved. Whilst there are many examples of conduct that may amount to bias, an allegation often relates to where a witness has taken a bribe or has very close relations with the party calling him or that he has a particular grudge against the cross-examining party. For example, in *R v Shaw* (1888) 16 Cox CC 503, a prosecution witness who denied in cross-examination that he had quarrelled with the accused and had threatened revenge, was allowed to have his evidence contradicted. In *R v Mendy* (1977) 64 Cr App R 4, the accused's husband, who was to be called as a defence witness, was waiting outside court until his turn to testify. He denied in cross-examination that he had spoken to a man who had been seen in the public gallery taking notes of the proceedings against the witness's wife. The court held that the prosecution was entitled to rebut the denial. In *Thomas v David* (1836) 7 C & P 350, where a witness denied that she was the mistress of the party, evidence to rebut the witness's answer was admitted. Finally, in *R v Busby* (1982) 75 Cr App R 79, a police officer was cross-examined about whether he had threatened a defence witness. This police officer denied the allegation and evidence was admitted that rebutted his denial.

A witness's previous convictions

As we shall see in Chapters 20 and 21, the defendant generally has a shield under section 1(f) of the Criminal Evidence Act 1898 against evidence of his convictions and past conduct being heard by the court. A person called as a witness in a criminal trial does not enjoy the same immunity and he may be asked questions in cross-examination about his character and convictions. Where the witness denies the fact of his conviction(s), the cross-examining advocate can prove the conviction. The position is governed by section 6(1) of the Criminal Procedure Act 1865:

> (1) A witness may be questioned as to whether he has been convicted of any felony or misdemeanour and upon being so questioned, if he either denies or does not admit the fact or refuses to answer it shall be lawful for the cross-examining party to prove the conviction.

Whilst a literal interpretation of section 6(1) appears to give the cross-examining party the right to prove any conviction against any witness whether the conviction has any relevance to the issues in the case or not, in practice, the operation of the subsection is constrained by a number of factors. First, the cross-examination will be subject to the *Practice Direction (QBD: Rehabilitation of Offenders Act 1974: Implementation: Reference to Spent Convictions during Trial)* [1975] 1 WLR 1065, which provides that no reference should be made to a 'spent' conviction under the Rehabilitation of Offenders Act 1974 if it can be 'reasonably avoided'. The question of whether the reference to the spent conviction can be 'reasonably avoided' is a matter for the judge to decide on the facts of the case. A failure to comply with the Practice Direction will not be a ground for quashing an otherwise proper conviction. In *R v Lawrence* [1995] Crim LR 815, the trial judge refused the defence application to cross-examine the victim in detail about his 20 previous 'spent' convictions, the majority of which were for dishonesty but did allow questions to be asked about four more recent dishonesty convictions. The Court of Appeal held that the effect of the Practice Direction was to give the judge a wide discretion and although cross-examination might have been permitted on one of the previous convictions for perverting the course of justice, it was not possible to say that the judge had exercised the discretion improperly. Secondly, cross-examining a witness on his previous convictions will also be subject to the general judicial discretion to prevent any questions that are unnecessary or improper as outlined in *R v Sweet-Escott* above.

Evidence of reputation for untruthfulness

In addition to the general right to prove a witness's convictions under section 6(1) of the Criminal Procedure Act 1865, it is also permitted during cross-examination to call a witness or to adduce evidence with the intention of undermining other aspects of the witness's character and credibility. The evidence is usually put in this way by the cross-examining advocate suggesting to the witness 'From your knowledge of X would you believe him on his oath?'

The practice and procedure for impugning the witness's reputation for speaking the truth is summarised by the comments of Lord Justice Edmund-Davies in *R v Richardson and Longman* (1968) 52 Cr App R 317:

> A witness may be asked whether he has knowledge of the impugned witness's general reputation for veracity and whether from such knowledge he would believe the impugned witness's testimony. The witness called to impeach the credibility of another witness may also express his individual opinion based upon his personal knowledge as to whether the latter is to be believed on his oath, and is not confined to giving an opinion based merely on reputation.

Under this provision it is quite common, for example, for the cross-examining party to produce evidence that seeks to undermine the witness's credibility in speaking the truth. The opposing party is allowed to cross-examine the witness in an attempt to repair any damage to the impugned witness's reputation. Where appropriate other witnesses may be called to redeem the witness's reputation. It is a question for the jury to decide how much weight (if any) it attaches to the allegations of untruthfulness.

Medical evidence relating to the unreliability of the witness's evidence

During cross-examination it is also permissible for the party to introduce medical evidence which may undermine the witness's credibility or the accuracy of his testimony. The leading case is discussed below.

Toohey v Commissioner of Police of the Metropolis [1965] AC 595

The accused was charged with others with assaulting M with intent to rob. The defence submitted that M had been drinking and that the defendant had merely been trying to help the victim, but that he became hysterical and alleged that he had been assaulted. The trial judge ruled as inadmissible the evidence of a doctor who had examined M shortly after the alleged assault which suggested that drink could cause hysteria, and that M was more prone to hysterical behaviour than a normal person. The House of Lords in quashing the conviction held that medical evidence was admissible not only because of its relevance to the facts in issue but also because it showed that the witness suffered from an abnormality that in some way affected the reliability of his evidence.

The principles developed in *Toohey* were applied in *R v Eades* [1972] Crim LR 99 where the prosecution was allowed to call psychiatric evidence to rebut the defendant's account of how he had suddenly discovered his memory about a fatal car crash in a way that was inconsistent with the prevailing medical opinion of the time. The law requires the evidence of unreliability to come from a recognised medical discipline. Medical evidence therefore means a medically qualified person, which includes a psychiatrist but not necessarily a psychologist.

RE-EXAMINATION

The third stage of witness testimony is re-examination, where the party calling the witness will be entitled to ask further questions. Re-examination will only be available where a witness has previously been examined in chief. Whether an advocate makes use of the opportunities provided by re-examination is a tactical consideration and should be considered where the evidence of the witness has been discredited in cross-examination or that some points in support of the witness's evidence need to be clarified. Re-examination is therefore available to repair the damage done to a witness's credibility during cross-examination and to explain any confusion or ambiguities in the witness's evidence. Leading questions are not permitted because, as with examination-in-chief, the advocate is dealing with his own witness. A witness may refresh his memory during re-examination subject to the same procedure and considerations as in examination-in-chief.

The most important general issue that may arise during re-examination is where the opposing advocate has suggested in cross-examination that the witness has recently made up or fabricated his evidence. This is a potentially serious attack on the witness's credibility. Where this occurs the cross-examiner is making an allegation against the witness of recent fabrication, ie that the witness has recently made up his evidence to assist the case of the party calling him, and in re-examination, the witness's advocate may take the following action.

Rebutting an allegation of recent fabrication

Where an allegation of recent fabrication has been made in cross-examination, the witness's previous consistent statement will be admissible in re-examination to rebut the allegation that the witness has only recently made his evidence up. The principle is illustrated in the following case.

R v Oyesiku (1972) 56 Cr App R 240

A police officer went to O's home to arrest him. The police officer testified that in the course of the arrest he was assaulted by O. O's wife had witnessed the incident, and before she had an opportunity to see or talk to her husband again, she told her solicitor that the police officer was the aggressor, and, that O, not knowing that the man in plain clothes, was a police officer, had merely tried to break free from his hold. When cross-examined she was accused of recently fabricating her evidence to match that of O. The defence wished to call O's solicitor to give his account of what Mrs O had said and when she had said it. The judge refused leave and O was convicted.

   On appeal against conviction, the Court of Appeal ruled that the judge had been wrong to refuse leave to adduce evidence of Mrs O's previous statement and quashed O's conviction. This was a classic example of an assertion of recent fabrication, and the solicitor's evidence, not only as regards the account of what Mrs O had said to him, but also the time at which she had said it, would have completely refuted the assertion put to Mrs O in cross-examination.

Two points should be noted about admitting the witness's previous consistent statement in these circumstances. First, the rule will not be invoked merely because the truthfulness of the witness's evidence has been questioned (*Fox v General Medical Council* [1960] 1 WLR 1017). Secondly, the effect of the rule is to allow the witness's previous consistent statement to be put before the court to prove the consistency of the witness's evidence and to repair any damage to his credibility arising out of the allegation of recent fabrication.

   As we noted in Chapter 15, both the Criminal Courts Review and the Law Commission in its report *Evidence in Criminal Proceedings: Hearsay and Related Topics* (1997) have recommended a number of reforms to the law of witness testimony which are relevant not only to examination-in-chief but also to cross-examination and re-examination. In its 1997 report, the Law Commission recommended that where a witness admits making a previous inconsistent statement or the previous inconsistent statement is proved under sections 3, 4 or 5 of the Criminal Procedure Act 1865, the statement should be admissible as evidence of any matter stated of which oral evidence by the witness would be admissible. A similar recommendation was proposed in relation to re-examination, where a witness's previous statement is used to rebut a suggestion of recent fabrication. If implemented, these reforms would reflect the position in civil proceedings under the hearsay provisions of the Civil Evidence Act 1995, which are considered in Chapter 29.

Further reading

Law Commission Final Report No 245 (1997) *Evidence in Criminal Proceedings: Hearsay and Related Topics*, HMSO.

Newark, M., 'Opening Up the Collateral Issue Rule' (1992) 42 Northern Ireland Legal Quarterly 166.

Pattenden, R., 'Evidence of Previous Malpractice by Police Witnesses and *R. v. Edwards*' [1992] Crim LR 549.

Wigmore, J.H. (1974; revised edn J.H. Chadbourn) *Evidence in Trials at Common Law*, Vol 5, Boston, Little, Brown & Co.

Chapter 17

CROSS-EXAMINATION OF THE COMPLAINANT IN A SEXUAL OFFENCE

INTRODUCTION

The issues that may properly be raised in the cross-examination of the complainant in a sexual offence have historically caused a dilemma for the law of evidence. It should always be remembered that the complainant appears as a witness in the proceedings and that it is the accused who is on trial and not the complainant. It is only appropriate therefore that the complainant should be treated as an 'ordinary' witness and that generally the rules of evidence that apply to the cross-examination of other witnesses should also apply to the complainant in proceedings for a sexual offence. On the other hand, the prosecution of a sexual offence frequently involves a number of unusual aspects that are generally not found in the prosecution of other offences. For example, the most commonly raised defence in cases of rape is consent, which in itself causes a number of evidential difficulties for the prosecution in proving the defendant's *mens rea*. These difficulties are further heightened where the complainant and the accused have previously engaged in a consensual sexual relationship. Also, many sexual offences are characterised by the absence of independent evidence, although with the rapid developments in forensic science such as DNA evidence, in some prosecutions, this problem can now be overcome. In many cases the only percipient witnesses who may testify at trial are the complainant and the accused. As result, the decisive factor in the prosecution of many sexual offences is how the fact finder assesses the complainant's credibility as a witness and whether, on the evidence presented to the jury or the magistrates, they believe the complainant's evidence. Therefore, as a recognition of the evidential value of the complainant's credibility in sexual offences, the rules relating to the questions that may be asked in the cross-examination of the complainant have evolved to deal with these difficult issues. They are the subject matter of this chapter.

THE POSITION AT COMMON LAW

At common law, the complainant in a rape offence could be cross-examined about her sexual history if the questions were directly relevant to a fact in issue such as consent or the perpetrator's identity or whether she was the kind of woman to make an allegation of rape. Clearly, questions about her previous sexual history that were not directed to proving a fact in issue were a collateral issue and as noted above in Chapter 16, the general rule is that a witness's answer to a collateral question is final. However, as in so many other areas of the law of evidence, a number of exceptions developed to the general rule where answers given by the complainant to questions about her previous sexual conduct did not fall within the finality rule so that the defence was permitted to put evidence before the court to rebut the complainant's answer. These exceptions applied in the following circumstances.

First, the complainant could be cross-examined about whether before the act complained of she had engaged in sexual intercourse with the accused as the law considered that such an act was relevant to the issue of consent. Where the complainant denied that intercourse had previous taken place between her and the accused, evidence could be introduced to rebut her denial (*R v Riley* (1887) 18 QBD 481). Secondly, by applying a very generous interpretation of the *res gestae* rule, evidence could be introduced about the surrounding circumstances in which the offence had occurred where it was relevant to proving that the complainant had behaved in a sexually provocative way immediately before the alleged offence was committed. Thirdly, evidence was admissible to show that the woman was a prostitute because the courts considered that this fact was relevant to the issue of consent as the defendant might reasonably have thought the woman was consenting to intercourse if she was a prostitute (R v Clay (1851) 5 Cox 146).

SEXUAL OFFENCES (AMENDMENT) ACT 1976

The operation of the common law rules proved to be unsatisfactory in a number of ways. First, in many cases the complainant's actions and character became the overriding issue at the trial rather than the culpability of the defendant's actions. The common law also failed to reflect society's changing views about sexual morality. The concept of the 'chaste' woman that had underpinned the operation of the former rules was inappropriate for the more sexually promiscuous era of the 1960s and 1970s. In the opinion of the Heilbron Committee (*Report of the Advisory Group on the Law of Rape*, Cmnd 6352 (1976)), which was set up to advise the government on the law of rape following the House of Lords' decision in *DPP v Morgan* [1976] AC 182, evidence of the complainant's sexual history was used in many cases to prejudice the jury against the complainant. In its report, the Committee recommended that legislation should be passed to limit the issues that may be raised in the cross-examination of the complainant. The government accepted the report, and its recommendations were put into statutory form by the Sexual Offences (Amendment) Act 1976. Section 2 of the 1976 Act regulated the issues that could be raised in the cross-examination of the complainant in a rape offence:

> (1) If at a trial any person is for the time being charged with a rape offence to which he pleads not guilty, then, except with the leave of the judge, no evidence and no question in cross-examination shall be adduced or asked at the trial, by or on behalf of any accused at the trial, about any sexual experience of a complainant with a person other than the accused.
>
> (2) The judge shall not give leave in pursuance of the preceding subsection for any evidence or question except on an application made to him in the absence of the jury by or on behalf of the defendant; and on such an application, the judge shall give leave only if and only if he is satisfied that it would be unfair to that defendant to refuse to allow the evidence to be adduced or the question to be asked.

Before considering the operation of section 2, two preliminary points should be noted. First, the statutory rules only applied to the complainant's sexual history with some-one other than the accused. The common law continued to govern the questions that could be asked in cross-examination about the sexual relationship between the accused and the complainant. Secondly, the section applied where the defendant had been charged with a 'rape' offence, which included rape, attempted rape and aiding and abetting rape or where non-consensual buggery had occurred with a man or a woman. The section did not include other sexual offences such as indecent assault and indecency with children.

In spite of Parliament's intentions, the interpretation and application of section 2 also proved to be problematic for the courts. The key to the section's application was the test to be applied to determine whether it would be 'unfair to the defendant' to refuse evidence to be heard about the complainant's sexual behaviour with men other than the accused. The leading case under section 2 of the 1976 Act is *R* v *Viola* below.

R *v* Viola (1982) 75 Cr App R 125

The accused was charged with raping the complainant in her flat about midnight on a Tuesday. At his trial, the defendant claimed that when he had called at the complainant's flat she made advances towards him, which led to consensual sexual intercourse. His counsel unsuccessfully sought to cross-examine the complainant about the allegation that she had had sexual intercourse with two other men who had called at her flat earlier on the day of the offence. The accused was convicted and appealed. The Court of Appeal held that on the facts, cross-examination should have been allowed because as the circumstances of the alleged acts of intercourse with the two men were so similar to the circumstances of the rape, it was relevant to the issue of consent and the jury might have taken a different view of the complainant's testimony if it had heard the evidence of the complainant's sexual conduct with the other two men.

In deciding whether cross-examination should be allowed under section 2, Lord Lane CJ in *R* v *Viola* suggested a two-stage test. First, were the questions that would be put to the complainant 'relevant' according to the ordinary common law rules of evidence and relevant to the case being put to the defendant? If the relevance test was satisfied, the second issue was whether the questions were permitted within the boundaries allowed by section 2. The section was aimed at excluding questions that merely went to impugn the complainant's credit by, for example, suggesting that the complainant was the kind of woman who had sex with men to whom she was not married and was therefore not the kind of woman to be believed when she alleged that she had been raped. Where however the cross-examination about the complainant's sexual experi-ence with people other than with the accused was directed at an issue in the case, the complainant could be cross-examined if the court gave leave. In giving this guidance the Court of Appeal recognised that these were not 'hard and fast rules' and that judgment about the application of section 2 should be taken on the facts of each case.

As a result of the guidance given in *R* v *Viola*, cross-examination on the following issues was generally permitted under section 2 of the 1976 Act:

1   The victim could be cross-examined where it was suggested that she had been extremely promiscuous and it was relevant to the issue that she was more likely to consent to sex with someone she had only just met.

2 Where the complainant had previously made false allegations of rape, this could be
   explored in cross-examination (*R v Cox* (1987) 84 Cr App R 132).
3 As illustrated by *R v Viola*, cross-examination should be allowed about the victim's
   sexual experience immediately before and/or after the rape on the basis of 'similar
   facts', so that it was relevant to show that she had been a willing participant in the
   offence.

In many cases, the operation of section 2 of the 1976 Act proved to be little more
satisfactory than the former position at common law. The legislation was considered
to be unnecessarily restrictive by applying to offences of rape only. Also, with the
section limiting cross-examination to the complainant's sexual experience with a
third party and not with the accused, issues were often raised at trial that were only
marginally relevant to deciding the guilt of the accused in the present offence and
placed undue emphasis on the issue of the complainant's credibility. The rules of evidence and procedure for dealing with victims of sexual crimes became the subject
of widespread public criticism following a number of high-profile cases that were
widely reported in the media. In one infamous case in 1997, the accused, Ralston
Edwards at his trial for rape, took advantage of the defendant's right to cross-examine prosecution witnesses personally, and spent six days cross-examining his victim,
Julia Mason. To the victim's torment, the accused wore the same clothes at the trial
that he had worn during the 16 hours that he had attacked her in her home (see *The
Times*, 7 May 1998). In another infamous case, the defendant had sacked his lawyer
at an early stage during his trial for rape, and subjected the two complainants in the
case to 'repetitious and irrelevant questions designed to intimidate and humiliate
them' (*R v Brown (Milton)* [1998] 2 Cr App R 364). At Brown's appeal, Lord
Bingham CJ suggested that if a similar situation arose in the future, the judge should
intervene to save the witness from humiliating, abusive or intimidating questions.
Finally, Home Office statistics quoted in *Speaking Up for Justice*, the report of the
Interdepartmental Working Group on the Treatment of Vulnerable or Intimidated
Witnesses in the Criminal Justice System (June 1998) showed that whilst women
were confident in reporting rapes, there was a high drop-out rate during the early
stages of the criminal justice process. In 1985, 24% of rapes reported to the police
resulted in a conviction but by 1996 the number of rape complaints to the police had
trebled but the conviction rate had fallen to 9%. This was partly explained by the
complainant's fear of being cross-examined in public about her past sexual history
and extensive questioning about whether she had consented to sex on previous
occasions were often used by the defence to distract the jury from the proper issues
at trial.

YOUTH JUSTICE AND CRIMINAL EVIDENCE ACT 1999

In response to these problems the Labour government gave priority to combating
public concern about the treatment of the victims of crime generally, and the
position of the complainant in a sexual offence in particular. The result of the
government's deliberations was the enactment of the Youth Justice and Criminal
Evidence Act 1999, which is largely based on the recommendations contained in

Speaking Up For Justice. The 1999 Act introduces changes to the law governing the cross-examination of the complainant in a sexual offence. The changes are set out in full below.

Complainant's entitlement to a special measures direction under section 19

The particular vulnerability of the complainant in a sexual offence is governed by section 17(4) of the 1999 Act where the complainant appears as a witness in the proceedings. Under this section, the witness will be entitled to a special measures direction under section 19 on the basis of her position as the complainant without having to satisfy any of the grounds that other witnesses are required to comply with. Under section 19, the court may make a special measures direction that includes screening the complainant from an accused under section 23 or allowing the complainant to give evidence by a live television link under section 24. The granting of a special measures direction is considered in detail in Chapter 18.

Preventing the accused from personally cross-examining the victim of a sexual offence (sections 34–36)

The general rule is that where he is not legally represented, the defendant may personally cross-examine all the witnesses called by the prosecution. However, as an exception to this general rule, section 34 of the 1999 Act introduces a mandatory ban on an unrepresented defendant charged with a sexual offence from personally cross-examining the complainant either in connection with the offence or in connection with any other offence with which that person is charged in the proceedings. Consider the following example.

Example

Bob, who is charged with rape and burglary, dismissed his barrister at the beginning of the trial. The operation of section 34 of the 1999 Act prevents him from personally cross-examining the complainant, Sylvia, about the offences of rape and burglary.

The protection afforded in cross-examination to certain categories of witnesses in a sexual offence is taken further by section 35 of the 1999 Act. Under section 35 no person charged with an offence to which this section applies may cross-examine in person a 'protected' witness. A 'protected witness' is a witness who:

- either is the complainant; or
- is alleged to have been a witness to the commission of the offence to which section 35 applies, and
- either is a child; or
- falls to be cross-examined after giving evidence-in-chief by means of a video recording made at a time when the witness was a child; or
- in any other way at any such time.

The offences to which the section applies are:

    (a) any offence under—
        (i) the Sexual Offences Act 1956,
        (ii) the Indecency with Children Act 1960,
        (iii) the Sexual Offences Act 1967,
        (iv) section 54 of the Criminal Law Act 1977, or
        (v) the Protection of Children Act 1978;
    (b) kidnapping, false imprisonment or an offence under section 1 or 2 of the Child Abduction Act 1984.

Consider the following example of the operation of section 35.

Example

Leonard is charged with three offences of indecency with children contrary to the Indecency with Children Act 1960. The prosecution alleges that the offences occurred in the changing room of the local swimming pool. The prosecution wishes to call Simon, aged 12, who saw Leonard take a group of children into the changing room at the time the alleged offences were committed. Although Leonard has dismissed his counsel, section 35 of the 1999 Act prevents him from personally cross-examining Simon, as the accused is charged with an offence to which section 35 applies and Simon is a 'protected' witness for the purposes of the section.

Cross-examination of a complainant in proceedings for a sexual offence (section 41)

At common law, at the accused's trial for rape, evidence of the complainant's consensual acts of sexual intercourse with the accused could be given on the basis that it made it more likely than not that on the occasion of the alleged offence, the complainant had consented. The issues that could properly be raised in the cross-examination of the complainant under the Sexual Offences (Amendment) Act 1976 related to her sexual experience with any person other than the accused where it was 'in the interests of justice' to do so. The first effect of section 41 of the 1999 Act is to abolish this distinction by applying to the complainant's sexual experience with both the accused and with third parties. Secondly, the ambit of the section has been widened to include not only rape offences, but also under section 62 of the 1999 Act:

- the prosecution of offences for burglary with intent to rape;
- an offence under sections 2–12 and 14–17 of the Sexual Offences Act 1956 including unlawful intercourse and indecent assault;
- an offence under section 128 of the Mental Health Act 1959;
- an offence under section 1 of the Indecency with Children Act 1960;
- an offence under section 54 of the Criminal Law Act 1977; or
- an inchoate offence in any of the above.

Thirdly, the provisions of section 41 apply not only to the trial of the matter but also to other proceedings including evidence at committal proceedings where the offence is triable either way, any other hearing between conviction and sentence and the hearing of the accused's appeal.

Section 41 provides:

(1) If at a trial a person is charged with a sexual offence, then, except with the leave of the court—
  (a) no evidence may be adduced, and
  (b) no question may be asked in cross-examination,
by or on behalf of any accused at the trial, about any sexual behaviour of the complainant.
  (2) The court may give leave in relation to any evidence or question only on an application made by or on behalf of an accused, and may not give such leave unless it is satisfied—
  (a) that subsection (3) or (5) applies; and
  (b) that a refusal of leave might have the result of rendering unsafe a conclusion of the jury or (as the case may be) the court on any relevant issue in the case.
  (3) This subsection applies if the evidence or question relates to a relevant issue in the case and either—
  (a) that issue is not an issue of consent; or
  (b) it is an issue of consent and the sexual behaviour of the complainant to which the evidence or question relates is alleged to have taken place at or about the same time as the event which is the subject matter of the charge against the accused; or
  (c) it is an issue of consent and the sexual behaviour of the complainant to which the evidence or question relates is alleged to have been, in any respect, so similar—
    (i) to any sexual behaviour of the complainant which (according to evidence adduced or to be adduced by or on behalf of the accused) took place as part of the event which is the subject matter of the charge against the accused; or
    (ii) to any other sexual behaviour of the complainant which (according to such evidence) took place at or about the same time as that event, that the similarity cannot reasonably be explained as a coincidence.
  (4) For the purposes of subsection (3) no evidence or question shall be regarded as relating to a relevant issue in the case if it appears to the court to be reasonable to assume that the purpose (or main purpose) for which it would be adduced or asked is to establish or elicit material for impugning the credibility of the complainant as a witness.
  (5) This subsection applies if the evidence or question—
  (a) relates to any evidence adduced by the prosecution about any sexual behaviour of the complainant; and
  (b) in the opinion of the court, would go no further than is necessary to enable the evidence adduced by the prosecution to be rebutted or explained by or on behalf of the accused.

For the purposes of section 41, 'sexual behaviour' is defined by section 42(1)(c):

'sexual behaviour' means any sexual behaviour or other sexual experience, whether or not involving any accused or other person, but excluding (except in section 41(3)(c)(i) and (5)(a)) anything alleged to have taken place as part of the event which is the subject matter of the charge against the accused...

The general effect of section 41

Section 41(1) establishes a general restriction on the evidence that (a) can be put before the court or (b) the questions that may be asked by the defence about the complainant's sexual behaviour. If the defence wishes the restriction to be lifted it will be necessary to apply to the judge for leave under section 43(1). The application will be heard in private and in the absence of the complainant. The judge will announce his decision in open court in the absence of the jury giving reasons for his decision. If leave is granted, section 43(2) requires the judge to indicate the extent of the evidence that may be adduced or the questions that may be asked about the complainant's sexual behaviour.

Granting leave by lifting the restriction under section 41

The restriction imposed by section 41(1) may be lifted where the court grants leave under section 41(2). Leave may only be granted where the judge is satisfied that one of the grounds under section 41(3) or section 41(5) considered below applies and that a refusal might render as unsafe a conclusion of the jury or the court on any 'relevant issue' as per section 41(2)(b).

The complainant is further protected by section 41(4). The section prohibits evidence from being adduced or question being asked about her sexual history where the purpose or the main purpose is merely to impugn the character of the complainant in order to persuade the jury that she ought not to be believed on oath. The application of section 41 has already caused difficulties as illustrated by the case of *R v A*.

R v A [2001] 3 All ER 1

The complainant began a sexual relationship with a friend of the defendant and she visited him at the flat that he was then sharing with the defendant. On the evening of 13 June 2000 the complainant and the friend had sexual intercourse at the flat when the defendant was not there. Later, when the defendant returned, the three of them went out for a picnic. The two men drank whisky and beer. When they got back to the flat the friend collapsed and was taken to hospital. Later, in the early hours of 14 June, the defendant and the complainant left the flat to go to the hospital. The prosecution's case was that as they walked along the route selected by the defendant, he fell down. When the complainant tried to help him, he pulled her to the ground and had sexual intercourse with her.

The defendant, A, was charged with rape, and claimed that the intercourse was part of a continuing consensual sexual relationship that he had been having with the complainant. His defence was that sexual intercourse had taken place with the complainant's consent or, alternatively, that he believed that she had consented.

Before the trial, at a preparatory hearing, A's counsel applied to cross-examine the complainant under section 41(3)(c) about an alleged sexual relationship between her and A during the three weeks before the alleged rape. The judge ruled that the complainant could not be cross-examined nor could evidence be led about the alleged relationship. In refusing the defence application, the judge relied on section 41 of the Youth Justice and Criminal Evidence Act 1999 which precluded the court from giving leave to adduce evidence of the complainant's sexual behaviour or allow cross-examination on it unless the court was satisfied that section 41(3) or (5) applied, and that a refusal of leave might have the result of rendering unsafe a conclusion of the jury or the court on any relevant issue. Section 41(3) applied if the evidence or question related to a relevant issue falling within one of the paragraphs of that subsection. The qualifying condition in section 41(3)(c) was that the issue was one of consent and that the sexual behaviour of the complainant, to which the evidence or question related, was alleged to have been, in any respect, so similar to any such behaviour of the complainant which took place as part of the event of the subject matter of the charge against the accused, or to any other sexual behaviour of the complainant which took place at or about the same time as the event, that the similarity could not reasonably be explained as a coincidence.

On A's appeal against the ruling at the preparatory hearing (which was reported as *R* v *Y (Sexual Offence: Complainant's Sexual History)* (2001) *The Times*, 13 February), the Court of Appeal held that the alleged previous sexual relationship was admissible in relation to A's belief in consent but not in relation to the issue of consent itself. The Court of Appeal took the view, however, that a direction to the jury that the evidence was relevant to the question of A's belief as to consent, but not to consent itself might breach A's right to a fair trial under Article 6 of the European Convention on Human Rights. The case was referred to the House of Lords on the following point of law of public importance:

> May a sexual relationship between a defendant and a complainant be relevant to the issue of consent so as to render its exclusion under section 41 of the Youth Justice and Criminal Evidence Act 1999 a contravention to the defendant's right to a fair trial?

Their Lordships held that by applying a purposive interpretation to section 41(3)(c) of the 1999 Act as required by section 3 of the Human Rights Act 1998, and always by paying due regard to protecting the dignity of the complainant in a sexual offence, the test of admissibility was whether the evidence, and the questioning relating to it, was relevant to the issue of consent and that to exclude it would endanger the fairness of the trial under Article 6 of the European Convention on Human Rights. If that test was satisfied, the evidence should not be excluded. The possibility of questioning the complainant about the alleged recent sexual relationship between her and A, and the admissibility of evidence on that point, were matters for the trial judge to decide.

Whilst the case of *R* v *A* was specifically concerned with the interpretation and application of section 41(3)(c), the House of Lords additionally provided useful guidance as to how the courts might interpret section 41(3)(a) and (b). These provisions also allow evidence to be adduced or questions to be asked about the complainant's sexual behaviour in specified circumstances. Paragraphs (a) and (b) of section 41(3) are considered below.

Lifting the restriction where it is relevant to an issue other than consent (section 41(3)(a))

Leave will be granted for evidence to be presented or questions to be asked about the complainant's sexual behaviour where it is relevant to an issue other than consent. Lord Hope in *R* v *A* identified a number of issues that might fall within this paragraph, for example:

- where the accused raises the defence of honest belief in that he may honestly but mistakenly have believed that the complainant was consenting to the sexual act; or
- where the complainant was biased against the accused; or
- where the complainant had a reason to fabricate her evidence; or
- where there was an alternative explanation for the physical conditions on which the Crown relies to establish that intercourse took place; or
- especially in the case of young complainants, that the detail of their account must have come from some other sexual activity before or after the event which provides an explanation for their knowledge of that activity.

In most cases the condition under section 41(3)(a) will be satisfied where the accused honestly but mistakenly believed that at the time of the offence the complainant was consenting but now acknowledges that the complainant did not in fact consent.

Example

After a night out 'on the town' Dean invites Gary back to the flat that Dean shares with his girlfriend, Susie. Dean asks Gary whether he wants to play this game which involves Dean watching whilst Susie has sexual intercourse with a stranger. Dean tells Gary not to worry if Susie appears to be resistant as this apparent reluctance adds to her sexual pleasure.

Gary has sexual intercourse with Susie, who appears distressed and screams at Gary to stop. Later that night Susie makes a complaint to the police and Gary is charged with rape. At trial, Gary's counsel seeks leave to cross-examine Susie that on a number of other occasions, she has engaged in consensual sexual intercourse with a number of men who Dean has met in town and taken back to their flat.

Leave may be granted under section 41(3)(a) for Susie to be cross-examined about her sexual experiences with these men, to support Gary's defence, that he honestly but mistakenly believed that Susie was consenting. In deciding the issue, the court must be satisfied that a refusal to grant leave might render any conviction unsafe.

Lifting the restriction where the evidence relates to sexual behaviour 'at or about the same time' as the subject matter of the charge (section 41(3)(b))

A second qualifying condition or 'gateway' is provided by section 41(3)(b) where evidence can be adduced or questions asked in the cross-examination of the complainant about her sexual behaviour where it relates to matters which are alleged to have taken place 'at or about the same time' as the event which is the subject matter of the indictment. Evidence put to the court under this provision will be relevant to the issue of consent.

According to Lord Steyn in *R v A* above, it would be appropriate to grant leave under section 41(3)(b) where it is alleged that the complainant invited the accused to have sexual intercourse with her earlier that evening. Lord Clyde acknowledged that whilst 'there is a degree of elasticity in this provision' it should be interpreted subject to the ordinary principles of remoteness. It is incumbent therefore on the judge to determine the permissible degree of remoteness to be determined on the facts of the particular case. Lord Clyde referred to a broadly similar, although a more generously drafted statutory test in Missouri law, which allows incidents to be heard which are 'reasonably contemporaneous' with the subject matter of the indictment. In *State of Missouri v Murray* 842 SW (2d) 122 (1992) it was held that incidents bearing on consent which had occurred three and a half and six and a half months before the alleged offence should have been admitted. Lord Hope concluded that whilst it might be possible to interpret the meaning of the phrase 'at or about the same time' to several minutes or to several hours, it may be difficult to extend to a period of several days.

Example

On the way home from a nightclub in a taxi, Julia makes sexually overt advances towards Tom, who is embarrassed by her conduct. A short while later, in her flat, Tom and Julia have sexual intercourse. Julia alleges that Tom raped her and makes a complaint to the police. Tom is charged with rape. At trial, his counsel seeks leave to adduce evidence about Julia's sexual behaviour at or about

the same time as the event in question on the ground that it is relevant to Tom's belief that Julia con-
sented. Leave will be granted where, on the facts, the ground under section 41(3)(b) is satisfied,
which on the facts is whether the advances made by Julia can be construed at or about the same
as the offence and that a refusal to grant leave might render any conviction unsafe. If granted, the
defence will call the taxi driver to give evidence about Julia's behaviour in her taxi or be allowed
to cross-examine Julia.

Applying the dicta of Lord Clyde in *R v A* and the Home Office guidelines to the issue of remoteness, a different conclusion is likely to be reached on the following facts.

On a Saturday night in February, Tom meets Julia in a nightclub and invites her back to his flat for
coffee. Some weeks before, Tom and Julia had met at a Christmas party and they had had con-
sensual sexual intercourse in the back of Julia's car. After coffee, Tom makes advances towards
Julia who appears to resist. Tom continues to behave in a sexually aggressive way and they have
sexual intercourse. The following day, Julia makes a complaint to the police and Tom is charged
with rape. At trial, the defence apply for leave under section 41(3)(b) to cross-examine Julia about
what had occurred between them after the Christmas party on the ground that it is relevant to
Tom's belief that Julia was consenting during the incident which is the subject of the indictment.
On the facts, leave is unlikely to be granted due to the remoteness in time between the acts of
consensual intercourse and the incident relating to the allegation of rape.

Lifting the restriction on the basis of 'similar' sexual behaviour (section 41(3)(c))

The issues that may be raised under section 41(3)(c) are also relevant to the issue of consent. Paragraph (c) allows evidence to be adduced or questions to be asked about the previous sexual behaviour of the complainant, which it is alleged was so similar to the subject matter of the charge that it cannot be explained as a coincidence. The complainant's 'similar' sexual behaviour can either have taken place as part of the event which is the subject matter of the charge against the accused, or at or about the same time as the event which is the subject matter of the charge. You will recall that the operation of section 41(3)(c) was the main focus of the House of Lords' deliberations in *R v A*.

If the similarities between the complainant's behaviour cannot be explained as a coincidence the court is required to adopt an approach that is based on the rules for admitting similar fact evidence. The test to be applied appears to lie between the test of 'high probative force' as laid down in *DPP v P* [1991] 2 AC 447, which in the context of section 41(3)(c) is considered to be too liberal, and the more restrictive ground of 'striking similarity' adopted in *DPP v Boardman* [1975] AC 421.

Lord Hope, in reiterating the tests under the similar fact evidence principle, stated that the similarities which the section permits may be expressed in two alternatives. The first, which was raised in *R v A*, relates to the complainant's sexual behaviour on some other occasion which took place as part of the event charged that cannot reasonably be explained on the basis of coincidence. The provision may be widely interpreted to include the complainant's sexual behaviour with the accused and with third parties and may also relate to sexual behaviour before as well as after the event charged. On this criteria, the complainant's behaviour in *R v A* did not satisfy the test to allow evidence to be adduced about the complainant's sexual behaviour or for her to be cross-examined under section 41(3)(c) as there was no similarity between the complainant's sexual behaviour with the respondent on a prior occasion and her behaviour which took place as part of the event charged except that it included occasions when she is alleged to have had sexual intercourse with him. According to Lord Hope, the type of allegations that the respondent had made in the present case about the complainant's sexual behaviour was one of the evils that the section had been designed to address – that simply because the complainant had had sexual intercourse with the respondent on a previous occasion she was more likely to have consented on this occasion. It, however, remained open to the respondent at trial, to support his contention that the similarity in the respondent's behaviour cannot simply be explained on the basis of coincidence.

The alternative to the 'similarity' test relates to the complainant's sexual behaviour on some other occasion which is alleged to be so similar to any other sexual behaviour of the complainant which took place 'at or about the same time' as the event charged that it cannot reasonably be explained as coincidence. As with the first alternative, the provision can apply to the complainant's sexual behaviour with the accused and with third parties and it may also relate to sexual behaviour before as well as after the event charged subject to the requirement that the similarity cannot reasonably be explained as a coincidence.

As an illustration of the operation of section 41(3)(c), consider the following examples. The first has been adapted from the speech of Lord Hutton whilst the second comes from Lord Steyn's speech.

Examples

Peter is charged with raping Angela. At his trial he wishes to give evidence that for a number of months prior to the alleged offence he had a close, intimate relationship with Angela and that they frequently had consensual sexual intercourse. Prior to the act of intercourse, Peter would passionately kiss Angela, who would then respond by passionately kissing Peter. On the night of the alleged offence, before having intercourse, the couple had kissed passionately as they had done on previous occasions.

The question to be asked is whether Peter can adduce evidence or cross-examine the complainant about what had occurred between them on the earlier occasions under section 41(3)(c). In deciding whether to grant leave, the judge must decide whether the behaviour on the prior occasions when consensual intercourse took place is 'so similar' to what occurred on the night of the alleged offence, that it cannot be explained as a mere coincidence. Also, as the alleged behaviour between Peter and Angela is normal behaviour between a man and woman, it cannot be said to satisfy the 'similarity' test.

After a night out, Denise and Robert go back to Robert's flat where Robert believes they have consensual sexual intercourse. As Robert takes Denise home in his car, Denise threatens Robert that unless he pays her £500 she will go to the police and allege that Robert has just raped her. If Robert is charged with rape, at trial, with the leave of the court, Denise could be cross-examined or evidence could be adduced that on a previous occasion, after Robert and Denise had intercourse, Denise had blackmailed Robert threatening that unless he paid her £200 she would complain to the police that he had raped her. On this occasion Robert had paid Denise £200 to keep her quiet.

This example is likely to fall within section 41(3)(c) as the similarity test between the two incidents appears to be satisfied and could not be explained as a coincidence.

Lifting the restriction to rebut assertions about the complainant's sexual behaviour (section 41(5))

The effect of section 41(5) is to provide the defence with the opportunity to rebut an assertion made by the prosecution about the complainant's sexual behaviour. In its effect, this provision is the reverse of the 'tit-for-tat' principle that where the defence falsely adduces evidence of the defendant's good character, both at common law and under the Criminal Evidence Act 1898, the prosecution may rebut the assertion of the defendant's good character. It would be appropriate for the defence to invoke section 41(5) in the following example.

Example

Tina, the complainant in a rape case, states in evidence-in-chief that she has only had sexual intercourse with her husband. The defence may apply to the court for evidence to be adduced or for Tina to be cross-examined about the fact that six months ago she had consensual sexual intercourse with Richard, the defendant's brother. It would also be possible for evidence to be adduced or for Tina to be cross-examined about the fact that 12 months ago she had consensual sexual intercourse with Dan, the accused.

In both situations described above, the defence is allowed to rebut the complainant's assertion about her sexual behaviour.

SECTION 41 AND THE HUMAN RIGHTS ACT 1998

The House of Lords' decision in *R v A* [2001] 3 All ER 1 is significant not only for identifying the range of issues that may be raised in accordance with section 41(3) of the 1999 Act in the cross-examination of the complainant in proceedings for a sexual offence, but also provides an instructive example of how the courts may approach the interpretative obligations imposed by section 3 of the Human Rights Act 1998, which are to ensure that domestic legislation complies with jurisprudence of the Convention and most notably the requirements of Article 6 (right to a fair trial).

As we noted above, whilst the specific question before their Lordships was whether evidence was admissible under section 41(3)(c), the House of Lords also took the opportunity to consider the overall effect of section 41(3), which is to create a blanket exclusion of all potentially relevant evidence about the alleged sexual experience between the defendant and the complainant, subject to a number of narrow exceptions. According to Lord Slynn, the restrictions placed on the court's powers to grant leave seriously limit the opportunities for cross-examination or the adducing of evidence on behalf of the accused, and are apparently incompatible with the defendant's right to a fair trial under Article 6 of the Convention.

Special status of the right to a fair trial under Article 6

In interpreting section 41 of the Youth Justice and Criminal Evidence Act 1999 in the context of the 'fair trial' provisions, the House of Lords acknowledged that Article 6 occupies a distinctive position in Convention jurisprudence. In *Van Mechelen v The Netherlands (Article 6)* (1998) 25 EHRR 647, the European Court of Human Rights held that, having regard to the place that the right to a fair administration of justice holds in a democratic society, any measures restricting the rights of the defence should be strictly enforced. A conviction obtained in breach of the fair trial provisions should not be allowed to stand.

The European Court of Human Rights further held that when it is necessary to consider whether Parliament has made excessive inroads into the right to a fair trial in a criminal statute, the first question the court has to ask is whether the statutory enactment interfered with a Convention right. At that stage the purpose of the legislation plays a secondary role. It is at the second stage, when the government seeks to justify the interference, that the legislative purpose of the statute becomes relevant. At that stage the principle of proportionality should be applied. As the right to a fair trial is absolute, the only balancing that is permitted to occur is in respect of what a fair trial entails. In assessing the compatibility of section 41 of the 1999 Act with the Human Rights Act 1998, account may be taken of the triangulation of the interests of the accused, the victim and society.

In this context proportionality has a role to play. In deciding whether a statutory enactment was arbitrary or excessive, the court should ask itself whether:

- the legislative objective was sufficiently important to justify limiting a fundamental right;
- the measures designed to meet that objective were rationally connected to it; and
- the means used to impair the right or freedom were no more than necessary to accomplish that objective.

The critical matter on this issue, was the third criterion. Given the centrality of the right to a fair trial in the scheme of the Convention, the question was whether section 41 made excessive inroads into the guarantee to a fair trial. A detailed explanation of the operation of the European Convention on Human Rights 1950 under the Human Rights Act 1998 is given in Chapter 2.

Approaches to interpreting section 41

In assessing the compatibility of section 41 with the 'fair trial' provisions, two processes of interpretation could be adopted. First, the ordinary rules of statutory construction could be applied in a purposive and contextual interpretation of the section, which might minimise the breadth of its provisions. If this approach did not produce the desired result under Article 6, the interpretative obligation contained in section 3 of the Human Rights Act 1998 might also be applied to ensure that, as section 3(1) requires:

> So far as it is possible to do so, primary legislation … must be read and given effect in a way which is compatible with the Convention rights.

Lord Steyn in *R* v *A* stated that according to ordinary methods of interpretation section 41(3)(c) was a statutory adoption of the strikingly similar test enunciated in *DPP* v *Boardman* [1975] AC 421, which meant that the gateway to adducing evidence of the sexual behaviour of the complainant would only be available in rare cases. Alternatively, section 41(3)(c) could be interpreted by applying the test of high probative value as stated in *DPP* v *P* [1991] 2 AC 447. Even in these circumstances, the threshold for the court granting leave under the section was very high and could not solve the problem that section 41 was *prima facie* in breach of the defendant's right to a fair trial under Article 6.

Where, as in *R* v *A*, the court concludes that Parliament has gone too far in diminishing the defendant's right to a fair trial, it must then consider whether the provisions can be interpreted compatibly with section 3 of the Human Rights Act 1998. (This view was not shared unanimously by the Law Lords – Lord Hope dissenting.)

In expressing the views of the majority in *R* v *A*, Lord Steyn described the duty under section 3 in the following way:

> ...the interpretative obligation under section 3 of the 1998 Act is a strong one...It is an emphatic adjuration...Section 3 places a duty on the court to strive to find a possible interpretation compatible with Convention rights. Under ordinary methods of interpretation a court may depart from the language of the statute to avoid absurd consequences: section 3 goes much further.

A majority of the House (Lords Steyn, Hutton and Clyde) concluded that by applying section 3 to section 41(3)(c), it was possible to read by implication into the section that the necessary evidence or questioning of the complainant which was required to achieve a fair trial under Article 6 should not be inadmissible. Lord Steyn described the interpretative process in this way:

> In my view section 3 requires the court to subordinate the niceties of the language of section 41(3)(c), and in particular the touchstone of coincidence, to broader considerations of relevance judged by logical and common sense criteria of time and circumstances. ... It is therefore possible under section 3 to read section 41 of the 1999 Act, and in particular section 41(3)(c), as subject to the implied provision that evidence or questioning which is required to ensure a fair trial under article 6 of the Convention should not be treated as inadmissible. The result of such a reading would be that sometimes logically relevant sexual experience between a complainant and an accused may be admitted under section 41(3)(c).

Further reading

Cook, K., 'Sexual History Evidence: The Defendant Fights Back' (2001) 151 NLJ 1133.

Geddes, A., 'The Exclusion of Evidence Relating to a Complainant's Sexual Behaviour in Sexual Offence Trials' (1999) 149 NLJ 1084.

Home Office (1998) *Speaking Up for Justice*, Report of the Interdepartmental Working Group on the Treatment of Vulnerable or Intimidated Witnesses in the Criminal Justice System.

Kibble, N., 'The Sexual History Provisions: Charting a Course between Inflexible Legislative Rules and Wholly Untrammelled Judicial Discretion' [2000] Crim LR 274.

Mirfield, P., 'Human Wrongs?' (2002) 118 LQR 20.

Temkin, J., 'Sexual History Evidence – The Ravishment of Section 2' [1993] Crim LR 3.

Young, G., 'The Sexual History Provisions in the Youth Justice and Criminal Evidence Act 1999 – A Violation to the Right to Fair Trial' (2001) 41 Medicine, Science and the Law 217.

Chapter 18

ORAL TESTIMONY OF VULNERABLE, INTIMIDATED OR UNRELIABLE WITNESSES

INTRODUCTION

A significant influence on the law of evidence has been the adoption of the adversarial system of fact adjudication by the English criminal trial. The characteristics of adversarialism, which were considered in Chapter 4, include an emphasis on the primacy of the trial and the principle of orality as the preferred and most highly probative means of giving evidence in a criminal trial.

In view of the primacy of oral evidence in the adversarial system, it therefore seems perverse that historically the English criminal trial has adopted an inflexible approach to the treatment of 'vulnerable' or 'intimidated' witnesses. The result has been that over the years many people who may be described as a 'vulnerable' or 'intimidated' witness such as children, young people and certain classes of adult witnesses, for example those with learning difficulties, have been ruled incompetent or have been incapable of giving coherent and credible evidence. The purpose of this chapter is to trace the development of the law in receiving the evidence of these witnesses and to consider the ways in which recent legislative changes introduced by the Criminal Justice Act 1988 and the proposed changes under the Youth Justice and Criminal Evidence Act 1999, which are due for implementation during 2002, have sought to deal with the problem. These provisions should also be read in conjunction with Chapter 17, which explains the rules relating to the cross-examination of a victim in proceedings for a sexual offence. A second related issue to the theme of witness testimony is to consider how the law approaches the evidence of certain other classes of witnesses whose evidence may be regarded as 'unreliable' for a number of different reasons or where, as a matter of law, in order for their evidence to be accepted by the court, it has to be supported by other independent evidence. This will be dealt with under the law relating to corroboration.

YOUTH JUSTICE AND CRIMINAL EVIDENCE ACT 1999

In its manifesto to the 1997 General Election, the Labour Party placed the issue of law and order in general and the workings of the criminal justice system in particular at the centre of its proposed legislative programme. In a response to well-versed public concerns about the criminal justice system favouring the interests of defendants over the welfare of the victims of crime and those appearing as witnesses in criminal trials, the manifesto promised 'greater protection...for those subject to intimidation including witnesses'. As well as the many complainants in rape trials whose trauma might be exacerbated by

giving evidence in court, other categories of vulnerable or intimidated witnesses were
identified as being in need of additional protection when testifying in court, in particular
children and certain adult witnesses. Adult witnesses may be classified as vulnerable due
to a number of factors such as anxiety and stress at being involved in criminal proceedings
or because there are personal circumstances that connect them in some way with the
defendant or because there is a threat of intimidation, which may have either prevented
them from reporting the offence or led them to refuse to give evidence at the trial.

To combat these problems in June 1997 the Home Secretary, Jack Straw, announced
the establishment of an interdepartmental working party to undertake a wide-ranging
review of the law relating to the treatment of vulnerable and intimidated witnesses giving evidence in the criminal justice system. In coming to its conclusions and making a
number of recommendations, the working group was required to take into account a
number of overriding principles. First, the terms of reference of the review did not distinguish between prosecution and defence witnesses. Secondly, the review was also
required to have regard to the 'interests of justice' in balancing the rights of the defendant
to a fair trial against the needs of a witness who should not feel traumatised or intimidated by his or her involvement in the criminal justice system. The terms of reference also
took account of the United Kingdom's obligations under the European Convention on
Human Rights. Finally, the working group was required to take into account the
National Standards of Witness Care in England and Wales, which were developed in
1996 by the Trials Issues Group an inter-agency group with the task of taking forward
certain initiatives and developing new policies in the criminal justice system.

The Report of the Interdepartmental Working Group on the Treatment of Vulnerable
or Intimidated Witnesses in the Criminal Justice System, *Speaking up for Justice*, was
published in June 1998. The report recommended a coherent and integrated scheme to
provide appropriate support and assistance for vulnerable or intimidated witnesses, with
proposals covering the investigation stage, pre-trial support, at the trial and after the
trial. The working group's proposals are incorporated into the Youth Justice and
Criminal Evidence Act 1999. The relevant provisions are described and discussed below.

Assisting intimidated or vulnerable witnesses to give evidence

Chapter 1 of Part II of the Youth Justice and Criminal Evidence Act 1999 introduces
a range of measures to assist witnesses who come within the definition of vulnerable
or intimidated witnesses to give evidence in criminal proceedings. The measures are:

- screening the witness;
- giving evidence by a live television link;
- giving evidence in private;
- the removal of wigs and gowns;
- admitting a video recording of an interview as the witness's evidence-in-chief;
- video recording the cross-examination and re-examination of a witness and admitting the recording as evidence of the witness under cross-examination and in
  re-examination;
- the examination of a witness through an intermediary; and
- the provision of appropriate aids to communication.

Witnesses who are eligible for assistance

The working group identified two categories of witnesses who may be eligible for assistance when giving evidence. The first classification, now contained in section 16 of the 1999 Act, applies to a witness (other than the defendant) who is vulnerable as a result of his personal characteristics. His vulnerability may arise from his age or as a result of a significant impairment of his intelligence and social functioning, mental disability, mental or physical disorder or a physical disability. Where a witness falls into this category he is automatically entitled to a special measures direction entitling him to a range of facilities to assist him in giving evidence.

The second classification, now contained in section 17 of the 1999 Act, applies to a witness who might be entitled to a special measures direction where his personal and/or social circumstances bring him within the operation of the 1999 Act. The personal and/or social circumstances that the court may take into account include whether the witness is likely to suffer emotional trauma or is likely to be intimidated or distressed and is unlikely to give his best evidence without the assistance of one or more of the special measures contained in the Act. In exercising its discretion whether to give a special measures direction for this class of witness, the court will have regard to:

1 the witness's age;
2 the witness's cultural/ethnic background;
3 the witness's relationship to the party in the proceedings;
4 the nature of the offence;
5 the dangerousness of the defendant or his family or his associates in relation to the witness; and
6 any other relevant factor including the views of the witness himself.

Witnesses eligible for assistance on the grounds of age or incapacity (section 16)

Section 16 establishes the criteria for a witness to be classified as eligible for assistance on the grounds of age or incapacity.

A witness will be eligible for assistance if–

- he is under 17 at the time of the hearing (section 16(1)(a)); or
- if the court considers that the quality of the evidence given by the witness is likely to be diminished by one of the factors identified in section 16(2) (section 16(1)(b)).

The grounds identified by section 16(2) are:

    (a) that the witness—
        (i) suffers from mental disorder within the meaning of the Mental Health Act 1983, or
        (ii) otherwise has a significant impairment of intelligence and social functioning;
    (b) that the witness has a physical disability or is suffering from a physical disorder.

A number of these important provisions require clarification. First, 'at the time of the hearing' means the time when the court has to make a decision about the eligibility of the witness under section 19(2) of the 1999 Act. Secondly, where the court in exercising its discretion under the Act is required to take into account 'the quality of the witness's evidence', the court will take into account the coherence and accuracy of the witness's evidence as well as his ability to answer questions put to him during his evidence. Thirdly, section 21 provides additional safeguards for a child witness. Where a witness gives evidence and is under the age of 17 and comes within section 16(1)(a), section 21(1)(a) creates a presumption in favour of a special measures direction being granted to permit the witness's examination-in-chief to be admitted as a video recording under section 27. If any of the child's evidence is not given by a video recording, the special measures direction will require the witness to testify through a live television link. Further protection is provided by section 21(1)(b), which applies to a child 'in need of special protection'. The provision will apply where the child witness is under the age of 17 and the offence to which the proceedings relates falls within one of a specified number of offences falling within section 35(3)(a) which includes a range of sexual offences or within section 35(3)(b), which includes offences of kidnapping or assault. Where a witness comes within section 21(1)(b) and a special measures direction is made in respect of the child's evidence-in-chief to be video recorded under section 27, the court must also provide a special measures direction under section 28 requiring the child's cross-examination and re-examination to be video recorded.

Example

Stella and Donald are to be called as prosecution witnesses at Matt's trial for kidnapping. Under section 16 of the 1999 Act, Stella, who is 14 years old, will be eligible to a special measures direction as of right due to her age.

A special measures direction may be made in respect of Donald, aged 23, who suffers from a mental impairment, provided the court is satisfied that the quality of his evidence will be diminished by reason of his disability.

Witnesses eligible for assistance on the grounds of fear or distress about testifying (section 17)

The protection afforded by section 17 may apply to all witnesses in criminal proceedings other than the accused where the court is satisfied that the quality of the witness's evidence will be diminished by reason of his fear or distress in connection with testifying in the proceedings. In deciding whether to give a special measures direction under section 19, section 17(2) requires the court to take into account certain factors including:

- the nature of and the alleged circumstances of the offence to which the proceedings relate;
- the age of the witness;
- where relevant, the social and cultural background and ethnic origin of the witness;

- the domestic and employment circumstances of the witness;
- any religious and political beliefs;
- behaviour towards the witness on the part of the accused, members of the accused's family or associates; or any other person who is likely to be an accused or a witness in the proceedings; and
- the views of the witness.

Example

Dawn is the main prosecution witness at Andrew's trial for a public order offence arising out of disturbances at Andrew's flat. Dawn, who is Andrew's neighbour, alleges that members of Andrew's family have made threats against her if she testifies against him. Dawn requests that a special measures direction be made in her favour. In view of this request, the circumstances of the offence, the alleged threats to Dawn and any other 'relevant' factor in section 17(2), the court is likely to make the direction under section 19, provided it is satisfied that the quality of Dawn's evidence will be diminished by reason of her fear or distress in connection with testifying at Andrew's trial.

Making a special measures direction (section 19)

Section 19 regulates the procedure for making a special measures direction. This may be done following an application by a party to the proceedings or it may be done by the court's own motion. Section 19(2) provides as follows:

> (2) Where the court determines that the witness is eligible for assistance by virtue of section 16 or 17, the court must then—
>> (a) determine whether any of the special measures available in relation to the witness (or any combination of them), would, in its opinion, be likely to improve the quality of evidence given by the witness; and
>> (b) if so—
>>> (i) determine which of those measures (or combination of them) would, in its opinion, be likely to maximise so far as practicable the quality of such evidence; and
>>> (ii) give a direction under this section for the measure or measures so determined to apply to evidence given by the witness.

An application to the court to make a special measures direction may be made by either the prosecution or by the defence or the court may make the order of its own motion. In deciding whether a direction should be made, the court must be satisfied that it will improve the quality of the witness's evidence. When a special measures direction is ordered, the court will announce which special measures are appropriate on the facts in the case and are relevant to the witness's personal characteristics. In interpreting the new statutory provisions it is likely that much of the case law that was developed in applying the provisions under the Criminal Justice Act 1988 and at common law will have at least persuasive authority when the court decides which range of facilities should be made available in accordance with a special measures direction under the 1999 Act.

The use of screens (section 23)

Under section 23(1), a special measures direction may provide that where a witness is being sworn or gives evidence he should be prevented from seeing the accused by the use of a screen or other arrangement. Section 23(2) provides that the screen should not prevent the witness from being seen and seeing the judge or justices and in Crown Court trials, the jury. The witness should also be seen by the advocates and any person who has been appointed to assist the witness. This final provision would include, for example, an interpreter appointed under section 29 of the 1999 Act.

The use of screens under section 23 builds on the reforms introduced by the common law. In some courts, which lack the necessary technology to allow evidence to be given through a television link or by video as provided by the Criminal Justice Act 1988, an alternative practice to protect a child witness is to allow him or her to give evidence from behind a screen erected between the witness box and the defendant sitting in the dock. The judge will allow this facility where, on the balance of fairness, it is appropriate for the witness to give evidence in this way. The 'balance of fairness' is determined by the judge weighing the public interest as represented by the prosecution in protecting the child witness from being intimidated whilst giving evidence against any prejudice to the accused. In protecting the accused against any potential prejudice, the judge is required to direct the jury accordingly. In R v X, Y and Z (1990) 91 Cr App R 36, the Court of Appeal approved the trial judge's direction that the use of a screen was to prevent the child from being intimidated by his surroundings as he might find coming before a court frightening. At the beginning of the trial the judge had told the jury not to allow the presence of the screen in any way to prejudice them against the defendant.

Whilst the use of screens was primarily directed towards protecting child witnesses, in a number of circumstances their use has been extended to protect vulnerable or intimidated adult witnesses. In R v Schaub [1994] Crim LR 53, the Court of Appeal stated that the use of screens to prevent the witness from having eye contact with the accused should only be used sparingly and where it was otherwise impossible to do justice. In R v Schaub the use of a screen to protect the witness from the accused in a prosecution for multiple rape was approved. Similarly, in R v Foster [1995] Crim LR 333, a differently constituted Court of Appeal allowed a 20-year-old witness to give evidence from behind a screen against her stepfather who was on trial for raping her. According to the Court of Appeal, the legal test to be applied was the duty to endeavour to see that justice was done and provided that the judge warned the jury about not drawing adverse inferences from the use of the screen, there was no real risk of prejudice to the accused.

The use of a screen was also approved in cases involving witnesses threatened with violence. In R v Watford Magistrates' Court, ex parte Lenman [1993] Crim LR 388, the Divisional Court upheld the magistrates' decision to allow witnesses to give evidence from behind a screen where they were afraid of reprisals. In R v Taylor [1995] Crim LR 253, the Court of Appeal approved the practice of allowing a schoolgirl witness in a murder trial to give evidence from behind a screen and went on to set out the grounds for the exercise of the court's discretion. It was held that it would be appropriate for a witness to give evidence from behind a screen where:

- there were real grounds for fearing the consequences if the witness's identity was revealed;
- the evidence was sufficiently relevant and important to make it unfair to the prosecution to proceed without it;
- the prosecution was able to satisfy the court about the creditworthiness of the witness;
- there was no undue prejudice to the defendant; and
- the court could balance the need for anonymity and protection of the witness against unfairness or the appearance of unfairness to the defendant in the particular case.

Of course, an alternative way an intimidated witness's evidence may be put before the court is where his evidence is contained in a 'document' and under section 23(3)(b) of the Criminal Justice Act 1988 he is not giving oral evidence through 'fear' or because he is 'being kept out of the way'. This provision is an important exception to the hearsay rule in criminal proceedings and is dealt with in more detail in Chapter 14.

Giving evidence by a live television link (section 24)

Under section 24(1), a special measures direction may allow the witness to give evidence by a live television link. The direction will be made where it appears to be 'in the interests of justice' to do so, and the previous practice and procedure under the Criminal Justice Act 1988 will be relevant in assisting the court when exercising its powers under section 24.

Section 32(1) of the Criminal Justice Act 1988 permits a 'child', with the leave of the court, to give evidence through a live television link where the defendant is charged with an offence which involved an assault on, or injury or a threat of injury to, a person; or the offence is one of cruelty to a child under 16 or a sexual offence against a child under the age of 14; or to an inchoate offence of any of the above. The provision applied to trials on indictment in the Crown Court, appeals to the Court of Appeal and to proceedings in the youth court. Section 32 removed the need for children to give evidence in open court where it might be intimidating or traumatic or embarrassing for them to do so. If leave was granted, the child witness would sit in a room adjacent to the court watching a television where he would see the talking head of the examining advocate or the judge. The child would not normally see any other person in the proceedings, including the accused.

Giving evidence in private (section 25)

A special measures direction may provide for the exclusion from the court of persons specified in the direction. The direction may only be made where the proceedings relate to a sexual offence or it appears to the court that there are reasonable grounds for believing that any other person other than the accused has sought or will seek to intimidate the witness in connection with testifying in the proceedings (section 25(4)).

Under the provisions, the following participants in the trial may not be excluded:

- the accused;
- the accused's legal representatives; or
- an interpreter appointed to assist the witness under section 25(2); or
- to a court reporter representing a news gathering organisation.

Removal of wigs and gowns (section 26)

A special measures direction may provide for the wearing of wigs or gowns to be dispensed with during the giving of a witness's evidence.

Video-recorded evidence-in-chief (section 27)

Under section 27(1) a special measures direction may provide for a video recording of an interview of the witness to be admitted as his evidence-in-chief. The court has the discretion not to allow the recording to stand as the evidence-in-chief, where in all the circumstances of the case it would not be in 'the interests of justice' to allow the recording (or part) to be admitted. In exercising its power under section 27(2), the court will have regard to any prejudice to the accused that might result from the witness's evidence being heard in this way as against the desirability of showing the recorded interview. Where the court considers that a recording ought to be admitted, this presumption may be rebutted under section 27(4), which provides that the recording will not be admitted where the witness is not available for cross-examination and the parties have not agreed that it is not necessary for the witness to be made available. If the witness's evidence has been given in chief by video, the witness may not give evidence in any way on matters that have been adequately dealt with by the recording unless the court gives its consent under section 27(5).

Section 32A of the Criminal Justice Act 1988 as amended by the Criminal Justice Act 1991 permits a child witness to give evidence by a video-recorded interview. The section was based on the recommendations of the Report of the Advisory Group on Video-Recorded Evidence (1989) and sought to address two common problems associated with a child's evidence. First, it was intended to reduce the distress experienced by the child during the proceedings. Secondly, the child's evidence could be given at a much earlier stage in the proceedings than at the trial when the events were clearly still fresh in the child's memory.

Section 32A permitted a 'child' witness to be interviewed by an adult and for that interview to be videotaped and with leave of the court, the recording could be put before the court as the child's evidence-in-chief. Leave would be given unless the child was not be available for cross-examination, or the rules of court, requiring disclosure of the circumstances in which the recording was made, had not been satisfactorily complied with, or the court was, of the opinion, having regard to all the circumstances, that in the interests of justice the recording ought not have been admitted. Section 32A applied to the same category of offences that allowed evidence to be given through a live television link.

As a matter of policy, the courts provided a broad interpretation of the range of offences to which section 32A applied. In *R v Lee (Robert Paul)* (1995) *The Times*, 28 December, the Court of Appeal held that a child could give evidence by video because of a threat of injury where the threat was to his mother and thus only indirectly to him.

It should be appreciated that the video recording is not the witness's actual evidence, but may only be used to assist the court in assessing the witness's consistency. In *R v Atkinson* [1995] Crim LR 490, the Court of Appeal held that it was not inappropriate for a jury in retirement to see videos of police interviews with the child victim of a sexual offence, where the defendant had made an issue of inconsistencies within the witness's evidence. The judge was also required to make it clear that the video was not evidence in itself but was available to assist the jury to compare the evidence with the previous statements on video, to assess their consistency and consider how the evidence had been obtained.

Video-recorded cross-examination or re-examination (section 28)

Where a special measures direction provides for the video recording to be admitted under section 27 as the witness's evidence-in-chief, the direction may also provide that any cross-examination or re-examination be video recorded. The recording must be made in the presence of the judge or justices and the legal representatives acting in the proceedings. The recording may be made in the absence of the accused.

Example

Stella is to be called as a prosecution witness at Matt's trial for kidnapping. Under section 16 of the 1999 Act, Stella, who is aged 14, will be eligible to a special measures direction as of right due to her age. Also, due to the presumption created by section 21, which is dealt with above, in addition to any other special measures direction, Stella's evidence-in-chief will be given in the form of a video-recorded interview under section 27. The special measures direction will also provide that Stella's cross-examination and re-examination could be video recorded (section 28).

Examination of a witness through an intermediary (section 29)

A special measures direction may provide for the witness to be examined through an interpreter or through any other person (an intermediary) as the court may direct. The intermediary is required to communicate questions to the witness and may give to the person asking the questions the witness's reply. The intermediary may also explain to the witness or to the advocate any question or answer that might have been given. The witness may be examined in the presence of the judge or justices and the legal representatives of each party. The witness may also be examined in the presence of the jury except in the case of a video-recorded interview. An intermediary or an interpreter is subject to the provisions of section 1 of the Perjury Act 1911.

Aids to communication (section 30)

A special measures direction may provide for the witness while giving evidence (whether in court or otherwise) to be provided with such device as the court considers appropriate with a view to enabling questions or answers to be communicated to or by the witness despite any disorder or disability or other impairment which the witness has or suffers from.

The law relating to the court's powers to make a special measures direction is at an early stage of development. As we noted above, until the opportunity arises for the Divisional Court and, more importantly, the Court of Appeal and the House of Lords to apply and interpret these provisions, the authorities under the Criminal Justice Act 1988 and under the common law will continue to be relevant.

Protection of witnesses from cross-examination by the accused in person (section 36)

Section 36 of the 1999 Act gives the court the power to prohibit an unrepresented defendant from personally cross-examining a witness in a non-sexual offence. A witness for the purpose of section 36 does not include any other person charged in the proceedings. An application for a direction to be made under section 36 may be made by the prosecutor or by the court by its own motion. There are three grounds to be satisfied before the court may make a direction under section 36:

1 it appears to the court that the quality of the evidence given by the witness in cross-examination is likely to be diminished if the cross-examination is conducted in person by the accused;
2 the quality of the cross-examination is likely to be improved if the direction was given; and
3 it would not be 'contrary to the interests of justice' to make a direction.

In exercising its powers under section 36, the court must have regard to a number of issues including:

- any views expressed by the witness;
- the nature of the questions likely to be asked;
- the accused's behaviour during the proceedings; and
- any relationship between the witness and the accused.

The court must state its reason(s) in court for making or refusing an application under section 36.

Where an order is made under section 36, the court should allow the accused to make arrangements for a legal representative to cross-examine the witness. Under the 'interests of justice' test contained in Schedule 3 to the Access to Justice 1999, the accused may be granted a representation order where it is in the interests of a third party for the defendant to be legally represented. This ground will cover the situation where the accused has been prevented by the court from personally cross-examining the witness. Where the accused refuses to co-operate, the court may make the necessary arrangements on behalf of the accused to appoint a legal representative.

Example

Randolph is charged with a street robbery against Vera, who is a frail 86-year-old. Randolph, who does not recognise the court proceedings, has been disruptive during the trial and is conducting his own defence. The prosecution wishes to call Vera to give evidence and makes an application under section 36 to prohibit Randolph from cross-examining Vera in person. The court may make the order where the court is satisfied that Vera's evidence in cross-examination will be diminished if she is cross-examined in person by Randolph and that the quality of the cross-examination would be improved if he was legally represented. Finally, the court has to be satisfied that it is 'not contrary to the interests of justice' to make the order.

In deciding whether to grant the prosecution's application the court will take into account such factors as the relationship between the parties and accused's behaviour during the proceedings. On the facts of the case, it is likely that the judge will grant the application and make an order under section 36 prohibiting Randolph from personally cross-examining Vera. The judge must announce the reasons for his decision in open court.

CORROBORATION – SUPPORTING THE EVIDENCE OF AN 'UNRELIABLE' WITNESS

An issue closely associated to witness testimony is the law relating to corroboration or the need for a witness's evidence to be supported by other independent evidence in the case. The general rule in criminal cases is that for evidence to be probative of a fact in issue, it does not have to be supported by other, independent evidence. In spite of Lord Morris's warning in *DPP v Hester* [1973] AC 296 that '(A)ny risk of the conviction of an innocent person is lessened if conviction is based upon the testimony of more than one acceptable witness', in the prosecution of a simple case, it may be possible for the defendant to be convicted on a single piece of evidence provided that evidence is probative of all the facts in issue in the case and satisfies the standard of proof of 'beyond reasonable doubt'.

However, as exceptions to this general rule, in the prosecution of some criminal offences, corroborative or supporting evidence is required as a matter of law before the accused can be convicted or in other situations where it is in the interests of justice for the court to proceed with caution in convicting the accused on the unsupported evidence of certain classes of witnesses. Before we consider these exceptions to the general rule about corroborative evidence, it is necessary to consider the meaning of corroboration.

The nature of corroborative evidence

Put simply, corroborative evidence is independent evidence which supports or confirms some other evidence in the case. The leading judicial definition of corroboration is to be found in *R v Baskerville* [1916] 2 KB 658, where Lord Reid CJ stated:

> ... evidence in corroboration must be independent testimony which affects the accused by connecting or tending to connect him with the crime. In other words it must be evidence which implicates him... which confirms in some material particular not only the evidence that the crime has been committed, but also that the prisoner committed it. The test applicable to determine the nature and extent of corroboration is thus the same whether the case falls within the practice at common law or within that class of offences for which corroboration is required by statute.

According to the test in *R v Baskerville*, the essential requirements for evidence to be corroborative are that:

* the evidence should be admissible in its own right;
* it must be independent of the evidence to be corroborated; and
* it must implicate the accused in a material way with the crime charged in not only suggesting that the offence was committed but also that it was committed by the accused.

Corroborative evidence can come from the oral testimony of another witness, documentary evidence, real evidence or circumstantial evidence. In certain situations it may even come from the conduct of the accused himself. Consider the following categories of evidence which have been held capable of corroborating or supporting other evidence in the case.

Circumstantial evidence

Depending on the facts of the particular case, circumstantial evidence may be capable of corroborating the prosecution or the defence case. In *R v McInnes* (1990) 90 Cr App R 99, the accused was charged with kidnapping and raping a seven-year-old girl. The girl had been picked up by a stranger and taken away in his car. She was then sexually assaulted. She was able to describe the person responsible for the offences and showed detailed knowledge of the inside of the defendant's car. The interior was said to be full of sweet wrappers, the base of the gear lever was torn and the knob of the gear lever was off-centre. The girl picked out the accused at an identification parade and was also able to recognise his car. The car's interior was found to match the description given by the victim. Whilst the accused denied that the child had ever been in the car, the prosecution submitted that she could not have known about the car's interior unless she had been in it. The Court of Appeal held that the victim's description of the car's interior amounted to circumstantial, independent evidence that identified the accused and therefore corroborated the girl's testimony in respect of the kidnapping charge.

Lies told by the defendant

Lies told by the defendant in an out-of-court statement or in a statement made in court are, in certain circumstances, capable of being corroborative evidence of his guilt. For example, in *R v Goodway* [1993] 4 All ER 894, lies told by the accused about his whereabouts at the time of the offence were used in support of the identification evidence adduced by the prosecution.

The rationale for the rule is that by lying the accused has something to hide and is trying to get out of trouble. In *R v Lucas* [1981] QB 720 the Court of Appeal restated the conditions that must be met for the defendant's lies to amount to corroboration:

1 the lie must be deliberate;
2 the lie must relate to a material issue in the case;
3 the lie must be motivated by a realisation of guilt and fear of the truth; and

4 the lie must be proved to be a lie by evidence other than that of the witness who is
   to be corroborated.

The Court of Appeal also stated that in appropriate cases the jury should be reminded
that some people may lie for reasons other than perhaps hiding their guilt for the
present offence, such as where the accused has lied out of shame or to bolster a defence
or out of a wish to conceal his disgraceful behaviour from his family.

  The court will proceed with caution when directing the jury on the evidential
significance of the defendant's lies. For reasons that are not always entirely clear or
logical to the lay person, a defendant will not always tell the truth during a criminal
investigation or during their trial. This occurs with consistent regularity even where lying
is clearly against the defendant's interests. In relation to the evidential significance of the
defendant's lies, the reasons for the need for caution were identified by the Court of
Appeal in *R v Burge, Hurst and Pegg* [1996] 1 Cr App R 163, where it was stated that:

> Defendants in criminal cases may have lied for many reasons, for example to bolster a true
> defence. They may feel that they are wrongly implicated and although innocent that
> nobody will believe them and so they just lie to conceal matters which look bad but which
> in truth are not bad. They may lie to protect someone else. They may lie because they are
> embarrassed or ashamed about other conduct of theirs which is not the offence charged.
> They may lie out of panic or confusion. All sorts of reasons.

The Court of Appeal held that when giving a direction to the jury about the evidential
value of the defendant's lies, the judge should tailor the direction to the circumstances
of the case; indicate that the lie should be proved beyond reasonable doubt and remind
the jury that the lie, in itself, is not evidence of guilt since the defendant might be lying
for an innocent reason that does not support the prosecution case. Consider the
following example.

Example

*Phillip, who is charged with murder, pleads provocation at trial. In cross-examination, he admitted
that he had lied during a police interview when he stated that he had never met the victim. The jury
may be directed that Phillip's lie may corroborate the prosecution case against him provided the jury
are directed that they must be sure that Phillip lied to conceal the fact that he had murdered the
victim.*

Other types of corroborative evidence

There are additional sources of evidence, which may, in appropriate circumstances,
amount to corroborative evidence. First, under section 62 of PACE, where a person
without good cause refuses to give consent to the taking of an intimate sample, this is
capable of amounting to corroboration of any evidence against him in relation to
which the refusal is material or in some other way significant to other evidence in the
case. Secondly, where the accused testifies in his own defence, his evidence in court,
may confirm the substance of the prosecution evidence or certain other circumstantial
evidence, and thus it is capable of being corroborative evidence. Finally, in the leading
case of *DPP v Kilbourne* [1973] AC 729, evidence of similar misconduct was held to

be capable of amounting to corroboration of later allegations. The defendant in this case faced a number of charges of indecency relating to schoolboys. The defence contended that any association was entirely innocent, and on appeal the House of Lords said that evidence of similar misconduct was admissible because it went to rebut the defence of an innocent association. (For a detailed discussion of the similar fact evidence rule see Chapter 20.)

CASES WHERE CORROBORATIVE EVIDENCE IS REQUIRED AS A MATTER OF LAW

Parliament has specified that the defendant cannot be convicted unless one piece of evidence is supported by other independent evidence in the following four situations. Under the relevant legislation, corroboration is required as a matter of law.

Speeding (Road Traffic Regulation Act 1984, s 89(2))

The effect of section 89(2) of the Road Traffic Regulation Act 1984 is that on a charge of driving a motor vehicle on the road at an excessive speed there can be no conviction on the opinion evidence of one prosecution witness only as to the speed of the vehicle. Section 89(2) states that:

> A person prosecuted for such an offence shall not be liable to be convicted solely on the evidence of one witness to the effect that, in the opinion of the witness, the person prosecuted was driving the vehicle at a speed exceeding the specified limit.

A conviction will only be founded where the opinion of one witness as to the vehicle's speed is corroborated by the opinion evidence of another witness. The evidence corroborating the witness's opinion is required to confirm the speed of the defendant's vehicle but not to prove the vehicle's registration number.

The section, which is also one of the exceptions to the general rule about the admissibility of non-expert opinion evidence, applies to evidence of opinion only and not to evidence of fact. The section is less important than formerly as in most modern prosecutions the speed of the vehicle is proved by an electronic device such as a radar gun or even an officer's own vehicle's speedometer reading. In *Nicholas v Penny* [1950] 2 KB 466, the magistrates had properly convicted the defendant on the evidence of a police officer who had checked the speed of the defendant's vehicle from the speedometer of his own car which was driven at an even distance behind the defendant's car.

Perjury (Perjury Act 1911, section 13)

Section 13 provides that:

> A person shall not be liable to be convicted of any offence against this Act, or of any other offence declared by any other Act to be perjury or to subornation of perjury, or to be punishable or subornation of perjury, solely on the evidence of one witness as to the falsity of any statement alleged to be false.

An accused cannot be convicted of any perjury on the evidence of one witness alone, as to the falsity of any statement he made which is alleged to be false. The corroborative evidence is required to prove the falsity of the statement and it is the only issue that the corroboration needs to address. For the evidence to be corroborative it does not have to come from another witness but may be in the form of documentary or other admissible evidence. For example, in *R v Threlfal* (1914) 10 Cr App R 112, a letter persuading another to commit perjury was held to be corroborative evidence of the prosecution case against the accused.

Treason (Treason Act 1795, section 1)

Section 1 of the Treason Act 1795 provides that an accused cannot be convicted of high treason (ie contriving the death or restraint of the Sovereign or her heirs) without the oaths of two lawful and credible witnesses. The requirement for credibility suggests that the jury must be satisfied that they would have been prepared to convict on the testimony of each witness alone. The Criminal Law Revision Committee (Eleventh Report, Cmnd 4991 (1972) paragraph 195) has recommended the abolition of this provision.

Attempts to commit speeding, perjury or treason (Criminal Attempts Act 1981, sections 1 and 2)

Section 2(2)(g) of the Criminal Attempts Act 1981 provides that 'all provisions whereby a person may not be convicted ... on the uncorroborated evidence of one witness (including any provision requiring the evidence of not less than two credible witnesses)' apply also to attempts to commit the offences in question. Therefore, under section 1 of the Criminal Attempts Act 1981, a requirement for corroborative evidence in proving the 'full' offence as explained above also applies where the accused is charged with attempting the offence.

WHERE A CORROBORATION WARNING OR A REQUIREMENT FOR SUPPORTING EVIDENCE MAY BE DESIRABLE IN THE INTERESTS OF JUSTICE

The common law treated the evidence of certain classes of witnesses such as children, the complainant in a sexual offence and accomplices with a degree of scepticism. The evidence of a child or young person was considered to be less reliable than the testimony of other witnesses, whilst it was suggested that allegations of sexual misconduct were easy to make but difficult to prove. An accomplice who gave evidence against another person charged in the offence was regarded as having an improper motive of his own to serve by giving tainted evidence. In *R v Beck* [1982] 1 WLR 461, it was held that the judge should warn the jury to proceed with caution where there was material to suggest that witness's evidence might be tainted, whilst Lord Taylor CJ in *R v Cheema* [1994] 1 All ER 639, suggested that a warning in suitable terms as to the danger of a witness having an axe to grind was desirable. In relation to the evidence of children, the complainants in a sexual offence and to accomplices, the judge was required, as a matter of law, to give a warning to the jury about the dangers of convicting the accused on the unsupported evidence of these witnesses. Where an appropriate warning was not given, there could be grounds for the defendant successfully appealing against his conviction.

In recent years this area of the law has been reformed as a result of the recommendations contained in the Report of the Royal Commission on Criminal Justice (the Runciman Commission, Cm 2263 (1993)) which, in turn, adopted the Law Commission Report, *Corroboration in Evidence in Criminal Trials* (Law Commission Report No 202 (1991)). In identifying the need for reform, it was suggested that the former regime had fallen into disrepute as it had proved to be not only inflexible and complex, but also had ceased to be appropriate to the purpose that it had intended to serve. Therefore, acting on these recommendations, Parliament passed section 34 of the Criminal Justice Act 1988, which abolished the requirement for a corroboration warning in respect of the unsworn evidence of a child and section 32 of the Criminal Justice and Public Order Act 1994, which abolished the requirement for the judge to give a warning to the jury about the dangers of convicting on the unsupported evidence of an accomplice or the victim of a sexual offence or of a child's unsworn evidence.

In the modern law of evidence whether a corroboration warning is required is a matter of judicial discretion to be exercised on the particulars facts and circumstances of each case. The leading case is *R v Makanjuola* [1995] 3 All ER 730, where Lord Taylor CJ provided guidance as to the circumstances in which a corroboration warning might be appropriate:

1 Section 32(1) of the Criminal Justice and Public Order Act 1994 abrogated the requirement to give a corroboration direction in respect of an alleged accomplice or a complainant in proceedings for a sexual offence, simply because a witness falls into one of these categories.
2 It is matter for the judge's discretion what, if any, warning he considers appropriate in respect of such a witness as indeed in respect of any other witness in whatever type of case.
3 In some cases, it may be appropriate for the judge to warn the jury to exercise caution before acting upon the unsupported evidence of a witness. This will not be so simply because the witness is a complainant in proceedings for a sexual offence, nor will it necessarily be so because the witness is an accomplice. There will need to be an evidential basis for suggesting that the evidence of the witness may be unreliable. An evidential basis does not include mere suggestion by cross-examining counsel.
4 If any question arises as to whether the judge should give a special warning in respect of a witness, it is desirable that the question be resolved with counsel in the absence of the jury before final speeches.
5 Where the judge does decide to give some warning in respect of a witness, it will be appropriate to do so as part of the judge's review of the evidence and his comments as to how the jury should evaluate it rather than a set-piece legal direction.
6 Where some warning is required, it will be for the judge to decide the strengths and terms of the warning. It does not have to be invested with the whole florid regime of the old corroboration warning.
7 Attempts to re-impose the straitjacket of the old corroboration rules are strongly to be deprecated.
8 The Court of Appeal will be disinclined to interfere with the trial judge's exercise of his discretion save in cases where that exercise is 'unreasonable' in the

Wednesbury sense as explained in *Associated Picture Houses Ltd* v *Wednesbury Corporation* [1948] 1 KB 223.

As a result of the decision in *R* v *Makanjuola*, the law relating to corroboration has been liberated from the application of the previous rigid requirements. It is no longer mandatory to give a warning simply because the witness is an accomplice, a child or the complainant in proceedings for a sexual offence. The decision whether a warning is given is a matter of judicial discretion to be exercised on the particular facts of the case. If the judge decides that a warning is appropriate it will form part of the judge's review of the evidence at the conclusion of the case. The words 'supporting evidence' have been taken not to include corroborative evidence in the strict meaning of *R* v *Baskerville* above. Following these important changes to the law what approach have the courts adopted to giving a corroboration warning?

Giving a corroboration warning after *R* v *Makanjuola*

The wholly discretionary approach to the giving of a corroboration warning outlined by Lord Taylor's guidelines in *R* v *Makanjuola* above was supported by the Court of Appeal in *R* v *Muncaster* [1999] Crim LR 409. The defendant was convicted of three counts of possession of LSD with intent to supply. Most of the drugs were discovered in a hire car when M was stopped for drink/driving. The car had been hired by K, who was M's co-accused and with whom M was staying. K's fingerprints were on the envelope in which the drugs were found and when the police searched K's home, more drugs were discovered in a room that was used by M. K was abroad at this time and on her return she visited M in prison. She gave evidence that M had told her that there were drugs in the house and that she should get rid of them. K took the drugs to the police but was arrested and charged with the offence. At trial, the co-defendants put forward cut-throat defences, and M, who had made a no comment interview at the police station, did not give evidence at trial. M was convicted and appealed on the ground that the judge had made an inadequate direction on the way the jury should approach evidence given by K that was detrimental to M and was not sufficiently clear.

In dismissing the appeal, the Court of Appeal declined to intervene in the trial judge's direction stating that the law relating to corroboration should be reconsidered following the implementation of section 32 of the Criminal Justice and Public Order Act 1994 and the case of *R* v *Makanjuola* by suggesting that section 32 applied to all cases where the judge was considering the matter of a discretionary warning. In the present case, the judge had recognised the need for caution by warning the jury in his summing up that K had 'an axe to grind'. As a result, it must have been wholly apparent to the jury that K's evidence should be looked at with caution in so far as it affected M. This did not absolve the judge from saying something to the jury about the matter, but where what he said was not a technical direction of law but merely an observation of common sense, the extent and detail in which he needed to go into the matter was very much a question for him, as was held in *R* v *Makanjuola*.

What is required when one defendant implicates another in evidence is simply to warn the jury of what may very often be obvious – namely that the defendant witness may have a purpose of his own to serve. As an application of the current law consider the following example.

Example

Tony is charged with causing grievous bodily harm with intent arising out of a fight outside a pub. The three other men who were involved in the fight were charged with, and at an earlier hearing, had pleaded guilty to affray. They give evidence for the prosecution at Tony's trial. In exercising his discretion, the judge in his summing up, may warn the jury about convicting Tony on the unsupported evidence of the three witnesses without independent, supporting evidence. The three prosecution witnesses may have a motive of their own to serve by giving evidence against Tony – perhaps in seeking to play down their role in the offence – and there is the possibility that they have concocted their evidence. It is a matter for the jury to decide the weight it gives to the evidence of the prosecution witnesses and to decide whether corroborative evidence is required. If the jury is satisfied about the cogency and the reliability of the witness's evidence, Tony may be convicted on their unsupported evidence.

Following the decision in *R v Makanjuola* above, it is a matter of judicial discretion whether the judge will give a corroboration warning in respect of the evidence of a child or a young person. The discretion will be exercised on the particular facts of the case and the witness's subjective characteristics such as age, maturity, understanding, his involvement in the alleged offence and whether he has given sworn or unsworn evidence. An example of the modern approach is provided by *R v L* [1999] Crim LR 489. The appellant had separated from the complainant's mother after each claimed to have been attacked by the other at a public house. Shortly afterwards, the complainant, J, who was then nine years old, complained to her mother that the appellant had indecently assaulted her. The appellant maintained that the complaint arose because of the mother's grievance against him about the incident in the public house, about which J knew. The indictment against the defendant contained allegations of indecent assault in counts 1–4; attempted rape in count 5; and indecent assault in preparation for rape in count 6.

When she gave evidence at trial, J could not be sure how many times she had been indecently assaulted by the appellant and the judge directed the jury that the appellant should be acquitted on counts 2, 3 and 4. The jury also acquitted him on counts 1 and 5, but found him guilty on count 6. He appealed against the conviction on the grounds that the judge had not directed the jury about how to approach the child's evidence and in particular that no warning had been given about the dangers of convicting if that evidence was not supported by other external evidence, which it was not. In addition, inappropriate comment by the judge wrongly stressed the reliability of the child's evidence and was a misdirection.

In dismissing the appeal, the Court of Appeal stated that following the decision of *R v Makanjuola* and Lord Taylor's CJ's summary of the law in that case, in exercising his discretion the judge should first, consider whether any warning was desirable, and if so, what direction would be appropriate, depended on the circumstances of the particular case, the issues raised and the content and quality of the witness's evidence. In this case, the judge had based his direction on that suggested in *R v Makanjuola* and was completely fair as his specific remark that children were very good witnesses had been taken out of context. The appellant had come nowhere near to persuading the court that the judge's exercise of his discretion to give this particular direction was *Wednesbury* unreasonable.

Further reading

Birch, D., 'A Better Deal for Vulnerable Witnesses' [2000] Crim LR 223.

Bull, R., 'Obtaining Evidence Expertly: The Reliability of Interviews with Child Witnesses' (1992) 1 Expert Evidence 5.

Elliott, D.W., 'The Risk of Over Persuasion' [2000] Crim LR 159.

Pigot QC, Judge Thomas (1989) *Report of the Advisory Group on Video-recorded Evidence*, HMSO.

Runciman of Doxford, Viscount (1993) *Report of the Royal Commission on Criminal Justice*, Cmnd 2263, HMSO.

Spencer, J.R. and Flin, R.H. (1993) *The Evidence of Children: The Law and the Psychology*, 2nd edn, Blackstone.

Chapter 19

OPINION EVIDENCE

INTRODUCTION

When deciding the issue of the defendant's guilt or innocence, the jury or the magistrates will base their decision on the whole of the evidence presented in the case by each party. In the prosecution of all but the most straightforward of cases, the fact finders will be required to consider the probative value and weight of different types of admissible evidence including documentary evidence, real evidence and exhibits produced in court, the written statements of 'absent witnesses' admitted as exceptions to the hearsay rule as well as the oral testimony of witnesses appearing at the trial. The general rule is that when testifying in court a witness may only give factual evidence from his personal knowledge as in the following examples:

Examples

'On the night of the offence I was walking along High Street.'

'I go to the pub at 10 o'clock every night.'

In each example the witness is stating a fact from his personal knowledge about an issue that is relevant to the case.

A witness however, is not generally permitted to give an opinion on an issue to be decided by the court. An opinion, for the purposes of the law of evidence includes where the witness gives a judgment or draws an inference or makes an assumption on a fact in the case. Consider the following as examples of inadmissible opinion evidence.

Examples

'When I saw the accused I knew that he was up to no good.'

'It was obvious to me that the defendant was guilty.'

'The defendant had drunk too much to have been able to drive safely.'

In the first two examples the witness is making an inference or an assumption from the facts within his personal knowledge about the identity of the person, who, in his opinion, committed the offence. In the third example the witness is making an assumption about the defendant's fitness to drive. Opinion evidence of this kind is regarded as being undesirable for a number of reasons. First, as we can see, in making these assumptions, the witness is usurping the function of the fact finder in the trial. It is the responsibility of the jury or the magistrates to form an opinion on the issue of the accused's guilt and not a witness. This rule is known as the ultimate issue rule, which is considered in more detail below. Secondly, it is suggested that if a witness was allowed to give his opinion it may mislead or confuse the court. Also, in many cases the witness's opinion is irrelevant to the outcome of the proceedings as a whole, as it will be based on his limited, subjective knowledge of the case whilst, in deciding the accused's guilt, the fact finder will have the benefit of having heard all the evidence from a number of witnesses and seen other types of evidence such as the exhibits and documents presented as part of either the prosecution or the defence case.

In spite of the well-established reasons for making opinion evidence inadmissible, there are two exceptions to the general rule, where, in a criminal case, a witness is permitted to go beyond merely giving factual evidence to the court. The first exception relates to those inferences that can be drawn from knowledge gleaned through the witness's general experience of life on an issue in the case not requiring expertise. The second exception allows an expert witness to give an opinion on any issue that goes beyond the ordinary competence of the court. In this context, the ordinary competence of the court includes the knowledge of the jurors or the magistrates. The purpose of this chapter is to examine the exceptions to the general rule that permit opinion evidence to be heard in criminal proceedings.

OPINION EVIDENCE ON AN ISSUE NOT REQUIRING EXPERTISE

Under this rule, when giving evidence, a witness may make certain inferences and assumptions from the facts within his personal experience on an issue not requiring expertise arising out of the events about which he is testifying. Depending on the facts in the particular case a witness will be permitted to make statements of opinion such as the examples below.

Examples

'The victim appeared to be in good health on the day of his death.'

'That is the knife I saw the accused carrying.'

'On the day I arrested the accused, his speech was slurred and his breath smelled of alcohol.'

In each of the above the witness is giving his opinion on matters within his personal knowledge and experience that do not require special expertise or training. The rule provides a convenient way of allowing a witness to convey a number of facts that led him to form that opinion. If the witness was not permitted to give evidence in this way he would have to list all the specific facts that led to him to draw these conclusions. This would be a laborious and time-consuming way of putting the evidence before the court. Also, without granting this concession, it might not be possible for the court to hear potentially relevant evidence that lies exclusively within the witness's knowledge and experience. In the Seventeenth Report of the Law Reform Committee, *Evidence of Opinion and Expert Evidence*, Cmnd 4489 (1970) the rationale for the rule was described in this way:

> Unless opinions, estimates and inferences which men make in their daily lives reach without conscious ratiocination as a result of what they perceive with their physical senses were treated in the law of evidence as if they were statements of fact, the witnesses could find

themselves unable to communicate to the judge an accurate impression of the events they were seeking to describe.

In modern criminal cases the most common example of this type of evidence relates to a witness's opinion about the identity of the accused, see examples below.

Whilst the admission of non-expert opinion evidence is largely a matter of judicial discretion to be exercised on the particular facts of each case, examples of the range of matters on which non-expert opinion evidence is admissible was provided by Lord MacDermott CJ in *Sherrard v Jacob* [1965] NI 151 CA. These include:

- the identification of handwriting, persons and things;
- a person's apparent age;
- the bodily plight or condition of a person, including death and illness;
- the emotional state of a person including whether he or she was distressed, angry or affectionate;
- the condition of things including whether it was worn or shabby, used or new;
- certain questions of value; and
- estimates of speed and distance.

As an application of the rule in action consider the following cases.

R v Deenik [1992] Crim LR 578

Deenik was convicted of being knowingly concerned with the importation of cannabis resin. Whilst being interviewed by customs officers, Deenik was overheard by another officer who identified his voice as that of a person she had spoken to by telephone when she was masquerading as the wife of a co-accused. At the trial, the witness was permitted to state that in her opinion she recognised the defendant's voice as belonging to the person she had spoken to on the telephone. The defendant was convicted and appealed. In dismissing the appeal, the Court of Appeal held that the evidence identifying the accused's voice was admissible and considerations of the manner in which the officer had heard the evidence were relevant in deciding the weight to be accorded to the evidence and not its admissibility.

Doe d Mudd v Suckermore (1837) 7 LJQB 33

The witness was allowed to give his opinion about the identity of the handwriting of someone who was known to him.

The position is now governed by section 8 of the Criminal Procedure Act 1865 which provides that:

> Comparison of a disputed writing with any writing proved to the satisfaction of the judge to be genuine shall be permitted to be made by witnesses; and such writings, and the evidence of witnesses respecting the same, may be submitted to the court and jury as evidence of genuineness or otherwise of the writing in dispute.

For the rule to apply the witness must be acquainted with the defendant's writing and will be liable to be cross-examined on the issue. The witness's acquaintance with the defendant's writing may have come about in a number of ways, by, for example, the witness receiving correspondence from the defendant or where he has seen the writing in other circumstances. Whilst section 8 does not expressly require that the comparison should be made by an expert, in *R* v *Tilley* [1961] 1 WLR 1309, the Court of Criminal Appeal held that a jury should not be left on its own to decide questions of disputed handwriting without the assistance of expert evidence – although this rule may be relaxed according to the facts of the particular case. Other examples include:

R v Beckett (1913) 8 Cr App R 204

The accused was charged with maliciously damaging a plate glass window worth more than £5. The value of the window was an essential ingredient in the offence, and, at the trial, the fact was proven by an assistant superintendent of the post office who testified as to the window's value. The Court of Appeal upheld the accused's conviction on the ground that the witness was permitted to give his personal opinion about the window's value.

R v Davies [1962] 3 All ER 97

The accused was charged with a drink/driving offence and at the trial, a lay witness had been permitted to state that he had formed the impression that the accused had been drinking. On the facts, the Courts-Martial Appeal Court held that such testimony was admissible as it was within the witness's personal knowledge and the inference the witness had drawn was not a matter that required expertise provided the witness described the facts which had formed the basis for his opinion.

The line drawn between what is an admissible statement of opinion and inadmissible opinion is not always easy to identify. In *R* v *Davies* above, whilst it was permissible for the witness to state to the court that he had formed the impression that the accused had been drinking, the Courts-Martial Appeal Court suggested that the witness would not have been allowed to go on to state that in his opinion the accused was too drunk to drive as such an assessment would have to be made by an expert witness.

ADMISSION OF EXPERT EVIDENCE IN CRIMINAL PROCEEDINGS

The second exception to the general rule about the admissibility of opinion evidence in criminal proceedings relates to expert evidence. Due to the complex nature of many issues that arise during the modern criminal trial, the court may need the assistance of an expert to help it to form an opinion on the facts of the case. Put simply, the opinion evidence of an expert witness will be admissible in criminal proceedings on an issue that goes beyond the ordinary competence of the court and is necessary to help the court reach a decision on the facts of the case. The phrase the 'ordinary competence of the court' means the ordinary knowledge of the fact finder – the jury or the magistrates. It is for the judge or the magistrates' adviser to decide on the facts of the case whether expert evidence is required.

In recent years the role of the expert witness in the criminal justice system has come under close scrutiny, as has also the role of the expert in the adversarial system. During the 1970s and 1980s, a number of high profile 'miscarriages of justice' were attributed, in part, to flawed expert evidence either through the undue reliance on scientifically unreliable methods or because of the expert's misperception of his role in the prosecution process. The most significant case involved Judith Ward (see *R* v *Ward* [1993] 2 All ER 577) where the Court of Appeal identified as one of the reasons for the appellant's 'unsafe' conviction was the role taken by the forensic scientists who improperly regarded their primary responsibility as helping the police to convict the alleged perpetrator of the offence rather than acting in an impartial, neutral way in assisting the court to reach its decision. A common tendency was to withhold disclosing to the defence, scientific and other forensic evidence that may have undermined the prosecution case or assisted the defence case. The Crown Court (Advance Notice of Expert Evidence) Rules 1987 (SI 1987 No 716) and the Magistrates' Courts (Advance Notice of Expert Evidence) Rules 1997 (SI 1997 No 705) now require both the prosecution and the defence to make a full disclosure of their expert evidence before trial. The rules supplement the prosecution's general duty of disclosure of all scientific evidence that it has in its possession.

In the context of expert evidence, another concern is that the rapid advances in scientific and technological innovation have placed new investigative techniques based on forensic science and DNA evidence in the public domain. This has led to a heightened public expectation that the application of these new methods of crime detection will lead to a dramatic increase in conviction rates. In practice, however, the public's perception is based more on media hype rather than the use of sophisticated forensic science being a common feature of the day-to-day investigation of criminal offences. In the Report by the Comptroller and Auditor General: *The Forensic Science Service* (HC 689, 1997–98), it was noted that forensic science is only used in 1.7% of notifiable offences. The under-utilisation of this potentially valuable resource is partly attributed to the finite resources that are available to all police forces as well as the common pattern in the detection of many crimes where the suspect's identity is known by the police or where the suspect is arrested at the scene of the crime and therefore the assistance of forensic science is not always required. There is no doubt, however, that where DNA evidence is available, it has become a potent weapon as part of the prosecution's evidence at trial.

The issues on which expert evidence may be required

The admission of expert evidence has long been recognised in English law, but Saunders J's comments in *Buckley v Rice-Thomas* (1554) 1 Plowd 118 confirm that it is not possible to provide an exhaustive list of the issues on which expert evidence may be heard. Whilst in *R v Clarke* [1995] 2 Cr App R 425, the Court of Appeal said there were no closed categories as regards what expert evidence may be placed before the jury, the following areas of expertise are often required by the court to assist in the decision-making process. A useful classification of the types of forensic evidence is provided by Ede and Shepherd in *Active Defence* (see Further reading below) in the following ways:

Forensic evidence from a natural (biological) source – includes expert testimony about the origin and type of samples of:

- pathology;
- hair;
- textile fibres;
- bloodstains on clothing and weapons;
- semen;

- saliva;
- urine;
- DNA evidence;
- fingerprints;
- ear prints; and
- blood splattering.

Evidence of this type may establish a link between the accused and the victim at the scene of the crime. This type of evidence is appropriate in cases of murder, manslaughter, rape and non-fatal offences against the person.

Forensic evidence from a non-biological source – includes expert testimony about the origin and type of samples of:

- paint;
- wood;
- glass;
- footprints;
- oil;
- tyre prints; and
- skid marks.

Evidence of this type is most likely to be heard in, for example, a burglary offence where the accused broke into the victim's home or other property, or in a 'hit and run' offence, where oil stains found on the victim's person may be analysed to compare with the type of oil used in the accused's vehicle. In *R v Abadom* [1983] 1 WLR 126, the defendant was charged with robbery and fragments of glass were found imbedded in his shoes. The fragments were thought to come from a window that had allegedly been broken during the robbery. At the trial, an expert witness was permitted to give evidence that the glass samples found in the defendant's shoes had an identical refracted index with the glass from the broken window.

Expert evidence on other issues – includes:

- psychiatric evidence about the defendant's state of mind at the time of the commission of the alleged offence and at the trial;
- psychological evidence about the state of the defendant's mind at the time of the commission of the alleged offence and at the time of the trial;
- analysis of documentary evidence;
- analysis of handwriting;
- interpretation of video evidence;
- voice identification;
- facial mapping;
- ballistic evidence;
- accident investigation;
- the value of property;
- the literary merit of an obscene book;
- the purpose of equipment found at a drug dealer's home; and
- issues of foreign law.

Who is an expert?

It is for the court to decide whether a witness is qualified to give expert evidence. In most modern cases the witness's competence to give evidence as an expert is decided by the court examining the witness's qualifications and professional experience. The party calling the witness has the legal burden of proving the witness's competence to testify as an expert. For example, a psychiatrist or a psychologist will provide evidence to the court of his qualifications and relevant experience to establish his expertise by questions put to him at the beginning of his evidence-in-chief. It is not always necessary for the witness to be formally qualified in the subject about which he is required to give his opinion.

R v Silverlock [1894] 2 QB 766

A solicitor was permitted to give expert opinion evidence on handwriting. He had no formal qualifications in the subject but had studied it as a hobby for some years and had also gained some relevant experience in his working life. In being satisfied of the witness's competence, the court stated that in order to give expert evidence a witness must, first, be skilled in the relevant area, and secondly, have adequate knowledge in the area of his expertise.

Affirming the defendant's conviction, Lord Russell CJ stated:

> There is no decision which requires that the evidence of a man who is skilled in comparing handwriting, and who has formed a reliable opinion from past experience, should be excluded because his experience has not been gained in the way of his business. It is, however, really unnecessary to consider this point; for it seems ... in the present case that the witness was not only peritus, but was peritus in the way of his business.

A similar conclusion was reached in *Ajami* v *Comptroller of Customs* [1954] 1 WLR 1405, in which a banker with 24 years' experience of Nigerian banking law gave evidence as a foreign law expert. The same two-stage test was applied in the more recent case of *R* v *Clare and Peach* [1995] 2 Cr App R 333 where the Court of Appeal held that a witness could become qualified as an expert through his experience at work. In *R* v *Clare and Peach* a police officer who had made a lengthy study of a poor quality video which the prosecution suggested showed the defendants committing a number of public order offences was allowed to give evidence about what, in his opinion, was occurring on the videotape. The police officer had acquired his expertise by viewing the video 40 times in stop and slow motion.

Conversely, there will be some situations where a witness with relevant academic or professional qualifications will not be considered to be competent to give expert evidence. In *R* v *Inch* (1990) 91 Cr App R 51, the Courts-Martial Appeal Court ruled that a medical orderly who had experience in the treatment of cuts and lacerations should not have been permitted to have given his opinion that the victim's wound was the result of a blow from an instrument and was not consistent with a clash of heads as the defence had submitted. The court ruled that the evidence should have been given by a witness who was properly qualified to give a medical opinion.

The expert's methodology

An issue closely related to the competence of a witness to give expert evidence is whether the methodology employed by the witness in reaching a conclusion on the facts of the case is well respected in his field of study. In the past, the courts have taken a relatively relaxed attitude to the academic or scientific rigour adopted by the expert by allowing the fact finder to give appropriate weight to the evidence or to ignore it altogether if there is other evidence that conflicts with it. For example, in *R v Robb* (1991) 93 Cr App R 161, an experienced lecturer in phonetics, who also held an PhD in the subject, gave evidence that in his opinion the voices he had heard on two different tapes was the voice of the same person. The court decided that the evidence was correctly admitted even though the methodology he had employed in coming to his conclusion was not generally respected in the field of phonetics. In an important recent case the Court of Appeal appears to be taking a more stringent line with regard to admitting expert evidence where it was based on a doubtful methodology.

R *v* Gilfoyle [2001] 2 Cr App R 5

In June 1992 the body of the appellant's pregnant wife, P, was found hanging in the garage of their home. At the appellant's trial for murder it became apparent that either P had killed herself or she had been murdered by her husband. The appellant did not adduce any evidence and he was convicted of his wife's murder. After unsuccessfully appealing against his conviction to the Court of Appeal, the case was later referred to the Criminal Cases Review Commission. At this stage the appellant sought to admit fresh evidence by a distinguished psychologist, whose main area of expertise was the systematic analysis of human behaviour in order to determine the dominant strands within that personality. In 1993 he had prepared a report that expressed the view that it was unlikely that P had committed suicide. At the original trial, the prosecution had sought to get the evidence admitted but it had been ruled as inadmissible. In August 1997 the witness had written to the appellant's solicitors stressing that at the time of his report in 1993, he was unaware of certain factors relating to P, and said that a much more thorough psychological report should be prepared. In a later report, written in 2000 and sent to the Criminal Cases Review Commission, he concluded that his initial report had been wrong and that there was convincing support for the proposition that P had killed herself.

In dismissing the appeal and declining to admit the fresh evidence, the Court of Appeal stated that the psychologist's evidence was not of the type of expert evidence that would be put before the court for a number of reasons:

1   He had never previously carried out the task that he had set himself, although that alone would not necessarily have been fatal to the admissibility of the evidence.
2   There were no criteria by which the quality of his opinions could be tested in that there was no substantial body of academic writing approving his methodology. The witness had made speculative conclusions that were not the stuff of which expert evidence was made.
3   The expert's views were based on one-sided information, most notably from the appellant and his family, who had not given evidence at the trial.
4   It was doubted that assessing levels of happiness or unhappiness were matters that properly should be decided by an expert. None of the points made by the expert about the suicide note were outside the experience of the jury.
5   Authorities from England, Canada and the United States pointed against the admission of such evidence.
6   If evidence of this kind were admissible in relation to the deceased, there could be no reason in principle for the rejection of evidence psychologically profiling a defendant. The roads of inquiry that would be opened up would be unending and of little or no help to the jury.

As we noted in *Gilfoyle* above, the decision in *R v Robb* (see also *R v Clarke* [1995] 2 Cr App R 425; *R v Stockwell* (1993) 97 Cr App R 260) reflected the courts' relaxed attitude to the admission of expert evidence which may be based on a less than rigorous methodology. This has led to a degree of uncertainty in the application of the standards to be met in some cases and therefore the Court of Appeal's decision in *R v Gilfoyle* is to be welcomed. Two factors were relevant to the court's rejection of the psychologist's evidence in *Gilfoyle*. First, whilst the report was relevant to an issue before the court, ie the cause of the victim's death, the expert witness had no direct expertise in the specific area of study – the carrying out of psychological autopsies. This clearly jeopardised his competence, as a matter of law to give expert evidence and therefore, on this basis, the Court of Appeal considered the psychologist's evidence to be irrelevant. A second related issue was the soundness of the scientific methodology that formed the basis of the psychologist's opinions. In his judgment Lord Justice Rose stated that 'his [the psychologist's] reports identify no criteria by reference to which the Court could test the quality of his opinions: there is no data base comparing real and questionable suicides and there is no substantial body of academic writing approving his methodology'. The court also referred to a number of English and North American authorities which pointed against the admission of such evidence. In the United States the guiding principle was found in *Frye v United States* 293 F 1013 (1923), which stated that evidence based on a developing new brand of science is not admissible until accepted by the scientific community as being able to provide accurate and reliable opinions, an approach that was also advocated in the English case of *R v Strudwick and Merry* (1993) 99 Cr App R 326. Therefore, in the present case the expert should have followed the advice of Lord President Cooper in *Davie v Edinburgh Magistrates* 1953 SC 34, by furnishing the court with 'the necessary scientific criteria for testing the accuracy of their conclusions, so as to enable the judge or jury to form their own independent judgment by the application of these criteria to the facts proved in evidence'. In failing to provide the necessary criteria by which the court could test the quality of the evidence or by failing to prove a database of comparable material against which to measure it and the lack of a substantial body of academic writing approving the methodology, the psychologist's report was inadmissible.

Proof of facts on which the expert's opinion is based

The facts on which the expert's opinion is based must be proved by admissible evidence. In *R v Turner* [1975] QB 834, Lord Justice Lawton stated:

> Before a court can assess the value of an opinion it must know the facts upon which it is based. If the expert has been misinformed about the facts or has taken irrelevant facts into consideration or has omitted to consider relevant ones, the opinion is likely to be valueless. In our judgment, counsel calling an expert, should in examination-in-chief ask his witness to state the facts upon which his opinion is based.

In some cases the expert will be able to prove the facts himself, where for instance he visited the scene of a burglary or examined the body of a homicide victim. However, in many cases the expert will not have the necessary knowledge as he did not visit the crime scene or examine the victim's body. This will not render the expert's evidence inadmissible but it will be necessary to put before the court other admissible evidence to prove these facts, which will normally be the evidence of other witnesses. For example, at a trial for murder, where the defence claim that the victim's wounds were self-inflicted, a witness, who had seen the deceased's body, may be asked to describe the wounds. It would then be open for the defence to call a surgeon who had not seen the body to give evidence of his opinion about how the victim had died, ie whether the wounds were self-inflicted or caused by a third party (*R* v *Mason* (1911) 7 Cr App R 67).

In forming his opinion, an expert is entitled to refer to other experts in the field and may refer to research papers, tests, experiments and other relevant matters. An issue that is commonly raised is that the expert in a criminal case cannot prove the facts upon which his opinion is based including where he refers to other work in the field. A strict interpretation of this approach would offend the hearsay rule, which is considered in detail in Chapters 12, 13 and 14. However, as a concession to the expert's role, the witness is entitled to rely on such facts as part of the process of forming his opinion and will not be subject to the hearsay rule as other witnesses would be. This point was raised in *R* v *Abadom* below.

R v Abadom [1983] 1 WLR 126

The defendant was charged with robbery and an important part of the prosecution case was whether fragments of glass found imbedded in the defendant's shoes had come from a window that had allegedly been broken during the robbery. At the trial, the expert gave evidence that based upon his personal analysis, the glass samples found in the defendant's shoes had an identical refracted index with the glass from the broken window. Having consulted unpublished statistics compiled by the Home Office Central Research Establishment, which showed that the index occurred in only 4% of all glass samples investigated, in his opinion there was a very strong likelihood that the glass in the shoes came from the window. The defendant was convicted and on appeal argued that the statistics were inadmissible as hearsay since the expert had no knowledge of the analysis on which the statistics had been based.

The Court of Appeal dismissed the appeal on the ground that the primary facts – the indices of the glass samples – had been proved by the expert by his own analysis of the glass samples – and that once the primary evidence on which an opinion is based is proven by admissible evidence, an expert is entitled to draw on the work of other experts in drawing his own conclusions. This did not involve a breach of the hearsay rule. A similar conclusion was reached in *R* v *Bradshaw* (1986) 82 Cr App R 79, where the issue at trial was the defence of diminished responsibility, it was held that whilst the doctors could not state what the accused had told them of his past symptoms as evidence of the existence of these symptoms, as this would offend the hearsay rule, they were permitted to give evidence about what the accused had told them which formed the basis of their conclusions about his mental condition.

Expert evidence required as a matter of law

Expert evidence will be admitted to assist the court on those issues that go beyond the court's ordinary competence and experience. In some instances, Parliament has specified that expert evidence will be required as a matter of law to prove an issue before the court. Consider the following two examples where Parliament has required expert evidence from two witnesses to confirm the defendant's state of mind satisfies the legal definition of insanity.

Criminal Procedure (Insanity and Unfitness to Plead) Act 1991, section 1

Section 1(1) of the Criminal Procedure (Insanity and Unfitness to Plead) Act 1991 provides:

> A jury shall not return a special verdict under section 2 of the Trial of Lunatics Act 1833 (acquittal on ground of insanity) except on the written or oral evidence of two or more registered medical practitioners at least one of whom is duly approved.

Criminal Procedure (Insanity) Act 1964, section 4

Section 4 of the Criminal Procedure (Insanity) Act 1964 provides that the issue of whether an accused is fit to be tried shall not be made by the jury except under section 4(6) on the 'written or oral evidence of two or more registered medical practitioners at least one of whom is duly approved'.

Expert evidence necessary to prove a fact in issue

In a number of other enactments Parliament has recognised that expert evidence may be necessary to assist the court in deciding a fact in issue.

The defence of 'public good'

Expert evidence may be heard where the accused puts forward the defence of 'public good' under section 4 of the Obscene Publications Act 1959.
   Section 4 provides that:

> (1) Subject to subsection (1A) of this section a person shall not be convicted of an offence ... if it is proved that publication of the article in question is justified as being for the public good on the ground that it is in the interests of science, literature, art or learning, or of other objects of general concern.
> (2) It is hereby declared that the opinion of the experts as to literary, artistic, science or other merits of an article may be admitted in any proceedings under this Act either to establish or to negative the said ground.

The effect of section 4(2) is that an expert's opinion may be heard by the court on the publication's literary, artistic or scientific merit in deciding whether the defence of 'public good' applies.

Admission of expert evidence as a matter of judicial discretion

The decision whether expert evidence is required and what weight will be attached to the evidence is a matter for the judge to decide on the particular facts and circumstances of each case. It is obviously important that the exercise of the discretion to admit expert evidence is taken on the correct grounds and its admission will only be lawful where the sole purpose is to assist the court in deciding an issue that is beyond its ordinary competence and experience. Expert evidence should not be admitted on an issue about which the court is capable of forming its own opinion. This important distinction was identified by the Court of Appeal in R v *Turner* below.

R v Turner [1975] 1 QB 834

Turner was charged with murdering his girlfriend by battering her to death with a hammer. He claimed that he had been provoked by her because she had been unfaithful and was pregnant with another man's child. The defence wished to adduce psychiatric evidence which suggested that the depth of the defendant's relationship with the victim was such that her admission of infidelity was likely to cause an explosive outburst of rage, and that the defendant's anger and grief was consistent with his personality. In upholding the trial judge's decision not to admit this evidence, the Court of Appeal stated that:

> If on the proven facts a judge or jury can form their own conclusion without help, then the opinion of the expert is unnecessary. In such a case if it is dressed up in scientific jargon it may make judgment more difficult. The fact that an expert has impressive scientific qualifications does not by that fact alone make his opinion in matters of human nature or behaviour within the limits of normality any more hopeful than that of the jurors themselves; but there is a danger that they may think it does.

In practice, the distinction referred to in R v *Turner* between questions of opinion and questions of fact is not always easy to ascertain – although in the context of expert evidence it is a vital distinction, as where the issue is a question of fact, that is a matter exclusively for the fact finders to decide from their own personal knowledge and experience. Where the issue is classified as an opinion, expert evidence may be properly admitted to assist the fact finder to decide the issue. An area where this important distinction has become clouded over the years is in relation to the admission of expert evidence to assist the court to decide an issue about an aspect of the defendant's state of mind.

Expert evidence and the defendant's state of mind

Where it is submitted that the defendant (or a witness) is suffering from a medically recognised mental illness or abnormality, this is an issue that goes beyond the ordinary competence of the court and expert evidence will be admitted to assist the court in deciding whether the condition existed or not. Consider the following cases:

R v Holmes [1953] 1 WLR 686

Expert evidence was admitted to assist the court to decide whether the accused was suffering from a disease of the mind within the *M'Naghten* Rules.

Toohey v Commissioner of Police of the Metropolis [1965] AC 595

Expert evidence was correctly admitted as to whether the accused had a mental disability that might render him incapable of giving evidence.

R v Bailey (1961) 66 Cr App R 31

When he was 17 the appellant met a young girl of 16 and apparently for no reason battered the girl to death. At trial he pleaded diminished responsibility and called three doctors to substantiate that plea. All three doctors gave evidence that at the time of the offence they considered that the appellant was suffering from an abnormality of the mind; that the abnormality was induced by disease, namely epilepsy and that the appellant's mental condition had been impaired. Whilst the Crown advocate cross-examined the doctors, the prosecution did not call medical evidence to contradict the medical witnesses nor was it suggested that there was any other evidence that would justify the jury coming to a conclusion other than that given by the medical witnesses.

R v Dix (1982) 74 Cr App 306

The admission of expert evidence in proving the defence of diminished responsibility was considered by the Court of Appeal. The court stated that whilst section 2 of the Homicide Act 1957 did not specifically require expert evidence to be adduced in cases involving diminished responsibility, it becomes a practical necessity if the defence is run at trial.

R v Silcott; R v Braithwaite; R v Raghip [1991] *The Times*, 9 December

Raghip was aged 19 but was of low IQ and had the reading age and functioning of a ten-year-old child. Raghip and the other two defendants were convicted for the murder of PC Blakelock during the Broadwater Farm riots which took place in October 1985. Their convictions were based on their admissions made in police interviews during which they were denied legal advice. In allowing his appeal against conviction, the Court of Appeal held that expert psychological or psychiatric evidence should have been admitted to show that Raghip was of lower than average intelligence and highly susceptible and that he suffered from a mental disorder that affected the reliability of his confession.

Hill v Baxter [1958] 1 QB 277

Expert evidence was permitted to establish the defence of automatism.

R v Smith [1979] 1 WLR 1445

The defendant was charged with murder. At his trial, the defence submitted that the accused stabbed the victim whilst he was sleepwalking in a state of automatism. The prosecution, in order to prove that the issue of automatism had only recently been conceived by the defence, sought to introduce evidence of the interviews that had taken place between the accused and two psychiatrists who had interviewed the defendant whilst he had been in custody. The defence submitted that as there was no question that the defendant had been suffering from diminished responsibility or insanity, the issue of automatism should have been left to the jury to decide from their own knowledge and experience. The Court of Appeal rejected this argument by stating that the type of automatism in question was not a condition that was within a juror's ordinary knowledge and experience and that, in order to decide the issue properly, the assistance of an expert was required.

The decision in R v *Smith* provides a useful explanation of the rationale for correctly allowing expert evidence to be heard. The key issue is that where fact finders are incapable of forming an opinion about an issue from their own knowledge and experience, expert evidence will be allowed. Where, conversely, the jurors are regarded as being capable of deciding an issue from their own knowledge and experience, expert evidence is deemed unnecessary. Some examples follow:

R v Turner [1975] QB 834

At his trial on a charge of murder, the defence wished to call a psychiatrist to give evidence on the issue of the accused's propensity to be provoked arsing out of the deep emotional relationship he had formed with the deceased that would have caused him to explode into a blind rage when told of her infidelity. The Court of Appeal, in upholding the trial judge's decision, stated that this was an issue on which expert evidence should not be heard as it was an issue that the jurors were capable of forming an opinion about from their 'ordinary human experience'.

R v Chard (1972) 56 Cr App R 268

The Court of Appeal approved the trial judge's refusal to permit the defence to call an expert to give evidence about the accused's intent to kill or to cause grievous bodily harm. In giving the judgment of the court, Roskill LJ stated that had the accused been suffering from insanity or diminished responsibility, it would have been appropriate for the medical evidence to have been heard. However, the issue of intention was entirely a matter that the jury could form its own opinion about without the need for expert evidence.

R v Masih [1986] Crim LR 395

The accused, who was charged with rape, did not suffer from a psychiatric illness but had an IQ of 72, which was just above the level of subnormality at 69. At the trial, the defence unsuccessfully applied to the trial judge to call a psychiatrist to assist the court on the issue of the defendant's state of mind, ie whether the accused was capable of knowing that the victim was not consenting or that he was reckless as to whether she was consenting. In upholding the exercise of the trial judge's discretion, the Court of Appeal held that provided the accused was above the level of subnormality it was not appropriate for an expert to be called unless the accused was suffering from a recognisable psychiatric condition.

R v Wood [1990] Crim LR 264

The accused was charged with murder and raised the partial defence under section 4 of the Homicide Act 1957 of acting in pursuance of a suicide pact. In supporting his defence and raising an analogy with diminished responsibility, the defence unsuccessfully attempted to introduce expert evidence to show that he suffered from a personality disorder. In upholding the trial judge's decision, the Court of Appeal stated that once the killing had been proved, the questions for the jury were questions of fact in deciding whether, first, the accused was acting in pursuance of a suicide pact and, secondly, whether the accused had an intention to die in the pact. As the 1957 Act did not introduce any medical or mental tests to assist the jury in deciding the issue, this was merely a question of fact that should be decided by the jury in the same way as other issues of fact.

Expert evidence and DNA samples

The admission of DNA evidence is undoubtedly the major modern advance in the scientific investigation of crime. DNA is the material in which genetic information is stored and passed from generation to generation. With the exception of identical twins, the DNA of an individual is unique. It is therefore possible for a human cell taken from samples of blood, saliva, semen or hair found at the scene of the crime to be compared from a sample (usually a mouth swab) taken from a person suspected of a crime. This will identify the individual's DNA or 'genetic fingerprint'. Where there is a match between the samples, there clearly is cogent evidence to link the accused with the offence charged. Whilst in law there is no requirement that prevents an accused from being convicted on the basis of DNA evidence alone, in most cases it will be supported by other independent evidence.

The technicalities associated with the interpretation of an accused's genetic fingerprint is clearly an issue that goes beyond the ordinary competence of the court and is a matter requiring expert evidence. However, the appropriate method to be adopted by the expert in explaining and evaluating the probative value of DNA evidence has caused the courts some problems. First, the courts are vigilant to ensure that the expert witness does not usurp the function of the fact finders by expressing a view on the accused's culpability even where there is a match between the DNA samples. Secondly, the expert must explain the scientific evidence in such a way that the fact finders understand it. As a safeguard against plunging the fact finders into an incomprehensible morass of theory and technicalities, some models of statistical analysis such as the Bayes Theorem should not be adopted as it is considered to be too complex for 'lay' people to understand, see *R v Adams* [1996] 2 Cr App 467. In the Court of Appeal decision of *R v Doheny and Adams* [1997] 1 Cr App R 369, Lord Justice Phillips gave an important judgment in which he set out the procedure to be adopted by the expert when explaining to the fact finders the conclusions to be drawn from a match between DNA profiles. His Lordship stated that the scientist who carried out the DNA profiling:

> ... will properly explain to the jury the nature of the match ('the matching DNA characteristics') between the DNA in the crime stain and the DNA in the blood sample taken from the defendant. He will properly, on the basis of empirical statistical data, give the jury the random occurrence ratio – the frequency with which the matching DNA characteristics are likely to be found in the population at large. Provided that he has the necessary data, and the statistical expertise, it may be appropriate for him then to say how many people with the matching characteristics are likely to be found in the United Kingdom – or perhaps in a more limited relevant sub group, such as, for instance, the Caucasian, sexually active males in the Manchester area. This will often be the limit of the evidence which he can properly and usefully give. It will then be for the jury to decide, having regard to all the relevant evidence, whether they are sure that it was the defendant who left the crime stain, or whether it is possible that it was left by someone else with the same matching DNA characteristics.
>
> The scientist should not be asked his opinion on the likelihood that it was the defendant who left the crime stain, nor when giving evidence should he use terminology which may lead the jury to believe that he is expressing such an opinion.
>
> It has been suggested that it may be appropriate for the statistician to expound to the jury a statistical approach to evaluating the likelihood that the defendant left the crime stain, using a formula which gives a numerical probability weighting to other pieces of evidence which bear on that question. This approach uses what is known as the Bayes Theorem. In the case of *Adams (Denis)* [1996] 2 Cr App R 467 this Court deprecated this exercise ...

Lord Justice Phillips went on to state that where there is a statistical match between the crime stain and the other sample, the jury should be directed along the following lines:

> If you accept the scientific evidence called by the Crown, that indicates that there are probably only four or five white males in the United Kingdom from whom that semen stain could have come. The defendant is one of them. The decision you have to reach, on all the evidence, is whether you are sure that it was the defendant who left that stain or whether it is possible that it was one of that other small group of men who share the same DNA characteristics.

The law requires therefore that a positive match between a DNA sample found at the crime scene and a sample taken from the accused should not necessarily be equated with irrefutable evidence of the defendant's guilt. As we noted above, in most cases, matching DNA samples will only be one piece of evidence forming part of the prosecution case. The prosecution may have also have a fingerprint match or the evidence of a witness who has positively identified the suspect at the crime scene, and the defence in cross-examination has failed to undermine the probative value of that witness's testimony. Even though the technicalities of DNA will have to be explained to the jury or magistrates by an expert witness, in the end the fact finders will give appropriate weight to such evidence on the basis of their common sense knowledge of the world.

To illustrate two other areas of law where expert evidence may be admitted as a matter of judicial discretion, consider the following cases which deal with the admission of expert evidence in some prosecutions for obscenity, and then where expert evidence may be admitted to assist the court in cases involving issues of foreign law.

Expert evidence in cases of obscenity

In a prosecution under the Obscene Publications Act 1959, expert evidence may be heard on the issue of the publication's artistic or literary merit where the defence of 'public good' is raised. The admission of expert evidence on this issue is, however, an exception to the general rule, as the courts have consistently held in cases involving allegations of obscenity or indecency that this is a matter for the jury to decide without the assistance of expert evidence as illustrated by the following cases:

R v Anderson [1972] 1 QB 304

Lord Widgery confirmed that the issue of whether a publication was obscene was a question of fact to be determined by the jury without the assistance of expert evidence.

R v Stamford [1972] 2 QB 391

The accused was charged with an offence of despatching packets containing indecent articles through the post (Post Office Act 1953, section 11). The Court of Appeal held that whether the articles were indecent or obscene was a matter for the jury without the assistance of an expert. The members of the jury were capable of deciding the question of whether the material was indecent or obscene from their general experience of life.

DPP v Jordan [1977] AC 699

The defendant was charged with an offence under section 2(1) of the Obscene Publications Act 1959; he raised the defence of 'public good' under section 4 of that Act. The court ruled that section 4 did not extend to allowing opinion evidence to be heard as to whether the publication of the obscene material would be of therapeutic benefit to members of the public with certain sexual tendencies. According to Lord Wilberforce this was not an issue for an expert but was a matter for the jury to decide as representing the views of the 'ordinary' man.

A similar approach to *R v Jordan* was taken in *R v Sumner* [1977] Crim LR 614 where it was held on behalf of the defence that the prosecution could not be allowed to put expert evidence before the court that the publication of the obscene article would tempt young people to read it.

As exceptions to the general rule, in the following 'obscenity' cases, expert evidence was held to be properly admitted because the expert's evidence related to an issue that was not capable of being decided by the jury.

R v Skirving and Grossman [1985] QB 819

The defendants were charged with having an obscene article for publication for gain under the Obscene Publications Act 1959. The publication was a pamphlet entitled 'Attention Coke Users. Free Base. The Greatest Thing Since Sex', which contained detailed explanations about how to take cocaine to obtain the maximum effect. The Court of Appeal held that expert evidence detailing the effects of taking cocaine had been correctly admitted at the trial as the characteristics of cocaine and the effect it had on the user went beyond the competence and experience of the ordinary person as they would not be expected to know the effect of taking the drug.

DPP v A and BC Chewing Gum Ltd [1968] 1 QB 159

In a case involving the publication of allegedly obscene material directed at young children, the Divisional Court held that the magistrates had improperly prevented the prosecution from introducing expert evidence in child psychiatry as to the likely effect of the material on children as this was not an issue on which the magistrates were capable of deciding from their personal experience.

Expert evidence and issues of foreign law

The admission of evidence on issues of foreign law is governed by section 15 of the Administration of Justice Act 1920, which requires that expert evidence should be given unless the issue could be agreed between the parties or no issue is taken. In *R v Okolie* (2000) *The Times*, 16 June, at trial it became clear that the Crown had not instructed an expert to prove the essential elements of a criminal offence under German law and the court refused an application to adjourn. On appeal, the Court of Appeal held that expert evidence was required to prove an issue and the trial judge had been correct in refusing to agree to the adjournment.

Expert evidence and the ultimate issue rule

At common law a witness was not entitled to give his opinion on the 'ultimate' issue. The ultimate issue in a criminal case is the defendant's guilt or innocence of the charge laid against him. Historically, the reason for not permitting a witness to give an opinion on the ultimate issue was that it would usurp the function of the jury or the magistrates. However, in recent years, the courts have been less inclined to enforce the ultimate issue rule strictly, and it has become common practice for an expert to give his opinion on the ultimate issue. The main proviso to this practice is that the actual words the expert uses should be different from those used when the court considers the same matter. The Criminal Law Revision Committee (Eleventh Report, Cmnd 4991 (1972) at paragraph 268) confirmed that a strict interpretation of the common law rule was no longer recognised by the courts. A leading authority on the more pragmatic approach is *R v Stockwell* (1993) 97 Cr App R 260 where the defendant was charged with robbery, which he denied. The main point of contention between the parties was whether the accused was the man whose image had been captured on a poor quality security video. The trial judge permitted the prosecution to call an expert on facial mapping to state that on the basis of the measurements he had carried out on the security photograph and the comparison he had made with the defendant's facial features, there was strong support to say that the robber and the defendant were the same man. Dismissing the defendant's appeal against conviction, Lord Taylor CJ said that the rule was more a matter of form than substance. It was permissible for an expert to give his opinion on the ultimate issue such as identification, provided that the jury were directed that they were not obliged to accept the expert's evidence.

Procedural requirements for the admission of expert evidence in criminal proceedings

There was a common law duty on the prosecution at a trial on indictment to disclose to the defence any evidence that it had not been given advance notice of so as not to catch the defence by surprise at trial by adducing undisclosed evidence. In criminal proceedings it was not until 1987 that provision was made for the pre-trial disclosure of expert evidence. The Crown Court (Advance Notice of Expert Evidence) Rules 1987 (SI 1987 No 716) impose the requirement that any party to proceedings before the Crown Court should disclose to the other parties any expert evidence that he intends to use at the trial, and, if required, to provide the other party with a copy of the facts, test and mode of analysis that was used by the expert witness. Where pre-trial disclosure is not made, the party who seeks to adduce the evidence during the course of the trial would not be able to do so without the leave of the court. In *R v Ward* [1993] 2 All ER 577, the Court of Appeal suggested that whilst the 1987 Rules are helpful, they do not detract from the prosecution's general duty of disclosure. This comment was particularly apposite in *Ward*, as one of the successful grounds of appeal was that government scientists had deliberately withheld potentially important material, which they believed might harm the prosecution case. The pre-trial disclosure of evidence that might undermine the prosecution case or assist the defence case has been codified by the Criminal Procedure and Investigations Act 1996.

Whilst the 1987 Rules covered the admission of oral expert evidence, they did not go as far as the equivalent civil rules allowing the admission of expert evidence as hearsay. This deficiency was remedied by section 30 of the Criminal Justice Act 1988, which provides that with the leave of the court an expert's report shall be admissible as evidence in criminal proceedings, whether or not the person making it attends to give oral evidence in those proceedings. In exercising its discretion under the Act, the court shall consider the contents of the report; the reasons why it is proposed that the person making the report shall not give oral evidence; any risk, having regard in particular to whether it is likely to be possible to controvert statements in the report if the person making it does not attend to give oral evidence in the proceedings, that its admission or exclusion will result in unfairness to the accused or, if there is more than one, to any of them; and to any other circumstances that appear to the court to be relevant. These grounds are similar to the exercise of the court's discretion under sections 25 and 26 of the Criminal Justice Act 1988. Where the court allows the evidence to be admitted, evidence of any fact or opinion of which the person making it could have given oral evidence will be admissible as hearsay. A similar provision for the pre-trial disclosure of expert evidence in summary proceedings between the parties is provided by the Magistrates' Courts (Advance Notice of Expert Evidence) Rules 1997 (SI 1997 No 705).

Using expert evidence in criminal cases – practical steps

There are a number of practical issues that lawyers should consider when using an expert witness in a criminal case. It is important to check the expert witness's credentials and experience of giving evidence in court. Expert witnesses are expensive and should be instructed early on in a case. It is important that lawyer works with the expert. The lawyer needs to fully understand the analytical basis of the expert's conclusion. In the case of a forensic expert, the lawyer will clearly need to understand the scientific and statistical basis of the expert's opinion. As we have already noted, expert evidence has to be disclosed prior to trial which means that each party's expert ought to be aware of the other's contrary opinion. The advocate may need to work with his own expert to plan the questions that need to be asked of the opposing expert witness in order to undermine the accuracy of the witness's opinion or his credibility. It is important to remember that in some instances the underlying primary facts on which an expert's opinion is premised have firstly to be proved to the satisfaction of the fact finder before relying on the expert's opinion.

Reforming expert evidence

As with Lord Woolf's report on civil justice in England and Wales, the Criminal Courts Review Report prepared by Lord Justice Auld devoted considerable time to considering a number of issues relating to expert evidence in criminal cases (see paragraphs 129–151). Many of the report's proposals are based on the reforms that have already been successfully implemented in civil cases.

The first proposal recommends the establishment of a self-governing body to oversee the setting of standards and to maintain a register for forensic scientists of all disciplines. It is suggested that the Council for the Registration of Forensic Practitioners would be a strong candidate to play this unifying role. Members would be subject to a Code of Conduct and there would be procedures to deal with complaints of professional misconduct, poor performance or ill health. The new body would have the power to withdraw the expert's name from the register. Lord Justice Auld expresses the hope that the courts would regard entry on the register as an indicator of a witness's competence, subject to the court's power to decide whether a witness is competent to give expert evidence on the facts of the particular case. New Criminal Procedure Rules should contain an equivalent provision to rule 35.3 of the Civil Procedure Rules that an expert's overriding duty is to the court and not to the party instructing him. As a recognition of the expert's objectivity, any statement or report prepared by the witness should contain a written declaration that his overriding duty is to the court. The control of expert evidence in the case would lie with the court and such evidence would only be allowed where it is reasonably required to resolve important issues in the proceedings. As under the Civil Procedure Rules, the judge or the magistrates would be required to apply the provisions rigorously. Unlike in civil cases, however, a criminal court would not have the power to appoint or select an expert, although the parties would be encouraged to resolve the matter by the appointment of a single, joint expert. Where experts are appointed for each side, the prosecution and the defence would normally require their experts to meet before trial to identify those issues on which they agree and those issues on which they disagree. Lord Justice Auld recognises the importance of modern technology in speeding up the trial process and extends the practice and procedures relating to expert evidence in this respect. Practitioners are recommended to use video-conferencing for communicating and conferring with experts before trial. Continued development of national facilities to enable experts to give evidence by a video link is a further recommendation.

Further reading

Alldridge, P., 'Forensic Science and Expert Evidence' (1994) 21 Journal of Law and Society 136.

Auld, Lord Justice (2001) *A Review of the Criminal Courts of England and Wales*, www.criminal-courts-review.org.uk.

Cooke, G., 'Are We Still Mis-using DNA Evidence?' (2000) 3 Archbold News 4.

Forensic Science – Special Feature, July 2001, The Legal Executive.

Jackson, J.D., 'The Ultimate Issue Rule: One Rule Too Many' [1984] Crim LR 75.

Roberts, P., 'Forensic Science Evidence after Runciman' [1994] Crim LR 780.

Roberts, P. and Willmore, C. (1993) *The Role of Forensic Science Evidence in Criminal Proceedings*, Royal Commission on Criminal Justice Research Study No 11, HMSO.

Runciman of Doxford, Viscount (1993) *Report of the Royal Commission on Criminal Justice*, Cmnd 2263, HMSO.

Steventon, B. (1993) *The Ability to Challenge DNA Evidence*, Royal Commission on Criminal Justice Research Study No 9, HMSO.

Woolf MR, Lord (1996) *Access to Justice, Final Report*, HMSO.

Chapter 20

CHARACTER EVIDENCE RELEVANT TO GUILT

INTRODUCTION

This chapter is largely concerned with the admissibility and evidential relevance of the defendant's bad character. Bad character is not confined simply to the fact that the defendant has one or more previous convictions. It is much wider and embraces such things as the defendant's reputation or disposition to act in a certain way, as well as character traits, predilections, and obsessive tendencies. In practice, it is any conduct capable of showing the defendant in a bad light.

Case scenario

Andrew is charged with causing death by dangerous driving. He denies the offence. The prosecution alleges Andrew was driving his vehicle much too fast in a built-up, busy area. Prosecution witnesses estimate his vehicle was travelling between 60–70 mph in a 30 mph area before impact. Andrew's car hit two pedestrians, a father and his daughter, who were attempting to cross the road. They died instantly. In his evidence, Andrew maintains he was not driving at such an excessive speed and was keeping a proper lookout at all times. He alleges the accident was caused by the unknown driver of a white transit van who emerged from a side street into his path, causing him not to see the pedestrians until it was too late. Andrew is unable to locate any witnesses who saw the white van, although its possible presence on the road at the time of the offence is put to prosecution witnesses who were at the scene.

Is Andrew guilty or not guilty? Essentially, this is a case which will be decided by whether Andrew's word can be believed. Is it relevant that Andrew has two previous endorsements for speeding on his driving licence and a conviction for careless driving and that he failed to tell his car insurance company about any of them? Should the jury reach its decision without knowing about Andrew's past?

As the above scenario illustrates, it is wrong to suggest evidence of bad character has no logical relevance in determining a defendant's guilt. It is commonly perceived that a person with a history of offending or behaving in a particular way is more likely to act in conformity with his past conduct. However, the fact that the defendant happens to have previous convictions, or exhibits certain character traits, does not mean that he is automatically guilty of the offence currently charged. His previous convictions do nothing more than show that the defendant has a predisposition to commit crime. The key difficulty for the law of evidence is to decide how much probative value should attach to bad character when determining the defendant's guilt in relation to the offence charged.

The general rule in English law is that evidence of bad character will not be admitted for the specific purpose of proving the defendant is guilty of an offence simply because he has committed offences on a previous occasion. In *Maxwell* v *DPP* [1935] AC 309, Viscount Sankey regarded this approach as 'one of the most deeply rooted and jealously guarded principles of our law'.

One of the major justifications for excluding such evidence is said to be that the prejudicial effect of such evidence outweighs its true probative value. However, we shall see that where evidence of bad character is sufficiently probative of the defendant's guilt, it may be admitted under the similar fact evidence rule as part of the prosecution's case.

The general rule prohibiting the admission of evidence of bad character has a sound rationale. It protects the defendant against the risk of prejudice by the fact finder. Prejudice is likely to arise in two ways: 'reasoning prejudice' and 'moral prejudice'. The former, often described as an example of 'forbidden reasoning', relates to the danger that jurors and lay magistrates will attach too much weight to the defendant's character and therefore give insufficient weight to other evidence having a more direct bearing on the defendant's involvement in the offence. The latter relates to the danger that the fact finders' judgment will be based to some extent on their moral reaction to the information on the defendant's character. The jury might be tempted to conclude: 'He's done it loads of time before, never mind the evidence. He's obviously guilty and deserves to be punished'. If such prejudicial reasoning were permitted, the requirement that the prosecution prove the defendant's guilt beyond reasonable doubt would be diminished and the risk of an innocent person being convicted would correspondingly increase. Furthermore, if the prosecution were routinely allowed to refer to a defendant's previous convictions during the trial, the temptation on the part of the police not to investigate a crime properly would be ever present. The police might believe that any weaknesses in the case could be ignored, as the available evidence, coupled with the knowledge of the defendant's previous convictions, would be enough to satisfy the fact finder of the defendant's guilt beyond reasonable doubt.

The widely held perception that jurors would be prejudiced by knowledge of a defendant's past has been borne out by research with mock juries commissioned as part of the Law Commission's review of the law in relation to previous misconduct of defendants (see Law Commission Consultation Paper No 141, Appendix C). The research findings concluded that jurors were more likely to convict a defendant whom they knew to have previous convictions. This was particularly so where the defendant's prior convictions were both recent and similar to the current charge or related to offences involving children. There are obvious limitations in conducting research on mock jurors in that the dynamics under which real juries operate are somewhat different. The risk of prejudice identified in the research however cannot be ignored. A further striking illustration of prejudice is provided by the case of *R* v *Bills* (1995) *The Times*, 1 March. The jury returned a verdict of not guilty on a more serious charge of wounding with intent to cause grievous bodily harm under section 18 of the Offences Against the Person Act 1861, returning instead a guilty verdict on the lesser charge under section 20. Before passing sentence the judge listed the defendant's previous convictions which included offences of robbery, assault and violence. A juror then told the court usher that the wrong verdict had been given. The jury was allowed to reconvene and convicted the defendant on the section 18 charge instead. The Court of Appeal reinstated the jury's earlier verdict. It is not difficult to infer that had the jury been made aware of the defendant's record in the course of the trial it is most likely that he would have been convicted of the section 18 offence.

The jury research findings mentioned above have been give more credence by the results of further research on the effect of revealing aspects of a defendant's bad character conducted on real magistrates. The research findings are explained in the Law Commission's Report No 273 (see Appendix A of the report and below) on the admissibility of bad character evidence and are comparable with the earlier study. They show that magistrates are equally adversely influenced by the knowledge that a defendant has previous convictions of a specific kind.

The general common law prohibition against admitting evidence of bad character contrasts markedly to the position in Continental justice systems where it is considered the court's right to know as much as possible about the person it is sitting in judgment of. Such knowledge would, of course, include the defendant's previous convictions and evidence of his disposition to act in a certain way.

Evidence of character is an extensive topic comprising a large amount of material. This chapter concentrates on the admission of bad character evidence relevant to the defendant's guilt. Chapter 21 deals with the conceptually different matter of bad character evidence admitted under the Criminal Evidence Act 1898, the evidential relevance of which goes to the question of whether the defendant's word on oath should be believed. Chapter 21 also includes consideration of the evidential use that can be made of the defendant's good character.

In July 1996, the Law Commission published Consultation Paper No 141, *Evidence in Criminal Proceedings: Previous Misconduct of the Accused.* An extensive review of the current law was undertaken in the consultation paper which identified a number of valid criticisms of the current law and suggested a number of options for reform. This was followed by Law Commission Report No 273, *Evidence of Bad Character in Criminal Proceedings* in October 2001. The report contains the Law Commission's final recommendations for reform of the law relating to the admission of bad character evidence at trial and is accompanied by draft legislation. The proposals for reform are considered in detail in Chapter 21.

SIMILAR FACT EVIDENCE

It is imperative to realise that evidence of bad character admitted within the similar fact evidence rule is not admissible for the general purpose of showing the court that the defendant is a person likely to act in conformity with his past but for the specific purpose of proving the defendant's guilt. The admission of such evidence is exceptional, requiring a high degree of probative force. The probative value gained from knowledge of the defendant's past exceeds the prejudice it is likely to cause because such evidence points the finger of guilt emphatically at the defendant. The issue to which similar fact evidence is directed differs from case to case. Sometimes the evidence is capable of rebutting a defence advanced by an accused; in other cases it has been used to help establish the defendant's motive or it has proved the defendant's identity as the person responsible for committing the crime.

The relevance of similar fact evidence to the assessment of the defendant's guilt is well illustrated in the cases of *Makin v Attorney-General for New South Wales* [1894]

AC 57 and *R* v *Straffen* [1952] 2 QB 911. *Makin* v *Attorney-General for New South Wales*, saw the first attempt to explain the nature of the reasoning process used to justify the admission of similar fact evidence.

The *Makin* era

Makin *v* Attorney-General for New South Wales [1894] AC 57

The defendants were charged with the murder of a baby whose skeleton had been discovered in their back garden. There was no indication of how the baby had died – whether by accident, wilful harm or natural causes. In return for a small fee paid by the baby's mother, the baby had been taken into the care of the defendants as part of an informal adoption arrangement. A search of two former residences of the defendants revealed the remains of several more babies. All of the babies had been informally adopted in return for a small fee. The issue for the court was whether this knowledge was admissible to prove the defendants were guilty of the murder of the baby for which they had been charged. The probative value of the evidence stemmed from the fact that it did more than show the defendants in an unfavourable light. It showed them to have acted in a very systematic way, by adopting the babies and murdering them. How else could the grim discoveries be accounted for? Such conduct went a considerable way to proving the defendants were guilty of the murder of the child who was the subject of the indictment.

Lord Herschell explained the nature of the reasoning process in *Makin* thus:

> It is undoubtedly not competent for the prosecution to adduce evidence tending to show that the accused has been guilty of criminal acts other than those covered by the indictment, for the purpose of leading to the conclusion that the person is likely from his criminal conduct or character to have committed the offence for which he is being tried. On the other hand, the mere fact that the evidence adduced tends to show the commission of other crimes does not render it inadmissible if it be relevant to an issue before the jury, and it may be so relevant if it bears upon the question whether the acts alleged to constitute the crime charged in the indictment were designed or accidental, or to rebut a defence which would otherwise be open to the accused.

Lord Herschell's first statement of principle refers to the risk of 'forbidden' reasoning outlined in the introduction to this chapter, namely the idea that the defendant is more likely to be found guilty of the offence with which he is charged where it is made known that he has previous convictions. The jury is forbidden to have such knowledge on this basis because its relevance is highly dubious having regard to the prejudice it might cause.

The second statement of principle refers to the defendant's propensity to commit crimes in a specific way, which is capable of being adduced as evidence of guilt because it is particularly relevant to an issue before the jury. The case of *R* v *Straffen* below provides an example.

R *v* Straffen [1952] 2 QB 911

The defendant was charged with the murder of a young girl on Broadmoor. The child had been strangled. She had not been sexually assaulted and no attempt had been made to conceal her body. There were no witnesses to the incident. It so happened that the defendant, an inmate at Broadmoor mental hospital, had escaped his confinement and was at large at the time the murder was committed. The defendant had been detained in Broadmoor following his conviction for two earlier murders. In both instances, the murder victims had been young girls. Both had been strangled, neither had been sexually assaulted nor had there been an attempt to conceal their bodies. Could these two previous convictions be used in evidence against the defendant on the current charge of murder? The Court of Appeal was firmly of the view that they could. The defendant's modus operandi was akin to him leaving his fingerprints at the scene of the crime. The probative value of the evidence was hugely compelling. It could not be explained on the basis of coincidence. It effectively pointed the finger of guilt at the defendant.

Difficulties with the principles stated in *Makin* v *Attorney-General for New South Wales* began to emerge. Courts increasingly looked for an issue in the case to which they could ascribe specific relevancy of the sort described by Lord Herschell. In other words, the evidence had to be directed at disproving accident or mistake or establishing proof of design on the part of the defendant. *Makin* was misinterpreted as forbidding the admission of any evidence to show a criminal propensity. In fact, as many of the decided cases, including *R* v *Straffen* show, the propensity of the defendant to act in a certain way can constitute highly relevant evidence of guilt.

Evidence of propensity has been particularly troublesome for the courts in relation to crimes of a sexual nature. Is the possession of sexual material of a pornographic or paedophiliac nature relevant to show the accused's guilt on offences of a sexual nature or does it merely show the accused has an unhealthy interest in this kind of material?

Thompson *v* R [1918] AC 221

The defendant had been arrested in connection with offences of gross indecency with boys. The offences were committed in public toilets. A trap was sprung in that his victims agreed to meet him at the same place and time for the same purpose. On this occasion, however, they brought the police with them. The defendant maintained the boys were mistaken in their identification of him and this became the main issue in the trial. On searching the defendant's living accommodation the police had found a powder puff and photographs of naked boys. The trial judge admitted this evidence in support of the boys' identification of the defendant. The House of Lords affirmed that the judge had been right to do so, with two of their Lordships maintaining that the articles showed the defendant to have the same 'abnormal propensities' as the man who had committed the offences against the boys. There was little doubting that the articles constituted relevant evidence, as they went some considerable way towards disproving the notion that the boys had been mistaken in their identification. However, in an unfortunate statement, which had the effect for some time of singling out homosexual acts for special treatment under the similar fact evidence rule, Lord Sumner stated:

> A thief, a cheat, a coiner or housebreaker is only a particular specimen of the genus rogue, and, though no doubt each tends to keep to his own line of business, they all alike possess the by no means extraordinary mental characteristic that they propose somehow to get their living dishonestly. So common a characteristic is not a recognisable mark of the individual. Persons, however, who commit the offences now under consideration seek the habitual gratification of a particular perverted lust, which not only takes them out of the class of ordinary men gone wrong, but stamps them with the hallmark of a specialised and extraordinary class as much as if they carried on their bodies some physical peculiarity.

The desire to formalise the principles and to look for specific pigeonholes in which to place similar fact evidence led to criticism and a review of the law in the leading case of *DPP* v *Boardman* below.

The *Boardman* era

DPP *v* Boardman [1975] AC 421

The defendant was a headmaster at an all-boys public school. He was charged with the attempted buggery of one pupil and incitement to commit buggery with another. Each boy testified that the defendant had individually approached him on separate occasions in the school dormitory in the early hours of the morning. Each boy described on oath how the defendant had whispered to him and asked him to participate in the act of buggery. In both cases the defendant had made it clear that he wanted the boys to assume the active role in the buggery whilst he took the passive role. The defendant asserted his innocence at trial and claimed the boys were lying and acting in collusion.

The defendant pleaded not guilty to both charges and sought to have a separate trial in respect of each allegation. The trial judge refused. At the time, the rules requiring a mandatory corroboration warning in relation to the evidence of victims of sexual offences were in force. They have since been abolished. As a consequence of the trial judge's decision, the jury was directed that if it accepted the evidence of the one boy, it could use it to corroborate the evidence of the other. The defendant appealed on the basis that the trial judge was in error.

The House of Lords unanimously dismissed the defendant's appeal.

Before considering the judgment of the House of Lords in *DPP* v *Boardman* it is necessary to consider the procedural rules relating to the joinder of offences as they have an important role to play in the context of similar fact evidence.

Under rule 9 of the Indictment Rules 1971 (SI 1971 No 1253), charges may be joined in one indictment and therefore tried at the same time, providing the charges arise out of the same facts or form part of a series of offences of the same or similar character. In such cases the judge must warn the jury to consider the evidence in relation to each charge separately. The trial judge must make it abundantly clear that the jury must not use the evidence in relation to one of the charges to lend support to the evidence in relation to the other charge. Whether jurors are capable of performing such mental gymnastics is subject to considerable debate. The established exception to this rule, however, is where the evidence in relation to one charge is sufficiently similar to the evidence in relation to the second charge as to amount to similar fact evidence. In this situation, the jury may take the evidence in relation to one charge and use it to evaluate the evidence in relation to a second charge. This is what the jury were permitted to do in *DPP* v *Boardman*. In the trial judge's view there were sufficient similarities between the two charges to justify this.

In *DPP* v *Boardman*, the House of Lords redefined the reasoning used to justify the admission of similar fact evidence. Whilst *Makin* v *Attorney-General for New South Wales* established the relevancy of the defendant's bad character as the criterion for admitting similar fact evidence, *DPP* v *Boardman* clarified the degrees of relevance required. The House of Lords held that if the similar fact evidence had sufficient probative force and could avoid the 'forbidden reasoning', evidence of bad character was admissible to prove the defendant's guilt. The probative force of such evidence had to come from striking similarities between the defendant's previous conduct and his behaviour in the present offence.

> The basic principle must be that the admission of similar fact evidence (of the kind now in question) is exceptional and requires a strong degree of probative force. This probative

force is derived, if at all, from the circumstance that the facts testified to by the several witnesses bear to each other such a striking similarity that they must, when judged by experience and common sense, either all be true, or have arisen from a cause common to the
witnesses or from pure coincidence. (*per* Lord Wilberforce)

Lord Salmon explained the test for admitting such evidence in the following terms:

The test must be: is the evidence capable of tending to persuade a reasonable jury of the
accused's guilt on some ground other than his bad character and disposition to commit the
sort of crime with which he is charged? In the case of an alleged homosexual offence, just
as in the case of an alleged burglary, evidence which proves merely that the accused has
committed crimes in the past and is therefore disposed to commit the crime charged is
clearly inadmissible. It has, however, never been doubted that if the crime charged is committed in a uniquely or strikingly similar manner to other crimes committed by the accused
the manner in which the other crimes were committed may be evidence upon which a jury
could reasonably conclude that the accused was guilty of the crime charged. The similarity
would have to be so unique or striking that common sense makes it inexplicable on the
basis of coincidence.

In a vivid illustration of how the probative value might be ascribed to evidence of bad
character, Lord Hailsham gave the following, famous example:

For instance, whilst it would certainly not be enough to identify the culprit in a series of
burglaries that he climbed in through a ground floor window, the fact that he left the same
humorous limerick on the walls of the sitting room, or an esoteric symbol written in lip-
stick on the mirror, might well be enough. In a sex case, to adopt an example given in argument in the Court of Appeal, whilst a repeated homosexual act by itself might be quite
insufficient to admit the evidence as confirmatory of identity or design, the fact that it was
alleged to have been performed wearing the ceremonial head-dress of a Red Indian chief or
other eccentric garb might well in appropriate circumstances suffice.

The central issue in *DPP* v *Boardman* was whether the boys had lied and the evidence
to be admitted under the similar fact rule was directed purely at this issue. Their
Lordships' speeches clearly indicate it to have been a borderline case in terms of the
admissibility of similar fact evidence. There were just sufficient similarities in the
accounts of the two boys to give the probative value needed to justify the evidence in
relation to one charge being used to evaluate the evidence in relation to the other
charge. Was it coincidence that both boys had described exactly the same method of
approach by their headmaster, who expressed the desire to play the passive role? If
believed, such similarities in the boys' account of what happened took the events outside the realm of coincidence.

The decision in *DPP* v *Boardman* did little to clarify the law. The need to find 'striking similarities' in the evidence started to assume too much importance, leading to
relevant evidence of guilt being too easily excluded. Had the *Boardman* principles
been applied to the facts in *Thompson* v *R* above, the discovery of the powder puff
and indecent photographs of boys in the defendant's flat would not have satisfied the
striking similarity test. In *R* v *Scarrott* [1978] QB 1016, Lord Justice Scarman
redefined the rule by stressing that something more was needed than the repetition of
what he termed 'commonplace facts' in order to give similar fact evidence the
necessary degree of probative value.

Hallowed though by now the phrase 'strikingly similar' is it is no more than a label. Like all labels it can mislead ... Positive probative value is what the law requires, if similar fact evidence is to be admissible. Such probative value is not provided by the mere repetition of similar facts; there has to be some feature or features in the evidence sought to be adduced which provides a link – an underlying link as it has been called in some cases. The existence of such a link is not to be inferred from the mere similarity of facts which are themselves so commonplace that they can provide no sure ground for saying that they point to the commission by the accused of the offence under consideration.

The limitations of the *Boardman* and *Scarrott* approach are illustrated by the Court of Appeal's decision in *R v Beggs* below – a decision which Jenny McEwan in her book *Evidence and the Adversarial Process: The Modern Law*, regards as a denial of common sense.

R v Beggs (1990) 90 Cr App R 430

B was arrested on suspicion of murdering O by slitting his throat during the night. B and O, both male students, had met at a club and B had offered O a bed for the night. In interview B maintained O had made unwanted sexual advances to him during the night. When he would not desist, B had acted in self-defence by lashing out with a razor he always carried with him. Forensic evidence suggested the injury had been deliberately inflicted, requiring O's head to be pulled back. After an extensive police investigation five more counts of wounding were added to the murder indictment. In counts 1 and 2, the victim S, another student, told the police how on one occasion he had been living in the same house as B and had woken up to find B attending a wound on his leg. A penknife belonging to B was protruding from the mattress under which S had lain. B had persuaded him that the injury had been caused by a bedspring. On another occasion S had occupied the same bed-sit as B and had woken up one night to find a superficial laceration to his leg and a razor lying close by. B had denied all responsibility. He had pointed to two lacerations on the back of his own leg and suggested intruders had entered the room during the night.

On count 3, another victim R told the police how he had occupied a room in the same property as B and had been out drinking with B one evening. He awoke in the night to find a four-inch laceration to his calf. B denied any knowledge and once again suggested it was a bedspring. On count 4, L, another resident in the property, described how on one occasion he had been drinking with B. On retiring to his own bed-sit he awoke the next morning to find his duvet covered with blood caused by a large gash to his leg, necessitating 13 stitches. No weapon was ever found.

On count 5, B was alleged to have wounded M, a much older man at M's house.

The trial judge had allowed counts 1–5 to be joined with the murder count because he accepted the prosecution's submission under the similar fact evidence rule that the evidence was probative by rebutting B's claim that he had acted in self-defence in relation to the murder count. B was convicted of murder.

B's conviction was quashed in the Court of Appeal. Applying the tests propounded in *Boardman* and *Scarrott*, the Court of Appeal concluded there were far more striking dissimilarities between the various accounts than striking similarities. All the wounds had been inflicted on non-vulnerable parts of the body. In the case of O, the wound had been to the throat. There was no consistency in the choice of victim. In one instance it appeared that a razor blade had been used in another, a penknife. In some of the attacks it was not clear what weapon had been used. The Court of Appeal considered that the joinder of the wounding counts to the murder charge in order to rebut O's defence was in error as it could find no legal authority in which similar fact evidence had been used for such a purpose.

The law was once more reviewed in the decision of *DPP* v *P* [1991] 3 WLR 161. This case is now regarded as the modern, definitive statement of the grounds for justifying the admission of similar fact evidence.

The *DPP v P* era

DPP *v* P [1991] 3 WLR 161

The defendant, P, was the father of two daughters who accused him of incest and rape. In each case it was alleged that he had engaged in incest over a long period of time, using force and threatening the girls about what he would do if they told anyone. He had paid for an abortion in relation to each daughter. The defendant sought separate trials in relation to the allegations made by each daughter. In argument, the defence maintained that to try the two cases together would greatly increase the defendant's risk of being convicted and was therefore highly prejudicial. The trial judge refused the defendant's application for separate trials. He took the view that the evidence in support of the charges fell within the principles of similar fact evidence and that the charges should be considered by the jury as a whole. The defendant was convicted on both counts. The Court of Appeal quashed the convictions on the ground that a separate trial in respect of each daughter's allegation should have been ordered by taking the view that there had been insufficient striking similarities between the girls' accounts to justify the evidence of one being used in support of the evidence of the other. The father's behaviour in relation to each sister was described as being no more than the stock-in-trade conduct of a typical paedophile or incestuous father.

The House of Lords restored the conviction and once more redefined the principles underpinning the admissibility of similar fact evidence. Playing down the emphasis on the need for striking similarities, the House of Lords categorically restated the test for the admission of similar fact evidence as one that involved weighing up the probative value of the evidence sought to be adduced as against its prejudicial effect. Whilst probative force could derive from similarities in the manner in which an earlier offence was committed, such evidence was not rendered inadmissible merely because striking similarities were not present. Lord Mackay, who delivered the leading judgment, explained the position as follows:

> From all that was said by the House in *Reg. v. Boardman* I would deduce the essential feature of evidence which is to be admitted is that its probative force in support of the allegation that an accused person committed a crime is sufficiently great to make it just to admit the evidence, notwithstanding that it is prejudicial to the accused in tending to show that he was guilty of another crime. Such probative force may be derived from striking similarities in the evidence about the manner in which the crime was committed and the authorities provide illustrations of that of which *Reg. v. Straffen* [1952] 2 QB 911 and *Rex v. Smith* (1915) 11 Cr. App. R. 229, provides a notable example. But restricting the circumstances in which there is sufficient probative force to overcome prejudice of evidence relating to another crime to cases in which there is some striking similarity between them is to restrict the operation of the principle in a way which gives too much effect to a particular manner of stating it, and is not justified in principle ... Once the principle is recognised, that what has to be assessed is the probative force of the evidence in question, the infinite variety of circumstances in which the question arises, demonstrates that there is no single manner in which this can be achieved. Whether the evidence has sufficient probative value to outweigh its prejudicial effect must in each case be a question of degree.

When the issues in *DPP* v *P* are analysed, the relevance of the evidence was directed to the question of whether one sister's evidence could be used to support the other sister's evidence, notwithstanding the prejudice this might cause to the defendant. In other words it was directed at the credibility of the victims as witnesses. In the view of the House of Lords, the probative value of the evidence derived from the fact that both girls had described a prolonged course of conduct against them. Their father had subjected each to threats and general domination. His behaviour had exhibited obsessive tendencies towards both girls as well as the desire to keep them to himself and he had paid for an abortion in each case. Although the similarities could not be described as striking or unique, taken together the evidence gave significant probative force to what each girl had to say, sufficient to overcome any prejudice.

DPP v *P* clearly establishes the modern-day test for the admission of similar fact evidence. In deciding the issue the judge or magistrates must determine whether the probative value of the evidence outweighs its prejudicial effect. The probative value of the evidence is not dependent upon the presence of striking similarities. The degree of probative value required will vary depending on the issues in the case. The test in *DPP* v *P* is easy enough to state. It is not however always easy to apply. This reflects the dynamic nature of this type of evidence. A judgment in a particular case as to whether the probative value of the evidence is sufficient to outweigh its prejudicial effect necessarily involves a degree of subjectivity and it is right that it should. Such judgments can be difficult and the inability of the law to lay down concrete principles and guidance is not surprising. *DPP* v *P*, however, has had the much-desired result of liberating the straitjacket effect of the decision in *DPP* v *Boardman*. All types of evidence are capable of assuming the necessary probative force, including evidence of disposition and the presence of incriminating articles such as those found in the defendant's flat in *Thompson* v *R*.

The benefits of the decision in *DPP* v *P* can be seen in the context of *R* v *Beggs* (1989) 90 Cr App R 430, described above. Reinterpreting this decision in light of the principles laid down in *DPP* v *P*, the outcome would surely have been different. The dissimilarities identified by the Court of Appeal in the various accounts given by the different victims are superficial at best and belie the fact that the evidence suggested that the defendant was peculiarly predisposed to inflicting knife wounds on men in the middle of the night. Such a propensity was surely relevant to B's denial of murder on the grounds of self-defence. Given his peculiar propensity, how likely was it that B should find himself the victim of unwanted sexual advances so that he had to defend himself with a sharp blade?

Two Court of Appeal decisions usefully illustrate the approach to similar fact evidence following *DPP* v *P*.

R v Black [1995] Crim LR 640

The defendant was convicted of three counts of murder and kidnapping. The offences spanned a period of six years. All the victims were pre-pubescent young girls. They had all been abducted from public places close to their homes, with their bodies being found many miles away in an area that became known as the 'Midlands Triangle'. A transit van was believed to have been used in all the abductions. The defendant was arrested in connection with the three murders following his conviction in Scotland for the abduction and indecent assault of a young girl. The girl had been pre-pubescent. She had been snatched from a playground and put into the back of the defendant's transit van. She had been indecently assaulted before being gagged and bound. It had been the defendant's intention to drive the girl south. His attempt was thwarted by police intervention.

The Crown led evidence at his trial for murder to the effect that the facts of the earlier conviction in Scotland bore a strong similarity to the modus operandi of the three murders, tantamount to the defendant having left his hallmark or signature at the crime scene. The prosecution contended that given the similarity of circumstances (choice of victim, use of a transit van, commission of the offence in a lay-by) between the Scottish abduction and the three murders, it was not difficult to conclude that they had to be the work of the same individual. If the defendant committed the abduction in Scotland and he had pleaded guilty to this, there was a very strong inference that he had also committed the three murders. This view was rejected by the defendant, who argued that the probative value of the evidence was much diminished as many of the features between the incidents were commonplace for this type of crime and there were dissimilarities in the way in which the offences had been carried out. The defendant argued the prejudice caused by admitting the Scottish conviction outweighed any probative value. The Court of Appeal disagreed. Whilst there were some dissimilarities between the circumstances of the abduction and the circumstances of the murders, there were many similarities, and it was right that the jury could take account of the conviction in Scotland in assessing the likelihood that the defendant was responsible for the three murders.

R v Groves [1998] Crim LR 200

It was alleged that the defendant had been involved in the illegal importation of drugs. The drugs were hidden in a car driven by one of the co-accused. The importation had been intercepted by Customs and Excise officers, one of whom took the place of the driver. The arrangement to meet another co-accused was executed by the undercover officer. At the rendezvous in a car park, the defendant was also present. He was arrested and found to be in possession of a quantity of cannabis and £500. At his flat a further £2,119 and further quantities of cannabis were found. At his trial, the defendant maintained his presence at the car park had been entirely innocent. He had been having a drink with his friends and no mention was made of drugs. The trial judge admitted the evidence of the cannabis found on his person and at his flat on the importation charge on the basis that its probative value in disproving his defence of innocent presence was strong enough to outweigh the prejudice it caused. On appeal, the defence argued that the evidence should have been excluded, in that there were no striking similarities between the drugs found in the defendant's possession and the circumstances of the alleged importation. The Court of Appeal rejected the argument, restating that similar fact evidence is not limited to the presence of striking similarities.

Although the decision in *Noor Mohamed* v *R* [1949] AC 183 considerably pre-dates *DPP* v *P*, its facts by contrast provide an example of a case in which the evidence purporting to satisfy the test for the admission of similar fact lacked sufficient probative value. The accused was charged with the murder of a woman he lived with. The prosecution alleged he had poisoned the woman with cyanide. The accused was a goldsmith and therefore had legitimate possession of the substance. There was no evidence suggesting that the woman had been forced to ingest the cyanide, although her death was regarded as suspicious. The defendant contended she had committed suicide. The defendant's wife had died some years earlier from cyanide poisoning. There was evidence that she had been tricked by the defendant into ingesting the cyanide as a cure for toothache. The defendant had never been charged with any offence arising out of his wife's death. An attempt by the prosecution to have the evidence of the circumstances surrounding the wife's death admitted under the similar fact evidence rules was rejected by the Privy Council, who regarded the evidence as having little probative weight and merely an attempt by the prosecution to bolster a weak case.

Having regard to the case scenario in the introduction to this chapter, it is unlikely that Andrew's two previous endorsements for speeding and his conviction for careless driving would be admitted as similar fact evidence on the charge of causing death by dangerous driving, based on the test propounded in *DPP* v *P*. The incidents are insufficiently probative of any issue in the case and would be regarded as severely prejudicial to Andrew, were they to be admitted on the issue of his guilt.

Is the issue of identification singled out for special treatment under the similar fact evidence rule?

The test for admitting similar fact evidence as set out in *DPP* v *P* above seems clear. However, Lord Mackay muddied the waters by singling out for special consideration similar fact evidence admitted for the purpose of proving the identification of the defendant as the culprit. He stated:

> Obviously, in cases where the identity of the offender is in issue, evidence of a character sufficiently special reasonably to identify the perpetrator is required and the discussion which follows in Lord Salmon's speech [*DPP* v *Boardman*, see quote reproduced above]... indicates that he had that type of case in mind.

Referring to what was asked of the similar fact evidence on the facts in *DPP* v *P*, and contrasting this with what is asked of similar fact evidence admitted in effect to prove the identity of the accused as the culprit, Lord Mackay went on to say:

> When a question of the kind raised in this case arises I consider that the judge must first decide whether there is material upon which the jury would be entitled to conclude that the evidence of one victim, about what occurred to that victim, is so related to the evidence given by another victim, about what happened to that other victim, that the evidence of the first victim provides strong enough support for the evidence of the second victim to make it just to admit it notwithstanding the prejudicial effect of admitting the evidence. This relationship, from which support is derived, may take many forms and while these forms may include 'striking similarity' in the manner in which the crime is committed, consisting of unusual characteristics in its execution the necessary relationship is by no means confined to such circumstances. Relationships in time and circumstances other than these may well be important relationships in this connection. Where the identity of the perpetrator is in issue, and evidence of this kind is important in that connection, obviously something in the nature of what has been called in the course of the argument a signature or other special feature will be necessary. To transpose this requirement to other situations where the question is whether a crime has been committed, rather than who did commit it, is to impose an unnecessary and improper restriction upon the application of the principle.

In many ways, the decision in *DPP* v *P* has relaxed the test for the admission of similar fact evidence. The threshold requirement of 'unique or striking similarities' is no longer a condition of its admissibility, but what did Lord Mackay mean by singling out identification evidence as requiring a 'signature or other special feature'? Are striking similarities a prerequisite of similar fact evidence admitted to prove an accused's identification in a case?

What Lord Mackay said in relation to identity and similar fact evidence was on a purely *obiter* basis. The preferred view is that his remarks were directed to the sort of case where the similar fact evidence effectively provides the main evidence of guilt against the defendant. In such a case, the probative value of the evidence would have to be considered very high to justify the prejudice of admitting it. Such strong probative value is likely to derive from striking similarities which effectively amount to the defendant's 'hallmark' or 'signature'.

This view is supported by the Court of Appeal's decision in *R v W (John)* [1998] 2 Cr App R 289. The defendant was charged with an offence of indecent assault on a woman and a further charge of attempting to indecently assault another woman. The attacks had occurred within two weeks of each other. The defendant denied any involvement. The victims' description of their attacker resembled the defendant who had been in the vicinity on both occasions. One of the victims described how she had fought with her attacker and ripped his jacket. A tear, consistent with this witness's evidence, was found on a jacket worn by the defendant. The Court of Appeal rejected a submission that the jury should be prevented from using the evidence on one count in determining the defendant's identification in the other. There was a sufficient relationship in time and circumstance to satisfy its admission as similar fact evidence. In the Court of Appeal's view, a 'hallmark' or 'signature' was needed only in those cases where similar fact evidence is the only evidence of any substance against the accused.

The decision in *R v W (John)* highlights a further problem associated with disputed identification, namely whether the fact finder should be invited to take a sequential approach to similar fact evidence of identification or a cumulative approach.

Suppose X is on trial for two offences committed against separate victims in the same and perhaps unusual way. Each victim's evidence of identification is insufficient but taken together the evidence points to X being responsible. Should the jury take a sequential approach to the evidence, deciding first whether the defendant committed the earlier offence on evidence other than that provided by the similar facts in the other case? Once the jury finds the defendant guilty of the earlier offence and comes to the conclusion that the two offences were the work of the same individual, the inference that the defendant is guilty of the second offence becomes irresistible. Or, should the jury be permitted to take a cumulative approach to an assessment of the overall evidence? This would allow the jury to look at the evidence of identification in respect of both allegations in order to see if the totality of the evidence points to the defendant being the culprit in both cases.

In *R v W (John)*, the Court of Appeal sanctioned the use of the cumulative approach to the evidence of identification in that case. This accords with two earlier Court of Appeal decisions.

R v Downey [1995] 1 Cr App R 547

Two robberies of a very similar nature were committed at petrol stations within minutes of each other. In each case the robber wore a black stocking mask and threatened the cashier with a handgun. A video camera had filmed the incident at the first petrol station and the jury was shown a still photograph of the robber taken from the video, which bore a strong resemblance to the defendant. The judge directed the jury that if it came to the conclusion that the same person had committed both robberies, which was obviously a very plausible inference in this case, it was entitled to pool the evidence of identification from each robbery in order to decide whether the defendant had been the robber on both occasions. The Court of Appeal endorsed the trial judge's approach.

R v Barnes [1995] 2 Cr App R 491

Two offences of indecent assault were committed on different victims in very similar circumstances. Identification of the defendant as the attacker was disputed. The defendant appealed on the basis that the judge should have told the jury that only if it was sure of guilt on one count could it then use the evidence of identification on that count in support of the identification evidence on the other count. The Court of Appeal rejected that argument. Logic dictated that if the jury was satisfied that the same man had committed both offences, based on evidence other than eyewitness identification, then it followed that both victims would have been seeking to identify the same person. Therefore there was no reason why their evidence should not be regarded as mutually supportive.

The direction to the jury in each of the above cases permitted it to take a cumulative approach to the evidence of the defendant's involvement. In contrast, a sequential approach to the evidence of identification was required in the case of *R v McGranaghan* [1995] 1 Cr App R 559. Three separate rapes had been committed in very similar circumstances. In none of the allegations of rape was the evidence of identification particularly strong. A major weakness in the prosecution's case was the lack of forensic evidence. The defendant maintained he had been mistakenly identified by his victims. He asserted an alibi in relation to one of the charges and called a witness on appeal who stated that the accused had had a beard at the time of one of the alleged rapes, which had not been mentioned by the victim. The trial judge had allowed the jury to take a cumulative approach to the evidence of identification, providing the jury was satisfied the rapes were the work of one man. The Court of Appeal quashed the conviction, concluding that the similar facts in this case went to show that the same man committed both offences but that it did not prove the defendant was that man. Before the jury could use similar fact evidence, it would firstly need to be satisfied as to the defendant's guilt on one count, without the assistance of similar fact evidence from the other counts.

The decision in *R v W (John)* above suggests that the sequential approach should be confined to those cases where the jury is invited to reason that because the defendant committed crime A, he also committed crime B. This involves not only proof of the similarity between the two offences but that the defendant did in fact commit offence A. Having regard to the circumstances in which the offences were committed, such an approach to the evidence was not required in *R v Barnes* nor in *R v W (John)*.

The use of the two different approaches in determining whether the defendant committed the offences charged in cases where the defendant faces more than one allegation and the evidence of the defendant's identity in relation to each is not certain reflects the nature of similar fact cases in general. The evidential dilemma that the court must address varies from case to case. Dictating a particular approach would be wrong in principle. Discretion is all-important as each case has to be decided on its own facts.

Cogency and collusion

The probative value of similar fact evidence is largely dependent upon its cogency. For similar fact evidence to possess probative value, it must be true. Where a defendant has already been convicted of the earlier offence forming the basis of similar fact evidence as in *R v Black* [1995] Crim LR 640 above, the evidence is capable of assuming a high degree of cogency. Where a defendant does not admit the earlier misconduct the question of the cogency of the earlier evidence arises. We have already seen some of the problems associated with this where similar fact evidence is required to prove the identity of the defendant based on a series of incidents, all of which the defendant denies. Where identification of the defendant is not disputed issues as to the cogency of evidence often arise where the evidence of similar facts is provided in the accounts of different witnesses. Where there is a risk of collusion between prosecution witnesses, doubts about the cogency of the similar fact evidence assume considerable importance. The leading authority on this matter is the decision of the House of Lords in *R* v *H*.

R v H [1995] 2 AC 596

The defendant in this case had been convicted of acts of gross indecency with his two stepdaughters, alleged to have been committed between 1987 and 1989. Neither girl had made a complaint until 1992, when one of the girls told her mother of the abuse. The mother then quizzed the other sister. At first she said nothing had happened, but later, after speaking to her older sister, she also made specific allegations. There had been an obvious risk of collusion between the two sisters. The judge had directed the jury to decide first whether they believed the sisters had collaborated in such a way as to concoct a false story against their father. If the jury believed the sisters to be telling the truth, then it would have been permissible for the jury, in accordance with the principles laid down in *DPP* v *P*, to have taken the evidence of one of the sisters and use it in support of the evidence of the other. The defendant appealed against his conviction.

At issue was whether it should be a condition of the admissibility of similar fact evidence that the judge should find that there had been no collusion, even innocent collusion, between witnesses, or whether this was a matter for the jury. The House of Lords took the view that, as a general rule, the issue of collusion between witnesses was a matter for the jury and that the judge should approach the question of admissibility on the basis that the similar facts alleged were true. To adopt the contrary approach would usurp the proper function of the jury in deciding the credibility of witnesses.

The principles which emerge from *R* v *H* are summarised in the judgment of Lord Mackay:

> Where there is an application to exclude evidence on the ground that it does not qualify as similar fact evidence and the submission raises a question of collusion (not only deliberate but including unconscious influence of one witness by another) the judge should approach the question of admissibility on the basis that the similar facts alleged are true and apply the test set out by this House in *Director of Public Prosecutions* v. *P* [1991] 2 AC 447 accordingly. It follows that generally collusion is not relevant at this stage.
>
> Secondly, if a submission is made raising a question of collusion in such a way as to cause the judge difficulty in applying the test referred to he may be compelled to hold a voire dire. The situations in which collusion is relevant in the consideration of admissibility would arise only in a very exceptional case of which no illustration was afforded in the argument on this appeal but I regard it as right to include this as a possibility since it is difficult to foresee all the circumstances that might arise. The present is certainly not a case in which the risk of collusion affects the application of the test.
>
> Thirdly, if evidence of similar facts has been admitted and circumstances are adduced in the course of the trial which indicate that no reasonable jury could accept the evidence as free from collusion the judge should direct the jury that it cannot be relied upon as corroboration or indeed for any other purpose adverse to the defence.

And fourthly, where this is not so but the question of collusion has been raised the judge must clearly draw the importance of collusion to the attention of the jury and leave it to them to decide whether, notwithstanding such evidence of collusion as may have been put before them, they are satisfied that the evidence can be relied upon as free from collusion and tell them that if they are not so satisfied they cannot properly rely upon it as corroboration or for any other purpose adverse to the defence.

The mandatory requirement of the judge to give a corroboration warning to the jury about the dangers of relying on the evidence of victims of sexual offences was in fact abolished by sections 32 and 33 of the Criminal Justice and Public Order Act 1994. The general principles of R v H as regards the issue of collusion, however, remain good law.

In its consultation exercise the Law Commission expressed some concerns about certain aspects of the decision in R v H. Drawing on research findings, it expressed scepticism as to whether the jury could comply with a direction from the judge to ignore similar fact evidence which had become seriously tainted in a case where evidence of collusion emerges during the trial, after the admission of the evidence. Although not expressing a final opinion, the Law Commission felt there was considerable merit in the judge being required to stop the trial if there was a danger of unfairness to the defendant occasioned by the prejudice caused or by the danger of the jury being misled. This is included as a specific recommendation in Law Commission Report No 273 and is given effect in clause 13 of the draft Criminal Evidence Bill.

Similar fact evidence stemming from conduct which is neither unlawful nor has resulted in a conviction

Providing the probative value of the evidence outweighs its prejudicial effect, similar fact evidence may be derived from conduct which is not unlawful in itself, or which has not resulted in a conviction for a particular offence, but where there are similarities in the circumstances leading up to the commission of the offence.

R v Butler (1987) 84 Cr App R 12

The defendant was charged with rape and indecent assault. The manner in which the rapist had carried out the attack, which took place inside the victim's car, was unsavoury and unusual. The defendant disputed the identification of him by the victim. Evidence was called from the defendant's previous girlfriend who testified to consensual unsavoury sexual acts performed on her by the defendant identical to those perpetrated on the victim. These consensual acts had also been committed in a car. The former girlfriend's consent meant that no criminal offence had been perpetrated on her. The prejudice engendered by the girlfriend's evidence was outweighed by the relevance her evidence had to the issue of disputed identification and was properly admitted under the similar fact evidence rule.

R v Barrington [1981] 1 WLR 419

The defendant was alleged to have indecently assaulted three girls. Each girl had been lured to the defendant's house on the pretext of babysitting. The defendant and the woman he lived with told the girls that they were professional photographers and that the girls could win cash prizes for posing nude. The girls were shown pornographic photographs and attempts were made to get them to pose nude. The defendant claimed the girls had concocted the evidence against him. The prosecution was permitted to call three other girls under the similar fact evidence rule, unconnected with the victims, to give evidence that they too had been lured to the defendant's house on the same pretext and had been shown pornographic photographs and asked to pose nude. However, in their cases no indecent assault had occurred. Notwithstanding that the evidence of the three witnesses did not disclose an indecent assault on them, it did disclose similarities in the surrounding circumstances. Such similar accounts could not be explained on the basis of coincidence and gave considerable support to the view that the girls were telling the truth about the indecent assault.

Similar fact evidence stemming from a previous acquittal

Where similar fact conduct stems from a case in which the defendant was acquitted, can it be used as evidence in a later case in which the defendant is charged with a similar offence but involving a different victim? The House of Lords has recently determined this very important question in a way that has implications for the rule relating to double jeopardy.

R v Z [2000] 3 WLR 117

The defendant was charged with rape. His defence was one of consent or mistaken belief that his victim had consented. The defendant had previously faced four separate trials, each involving allegations of rape. In each instance, the defendant had said his victims had consented. He was convicted in one of the cases but acquitted in the other three. It was accepted that there were a number of similarities in the conduct of the defendant alleged by the victim in the present case and the other four complainants in the earlier rape trials. Such evidence, if admitted, had significant probative value in that it tended to refute the defendant's assertion that he thought his victim was consenting or that he was mistaken as to her consent on this particular occasion. To be mistaken on one occasion as to the victim's consent can plausibly be explained but to have been mistaken on four separate occasions and again in this instance surely defies belief?

The prosecution sought a ruling from the trial judge to use the previous conviction and the previous acquittals as similar fact evidence in support of the prosecution's case. The defendant opposed the application on the ground that it would cause his defence undue prejudice and would be contrary to the long-established rule which prevents the defendant from being placed in double jeopardy.

To understand the implications of the decision in R v Z, it is necessary to digress slightly and consider the history of the double jeopardy rule. In its strictest sense, the rule prevents an accused from being tried for the same or substantially the same offence as one for which he has already been acquitted. It is sometimes referred to as a plea of *autrefois acquit*, and is more like a rule of substantive law than a rule of evidence. The rationale for the rule is based on the notion of fairness, the need for finality in criminal litigation and the need to encourage the efficient investigation of criminal offences.

The defendant placed reliance on the Privy Council's decision in *Sambasivam* v *Public Prosecutor of Malaya* [1950] AC 458 in which Lord MacDermott widened the application of the double jeopardy rule when he stated in his speech that:

> The effect of a verdict of acquittal pronounced by a competent court on a lawful charge and after a lawful trial is not completely stated by saying that the person acquitted cannot

be tried again for the same offence. To that it must be added that the verdict is binding and conclusive in all subsequent proceedings between the parties to the adjudication.

Sambasivam was taken to have expanded the ambit of the double jeopardy rule beyond the risk of an accused being convicted of an offence of which he had previously been acquitted to prohibiting a collateral attack on an acquittal in subsequent proceedings. The prosecution may not rely in a later case on evidence, the relevance of which is enhanced, by the assumption that the accused was in fact guilty of the earlier offence of which he had been acquitted.

In R v Z, the Court of Appeal felt constrained to follow the rule in *Sambasivam*, despite being critical of it since it stood in the way of admitting cogent similar fact evidence. As Roberts, [2000] Crim LR 952 at 958, comments:

> It is one thing to provide, as the *autrefois* pleas do, that a jury's determination of guilt or innocence in relation to offences charged in the proceedings shall be final. It is quite another to say, with *Sambasivam*, that a jury's factual determinations irrevocably fix the meaning of any evidence supporting its verdict, so that courts in future litigation must take that meaning as read, even though a new factual matrix casts doubt on the original determination, and perhaps even suggests a different interpretation of the evidence altogether. The notion of fixing evidential meaning for all time runs counter to the established conception of probative value, which stresses the contextual nature of both relevance and weight.

In upholding the defendant's conviction in R v Z, the House of Lords concluded the decision in *Sambasivam* was correct on the facts in that case, in that the legal process had twice exposed the defendant to the risk of being convicted of the same crime, as the two offences were founded on one and the same incident. As such, trying the defendant for a second offence was manifestly inconsistent with his previous acquittal on the first offence on the same facts. However, it ruled that the application of the rule against double jeopardy applied only to a situation in which the accused is 'put on trial again for an offence of which he has been acquitted ... or may result in the punishment of the accused on some other ground for the same offence'. The rule prohibiting double jeopardy of the accused 'is not infringed if what the prosecutor seeks to do is to lead evidence which was led at a previous trial, not for the purposes of punishing the accused in any way for an offence of which he has been acquitted, but in order to prove that the defendant is guilty of a subsequent offence which was not before the court in the previous trial'.

By restricting the ambit of double jeopardy in this way, the application of similar fact principles is unimpeded by the presence of a previous acquittal. The law's position in this respect is summed up in the words of Lord Hobhouse in R v Z:

> The correct answer to be given in this case is clear. It was a case of similar facts. Similar facts are admissible because they are relevant to the proof of the defendant's guilt. The evidence relating to one incident taken in isolation may be unconvincing. It may depend upon a straight conflict of evidence between two people. It may leave open seemingly plausible explanations. The guilt of the defendant may not be proved beyond reasonable doubt. But, when evidence is given of a number of similar incidents, the position may be changed. The evidence of the defendant's guilt may become overwhelming. The fact that a number of witnesses come forward and without collusion give a similar account of the defendant's behaviour may give

credit to the evidence of each of them and discredit the denials of the defendant. Evidence of system may negative a defence of accident. This is the simple truth upon which similar fact evidence is admitted: it has probative value and is not merely prejudicial ... It is not disputed that the jury may hear about similar incidents which have not been the subject of a previous trial. The dispute is whether the jury may hear about similar incidents which have been the subject of earlier trials at which the defendant was acquitted. It would be a denial of the principle upon which similar fact evidence is admitted that such evidence should be treated as inadmissible. As I will stress, there will always be a question whether the trial judge should exercise his discretion to exclude the evidence under section 78 of the Police and Criminal Evidence Act 1984. But as regards admissibility, it is in principle admissible.

The decision in *R v Z* is to be welcomed. It provides confirmation that there is no longer any objection in principle to the admission of similar fact evidence stemming from a previous acquittal providing the test which requires the probative force of the evidence to be weighed against its prejudicial effect has been properly undertaken and the court has concluded that the evidence assumes the necessary degree of relevance to the issues in the particular case.

Similar fact evidence – proposals for reform

The Law Commission's specific criticism of the rules admitting similar fact evidence was that it gave a trial judge too much discretion leading to uncertainty about the precise application of the principles (Consultation Paper No 141). The Law Commission commented that:

> Although, as we have seen, the House of Lords' decisions in *Boardman* and in *DPP v P* have advanced the common law considerably, if one tried to formulate a test for the admissibility of all evidence of bad character on the basis of those two decisions, there would still be gaps. The extent of the rule, the degree to which there is any room left for a discretion to exclude prejudicial evidence after the rule has been applied, how the rule is to be applied where identity is in issue: these are currently unclear. Moreover, it is arguable that the case law is not clear on the essential point: when is it just to admit evidence of bad character. (paragraph 10.21)

It is a criticism endorsed by the Law Commission in its Report No 273. The Commission criticises the test in *DPP v P* as being too vague in that it 'does not settle the question of how much the probative value of the evidence ought to relate to the prejudicial effect in order for it to be admitted'.

Consideration of the Law Commission's final recommendations for the reform of the similar fact evidence rule are deferred until Chapter 21, when they are considered in the context of the Law Commission's overhaul of the entire law relating to the admission of bad character evidence.

Can similar fact evidence be adduced by a defendant against his co-accused?

Whilst the decision to admit similar fact evidence as part of the prosecution's case is fraught with complexity, the decision to admit it in relation to a co-accused is relatively straightforward. Providing it is relevant to the defence of co-accused X to adduce evidence of the character of a co-accused Y, the judge has no discretion to refuse to admit the evidence even though it is bound to cause considerable prejudice to Y. The decision to admit the evidence is not dependent upon the probative value versus prejudicial effect test, but purely on the relevance of the evidence. Character in this instance would include previous convictions, misconduct and evidence of a disposition to act in a certain way. The safeguard, however, is in relation to the notion of relevance and in this respect the courts have chosen to define relevance very tightly. In effect co-accused X would have to show that the guilt of his co-accused Y effectively proves X's innocence. This is more likely to be the case where the evidence points to the commission of the offence by one or the other.

Lowery v R [1974] AC 85

Lowery was jointly tried for the motiveless, sadistic murder of a girl. The evidence pointed to the fact that one or both of the accused had carried out the killing. Each blamed the other. Lowery's co-accused was permitted to call evidence from a psychologist who testified it was more likely that Lowery had committed the offence because Lowery had an aggressive personality and was more predisposed to act in such a way. Both were convicted of murder. In the view of the Privy Council, the evidence was rightly admitted as it showed Lowery was the one more likely to have acted in this way because of his disposition and this in turn was relevant to the defence of his co-accused.

The outcome of the *Lowery* case contrasts with that in *R v Neale* (1977) 65 Cr App R 304. The defendants, X and Y, were jointly charged with arson and manslaughter. X claimed he was not present when Y started the fire and put forward the defence of alibi. X sought to have admitted in evidence the fact that Y had a fixation with fire and had previously started several other fires. Such evidence was indicative of Y's guilt, but it assumed no relevance to X's defence and the Court of Appeal held that it should not have been admitted.

R v *Douglass* (1989) 89 Cr App R 264 is authority for the proposition that, where A makes his or his co-accused's tendency to behave in a certain way an issue as to his likely guilt, his co-accused B may adduce evidence in rebuttal. In this case, A and B were charged with causing death by dangerous driving. The prosecution's case was that A and B were vying with each other on the road in order to gain an advantage. There was evidence to suggest that A had been drinking. It had been B's vehicle which had collided head on with a car coming in the opposite direction. B had been attempting to overtake A's vehicle at the time. A gave evidence that he had not forced B into the path of the oncoming vehicle and that in attempting to overtake, B had lost control of his vehicle. This was denied by B, who did not give evidence in his defence. At trial, however, B's counsel asked B's girlfriend about his drinking habits. She gave evidence that in the two years she had known him, B had never consumed alcohol. The purpose of the evidence was to suggest that, by virtue of this fact, B was less likely to have driven aggressively or badly, in contrast to A. The trial judge permitted A to make known to the jury the fact that B had previous convictions for various offences, including drink/driving. Both A and B were convicted of causing death by dangerous driving. Following the decision in *R v Lowery*, the Court of Appeal held that A should have been allowed to adduce evidence of B's previous convictions, including the two convictions for drink/driving offences. The jury needed to know the type of person B was.

B's propensity not to have driven as alleged, which was something he had brought into issue, became relevant to deciding A's guilt or innocence.

Statutory admission of similar fact evidence

There are two instances in which Parliament has expressly authorised the use of similar fact evidence. One is under section 1(2) of the Official Secrets Act 1911. The other, more commonly used, is under section 27(3) of the Theft Act 1968, which aids the proof of *mens rea* in relation to the charge of handling stolen goods. Where a defendant denies knowledge or belief that the goods of which he was found in possession are stolen, the prosecution may adduce evidence of the defendant's criminal disposition by proving the defendant has previously been in possession of stolen goods or that he has a previous conviction for handling stolen goods or theft in the preceding five years. Such evidence is capable of casting serious doubt on the defendant's assertion that he did not know the goods were stolen or that he did not believe them to be so. Section 27(3) can create prejudice and as a result is used sparingly by prosecutors. Furthermore, the provisions in the Criminal Justice and Public Order Act 1994 permitting the fact finder to draw an adverse inference in circumstances where a defendant has remained silent at the police station or has refused to answer questions on oath, put pressure on a defendant to answer questions as to his knowledge in interview and to give evidence on oath and therefore make section 27(3) less justifiable. The Law Commission has advocated its repeal.

Bad character necessarily forming part of the prosecution's case

Sometimes bad character is incidental to proving the prosecution's case. For example, where an accused commits a criminal offence whilst serving a sentence of imprisonment, this necessarily alerts the court to the fact that the accused has a previous conviction. A further example is the offence of absconding whilst on bail, under section 6(1) of the Bail Act 1976. It obviously implies the defendant has previously been arrested and charged with an offence. In these circumstances the jury must be instructed and the magistrates must warn themselves not to be influenced by such knowledge when considering the evidence on the charge before them.

Occasionally, the fact of a previous conviction forms part of the definition of the offence. Under section 21 of the Firearms Act 1968 it is an offence for a person previously convicted of an offence for which he was given a custodial sentence to be in possession of a firearm. In such a case, the jury must be instructed that this is part of the definition of the offence and is irrelevant to any wider issues of guilt.

ADDUCING THE CONVICTION OF OTHERS RELEVANT TO PROOF OF A DEFENDANT'S GUILT IN SUBSEQUENT PROCEEDINGS (PACE, SECTION 74)

Section 74 of PACE relates to the conviction of a person other than the accused in circumstances where that person's conviction assumes relevance to the guilt of the accused. The section provides:

(1) In any proceedings the fact that a person other than the accused has been convicted of an offence by or before any court in the United Kingdom ... shall be admissible in evidence for the purpose of proving, where to do so is relevant to any issue in those proceedings, that that person committed that offence, whether or not any evidence of his having committed the offence is given.

(2) In any proceedings in which by virtue of this section a person other than the accused is proved to have been convicted of an offence ... he shall be taken to have committed that offence unless the contrary is proved.

Section 74 has a similar effect in criminal proceedings as section 11 of the Civil Evidence Act 1968 has in civil proceedings (see Chapter 30).

Section 74 has considerable practical application in relation to offences of theft and handling stolen goods. Every charge of handling requires proof that the goods have been stolen. Where, for example, at the trial of X for handling stolen goods, it is relevant to prove that Y (the thief) has been convicted of the theft of the goods, Y's conviction can be proved to the court under section 74. An element of the offence with which X is charged is provided for in the commission of an offence by Y. In these circumstances, it benefits the prosecution to be able to produce a certificate of Y's conviction to this effect. In *R* v *Pigram* [1995] Crim LR 808 an element of the offence charged against the defendant was supplied by the conviction of his co-accused. The defendant was jointly charged in connection with an offence of handling stolen goods. His co-accused's guilty plea was used by the prosecution under section 74 PACE to prove the defendant's knowledge that the goods were stolen.

The section is not confined to proof of the elements of an offence as a precondition to the prosecution of the accused. The conviction, on which the prosecution seeks to place reliance, may be relevant simply to an issue in the proceedings. In other words, the conviction of others may go some way to proving relevant underlying facts in the case against the accused. The key word to the operation of section 74, is 'relevant'. The section has been used in cases involving allegations of a joint enterprise by more than one accused, whether charged as a conspiracy or as a substantive offence. Section 74 is often utilised where two co-defendants are tried separately and one or other of the co-accused has been convicted, usually on a guilty plea before the other accused is tried. The conviction of the other co-accused may be relevant to show an offence was jointly committed or that there was a conspiracy in operation. Notwithstanding that the prosecution satisfies the condition that proof of a conviction is relevant to any issue in the proceedings, the judge is required to consider whether in exercising his discretion under section 78 of PACE, the admission of the evidence would have an 'adverse effect on the fairness of the proceedings'. The application of section 78 of PACE is considered at length in Chapter 5.

R v O'Connor (1987) 85 Cr App R 304

The defendant was charged with conspiracy to obtain property by deception. His co-accused B had previously pleaded guilty to the charge the accused was facing. The prosecution was permitted to adduce evidence of B's conviction for the purpose of proving the existence of a conspiracy. The Court of Appeal held that this had been wrong. In this case there had only been two parties to the conspiracy. By using B's conviction in this way, the defendant effectively had to prove his innocence.

B was not in court to be cross-examined. Accordingly, the admission of the evidence had an adverse effect on the fairness of the proceedings and ought to have been excluded.

R v Robertson [1987] 3 All ER 231

The defendant was charged with offences of burglary and conspiracy to burgle. The defendant's co-accused, L and P, had previously pleaded guilty to individual counts of burglary. The defendant did not dispute these. The prosecution was allowed to adduce in evidence the fact of P and L's convictions as evidence of a conspiracy between them. An eyewitness was able to give evidence that the defendant had been with them both at the time. Taken together, the evidence pointed to a joint plan. Section 78 of PACE was not felt to have been applicable on the facts, however Lord Lane cautioned:

> It only remains to add this. Section 74 is a provision which should be sparingly used. There will be occasions where, although the evidence may be technically admissible, its effect is likely to be so slight that it will be wiser not to adduce it ... Secondly, where the evidence is admitted, the judge should be careful to explain to the jury the effect of the evidence and its limitation.

Lord Lane's cautionary note serves as a warning of the dangers surrounding section 74(1) of PACE. The fact that someone other than the defendant stands convicted in connection with the offence does not automatically mean the defendant is guilty as it merely establishes the commission of the offence by the convicted person alone. This needs to be made very clear to the jury.

The decision in R v Mahmood and Manzur [1997] 1 Cr App R 414 affords a useful illustration of the discretion that can be exercised under section 78 in this connection. The appellants, KM and NM, and a co-defendant, L, were indicted on a separate count of raping the same girl. The girl had been drunk. The appellants maintained she had consented or they believed her to have consented to sexual intercourse. L pleaded guilty before the appellants' trial. The appellants were convicted and appealed on the ground that the judge had erred in admitting evidence before the jury of L's guilty plea under section 74(1) of PACE. Quashing the convictions and ordering a re-trial, the Court of Appeal held that, in deciding whether a conviction ought to be admitted under section 74, the court must have regard to section 78 of PACE. The judge had to apply a two-fold test. He had to ask himself:

1   whether the conviction sought to be relied on by the prosecution was clearly relevant to an issue in the trial of the defendant/s; and
2   if it was relevant, whether there is any prejudice to the defendant/s in respect of the fairness of the proceedings. If there is, the judge must exercise his discretion under section 78 accordingly.

The Court of Appeal regarded as essential that the trial judge should have been told the basis on which L had pleaded guilty, so that the judge could identify the issue at the appellants' trial to which it was relevant. L could have pleaded guilty on the basis of any number of different issues. His reasons for pleading guilty may or may not have been relevant to the issues the appellants had raised. In view of this, the convictions could not be considered safe. The case confirms that the judge must direct the jury in very clear terms as to why the evidence is being placed before it and what its true evidential value is, ie what the jury can and cannot do with it.

Further reading

Dennis, I.H. (1999) *The Law of Evidence*, Sweet & Maxwell.

Law Commission (1996) *Evidence in Criminal Proceedings: Previous Misconduct of a Defendant*, Law Commission Consultation Paper No 141, HMSO.

Law Commission (2001) *Evidence in Criminal Proceedings: Previous Misconduct of a Defendant*, Law Commission Report No 273, HMSO.

McEwan, J., 'The Law Commission Consultation Paper on Previous Misconduct: (2) Law Commission Dodges the Nettle on Consultation Paper No 141' [1997] Crim LR 93.

McEwan, J. (1998) *Evidence and the Adversarial Process: The Modern Law*, 2nd edn, Hart Publishing.

Mirfield, P., 'Proof and Prejudice in the House of Lords' (1996) 112 LQR 1.

Munday, R., 'Similar Fact Evidence and the Risk of Contaminated Testimony' [1995] Camb LJ 522.

Pattenden, R., 'Similar Fact Evidence and Proof of Identity' (1996) 112 LQR 446.

Roberts, P., 'Acquitted Misconduct Evidence and Double Jeopardy Principles – From *Sambasivam to Z*' [2000] Crim LR 952.

Zuckerman, A., 'Similar Fact Evidence: The Unobservable Rule' (1987) 103 LQR 187.

Chapter 21

CHARACTER EVIDENCE RELEVANT TO THE CREDIBILITY OF THE DEFENDANT AS A WITNESS

INTRODUCTION

We saw in the previous chapter that character evidence admitted as part of the prosecution's case under the similar fact evidence rule is relevant to proving the defendant's guilt on the charge for which he is being tried. This chapter examines the statutory rules dealing with aspects of the defendant's character that may be revealed during his cross-examination, which may be relevant to the issue of his credibility as a witness. The chapter also includes a separate examination of the law dealing with the evidential value of the defendant's good character.

The defendant may only be cross-examined if he has elected to give evidence on oath, as the Criminal Evidence Act 1898 makes the defendant a competent but not a compellable witness in his own defence. As we noted in Chapter 16, one of the purposes of cross-examination is to undermine the credibility of the witness who gives evidence on oath. In undermining a witness's credibility, questions may be directed at a witness with a view to attacking his moral integrity and credibility, for example, by accusing the witness of lying or by putting questions to him about his previous convictions.

Having elected to give evidence is the defendant to be treated in cross-examination like any other witness given that such questioning would expose the defendant to a real risk of prejudice? In enacting the Criminal Evidence Act 1898, Parliament sought to deal with this dilemma by a compromise contained in section 1(e) and (f) of the Act.

EVIDENCE OF BAD CHARACTER (CRIMINAL EVIDENCE ACT 1898, SECTION 1)

Section 1(e) and (f) of the Criminal Evidence Act 1898, as amended, provides:

(e) A person charged and being a witness in pursuance of this Act may be asked any question in cross-examination notwithstanding that it would tend to criminate him as to the offence charged:

(f) A person charged and called as a witness in pursuance of this Act shall not be asked, and if asked shall not be required to answer, any question tending to show that he has committed or been convicted of or been charged with any offence other than that wherewith he is then charged, or is of bad character, unless—

(i) the proof that he has committed or been convicted of such other offence is admissible evidence to show that he is guilty of the offence wherewith he is then charged; or

(ii) he has personally or by his advocate asked questions of the witnesses for the prosecution with a view to establish his own good character, or has given evidence of his good character, or the nature or conduct of the defence is such as to involve imputations on the character of the prosecutor or the witnesses for the prosecution, or the deceased victim of the alleged crime; or

(iii) he has given evidence against any other person charged in the same proceedings.

These provisions are unwieldy and just to confuse matters they will be relabelled when section 67 of the Youth Justice and Criminal Evidence Act 1999 comes into force. Section 1(e) will become section 1(2) and section 1(f)(i), (ii) and (iii) will be relabelled as section 1(3)(i), (ii) and (iii). The general effect of section 1(f) is to give the defendant the protection of a shield against his bad character being disclosed to the fact finder. However, his shield can be thrown away in the circumstances prescribed in section 1(f)(ii) and (iii). Where the shield is thrown away, the defendant's bad character is relevant only to undermining the defendant's credibility as a witness in his own defence. Crucially, bad character in these circumstances must not be considered as evidence of the defendant's guilt and in a Crown Court trial, the jury must be directed accordingly. This is the critical evidential difference between character admitted under the similar fact evidence rule and character revealed as a consequence of the defendant throwing away his shield. Whether the jury can always make the distinction between relevance to credibility and relevance to guilt is a matter of some considerable controversy.

Interpreting section 1(e) and (f)

Section 1(e) makes it clear that, having decided to give evidence, the defendant will be expected to answer any questions put to him in cross-examination which would tend to incriminate him on the charge or charges he presently faces. However, section 1(f) protects the defendant from being asked any questions that would tend to show that he:

* has committed,
* has been charged with,
* has been convicted of any offence other than the charge he is on trial for, or
* is of bad character.

In *Maxwell v DPP* [1935] AC 309, the House of Lords held the word 'charged' in section 1(f) extends to a charge in respect of which the defendant was acquitted. The defendant was a doctor. He was accused of manslaughter having carried out an illegal abortion. In evidence he asserted he was of good character. The prosecution sought to ask him about a previous charge of manslaughter he had faced in respect of a patient, of which he had been acquitted. The House of Lords concluded that, on the facts, such questioning was irrelevant to the issue of the defendant's credibility in this case and to the likelihood that he had committed the offence and therefore should not have been asked.

Maxwell v DPP is a pertinent reminder of the importance of the fundamental requirement that to be admissible, evidence must be relevant. As explained later in the chapter, the Criminal Evidence Act 1898 permits the prosecution to ask questions of the accused that are normally prohibited under section 1(f). However, the questions permitted under the exception to section 1(f) must fulfil the fundamental requirement of being relevant to an issue in the case. For this reason, the decision in *Maxwell* is not authority for the proposition that a previous acquittal can never be relevant to the defendant's credibility on oath, or indeed his guilt in relation to an offence charged.

Example

The defendant is charged with being in possession of a controlled drug, contrary to section 5(3) of the Misuse of Drugs Act 1971. The defendant is found in possession of a sealed box. The box contains drugs. The defendant says he was minding the box for a friend and that he had no reason to suspect the box contained anything illegal. If this assertion cannot be disproved by the prosecution, the defendant is entitled to be acquitted of the offence for which he has been charged (see R v Lambert [2001] 3 All ER 577, Chapter 11). On oath, the defendant asserts his good character. In doing so, he throws away his shield and is liable to cross-examination under section 1(f)(ii). In order to rebut the assertion that, by virtue of his good character the defendant is less likely to have committed this offence, the prosecution seeks to question the defendant about a similar charge of possession he faced a couple of years ago, in respect of which he was acquitted. In the earlier trial, the defendant advanced the same defence. Such questioning would arguably satisfy the criterion of relevance, as it has a bearing on the issue of the defendant's guilty knowledge as to the probable contents of the box.

In *Stirland v DPP* [1944] AC 315, the House of Lords confirmed 'charged' meant, 'brought before a court'. The defendant faced a charge of forgery. He gave evidence that he had not been charged with any offence of forgery before. The prosecution sought to ask questions about his dismissal from his employment on suspicion of forgery. This did not constitute being brought before a criminal court and, as such, it assumed no relevance to the rebuttal of the defendant's assertion of good character.

The relationship between section 1(e) and (f)

A common source of confusion is the relationship between section 1(e) and (f). Section 1(e) would appear to permit the defendant to be asked in cross-examination any question that would tend to incriminate him as to the offence with which he is presently charged:

> (e) A person charged and being a witness in pursuance of this Act may be asked any question in cross-examination notwithstanding that it would tend to criminate him as to the offence charged.

This seems to contradict the wording of section 1(f):

> (f) A person charged and called as a witness in pursuance of this Act shall not be asked, and if asked shall not be required to answer, any question tending to show that he has committed or been convicted of or been charged with any offence other than that wherewith he is then charged, or is of bad character, unless—

Does section 1(f) suggest questions cannot in fact be asked of the accused, notwithstanding that they might have a bearing on his guilt, if they incidentally reveal an aspect of his bad character? If so, what is its relationship with section 1(f)(i) which provides that the prohibition in section 1(f) has no application to:

(i) the proof that he has committed or been convicted of such other offence is admissible evidence to show that he is guilty of the offence wherewith he is then charged; ...

The clear wording of proviso (f) appears to be in conflict with section 1(f)(i) which permits the prosecution to ask questions of the accused about his having committed or been convicted of other offences (separate from those with which he is now charged), providing those offences are admissible as evidence of guilt.

The opportunity to provide some clarification on the apparent conflict within the sections was given to the House of Lords in *Jones* v *DPP* below.

Jones *v* DPP [1962] AC 635

The accused was charged with the murder of a girl guide. He had a previous conviction for the rape of a girl guide some months before the victim's death. Although there were similarities between the two attacks, the prosecution did not rely on similar fact evidence as part of its case as it did not want the girl to have to go through the ordeal of giving evidence again. When the defendant was first interviewed about the murder, he gave a false alibi, saying that he had been using the services of a prostitute at the time of the murder. In his examination-in-chief, his counsel asked him about the false alibi. In his evidence, the defendant said that the reason for lying to the police was that he had been in trouble with the police before and did not want to get involved with them again. He then gave fresh alibi evidence, which was identical to the alibi he had attempted to use at his previous trial for rape. The judge gave leave for the prosecuting counsel to cross-examine the defendant about the remarkable similarity between this new alibi and the one he had adduced on the other occasion when he had been 'in trouble'. No details were given to the jury of his previous conviction. The defendant was convicted. The House of Lords unanimously dismissed his appeal.

The reasoning of the Law Lords in *Jones* v *DPP* was less than unanimous. Lord Devlin and Lord Denning were of the view that the questioning fell within the meaning of section 1(e). The questioning was relevant to the defendant's guilt. The remarkable similarities in the alibi details suggested the alibi on this occasion had been concocted. Both their Lordships considered that such cross-examination would have been permissible irrespective of whether the defendant himself had made the jury aware of the earlier occasion on which he had been in trouble with the police.

Lord Morris felt section 1(f) prevailed over section 1(e) in that notwithstanding the questioning was relevant to guilt, it could not be pursued if it raised a matter prohibited under section 1(f). The only circumstances in which the prohibition could be lifted were set out in section 1(f)(i), (ii) and (iii).

Lord Reid and Viscount Simmonds held that section 1(e) only permitted questioning that was directly relevant to the issue of guilt. In this case the questioning in relation to the false alibi was of indirect relevance to guilt. This takes a very narrow view of relevance to guilt within the meaning of section 1(e).

Ultimately, the decision of the majority in this case was based solely on the wording of section 1(f). In conducting his defence, the defendant had already disclosed to the jury that he had been in trouble with the police before as a way of explaining away the false alibi he had given to the police in interview. Consequently cross-examination of him as regards the alibi he had given on the prior occasion was permitted because the questioning did not 'tend to show', within the meaning of section 1(f), any prohibited matter which the jury did not already know about.

Unfortunately, the decision in *Jones* v *DPP* provides little clarification of the relationship between section 1(e) and (f). It does represent, however, a pragmatic solution to an unresolvable conflict identified in the drafting of the two paragraphs of section 1. The conflict mirrors the difficulty already identified as to how much latitude the prosecution should be given to cross-examine the defendant on an issue as to guilt, of which his credibility is a key component without causing the defendant undue prejudice.

The pragmatic approach adopted by the House of Lords in *DPP* v *Jones* is further illustrated by the decision in *R* v *Anderson* [1988] QB 678. The defendant was a member of the IRA. She was charged with conspiracy to bomb a hotel in Brighton which was hosting the Conservative Party Conference. In her examination-in-chief, she explained her possession of false identity documents by stating that she was involved in an attempt to smuggle IRA members out of Ireland into Europe. The prosecution did not believe her account and were given leave to cross-examine her about other terrorist activities for which the police wished to interview her. The questions were directed towards showing that as a 'wanted' person in Ireland, the defendant would be a most unsuitable person to assist such a smuggling operation. On her appeal, it was held that her involvement in other offences was not a revelation to the jury, and so eliciting the evidence under cross-examination did not contravene section 1(f).

What is the purpose of section 1(f)(i)?

The wording of section 1(f)(i) would seem to permit the defendant to be cross-examined about his commission of or conviction for other offences. As such, it is in conflict with the general prohibition under section 1(f). The effect of the section is in fact to permit the prosecution to cross-examine the defendant on any previous offending which would satisfy the conditions of admissibility as similar fact evidence, discussed in the previous chapter. Whilst section 1(f)(i) refers to conviction and commission of offences only, at common law, similar fact evidence can also include the defendant's misconduct which falls short of being unlawful and any previous acquittals. The omission in section 1(f)(i) is less problematic than it appears, largely due to the decision in *Jones* v *DPP*, which held that the prosecution may only question the defendant on oath regarding his commission or conviction for offences relevant to guilt, where those offences have already formed part of the prosecution's case in chief. As such, the jury will already know details of the defendant's past. Section 1(f), which contains the general prohibition on questions about misconduct and other charges, will not apply in these circumstances as further questioning in cross-examination would not 'tend to show' something the jury were unaware of.

Admitting evidence of the defendant's character (section 1(f)(ii))

The defendant may lose his shield against cross-examination on the matters prohibited by section 1(f) if:

(ii) he has personally or by his advocate asked questions of the witnesses for the prosecution with a view to establish his own good character, or has given evidence of his good character, or the nature or conduct of the defence is such as to involve imputations on the character of the prosecutor or the witnesses for the prosecution, or the deceased victim of the alleged crime; ...

As can be seen, section 1(f)(ii) identifies two grounds where the accused may be cross-examined about his character and convictions: where he asserts evidence of his own good character and where imputations are made against the character of a prosecution witness or the deceased victim of the crime.

Asserting good character

What constitutes an assertion of good character?

The defendant can make an assertion of good character under the first limb of section 1(f)(ii) of the 1898 Act and at common law (see later) by declaring he has no previous convictions. However, the assertion need not be so explicit. In past cases a statement by the accused that he regularly attends church or is a happily married man in regular employment have been held to amount to an implicit assertion of good character. However, in *R v Robinson* [2001] Crim LR 478, the Court of Appeal held it had been wrong for the trial judge to have taken the view that the waving of a Bible at the jury by a rather excitable and verbose defendant amounted to an assertion of good character given the judge had failed to warn the defendant of his behaviour.

Not every assertion will amount to a claim of good character. The defendant's shield will not be lost where a defence witness voluntarily deposes to the virtues of the defendant, either whilst giving evidence-in-chief or in response to a question in cross-examination. This is made clear by the decision in *R v Redd* [1923] 1 KB 104. Nor will the defendant lose his shield if, as was the case in *R v Stronach* [1988] Crim LR 48, he is led in cross-examination by the prosecution to make an assertion of his good character.

The decision in *R v Ellis* [1910] KB 746 confirms an assertion of good character is not made where the defendant does no more than assert his innocence. In this case, the defendant referred to a course of business dealings that he had had with the victim all of which had been legitimate, in order to refute a charge of dishonesty in relation to a further course of dealings.

Also, evidence that reflects well on the accused and is confined to the facts in issue will not amount to an assertion. In *Malindi v R* [1957] 1 AC 439 the accused was charged with conspiracy to commit arson. The accused gave evidence that at a political meeting (which was central to the case) he had spoken against the use of violence. The trial judge ruled that this was an assertion of good character. The Privy Council took a different view, deeming the evidence to relate directly to an issue of fact in the case.

The indivisibility of character evidence

As with the common law rules relating to evidence of good character, which are consi-dered later in this chapter, character evidence is indivisible under the Criminal Evidence Act 1898. Asserting but one aspect of good character, however relevant that might be to refuting the charge faced by the accused, exposes the accused to the risk of cross-examination on all aspects of his character for the purpose of rebutting the assertion.

R v Winfield (1939) 27 Cr App R 139

In defence of a charge of indecent assault on another man, the defendant gave evidence on oath that he was a heterosexual man and that, for this reason, he was unlikely to have committed the offence. The prosecution was entitled to rebut this assertion of good character by adducing evidence of the defendant's convictions for dishonesty. The defendant had not in fact put his credibility as a witness directly in issue, nevertheless, because the courts regard character as being indivisible, his previous convictions for dishonesty were admitted.

The rule on the indivisibility of character evidence has been criticised in many academic quarters for its potential to cause injustice. What would, for example, be the point of allowing the prosecution to adduce evidence of the defendant's previous conviction for soliciting if he were to assert his honesty and general integrity in relation to a charge of theft? Such evidence is potentially prejudicial and bears little relevance to the question of how truthful the defendant is likely to be on oath. The Law Commission has recommended the abolition of the rule on indivisibility so as to 'avoid the injustice that may arise where the defendant truthfully asserts that he or she has a good character in a certain respect, and may then be cross-examined on discreditable conduct which has no bearing on the assertion made' (Law Commission Consultation Paper No 141).

The aspects of character revealed under the first limb of section 1(f)(ii) are relevant to the defendant's credibility as a witness on oath and must not be taken by the jury or the magistrates as evidence of the defendant's guilt on the matter. It is not always easy for the fact finder to draw a clear distinction between relevance to the defendant's credibility as a witness, as opposed to relevance in relation to an assessment of his guilt. Where the trial judge is persuaded that it would be impossible for the jury to make the distinction, the judge may prohibit or restrict the questioning of the defendant as regards his bad character in the exercise of his discretion to ensure a fair trial. The use of judicial discretion in this regard is considered later in this chapter.

Casting imputations on prosecution witnesses

(ii) ... the nature or conduct of the defence is such as to involve imputations on the character of the prosecutor or the witnesses for the prosecution, or the deceased victim of the alleged crime; ...

The accused loses his shield under the second limb of section 1(f)(ii) if he or his advocate casts an imputation on a witness for the prosecution or on the deceased victim of the alleged offence. An imputation is a comment or a question intended to denigrate the character or credibility of a prosecution witness or the deceased victim of a crime. The decision of the Court of Appeal in *R v Miller* [1997] 2 Cr App R 178 confirms the ambit of section 1(f)(ii) extends to 'paper witnesses', which would include a witness whose evidence is given in deposition form or in documentary form under an exception to the rule against admitting hearsay evidence.

There are said to be three justifications for admitting evidence prejudicial to the defendant under the second limb of section 1(f)(ii): fairness, deterrence and credibility.

Fairness

The second limb of section 1(f)(ii) invokes the 'tit-for tat' principle as a measure of fairness. Where an accused with previous convictions impugns the character of a prosecution witness for the purpose of leading the court to conclude the witness's evidence is not to be believed, it is only fair that the fact finder is made aware of the character of the person who is casting such an imputation. Were this not the case, how could the fact finder properly determine where the truth might lie as between the witness and the accused?

Deterrence

Public interest demands the protection of witnesses against gratuitous attacks in a way that ensures that the fact finder does not have a distorted impression of the witness. The defendant is deterred from making assertions because of the evidential consequences that can stem from the loss of his shield. The deterrent effect however is lost where the defendant decides not to testify himself. It is therefore somewhat illogical that the defendant can attack the character of a prosecution witness with impunity without fear of losing his shield if he chooses not to give evidence on oath in support of his own defence.

R v Butterwasser [1947] 2 All ER 415

The defendant, who was on trial for wounding, had previous convictions for violence. The defendant's advocate cross-examined a number of prosecution witnesses on their previous convictions for violence with a view to destroying their credibility. The defendant did not give evidence himself. The Court of Criminal Appeal held the defendant had not put his character in issue by reason of the fact that he had attacked the credibility of prosecution witnesses. As he had not given evidence on oath he was not liable to cross-examination on his character, as his credibility had not been called into question under the 1898 Act.

Credibility

The defendant invites comparison with his own character when he attacks the character of a prosecution witness on oath. Loss of the defendant's shield helps the fact finder to make an informed assessment of the defendant's credibility as a witness.

Relevance to the defendant's credibility only

Character revealed under the second limb of section 1(f)(ii) is relevant only to an assessment of the accused's credibility as a witness giving evidence on oath. It cannot be used as evidence of the defendant's guilt on the matter with which he is charged. This must be made absolutely clear to a jury in a Crown Court trial and magistrates should be reminded of this when adjudicating in a summary trial. The court is under an obligation to ensure the defendant has a fair trial. Where there is a danger that the jury, in particular, might be unable to make the distinction between relevance to credibility and relevance to guilt, the court has a discretion, both at common law and under section 78 of PACE, to limit or prohibit the prosecution in the questions it asks under section 1(f)(ii). The position is neatly summed up by the dictum of Lord Sankey in

Maxwell v *DPP*: 'The question whether a man has been charged, convicted or acquitted even if it goes to credibility ought not to be admitted if there is any risk of the jury being misled into thinking that it goes not to credibility but to the probability of his having committed the offence with which he is charged.'

What constitutes casting an imputation?

Some latitude is given to the courts in determining what amounts to casting an imputation under the second limb of section 1(f)(ii). If it were otherwise, any denial of guilt, including a not guilty plea, which has the effect of implying witnesses might be prepared to perjure themselves on oath, would fall within the literal meaning of the words used in the section.

Almost any statement which impugns the character of a prosecution witness by suggesting specific discreditable or disgraceful conduct will cause the defendant to lose his shield. It matters not that the imputation is indispensable to the conduct of the accused's defence. Indeed, the defendant may not want to cast an imputation but may be forced to in order to answer the allegations made against him.

R v Bishop [1975] QB 274

The defendant was charged with burglary, namely that he entered premises as a trespasser and stole property. He denied the offence. Evidence was given that the defendant's fingerprints had been found on several items in the victim's room. The defendant explained the presence of his prints by stating he had visited the victim's property on many occasions because he had had a homosexual relationship with him. The victim denied this. The allegation of a homosexual relationship was probably true and was necessary to explain the defendant's innocent presence at the property. However, it was held to constitute an imputation against the character of the victim.

To mitigate the hardship caused by a literal interpretation of the section, a distinction is drawn in the case law between a denial of guilt, even an emphatic denial on the one hand, and any assertion or implied assertion which is an attack on the character of prosecution witnesses or the deceased victim on the other. The former should not result in the defendant's loss of shield, the latter almost certainly will. In *R* v *Rouse* [1904] 1 KB 184, the accused shouted out to a prosecution witness: 'you're a bloody liar!' This was deemed to be an emphatic denial of guilt as opposed to an imputation. The two leading cases on casting imputations are *Selvey* v *DPP* and *R* v *Britzman and Hall* below. Both cases illustrate the difficulty of dividing a clear line between what constitutes an emphatic denial of guilt and what amounts to casting an imputation.

Selvey v DPP [1970] AC 304

The defendant was charged with buggery. He denied the offence had taken place. The victim was cross-examined along the lines that he was a male prostitute and had offered sexual services to the defendant for money. The defendant claimed that his refusal of the offer had resulted in a false allegation of buggery being made against him. The defendant had argued that as the imputation was a necessary part of his defence, he should not be deemed to have thrown away his shield and that, even if he had thrown away his shield, the trial judge should have exercised his discretion to disallow cross-examination on his criminal record. Notwithstanding that the allegation was a necessary part of his defence, the House of Lords concluded that by alleging the victim was a male prostitute the defendant had cast an imputation within the meaning of the words in the statute.

R v Britzman and Hall [1983] 1 WLR 350

An imputation was made against investigating officers. On oath, officers testified that the defendant had made incriminating statements in the course of a long interview with them. The defendant denied the words attributed to him, although he did not actually accuse the police of impropriety. The Court of Appeal held that in the circumstances of the case, for the defendant to have denied the conversation ever took place was to impliedly accuse the officers of fabricating confession evidence in order to obtain a conviction.

It is of course not uncommon for defendants to make allegations of police impropriety in the way in which evidence is gathered during the investigative process. This case is therefore particularly important in that the judgment of Lord Justice Lawton lays down some useful guidance on what constitutes casting an imputation in general and in particular against investigating officers:

> A defence to a criminal charge which suggests that prosecution witnesses have deliberately made up false evidence in order to secure a conviction must involve imputations on the characters of those witnesses with the consequence that the trial judge may, in the exercise of his discretion allow prosecuting counsel to cross-examine the defendant about offences of which he has been convicted. In our judgment this is what Parliament intended should happen in most cases. Where allegations of the fabrication of evidence are made against prosecution witnesses, as they often are these days, juries are entitled to know about the characters of those making them...
>
> We hope that it will be useful for both judges and counsel to set out some guidelines for the exercise of discretion in favour of defendants. First it should be used if there is nothing more than a denial, however emphatic or offensively made, of an act or short series of acts amounting to one incident or in what was said to have been a short interview. Examples are provided by the kind of evidence given in pickpocket cases and where the defendant is alleged to have said: 'Who grassed me this time?' The position would be different however if there were a denial of evidence of a long period of detailed observation extending over hours and just as in this case where there were denials of long conversations...
>
> Second, cross-examination should only be allowed if the judge is sure that there is no possibility of mistake, misunderstanding or confusion and that the jury will inevitably have to decide whether the prosecution witnesses have fabricated evidence. Defendants sometimes make wild allegations whilst giving evidence. Allowance should be made for the strain of being in the witness box and the exaggerated use of language which sometimes results from such strain or lack of education or mental instability. Particular care should be used when a defendant is led into making allegations during cross-examination. The defendant who, during cross-examination, is driven to explaining away evidence by saying it has been made up or planted on him usually convicts himself without having his previous convictions brought out. Finally, there is no need for the prosecution to rely upon section 1(f)(ii) if the evidence against a defendant is overwhelming.

Having regard to the decisions of *Selvey* and *Britzman and Hall*, are there instances when it can confidently be predicated that an accused's shield will be lost?

It will almost certainly be lost where the defendant:

- alleges that a prosecution witness is biased;
- makes an allegation that the police have fabricated evidence;
- cross-examines a prosecution witness on any previous convictions they might have;
- accuses a prosecution witness of perjury;
- accuses the investigating officers of deliberately flouting PACE and the Codes of Practice.

It will probably not amount to an imputation where the defendant puts it to a prosecution witness that:

- he or she is mistaken, confused or simply wrong;
- the police have got some aspect of the Codes of Practice wrong;
- he or she is lying, though this depends on what latitude the court gives to an accused in accordance with the decision in *R v Britzman and Hall*.

The decision in *R v Britzman and Hall* provides guidance and a measure of protection for the accused. Courts must give an accused a degree of latitude in the witness box and must make allowance for the stresses and strains associated with giving evidence on oath. However, section 1(f)(ii) of the 1898 Act still presents a significant obstacle to a defendant who has previous convictions but who maintains his confession was fabricated or obtained in blatant breach of the Codes of Practice, or who believes the evidence that the police claim to have obtained has been planted by them. Such a defendant is in a 'no-win' situation: if the defendant testifies his previous convictions will almost certainly be revealed and the risk of conviction is increased. If the defendant does not testify, the assertion put by his advocate that his confession was fabricated is robbed of significant probative force.

Can the operation of section 1(f)(ii) be said to violate the defendant's right to a fair trial where the defendant feels he is unable to conduct his defence in an unfettered manner? Arguably it does and the provision must be considered to be vulnerable to a challenge under Article 6 of the European Convention on Human Rights. One of the principal criticisms of the operation of section 1(f)(ii) identified in the Law Commission's Consultation Paper is the unfairness of the provision which inhibits an accused from giving evidence for fear of losing his shield in circumstances where an imputation is a necessary part of the accused's defence.

The Law Commission provisionally recommended that the law be changed so that no imputation could be regarded as having been made where the accusations put to a witness relate to the witness's conduct in the incident or the investigation which followed it. The Law Commission's final proposals for reform are considered later in the chapter.

Exercise of judicial discretion where shield has been lost

Where an accused has lost his shield under the second limb of section 1(f)(ii), the court has discretion to prevent or to restrict the cross-examination of the accused on his previous criminal record where the prejudicial effect of his record would outweigh its probative value. The sole purpose of cross-examination under this limb is to attack the defendant's credibility as a witness in his own defence. If the judge concludes that by reason of the knowledge imparted to the court as a result of the defendant losing his shield, it will be impossible for the jury not to infer the defendant's guilt, he should exercise his discretion to refuse to allow cross-examination of the defendant. With this in mind, should the judge confine questioning of the defendant to offences relevant to his credibility, ie convictions for perjury or dishonesty? Where a defendant is being tried for an offence of indecent assault and throws away his shield should his previous conviction for indecent assault be revealed? How can such a conviction be regarded as being relevant purely to an assessment of the defendant's credibility as the section demands that it should be? Where the prosecution is allowed to cross-examine the defendant how much detail is it allowed to go into as regards the defendant's previous convictions? Can reference be made to spent convictions?

Restricting the nature of the questions asked in cross-examination was endorsed on the facts and the decision in R v *France* below.

R v France [1979] Crim LR 48

The defendant was charged with theft from a jeweller's shop. It was alleged he had distracted the shop assistant and taken the goods. At his trial the defendant lost his shield by casting imputations on the character of one of the prosecution witnesses. In his cross-examination, the defendant was asked not only about the fact that he had previous convictions for theft and other crimes involving dishonesty, but also about the method he had used in committing his previous offences of theft. This included deliberate distraction of the shop assistant in order to facilitate the theft. The Court of Appeal quashed his subsequent conviction for theft, because there was no question of the prior misconduct amounting to similar fact evidence. Section (1)(f)(ii) was not to be used in such a way. If the evidence satisfied the test for admission as similar fact, it had been open to the prosecution to present it as part of its case. The Court of Appeal took the view that simply to make the jury aware that the defendant had previous convictions for theft would have been sufficient in itself to enable the jury to carry out an assessment of the defendant's credibility. Questioning the defendant about the detail behind his convictions went far beyond the bounds of relevance to his credibility as a witness.

The high-water mark of concern for the defendant came in the decision of the Court of Appeal in R v *Watts* [1983] 3 All ER 101. In this case, the defendant faced an allegation of indecent assault on a woman. The defendant was of low intelligence. He denied the offence. At his trial, he asserted the police had fabricated an oral confession he was alleged to have made. Having thrown away his shield, he was cross-examined on previous convictions for indecent assault involving young girls. The trial judge quite properly directed the jury not to use the fact of the previous convictions as evidence of guilt. Unsurprisingly, the defendant was convicted. His conviction was quashed in the Court of Appeal for reasons explained by Lord Lane CJ:

> The prejudice which the appellant must have suffered in the eyes of the jury when it was disclosed that he had previous convictions for offences against young children could hardly have been greater. The probative value of the convictions, on the sole issue on which they were admissible, was, at best, slight. The previous offences did not involve dishonesty. Nor were they so similar to the offence which the jury were trying that they could have been admitted as evidence of similar facts on the issue of identity...

Was Lord Lane CJ right to suggest that the previous convictions had little probative value on the issue of the defendant's credibility? Did not the fact that the defendant had previous convictions for a similar offence make it logically less likely that he was telling the truth when he stated on oath that he did not commit the offence? Arguably it did, but the obvious risk of prejudice to the defendant in admitting his convictions as being relevant to his credibility only was quite properly identified by Lord Lane CJ. If such evidence would not have been admitted as similar fact evidence because its prejudicial effect was greater than its probative value, can it be said that that prejudice can safely be ignored by instructing the jury to use only the evidence in its assessment of the defendant's credibility?

The decision in R v Watts must now be read in conjunction with the subsequent decision in R v Powell [1985] 1 WLR 1364, in which Lord Lane CJ once again delivered the leading judgment. The defendant was charged with living off the earnings of a prostitute. He maintained the prosecution's case was a total fabrication. He also falsely made an assertion of his good character. The prosecution sought leave to cross-examine the defendant about a previous conviction for allowing premises to be used as a brothel. The trial judge faced a dilemma and following the decision in R v Watts, he permitted the cross-examination to rebut the assertion of good character and not on the basis that an imputation had been cast against prosecution witnesses.

In affirming the conviction, the Court of Appeal held that the only mistake the judge had made was not to have permitted the cross-examination on the basis that the defendant had cast an imputation. Lord Lane CJ observed that in R v Watts he had overlooked the 'tit-for-tat' principle behind the legislation and had paid too much attention to offences of dishonesty as touching on the matter of credibility. He admitted he had not given due weight to the decision in Selvey v DPP, which clearly did not prevent offences of a similar kind from being admitted in circumstances where the shield had been thrown away. In summary, Lord Lane CJ concluded that where there has been a deliberate attack on the conduct of a prosecution witness calculated to discredit him, the jury was entitled to know the previous convictions of the individual making the attack. The fact that the previous convictions happen to be similar is a matter for the judge to take on board when exercising his discretion, but was not a bar to cross-examination.

The two principal cases providing guidance on the ability of a court to prohibit or restrict cross-examination where the shield has been lost under section (1)(f)(ii) are R v Burke (1986) 82 Cr App R 156 and R v McLeod [1994] 3 All ER 254. In the former case, Lord Ackner laid down the following guidelines:

1. The trial judge must weigh the prejudicial effect of the questions against the damage done by the attack on the prosecution's witnesses, and must generally exercise his discretion so as to secure a trial that is fair to both the prosecution and the defence...

2. Cases must occur in which it would be unjust to admit evidence of a character which is gravely prejudicial to the accused, even though there may be some tenuous grounds for holding it technically admissible ... Thus, although the position is established in law, still the putting of the questions as to the character of the accused person may be fraught with results which immeasurably outweigh the result of questions put by the defence and which make a fair trial of the accused almost impossible.

3. In the ordinary and normal case the trial judge may feel that if the credit of the prosecutor or his witnesses has been attacked, it is only fair that the jury should have before them material on which they can form their judgment, whether the accused person is any more worthy to be believed than those he has attacked. It is obviously unfair that the jury should be left in the dark about an accused person's character if the conduct of his defence has attacked the character of the prosecutor or the witnesses for the prosecution.

4. In order to see if the conviction should be quashed, it is not enough that the court thinks it would have exercised its discretion differently. The court will not interfere with the exercise of a discretion by the judge unless he has erred in principle, or there is no material on which he could properly have arrived at his decision.

The most recent guidance on the exercise of discretion is provided by the Court of Appeal in *R v McLeod* below.

R v McLeod [1994] 3 All ER 254

The defendant was convicted of armed robbery which involved the use of stolen cars. At the police interview, he made a confession, but in evidence he denied being involved in the robbery and maintained the police had created the case against him, including fabricating his confession. Anticipating that by running this defence his shield would be lost, defence counsel briefly asked his client about his previous convictions. In cross-examination the defendant was asked detailed questions concerning a previous robbery in relation to which he had pleaded not guilty, having relied on a defence of alibi. He was asked further questions about other offences of theft and the handling of a car with false registration plates. The defence objected to these questions only after they had been asked. On appeal, it was submitted that these questions should not have been asked. The appeal was dismissed.

The Court of Appeal set out the following guidelines in *R v McLeod*:

(1) The primary purpose of cross-examination as to previous convictions and bad character of the accused is to show that he is not worthy of belief. It is not, and should not be, to show that he has a disposition to commit the type of offence with which he is charged. But the mere fact that the offences are of a similar type to that charged or because their number and type have the incidental effect of suggesting a tendency or disposition to commit the offence charged will not make them improper.

(2) It is undesirable that there should be a prolonged or extensive cross-examination in relation to previous offences. This is because it will divert the jury from the principal issues in the case, the guilt of the accused in the instant offence, and not the earlier ones.

(3) Similarities of defences which have been rejected by the juries on previous occasions, for example false alibis or the defence that an incriminating substance had been planted and whether or not the accused pleaded guilty or was disbelieved having given evidence on oath, may be legitimate matters for questions. These matters do not show a disposition to commit the offence in question but are clearly relevant to credibility.

(4) Underlying facts that show particularly bad character over and above the bare facts of the case are not necessarily to be excluded. However the judge should be careful to balance the gravity of the attack on the prosecution with the degree of prejudice to the defence which will result from the disclosure of the facts in question.

(5) If objection to a particular line of cross-examination about the underlying facts of a previous offence, it should be taken as soon as it is apparent to defence counsel that it is in danger of going too far.

(6) While it is the duty of the judge to keep cross-examination within proper bounds, if no objection is taken at the time it will be difficult thereafter to contend that the judge has wrongly exercised his discretion. In any event this Court will not interfere with the exercise of the judge's discretion save on well-established principles.

(7) In every case where the accused has been cross-examined as to his character and previous offences, the judge must in his summing up tell the jury that the purpose of the questioning goes only to credit and they should not consider that it shows a propensity to commit the offence they are considering.

The above guidelines demonstrate two important points:

1 convincing the court to exercise its discretion to prohibit or restrict questioning is not easy; and
2 persuading the Court of Appeal to overturn a conviction where a judge has refused to exercise discretion is much the same.

The onerous nature of section 1(f)(ii) is illustrated by the decision in *R v Wainwright* below.

R *v* Wainwright [1998] Crim LR 665

The defendant was a serving prisoner charged with the murder of a fellow inmate, T. There was some evidence of bad feeling between the defendant and the deceased. The defendant maintained he had acted in self-defence. The prosecution accepted the deceased inmate had a bad reputation for violence. The ambulance men who attended the deceased had found him to be in possession of a knife. Prison officers, by contrast, gave evidence that the defendant was unusually friendly and had made good progress. The prosecution argued that the defendant had thrown away his shield by casting imputations and asserting his 'good' character. This was conceded by the defendant's counsel who sought to limit cross-examination to his client's previous convictions for dishonesty and not the fact that he was serving a sentence for a grave offence of violence. The trial judge refused to limit the cross-examination and the defendant was convicted of manslaughter. On appeal, it was argued that the appellant had not cast imputations as the prosecution had conceded the deceased victim was of bad character and had a reputation for violence. The Court of Appeal rejected this argument. As for discretion to limit cross-examination, counsel for the defendant pointed to the fact that the deceased's bad character had not been disputed and the prejudicial effect of the defendant's convictions had been great. Placing reliance on *R v Burke* and *R* v *McLeod*, the Court of Appeal concluded it had been the only way for the jury to get a balanced picture of the two men.

By contrast, two recent decisions of the Court of Appeal show instances where discretion should have been exercised in favour of the defendant.

R *v* Davison-Jenkins [1997] Crim LR 816

The defendant was caught stealing cheap cosmetics at the pharmacy retailer, Boots. She denied an intention to steal. The defendant had a psychiatric history, which resulted in her taking valium and occasionally suffering panic attacks. At her trial, she gave evidence about her job as a manager; about her good schooling and university education; that the wealthy father of her son, who owned three houses, was in Italy and had taken her son there and had not returned him. Her evidence was sufficient to put her character in question and permission was granted to allow the prosecution to cross-examine her on her previous convictions, which included shoplifting. The defendant was convicted and appealed on the ground that she should not have been cross-examined on her convictions. In allowing the appeal, the Court of Appeal concluded that the recorder's summing up in relation to what her previous convictions were for, including specific references to the fact that one was for shoplifting cosmetics and clothes, made it highly unlikely that the jury would be able to put these factors out of its mind in assessing the defendant's guilt. The prejudice to the accused of this direction outweighed any marginal relevance to the issue of the accused's credibility. Furthermore, it had been wrong to go into the detail of the defendant's previous offending.

R v Barratt [2000] Crim LR 847

The defendant was charged with possession of an offensive weapon. He threw away his shield by casting an imputation on the character of a prosecution witness. Leave was given to cross-examine the defendant on a spent conviction for possession of an offensive weapon dating back to 1985. The Court of Appeal quashed the conviction, because it felt the judge should have exercised his discretion to refuse leave. He had failed to weigh up the fact that the offence was long spent and would therefore have little impact on the defendant's credibility, as compared with the substantial risk of prejudice the revelation must have caused.

The Rehabilitation of Offenders Act 1974 provides that a person, whose conviction is spent within the definition of the Act, is to be treated as having not committed the offence. Section 7 of the 1974 Act, however, excludes criminal proceedings from its operation. Does this mean that a defendant can routinely refer to a prosecution witness's spent convictions in an effort to discredit the witness or that a defendant's spent conviction can be adduced in accordance with the operation of the Criminal Evidence Act 1898? A means of protection is afforded in each of the above cases by *Practice Direction (QBD: Rehabilitation of Offenders Act 1974: Implementation: Reference to Spent Convictions during Trial)* [1975] 1 WLR 1065. The Practice Direction requires all courts in criminal proceedings to have regard to the spirit of the Rehabilitation of Offenders Act 1974 and not to allow mention of spent convictions except with the authority of the judge and only when it is in the interests of justice to do so. Note should also be taken of the operation of section 16 of the Children and Young Persons Act 1916. This section absolutely prohibits any mention, in a criminal trial of an accused aged over 21, of any previous convictions the accused might have for offences committed whilst under the age of 14.

PRACTICAL STEPS – A TACTICAL DILEMMA

For many defendants, the second limb of section 1(f)(ii) creates a considerable tactical dilemma, in that it can hamper the way in which a defence is constructed. In some cases it will be necessary for the defendant to impugn the character of a prosecution witness in an attempt to establish his innocence. Having had to throw away his shield in such circumstances, the defendant will be at serious risk of having aspects of his bad character revealed to the court. The defendant could of course choose not to give evidence

on oath, in which case he would not be liable to have his previous convictions exposed
under the 1898 Act. However, in so choosing, his silence at trial could well result in an
adverse evidential inference being drawn against him under section 35 of the Criminal
Justice and Public Order Act 1994. In *R v Cowan* [1995] 3 WLR 818, the Court of
Appeal firmly rejected an argument that no adverse inference should be drawn under
section 35 where giving evidence on oath exposes a defendant to the very real possibility of cross-examination on his criminal record under the 1898 Act. Section 35
undoubtedly increases the pressure on the defendant to testify (see Chapter 7).

As a matter of tactics, it is common practice in appropriate circumstances for a
defence advocate to ask his client to confirm his previous convictions on oath before
giving evidence. By stealing the prosecution's thunder in this way, a certain amount of
damage limitation is achieved in that the element of drama and surprise such a revelation would cause if it were brought out in cross-examination of the defendant is lost.
Where a defendant has pleaded guilty to the vast majority of his previous offences, this
too ought to be pointed out to the court. It implies the accused fully understands the
advantages in pleading guilty, but chooses not to do so on this occasion because he is
innocent of the charge.

Defendants need to be carefully prepared for the experience of giving evidence on
oath. Express or implied false assertions of good character must be avoided. The
defence advocate is assisted in this regard by *Practice Direction (Crime: Antecedents)*
[1993] 1 WLR 1459 requiring the prosecution to disclose any previous convictions the
defendant may have. The defendant should be counselled as to the importance of not
unnecessarily impugning the character of a prosecution witness, even though he might
feel wound up under the pressure of cross-examination. The advocate should carefully
plan his strategy for the cross-examination of all witnesses in the case in order to
decide if an imputation is absolutely necessary. In a case where the defendant denies
being at the scene of the crime all that may be necessary to raise a reasonable doubt is
to accuse an eyewitness of being mistaken rather than lying. The advocate should
always be prepared to mount a submission that the nature of questions asked in cross-
examination should be restricted or that certain previous convictions should be withheld on the basis that it would prejudice the defendant's right to a fair trial.

The case of *R v Taylor and Goodman* [1999] Crim LR 407 gave the Court of Appeal
an opportunity to review the procedure to be adopted in cases where a fellow co-
defendant chooses to plead guilty and to give evidence for the prosecution. The facts
involved a conspiracy to commit robbery. There were three accused, M, T and G. M
pleaded guilty, 'turning Queen's evidence', thereby becoming competent to give evidence for the prosecution as an accomplice. At the request of the defence, the prosecution did not make known to the jury the fact of M's extensive criminal record.
Counsel for G and T did not wish to cross-examine M on his criminal record for fear
that it would lead to G and T being cross-examined on their criminal records. In the
course of his evidence, G accused both M and the investigating officer of lying and
falsely implicating G and T in the involvement of a fictitious crime to cover up M's
misconduct. Counsel for the prosecution sought to cross-examine G on his extensive
criminal record. G's counsel maintained his client had done no more than to mount a
vigorous denial of the allegations. The judge concluded that the line of questioning
went beyond an emphatic denial and permitted the prosecution to adduce evidence of

G's previous convictions. Both T and G were convicted. G appealed on the basis that the jury had not been made aware of M's previous convictions and was therefore not in a position to make a proper evaluation as to where the truth might lie. T appealed on the basis that, although his previous convictions were not revealed to the jury, the jury might have been influenced by its knowledge of G's previous convictions.

The Court of Appeal affirmed both convictions. In doing so, however, it considered it was doubtful whether any judge would regard cross-examination on an accomplice's criminal record as justification for permitting the defendant's previous convictions to be adduced in evidence:

> We believe that in many parts of the country nowadays, unless counsel for the defence indicates otherwise, information about an accomplice's previous convictions is normally given to the jury at the outset of the case by counsel for the prosecution, not only so that the jury may be informed of the actual facts, but also for the forensically sensible reason that a jury might well react adversely to the sudden emergence of such facts about someone who is in any event disreputable. Where this is not the practice, the practice should be altered so that normally counsel for the prosecution should offer to disclose such convictions to the jury unless invited not to do so by counsel for the defence, for whatever reason may seem appropriate at that time, counsel for the prosecution should open the case and tell the jury about them at the outset.

The practice sanctioned by the Court of Appeal in *R v Taylor and Goodman* of disclosing at the start of the trial the convictions of accomplices who are giving evidence for the prosecution is important in that it means that cross-examination of such witnesses on their criminal record will not lead to the defendant losing his shield under section 1(f), as that information will have already been disclosed to the fact finder. The decision of the Court of Appeal is welcome and goes some way to mitigating the potential hazards for the defendant under the current law.

The dilemmas posed by the operation of section 1(f)(ii) are illustrated in the context of the death by dangerous driving case scenario involving Andrew in the introduction to Chapter 20. If Andrew were to give evidence and was foolish enough to assert his good character or to cast an imputation on a prosecution witness, he would throw away his shield under section 1(f)(ii) and risk cross-examination on both his driving record and his failure to inform his insurance company of his driving misdemeanours.

Is it relevant to an assessment of Andrew's credibility to make the fact finder aware of his previous driving offences? Arguably, the only wrongdoing relevant to his credibility as a witness is his failure to tell his insurance company of his previous convictions, implying a willingness on his part to lie or to at least be economical with the truth. His advocate might argue that Andrew is entitled to make an assertion of good character, so long as he does not suggest that he has an exemplary driving record. Given the indivisibility of character however, it seems doubtful that such a submission would succeed. In any event, the prosecution would be entitled to cross-examine Andrew on his failure to inform his insurance company of his convictions in order to rebut his assertion of good character and this, in turn, would alert the fact finder to the fact that Andrew does not have a clean driving licence.

In the event of Andrew's shield being lost, his advocate might seek to persuade the judge to exercise his discretion not to allow cross-examination on his client's driving record, or to restrict the nature of such cross-examination, having regard to the prejudice it would cause. The disclosure of a previous conviction for careless driving and two previous endorsements for speeding in a case where dangerous driving (in which, speed is alleged to be factor) would make an acquittal unlikely. The best course of action for Andrew would be to be extremely cautious in the witness box and not to say or do anything that is likely to result in the loss of his shield.

Criticisms of section 1(f)(ii)

The Law Commission identified a number of specific criticisms of the second limb of section 1(f)(ii) of the Criminal Evidence Act 1898 (see Law Commission Consultation Paper No 41 and Report No 273).

1 It makes no allowance for the fact that casting an imputation on a prosecution witness may be a necessity for the defendant.
2 It inhibits a defendant from testifying in support of his own defence and consequentially subjects him to the risk of an adverse inference under section 35 of the Criminal Justice and Public Order Act 1994. Revelation of the accused's previous convictions makes conviction on the current charge more likely. Where the allegation against a prosecution witness is true and is a necessary part of an accused's defence, a defendant with previous convictions is in a no-win situation.
3 It is both illogical and unrealistic to expect fact finders to draw a distinction between relevance as to credibility and relevance as to guilt.
4 Notwithstanding the loss of shield under the second limb of section 1(f)(ii), a court must exercise its judicial discretion where it concludes that the prejudicial effect of the cross-examination would exceed its probative value. Such an assessment is not easily made and can have the effect of undermining the intent behind the second limb, whilst leading to uncertainty.

The Law Commission was highly critical of the rationales behind the operation of the second limb of section 1(f)(ii). So far as assisting the fact finder in an assessment of the defendant's credibility, the Law Commission relied on psychological research undertaken as part of the Law Commission's review, which showed that the knowledge of a defendant's previous convictions had very little effect on a fact finder's assessment of the defendant's credibility as a witness in his own defence. This is compounded by the indivisibility rule which often means the revelation of aspects of the defendant's bad character that have little or no relevance to his truthfulness as a witness.

The research conducted on mock jurors confirmed that fact finders have great difficulty in distinguishing between the defendant's credibility as opposed to his guilt (Law Commission Consultation Paper No 141, Appendix C). The research found that when it was made known to jurors that a defendant had previous convictions for dishonesty or assault, they did not significantly find the defendant a less credible witness as a consequence. Furthermore, where evidence of bad character was admitted, jurors were unlikely to restrict its use to an assessment only of the accused's credibility on oath even when instructed to do so by the judge. Most interestingly, it was only in situations where the jury were told the defendant had a previous conviction for an indecent assault on a child or had a recent previous conviction similar to the offence for which the defendant was being tried, that the jury was more likely to find the defendant to be significantly less believable on oath. The latter finding surely accords with common sense. However, this is to permit the 'forbidden reasoning' from propensity to guilt discussed in the introduction to Chapter 20. The jury might well reason that in the light of the defendant's previous convictions he has a predisposition to commit that type of crime and therefore he is not to be believed on oath when he says he is not guilty of the current similar charge.

The fairness of admitting the defendant's previous convictions was criticised because the fairness to the impugned witness is gained at the expense of fairness to the defendant. It must not be forgotten that the effect of the second limb of section 1(f)(ii) is to allow the admission of bad character evidence which would never have passed the similar fact evidence test, and which is as a consequence more prejudicial than probative. Although the fact finder is directed not to treat the evidence as having a bearing on the defendant's guilt, the point has already been made that it is often difficult, if not impossible, for the fact finder to achieve, especially where the previous convictions are similar to the offence presently under consideration.

The deterrent argument was also criticised. The Law Commission was firmly of the view that the second limb was not the best way of securing protection from unfair and irrelevant cross-examination of prosecution witnesses. Whilst the defendant should be discouraged from making spurious attacks on a prosecution witness, the Law Commission observed that he too is entitled to be protected from the risk of a wrongful conviction. Furthermore, as we saw from the case of *R v Butterwasser* [1947] 2 All ER 415, the deterrent effect has no application to the situation in which the defendant attacks the character of a prosecution witness but chooses not to give evidence himself.

Overall, the Law Commission concluded that the whole of the second limb of section 1(f)(ii) was flawed in that it can lead to difficult choices for some defendants who have previous convictions but who feel they must give evidence in an attempt to establish their innocence. The exercise of a wide-ranging discretion had tempered some of the harsher aspects, but it had also led to a lack of clarity and a degree of uncertainty as to what amounted to an imputation and as to when discretion was likely to be exercised. This imposed practical difficulties on defence advocates in trying to advise their clients appropriately.

Cross-examination of the accused under section 1(f)(iii)

(iii) he has given evidence against any other person charged in the same proceedings.

Section 1(f)(iii) provides that the shield will be lost by an accused (D1) who has given evidence against any other person charged (D2) in the same proceedings. It is not necessary for D1 to attack D2's character. It is sufficient that D1 gives evidence which strengthens or supports the prosecution's case against D2 or undermines D2's case, so making his conviction more likely. For the purposes of section 1(f)(iii), it does not matter that D1's attack on D2's character was unintentional.

The purpose of permitting D2 to cross-examine D1 on aspects of D1's character is to enable D2 to discredit D1 where D1 has given evidence against him. Section 1(f)(iii) affords the opportunity of running a 'cut-throat defence' with often devastating consequences.

Example

D1 and D2 are jointly charged. D2 knows that D1 has an extensive history of past misconduct. D2 has no previous convictions. D2 knows that if he gives evidence on oath putting the blame on D1, D1 will be faced with two stark options. Option 1 would be for D1 not to give evidence on oath. Option 2 would be for D1 to give evidence harmful to D2. By taking Option 1, D1 would risk an adverse evidential inference being drawn against him under section 35 of the Criminal Justice and Public Order Act 1994. By taking Option 2, which D1 is effectively compelled to do, D1 knows he will throw away his shield under section 1(f)(iii) and will be cross-examined on his record of previous convictions. In such a case, as a matter of tactics D2 has nothing to lose and potentially much to gain. Where both D1 and D2 have previous convictions, the decision to run a 'cut-throat defence' usually results in the conviction of both!

There is one fundamental difference between the operation of section 1(f)(ii) and (iii). Paragraph (ii) confers discretion on the court to limit and restrict cross-examination, whilst paragraph (iii) does not. Under section l(f)(iii), a court cannot refuse leave to cross-examine where the conditions permitting cross-examination are made out. The rationale in support of the lack of any judicial discretion is summed up in the words of Lord Donovan in *Murdoch* v *Taylor* [1965] AC 574:

> [The accused] seeks to defend himself; to say to the jury that the man who is giving evidence against him is unworthy of belief; and to support that assertion by proof of bad character. The right to do this, in my opinion, cannot be fettered in any way.

Having regard to the example above, the absence of any judicial discretion to prohibit or restrict cross-examination under section 1(f)(iii) has the potential for causing considerable prejudice to a co-accused, particularly where D2 has little to lose because he has no criminal convictions or his convictions are of a trivial nature.

Where character is revealed in accordance with section 1(f)(iii), it is relevant only to an assessment of the defendant's credibility as a witness on oath and should not be utilised as evidence of his guilt in the matter with which he is charged. In a jury trial the judge must carefully and clearly instruct the jury in this regard.

The principles behind section 1(f)(iii) were extensively reviewed in two leading cases.

Murdoch *v* Taylor [1965] AC 574

The accused (D1) was charged, together with another (D2), with handling stolen goods. D1 testified that he had no knowledge as to what was in a box he had received, because the contents of the box were nothing to do with him but were the sole responsibility of D2. The trial judge ruled D1 had lost his shield under section 1(f)(iii) and that therefore D2 had the right to cross-examine D1 on his previous convictions. D1 appealed against his conviction, contending he had not given evidence against D2 and that he had not intended to shift the blame from himself onto D2. Affirming the conviction, the House of Lords held that, notwithstanding D1's motive, his evidence had strengthened the prosecution case against D2 and had by implication alleged that it was D2 and D2 only who was the handler of stolen goods.

In *Murdoch* v *Taylor* the House of Lords confirmed that:

(a) section 1(f)(iii) applies whether the evidence against a co-accused is given as examination-in-chief or cross-examination; and

(b) a statement by one co-accused which does no more than contradict the evidence of another co-accused without further advancing the prosecution case in any significant degree, will not invoke the operation of section 1(f)(iii).

This latter proposition gave rise to some difficulty in *R v Bruce* [1975] 3 All ER 277. The accused (B) was charged jointly with M and others with robbing the victim by surrounding him and threatening him so that he handed over his property. M's defence was that there had been a plan to rob the victim but that he, M, had not been a party to it. B, in his defence, asserted that there had never been any plan at all. The trial judge had ruled that M was entitled to cross-examine B on his previous convictions in accordance with section 1(f)(iii) of the 1898 Act. All of the co-accused were convicted of theft, not robbery. The Court of Appeal held that the judge had been wrong to allow the cross-examination, because B had not given evidence against M within the meaning of the paragraph. B's evidence was a total contradiction of M's, but it did not undermine M's defence, nor did it strengthen the prosecution case against M. In fact, it had quite the reverse effect, because if the co-accused were not acting in concert in accordance with some prior plan, it was more likely that M would be acquitted.

The opportunity to restate the principles behind section 1(f)(iii) was taken by the Court of Appeal in the other leading case – *R v Varley* [1982] 2 All ER 519. A and B were jointly charged with robbery. A gave evidence to the effect that he had taken part in the robbery under duress as B had made serious threats on A's life unless he joined in. B testified that A's evidence was false, and that he, B, had not been a party to the offence. The judge ruled that A was entitled to cross-examine B on his previous convictions, as B had given evidence against him within the terms of section 1(f)(iii). B appealed against his conviction on the ground that the judge had erred in allowing the cross-examination. His conviction was upheld, and the Court of Appeal laid down the following guidelines:

1 If it is established that a person jointly charged has given evidence against the co-defendant that defendant has a right to cross-examine the other as to previous convictions and the trial judge has no discretion to refuse an application.
2 Such evidence may be given either in chief or during cross-examination.
3 It has to be decided objectively whether the evidence either supports the prosecution case in a material respect or undermines the defence of the co-accused.
4 If consideration has to be given to the undermining of the other's defence, care must be taken to see that the evidence clearly undermines the defence. Inconvenience to or inconsistency with the other's defence is not of itself sufficient.
5 Mere denial of participation in a joint venture is not of itself sufficient to rank as evidence against the co-defendant. For the proviso to apply, such denial must lead to the conclusion that if the witness did not participate then it must have been the other who did.
6 Where the one defendant asserts or in due course would assert one view of the joint venture, which is directly contradicted, such evidence may be evidence against the co-defendant.

Although the guidelines make reference throughout to 'jointly charged' and 'co-defendant', this must not be taken to mean that they must be charged with the same offence; it is sufficient that the co-accused are jointly tried, albeit for different offences.

There may be circumstances where the court has to proceed with caution in deciding whether a co-accused has given evidence against another co-accused. In *R v Kirkpatrick* [1998] Crim LR 63, K was convicted of indecent assault on a woman aged 19. His co-defendant, B, was also convicted, and a third man, L, pleaded guilty. The complainant alleged that after meeting L in a nightclub, she went back to a flat with K, B, L and a fourth man, where each indecently assaulted her. B, the first defendant, stated that L and the woman had gone into the bedroom after having kissed and cuddled on the settee. B, who had fallen asleep, was woken up by screams coming from the bedroom. He saw K and the fourth man giggling in the doorway. B denied participating in the indecent assault. Counsel for K applied to cross-examine B under section 1(f)(iii) on his previous convictions, on the ground that he had given evidence against K. The judge refused the application, holding that B's evidence did not impugn K. On appeal, it was submitted that the judge's reasoning was wrong. In dismissing the appeal, it was held that B's evidence did not undermine K's defence or implicate him in the offence charged. B's evidence only sought to exculpate B and was, at best, inconsistent with K's evidence. It implicated L only and most significantly, B's evidence did not prevent the jury from acquitting K. Making the distinction identified in *R v Varley*, between giving evidence inconsistent with a defence of a co-accused and giving evidence which undermines the defence of a co-accused, presents difficulties for the courts. The decisions in *R v Kirkpatrick* and *R v Bruce* above each highlight this.

The Law Commission's principal criticism of section 1(f)(iii) is the complete lack of any judicial discretion to prevent or restrict cross-examination. The tendency for the fact finder to confuse credibility with guilt under the provision and thereby embark on the route of 'forbidden reasoning' is likely for the reasons identified in relation to the second limb of section 1(f)(ii) above. The lack of judicial discretion under section 1(f)(iii) further accentuates this problem. The loss of shield under section 1(f)(iii) can result in the admission of marginally or barely relevant evidence of a co-accused's past misconduct.

A further criticism of the operation of section 1(f)(iii) by the Law Commission is that it inhibits some defendants from testifying, particularly where D1 would be compelled to give evidence in a way that will undermine D2's defence. Should the loss of D1's shield be automatic in these circumstances? In Consultation Paper No 141 the Law Commission favoured giving the court a discretion to prohibit or to restrict cross-examination and proposed reform to ensure that D1's shield would not be lost where D1's challenge to D2's character relates to D2's conduct in the incident in question or the investigation of it.

Proposals for reform

In Law Commission Report No 273, the Law Commission identified some of the principal defects of section 1 of the Criminal Evidence Act 1898 as follows:

- The statutory rules are supposed to have the effect that only bad character evidence which goes to credibility should be admitted in cross-examination of a defendant who 'loses the shield', but the courts can and do admit evidence which does not relate to credibility.

- The rule that bad character evidence on the 'tit-for-tat' basis may only be adduced in cross-examination means that witnesses are inadequately protected from irrelevant cross-examination on their character.

- The fear of 'losing the shield', which should deter a defendant from making gratuitous attacks, does not bite where that defendant does not testify, or has no criminal record to be revealed. This puts a premium on tactical decisions and distorts the process.

- Defendants may be inhibited from putting their true defence on the central set of facts for fear of their character going in.

- The statute does not preclude evidence of the defendant's bad character being admitted even where its prejudicial effect outweighs its relevance to the defendant's credibility.

- There is no power to prevent the record of a defendant being admitted where that defendant has undermined the defence of a co-accused. Unfairness can result. (paragraph 4.1)

A further criticism of the current law identified by the Law Commission is the real risk of fact finder speculation. Given the increasing knowledge of jurors as to the operation of legal rules within the criminal justice system, there is a danger that jurors who are not told that a defendant has previous convictions will assume that he has. This raises the question of whether it would be better to inform fact finders as to the true position at the outset of the trial in order to prevent speculation.

Overall, the law in relation to the admissibility of bad character evidence is characterised as being:

> a haphazard mixture of statute and common law rules which produce inconsistent and unpredictable results, in crucial respects distort the trial process, make tactical considerations paramount and inhibit the defence in presenting its true case to the fact-finders whilst often exposing witnesses to gratuitous and humiliating exposure of long forgotten misconduct.

In Consultation Paper No 141, the Law Commission set out six general approaches to reform. The approaches ranged from automatically adducing the defendant's criminal record at the start of the trial through to the current position of an exclusionary rule with separate exceptions for evidence admissible as part of the prosecution's case and subsequently in the proceedings depending on the course of events.

The Law Commission concluded that the dangers of prejudice identified in the research findings cannot be ignored and that whilst the automatic admission of a defendant's record at the start of the trial would make for a simplistic approach, at least on the face of it, such simplicity must not be achieved at the expense of justice.

In formulating recommendations for reform, the Law Commission foresaw no easy solution to a problem characterised by great complexity and a variety of factual situations to which rules must apply. Ultimately, the Law Commission is in favour of reform on the basis of an exclusionary rule incorporating specified statutory exceptions, with rules restricting the use of bad character evidence applying to all participants in the trial process and not being confined solely to the defendant.

The proposals for reform contained in Law Commission Report No 273 are as comprehensive as they are ambitious and appear complex at first glance. However, the Law Commission is to be commended in many respects. In answering all the criticisms identified in the operation of the current law in one comprehensive single statutory framework, which would bring about the repeal of the common law and the Criminal Evidence Act 1898, the Law Commission leaves no stone unturned.

In Chapter 5 of Report No 273, the Law Commission sets out guiding principles for reform in this area, including:

5.2   The rules of evidence should so far as is consistent with fairness be simple, accessible and readily understood.

5.3   The rules should be capable of being applied predictably and consistently by the courts but be sufficiently flexible to cater for the infinite variety of factual situations to which they will apply.

5.4   Where arbiters of law are called on to decide questions of admissibility, as they must be from time to time, the rules of evidence must give clear guidance on the proper approach to the decision so that its correctness may be judged on appeal.

5.5   Where a court decides questions of admissibility of evidence, reasons for the decision must be given.

5.6   Fact-finders are, prima facie, entitled to have placed before them all the relevant evidence which is available.

5.7   'Relevant', in this context, means having some probative value on a matter in issue in the proceedings.

5.8   Such probative value may be direct, in the sense of bearing upon the matters in issue, or indirect, in the sense of bearing upon the truthfulness of a witness's account of matters in issue.

5.9   The rules for the admission of evidence should be such that they preclude fact-finders being unnecessarily misled or left in the dark.

5.10 The rules for the admission of evidence should be such that they avoid deterring people who have relevant evidence to give from giving it.

5.11 Any person, whether a defendant, a witness, or otherwise involved, may only have their bad character referred to in evidence if it is relevant for the fact-finders to be aware of it for the performance of their task.

5.12 In any particular case certain instances of previous misconduct may be relevant and certain other instances of the same person's conduct may not. Where it is sought to adduce evidence of bad character it may only be admitted to the extent that it is relevant to the matters in issue in the proceedings.

5.13 A defendant may only be convicted on what he or she is proved to have done, and not merely on his or her character or past conduct on an occasion other than that the subject of the charge.

In clause 1 of the Law Commission's draft Criminal Evidence Bill, evidence of bad character is defined as 'evidence which shows or tends to show that – (a) a person has committed an offence, or (b) he has behaved, or is disposed to behave, in a way that, in the opinion of the court, might be viewed with disapproval by a reasonable person.'

Fundamental to the Law Commission's proposed legislative scheme is drawing and maintaining a distinction between aspects of bad character which are central to the facts in the case and aspects of bad character which fall outside the central facts. Where a party (which would include the prosecution, defendant or co-defendant) seeks to adduce evidence of another person's bad character (whether defendant, witness or co-defendant) which goes outside the central facts of the case, leave of the court must be obtained. Where the evidence relates to the central facts however, leave need not be sought and the evidence can be admitted automatically. For the defendant, this would mean no loss of his shield.

What would constitute evidence of bad character central to the facts of the case? This is defined in clause 2 of the draft Criminal Evidence Bill as evidence that pertains to the alleged facts of the offence with which the defendant is charged or which is evidence of misconduct in connection with the investigation or prosecution of the offence. This would include evidence of misconduct in the course of the offence or close to that offence, in time, place or circumstances.

Thus, in a prosecution for robbery, the prosecution would be entitled to ask the defendant about any evidence that tends to suggest he is guilty of the offence charged. Evidence that the defendant has previously committed an offence of robbery would not be automatically admissible, as it would not fall within the central facts of the case. Under the definition of central facts, the prosecution would be free to question the defendant about the theft of a car alleged by the prosecution to have been used in the robbery, or that the defendant had intimidated a witness in the course of the proceedings. The latter would be evidence of misconduct in connection with the prosecution of the offence.

For the defendant such a reform would mean that an allegation could be put to a prosecution witness that he or she was lying about the defendant's involvement in the offence or that a police officer deliberately destroyed evidence of the defendant's innocence. The latter would be evidence connected to the investigation of the offence. Such a reform would answer a major criticism of the current law, namely that a line of questioning essential to the accused's defence currently results in the loss of his shield under the tit-for-tat principle.

Bad character evidence would also be automatically admitted under the Law Commission's proposals where all parties are in agreement that it should be admitted or where the defendant chooses to adduce evidence of his previous misconduct.

Where a party sought to adduce evidence of another's bad character falling outside the central facts of the case, as defined above, leave of the court would have to be obtained. Leave can only be granted under the Law Commission's proposals where a test of *enhanced relevance* is met. To fulfil the criteria of enhanced relevance, the party (defendant, prosecutor or co-defendant) seeking to adduce the evidence would have to prove that the evidence had substantial probative or explanatory value in relation to the issues in the case.

Notably, where the prosecution seeks to adduce aspects of the defendant's bad character which fall outside the central facts of the case then, in addition to the enhanced relevance test, an interests of justice test must additionally be met.

Questioning a non-defendant on aspects of his bad character which fall outside the central facts of the case

The Law Commission recognised that questioning a prosecution witness about his bad character raises a number of issues in the trial context similar to those involving the defendant. The previous misconduct of the witness may in fact have very little bearing on the witness's general credibility. The knowledge that the fact finder acquires may unduly prejudice the witness in its eyes and consequently distort the verdict in a case. Furthermore, the risk of a certain line of questioning may dissuade the witness from testifying. The Law Commission gave the following example at paragraph 9.20 of its report:

> *W is a middle-aged woman, who is raped by an acquaintance. D says she consented. The police explain to her that, when she gives evidence, which she must for the prosecution to succeed, she might be asked about a 20-year old shoplifting conviction. Neither her husband nor her children nor her friends know about this conviction. The fear that it would be mentioned in public is enough to dissuade her from giving evidence.*

Under the Law Commission's proposals, witnesses are entitled to a measure of protection in relation to questions asked about their bad character which fall outside the central facts of the case or the investigation or prosecution of the offence. The protection is afforded by the requirement of the court to grant leave. Leave will only be granted where the test of enhanced relevance is met. Such enhanced relevance is established in one of two ways. First, where the evidence sought to be adduced has either substantial probative value (clause 5 of the draft Criminal Evidence Bill) in relation to a matter which is a matter in issue in the proceedings and is of substantial importance in the context of the case as a whole or, secondly, where it has explanatory value (clause 4 of the draft Criminal Evidence Bill) such that, without it, the court or jury would find it impossible or difficult properly to understand other evidence in the case, and its value for understanding the case as a whole is substantial.

Substantial probative value

In assessing the probative value of the bad character evidence sought to be adduced, clause 5(2) of the draft Criminal Evidence Bill requires the court to have regard to:

(a) the nature and number of the events, or other things, to which the evidence relates;
(b) when those events or things are alleged to have happened or existed;
(c) where—
    (i) the evidence is evidence of a person's misconduct, and
    (ii) it is suggested that the evidence has probative value by reason of similarity between that misconduct and other alleged misconduct,
the nature and extent of the similarities and the dissimilarities between each of the alleged instances of misconduct;
(d) where—
    (i) the evidence is evidence of a person's misconduct,

(ii) it is suggested that that person is also responsible for the misconduct charged, and

(iii) the identity of the person responsible for the misconduct charged is disputed,

the extent to which the evidence shows or tends to show that the same person was responsible each time.

The test of enhanced relevance is not easy to define in the abstract. The Law Commission includes the following examples in Report No 273 at paragraph 9.32:

> D is charged with theft. W, who was D's employee at the time of the alleged offence, is a witness who will give incriminating evidence which a jury could hardly accept without convicting D. The bad character evidence in question is the fact (not disputed by the prosecution) that, in her previous job, four years before the time of D's alleged offence, W was dishonest in her expenses claims. D says that the witness is incompetent and therefore mistaken. It is hard to conceive that the evidence would be admissible under our enhanced test.

> Alternatively, D is charged with theft, and wishes to ask W about an allegation that she was dishonest in her previous job. In this example, D's case is that W is lying, not incompetent. The fact that in the relatively recent past she has been guilty of dishonesty at the work place might well surmount the test of enhanced relevance.

> A third variation: D is charged with theft and wishes to ask W about an allegation of dishonesty 10 years previously, or in a non-work context. The court might well take the view that it did not pass the enhanced relevance test.

Where a defendant is given leave to adduce a witness's bad character under clause 5 of the draft Criminal Evidence Bill, thereby inviting the fact finder to make a comparative assessment of his credibility, the defendant will be at risk of having aspects of his bad character revealed under clause 9 which is considered later.

If a defendant is refused leave to adduce evidence of a witness's bad character because it lacks substantial probative value in the court's view, would there not be a risk of prejudicing the defendant's right to a fair trial? The Law Commission does not think so. It suggests a court can approach the question of whether particular evidence has substantial probative value by asking itself whether the defendant can have a fair trial if the evidence is excluded. A negative answer to this would inevitably mean that the evidence does have sufficient relevance to be admitted.

Explanatory value

Evidence of a witness's bad character having explanatory value makes available to the fact finder background evidence which he needs to be aware of in order to understand the nature of what is alleged. In other words, it helps explain other evidence in the case and is important for the fact finder in understanding the case as a whole. Where such background evidence raises an aspect of a witness's bad character, it can only be admitted with leave of the court if it has substantial explanatory value. This is defined in clause 4 of the draft Criminal Evidence Bill as evidence which, without it, the court or jury would find it impossible or difficult properly to understand other evidence in the case, and its value for understanding the case as a whole is substantial.

Questioning a defendant on aspects of his bad character which fall outside the central facts of the case

Evidence of bad character of the defendant that falls outside the central facts in the case can only be admitted with leave of the court for one of four specific evidentiary purposes:

1 that the evidence has explanatory value (the explanatory exception);
2 that the evidence goes to a matter in issue (the incriminatory exception);
3 that the evidence goes to the credibility of the defendant (the credibility exception);
4 that the evidence has a corrective value (the corrective exception).

Under the Law Commission's proposals for reform, the prosecution will only be able to adduce evidence of the defendant's bad character if it is able to satisfy the test of enhanced relevance in relation to one of the specific evidential purposes outlined above and the interests of justice require it to be admitted. We will briefly consider each exception.

The explanatory exception

Evidence having substantial explanatory value is defined above (clause 4 of the draft Criminal Evidence Bill) in the context of non-defendant witnesses. Where this exception is relied upon by the prosecution to admit evidence of the defendant's bad character, an additional interests of justice test must be met. The interests of justice are met where the evidence sought to be admitted carries no risk of prejudice to the defendant, or where it does, the value of the evidence for understanding the case as a whole is such that, taking account of the risk of prejudice, the interests of justice nevertheless require the evidence to be admitted.

The incriminatory exception

The provisions in clause 8 of the draft Criminal Evidence Bill seek to admit similar fact evidence. In doing so the prosecution would have to satisfy two conditions: first, that the evidence has substantial probative value in relation to a matter which is a matter in issue in the proceedings and is of substantial importance in the context of the case overall and, secondly, that where the evidence sought to be adduced carries a risk of prejudice, the interests of justice require the evidence to be admitted in view of:

   (i) how much probative value it has in relation to the matter in issue,
   (ii) what other evidence has been, or can be, given on that matter, and
   (iii) how important that matter is in the context of the case as a whole.

In determining these two conditions the court is further required to have regard to the factors listed in clause 5(2), set out above.

The proposed rules to regulate the admission of similar fact evidence are extremely detailed, but are, in the Law Commission's view, 'sufficiently flexible' to cater for the infinite variety of factual situations likely to occur before a court.

The credibility exception

This exception is comparable to the second limb of section 1(f)(ii) of the Criminal Evidence Act 1898. In certain circumstances, the Law Commission considered it would be in the interests of justice to admit evidence of the defendant's bad character which shows a propensity on the defendant's part to be untruthful. Such evidence would only be admissible under clause 9 of the draft Criminal Evidence Bill with leave of the court, where the test of enhanced relevance is met and it is in the interests of justice to admit it. To satisfy the enhanced relevance test the prosecution would need to show that:

1   the evidence has substantial value in showing that the defendant has a propensity to be untruthful,
2   the defendant has suggested that another person has a propensity to be untruthful,
3   the evidence adduced in support of that suggestion does not have to do with the offence charged, and is not evidence of misconduct in connection with the investigation or prosecution of that offence,
4   without the evidence of the defendant's bad character the fact finder would get a misleading impression of the defendant's propensity to be untruthful in comparison with that of the other person.

The interests of justice test as regards the credibility exception would require the evidence to be admitted if it was unprejudicial or so probative that, even taking account of the risks of prejudice, the interests of justice require it to be admissible. In assessing the probative value and prejudicial effect, the court would be required to have regard to a further list of statutory factors set out in clause 9(7) of the draft Criminal Evidence Bill which include consideration by the court of the nature and number of attacks made by the defendant and how important the defendant's and the witness's propensity to be untruthful is in the context of each side's case. Only evidence of bad character strictly relevant to the defendant's credibility would be admitted under this exception.

The defendant would remain free to pursue the questioning of a witness falling within the definition of the central facts of the case, as defined earlier. The defendant would only be liable to cross-examination on his criminal convictions under the credibility exception if he had called a witness's general propensity for untruthfulness into question. Such an attack, under the Law Commission's proposals would not need to be made personally by the defendant and could be made by the defendant in an out-of-court statement which is admitted into evidence, such as what he was heard to say on being cautioned following his arrest.

The corrective exception

The corrective exception is comparable to the first limb of section 1(f)(ii) – a false or inaccurate assertion of good character by the defendant. Under the Law Commission's proposals, an assertion of good character could be made even though the defendant has chosen not to testify at all. An assertion of good character is given a wide definition in clause 10(5) of the draft Criminal Evidence Bill.

Leave would only be granted to allow the prosecution to admit evidence of the defendant's bad character under the corrective exception if three grounds were established:

1   The defendant was responsible for making an express or implied assertion which created a false impression.
2   The evidence in rebuttal had substantial probative value in correcting the impression.
3   The interests of justice require the evidence to be admitted having taken account of its potentially prejudicial effect.

The interests of justice test under this exception would require the court to have regard to a list of statutory factors set out in clause 10(4) which includes a consideration of how much probative value the evidence has in correcting the false impression and whether such an impression can be corrected in some less prejudicial way. It may be that the evidence created by the defendant is of very little relevance in the context of the case as a whole, in which case, leave is unlikely to be granted.

Where evidence is adduced under this exception, the Law Commission concurred with the criticism of the current law which allows the evidence to assume relevance only as to the defendant's credibility. If good character evidence has relevance to both the defendant's credibility and his propensity to have committed the crime, the Law Commission considered it illogical that such rebuttal evidence of a defendant's good character should have its evidential use confined solely to an assessment of the defendant's credibility. It recommended that where the evidence is capable of being used by the fact finder as evidence of the defendant's guilt, this is a factor the court must have regard to in deciding whether or not to give leave. Where leave is given in these circumstances, however, it would serve no purpose to tell the jury that it is irrelevant to the issue of guilt.

The co-defendant exception

Having identified numerous criticisms of the current law in relation to section 1(f)(iii) of the Criminal Evidence Act 1898, the Law Commission would reform the existing law in such a way that, providing a co-defendant's attack fell within the central facts of the case, leave of the court to adduce evidence of a fellow co-accused's bad character would not be required and the defendant adducing the evidence would have nothing to fear. If a co-defendant wished to adduce evidence of his co-accused's bad character outside the central facts of the case, leave would be required. To obtain leave, the test of enhanced relevance would have to be met: the evidence would have to be of substantial probative value to an issue between the defendants and that issue would need to be of substantial importance in the context of the case as a whole.

According to the Law Commission, the advantage of such reform would be the imposition on the defendant of a requirement for him to justify the introduction of such evidence, thereby preventing the admission of evidence of bad character which has only minimal relevance to the issues in the case. Where one co-defendant seeks leave solely to adduce evidence showing that his fellow co-defendant has a propensity for untruthfulness, leave will only be given where the enhanced relevance test is met and the nature of D1's defence is such as to undermine D2's defence. In assessing the probative value of the evidence to be adduced, the court would once more be required to have regard to the factors listed in clause 5(2) of the draft Criminal Evidence Bill.

The Law Commission illustrated the operation of its co-defendant exception with the following examples. (In considering the examples, assume that D1 has several previous convictions for robbery and that D2 is of good character.)

> *D1 and D2 are jointly charged with robbery. D1's defence is that D2 did it on her own. In order to get D1's criminal record admitted under the co-defendant exception on the basis that D1 has undermined D2's case, D2 must show that his convictions show he is likely to lie on oath. What is in issue is D1's propensity to tell the truth not his propensity to rob.*

14.50 The evidence is less likely to be admitted in relation to credibility than under the current law. It would be clearer than it is under the current law that *only* evidence of D1's bad character which was relevant to his credibility would be admissible, and there would be no danger of bad character evidence of little probative value (but significant prejudicial effect) being admitted.

> *D2 might seek to have D1's convictions admitted on the basis that they are substantially relevant directly to the issue of who committed the robbery. If D1 has recent convictions for robbery, they are more likely to be admissible on this basis, whereas other kinds of dishonesty offence might not be sufficiently relevant.*

14.51 It may be that the evidence of D1's previous convictions is directly relevant to the central issue of who committed the robbery even though it could have a similar prejudicial effect to that described by the respondent. However, the evidence would have to be substantially probative to be adduced, rather than creep in under the guise of credibility.

Other evidential and procedural safeguards

A number of further evidential and procedural safeguards are included in the Law Commission's proposed legislative scheme.

Clause 13 of the draft Criminal Evidence Bill makes provision for a judge to stop a trial where evidence of the defendant's bad character had been admitted with leave, but had subsequently become contaminated, perhaps by reason of proven collaboration or collusion between witnesses.

Clause 14 provides that the probative value of bad character evidence is to be assessed on the assumption that it is true, except where it appears that no court or jury could reasonably find the evidence tendered to be true. This would have the effect of placing *R v H* [1995] 2 AC 596 (discussed in Chapter 20) on a statutory footing.

Clause 15 requires a court to give recorded reasons where it:

- rules on whether bad character evidence is admissible only with leave,
- gives or refuses leave, or
- rules on an application to stop the trial under clause 13.

In accordance with clause 16, a party seeking to adduce evidence of the defendant's bad character would have to serve a notice of intention to do so.

The Law Commission gave two situations in which a judge might be required to give a warning to a jury. The first is where no evidence has been adduced about the defendant's bad character and there is a danger that the jury might speculate what information has been withheld from it. In such a case, the judge might wish to warn the jury not to speculate on any matter upon which it has not heard evidence. The second situation in which a warning might be appropriate would be where there is a danger that the jury may give undue weight to bad character evidence which has been admitted. Unlike the Criminal Evidence Act 1898, where evidence admitted consequent upon the defendant's loss of shield, has relevance to the defendant's credibility only, under these proposals the judge would remain free to advise the jury as appropriate. However, in such cases the judge must commence by pointing out the way in which the evidence is said to be relevant, ie under the corrective or credibility exception. The application of the interests of justice test will already have considered the risk of prejudice, but the trial judge might still wish to warn the jury, particularly where misconduct admitted under the credibility exception happens to be similar to the offence charged.

The recommendations in the Law Commission Report No 273 are put forward as making the law on the admission of bad character evidence fairer in the following ways:

(1) All the rules will be in one statute and will therefore be accessible.
(2) They will give greater protection for non-defendants.
(3) They will result in the elimination of 'tit-for-tat' unfairness thereby giving greater protection for defendants.
(4) A co-defendant with a criminal record is less likely to suffer the admission of that record where it is not warranted.
(5) Judges will have to give and juries seek to comply with fewer nonsensical directions drawing bizarre and unreal distinctions between credibility and propensity.
(6) The establishment of consistent statutory tests coupled with guidance for courts when ruling on admissibility will result in greater consistency of decisions. (paragraph 1.9)

If implemented, the Law Commission's recommendations would solve most of the complaints regarding the current law. Evidence of bad character would only be admitted on the basis of a searching examination as to its true relevance and, in the case of a defendant, only if the interests of justice require it to be admitted. Advocates would be forced to identify the evidential basis on which they seek to have the evidence admitted and to justify their reasons for wanting to adduce the evidence by careful and considered articulation of a considerable number of statutory factors. The rule on the indivisibility of character evidence would also cease to have any further application.

The proposals do serve the ends of justice in that they would offer protection to witnesses against gratuitous attacks on their character and only highly relevant evidence of bad character would be adduced. Tactics would assume less importance in trials and the defendant would not need to feel inhibited about testifying where an attack on a prosecution witness or a co-defendant was necessary to enable him to mount an effective defence. In each instance the prejudicial effect of the evidence would have to be weighed up in determining where the interests of justice lie. Where an aspect of the defendant's bad character stood to be admitted, the court would be required to undertake a careful, consistent and structured balancing exercise.

However, on the negative side, the proposals are lengthy and very technical. It is not difficult to foresee that considerable time would be taken up in legal argument on the finer points of relevance and what constituted a central fact in the case. No doubt a considerable number of appeals would ensue giving rise to the distinct danger that, as case law developed, greater complexities would arise.

Unlike the Law Commission's proposals, in the Criminal Courts Review Report, Lord Justice Auld is keen to move away from technical rules of evidence in favour of placing a higher degree of trust in fact finders. In relation to the future reform of this area of law, Lord Justice Auld would prefer to see a system that is simple and more honest. This would be best achieved by informing the fact finder of the accused's criminal record, if he has one, at the start of the trial and trusting the fact finder to give the evidence an appropriate degree of weight.

The issue of the admissibility of a defendant's bad character is currently a matter of political debate. It its election manifesto, the Labour government was eager to ensure the disclosure of a defendant's previous convictions where relevant as the current law is perceived to be an obstacle to securing the conviction of greater numbers of guilty individuals. The Law Commission conceded that it could not predict whether its proposals would result in a significant increase in the number of occasions on which a fact finder would be told of a defendant's previous convictions. It rightly made no apology for this because an assessment of whether a defendant's previous convictions should be disclosed involves a very careful balancing exercise which has to be undertaken in the context of each case. As Lord Justice Auld himself concedes, the law in relation to the admission of bad character evidence is complex and there are no straightforward answers. It remains to be seen whether the government adopts the Law Commission's recommendations or chooses a more radical approach.

EVIDENCE OF THE DEFENDANT'S GOOD CHARACTER

We have considered the defendant's bad character at some length, but what of those defendants whose character is without blemish – what is the evidential effect of the defendant's good character being disclosed to the court?

Evidence of good character can be tendered at trial by the oral or written testimony of witnesses, by the defendant himself in examination-in-chief or by answers to questions in cross-examination of prosecution witnesses. The evidence is tendered in the hope of persuading the jury or magistrates that by virtue of never having been in trouble before the defendant is an individual less likely to have committed the offence with which he is now charged. The knowledge that the defendant has an unblemished character might also make the fact finder morally less resistant to acquitting him.

What constitutes evidence of good character?

To answer this question, it is necessary to consider the archaic and somewhat baffling rule expressed in *R v Rowton* [1861–73] All ER 549, which confines a witness as to good character to giving evidence of the accused's good character based on his knowledge of the defendant's reputation in the community. The rule, which is arbitrary in many ways, prevents the witness from giving his opinion of the defendant's disposition, as well as evidence of the defendant's good conduct on specific occasions. A person's reputation may well be based, in part, on his disposition to act in a certain way. The dividing line between the two is not easy to draw. The rule ignores this fact and the evidential relevance that disposition evidence can have to the defence of the accused.

The rule as expressed in *R v Rowton* is unduly restrictive and has consistently been ignored in practice. Where witnesses are called to give evidence of good character, they frequently depose to their opinion of the defendant based on their experience and impression of the defendant as determined by the context of their dealings with him. Having said this, the rule was reaffirmed in the much later decision of *R v Redgrave* (1982) 74 Cr App R 10. In this case the defendant was charged with importuning for immoral purposes in a gentleman's public toilet. He sought to adduce in evidence various love letters and valentine cards indicating his sexual proclivity was heterosexual and not homosexual, for the purpose of showing he was less likely to have committed the offence with which he was charged. The judge refused to admit the evidence as the defendant was seeking to adduce evidence of particular acts to show his heterosexual disposition instead of confining his evidence to his general reputation not to act in such a way, as prescribed by the rule in *R v Rowton*.

The Court of Appeal held the trial judge had acted correctly. It would, however, have permitted evidence showing the defendant was generally reputed to be a happily married man, had he in fact been married! The application of the rule in *R v Rowton* totally ignores the fact that the evidence of disposition in the case was not relevant to the issue of his credibility as a witness, but to his complete denial of the offence. The fact of his heterosexual disposition, in other words, made it less likely that he had committed the offence.

What is the evidential effect of good character?

Prior to the decision of the Court of Appeal in *R v Vye*; *R v Wise*; *R v Stephenson* [1993] 3 All ER 241, the case law was in a state of conflict and confusion as to the evidential relevance that good character evidence could assume. Could good character be relevant to the likelihood that the defendant had committed the offence for which he was on trial, or was it merely relevant to an assessment of his credibility as a witness giving evidence on oath, always assuming he had chosen to give evidence? In *R v Vye*, Lord Taylor CJ laid down the following important guidelines for the conduct of future cases:

1   When an accused has given evidence, a direction should be given as to the relevance of his good character to his credibility as a witness.

2   If the accused does not give evidence, but before the trial made an exculpatory statement to the police, then a direction should be given that his good character must be considered when assessing his credibility regarding that statement.

3   Where the accused has neither given evidence nor made any pre-trial statement, no direction can be given as to his credibility being affected by his good character, but the judge should direct the jury on the effect of the accused's good character on the likelihood of his having committed the offence(s) with which he is charged; and this direction should be given after any direction as to credibility in cases where the accused testifies or makes a pre-trial exculpatory statement.

4   Where there are two or more accused and not all of them are of good character, there is a danger (when the full direction is given) of the good character of those with unblemished records suggesting, by inference, that the others are of bad character. Furthermore, where good character is relevant to innocence, those without any mention of their character being made are, by implication, assumed to be of bad character. There is then a danger that this can be held against them when their guilt or innocence is considered. An accused with good character is entitled to the full direction, and it is a matter for the trial judge whether he gives a direction in respect of the co-accused with no previous good character; he may do this by telling the jury that it must try the case on the evidence it has heard and must not speculate on an accused's character in the absence of any mention of it. Of paramount importance is the avoidance of prejudice to any co-accused who is not of previous good character.

R v Vye confirms that good character is always relevant to the likelihood of the defendant having committed the crime. It may therefore be used by the jury or by magistrates, when assessing the evidence in the case before them, to infer the defendant is less likely to be predisposed to committing criminal offences. This is the position irrespective of whether the defendant gives evidence at his trial and the judge must direct the jury accordingly. Additionally, where the defendant takes the stand, he is entitled to the additional direction that his good character is relevant to his credibility on oath. In other words, the court may consider that the absence of a criminal record makes it more likely that he is speaking the truth when he asserts his innocence on oath. Even where the defendant does not give evidence, if he has answered questions at the police station and has put forward a defence which he maintains at trial, he is still entitled to a credibility direction in relation to this fact.

In promulgating the guidelines in *R v Vye* Lord Taylor CJ tackled the problematic issue of what to do with two or more co-accused, only one of whom is without previous convictions. It would seem that whether the judge chooses to draw attention to this fact or not is a matter for his discretion. In *R v Vye*, the declaration of the principles as regard a co-accused were predicated on the assumption that no comment has been made on the co-accused's character. Where a co-accused's criminal record has been made known to the jury in the course of the proceedings, *R v Cain* [1994] 1 WLR 1449 makes clear the direction that the judge must give. He must instruct the jury that any previous convictions are relevant only to the co-accused's credibility as a witness (assuming he has given evidence on oath, or at least made a statement denying his guilt when interviewed at the police station). Such convictions may not be used for the purpose of inferring the co-accused is more likely to be guilty.

Further clarification on the law as regards good character is provided by the decision of the House of Lords in *R v Aziz* [1995] 3 WLR 53. The decision provides confirmation that the absence of previous convictions is not necessarily indicative of good character. The two accused in this case were on trial for conspiracy to evade the payment of VAT. Both pleaded not guilty and relied on the fact that they had no previous convictions. In evidence, however, they admitted to other acts of dishonesty as regards Customs and Excise. In the circumstances, were they entitled to a good character direction? On the facts in this case, the House of Lords considered both defendants were entitled to a *Vye* direction. In other circumstances, however, it is a matter for the judge as to whether a *Vye* direction should be given, having regard to admitted criminal or quasi-criminal conduct. In some circumstances it may be appropriate for the judge to refuse to give the direction at all when it would be an affront to common sense. In the words of Lord Steyn, who delivered the leading judgment:

> A good starting point is that a judge should never be compelled to give meaningless or absurd directions. And cases occur from time to time where a defendant, who has no previous convictions, is shown beyond doubt to have been guilty of serious criminal behaviour similar to the offence charged in the indictment. A sensible criminal justice system should not compel a judge to go through the charade of giving directions in accordance with *Vye* in a case where the defendant's claim to good character is spurious. I would therefore hold that a trial judge has a residual discretion to decline to give any character directions in the case of a defendant without previous convictions if the judge considers it an insult to common sense to give directions in accordance with *Vye*.

As to the nature of the judge's discretion, Lord Steyn observed:

> Discretions range from the open-textured discretionary powers to narrowly circumscribed discretionary powers. The residual discretion of a trial judge to dispense with character directions in respect of a defendant of good character is of the more limited variety. Prima facie the directions must be given. And the judge will often be able to place a fair and balanced picture before the jury by giving directions in accordance with *Vye* [1993] 1 WLR 471 and then adding words of qualification concerning other proved or possible criminal conduct of the defendant which emerged during the trial. On the other hand, if it would make no sense to give character directions in accordance with *Vye*, the judge may in his discretion dispense with them.

The subsequent decision in *R v Hickmet* [1996] Crim LR 588 has affirmed the *Vye* direction may still be given, albeit in a possibly qualified form, in situations where any previous convictions of the defendant are spent within the definition of the Rehabilitation of Offenders Act 1974 or are still current but are of a trivial or unrelated nature.

How can evidence of good character be rebutted?

Good character evidence can be rebutted by the prosecution both at common law and under statute. Where the defendant himself asserts good character on oath, rebuttal is provided for, as we saw earlier in this chapter, under section 1(f)(ii) of the Criminal Evidence Act 1898. Where the defendant asserts his good character otherwise than whilst giving evidence on oath, the prosecution is entitled to rebut the evidence under principles developed at common law.

Evidence of good character can be rebutted by adducing evidence of the defendant's previous convictions or other discreditable conduct. At common law, as under the Criminal Evidence Act 1898, evidence of character is indivisible. The defendant may have put in issue merely one facet of his good character but in doing so the prosecution is entitled to rebut all aspects. According to Humphreys J in the case of *R v Winfield* (1939) 27 Cr App R 139 '... there is no such thing known to our procedure as putting half your character in issue and leaving the other half out'. The facts in *R v Winfield* were considered earlier in the chapter.

The rule on the indivisibility of character has been criticised in many academic quarters for its potential to cause injustice. The Law Commission recommended its abolition in Consultation Paper No 141. Consideration of the Law Commission's final proposals on this point were dealt with above under the heading 'The corrective exception'.

Further reading

Dennis, I.H. (1999) *The Law of Evidence*, Sweet & Maxwell.

Derbyshire, P., 'The Law Commission Consultation Paper on Previous Misconduct: (3) Previous Misconduct and Magistrates' Courts – Some Tales from the Real World' [1997] Crim LR 105.

Elliott, D.W., 'Cut Throat Tactics: The Freedom of an Accused to Prejudice a Co-accused' [1991] Crim LR 5.

Law Commission (1996) *Evidence in Criminal Proceedings: Previous Misconduct of a Defendant*, Law Commission Consultation Paper No 141, HMSO.

Law Commission (2001) *Evidence in Criminal Proceedings: Previous Misconduct of a Defendant*, Law Commission Report No 273, HMSO.

Lloyd-Bostock, S., 'The Effects on Juries of Hearing about the Defendant's Previous Criminal Record: A Simulation Study' [2000] Crim LR 734.

McEwan, J., 'The Law Commission Consultation Paper on Previous Misconduct: (2) Law Commission Dodges the Nettle on Consultation Paper No 141' [1997] Crim LR 93.

McEwan, J. (1998) *Evidence and the Adversarial Process: The Modern Law*, 2nd edn, Hart Publishing.

Munday, R., 'The Paradox of Cross-examination to Credit – Simply Too Close for Comfort' [1994] Camb LJ 303.

Roberts, P., 'The Law Commission Consultation Paper on Previous Misconduct: (1) All the Usual Suspects: A Critical Appraisal of Law Commission Consultation Paper No 141' [1997] Crim LR 75.

Zuckerman, A. (1989) *The Principles of Criminal Evidence*, Clarendon Press.

Part 3

CIVIL EVIDENCE

Chapter 22

THE RULES OF CIVIL EVIDENCE AND PROCEDURE

INTRODUCTION

Part 3 examines the application and interpretation of the rules of evidence in 'mainstream' civil proceedings. Civil actions, which mainly involve issues of contractual or tortious liability or on a litigant's claim to property rights, are heard in the High Court or in the county court. Where relevant, reference will also be made in the following chapters to other forms of proceedings under the Children Act 1989 and the the rules of evidence and procedure in tribunals.

As we explained in Chapter 1, one of the reasons for treating the laws of criminal and civil evidence as two distinct bodies of rules is the different approach taken in each jurisdiction to the process of proof. You will recall that the phrase 'the process of proof' relates to the way in which a party in a case is required, by the rules of evidence and procedure, to prove its version of the facts and interpretation of the law to the fact finder. The reasons for this distinctive approach should be apparent and are based on the different purposes, philosophy, evidential and procedural rules that apply between civil and criminal cases. Civil litigation concerns disputes between private individuals who are seeking to assert and enforce their legal rights against each other. The purpose of a claimant taking a case to a civil court is to seek compensation for any physical and/or pecuniary loss that has been caused by the defendant's acts or omissions. The concept of punishment and deterrence, important factors in the prosecution of a criminal case, play a minor role in civil litigation as does the role of the State and its institutions, who are the major actors in the criminal justice system.

As a result, in many civil cases, there is likely to be a greater equality in resources between the claimant and the defendant, even with the significant reduction in the availability of publicly funded legal representation. This is compared to the potentially great resources that are available to the State when it prosecutes a criminal offence against a private individual as the defendant. Therefore, the court's general duty to ensure the accused enjoys a fair trial in criminal proceedings, which seeks to redress this imbalance and which underpins many of the exclusionary rules of criminal evidence, has little application in civil cases. Also, the social stigma that attaches to an accused who has been found guilty of a criminal offence does not apply to an unsuccessful litigant in a civil action – although losing a high-value commercial action may adversely affect the party's reputation and standing in the business community. For these reasons and because of the non-involvement of lay people in the judicial process, in civil cases there is a much freer science of proof as opposed to many of the exclusionary rules that apply in criminal evidence.

THE CIVIL PROCEDURE RULES

In introducing the laws of civil evidence it is necessary to have some understanding of the procedural context in which the evidential rules operate. This comment has been especially true since 26 April 1999, when the Civil Procedure Rules 1998 (SI 1998 No 3132), together with the Practice Directions and forms which supplement the Rules, came into force, fundamentally changing the procedure and management of civil litigation. The introduction of the Civil Procedure Rules came against a background of widespread dissatisfaction with the civil justice system. Expressions of dissatisfaction came from a number of influential sources including lawyers, the judiciary, politicians and from many litigants who highlighted a number of problems with the 'old' system of civil litigation that led to unacceptable delays, high expense, great complexity, and uncertainty. In practice, the former procedural regime under the Rules of the Supreme Court 1965 (RSC) and County Court Rules 1981 (CCR) had become cumbersome, slow and expensive to operate.

In response to these problems, on 28 March 1994 Lord Woolf MR was appointed by the then Lord Chancellor, Lord Mackay, to review the rules and procedures of the civil courts. The aims of the review were to improve access to justice and to cut the costs of litigation; to reduce the complexity of the rules; to modernise the terminology of civil litigation and to remove the unnecessary distinctions between practice and procedure.

The problems with the operation of the RSC and the CCR were clearly apparent to Lord Woolf and his team of assessors who toured the country holding a number of access to justice seminars. Such concerns were well documented in the *Access to Justice, Interim Report* (June 1995), where Lord Woolf observed:

> The key problems facing civil justice today are cost, delay and complexity. These three are inter-related and stem from the uncontrolled nature of the litigation process.

In addition to the problems caused by the costs, delay and complexity, Lord Woolf concluded that the existing procedural rules in part contributed to the perceived imbalance between the resources available to a wealthy litigant and the under-resourced litigant; they were too vague and uncertain in their application which caused difficulties in estimating costs and the duration of cases, and they were too fragmented in the way in which pre-trial and trial procedures were organised. The system was also excessively adversarial. Cases were managed by the parties in a partisan way whilst the rules of the court were not only often ignored by the parties but were not enforced by the courts.

In providing an opportunity for careful consideration and debate of his findings Lord Woolf's report was published in two stages – the *Interim Report*, and *Access to Justice, Final Report* (July 1996). In total, the *Interim Report* and the *Final Report* contained over 300 separate recommendations to improve and streamline the civil justice system. Lord Woolf's stated objectives were to improve access to justice and to provide a more efficient and a less costly method of resolving disputes. More specifically a number of principles were identified that would underlie the system of civil litigation in England and Wales. These principles include:

- involving the courts would be viewed as a last resort for dispute resolution;
- litigation should be less adversarial and more co-operative;

- litigation should be less complex;
- the timescale of litigation should be shorter and more certain;
- the costs of litigation should be more affordable and more proportionate to the value or the complexity of the individual case;
- the structure of the courts and the allocation of judges should be designed to meet the needs of litigants;
- judges should be deployed effectively so that they can manage litigation in accordance with the new rules and protocols.

Lord Woolf's recommendations were incorporated into the Civil Procedure Act 1997, under which the Civil Procedure Rules 1998 were implemented in April 1999, and provided the most radical changes to civil procedure in England and Wales since Lord Selborne's reforms of the 1870s. Not only did the Civil Procedure Rules create a new set of civil procedural rules but they also introduced an entirely new philosophy and ethos that now govern the conduct of civil cases by the parties, their lawyers and witnesses, and the judiciary. The Rules constitute a unified code that applies to all civil courts, ending the artificial distinction in practice and procedure between the High Court and the county court that had existed under the Rules of the Supreme Court and the County Court Rules.

CIVIL LITIGATION IN THE 'NEW LEGAL LANDSCAPE'

The Civil Procedure Rules (CPR) are divided into Parts. Each Part covers a general step in the proceedings and is supplemented by a Practice Direction. For example, the Practice Direction to Part 32 sets out the rules relating to witness statements. The overriding objectives contained in CPR Part 1 set out the ethos and philosophy for dealing with all civil cases to which the Rules apply and are highly relevant to the operation of the rules of evidence in civil proceedings.

The ethos of civil litigation (CPR Part 1)

Part 1 sets out the overriding objective of the Civil Procedure Rules. CPR rule 1.1(1) provides:

(1) These Rules are a new procedural code with the overriding objective of enabling the court to deal with cases justly.

CPR rule 1.1(2) provides that dealing with a case 'justly' includes, so far as is practicable:

(a) ensuring that the parties are on an equal footing;
(b) saving expense;
(c) dealing with the case in ways which are proportionate—
    (i) to the amount of money involved;
    (ii) to the importance of the case;
    (iii) to the complexity of the issues; and
    (iv) to the financial position of each party;
(d) ensuring that it is dealt with expeditiously and fairly; and
(e) allotting to it an appropriate share of the court's resources, while taking into account the need to allot resources to other cases.

CPR rule 1.2 requires that:

> The court must seek to give effect to the overriding objective when it—
>
>> (a) exercises any power given to it by the Rules; or
>> (b) interprets any rule.

CPR rule 1.3 provides that the parties are required to help the court to further the overriding objective.

Before the introduction of the Civil Procedure Rules, the speed at which a case progressed and the way in which the party proved its case was largely determined by the parties' lawyers. Under CPR rule 1.4(1):

> (1) The court must further the overriding objective by actively managing cases.

Under CPR rule 1.4(2) active case management includes:

- encouraging the parties to co-operate with each other in the conduct of the proceedings;
- identifying the issues at an early stage;
- deciding in which order the issues should be resolved;
- encouraging the parties to use alternative dispute resolution;
- helping the parties to settle the whole of the case or part of it;
- fixing timetables or otherwise controlling the progress of the case;
- dealing with the case without the parties attending court;
- giving directions to ensure that the trial of a case proceeds quickly and efficiently.

The importance of these general principles should not be underestimated. The courts and the parties are required to apply these general principles at all stages of the litigation. They are designed to:

- achieve a just result to the civil litigation;
- ensure that the parties receive fair treatment;
- keep costs within reasonable bounds; and
- avoid delay.

'Justice' is achieved through the application of the principles of 'equality, economy, proportionality and expedition'. 'Equality' requires that all parties will be treated equally irrespective of their financial resources. Proportionality requires that only those resources that are appropriate to the sum claimed and/or the complexity and importance of the case should be expended on a particular case. 'Fairness' requires that all litigants will co-operate with the other party in the case and with the court. Pre-litigation protocols, such as in personal injury litigation, are intended to secure the early exchange of information. A party's case now has to be fully stated and the traditional forms of pleading are inappropriate. Lack of co-operation may be met with sanctions imposed by the court, which are usually costs sanctions or penalties.

The Civil Procedure Rules apply to all proceedings in the county court, the High Court and the Civil Division of the Court of Appeal, except cases of insolvency, family proceedings, proceedings within the meaning of the Mental Health Act 1983 and non-contentious probate matters.

Several themes can be distilled from the overriding objective. First, there is an emphasis on much greater judicial management of cases. The parties no longer have control of a case as was the situation under the former rules. The judiciary, as part of its case management responsibilities, sets strict timetables for each stage of the proceedings including trial. All the parties are expected to comply with the set timetable. Secondly, each party's lawyer is required to identify key issues of liability, quantum and evidence at an early stage in the proceedings and to consider the possibility of seeking a negotiated settlement.

The terminology of the Civil Procedure Rules

An important consequence of Lord Woolf's modernisation of the civil justice system is the abolition of many of the traditional, archaic phrases and jargon, which are replaced by modern terminology. In studying pre-Civil Procedure Rules decisions on the principles of civil evidence, you will come across the old terms. Some of these are set out below together with their CPR equivalent.

- 'plaintiff' to 'claimant';
- 'writ' to 'claim form';
- 'pleading' to 'statement of case';
- 'statement of claim' to 'particulars of claim';
- 'interlocutory' to 'interim';
- 'interrogatories' and 'further and better particulars' to 'requests for information';
- 'discovery' to 'disclosure';
- 'leave of the court' to 'permission of the court';
- 'minor or infant' to 'child';
- 'in camera' or 'in chambers' to 'in private';
- 'subpoena' to 'witness summons';
- *inter partes* to 'on notice';
- *ex parte* to 'without notice'.

THE CIVIL COURTS AND THE RULES OF EVIDENCE

It is important to be aware that different rules of civil evidence apply depending on whether the court is sitting as a trial court or as an appellate court. A further important influence on the operation of the evidential rules is the case management tracks introduced by the Civil Procedure Rules.

The jurisdiction to try civil cases in England and Wales is shared between the High Court, the county court and the magistrates' court. The High Court comprises three divisions: the Queen's Bench Division, the Chancery Division and the Family Division. The allocation of business between the Divisions is prescribed by section 61 of the Supreme Court Act 1981. The main civil work of the Queen's Bench Division is in contract and tort whilst the Division also exercises the High Court's inherent jurisdiction in judicial review and, in criminal cases, it hears appeals by way of case stated from the magistrates' courts, the High Court and tribunals. In addition to this general allocation of work, a number of specialist courts work as jurisdictions of the Queen's Bench Division, including the Technology and Construction Court, the Commercial Court, the

Family Division and the Companies Court. Each court has its own rules of procedure and evidence. The work of the Chancery Division relates primarily to matters concerning the ownership of and interests in land, mortgages, bankruptcy and the administration of trusts. The jurisdiction of the Family Division includes matters relating to minors, legitimacy, adoption and proceedings under the Children Act 1989. In London, the High Court is based at the Royal Courts of Justice and at the 130 district registries situated in the major towns and cities in England and Wales. Most trials in the High Court are conducted by High Court judges, whilst interim applications dealing with pre-trial are heard by district judges in the provinces and by masters in London. In 2000/01 5,541 claims were lodged in the Queens Bench Division of the High Court, whilst during the same period 5,715 claims were lodged in the Chancery Division.

The county courts are a creation of statute, principally under the County Courts Act 1984. There are approximately 230 county courts in England and Wales, although under a policy of rationalisation the Lord Chancellor's Department is seeking to close some of the smaller courts situated in rural areas. Each county court is limited to exercising its powers within a defined geographical area. For administrative purposes, certain county courts in an area are designated as trial centres to deal with the more complex or high value civil cases, known as multi-track cases. Each civil trial centre is presided over by a circuit judge, who is responsible for the organisation of the civil trial court and its satellite courts. As well a circuit judge, the other judicial officers in the county court are district judges who hear most interim applications and try cases allocated to the fast track (see below) and some multi-track cases. In 2000/01 1,563,149 claims were lodged in the county court. During this period there were 58,730 hearings on the small claims track and 14,574 trials were held in open court.

Since the introduction of the civil justice reforms, the traditional jurisdictional distinction between the county court and High Court has become much less significant as the Civil Procedure Rules have created an alternative way of allocating cases by introducing, under CPR Part 26, a new system of case management.

A case will now be allocated by the judge to one of the three case management tracks, known as the small claims track, the fast track or the multi-track as part of his case management responsibilities. The case will be allocated to one of the three tracks after the judge has considered allocation questionnaires completed by the parties within 14 days of their receipt and/or by taking into account any relevant matter. The questionnaires are sent to the parties in most actions after the filing of the defence.

In allocating a case to the appropriate track, the following criteria are important:

- the financial value of the claim;
- the nature of the remedy sought;
- the complexity of the facts, law and evidence;
- the number of parties involved;
- the amount of oral evidence to be heard and the views of the parties.

The small claims track

The small claims track replaced the small claims procedure in the county court and is generally for cases with a financial limit of not more than £5,000 for general actions in contract and tort. Personal injury claims of up to £1,000 and housing disrepair cases will also usually be allocated to the small claims track. Cases on the small claims track will proceed in a similar way as under the former small claims arbitration procedure. The hearing will normally be informal and the strict rules of evidence will not apply. Evidence is not normally given on oath and the cross-examination of witnesses may be limited as there is an emphasis towards excluding oral evidence and placing greater reliance on 'paper' evidence.

The fast track

The fast track is suitable for dealing with straightforward actions as quickly as possible. This track handles cases valued between £5,000 and £15,000, and also personal injury actions where the claim for damages exceeds £1,000. An important point to note is that it is the court's valuation of the claim that decides the allocation and not the parties. As soon as the case is allocated to the fast track, a timetable is set by the court with a trial date which will normally be within 30 weeks from the date on which the court gives its initial directions in the case. There will be few if any pre-trial hearings. Standard directions will be given relating to the disclosure of documents, service of witness statements and expert evidence. The witness statements will stand as evidence-in-chief and where the matter proceeds to trial, the trial should not last more than one day. The parties and the witnesses will be present in court – even before testifying. The opportunity to give oral evidence will be limited and, where it is allowed, evidence will be given on oath or affirmation.

In a fast track case, it is usual for the judge to give a full judgment immediately after the party's closing speeches. However, this is not a mandatory requirement and the judge may reserve his judgment or give a short judgment but delay giving reasons until a later date.

The multi-track

The majority of commercial cases fall into this track as it is designed for cases worth over £15,000. Where the case is worth less than £15,000, it may be allocated to the multi-track where other factors are present including the complexity of the case; the number of parties involved or a point of law of public interest is raised. Important and complex personal injury actions as well as 'class' actions will be allocated to the multi-track.

A case that has been allocated to the multi-track will be managed by the court, but there is greater opportunity for the parties to influence the case management process than under the fast track or the small claims track. Litigants complete questionnaires to assist the court in preparation for the 'case management conference'. Strict timetables are imposed on the parties including the publication of the trial date, which litigants and the lawyers are expected to comply with.

PROCEDURAL STEPS IN A DEFENDED CIVIL CASE

As with criminal cases, the early stages of a civil case will involve the lawyer meeting with his client to take instructions and take a preliminary proof of evidence. A major difference between the criminal and civil jurisdictions is that in a civil case, the respon-sibility for investigating and collating the evidence rests with each party's lawyer and not with a State agency such as the police, Customs and Excise or a local authority. When investigating his client's case the lawyer will sometimes seek the assistance of a specialist third party such as an inquiry agent, a credit reference agency or an expert witness. In advising the client and preparing for trial, the case will proceed in the following way.

Advising the client – the preliminary steps

The initial advice to the client will concern a number of preliminary issues such as how the case is to be funded and ensuring that the action can be commenced within the permitted limitation periods as prescribed by the Limitation Act 1980. The main requirement at this stage is to obtain a more detailed proof of evidence from the client and from any potential witnesses.

The client's proof of evidence should be as comprehensive as possible and support his version of the facts. Where the lawyer is acting for a claimant he will always be aware of the general rule that the claimant will have the legal and evidential burdens of proving his case both in terms of liability and quantum. This requirement will have to be reflected in the claimant's witness statement. At an early stage in the proceedings, the client's proof of evidence will probably contain factual evidence which, although useful to his case, may be technically inadmissible if it proceeds to trial. Before the exchange of witness statements the client's statement will need to be edited to exclude any inadmissible material.

The lawyer, whether acting for the claimant or the defendant, will also need to take a statement from any potential witnesses of fact. There is no property in a witness and the lawyer may request an interview with anyone who might have factual knowledge of the case. It is important that a witness should be interviewed as soon as possible in the proceedings and whilst the events about which he may be required to testify are fresh in his memory. One problem that might be encountered is where the witness refuses to give a statement. Unlike in a criminal case, where the police have consider-able powers to coerce a reluctant witness to co-operate with the investigation, there is little that can be done in a civil action where a witness does not want to become involved in a case. Where the reluctant witness's evidence could have been crucial to the party's case, the lawyer will have to consider carefully whether, if the case proceeds to trial, the party will be able to prove its case.

As well as taking a statement from each witness, the lawyer should assemble the documentary evidence in the case. Not only does documentary evidence have consid-erable probative value in many civil cases, as a matter of professional conduct and as an obligation prescribed under the Civil Procedure Rules, the party will have to disclose all the documents in its possession that are relevant to the case including documents that may prove harmful to the party's own case or assist the other party's case. The rules of evidence governing the practice and procedure of disclosure are dealt with in Chapter 25.

In investigating the case and collating the evidence, the lawyer may have to visit the site where the cause of action arose. This may involve, for example in an industrial personal injury action, the lawyer inspecting the workplace where his client was hurt. In litigation arising out of a road traffic accident, the scene of the accident will be a priority. Site visits are important for taking photographs or for making plans. These important pieces of evidence will be admissible at trial, and where necessary, the person who took the photographs or drew the plan may be called as a witness. The practice and procedure for admitting plans and photographs at trial are considered in Chapter 29.

Even at this early stage, it may be necessary to instruct an expert to advise the lawyer on an issue that goes beyond the lawyer's knowledge. The most common example will be in a personal injury case, where a doctor's opinion about the extent of the claimant's injuries will have to be obtained. The law relating to expert evidence is discussed at Chapter 30.

A number of other tasks should be considered at the pre-action stage that may be relevant as to how a party discharges its legal and evidential burdens at trial. First, it may be necessary to instruct counsel to advise on the issue of liability or quantum, ie the total value of the party's claim, or to advise on any evidential issues that need to be considered.

Secondly, it may be necessary to apply to the court for pre-action disclosure. An application for pre-action disclosure will be appropriate where another potential party in the case holds documents that may be relevant in deciding whether or not to take proceedings. The application is permitted under section 33 of the Supreme Court Act 1981 or under section 52 of the County Courts Act 1984. The procedure to be followed is prescribed by CPR rule 31.16(3).

Thirdly, the parties may have to comply with the requirements of a pre-action protocol, which formally apply in the following actions:

- personal injury claims;
- clinical negligence claims;
- construction and engineering disputes;
- professional negligence claims; and
- defamation actions.

The protocols are designed to achieve a settlement in the case without the parties resorting to litigation. Significantly, even in those types of cases where a protocol has yet to be issued by the Lord Chancellor's Department, the parties are expected to behave in their pre-action preparations as if a protocol were in force. Costs penalties will be imposed where a party fails to comply with the 'spirit' of the pre-action code of conduct.

Commencing the action

Where it has not been possible to reach a negotiated settlement with the other side, the claimant will formally commence the proceedings. In some cases, the claimant's lawyer will have a choice in which court to start the proceedings. The general rule is that county courts have unlimited jurisdiction to hear all contract and tort cases. Specifically, however, where the value of the case is below £15,000, it must be started in the county court. If the value exceeds £15,000, the case may be commenced in the

High Court. A special rule applies to personal injury actions. The action must be commenced in the county court unless the value of the action is £50,000 or more. The practice under the Civil Procedure Rules is that where the value of the claim is under £50,000 the case should be commenced in the county court. Where the action is worth more than £50,000, both the High Court and the county court have jurisdiction, but in most cases the High Court will be the appropriate forum.

The action will be formally commenced by completing a claim form and either by lodging it in the court office or sending it by post together with the appropriate fee. The details of the claimant's action must either be set out in the claim form or in a separate document containing the particulars of claim. The particulars should contain a concise statement of facts on which the claimant relies.

On receiving the particulars of claim, the defendant may respond by filing an acknowledgement of service or file a defence. In a defended action, a defence must be filed within 14 days of the service of the particulars of the claim or within 28 days if a form of acknowledgement of service has been filed. After having been informed of the claimant's allegations and receiving the letter of claim, it is likely that the defence lawyer will already have gone through many of the preparatory stages of investigation and will therefore be in a position to comply with the prescribed time limits in the case.

Allocating the case

The next stage in the proceedings is the allocation of the case by the judge to a case management track and, unless the parties settle, the case will be listed for trial in either a county court or in the High Court. The practice and procedure in preparing for a civil trial and the evidential issues that arise at the trial are considered in Chapters 27 and 28.

THE RULES OF CIVIL EVIDENCE – AN OVERVIEW

As Lord Woolf intended, the introduction of the Civil Procedure Rules has not only reformed the practice and procedure in civil cases but has also completely changed the philosophy of civil litigation, the role of the parties, their legal advisers and the duties of the judiciary. It is therefore unsurprising that the rules of civil evidence, which are largely found in CPR Parts 32 and 33, have also changed. For example, it is probably no longer correct to describe the civil process of fact adjudication as 'adversarial'. The claimant and the defendant are now under a duty to co-operate and the judge is no longer required to play the role of a neutral, impartial umpire as the rules of criminal evidence require. As part of his case management responsibilities, the judge plays a proactive role in controlling every aspect of the case. It is more appropriate to describe the post-Woolf system of civil litigation as a 'managed' system of fact adjudication as opposed to an 'adversarial' system that prevails in the criminal jurisdiction.

Importantly, the Civil Procedure Rules requires the court to exercise strict control over the evidence at all stages of the litigation. This is particularly significant in relation to the disclosure of documents (formerly the discovery stage), the conduct of the trial and the role of expert witnesses. As part of his case management responsibilities, the judge can control the number of witnesses in the case, the issues upon which evidence is required and the way in which the evidence is presented at trial. The wide autonomy granted to a party in a criminal case as to how it presents its case to the court is not available to the parties in a civil action. The wide powers of case management given to judges is illustrated by CPR rule 32.1, which provides that otherwise admissible evidence may be excluded where 'it is in the interests of justice' to do so. If a similar provision was applied to defence evidence in a criminal case, it is likely that an appeal against conviction would succeed on the ground that the conviction was 'unsafe' under the Criminal Appeal Act 1968.

The Civil Procedure Rules also undermine the common law's dependence on oral testimony as the preferred means of giving evidence in court proceedings. Oral evidence will not always be heard at a civil trial as it is common for a witness's written statement to stand as his examination-in-chief. Oral evidence will only be heard with the leave of the judge exercising his discretion in accordance with the overriding principles of the Civil Procedure Rules. The opportunity for cross-examination is closely controlled especially in fast track cases where the timetable drawn up by the judge may specify how long each party has to cross-examine the other side's witnesses.

The procedure controlling the pre-trial disclosure of documents has also changed. Automatic disclosure is not recognised by the Civil Procedure Rules, as a court order is required before disclosure is allowed. Where disclosure is ordered, the parties' conduct is subject to the overriding duty of honesty.

The practice and procedure in relation to expert evidence was identified by Lord Woolf as one of the major causes of escalating costs in civil litigation. Expert evidence is governed by CPR Part 35, which requires the parties to co-operate and, where appropriate, appoint a jointly instructed expert. No party may adduce expert evidence without the permission of the court. The expert is required to acknowledge that his primary duty is to assist the court and not to take the partisan approach – a feature prevalent in the former system of civil litigation. Generally, an expert will not give oral evidence in a fast track case, although in a multi-track case it may be necessary for each party to instruct its own expert. Where this occurs each party will have the right to serve questions on the other side's expert requiring him to clarify certain points and/or giving him an opportunity to reply to opposing views. Where there are two experts the courts will usually require those experts to identify areas of agreement between them and to substantiate their opinions about any areas of disagreement.

In spite of these important changes, some familiar evidential issues still arise in all civil cases. These include issues relating to which party has the legal and evidential burdens of proof, the appropriate standard of proof, the law relating to a witness's competence and compellability, the operation of legal professional privilege, the application of public interest immunity and the admission of expert evidence. Also, a more traditional adversarial contest is retained in those multi-track cases that reach trial. Questions concerning the admission of hearsay evidence are more commonly encountered in civil litigation than in criminal cases. As Chapter 29 confirms, the rules on the admission of hearsay evidence under the Civil Evidence Act 1995 are much more relaxed than in criminal cases. Finally, although less common in civil cases than in criminal litigation, issues can arise as to a party's or a witness's character and convictions both at common law and under statute. Each of these important evidential topics are dealt with in the following chapters.

RULES OF EVIDENCE IN 'OTHER' CIVIL CASES

As noted in the introduction to this chapter, Part 3 of this text examines primarily the rules of evidence in mainstream civil proceedings in the county court and the High Court. It should not be forgotten however that the general term 'civil litigation', also covers, for example, proceedings in magistrates' courts, employment tribunals, the Lands Tribunal and social security tribunals. These have their own rules of practice and evidence. The overall jurisdiction, composition and procedure of tribunals is governed by the Tribunals and Inquiries Act 1992. Generally, in tribunals the rules of strict evidence do not apply and the way in which a party proves its case is governed by the specific rules of procedure and evidential provisions for the tribunal in which the case is heard.

Rules of evidence in proceedings under the Children Act 1989

Proceedings under the Children Act 1989 concern applications for court orders regarding children such as parental responsibility orders, contact orders and residence orders. The rules of evidence have developed to deal with the specific requirements of this important jurisdiction. Proceedings under the Children Act 1989 may be conducted in the High Court or in the county court or in the magistrates' court and, as a result, the traditional distinction between the rules of civil and criminal evidence has largely been abolished in these proceedings. Whilst the general rules of evidence apply to proceedings under the Children Act 1989, they are subject to certain modifications for two reasons. First, proceedings under the Act adopt an inquisitorial style of fact adjudication as opposed to the managed system that applies in proceedings in the High Court or in the county court. Secondly, in most proceedings under the Act, the court is required to act in compliance with the 'child welfare' principle as defined in section 1(1) of the 1989 Act. Therefore some of the rules of evidence that apply in mainstream civil proceedings would be out of place. For example, under section 98 of the Children Act 1989, no person can be excused from giving evidence or answering questions on the ground that the answer might incriminate him in a criminal charge in respect of himself or his spouse in proceedings seeking a care and supervision order or in a case involving the protection of children. The privilege against self-incrimination has no application to such proceedings.

Further reading

Woolf MR, Lord (1995) *Access to Justice, Interim Report*, Lord Chancellor's Department.
Woolf MR, Lord (1996) *Access to Justice, Final Report*, HMSO.

Chapter 23

THE BURDENS OF PROOF

INTRODUCTION

Unless the defendant admits the claimant's case or the claimant admits the defendant's counterclaim, all civil litigation involves allegations of disputed facts and the parties interpretations of the substantive law to those disputed facts. Where the case proceeds to a civil trial, the judge, or very occasionally the jury, will decide the case on the basis of the admissible evidence presented by each side in order to persuade the tribunal of fact of the truth of their case. As we saw in Chapter 1, a fundamental purpose of the law of evidence is to provide the ground rules for the process of litigation by identifying the facts in issue that each litigant has to discharge in order to prove its case to the court. This purpose is seen most clearly with respect to the rules on the legal and evidential burdens of proof. The rules indicate to a party bringing the case or defending the action the facts in issue that each side will have to prove to be successful at trial; the way in which facts will be proved and the appropriate standard of proof that will have to be satisfied if the legal and evidential burdens are to be successfully discharged. These rules may be described as the legal burden of proof; the evidential burden of proof and the standard of proof. The purpose of this chapter is to examine the way in which these rules operate in the context of a civil case.

THE LEGAL BURDEN OF PROOF – GENERAL RULE

The legal burden of proof is described in a number of ways including the 'probative burden' or the 'ultimate burden' or the 'burden of proof on the proceedings' or the 'persuasive burden'. A more satisfactory approach is to define the legal burden of proof in civil proceedings as 'the onus on one party to prove or disprove certain facts in issue'. The general rule in civil proceedings is that the party that bears the legal burden also has an evidential burden.

Whilst the rules of civil evidence do not incorporate the same enshrined principle as that expressed in the criminal case of *Woolmington v DPP* [1935] AC 462 (the accused in a criminal trial is presumed innocent unless proved guilty by the prosecution), the well-established general rule about the incidence of the legal burden of proof in civil proceedings is that 'he who asserts must prove'. Put simply, the legal burden of proving a fact in issue in a civil trial is on the party that asserts that fact. This principle is generally made clear in the pleadings, ie the statement of case and the defence and/or the counterclaim. As with criminal cases, the facts in issue in civil proceedings are a question of law to be determined by reference to the common law or to the statute creating the cause of action.

Examples

Javinder, as the claimant, is suing Anne, the defendant in negligence. Anne is defending the action by denying liability. To succeed in the action, under the principle of 'he who asserts must prove', Javinder has the legal burden of proving the following facts in issue:

- *Anne owed Javinder a duty of care;*
- *Anne breached the duty of care; and*
- *as a result of the breach, Javinder suffered damage or injury.*

John, the claimant, is suing Brogan Cars Ltd, the defendant for breach of contract. Brogan Cars are defending the action by denying liability. Under the principle of 'he who asserts must prove', to succeed at trial, John has the legal burden of proving the following facts in issue:

- *the existence of the contract between the parties;*
- *the terms of the contract;*
- *that the defendant breached the contract; and*
- *as a result of the defendant's breach, he, the claimant, has suffered loss.*

The legal burden is placed on the claimant in each of these situations as the claimant is making an assertion, and therefore he has the legal burden or the responsibility in law to prove that assertion.

In the first example, Javinder, as the claimant is asserting that the defendant owed him a duty of care, that the duty of care was broken and, as a result of the breach of the duty of care, he suffered damage and/or injury.

In the second example, John is making the positive assertion that a contract existed between himself and the defendant, Brogan Cars Ltd, and is also asserting the terms of the contract, that the defendant breached the contract and that as a result of the defendant's breach he has suffered the losses as pleaded.

In each example, as the defendant is merely denying the allegation pleaded in the claimant's statement of case, ie that they were not negligent as alleged or that the contract was not breached, the defendant has nothing to prove because the general maxim of 'he asserts must prove' applies.

Where the defendant, in denying liability, makes an assertion on the facts of the case, ie in an action for negligence that the claimant was contributorily negligent, or in an action for breach of contract that the operation of the contract was frustrated, or in defamation proceedings that the defamatory statement attracts the defence of 'justification' or that it is covered by 'fair comment' or absolute or qualified privilege, then the defendant will bear the legal burden of proving that fact in issue. Once again, the general maxim applies that the party that asserts a fact has the legal burden of proving that fact.

In the examples given above, once Javinder has discharged the legal and evidential burdens of proving the essential elements of negligence, Anne then has the legal and evidential burdens of proving that Javinder was contributorily negligent. In the action for breach of contract, when John has discharged the legal and evidential burdens of proof with regard to the existence of the contract, its terms and the alleged breach, Brogan Cars Ltd has the legal and evidential burdens of proving that the contract was frustrated.

Where each party discharges its legal and evidential burdens of proof, the judge will decide the case on the persuasiveness and probative value of the evidence presented to him in support of each party's version of the facts and the interpretation of the law to those facts.

A simple illustration of the operation of the rule relating to the incidence of the legal burden of proof is provided by *Wakelin v London and South Western Railway Co* (1887) 12 App Cas 41. An action in negligence was brought by the plaintiff following the death of her husband, whose body was found by the side of a railway line. The railway line crossed a public footpath that was guarded by hand gates. During the day the railway company employed a watchman to take charge of the gates, but at night-time the watchman was withdrawn. The dead body of the plaintiff's husband was found on the line near to the level crossing at night. He had been killed by a train. No evidence was given as to how the plaintiff's husband had got onto the line. At the trial, the jury gave judgment for the plaintiff. The Divisional Court set aside the verdict and the case went to the Court of Appeal. In giving the leading judgment, Lord Halsbury LC reaffirmed the principle that it was incumbent on the plaintiff to prove that her husband's death had been caused by the defendant's negligent act or negligent omission, which could be attributed as the cause of her husband's death. The plaintiff was held to have failed to discharge the legal and evidential burdens in proving the essential elements of the tort of negligence and therefore her action failed.

Even where a party in its pleadings makes a negative assertion, the principle remains that 'he who asserts must prove'. For example, in *Abrath v North Eastern Railway Co* (1886) 11 App Cas 247, an action for malicious prosecution, the judge directed the jury that it was for the plaintiff to establish 'a want of reasonable and probable cause and malice', and that it lay on the plaintiff to show that the defendants had not taken reasonable care to inform themselves of the true facts of the case. The House of Lords affirmed that this was a correct direction even though the assertions amounted to proving a negative.

It is sometimes suggested that during the course of the trial the burden will shift between the claimant and the defendant. A useful explanation of the meaning of the phrase the 'shifting burden' in a civil trial was provided by the Court of Appeal in *Brady v Group Lotus Car Companies plc* [1987] 3 All ER 1050. In his judgment, Lord Justice Dillon stated that the phrase has more than one meaning. First, it indicates that in order to reach a conclusion on the entire dispute, the court must successively decide two or more issues in respect of which the burden is not always on the same party. For example, the legal burden will shift between the parties where one party pleads a rebuttable presumption of law. A rebuttable presumption of law applies where a party proves one or more basic facts, the court may presume another fact to be established unless the other party produces evidence to rebut that presumption. (A detailed examination of presumptions can be found in Chapter 24.) For example, in an action for negligence arising out of a road traffic accident in which a car driven by the defendant hits the claimant causing the claimant personal injuries, where the claimant pleads the presumption of negligence (which is a rebuttable presumption of law) the claimant has the legal burden of proving that the car was under the defendant's exclusive control and that in the ordinary course of things the accident would not have happened if the defendant had not been negligent. Where the claimant proves these primary facts the legal burden then shifts to the defendant to prove that, on the balance of probabilities, he was not negligent. The decision as to whether the legal burden has been satisfactorily discharged can only be made by the judge at the end of the case after having heard all of the evidence.

The second situation where the burden may shift is commonly referred to as an evidentiary burden of proof. This connotes that during the trial an issue of fact will often be part of both parties' cases. The judge may consider at any stage of the trial that if no further evidence were to be heard in support of that fact, a particular party would have proven that fact to his satisfaction. The party to whom the principle applies may change several times during the course of the trial.

LEGAL BURDEN OF PROOF – EXCEPTIONS TO THE GENERAL RULE

In providing the rationale for the general rule of 'he who asserts must prove', Lord Maughan in *Josephine Constantine Steamship Line Ltd* v *Imperial Smelting Corp Ltd* [1942] AC 154, stated that the principle was 'founded on considerations of good sense [which] should not be departed from without strong reason'. In spite of Lord Maughan's confident assertion about the incidence of the legal burden in civil cases, as we stated earlier, it would be wrong to suggest that the principle is firmly enshrined in civil evidence as Lord Sankey's 'golden thread' is in criminal cases (*Woolmington* v *DPP* [1935] AC 462) – even after taking account of the recognised exceptions. Therefore, there are a number of exceptions under statute and at common law to the general rule in civil proceedings that where a party makes a positive assertion, it has the legal burden of proving that fact in issue. In a number of situations the incidence of the legal burden is determined by other factors.

Where the legal burden of proof is fixed by statute

As in statutes regulating the criminal law, when passing legislation to be applied in civil cases, Parliament may expressly or by implication place the legal burden on one or more issues on the defendant. The best known example is provided by section 171(7) of the Consumer Credit Act 1974, so that where a debtor alleges that a credit agreement is extortionate within the meaning of sections 137 and 138 of the 1974 Act, the legal burden of proof is put on the creditor to prove the credit agreement is not 'extortionate' (see *Coldunell Ltd* v *Gallon* [1986] 1 All ER 429).

Similarly, under section 98 of the Employment Rights Act 1996, in a claim for unfair dismissal, the legal burden is placed on the applicant (the former employee) to prove that he was dismissed. Once this legal burden has been discharged, the employer then has the legal burden of proving that the applicant's dismissal was fair by proving the dismissal was for one or more of the reasons recognised in the Act. Where the employer fails to discharge this legal burden, the applicant's claim will succeed. Consider the following example.

Example

Dale is suing his employer, the Goodbuy Motor Company, in the employment tribunal for unfair dismissal. Under the Employment Rights Act 1996, Dale has the legal burden of proving that he was dismissed. If this burden is successfully discharged, the legal burden passes to Goodbuy as the employer to prove that the reason for the dismissal was 'fair' within one of the statutory reasons, for example, that Dale was dismissed on the ground of his capability or conduct. Each party then has the burden to persuade the tribunal that the procedure adopted by the employer was 'fair' or 'unfair'.

In Chapter 11, in discussing the rules relating to the legal burden of proof in criminal cases, we saw how, as a matter of statutory construction and interpretation, the Court of Appeal in *R v Edwards* [1974] 2 All ER 1085 and the House of Lords in *R v Hunt* [1987] AC 352 provided guidance to the courts where, by implication, parliamentary legislation places the legal burden on the prosecution or on the defence. In *Nimmo v Alexander Cowan & Sons Ltd* [1968] AC 107, the House of Lords was required to adopt a similar approach in the context of a civil case. The plaintiff, an injured workman, alleged that his injuries were caused by his employer's breach of section 29(1) of the Factories Act 1961 which provided that '... every place at which at any time anyone has to work ... shall so far as is reasonably practicable be made and kept safe for any person therein'. The plaintiff proved that his workplace was unsafe but did not adduce any evidence that it had been 'reasonably practicable' to keep the workplace safe.

By a majority, the House of Lords decided that the plaintiff did not have the legal burden to prove the issue that it was 'reasonably practicable' to keep the premises safe. The legal burden lay with the defendant employer as it was much better placed to prove the facts as the fact in issue was within its peculiar knowledge as to the precautions that had been taken to keep the premises safe. The principle of imposing the legal burden on the employer to prove the 'reasonable practicability' test is a common requirement in many health and safety enactments contained in both primary and secondary legislation. For a detailed judicial consideration of the principle see *Edwards v National Coal Board* [1949] 1 All ER 743 and more recently the Court of Appeal's decision in *Furness v Midland Bank PLC* [2000] (unreported), which concerned an action for breach of statutory duty brought under the Workplace (Health, Safety and Welfare) Regulations 1992.

Therefore, in many civil cases where it is unclear on which party the legal burden has been imposed, as a matter of statutory construction, the courts will generally decide the issue on the basis of which party can most easily prove the fact in issue.

Where the legal burden of proof is fixed by agreement between the parties

A second exception to the general rule on the legal burden of proof relates to where the parties agree between themselves as to where the legal burden should lie on a particular issue. It is quite common, for example, where two parties enter into a contract for the contract itself to stipulate where the legal burden of proof should lie on specific facts in issue, should the contract become the subject of legal proceedings (*Chappell v National Car Parks* (1987) *The Times*, 22 May).

Where the parties' intentions at the time of making the agreement are unclear, in deciding which party bears the legal burden on a certain issue, the court will interpret the specific terms of the agreement between the parties. The approach taken by the courts is illustrated by the following cases.

Hurst v Evans [1917] 1 KB 352

The defendant underwriters insured the plaintiff, who was a jeweller, against loss of or damage to jewellery arising from any cause whatsoever except breakage and loss by the theft or dishonesty of any of the plaintiff's employees. The action by the plaintiff was founded on the terms of the policy after it came to light that one of the plaintiff's servants had stolen some jewellery. In interpreting the terms of the contract, the court held that the plaintiff had the legal burden of proving than some person other than one of his servants had stolen the jewellery, and that as he had failed to discharge this burden, his action would fail.

Levison v Patent Steam Carpet Cleaning Ltd [1978] QB 69

The plaintiff took an expensive Chinese carpet to the defendants to be cleaned. The contract entered into was subject to certain exclusion and limitation clauses, one of which stated that 'all merchandise is expressly accepted at the owner's risk'. The defendant company were unable to return the carpet as it had 'disappeared' and the company was unable to give any reason to account for the disappearance. The court held that the legal burden was on the defendant to show that there had been no fundamental breach of the contract, and not for the plaintiff to show that there had been a breach.

Rhesa Shipping Co SA v Edmunds [1985] 1 WLR 948

The plaintiff claimed for breach of an insurance contract when the defendant insurance company failed to pay under the policy when the plaintiff's ship sank. The plaintiff submitted that the ship had sunk as a result of a 'peril of the sea' after being hit by a submarine. The defendant argued that the ship had sunk as a result of 'wear and tear', which would have excluded the loss of the vessel from being covered by the policy. At trial, the judge was unconvinced by either of the party's submissions but gave judgment to the plaintiff on the basis that its evidence had more persuasive value than the defence case. In allowing the defendant's appeal, the House of Lords held that the judge's approach was wrong as the court's decision had to be based on which party successfully discharged its respective legal burdens. If the way in which the ship sank was part of the terms of the contract between the parties, which, the plaintiff asserted had been breached, the plaintiff would have the legal burden of proving the breach. However, if the issue of the ship sinking was part of an affirmative defence and that such an event came, for example, within the operation of an exclusion clause, the legal burden would lie with the defendant.

On the facts of the case, the House of Lords concluded that the plaintiff had the legal burden of proving that the ship had sunk as a result of a 'peril of the sea', and as the plaintiff had failed to discharge that burden on this issue, the case was lost.

Munro, Brice & Co v War Risks Association [1918] 2 KB 78

A ship had disappeared for reasons unknown and a claim was made under a policy of insurance which covered the ship subject to an exemption clause in respect of loss by capture or in consequence of hostilities. The issue before the court was whether the claimant had to prove that the ship was not lost as a result of enemy action. The court found in favour of the plaintiff on the basis that the legal burden lay with the defendant to prove that the facts fell within the exemption clause, which the defendants had failed to do.

Where the legal burden of proof is ascertained by reference to construction and policy considerations

As we noted above if it is unclear from the pleadings where the legal burden of proof should lie, the courts will resort to statutory interpretation and construction in order to determine the issue (*Nimmo* v *Alexander Cowan & Sons Ltd* [1968] AC 107). As in *Nimmo*, the general principle to emerge from the case law is that the burden will be put on the party who would be expected to discharge the legal burden with the least difficulty. As an illustration of the way in which the courts approach this issue consider the following cases.

Soward *v* Leggat (1856) 7 C & P 613

The plaintiff landlord claimed that the tenant had not repaired the leased premises (a negative assertion), the defendant tenant claimed that he had taken reasonable care of the premises and maintained them to a sufficiently high standard (a positive assertion). The court held that in deciding where the legal burden of proof should lie was not an exercise in semantics but a matter of deciding what, in essence, was being asserted. In this case, clearly what the plaintiff was asserting was that the defendant tenant had breached his covenant to maintain the premises; the defendant was merely denying that assertion. Therefore, the defendant had no burden of proof; it was for the plaintiff to prove his assertion.

Glendarroch, [1894] P 226

A contract for the carriage of goods by sea was subject to an exclusion clause in the carrier's favour that no liability would be incurred by it if the goods were lost or damaged by the perils of sea, provided that there was no negligence on the part of the carrier, its employees, or its agents. The owners sued for non-delivery of goods; the carriers said that this was due to the perils of the sea. The court decided that the parties should bear the following legal burdens of proof: first, it was for the owners to show the breach of the contract term, ie the non-delivery of the goods. If the first point was established satisfactorily, then, secondly, it was for the carrier to establish that this was a result of the perils of the sea. If the second issue was established satisfactorily, thirdly, it would be for the owners to establish that the loss was due to the negligence of the carrier, its employees, or its agents. In this case, there was not merely a denial of the plaintiffs' assertion by the defendant, but the defendant was asserting another fact in issue and thus had the legal burden of proving that fact if it were not to lose the case. If the defendant discharged that burden, it was then for the plaintiffs to discharge the legal burden of proving their assertion that the defendant was negligent if the plaintiffs were to succeed at trial.

Joseph Constantine SS Line *v* Imperial Smelting Corporation [1942] AC 154

The plaintiffs were claiming damages against the defendants for their failure to load goods after a ship on charter was destroyed by an explosion. There was no evidence to establish the cause of the explosion. The defendants pleaded frustration of the contract as their ship had exploded. At trial, the plaintiffs submitted that the defendants could not rely on frustration unless they proved that the explosion was not caused by their fault. In turn, the defendants submitted that the plaintiffs could not rely on frustration unless the plaintiffs showed that the cause of the explosion was the defendant's fault. The outcome of the case therefore turned on which party had the legal burden of proving the issue of frustration. Did the plaintiffs bear the legal burden of showing, on the balance of probabilities, that the explosion was due to some fault or negligence on the part of the defendants, or did the burden rest on the defendants to show that it was not caused by any fault on their part?

The House of Lords held that the legal burden should rest on the plaintiffs to prove that the defendants were at fault as it is generally easier to prove a positive than a negative assertion, ie it is easier to show why something is the fault of a party, than for a party to establish satisfactory reasons why it is not the fault of itself or its employees.

Therefore, an assertion by a party may be couched in affirmative or negative terms, but the court will determine exactly what is being alleged and then decide on which party the legal burden of proof lies. If the decision is that the assertion is truly a negative one, then this may, but will not always, be the conclusive factor. Although usually it is easier to prove a positive rather than a negative assertion, there may be reasons why a negative has to be proven. It may be, that the ease with which a party can discharge a burden of proof is a major factor – and on occasion the negative may be easier to prove than the positive; but, in addition, there may be a rule of substantive law involved which carries greater weight than evidential guidelines.

CASE PREPARATION AND THE LEGAL BURDEN OF PROOF

The rules relating to the incidence of the legal burden of proof in a civil case are not something that lawyers should ignore until the case reaches trial. Under the Civil Procedure Rules the requirement for a party to disclose its case much earlier in the proceedings makes it necessary for the parties' lawyers to assess the strength and the probative value of the evidence at an early stage. The practical consequences of the operation of the rules relating to the legal burden run throughout the whole proceedings from the investigation stage, to providing initial advice to the client, to drafting the pleadings, to negotiating with the other side and, finally, at the trial.

At the investigation stage, the client's lawyer has the responsibility for collecting the evidence in support of his party's case. He will need to identify the facts in issue and when acting for the claimant, assess whether the evidence has sufficient weight and probative value for the claimant to be able to satisfy his legal burden of proof at trial. The defence lawyer must also be aware that unless his client is denying liability, the court will expect the defendant to produce some evidence in support of the denial and/or to challenge the claimant's case. Also, when providing initial advice to the claimant or to the defendant about the strength of his own case and the other party's case, the lawyer may have to recommend a negotiated settlement where the party's evidence does not have sufficient probative force to discharge its legal burden.

When drafting the pleadings, the claimant's statement of case must incorporate the rules relating to the legal burden, by including relevant points of law or by referring to points of evidence in support of the claimant's case. Where, for example, the case is based on a written agreement such as a contract, a copy of the document or the relevant parts of it should be served with the particulars of claim. Where the action is defended, the defence must state which of the allegations contained in the particulars of claim are admitted and which are denied and must also give reasons for denying any allegation contained in the claimant's pleadings.

If the case proceeds to trial, under CPR rule 22.1 any statement of case and any witness statement must be verified by a statement of truth. This obligation means that legal representatives will need to be confident that any issue raised in the party's pleadings can be supported by evidence. A party failing to satisfy its legal burden at trial is likely to have a punitive costs order made against it, as well as the party's lawyer suffering serious damage to his professional reputation.

THE EVIDENTIAL BURDEN

As with criminal cases, the evidential burden is the practical way in which a party discharges its legal burden, by putting evidence before the court. In most cases this will include calling witnesses to give oral evidence, expert evidence, tendering hearsay evidence under the Civil Evidence Act 1995 and/or the production of documents and real evidence. As with the legal burden, the evidential burden is referred to in a number of ways including 'the duty of passing the judge' and 'the burden of adducing evidence'. Defined simply, the evidential burden is 'the onus on one party to adduce sufficient evidence to put a fact or facts in issue before the court'. In civil trials the general principle applies that the party bearing the legal burden also has the evidential burden to adduce sufficient evidence relating to the facts in issue to discharge its legal burden. It is unusual for a party in a civil case not to discharge its evidential burden as one of the main purposes of pre-trial procedures is to ensure that there is an issue to be tried at trial, and where a party fails to discharge its evidential burden, it would suffer considerable financial penalties with costs being awarded against it.

As well as being the 'practical' way in which a party discharges its legal burden, the incidence of the evidential burden has an additional purpose in a civil case by identifying which party is entitled to put its evidence first to the court. Usually, the claimant will have the right to begin, but where, for example, the defendant has the evidential burden on all the issues, the defendant will put his case first to the court.

THE STANDARD OF PROOF

The general rule is that where any fact in issue has to be proven in a civil trial, whether by the claimant or by the defendant, the standard required to discharge that burden is 'on the balance of probabilities'. It may also be referred to as 'proof on a preponderance of probabilities'.

According to Denning J in *Miller* v *Minister of Pensions* [1947] 2 All ER 372 the phrase has the following meaning:

> It must carry a high degree of probability, but not so high as is required in a criminal case. If the evidence is such that the tribunal can say, 'We think it more probable than not', the burden is discharged, but, if the probabilities are equal, it is not.

More recently, the meaning of the phrase 'on the balance of probabilities' was the subject of judicial consideration by the House of Lords in *Re H (Minors) (Sexual Abuse: Standard of Proof)* [1996] 1 All ER 1. Lord Nicholls in the leading judgment suggested the following meaning:

> The balance of probability standard means that a court is satisfied an event occurred if the court considers that, on the evidence, the occurrence of the event was more likely than not.

To successfully discharge the legal burden of proof in civil proceedings a party must prove to the court that it is more likely than not that its version of the facts is correct. Put crudely, proof on the balance of probabilities means in theory that if there is a 51% chance of the claimant's version persuading the court that it is the truth, the claimant will win the case. Whilst it is extremely difficult to quantify the standard of proof precisely in this way, there will be cases where the evidential scales are tipped marginally in favour of one side or the other.

The standard of proof – exceptions to the general rule

There are two well-established exceptions in civil cases where the 'balance of probabilities' is not the appropriate standard of proof. First, the standard of proof in committal proceedings for civil contempt of court is that of beyond reasonable doubt. In *Dean* v *Dean* [1987] 1 FLR 517, a case concerning contempt of court where the husband in a matrimonial dispute breached the undertakings he had given not to interfere with his wife and child, the Court of Appeal held that contempt of court, whether civil or criminal, was a common law misdemeanour and that it had long been established that the case against the alleged contemnor must be proved to the criminal standard of beyond reasonable doubt.

Secondly, a party may be under a statutory requirement to prove a fact in issue to the criminal standard of 'beyond reasonable doubt' and not on the balance of probabilities. In *Judd* v *Minister of Pensions and National Insurance* [1966] 2 QB 580, the claimant had fallen and injured himself whilst on an army exercise and over several years had suffered back pain that he attributed to the fall. Judd made a claim under article 4(2) and (3) of the Royal Warrant Act 1949 that he was entitled to a war pension in respect of his injury. The Minister refused his application and Judd appealed to the Pensions Appeal Tribunal, which concluded that to rebut the claimant's application for a war pension successfully, the Minister had to show on the balance of probabilities, that the claimant's injury had not been caused or aggravated by his army service.

In rejecting this interpretation of the provision, the Divisional Court held that Parliament had made it clear when passing the legislation that, in every pension claim, the Minister needed to be satisfied beyond reasonable doubt that the evidence did not support the applicant's claim even though a war pensions claim was a civil action.

In addition to the above, other exceptions have been identified judicially where the common standard of proof, 'on the balance of probabilities', has in a number of judicial pronouncements been held not to be sufficient for a party to prove its case in civil proceedings. These are allegations of criminal conduct in a civil case and certain family law and matrimonial proceedings.

Allegations of criminal conduct

Where civil proceedings involve allegations of a 'serious' nature, such as of a crime, the presumption has arisen that the more serious the allegation, the higher the degree of probability is required to prove those allegations. There has been a line of authorities which suggest that in order for a party to prove allegations of the commission of a crime in civil proceedings it is necessary to prove those allegations to the criminal standard of beyond reasonable doubt. This view was expressed in *Hurst* v *Evans* [1917] 1 KB 352, which involved allegations of theft against one of the parties, and in *Slattery* v *Mance* [1962] 1 QB 676 where there were allegations of arson in an action concerning an insurance policy. More recently, in *Bahai* v *Rashidian* [1985] 1 WLR 1337, the court adopted a similar approach where serious misconduct was alleged against a solicitor. This was followed by *Miles* v *Cain* (1989) *The Times*, 15 December, which was a civil action for sexual assault after the police had declined to prosecute the defendant in criminal proceedings.

However, a more satisfactory and consistent approach can be seen in the following line of cases that confirm the traditional formulation relating to the standard of proof.

Hornal *v* Neuberger Products Ltd [1957] 1 QB 247

The plaintiff claimed damages for breach of warranty and/or fraud against the defendant company's director. The defendant company had sold a lathe to the plaintiff, which the director had represented as being 'Soag reconditioned'. The plaintiff alleged that the director had made a false representation because he knew that the lathe had not been reconditioned. The question before the court was whether the representation had been made or not. Dismissing the claim for damages for breach of warranty, the trial judge said that he was satisfied on the balance of probabilities that the statement had been made, and awarded damages to the plaintiff. The defendant appealed.

On appeal, the Court of Appeal held that where an allegation of a crime is made in civil proceedings, the appropriate standard of proof was on the balance of probabilities and not beyond reasonable doubt. Lord Denning was of the view that there were degrees of probability within the same standard in that the more serious the allegation, the higher degree of probability was required. Lord Morris in concurring with this view explained the position in this way:

> Though no court and no jury would give less attention to issues lacking gravity than to those marked by it, the very elements of gravity become a part of the range of circumstances which have to be weighed in the scale when deciding as to the balance of probability.

In the opinion of Lord Morris, the balance of probability does not change but the cogency of the evidence will need to vary according to the seriousness of what is alleged. In other words, a court would need greater convincing to be satisfied on the balance of probability. Many may argue that this is the same thing as saying that there is in fact a sliding scale of proof.

The advantage of Lord Morris's approach is best summed up in the words of Lord Nicholls in the case of *Re H (Minors) (Sexual Abuse: Standard of Proof)* [1996] 1 All ER 1, which is considered in detail below:

> It provides a means by which the probability standard can accommodate one's instinctive feeling that even in civil proceedings a court should be more sure before finding serious allegations proved than when deciding less serious or trivial matters...

In *Re H*, the House of Lords considered the question of sliding scales of proof. The case involved care proceedings and confirms that the civil standard of proof applies to family proceedings. The stepfather was alleged to have assaulted one of the children of the family over a long period of time. He had previously been charged and acquitted of the rape of the child. The court had power to order the remaining children of the family be taken into care if it was satisfied that the children were likely to suffer significant harm. The trial judge had made it clear that he did not trust the evidence of the child's mother and her stepfather. However, he had reservations about the child's evidence too. Whilst there was, in his view, some truth in what she had said, given the high standard of proof required in allegations of sexual abuse, he did not feel the local authority had discharged its legal burden to the required standard. If the local authority were not able to prove on the balance of probability that the stepfather had sexually abused his stepdaughter or that there was a substantial risk that he might have, a care order could not be made. The House of Lords followed the principle laid down in *Hornal* v *Neuberger Products Ltd* above, namely that there is but one standard of proof, on the balance of probability. This case is of interest however for the gloss put on the *Hornal* principle by Lord Nicholls.

> The balance of probability standard means that a court is satisfied an event occurred if the court considers that, on the evidence, the occurrence of the event was more likely than not. When assessing the probabilities the court will have in mind as a factor, to whatever extent is appropriate in the particular case, that the more serious the allegation the less likely it is that the event occurred and, hence, the stronger should be the evidence before the court concludes that the allegation is established on the balance of probability ... A stepfather is usually less likely to have repeatedly raped his under age stepdaughter than on some occasion to have lost his temper and slapped her. Built into the preponderance of probability standard is a generous degree of flexibility in respect of the seriousness of the allegation ... It means only that the inherent probability or improbability of an event is itself a matter to be taken into account when weighing the probabilities and deciding whether, on balance, the event occurred.

Lord Nicholls rejected a third standard of proof, higher than on the balance of probability but lower than beyond reasonable doubt on the basis that it would add little to the existing law and would only serve to confuse. He observed the balance of probability test is 'unsatisfactorily vague because there are degrees of probability'. In his view, the current test however has the advantage of incorporating a degree of flexibility to deal with the nature of the proceedings in a given case.

A similar question arose in relation to the appropriate standard of proof in a civil case involving allegations of unlawful homicide. In *Re Dellow's Will Trusts* [1964] 1 WLR 451, Dellow, the testator, left his whole estate to his wife with gifts should she not survive. Dellow suffered a number of strokes that left him severely disabled. His wife who provided constant care became acutely depressed and both Dellow and his wife were found dead in a gas-filled room after having taken sleeping tablets. The issue before the court was whether Dellow had been unlawfully killed by his wife or whether they had died in pursuance of a suicide pact. If the court found that he had been unlawfully killed his estate would pass to the subject of his gifts; if Dellow had died in a suicide pact, his estate would have passed to his wife's and then to her beneficiaries. It was held that even though the crime alleged in the civil proceedings was murder, the standard of proof required did not have to reach the very high standard of beyond reasonable doubt.

More recently in *Francisco* v *Diedrick* (1998), *The Times*, 3 April, Allot J reaffirmed the position that the appropriate standard of proof in a civil action alleging murder was the civil standard on the balance of probabilities.

In light of the above decisions, it would seem that there is some confusion in the law and that whilst the authorities maintain there is no sliding scale of proof, the more serious the allegation, the stronger or more cogent the evidence is required to prove the allegation. However, any attempt to articulate the cogency of evidence test in words has not materialised and until the judiciary takes the opportunity to do so, an element of uncertainty will continue.

Family law and matrimonial cases

It is also uncertain whether a higher standard of proof is required to prove a fact in issue in family and matrimonial proceedings. In *Ginesi* v *Ginesi* [1948] P 179, the Court of Appeal held that an allegation of adultery must be proven to the criminal standard. This formulation was endorsed in *Bater* v *Bater* [1951] P 35 where the Court of Appeal upheld the trial judge's direction that on a petition for divorce alleging cruelty, the petitioner was required to prove the case beyond reasonable doubt. The same view was taken in *Bastable* v *Bastable* [1968] 1 WLR 1684, where it was suggested that an allegation of adultery is a serious matrimonial offence, and calls for a higher standard of proof than on the balance of probabilities. In *Preston-Jones* v *Preston-Jones* [1951] AC 391, a husband petitioned for divorce on the basis that his wife had given birth 360 days after the last opportunity he could have had intercourse with her. The House of Lords upheld the trial judge's direction that adultery had to be proved beyond reasonable doubt.

In the main these decisions can be explained as reflecting the moral and religious attitudes of the day to divorce and infidelity in marriage and that before the passing of the Divorce Reform Act 1969, the grounds for divorce were based on the idea of 'fault' by one of the parties to the marriage and the sense of responsibility that was attached to allegations of infidelity in marriage required such allegations to be proven to the criminal standard of beyond reasonable doubt. The modern view is that it is probably correct to state that in civil proceedings where allegations are made of criminal conduct and in family law and matrimonial cases, there is only one standard of proof. To succeed at trial a party is required to prove a fact in issue on the balance of probabilities (*Re H (Minors) (Sexual Abuse: Standard of Proof)* [1996] 1 All ER 1). Nevertheless, the more serious the allegation, the more cogent the evidence required to convince the court of the likelihood of that party's version of events being the truth.

Further reading

Hamer, D., 'The Civil Standard of Proof Uncertainty: Probability, Belief and Justice' (1994) Sydney Law Review 506.

Kaye, D.H., 'Clarifying the Burden of Persuasion: What Bayesian Decision Rules Do and Do Not Do' (1998) 2 E & P 1.

Pugh, C., 'Poisoning and Civil Compensation' (1996) Journal of Personal Injury Litigation 192.

Stone, J., 'Burden of Proof and the Judicial Process: A Commentary on *Joseph Constantine Steamship Ltd v Imperial Smelting Corporation Ltd*' (1944) 60 LQR 262.

Chapter 24

THE REQUIREMENT FOR PROOF – EXCEPTIONS TO THE GENERAL RULE

INTRODUCTION

The general rule in civil proceedings, as in criminal cases, is that where a party has the legal and evidential burden of proof on a fact in issue, the fact has to be proven by relevant and admissible evidence. This takes the form of a party proving its case in the way indicated by the court in accordance with its case management powers under the Civil Procedure Rules. This normally requires evidence to be tendered either by a witness giving oral testimony in court or by a written statement being given as the witness's evidence-in-chief or by the witness's written or oral statement tendered as hearsay evidence under the Civil Evidence Act 1995. In addition a party may also discharge its legal and evidential burdens by putting documentary evidence and/or of real evidence before the court.

There are three exceptions to the general rule requiring evidence to be adduced to discharge a legal or an evidential burden where the court may treat a fact as proven without the need for the party bearing the legal and evidential burdens to put evidence before the court in respect of that fact. The first exception applies where a party admits a fact by making a formal admission either before the trial or at the trial. The second exception applies where the proof of the fact in issue may be presumed by the court from an inference drawn from one or more primary facts. The third exception to the general rule is dealt under the doctrine of judicial notice. Judicial notice covers those facts that are so well known and notorious that it is not necessary for a party to prove that fact formally to the court.

FORMAL ADMISSIONS

Where a party formally admits the truth of a fact in issue in the case, the fact ceases to be in dispute between the parties, and, as such, any evidence to prove the fact will be ruled as inadmissible on the ground that it is irrelevant. There are a number of ways in which a fact in issue can be formally admitted by a party in a civil case.

Formal admissions before trial

In the pleadings

A party may formally admit a fact in the pleadings in the case, ie in a statement of case or in a defence or in a counterclaim or in a reply.

Example

In an action for breach of contract, the claimant may plead in his statement of case the existence of the contract between the parties and the allegation of the defendant's breach. In his defence, the defendant may admit the existence of the contract but deny that the contract has been breached. At the trial, the claimant is relieved of discharging the legal and evidential burdens of proving the existence of the contract as the defendant has formally admitted the fact. The parties will therefore be free to deal with the issue of the breach as this fact remains in dispute between them.

In response to a notice to admit facts

Under CPR rule 32.18, where a party wishes his opponent to admit a fact in issue without the need to call evidence to prove the fact at trial, a party may serve a 'notice to admit facts' on the other side no later than 21 days before trial, specifying the fact to be admitted. Where the fact is admitted, the opposing side is relieved of calling evidence in support of that fact at the trial. This procedure is appropriate where the fact to be admitted is uncontroversial or the party wishes to save expense by not having to call a particular witness to give evidence to prove the fact. Where the fact is not admitted, it remains in dispute and the party on whom the legal burden is vested must discharge the legal and evidential burdens of proving that fact. If the fact is subsequently proven at trial, the party who refused to admit the fact, may incur a costs penalty of proving the fact at trial.

By letter

Before the trial, a formal admission may be made by the party's legal adviser in a letter or otherwise in writing (CPR rule 14.1(2)). In *Ellis* v *Allen* [1914] 1 Ch 904, the High Court ruled that where the defendant had made an admission in a letter which had been sent to the plaintiff, the defendant was bound by the admission and the plaintiff was entitled to enter judgment on the basis of the admissions made in the letter.

Formal admissions during pre-trial trial hearings and at the trial

A formal admission may be made at a pre-trial hearing such as the case management conference or at the pre-trial review or by the party's advocate during the trial. A modern illustration of the rule is provided by the case of *Worldwide Corporation Ltd* v *Marconi Communications Ltd* (1999) *The Times*, 7 July. In an application to amend in order to set up a new cause of action, counsel for the claimant made a number of formal admissions at trial, the effect of which was to abandon the original action.

It may also be possible to make a formal admission by default, where a party fails to deal with one of the other party's allegations. In this situation, under the normal rules of witness testimony, where a party in cross-examination fails to challenge the other side's witness's evidence on a particular fact, the court will deem the cross-examining party to admit that fact.

INFORMAL ADMISSIONS

An informal admission is a written or an oral statement made by a party or by a person connected with the party that is adverse to that party's interests and is most commonly made in a letter, fax or an e-mail. An informal admission may also be made orally in a witness's answer to a question asked in cross-examination. Where an informal admission has been made, it may be disproved or explained by other evidence at the trial and it is at the court's discretion to decide how much weight should be attached to the statement.

An informal admission may also be made spontaneously by a person in response to the events giving rise to the cause of action. A common example of this type of informal admission will be where a witness accepts responsibility for causing a road traffic accident by stating, for example that 'It was all my fault. I didn't see the other vehicle coming. The next thing I knew his vehicle hit mine.' This admission would be admissible at trial as hearsay evidence under section 7 of the Civil Evidence Act 1995 and is dealt with in Chapter 29.

PRESUMPTIONS

The second situation where a party is relieved of the legal burden of proving a fact in issue is where the fact comes within the operation of a presumption. A presumption is an inference made about one fact from which the court is entitled to presume certain other facts without having those facts directly proven by evidence. The following example shows the operation of the common law presumption of legitimacy.

Example

There is a dispute between Stan and Gerald, who are brothers, about whether Arthur, who Stan believes to be his son from his marriage to Hilda, is entitled to a share in the estate of Frank, their deceased father.

In his will, Frank made the following testamentary disposition: 'The beneficiaries of my estate shall include all the legitimate children of my sons, Stan and Gerald.'

Gerald believes that Arthur is not Stan's legitimate child and is therefore not entitled to be a beneficiary under Frank's estate.

The presumption of legitimacy operates so that on proof of the basic fact (or primary fact) that Hilda gave birth to, or conceived, Arthur whilst she was married to Stan, the court will presume that Arthur is their legitimate child.

As the presumption of legitimacy is a rebuttable presumption of law, once the primary fact has been established, the legal burden then passes to Gerald to disprove that Arthur is not Stan and Hilda's legitimate child.

Whilst presumptions apply to both civil and criminal law, they operate primarily in civil cases as their operation may conflict with the general principle relating to the incidence of the legal burden of proof found in *Woolmington* v *DPP* [1935] AC 462 and they are not covered by the exceptions to the general rule found at common law or as expressly or impliedly required by statute.

Whilst this area of the law of evidence is beset by terminological difficulties, the traditional classification identifies three categories of presumptions:

- irrebuttable presumptions of law;
- rebuttable presumptions of law; or
- presumptions of facts.

Irrebuttable presumptions of law

An irrebuttable presumption of law operates so that on the proof of a basic fact, another fact must be presumed and the party against whom the presumption operates is barred from tendering any evidence in rebuttal. The following provisions are irrebuttable presumptions of law.

Section 50 of the Children and Young Persons Act 1933 provides that:

> It shall be conclusively presumed that no child under the age of ten years can be guilty of an offence.

Therefore, in a criminal case where the defence offers evidence that the accused is a child under ten, the prosecution is prevented from adducing evidence to rebut the presumption. In this sense the presumption that the child is not considered to be capable in English law of committing a criminal offence is irrebuttable, ie it cannot be disproved by any other evidence.

A provision with a similar evidential effect is found in section 13(1) of the Civil Evidence Act 1968, which provides that:

> In an action for libel or slander in which the question whether the plaintiff did or did not commit a criminal offence is relevant to an issue arising in the action, proof that, at the time when that issue falls to be determined, he stands convicted of that offence shall be conclusive evidence that he committed the offence; and his conviction thereof shall be admissible in evidence accordingly.

Section 13, which applies to defamation proceedings, creates a conclusive, irrebuttable presumption that the claimant committed the criminal offence. Once the fact of the conviction is proved, the court will presume that the claimant was convicted and that no evidence will be allowed to rebut the presumption.

Therefore, in a defamation action, the case will be struck out where the defendant's defamatory statement only contains an allegation that the claimant was convicted of the criminal offence to which section 13 applies as the claimant will not be permitted to rebut the presumption's operation that he was convicted by a criminal court as alleged by the defendant.

Rebuttable presumptions of law

A rebuttable presumption of law operates where, on the proof or admission of a primary fact, and in the absence of further evidence, another fact must be presumed. The party relying on the presumption bears the legal and evidential burden of proving the primary fact. Once the party has adduced sufficient evidence to establish the presumed fact, the presumption will apply unless the other party successfully discharges its legal and evidential burden to rebut the presumption. The standard of proof required to rebut the presumption is determined by the area of substantive law in which the presumption operates. In a civil case, the party that has the legal burden of rebutting the presumption is required to prove the issue to the normal standard of 'on the balance of probabilities'. The most important rebuttable presumptions of law are:

- the presumption of marriage;
- the presumption of legitimacy;
- the presumption of death;
- the *commorientes* rule;
- the presumption of regularity; and
- the presumption of negligence (*res ipsa loquitur*).

Presumption of marriage

There are two presumptions which operate in respect of marriage: a presumption of the formal validity of a marriage and a presumption of the essential validity of a marriage.

Formal validity of the marriage

The formal validity of marriage requires that the procedures prescribed by the domestic law of a country for a couple to be lawfully married have been properly complied with. In English law, for example, this includes the reading of banns before the ceremony or the obtaining of a special licence. The law will presume that on proof of the primary facts that the parties intended to marry, a marriage ceremony was performed and the appropriate procedures were followed and the marriage is legally valid. The leading English authority on the operation of the presumption of the validity of marriage is *Piers* v *Piers* [1843–1860] All ER Rep 159. The couple had their marriage ceremony in a private house. It was clear that they wished to be married, but there was no evidence that the parties had the special licence that was required before they could be married in a private house. It was held that upon proof of the two primary facts that the parties wished to be married and that a marriage ceremony had been performed, all the necessary formalities had been complied with. Once the court has accepted the existence of the primary facts, the legal and evidential burden then shifts to the party seeking to rebut the operation of the presumption.

The presumption will also apply to marriages performed under the terms of foreign law. In *Mahadervan* v *Mahadervan* [1964] P 233, a marriage ceremony had been celebrated between the couple in Ceylon (Sri Lanka). Two of the requirements of the local law were, first, the solemnisation of the ceremony by a Registrar either in his office or in another authorised place and, secondly, during the ceremony, the Registrar was required to address the parties. The parties lived as man and wife for seven years after the ceremony before the husband left for England and married another woman in England. At this time the validity of the man's first marriage was questioned. It was clear from the certificate to the first marriage that the ceremony had been solemnised by the Registrar in his office but there was no evidence that he had given the necessary address to the couple. For this reason, the husband's counsel submitted there was no presumption in favour of the marriage and that the husband had been free to marry in England. The court held that the presumption of the formal validity of marriage applied and that the foreign marriage was valid.

Essential validity of the marriage

Under English law a marriage may be void where the parties lacked the legal capacity to marry. This requires that the parties were free to marry, that they had the legal capacity and that they consented to marry, ie they were over 16 years old, not already validly married, and were not subjected to duress nor were they so intoxicated, or of such unsound mind, as to invalidate any consent given. The law will presume the essential validity of the marriage according to Barnard J in *Russell* v *Attorney-General* [1949] P 391, who explained the operation of the presumption in this way, '[W]here there is evidence of a ceremony of marriage having been performed, followed by a cohabitation of the parties, the validity of the marriage will be presumed, in the absence of decisive evidence to the contrary'.

A party who wishes to rebut the presumption will have the legal and evidential burden of proving that one of the parties lacked the capacity to marry. Consider the following example.

Example

In a dispute about Tony's entitlement to a share in property owned by Sandra, evidence is put forward that Dave and Sandra were married in June 2001, which the law will presume to be a valid marriage. Tony, who alleges that he married Sandra in May 1999, and that the marriage was still subsisting at the time of the ceremony between Dave and Sandra, will have the legal and evidential burden of proving that in June 2001 Sandra did not have the capacity to marry Dave as she was already married to him (Tony).

Rebutting the presumption of marriage – standard of proof

Before leaving the operation of the presumption of marriage, two further points need to be considered. First, there has been some judicial discussion over the years about the appropriate standard of proof that a party would have to reach in order to rebut the presumption. For example, in *Morris* v *Davies* (1837) 5 Cl & Fin 163, Lord Lyndhurst stated that '[T]he presumption of law is not lightly to be repelled. It is not to be broken in upon or shaken by a mere balance of probabilities. The evidence for the purpose of repelling it must be strong, distinct, satisfactory and conclusive'. These words were cited with approval by Lord Cottenham in *Piers* v *Piers* above. Later, in *Mahadervan* v *Mahadervan* above, Sir Jocelyn Simon P said that to rebut the presumption of the formal validity of marriage, it was necessary for the evidence to satisfy the test of beyond reasonable doubt. In spite of the formidable persuasive force of these judicial pronouncements, it is unlikely that this dicta continues to apply in modern law and, as noted in Chapter 23, the trend in recent years has been to apply the civil standard 'on the balance of probabilities' to cases involving allegations of matrimonial infidelity even though the cogency of the evidence required to rebut the presumption might be higher than in some other civil actions.

A second issue that has arisen out of the presumption's operation was the means by which a party could discharge its legal burden. An obvious way in which a party could prove that he or she had been through a valid marriage ceremony was to produce the marriage certificate. Yet, as a throwback to the common law's dread of manufactured evidence, the courts concluded in a number of cases that a marriage certificate had little value because under the relevant statute at the time, the Marriages Act 1836, which provided for the registration of marriages, the Registrar was not under any duty to require proof that the parties were capable of being married. An illustration of the problems that this approach led to is provided by the following case:

Peete (Deceased), Re, sub nom: Peete v Crompton [1952] 2 All ER 599

The plaintiff claimed to be the widow of the testator and, as such, she asked for provision under the Inheritance (Family Provision) Act 1938. In order to prove that she was the widow of the deceased she produced a certificate which showed that she went through a proper ceremony of marriage with the deceased on 23 June 1919. In that certificate she was described as a widow. In her evidence she stated that her first husband, Arthur Frederick Skinner, died in 1916. However she was unable to produce a certificate of his death. Her explanation was that he had died in an explosion at Nobel's Factory at Caversham and that she had learnt of his death a week later. Due to the cause of death it had been impossible to identify his body. In finding against the plaintiff, the court held that if the production of the marriage certificate and the statement that her former husband had died in 1916 had gone unchallenged and no evidence had been called to make the court doubt that fact, it would have been right and proper to call the plaintiff the widow of the deceased. However, once the issue had been put before the court that suggested a doubt about the widow's claim, the certificate was of little value and accordingly her application was dismissed.

Although there is no direct authority on the issue, it is suggested that the two presumptions of marriage do apply in criminal cases as well as in civil cases. So, for example, at a trial for bigamy, it will be necessary for the prosecution to prove that at the time of the second marriage, the defendant had already gone through a marriage that complied with the requirements of formal and essential validity.

Presumption of legitimacy

As we noted in the earlier example, a person will be presumed to be legitimate where the primary fact is proven that he was born or conceived during the period of his parent's lawful married life. As a matter of public policy the law provides a broad interpretation of the phrase 'married life' so that the presumption will apply even where the marriage continues to exist in unconventional circumstances. The law will therefore recognise the presumption where there is a maintenance order in force against the husband, unless it contains a non-cohabitation clause as in *Bowen v Norman* [1938] 1 KB 689, and even where the parties are living apart as held in *Ettenfield v Ettenfield* [1940] P 96. The presumption will also apply where the child is born so soon after the parent's wedding that pre-marital conception is indicated, see the *Poulett Peerage Case* [1903] AC 395. Finally, a child will presumed to be legitimate where the child was born soon after the termination of the parent's marriage provided that it could proved that conception took place during the subsistence of the marriage (*Maturin v Attorney-General* [1938] 2 All ER 214). For an illustration of the broad interpretation of the presumption, consider the following example based on *Overbury (Deceased), Re, sub nom: Sheppard v Matthews* [1955] Ch 122.

Example

Six months after her first husband died Julie remarried and two months later gave birth to a girl. The law will presume that the child is the legitimate daughter of Julie's first husband as conception appears to have occurred during the subsistence of this marriage.

Where a party seeks to rebut the presumption, he will have to discharge the legal burden of proof to the standard contained in section 26 of the Family Law Reform Act 1969 which provides:

> Any presumption of law as to the legitimacy or illegitimacy of any person may in civil proceedings be rebutted by evidence which shows that it is more probable than not that the person is illegitimate or legitimate, as the case may be, and it shall not be necessary to prove that fact beyond reasonable doubt in order to rebut the presumption.

In discharging the legal and evidential burdens under section 26, a party seeking to rebut the presumption of legitimacy may, for example, introduce evidence proving that sexual intercourse occurred between the child's mother and a man other than her husband, see *R* v *King's Lynn Magistrates' Court, ex parte Moore* (1988) 18 Fam Law 393 and *Jenion, Re sub nom: Jenion* v *Wynne* [1952] Ch 454. Evidence may also be admitted proving the husband's impotence at the time of the conception (*Legge* v *Edmonds* (1855) 25 LJ Ch 125) or evidence may be tendered about the husband's absence at the time of the child's conception. Expert evidence may be adduced from blood tests, DNA or by other scientific methods.

Presumption of death

Generally, the law will presume a person to have died where there has been no affirmative evidence that he was alive at some time during a continuous period of seven years or more. The party seeking to make use of the presumption has the legal burden of proving the following primary facts:

1 that the person has been absent for a continuous period of seven years;
2 that during those years there has not been any acceptable evidence that the person is alive;
3 that there are people who are likely to have heard from him and they have not; and
4 that all due inquiries have been made of his whereabouts and well-being, without success.

Where these primary facts are proven the court will presume that the person died at some time within the seven-year period.

The following cases indicate the way in which the courts interpret and apply the requirements of proving the primary facts in the presumption of death.

Chard *v* Chard [1955] 3 All ER 721

Mr Chard and his wife separated in 1909. No one could be found who had seen or heard of Mrs Chard since 1917. In 1933 Mr Chard remarried. Some years later Mr Chard and his second wife sought a decree of nullity, which would be granted only if his first wife had been alive at the time of the second marriage. The issue, therefore, was whether in 1933 the first Mrs Chard could have been presumed dead. The court held that the first Mrs Chard could not be presumed dead, as there were good reasons for her to conceal her whereabouts from Mr Chard and all due inquiries had not been made of her whereabouts or well-being.

Prudential Assurance Co v Edmonds (1877) 2 App Cas 487

A claim was made on a life insurance policy. It was alleged that one of the lives assured, Robert Nutt, was not dead. Members of the family gave evidence that they had not heard from him for more than seven years but knew that his niece had thought that she had seen Mr Nutt in Melbourne, Australia. The niece gave evidence that when she was aged 20, she had seen a man in a crowded street who she thought she recognised as her uncle from their last meeting five years earlier. The House of Lords held that it was up to the tribunal of fact to decide whether to accept the niece's evidence and that if they believed that she had been mistaken, the basic facts giving rise to the presumption would have to be proven. It should be decided on the particular facts of each case whether the relatives or friends were people who were likely to have heard from the absent person. If it could be established that the absent person had a reason not to contact the person, the fact of the non-communication could not be adduced in evidence in the case.

Bradshaw v Bradshaw [1956] P 274

Mrs Bradshaw had married in 1916 in India. She sought a decree of nullity of this marriage. It was granted in India in 1921 and she returned to England. In 1922 the nullity decree was rescinded in India but Mrs Bradshaw was unaware of this. Mr and Mrs Bradshaw married in 1940 and later separated. Mr Bradshaw, who was ordered to pay maintenance later discovered that the decree of nullity had been rescinded, and he applied for a decree of nullity of his marriage on the ground that his wife was already married at the time. Mrs Bradshaw had not heard from her first husband since she left India. It was held that the presumption of death of Mrs Bradshaw's first husband did not apply, as she had failed to make all due inquiries and the second marriage was therefore void.

Where circumstances such as those in *Bradshaw* exist, it might be thought that a spouse may be in danger of being the subject of criminal proceedings for bigamy. However, section 57 of the Offences Against the Person Act 1861 provides:

> a person marrying for the second time whose spouse shall have been continually absent for a period of seven years and shall not have been known by that person to have been living within that time ... shall not be guilty of the offence of bigamy.

The operation of the common law presumption of death has been codified in family proceedings by section 19 of the Matrimonial Causes Act 1973. Under the section a spouse may apply to the court for a decree presuming the death of his or her partner and dissolution of the marriage, where he or she has not been heard of for a continuous period of seven years or more and the applicant has no reason to believe that he or she has been alive during that period.

The presumption of death is limited in its application in two ways. First, on proof of the primary facts, the court will only presume that death occurred within the seven-year period. There is some conflict between the authorities as to whether the court will decide a specific date of death. The decision in *Re Phene's Trusts* (1870) LR 5 Ch App 139 suggests that the court will presume death at the date of the proceedings, but in *Chipchase v Chipchase* [1939] P 391, the court was prepared to presume death at the end of the seven-year period. The position continues to remain unclear. Secondly, the court will only presume the fact of the person's death and the presumption does not extend to proving any further related issue about the deceased. So, where the party seeks to establish that the party died unmarried or without next-of-kin, additional evidence will have to be tendered (*Jackson, Re, sub nom: Jackson v Ward* [1907] 2 Ch 354).

The commorientes *rule*

An issue closely related to the presumption of death is the operation of the *commorientes* rule (a statutory presumption under section 184 of the Law of Property Act 1925). The rule most commonly covers the situation where two or more people, who are usually related to each other, die together, for example in a car accident or in a plane disaster, and it is unclear in which order the people died. Section 184 of the Law of Property Act 1925 provides that, for all purposes affecting title to property, where persons die simultaneously the deaths are presumed to have occurred in order of seniority, ie that the oldest died first. The presumption under the *commorientes* rule was held to apply in *Hickman v Peacey* [1945] AC 304. Four people were killed when their London house received a direct hit by a German bomb. Two of them had made bequests benefiting others and for the purpose of succession under their wills the House of Lords held that those two died in order of seniority.

The *commorientes* rule was applied in *Hickman v Peacey* on the basis of a 'common disaster', but that is not essential for the presumption to apply. The basic fact that is required for the rule to apply is that the deaths should have occurred at approximately the same time, with no evidence as to who survived the other(s). Once these primary facts are proven the sequence of the deaths in order of seniority must be applied by the court in any proceedings affecting title to property. Finally, section 184 does not apply where one spouse or both die(s) intestate, in which case the position is governed by section 1(4) of the Intestates' Estates Act 1952.

Presumption of regularity

On proof of the primary fact that someone has acted as the holder of a public office, for example a police officer or a local council official, it will be presumed, unless evidence to the contrary is presented that he was properly appointed to that office and that the person has acted properly in discharging his duties as a public servant. This presumption is also known by the maxim *omnia praesumuntur rite esse acta*, which means that all acts are presumed to have been duly done. Cases where the presumption has been applied to the holders of a public office include:

- a police officer (*R v Gordon* (1789) 1 Leach 515);
- a judge (*R v Roberts* (1878) 38 LT 690); and
- a health and safety inspector (*Campbell v Wallsend Slipway & Engineering Co Ltd* [1978] ICR 1015).

In *TC Coombs & Co v IRC* [1991] 3 All ER 623, a tax inspector with the consent of a General Commissioner had served a notice under section 20 of the Taxes Management Act 1970 requiring stockbrokers to deliver documentary information that was relevant to determine the tax liability of one of their former employees. The court was entitled to presume that in the absence of evidence to the contrary the tax inspector and the General Commissioner had acted honestly and within the limits of their authority.

Presumption of negligence (res ipsa loquitur)

The presumption of negligence can be defined as 'the thing speaks for itself' and will arise on the proof of three primary facts:

1 there must be an absence of explanation as to how the harm occurred;
2 the harm must be a kind which would not in the ordinary course of things have occurred without negligence;
3 the 'thing' causing the harm must be under the exclusive management and control of the defendant or his employees.

The rationale for the presumption is that since the activity giving rise to the injury sustained by the claimant is under the exclusive management and control of the defendant or his employees and does not arise in the normal course of conduct, it may be presumed that unless evidence is presented to rebut the presumption, that the claimant's injury was caused by the defendant's negligence. The principle is illustrated by *Scott v London & St Katherine Docks Co* (1865) All ER 1861–1873 246, where the plaintiff was walking along a thoroughfare in the docks when a large sack of sugar fell from a crane and injured him. The defendants called no evidence as to their care or lack of it; the plaintiff had no evidence as to how the incident had occurred. The court held that the defendants were liable in negligence. Lord Erle CJ stated:

> Where the thing is shown to be under the management of the defendant or his servants, and the accident is such that in the ordinary course of things does not happen if those who have the management use proper care, it affords reasonable evidence in the absence of explanation by the defendant, that the incident arose from want of care.

As examples of the operation of the presumption of negligence, consider the following cases.

The Kite [1933] P 154

The plaintiffs were the owners of cargo on a barge, which collided with a bridge while being towed by a tug. The plaintiff claimed damages from the owners of the tug. The court held that once the presumption of negligence arose the defendants must discharge the legal burden or they would be liable. The burden would be discharged if the defendants gave a reasonable explanation, which was equally consistent with the accident happening without their negligence. If the defendants successfully discharged the burden, it shifted back to the plaintiff, and then, to succeed in the action, the plaintiff must prove the defendants' negligence.

Barkway v South Wales Transport [1948] 2 All ER 460

The plaintiff was injured when the defendants' bus, in which he was a passenger, veered off the road and rolled down an embankment. He brought an action in negligence, which succeeded when it was proved that the cause of the incident was a defective tyre (of which the defendants ought to have been aware) which burst and in consequence the driver lost control of the vehicle. What was said about the presumption of negligence was therefore *obiter*, but is nevertheless of persuasive authority:

If the defendants' bus leaves the road and falls down an embankment, and this without more is proved, then *res ipsa loquitur*, there is a presumption that the event is caused by the negligence on the part of the defendants, and the plaintiff succeeds unless the defendants rebut the presumption. It is no rebuttal for the defendants to show that the cause of the omnibus leaving the road is a burst tyre, since a tyre bursting, *per se*, is a neutral event equally consistent with negligence or due diligence on the part of the defendants. When a balance has been tilted one way it cannot be redressed by adding an equal weight to each scale, for the depressed scale will remain down. To rebut the presumption, the defendants must go further and prove either (a) that the tyre-burst was due to a specific cause which does not connote negligence on their part but points to its absence as more probable, or (b), if they can point to no such specific cause, that they had used all reasonable care in the management of their tyres.

Widdowson *v* Newgate Meat Corporation (1997) *The Times*, 4 December

The plaintiff was knocked down by a van driver, who was an employee of the defendant company. Neither the plaintiff nor the driver gave evidence at the trial. All that was known with any degree of certainty was that the plaintiff wearing darkish clothing, was walking along the unlit northbound carriageway of the A618, shortly before midnight on a fine, July evening, when he was hit by the van. It was a glancing blow which left the plaintiff lying in the middle of the nearside lane. In holding the defendant company liable, the Court of Appeal stated that the plaintiff could rely on the doctrine of *res ipsa loquitur*. The van was under the control of the defendant's employee who was under a duty to drive it with due care and attention for other road users. On the evidence, it was more likely than not that the defendant company's driver was the effective cause of the accident. The defendant company did not offer a plausible explanation, consistent with the absence of negligence on its part. In the absence of such evidence to rebut the inference of negligence on the part of its driver, the defendant was liable subject to the plaintiff's contributory negligence assessed at 50%.

Widdowson confirms that the presumption of negligence will apply where a party in the claimant's position establishes a *prima facie* case that the defendant was negligent even though it is not possible for him to prove precisely what was the relevant act or omission which set into effect the train of events leading to the accident.

In order to rebut the presumption of negligence, the defendant must follow Lord Griffiths' dictum in *Ng Chun Pui* v *Lee Chuen Tat* [1988] RTR 298 where there is 'loosely speaking' a burden on the defendant to show that he was not negligent. In practice, this only means that, faced with a *prima facie* case of negligence, the defendant will be found negligent unless he produces evidence that is capable of rebutting the *prima facie* case.

Presumptions of fact

Presumptions of fact are not true presumptions although, unlike some presumptions, they can be rebutted, and unlike others, they require proof of a basic fact. Nevertheless if a presumption of fact arises and the other side calls no evidence in rebuttal, the court is not bound to reach the conclusion indicated as it is in the case of true presumptions.

Continuance of life

On the proof or admission of the basic fact that a person was alive on a certain date, it may be presumed, unless there was evidence to the contrary, that the person is alive on a subsequent date. Consider the following example.

Example

On proof of the basic fact that Debbie was alive on 1 April 2000 there is a presumption of fact that she is still alive on some later date, for example 1 October 2001, when the court is invited to conclude that Debbie is still alive. However, even though no evidence is adduced to rebut that presumption, the court is not bound to draw the conclusion that Debbie is still alive. It remains a matter for the fact finder to decide whether to accept the evidence or not. If, for example, one of the parties adduces evidence that Debbie was suffering from an incurable illness in April 2000, the fact finder may be persuaded to believe that Debbie is not alive on 1 October 2001.

CONFLICTING PRESUMPTIONS

A situation sometimes arises where there are two presumptions in operation: one assisting the defendant, the other assisting the claimant. If the conflicting presumptions are of equal weight the court will decide that they cancel each other and that the parties must discharge their respective burdens by admissible evidence (see *Monckton v Tarr* [1930] 23 BWCC 504). Occasionally, public policy may play a part in the court's decision, as in *Taylor v Taylor* [1965] 1 All ER 872, where it was held that where conflicting presumptions regarding the validity of a current and an earlier marriage have equal effect then public policy would dictate that the current marriage should be the one which subsists.

JUDICIAL NOTICE

As we noted with respect to presumptions on the proof of specified primary facts, the court will presume the existence of other related facts without the court having direct evidence in support. The law relating to judicial notice takes the principle a stage further in that where the rule applies, in both civil and criminal proceedings, the court will accept the existence of a fact in issue without any proof at all. When this occurs, it is said that judicial notice is taken of that fact. The law recognises two forms of judicial notice – judicial notice without inquiry and judicial notice after inquiry. The rationale and purpose of judicial notice was explained by Lord Sumner in *Commonwealth Shipping Representative v Peninsular and Oriental Branch Service* [1923] AC 191 where he stated: 'Judicial notice refers to facts, which a judge can be called upon to receive and to act upon, either from his general knowledge of them, or from enquiries to be made by himself for his own information from sources to which it is proper for him to refer'.

Judicial notice without inquiry at common law is taken in respect of those facts that are so much part of common knowledge that they require no proof and cannot be rebutted in evidence. Facts that fall into this category include:

- criminals lead unhappy lives (*Burn v Edman* [1970] 2 QB 541);
- a fortnight is too short a period for human gestation (*R v Luffe* (1807) 8 East 193);
- the duration of human gestation is nine months (*Preston-Jones v Preston-Jones* [1951] AC 391);

- cats are ordinarily kept for domestic purposes (*Nye* v *Niblett* [1918] 1 KB 23); and
- the contents of all public Acts passed before 1851.

The court may also take judicial notice without inquiry of certain facts as required by statute relating to court documents and the contents of Acts passed after 1850. Under the rule, evidence is not required to prove the following:

- a judicial or official document signed by a judge of the Supreme Court as required by section 2 of the Evidence Act 1845;
- summonses and other documents issued in the county court that have been stamped or sealed by the court under section 134(2) of the County Courts Act 1984;
- all United Kingdom statutes passed after 1850 (unless the contrary is expressed in the Act) as required by section 3 of the Interpretation Act 1978;
- all European Community Treaties, the *Official Journal of the European Communities* and the decisions or the opinions of the European Court of Justice under section 3(2) of the European Communities Act 1972.

Judicial notice after inquiry applies to those facts that are not so notorious or part of common knowledge, of which notice may be taken by the judge after he has made appropriate inquiries. The inquiry may include referring to textbooks, works of reference, certificates from Ministers and government officials and oral statements from witnesses. For example, in *McQuaker* v *Goddard* [1940] 1 KB 687, the plaintiff had been bitten by a camel whilst feeding the animal at the defendant's zoo. The question arose whether the camel was a wild or domestic animal. Evidence was sought from a number of experts and works of reference. On the basis of these inquiries the judge concluded that camels were domestic animals!

In practice, most cases which fall into this category of judicial notice relate to facts of a political or historical nature or matters of custom or professional practice. In *Read* v *Bishop of Lincoln* [1892] AC 644, judicial notice was taken after appropriate inquiries were made in relation to the historic basis of church practice. Judicial notice may be taken in respect of the extent of a State's territorial sovereignty, the existence of a state of war, or the imposition of military rule. In *Secretary of State for Defence* v *Guardian Newspapers Ltd* [1984] 3 All ER 601, it was held that the classification of 'secret' appearing on a document originating in a government department was a matter of political record of which the House of Lords was entitled to take judicial notice.

Further reading

Bridge, N., 'Presumptions and Burdens' (1949) 12 MLR 273.

Campbell, E., 'Does the Presumption Survive Today?' (2000) 17 Trusts and Estates Law Journal 4.

Denning, A.T., 'Presumptions and Burdens' (1945) 61 LQR 379.

Harris, D., 'The Quick and the Dead' (1995) 4 British Tax Review 390.

Munday, R., 'Does Latin Impede Legal Understanding? The Case of "res ipsa loquitur" ... Apparently' (2000) Justice of the Peace and Local Government Law 995.

Wignall, G., 'Handling Boundary Disputes: Point of Evidence' (1998) 142 Solicitors Journal 626.

Chapter 25

DISCLOSURE

INTRODUCTION

In Chapter 9 we explained the prosecution's duty in a criminal case to disclose to the defence at a number of stages before the trial, the evidence and other material that it will rely on at trial and also to disclosing 'unused' evidence that either undermines the prosecution case or assists the defence case. The pre-trial disclosure of evidence is also an important stage in the preparation for trial in civil proceedings. Part 31 of the Civil Procedure Rules (CPR) and the Practice Direction to Part 31 regulate the practice and procedure of disclosure in fast track and multi-track cases but has no application to the small claims procedure. On the small claims track, disclosure will be ordered by the court in a special direction and will cover only the evidence on which the claimant or the defendant intends to rely on at trial. (Prior to the introduction of the Woolf reforms, the disclosure stage was known as 'discovery' and is referred to in this way in the older authorities cited below.)

'Disclosure' is the stage in civil proceedings where the parties are required to put 'their cards on the table' in revealing to the other side the documents that are or have been in their possession and to allow the other party to inspect some or all of those documents. In a complex commercial action, disclosure may include many thousands of documents whilst in a 'simple' contract action, each party may only have a small number of documents to disclose. Disclosure also recognises that in the good administration of justice, the court should make its decision on all the available evidence, as well as enabling the parties to assess the strengths and weaknesses of their own and their opponent's cases before the trial and to assist in the early settlement of the action.

The main theme of this chapter is examine each party's duty of disclosure in a civil case and to consider, as an exception to the general rule, where this duty might be superseded by the operation of the principles of public interest immunity.

THE DUTY OF DISCLOSURE

As with a number of other areas of civil litigation and evidence, the Civil Procedure Rules introduced a radical new procedural regime to the pre-trial disclosure of evidence. Under the new Rules the obligation to give disclosure is not automatic but in the vast majority of cases disclosure will be ordered by the court when the case is allocated to either the fast track or to the multi-track. The parties may also voluntarily agree to undertake disclosure.

The meaning of disclosure

The meaning of disclosure is provided by CPR rule 31.2, which states:

A party discloses a document by stating that the document exists or has existed.

In most cases, a party's obligations will be limited to 'standard disclosure' under CPR rule 31.5. CPR rule 31.6 provides that under 'standard disclosure' a party is required to disclose:

- the documents on which he relies; and
- the documents which adversely affect his own case:
- the documents which adversely affect another party's case;
- the documents which support another party's case; and
- all documents that are required to be disclosed under a Practice Direction.

The procedure for standard disclosure

CPR rule 31.10 sets out the procedure to be adopted for standard disclosure:

(1) The procedure for standard disclosure is as follows.
(2) Each party must make, and serve on every other party, a list of documents in the relevant practice form.
(3) The list must identify the documents in a convenient order and manner and as concisely as possible.
(4) The list must indicate—
  (a) those documents in respect of which the party claims a right or a duty to withhold inspection; and
  (b) (i) those documents which are no longer in the party's control; and
     (ii) what has happened to those documents.

Where an order for standard disclosure has been made, each party must make and serve a list of documents using the prescribed practice form (form N265). Paragraph 3.2 of the Practice Direction to Part 31 provides that it will normally be necessary to list the documents in date order, to number them consecutively and to give a concise description of each document, ie identifying whether the document is a letter or a fax or an e-mail.

The list is in three parts. The first part of the list itemises the documents that are in the party's control and for which there is no objection to the other party inspecting them. The second part of the list sets out the documents over which the party has control but objects to the other party inspecting them. The objection will most commonly be on the ground of public interest immunity or that the document is privileged. The third part of the list consists of those documents that a party has had but which are no longer in its control. Where the opponent wishes to inspect a document that is no longer in the party's control, the opponent must apply to the court to force the disclosing party to recover the original document or a copy of the original document.

The meaning of a 'document'

The word 'document' is widely defined by the Civil Procedure Rules. CPR rule 31.4 defines a document as 'anything in which information of any description is recorded'.

As well as traditional paper-based sources, modern forms of information recording formats are recognised to include audiotapes and computer databases. The following have been held to be a 'document' for the purpose of disclosure or discovery:

- audiotapes (*Wallace Smith Trust Co Ltd (In Liquidation)* v *Deloitte Haskins & Sells* [1996] 4 All ER 403);
- film/videotape and cassettes (*Senior* v *Holdsworth, ex parte ITN* [1975] 2 All ER 1009);
- microfilm (*Grant* v *Southwestern & County Properties Ltd* [1974] 2 All ER 465);
- photographs (*Lyell* v *Kennedy (No 3)* (1884) 27 Ch D 1);
- computer programs (*Derby & Co Ltd* v *Wheldon (No 9)* [1991] 1 WLR 652).

The right of inspection

Where a document has been disclosed, CPR rule 31.3 gives the other party the right to inspect the document unless:

(a) the document is no longer in the control of the party who disclosed it;
(b) the party disclosing the document has a right or a duty to withhold inspection of it; or
(c) a party withholds inspection on the ground that it is considered disproportionate to the issues in the case to make it available for inspection.

Where the right of inspection applies, the inspecting party must give notice of his intention to inspect and the party who disclosed the document must permit inspection within seven days after the date on which he received the notice. If 'personal' inspection is not convenient, a party may request a copy of the document, provided the party also undertakes paying the copying costs. The party who disclosed the document must supply a copy to the other side not more than seven days after the date on which the request is received.

Withholding inspection or disclosure of a document

The Civil Procedure Rules recognise certain grounds on which a party may refuse to disclose a document including that where it would be 'disproportionate' to the issues in the case to permit the inspection of the document (CPR rule 31.3(2)).

CPR rule 31.19 deals with the ground where a party claims the right to withhold inspection where disclosure would not be in the public interest. CPR rule 31.19(1) provides that:

> A person may apply, without notice, for an order permitting him to withhold disclosure of a document on the ground that disclosure would damage the public interest.

The usual reason for a party refusing to disclose a document where disclosure would 'damage the public interest' is if it is claimed that the document is covered by public interest immunity or by legal professional privilege. The law relating to legal professional privilege is considered in Chapter 26; public interest immunity in civil cases is explained below.

PUBLIC INTEREST IMMUNITY

As we noted above, CPR rule 31.19(1) recognises that a document can be withheld from inspection on the ground that it is covered by public interest immunity. The application may be made either by a party in the case or by a non-party and will usually be heard at the disclosure stage, although the claim may also be made during the trial. Public interest immunity is also variously referred to as 'Crown privilege', 'public policy' or as a 'gagging order'. The rule has been recognised at common law since at least 1784, where in *R v Hardy* (1794) 24 St Tr 199, it was held to be in the public interest to protect an informer's identity from being disclosed in court proceedings.

Public interest immunity is a rule of law that recognises that in exceptional circumstances it is considered to be in the higher public interest that a document should not be inspected by another party in the case, in order to maintain the confidentiality of certain categories of information, safeguarding, for example, State secrets or State security or the efficient operation of government or public services, or the investigation of crime. Claims for public interest immunity in civil proceedings have been made in respect of the following types of documents:

- Cabinet papers;
- advice to Ministers;
- foreign office despatches;
- internal police disciplinary reports;
- sources of confidential information;
- documents relating to the security of the State;
- documents relating to the development of high-level domestic policy;
- papers dealing with the integrity of the criminal investigation process;
- high-level interdepartmental minutes and correspondence; and
- documents relating to the general administration of the military.

The evidential effect is that where public interest immunity applies it prevents otherwise relevant and admissible evidence from being put into the public domain of a civil trial. Unlike the operation of private privilege, it also prevents the evidence withheld under the public interest immunity rule from being proven under the secondary evidence rule by using copies of the original document or by the court hearing oral evidence of the document's contents.

Historical development of public interest immunity

The modern law of public interest immunity is the product of a long period of judicial law-making, which has been developed against the background of wide-ranging debates about the transparency and openness of the British State and its government. Until 1973 public interest immunity was known as 'Crown privilege' and was historically part of the legal privileges and immunities enjoyed by the Crown in civil proceedings. As a matter of constitutional law, the 'Crown' not only includes the person of the monarch but also central government departments conducting the affairs of state in the monarch's name.

The traditional operation of Crown privilege is shown by the case of *Duncan v Cammell Laird & Co* below.

Duncan v Cammell Laird & Co [1942] AC 624

In 1939 HM Submarine *Thetis*, which had been built by the defendant company set out on sea trials with both Royal Navy personnel and civilians on board. The submarine sank and all of the 99 members of the ship's company were lost. The plaintiff, whose husband was one of the civilian casualties, brought an action against the defendants under the Fatal Accidents Act 1846, alleging negligence on its part in the design of the submarine. To prove her case at trial she needed to put evidence before the court of the vessel's design and construction. When she applied for discovery of the contractual documents, the defendant, acting under instructions from the Admiralty as the representative of the Crown, objected to the inspection of the evidence on the ground of 'Crown privilege'. The judge held that the documents should not be disclosed on the ground of national security as *The Thetis* had been a new design of submarine and the nation was at war.

The plaintiff's appeal against the non-disclosure of the documents went to the House of Lords, which upheld the judge's ruling and stated that the certificate from the Admiralty ordering the defendants not to disclose the documents was conclusive, ie it could not be challenged by the courts.

As well as ruling on the facts, Viscount Simons LC in *Duncan* v *Cammell Laird* went on to consider the general principles to be applied in cases where Crown privilege was claimed.

First, the House of Lords confirmed that it was open to assert Crown privilege where it was not considered to be in the public interest for particular documents to be disclosed in litigation. The privilege could apply to the contents of a particular document, known as a 'contents' claim, or to documents belonging to a particular class of documents which the public interest required should remain confidential whether or not the document contained anything to prejudice the public interest.

Secondly, where Crown privilege was claimed, properly executed ministerial affidavits or certificates declaring that the disclosure of the documents would be prejudicial to the public interest would be regarded as final and conclusive. The courts would not inquire further into the assertion of Crown privilege.

Whilst the decision to withhold inspection of the documents in *Duncan* v *Cammell Laird* and the apparent blanket immunity enjoyed by Ministers was justified at the time on the facts of the case as being necessary to protect State interests during a time national emergency, it led in a number of cases to government Ministers taking advantage of the court's apparent reluctance to keep a check on the powers of the Executive.

Ellis v Home Office [1953] 2 QB 135

The plaintiff, an inmate at Winchester prison, had been attacked by another prisoner while in the prison's hospital wing. He brought an action in negligence on the grounds that the attacker, who was known to be dangerous, had been allowed to move around the wing unsupervised. The Home Office successfully claimed Crown privilege to prevent the disclosure of police and medical records concerning the mental condition of the prisoner who had assaulted the plaintiff. All three judges in the Court of Appeal expressed regret of being bound by the decision in *Duncan v Cammell Laird* and suggested that in the present case, it was unlikely that serious damage to the interests of the State would have resulted from the production of the documents.

Broome v Broome [1955] P 190

In proceedings for divorce between a member of the armed services and his wife, the Secretary of State for War intervened to prevent the inspection of documents concerning the attempts to reconcile the parties made by the Soldiers', Sailors' and Airmen's Families' Association, which was a military service welfare organisation.

Following a period of sustained academic criticism, some of the judicial and political attitudes reflected in the decision of *Duncan* v *Cammell Laird* to grant State bodies apparent immunity against allowing sensitive and confidential material to be inspected under Crown privilege began to change. In 1956 the Lord Chancellor announced that Crown privilege would not be claimed in respect of certain classes of documents including medical reports of prison doctors in negligence actions against the Crown and documents relevant to the defence in a criminal charge. In *Glasgow Corporation* v *Central Land Board* 1956 SC (HL) 1, the House of Lords stated that the Scottish courts had the inherent power to override the Crown's objections to the documents being inspected. A similar pronouncement about the law in England and Wales was made by the Court of Appeal in *Re Grosvenor Hotel, London (No 2)* [1965] Ch 1210. This sense of judicial unease with regard to the operation of Crown privilege culminated in the landmark decision of the House of Lords in *Conway* v *Rimmer*.

Conway v Rimmer [1968] AC 910

The plaintiff, who had been a probationary police constable, was dismissed as being unlikely to perform efficiently as a police officer. During his probationary period he had been charged with the theft of a torch from a colleague's locker, but had been acquitted. He brought an action in malicious prosecution against the Chief Constable, and applied for discovery of reports made on his performance as a police constable which were relevant to proving the issue of malice. The Home Secretary immediately issued a ministerial certificate claiming that the documents should not be disclosed on the ground of public policy.

The House of Lords ordered that the documents should be admitted in evidence as, having examined them, their Lordships decided that there was no conceivable reason why their disclosure was prejudicial to the public interest. The documents were routine reports – they did not contain the names of police informants or anything at all which was of a sensitive nature which could justify their exclusion. A Minister's certificate was not conclusive and the courts were entitled to examine any evidence in respect of which it was asserted that public policy dictated exclusion.

In overruling *Duncan* v *Cammell Laird*, the House of Lords in *Conway* v *Rimmer* established a number of important principles on the operation of Crown privilege.

First, whilst unanimously agreeing that *Duncan* v *Cammell Laird* had been correctly decided on the facts in order to preserve national security at a time when the country was at war, the decision whether the Crown could withhold evidence was a matter of law to be decided not by a Minister but by the courts. Whilst the Minister's opinion would be given full weight in deciding the issue, the Minister was not the final arbiter of the decision. The court also had the power to seek clarification or amplification of the Minister's objection and to inspect the document in question in spite of the Minister's objections. According to Lord Reid:

> I would therefore propose that the House ought now to decide that courts have and are entitled to exercise a power and duty to hold a balance between the public interest, as expressed by a Minister to withhold certain documents or other evidence and the public interest in ensuring the proper administration of justice. That does not mean that a court would reject a Minister's view: full weight must be given to it in every case, and if the Minister's reasons are of a character which judicial experience is competent to weigh, then the Minister's view must prevail.

Secondly, the test to be applied in deciding whether the objection should be upheld required the court to balance two public interests – the interests of the State or public service in not disclosing the material and that of the proper administration of justice in disclosing the evidence. Their Lordships drew a distinction between the approach to be taken in a class claim and in a contents claim. In a contents claim the judicial discretion to inspect the documents would be used sparingly. In a class claim, certain classes of documents containing high-level information such as Cabinet minutes, Foreign Office dispatches, documents containing high-level interdepartmental minutes, documents relating to national security and information relating to the general administration of the armed forces or high-level Crown personnel should hardly ever be disclosed, whatever their contents. Lord Reid suggested that:

> There were certain classes of documents which ought not to be disclosed whatever their content might be. To my mind the most important reason is that such disclosure would create or fan ill-informed or captious public or political criticism. The business of government is difficult enough as it is, and no government could contemplate with equanimity the inner workings of the government machine being exposed to the gaze of those ready to criticise without adequate knowledge of the background and perhaps with an axe to grind.

Thirdly, in other cases – usually where immunity was claimed on the basis of the class to which the documents belonged and the basis of the Minister's claim appeared to be inadequate or was unclear – the court should be prepared to exercise its power of inspection to decide whether the evidence should be disclosed.

The significance of the decision in *Conway v Rimmer* in the development of the modern law of public interest immunity should not be overestimated. The case established a number of overriding principles which still form the basis of the modern law. It was for the courts to decide if a document should be disclosed. In most cases this decision could only be taken after the document has been inspected by the judge. Whilst the Minister's argument that it was not in the public interest for the documents to be disclosed would be taken into account, it was no longer decisive as it had been under the reasoning of *Duncan v Cammell Laird*. In deciding the issue, the judge should strike a balance between damage to the public interest if the document was released against the damage to the claimant's case if the document was withheld.

The development of the modern law continued with the decision in *Rogers v Home Secretary* [1973] AC 388, in which the House of Lords expressed disapproval of the term 'Crown privilege' and suggested that the right to withhold the disclosure of documents to protect the public interest should not be confined to the Crown.

Rogers v Home Secretary [1973] AC 388

Rogers applied to the Gaming Board for licences for a number of bingo clubs. The Gaming Board asked the local police for information about the applicant's character and suitability to hold a licence. The police reply was prejudicial to the application, which the Gaming Board refused. Rogers later came into possession of a copy of the letter written by the local police to the Gaming Board, which, he alleged, contained defamatory material about him. Rogers commenced an action in criminal libel against the Chief Constable of Sussex and sought discovery from the police of the report containing the information it had submitted to the Board.

The application for discovery was challenged by both the Gaming Board and the Home Secretary on the ground that disclosing the document would be prejudicial to the public interest. The application for discovery was refused by the Divisional Court, a decision that was later upheld by the House of Lords. According to the House of Lords, in applying a 'balancing exercise', the dangers of disclosure outweighed the risk of injustice to Rogers as a breach of confidentiality might have undermined the effectiveness of the Gaming Board's statutory duties if organisations or individuals were reluctant or refused to supply the Board with relevant information out of a fear that such information might be disclosed in litigation.

The House of Lords also suggested that the term 'Crown privilege' was inappropriate as it should be open to any public or private organisation to seek to protect the disclosure of certain information in the public interest. Lord Reid stated:

> The ground put forward has said to be Crown privilege. I think that expression is wrong and may be mis-leading. There is no question of any privilege in the ordinary sense of the word. The real question is whether the public interest requires that the letter should not be produced and whether the public interest is so strong as to override the ordinary right and interest of a litigant that he shall be able to lay before a court of justice all relevant evidence. A Minister of the Crown is always an appropriate and often the most appropriate person to assert this public interest, and the evidence or which advice he gives to the court is always valuable and may sometimes be indispensable. But in my view, it must always be open to any per-son interested to raise the question and there may be cases where the trial judge should himself raise the question if no-one else had done so.

In *Rogers* v *Home Secretary*, the House of Lords held that it was open to both public and private organisations to withhold disclosing documents where it was considered to be in the public interest. An important case which confirmed the operation of the rule beyond government departments, the police and local authorities to private organisations performing 'public' duties is *D* v *NSPCC* below.

D v NSPCC [1978] AC 171

The plaintiff was a mother who was confronted by a uniformed NSPCC officer at her door who stated that he was investigating a report that she was abusing her child. D suffered nervous shock as the allegation was totally without foundation. She brought an action in negligence against the NSPCC alleging that they had not exercised reasonable care in properly investigating the complaint before accusing her. To pursue her action she sought discovery of the source of the complaint, and on this issue the case eventually reached the House of Lords.

The House of Lords confirmed that it was accepted that the exclusion of evidence on the ground of public policy extended beyond the workings of government departments to any organisation and included a voluntary organisation such as the NSPCC, where it discharged a public duty. Whilst confidentiality is not in itself a sufficient ground for non-disclosure, in the instant case the confiden-tiality of informants should be protected if the NSPCC is to function properly in protecting children who may be at risk of abuse or neglect. Since most of their information derives from members of the public, the public must be certain that their identity will not be revealed. Consequently, the iden-tity of even a potentially malicious informant must be protected, and that outweighed D's interest in discovering the source of the baseless, or even malicious, report.

The reasoning of some of the Law Lords in the *NSPCC* case, including Lord Diplock, drew an analogy to cases involving the identity of police informants, without whom the proper functioning of the police in detecting crime and apprehending offenders would be substantially impaired. Lord Hailsham took a more expansive approach by suggesting that the categories of public interest immunity were not closed, and that new organisations might seek properly to withhold the disclosure of documents on the ground of public interest immunity as social conditions and social legislation developed.

Applying the principles of public interest immunity

As the cases above illustrate, the law relating to public interest immunity in civil cases is a difficult and challenging subject. One reason for this difficulty is that cases are not only decided on their own facts but also involve complex issues of political, diplomatic or economic policy. In spite of this observation, it appears that a number of overriding principles can be identified from the case law.

A class claim or a contents claim

In *Duncan v Cammell Laird & Co* [1942] AC 624, Lord Sankey stated that a claim to withhold documents on the ground of public policy could be made on the basis of a class claim or a contents claim. In a claim for class immunity, all documents falling within a specified class will be withheld from disclosure irrespective of the document's contents. The types of documents that may be the subject of a class claim include:

- advice to Ministers;
- national security matters;
- documents dealing with international relations;
- details of police informers; and
- documents dealing with criminal investigations.

A contents claim is based on the actual information contained in a particular document, as illustrated by *Duncan v Cammell Laird*, where the disclosure of the contents of the document would, for example, prejudice State security or high-level diplomatic communications or police operations. Documents that fall within a contents claim are most likely to deal with issues of high-level government policy and, as a result, the courts have been less vigilant in exercising control over a contents claim than over a class claim.

According to Lord Reid in *Conway v Rimmer* the disclosure of documents over which a contents claim has been asserted would 'create or fan ill-informed or captious public or political criticism' and it would rarely be proper for the court to question the Minister's decision not to disclose a document on the basis of its contents as the Minister was in a better position to assess the harm to the public that disclosure would engender than the court. In concurring with Lord Reid, Lord Hodson suggested that such documents required absolute protection whilst Lord Pearce was of the opinion that their production would never be ordered.

The courts have traditionally exercised greater vigilance over class claims as a class claim provides greater potential for government Ministers and other public servants to take advantage of the blanket immunity to all documents falling within a specified class. The reason for the courts' vigilance is that many of the documents which fall within the protected class may not contain any information that would be prejudicial to the public interest if they were disclosed.

An important justification in support of non-disclosure on the basis of a class claim has been the need to promote 'candour' in those public servants who write confidential reports and other similar documents. The candour argument suggested that if public servants knew that their communications were to be disclosed in court proceedings they would be inhibited from dealing with these matters in an honest and open way.

In recent years the candour argument has not attracted unqualified judicial support. In *Conway* v *Rimmer*, Lord Reid gave little weight to the idea that public servants would be inhibited if they thought their communications would be put into the public domain, whilst in *Burmah Oil Co Ltd* v *Bank of England* [1980] AC 1090, Lord Keith described the candour argument as utterly unsubstantial, although it should not be forgotten that in the same case Lord Wilberforce provided a powerful argument for suggesting that it should not be lightly dismissed.

In *R* v *Chief Constable of the West Midlands Police* [1995] 1 AC 274, Lord Woolf stated that the recognition of a new class-based public interest immunity requires clear and compelling evidence. In overruling a number of Court of Appeal decisions, the House of Lords held that there was no justification for imposing a general class immunity on documents generated during an investigation against the police under Part IX of the Police and Criminal Evidence Act 1984. This does not mean that in all cases a claim for class immunity will fail. The courts may draw a distinction in a class claim between documents dealing with low-level policy and those concerned with high-level policy. It is likely, for example, that the candour argument would be more sympathetically considered in relation to matters of high-level policy. It would also be open to the Minister to submit that the document should not be disclosed on the basis of a contents claim, where it would be appropriate to do so.

A further development that has undermined the sustainability of a class claim was Sir Richard Scott's report arising out of the scandal of the Matrix Churchill case (see Further reading below). In his report, Sir Richard Scott stated that documents should be disclosed unless they would cause 'real damage of harm to the public interest' and was highly critical of the government's unnecessary use of class claims. In response to the criticisms contained in the Scott report, on 18 December 1996, the Lord Chancellor and the Attorney-General announced to Parliament that the government was committed to the principle of the maximum disclosure of evidence in legal proceedings consistent with protecting the public interest. In asserting a claim for public interest immunity, Ministers would no longer issue certificates for whole classes of documents and that any applications for immunity would only be made where they believed that disclosure would damage the public interest.

The balancing exercise

CPR rule 31.19(2) lays down the procedure for claiming public interest immunity. The hearing before the judge may either be without notice or on notice. It is a matter of judicial discretion whether the document in question is available for inspection by the court.

At the hearing to decide whether the document should be disclosed the court will generally apply Lord Reid's dicta in *Conway* v *Rimmer* that the judge should engage in a balancing exercise of weighing up the competing claims to withhold or compel disclosure by considering the interests of all the parties in the case. In *Campbell* v *Tameside MBC* [1982] QB 1065, Lord Justice Ackner identified a number of 'basic' principles relating to the balancing process in deciding whether a claim for public interest immunity could be sustained. A decision to exclude otherwise admissible and relevant evidence always called for a clear justification and where there is a question of public interest immunity, the proper approach is to weigh up two public interests, that of the nation or public service in non-disclosure and that of justice in the production of the document. The party resisting disclosure has the burden of proving that the documents are covered by public interest immunity. This will normally be satisfied by the production of a ministerial certificate, which, as we have seen is likely to be conclusive in a contents application.

Where the court does not accept the certificate as conclusive in a contents claim or more generally in a class claim, the party seeking disclosure will have to persuade the court to inspect the documents. The test to be satisfied is whether the documents are reasonably required to dispose of the case fairly. In deciding this issue, the judge will consider the status of the documents in question, whether their absence will result in a complete or partial denial of justice to one or other of the parties or to both, and the importance of the particular litigation to the parties and the public. The decisions of the House of Lords in both *Burmah Oil Co Ltd v Bank of England* [1980] AC 1090 and *Air Canada v Secretary of State for Trade (No 2)* [1983] 1 All ER 910 confirm that the key test is having decided that the documents are necessary to dispose of the case fairly, the court should inspect the documents.

On inspecting the documents, the court may come to a number of different conclusions. First, as we note in *Burmah Oil Co Ltd v Bank of England* below, the court may conclude that the documents would not materially assist the party and therefore disclosure would not be ordered under the normal rules of evidence that the document is not relevant to a fact in issue. Alternatively, if the court concludes that disclosing the documents would assist the applicant, the court must balance the competing public interest in disclosing the documents against the public interest in non-disclosure. According to Lord Reid in *Conway v Rimmer*, non-disclosure of documents in a class claim would only be justified if it was really necessary for the proper functioning of the public service.

Grounds for applying for public interest immunity

Whilst it is not possible to provide an exhaustive list of issues that may be the subject of a claim for public interest immunity in civil litigation, the following grounds are most commonly raised.

Affairs of State and national security

As the decision in *Duncan v Cammell Laird* illustrates, it is clearly in the public interest that the high-level workings of government and the diplomatic service will almost always be protected from disclosure.

Burmah Oil Co Ltd *v* Bank of England [1980] AC 1090

The plaintiff had been rescued by the defendant bank when the value of its shares ran into difficulties. The rescue plan undertaken by the bank involved purchasing a number of shares in the plaintiff company, at a price which the plaintiff later alleged was 'unconscionable'. In proceedings to have the sale set aside, the plaintiff sought discovery of various memoranda of meetings attended by government Ministers, and other documents that would have revealed the inner workings of high-level government. After inspecting the documents, the House of Lords refused discovery on the ground that the documents would not assist the plaintiff in proving its case.

Air Canada v Secretary of State for Trade (No 2) [1983] 1 All ER 910

It was alleged that in 1979 and 1980 the Secretary of State had acted *ultra vires* the powers given to him by the Airports Authority Act 1975 in directing the British Airports Authority to increase landing charges at Heathrow Airport. It was further alleged that the increased charges, which were excessive and discriminatory in their effect, had been imposed to reduce the public sector borrowing requirement rather than for the purpose intended by Parliament when it had passed the 1975 Act which was concerned with the efficient management and administration of airports under the British Airports Authority's control. The plaintiffs sought discovery of documents in the possession of the Secretary of State and the British Airports Authority which contained details of high-level ministerial discussions. The Secretary of State claimed immunity from disclosure in the public interest. Whilst the High Court ordered the documents to be inspected, the decision was overturned by the Court of Appeal and the case went on appeal to the House of Lords.

In upholding the decision of the Court of Appeal, the House of Lords stated that the party seeking the production of the documents had to show that there was a reasonable probability that the information was likely to assist its case or damage its adversary's case, and further, that the documents were likely to be needed for a fair disposal of the case. It was not enough, as in this case, for the court to order the documents to be inspected on the basis of the plaintiffs' speculative belief that the information contained in the documents was likely to assist their case.

Complaints against the police and police disciplinary proceedings

Civil actions against the police for assault and battery and for malicious prosecution have generated considerable judicial activity in the field of public interest immunity. Many decisions have focused on the legal status of internal police disciplinary reports compiled against officers as a result of a complaint by a member of the public. The development of the law in this area is illustrated by the following cases.

Neilson v Laugharne [1981] 1 QB 736

The plaintiff sued a Chief Constable in false imprisonment, assault and trespass regarding an allegedly illegal search of his property. He applied to the court for discovery of statements made in a police internal inquiry which was a consequence of his initial complaint to the police. It was held that disclosure of such documents in a civil trial would impede full co-operation by those involved in such internal inquiries, and that it would not be in the public interest for the statements to be put in the public domain.

Peach v Metropolitan Police Commissioner [1986] QB 1064

The plaintiff's son died during a demonstration which was broken up by the police. His mother was informed by some of the bystanders that her son was not one of the protestors and that without provocation, he was struck about the head by police officers wielding batons. Mrs Peach brought a civil action against the Metropolitan Police Commissioner and sought discovery of documents which were used in the internal police inquiry into the incident. The Court of Appeal stated that *Neilson* v

Laugharne was not authority for non-disclosure of relevant documents in every police inquiry. Public interest in the proper administration of justice demanded that there should be disclosure of all relevant documents in order that justice could be done in the ensuing civil trial.

The decision in *Neilson* v *Laugharne* was expressly overruled by *R* v *Chief Constable of West Midlands, ex parte Wiley* below.

R v Chief Constable of West Midlands, ex parte Wiley [1994] 3 WLR 433

W, along with S who was suing the Chief Constable of Nottinghamshire, each alleged that they had been mistreated whilst in police custody and made a formal complaint under Part IX of the Police and Criminal Evidence Act 1984 and brought an action in civil proceedings for damages. During the complaints procedure W and S refused to make any statements without an undertaking from the Chief Constables that they would not use the documents or rely on the information in the statements in the civil proceedings. The undertakings were refused and the investigation into W's complaint was discontinued. The investigation of S's complaint did proceed and a file of documents was produced. On the ground that public interest immunity attached to police complaints documents as a class, S and W obtained declarations that the Chief Constables had acted unlawfully in refusing to give the undertakings, and S was granted an injunction restraining the Chief Constable from using the information in the file for any purpose in any proposed civil proceedings. The Chief Constable unsuccessfully appealed to the Court of Appeal against the judge's ruling and then to the House of Lords.

The House of Lords held, in allowing the appeal, that the Chief Constables had not acted unlawfully in not giving the undertakings. Although the contents of individual contents might be covered by public interest immunity, there was no justification for imposing a general class of public interest immunity on all documents produced by an investigation under the complaints procedure.

The decision in *Ex parte Wiley* distinguishes the earlier cases on the privileged status of internal police documents as illustrated in *Neilson* v *Laugharne* by explaining that the earlier cases had been concerned with section 49 of the Police Act 1964. Section 49 of the 1964 Act had been repealed by Part IX of the Police and Criminal Evidence Act 1984, 'Police Complaints and Discipline', under which there could be no 'blanket immunity' from disclosure of documents used in internal inquiries by the police. Dependent upon the facts of any particular case, a balancing exercise may be necessary between the proper functioning (including disciplinary matters) of the police service and the public interest in the proper administration of justice. The basic guidance as to whether public interest immunity should be granted in either civil or criminal proceedings was given by Lord Templeman in *Ex parte Wiley*:

- if a document was not relevant and material, it need not be disclosed;
- where there is a doubt as to the document's relevance, the directions of the court can be obtained before trial;
- if a document is relevant and material, it must be disclosed unless it is confidential and a breach of that confidentiality would cause harm to the interest of justice, by non-disclosure;
- if there is doubt as to whether substantial harm could be caused by disclosure the matter can be referred to the court;
- if the holder decides that a document should not be disclosed, that decision can be upheld or set aside by the judge.

The identity of informers in criminal investigations

The general rule in civil proceedings is that the identity of an informer in a criminal investigation is protected from disclosure, as there is an overriding public interest in preserving the anonymity of informants. The basis of the modern law is to be found in a nineteenth century case.

Marks v Breyfus (1890) 25 QBD 494

The plaintiff claimed damages for malicious prosecution. In the course of the trial he asked the Director of Public Prosecutions to identify the informants but the judge disallowed the question. This ruling was upheld by the Court of Appeal on the ground that the prosecution was considered to be for a public object and that the information ought not be disclosed on the ground of public policy. According to Lord Esher the only exception to this general rule is where disclosing the informant's identity would prove the defendant's innocence.

The principles outlined in *Marks* v *Breyfus* were applied in the following case:

Alfred Crompton Amusement Machines Ltd v Commissioners for Customs and Excise (No 2) [1974] AC 405

The Commissioners for Customs and Excise had obtained information from the defendant company's customers which was relevant to assessing the company's liability for purchase tax. The House of Lords held that the Commissioners were entitled to withhold disclosure of the documents identifying the informers because if it became known that sources of information could not be kept secret, the workings of the Commissioners in relation to tax matters would be undermined (see *Rogers* v *Home Secretary* [1973] AC 388 above for similar reasoning).

The general mandatory rule protecting the anonymity of a police informant in *Marks* v *Breyfus* may be the subject of an exception where the informer himself voluntarily waives his right to remain anonymous. In *Savage* v *Chief Constable of Hampshire* [1997] 1 WLR 1061, the plaintiff commenced proceedings against the defendant to recover a contractually agreed sum for his services as a police informer. As the plaintiff's claim as pleaded was struck out for being frivolous and vexatious, the issue was not fully considered, but the Court of Appeal stated that it was possible for an informer to waive his right to remain anonymous. If this argument were accepted, it would have the effect of requiring the court to achieve a balance between the two competing public interests of disclosure and non-disclosure.

Further reading

Allan, T.R.S., 'Public Interest Immunity and Ministers' Responsibilities' [1993] Crim LR 660.

Forsyth, C., 'Public Interest Immunity: Recent and Future Developments' [1997] Camb LJ 51.

Scott, R. (1995–96) *Report of the Inquiry into the Export of Defence Equipment and Dual-use Goods to Iraq and Related Prosecutions*, House of Commons Paper 115.

Scott, R., 'The Acceptable and Unacceptable Use of Public Interest Immunity' [1996] Public Law 427.

Chapter 26

THE OPERATION OF PRIVATE PRIVILEGE

INTRODUCTION

The term 'private privilege' covers a number of separate privileges that may be claimed by a legal entity acting in its personal capacity. A private legal entity includes an individual or a company and even a public body such as a local authority where it acts in its private legal capacity. Where the privilege applies, it prevents a party to the action or a witness from having to answer certain questions at trial or to disclose certain documents or to produce certain items of real evidence. The term 'private privilege' includes legal professional privilege, the privilege against self-incrimination and 'without prejudice' negotiations.

The effect of the application of the doctrine of 'private privilege' is similar to where public interest immunity is successfully claimed, in that it prevents a witness's written or oral statement or documentary evidence, which is otherwise relevant and admissible, from being disclosed either at the pre-trial stage or at the trial. The rules of private privilege apply out of the due recognition that in the proper administration of justice it is in the wider public interest to protect the confidential relationships between lawyer and client and/or a third party or out of respect to genuine attempts to settle a civil dispute without resort to litigation through the operation of the 'without prejudice' rule. Two other associated topics are also considered in this chapter – the disclosure of confidential information and the operation of journalistic privilege in civil proceedings.

LEGAL PROFESSIONAL PRIVILEGE

The general rule is that:

(a) any communication between a legal adviser and his client; or
(b) between a legal adviser and a third party for the purpose of pending or contemplated litigation

is privileged and therefore does not have to be disclosed in civil proceedings. The legal profession is the only profession to which this privilege applies and no similar provision applies, for example, between a social worker and client or between a doctor and his patient or between a priest and his penitent.

The rationale for the special immunity granted to the lawyer/client relationship was explained by Sir Richard Scott V-C in *Re Barings plc* [1998] 1 All ER 673 where he stated 'that individuals should be able to consult their lawyers in the certain knowledge that what they tell their lawyers and the advice they receive from their lawyers, whether orally or in writing, will be immune from compulsory disclosure'.

Communications between client and legal adviser

A communication between a lawyer and his client will be privileged from disclosure where it was made confidentially and for the purpose of giving legal advice. The word 'communication' relates to both oral and written statements made by the client or by the legal adviser and will cover all modern forms of communication including fax and e-mail. In a typical case this includes written material such as letters, proofs of evidence from the client and memoranda of advice given. As a matter of policy the courts construe the phrase 'for the purposes of legal advice' broadly. In *Balabel* v *Air India* [1988] Ch 317, the Court of Appeal stated that it would be far too narrow to limit the operation of legal professional privilege to communications specifically conveying or seeking legal advice. Legal professional privilege extends to all documents that can properly be said to be part of that necessary exchange of information whose object is the giving of legal advice as and when appropriate. In deciding the issue, the crucial question is what is the aim or purpose of the communication. If the purpose of the communication can properly be said to be part of the process of obtaining or giving legal advice, it will be privileged and will not have to be disclosed. Therefore communications between a legal adviser and his client such as draft documents, working papers, attendance notes recording client meetings, memoranda, internal communications within the client's organisation, such as a company, will also be protected where the object of the communication is to enable legal advice to be given or sought.

The operation of legal professional privilege is not simply confined to a document containing legal advice by informing the client about the law but also includes a number of related matters covered by the communication. In *Nederlandse Reassurantie Groep Holding NV* v *Bacon & Woodrow* [1995] 1 All ER 976, a communication between a solicitor and a client about the commercial wisdom of entering into a contract was held to be privileged. In *Re Sarah C Getty Trust* [1985] 2 All ER 809, information received by a lawyer in his professional capacity from a third party which was passed to the client was also held to be privileged. In *Minter* v *Priest* [1930] AC 558 (see below), the House of Lords recognised that conversations between a solicitor and a prospective client with a view to the client obtaining a loan for the deposit on the purchase of real estate were privileged from disclosure as the 'business' was 'professional business' within the ordinary scope of the solicitor's employment. The privilege will apply whether or not the lawyer accepts the client's instructions.

The application of the privilege, is not however, without limitations. Where the communication does not come within the phrase 'the giving of legal advice', it will not be privileged and will have to be disclosed in the normal course of the proceedings.

Minter *v* Priest [1930] AC 558

The appellant had agreed with S to purchase a house which the appellant owned subject to two mortgages. It was further agreed that a third person T would take a share of the profits when the house was sold. S arranged to attend a meeting with Priest, the respondent, who was a solicitor, and T. At the meeting S suggested that the respondent should find the money to pay the deposit on the house and that, in any event, the respondent should act as the solicitor to the house purchase. The respondent refused, and in giving his reasons for the refusal slandered the appellant, with whom he had had previous dealings. The respondent then suggested to S and T that he should purchase the house on their behalf with the connivance of the first mortgagee for the amount due on the mortgage with a view to reselling the house for profit to be divided between the respondent, S and T. T repeated the slander to the appellant and gave an account of the interview. In an action by the appellant against the respondent for slander, the respondent claimed that the slanderous comments had been made on an occasion that was covered by legal professional privilege. At the trial of the action the judge ruled that the statement was not so privileged.

In concurring with the trial judge's decision, the House of Lords agreed that the respondent's statement was rightly put in evidence and was not covered by legal professional privilege. In giving the leading speech, Lord Buckmaster suggested that when the respondent had made the statement, a solicitor/client relationship did not exist between the parties and that the respondent never undertook the duty of solicitor 'but that the conversation from first to last was nothing but the disclosure of a malicious scheme to deprive the appellant of the chance of effecting a contract with a view to the respondent making and sharing a profit on another disposition of the property'.

According to the House of Lords in *Minter* v *Priest*, legal professional privilege will not extend to a communication in which the solicitor is advising in some other capacity unrelated to giving professional legal advice.

Whilst the law broadly interprets the ambit of the information that can be contained in a 'privileged' document, a similarly broad view is taken about the meaning of a 'legal adviser'. The phrase is not restricted to advice given by a solicitor, but also includes counsel and salaried people from whom legal advice is sought including legal executives, paralegals, trainee solicitors, counsel and the staff of a company's legal department where advice is sought by the company's officials (*Alfred Crompton Amusement Machines* v *Customs and Excise Commissioners (No 2)* [1973] 2 All ER 1169).

Communications with third parties for the purpose of pending or contemplated litigation

The second head of legal professional privilege relates to where the communication is between the legal adviser (or client) and a third party where the communication was made for the purpose of pending or contemplated litigation between the client and another person. A typical situation is where the legal adviser has been in communication with an expert witness, for example, a medical expert or motor engineer, to obtain his opinion on the issue of liability or quantum with a view to pending or contemplated litigation.

The requirement that the privilege may only apply to communications that have been created for pending or contemplated litigation is strictly observed by the courts. In *Wheeler* v *Le Marchant* (1881) 17 Ch D 675, it was held that communications between the solicitor and a surveyor were not privileged even though they were relevant to the matter being litigated, because they were made when there was no litigation contemplated by the client.

In *Ventouris* v *Mountain; The Italia Express* [1991] 3 All ER 472, the plaintiff sued the defendant underwriter in respect of a maritime policy relating to a ship owned by the plaintiff. The defendant had refused to pay out on a claim by the plaintiff after explosions occurred on the ship while berthed in Piraeus. The defence was based on information received from the plaintiff's cousin to the effect that the plaintiff had conspired with others to destroy the ship and that, accordingly, the plaintiff's claim had been made fraudulently. On discovery (now known as disclosure under the Civil Procedure Rules), the defendant claimed privilege in respect of documents which had come into being before the litigation but which had been supplied by the plaintiff's cousin to the defendant's solicitors during the litigation. The Court of Appeal held that the documents were not privileged. The central issue must be the purpose for which the document came into being. If it came into being prior to the litigation for some purpose unconnected with the litigation, the fact that the solicitor subsequently obtains it for litigation does not of itself render it privileged.

The key point in deciding the issue is: was the document created for the dominant purpose of litigation? An important example of the approach taken by the courts is provided by *Waugh* v *British Railways Board* below.

Waugh *v* British Railways Board [1980] AC 521

The plaintiff's husband was an employee of British Rail who had been killed in an accident at work. In accordance with its usual practice the British Railways Board had compiled a report two days after the accident headed 'For the Information of the Board's Solicitor'. The plaintiff sought discovery of this report to use its contents in her action in negligence against British Rail. The Board claimed that the report was privileged. The House of Lords held that the document had been created for two purposes: that of establishing the cause of the accident so that any appropriate safety measures could be taken to prevent a recurrence; and, secondly, that of enabling the Board's solicitors to advise in any litigation which would inevitably follow. Their Lordships stated that the former of the two purposes was the dominant one and therefore the report was not privileged.

Compare the decision in *Waugh* with *Guinness Peat Properties Ltd* v *Fitzroy Robinson Partnership* [1987] 1 WLR 1027. In the *Guinness* case, the plaintiffs, who were building developers, alleged negligence on the part of the defendant architects. The architects had sent a report on the matter to their insurers in accordance with their professional indemnity policy. The plaintiffs sought discovery of the document on the grounds that the dominant purpose of the document was to comply with the indemnity insurance and not for the purpose of giving advice on pending or contemplated litigation. It was held that the document was privileged as it had been created for the 'dominant' purpose of contemplated or existing litigation.

In practice, the 'dominant purpose' principle is assessed objectively on the particular facts of the case and not subjectively on the intentions of the party creating and sending the document. In particular the genesis of the communication has to be considered, which in the *Guinness* case had been prepared following a requirement from the insurers, so that they would have information on which they would be able to seek advice for pending or contemplated litigation.

Legal professional privilege and the courts

The general principle is that the courts will uphold the sanctity of legal professional privilege. An illustration of this strict approach is to be found in the criminal case described below.

R *v* Derby Magistrates' Court, ex parte B [1996] Crim LR 190

A sixteen-year-old girl was murdered. The appellant was arrested and made a statement to the police that he alone was responsible for the murder. He later retracted the statement and alleged that although he had been present at the scene of the crime, it was his stepfather who had killed the girl. Relying on this second statement, the appellant was acquitted in the Crown Court. Subsequently his stepfather was charged with the murder. At the latter's committal proceedings before a stipendiary magistrate, the appellant was called as a witness for the prosecution and repeated the statement that his stepfather had killed the girl. He was cross-examined by the defence about the instructions he had given to his solicitor concerning the murder. The appellant claimed legal professional privilege but the magistrate, on application by the stepfather under section 97 of the Magistrates' Courts Act 1980, issued a summons directing the appellant and his solicitor to produce the relevant proofs of evidence on the ground that they would be 'likely to be material evidence' within section 97. In an application for judicial review, the Divisional Court upheld the magistrates' decision but certified that the case should be heard by the House of Lords.

The House of Lords held, allowing the appeal, that a witness summons could not be issued under section 97 to compel the production of documents protected by legal professional privilege unless the privilege had been waived, which in the instant case, it had not. It was an established principle that a client must be able to consult his lawyer in confidence, otherwise he might hold back the truth. Legal professional privilege was a fundamental condition on which the administration of justice rested.

Lifting the veil of legal professional privilege

Whilst the courts strictly enforce the sanctity of legal professional privilege, there are a number of situations where the veil of legal professional privilege will be lifted and the evidence over which the privilege has been claimed will be disclosed.

Waiver

Legal professional privilege cannot be relied on where the privilege is waived by the client in whom it vests. Legal professional privilege belongs to the client and can only be expressly or impliedly waived by the client. Waiver will occur where, for example, privileged evidence is disclosed by the service of a hearsay notice under section 2 of the Civil Evidence Act 1995 or by the service and use of a witness statement at trial. Privilege is also waived where privileged evidence is used at an interim application before the trial. In *Derby & Co Ltd* v *Weldon (No 10)* [1991] 1 WLR 660, the High Court held that where a party used evidence covered by legal professional privilege at an interim hearing dealing with an application for a freezing injunction against the defendant's assets, that party waived the right to assert privilege over the same material at the subsequent trial.

Also, where a client sues his former solicitor in negligence, any privilege subsisting over the relevant evidence will be waived. In *Lillicrap* v *Nalder & Son* [1993] 1 WLR 94, the plaintiffs, who were property developers, sued their solicitors in negligence for failing to advise them on rights of way that were material to the title of a property. The Court of Appeal held that where a solicitor is sued by his client, the client impliedly waives his privilege and right to confidence in respect of all matters that were relevant to a fact in issue before the court.

Where the privilege has been used in the commission of a crime

The courts will also lift the veil of legal professional privilege where it is suggested that the privilege has been used for the commission of a crime (R v *Cox and Railton* below).

R v Cox and Railton (1884) 14 QBD 153

The defendants had consulted a solicitor for advice on how a judgment against them in a civil action could be set aside without their having to comply with it. The solicitor advised them that it could not lawfully be done given the lapse of time. The defendants then executed a fraudulent document that they backdated to achieve their unlawful purpose. At the defendants' criminal trial, the solicitor was called as a prosecution witness and repeated in evidence his advice to the defendants. The court held that no privilege attached to the conversation between the solicitor and the defendants as the purpose was to facilitate the commission of a crime.

In *Nationwide Building Society* v *Various Solicitors (No 1)* (1998) *The Times*, 5 February, the plaintiff brought an action against a number of firms of solicitors in relation to conveyancing transactions in which the defendant firms had acted for both Nationwide and the borrowers. Nationwide claimed that in breach of duty, the defendants had failed to advise them of certain matters of which they knew or ought to have known, for example, that the contract price that the borrower was paying for the property was less than that specified by him in his mortgage application; or that the purchase was by way of a sub-sale. At the pre-trial review, the court was required to decide a number of issues concerning the application of legal professional privilege. The High Court held that legal professional privilege existed over confidential communications between solicitor and client in relation to a conveyancing transaction. However, the privilege could be overridden on the lender's application for discovery where the borrower had made misrepresentations to the lender in order to secure an advance, provided that bad faith or impropriety had been pleaded and there was sufficient foundation of fact to support the allegation.

Proving the accused's innocence to a criminal charge

Where the privileged material goes to prove the innocence of an accused in a criminal case, the interests of the proper administration of justice will outweigh the claims of legal professional privilege and the evidence will generally be disclosed.

Inadvertent disclosure of privileged documents

Where by accident a privileged document falls into the possession of another party in the case, a number of consequences may follow. First, it may be possible to seek an injunction to prevent the document's use at trial provided the 'error' is discovered in time for the matter to be heard. This course of action was taken in *Goddard* v *Nationwide Building Society* [1987] QB 670, where the plaintiff submitted that a note which had come into the possession of the defendants was privileged and applied for an injunction preventing its use. The Court of Appeal granted the injunction requiring the defendant to deliver up the note and restraining its use or disclosure. Where there is insufficient time to seek an injunction, a party may rely on the Civil Procedure Rules. CPR rule 31.20 states:

> Where a party inadvertently allows a privileged document to be inspected, the party who has inspected the document may use it or its contents only with the permission of the court.

The position under CPR rule 31.10 was considered in *Breeze* v *John Stacey & Sons Ltd* (1999) *The Times*, 8 July. The defendant's solicitors inadvertently attached several documents covered by legal professional privilege to an affidavit served on the claimant's solicitors. The Court of Appeal held that on the inadvertent disclosure of privileged documents there is no requirement to inquire whether privilege has been waived in the absence of an obvious mistake. The court went on restate the principles that were long established under the 'old' Rules prior to the introduction of the Civil Procedure Rules. If the mistake was obvious and it was clear that the documents had been inadvertently disclosed, the privileged material should be returned. If the mistake was not apparent, then it must be decided if a reasonable, hypothetical solicitor would have concluded that disclosure must have occurred as a result of a mistake. If so, the documents should be returned.

Legal professional privilege and the secondary evidence rule

The veil of legal professional privilege may be lifted by the other party to the action producing copies of the original documents over which privilege is claimed. The leading authority on the point is *Calcraft* v *Guest*.

Calcraft *v* Guest [1898] 1 QB 759

In 1887 certain documents came into existence over which the owner of a fishery in Dorset claimed legal professional privilege. In 1898 his successor in title to the fishery, Calcraft, brought an action for trespass to the fishery. Calcraft succeeded in his action at trial but one of the defendants appealed. Between the trial and the appeal the documents made in 1787 came to light and the appellant's solicitor took copies of the originals before they were handed back to the plaintiff in the main litigation. On the appeal of the action, the appellant sought to put in evidence copies of the original documents. This gave rise to two questions for the Court of Appeal to consider. First, were the original documents privileged from disclosure and, secondly, if they were privileged, could the copies be used as secondary evidence of their contents? The Court of Appeal held that the original documents were privileged in 1787 and had remained privileged ever since. In relation to the second question, the copies of the document were not privileged and were admissible in evidence at the trial as secondary evidence.

Whilst the principle in *Calcraft* v *Guest* and the secondary evidence rule appears to be clear, in practice its operation is restricted. For example, if the privileged document was obtained by a trick, it is open to the tricked party to seek an injunction to prevent the copy (or the original) from being used. In *Ashburton* v *Pape* [1913] 2 Ch 469, Pape was a bankrupt, whose discharge from bankruptcy was opposed by the plaintiff. By a trick, Pape obtained several privileged letters written between the plaintiff and the plaintiff's solicitors. Pape arranged for some copies to be made. The plaintiff successfully applied to the court for an order preventing the use of the copies and requiring Pape to surrender the documents to the plaintiff's solicitor.

Where copies of the privileged documents have been obtained inadvertently, before their use at trial, the party may also apply to the court for an injunction preventing their use.

Finally, where the secondary evidence has come into the solicitor's possession by nefarious or unconventional means, the Solicitors' Practice Rules (which place an obligation on solicitors to maintain the good reputation of their profession and to do nothing that will compromise the independence and integrity of its members) should persuade the solicitor that it would be inappropriate for the secondary evidence to be used at trial.

THE PRIVILEGE AGAINST SELF-INCRIMINATION

In criminal proceedings, the accused may be asked questions about the offence for which he is being tried under section 1(e) of the Criminal Evidence Act 1898, but he is entitled to refuse to answer any question if his answer would tend to expose him to a criminal charge other than the one he currently faces. In civil proceedings, a witness may claim the privilege against self-incrimination if his answer or disclosure of any document would tend to expose him or his spouse to a criminal charge or to a penalty or to forfeiture. The privilege against self-incrimination has been recognised at common law since at least 1847, and provides that no one shall be forced to incriminate himself out of his own mouth. A leading explanation of the principle is to be found in Goddard LJ's statement in *Blunt v Park Lane Hotel Ltd* [1942] 2 All ER 187, in which he made the following observation:

> The rule is that no one is bound to answer any question if the answer thereto, would in the opinion of the judge, have a tendency to expose the defendant to any criminal charge, penalty or forfeiture which the judge regards as reasonably likely to be preferred or sued for.

The privilege can be claimed both during the pre-trial disclosure stage and at the trial. The privilege at the disclosure stage can be claimed if the documents to be disclosed would expose one of the parties to the possibility of a criminal prosecution. The privilege at the trial can be claimed by a witness to prevent him being forced to answer a question or to disclose documents that may lead to him being prosecuted for a criminal offence.

The modern law in civil proceedings is governed by section 14 of the Civil Evidence Act 1968 which provides:

> The right of a person in any legal proceedings other than criminal proceedings to refuse to answer any question or produce any document or things if to do so would tend to expose that person to proceedings for an offence or for the recovery of a penalty—
> > (a) shall apply only as regards criminal offences under the law of any part of the United Kingdom and the penalties provided for by such law...

The effect of section 14 is that no witness can be required to answer any question or produce any document or thing if to do so would expose that person or that person's spouse to proceedings for any criminal offence in the United Kingdom or to European Community sanctions or penalties (*Rio Tinto Zinc Corporation v Westinghouse Electric Corporation* [1978] AC 547). Whilst the privilege has to be claimed by the witness, it is the judge's responsibility to decide whether the witness's answer would tend to expose the witness or his spouse to a criminal charge or incur a sanction or a penalty. It is important to note that the fear must not be fanciful or theoretical. As Lord Lowry stated in *AT & T Istel Ltd* v *Tully* [1992] 3 All ER 523:

> ... there is no absolute privilege against answering incriminatory questions: the privilege is against exposing oneself to the reasonable risk of prosecution.

Where the judge decides that such a danger exists, the witness is excused from answering the question. In the *Istel* case, the House of Lords held that the privilege could not be relied on in refusing to obey a court order to file an affidavit disclosing all dealings with certain monies and assets derived from them, as long as the order contained a proviso stating that no disclosed material would be used in any prosecution of a person required to make the disclosure. It had to be shown that the prosecuting authorities were prepared to comply with the undertaking.

Exceptions to the privilege against self-incrimination

In modern civil proceedings the operation of the privilege against self-incrimination is not absolute. In a number of enactments Parliament has either modified or abrogated the privilege's operation.

Where Parliament has modified the operation of the privilege

Theft Act 1968, section 31(1)

Section 31(1) provides that:

> A person shall not be excused, by reason that to do so may incriminate that person or the wife or husband of that person of an offence under this Act—
>> (a) from answering any question put to that person in proceedings for the recovery or the administration of any property, for the execution of any trust or for an account of any property or dealings with the property; or
>> (b) from complying with any order in any such proceedings.

The effect of the section is that a witness may not refuse to answer any questions in proceedings for the recovery or administration of property or for the execution of a trust on the ground that to do so might incriminate him or his spouse in an offence under the 1968 Act, including an offence of false accounting under section 17 of that Act.

The provision is subject to the important limitation that the witness's answers are not admissible against him or his spouse in subsequent proceedings under the 1968 Act. Therefore, any evidence obtained in the civil court cannot be directly used in any criminal proceedings although the evidence a witness gives in these proceedings may put the prosecuting authorities on notice that the witness may have behaved dishonestly in connection with the administration of the trust.

Supreme Court Act 1981, section 72

The rapid growth of information technology has required that the law should effectively respond to allegations of infringement of copyright, which often involves allegations of fraud. Under section 72(1), in any proceedings in the High Court for the infringement of intellectual property rights, including copyrights, patents, registered designs, technical information or passing off, the witness cannot refuse to answer questions on the basis of incriminating himself or his spouse. The witness's answers are inadmissible in any subsequent proceedings except, under section 72(4), in cases of perjury and contempt.

Where Parliament has abrogated the operation of the privilege

Whilst for example the provisions under the Theft Act 1968 make some inroads into the traditional operation of the privilege against self-incrimination by allowing certain questions to be asked that are *prima facie* in breach of the privilege's traditional limits, the witness's answers cannot be used in other proceedings. There is however a second group of statutes which permit not only potentially incriminating questions to be asked but also permit the witness's answers to be used against him in later proceedings. In the main, these statutes are part of the regulatory framework that give wide legal powers to the police and other law enforcement officers when investigating allegations of fraud and other malpractice in the running of companies.

Proceedings under the Insolvency Act 1986

In *Bishopsgate Investment Management Ltd v Maxwell* [1992] 2 All ER 856, it was held that the privilege did not apply to investigations under section 236 of the Insolvency Act 1986 subject to the discretion of the trial judge to relieve the respondent of any oppression. In the later decision of *Re Arrows Ltd (No 4)* [1995] 2 AC 75, the House of Lords held that the Director of the Serious Fraud Squad could make full use in any prosecution of transcripts of examinations carried out under section 236 of the Insolvency Act 1986, whilst confirming the trial judge's discretion to exclude any evidence where admitting it would have a sufficiently adverse effect on the fairness of the trial.

The privilege against self-incrimination is also excluded under the 1986 Act:

- in relation to the private examination of an insolvent individual (section 366);
- in relation to the public examination of an officer of a company by the liquidator (section 133);
- in relation to the public examination of an insolvent individual (section 290).

Banking Act 1987, section 42

Under section 42 of the Banking Act 1987 the privilege against self-incrimination is abrogated where a person has been charged with deception and anticipates further prosecution under the Act (*Bank of England v Riley* [1992] 1 All ER 769).

Companies Act 1985, sections 434–436

These provisions are part of the general regulatory framework referred to above that confers wide-ranging powers on State officials to question witnesses and to seize documents and other 'relevant' material in the investigation of fraud in the running of companies.

Section 434 permits Board of Trade inspectors appointed to investigate suspected fraud in the conduct or management of a company to require an officer of the company or any person possessing relevant information to produce any documents relating to the company and to answer any questions put by the inspectors. The use that may be made of the person's answers depends upon the nature of the proceedings that are subsequently taken as a result of the investigation. For example, section 434(5A) and (5B) of the Companies Act 1985 provides that no evidence of the answers given by a person to an inspector questioned under section 434 may be used in evidence by the prosecution against him in criminal proceedings unless the evidence is adduced or the question is asked on behalf of the person charged. The accused cannot therefore be compelled to answer questions or to disclose the answers that he gave to the inspectors, unless as an exception to the general rule, he is being prosecuted for an offence under section 2 or 5 of the Perjury Act 1911. For a fuller discussion on the application of the operation of privilege against self-incrimination under the Companies Act 1985 and the challenges that have been made against the provisions under the European Convention on Human Rights, see Chapter 10.

Children Act 1989, section 98

As an exception to the general proposition that the privilege against self-incrimination has been abrogated in statutes concerned with preventing fraud in the running of companies, section 98 of the Children Act 1989 provides that in proceedings in which a court is hearing an application relating to a care, supervision or protection order in respect to a child, no person shall be excused from answering any question that might incriminate him and his spouse.

OPERATION OF PRIVATE PRIVILEGE AND THE PRE-TRIAL DISCLOSURE OF EVIDENCE

Although the Civil Procedure Rules do not specifically refer to the word 'privilege', it is well established that under CPR rule 31.3(1)(b), a document can be withheld from being inspected where a party successfully claims that it is covered by legal professional privilege or that its disclosure will offend his privilege against self-incrimination. CPR rule 31.3(1) states:

> A party to whom a document has been disclosed has a right to inspect that document except where—
>
> ...
>
> (b) the party disclosing the document has a right or a duty to withhold inspection of it...

The claim that a document is privileged from inspection by the other side may be made in the list of documents required by CPR rule 31.19(4) or by serving a formal notice or by applying to the court to give effect to the claim to privilege. Where the other side disputes the claim, it may also request the court to decide the issue. The application is likely to be made without notice. In deciding the issue, the court may require the production of the document and, where appropriate, invite representations from the claimant or from the defendant and from any relevant third parties.

NEGOTIATIONS AND 'WITHOUT PREJUDICE' COMMUNICATIONS

As one of the major aims of the Civil Procedure Rules and pre-trial proceedings in civil cases is to assist the parties to settle their disputes without a full trial, attempts to negotiate a settlement between the parties are encouraged. Therefore, where a communication between the parties for the purpose of attempting to settle the litigation is made on a 'without prejudice' basis, it is privileged from being disclosed if the case reaches trial. The ambit of the rule renders inadmissible evidence in those proceedings of any statement made in negotiations between the parties in a genuine attempt to settle their dispute. The purpose of 'without prejudice' communications is to enable the parties to negotiate freely, without any fear that statements made during those negotiations may be used against them if the parties fail to settle the case without recourse to litigation.

In most cases, oral negotiations will be specifically made on a 'without prejudice' basis whilst, to attract the privilege, letters and other permanent forms of communication that contain offers of settlement will be actually marked 'without prejudice'. This, however, is not an essential pre-requisite for protection. The clearest statement of the law is to be found in Lord Griffiths' speech in *Rush & Tompkins v Greater London Council* [1988] 3 All ER 737:

> A competent solicitor will always head any negotiating correspondence 'without prejudice' to make clear beyond reasonable doubt that in the event of the negotiations being unsuccessful they are not to be referred to at the subsequent trial. However, the application of the rule is not dependent on the use of the phrase 'without prejudice' and if it is clear from the surrounding circumstances that the parties were seeking to compromise the action, evidence of the content of these negotiations will not be admissible at the trial and cannot be used to establish an admission or partial admission.

The actual words used in the communication are less important than the appearance of the party's intention. If it is clear from the letter or the words spoken that the party intended the communication to be a bona fide attempt to settle the dispute, the court may regard the communication as privileged. The protection afforded to a 'without privilege' communication may therefore arise by implication. In *Pool v Pool* [1951] 2 All ER 563, the wife had filed a petition for divorce. Prior to the trial, meetings had been held at the chambers of Mrs Pool's counsel attended by her solicitor, her husband's solicitor and barrister. Nobody at the meetings actually used the words 'without prejudice'. However, the sole purpose of the meetings was to effect a reconciliation between the parties. The judge inferred on the facts of the case that there was a tacit understanding that the conversations were made without prejudice. In the same way, it is not always conclusive that a communication will be privileged where it is marked 'without prejudice'. A letter of acknowledgement of receipt of earlier correspondence is not protected by the doctrine even if the writer heads it 'without prejudice'.

In *South Shropshire District Council v Amos* [1987] 1 All ER 340, Parker LJ in the Court of Appeal said:

> In order to avoid any possibility of future unnecessary disputes about such matters we conclude by stating that we agree with the judge (a) that the heading 'without prejudice' does not conclusively or automatically render a document so marked privileged, (b) that, if

privilege is claimed but challenged, the court can look at the document so headed in order to determine its nature.

It is important to note the difference in the legal status between an 'off the record' or a 'confidential' communication and a 'without prejudice' communication. The general rule appears to be that statements made 'off the record' have no legal significance and therefore will not attract the privilege afforded to 'without prejudice' negotiations. It was suggested by Lord Megarry in *Chocoladefabriken Lindt & Sprungli AG v Nestlé Co Ltd* [1977] RPC 287, that informal conversations may, at best, assist in showing the court that the discussions were to be made 'without prejudice' but the precise legal status of such a conversation will be decided on the facts and the surrounding circumstances of the particular case.

Scope of the 'without prejudice' rule

At one stage, the scope of the rule was narrowly interpreted by the courts as illustrated by the decision in *Re Daintry, ex parte Holt* [1893] 2 QB 116. In recent years the application of the rule has been widened by a number of Court of Appeal decisions including *South Shropshire District Council v Amos* and *Rush & Tompkins v Greater London Council* above. A useful exposition of the present law was provided by Lord Justice Hoffmann in *Forster v Freidland* (Unreported, November 10, 1992) in which he stated:

> It seems to me ... that there is no basis in authority or in principle for limiting the rule to negotiations aimed at resolving the legal issues between the parties. There must be many without prejudice negotiations which do not address the issues at all. They are attempts to find an agreed solution which will make it unnecessary for the issues to be debated in negotiation or in court.

Lifting the veil of 'without privilege' communications

As with legal professional privilege, the law recognises a number of situations where the veil of privilege will be lifted and 'without prejudice' communications will be admissible in evidence. The court will inquire into the status of the negotiations and any supporting documentation in deciding whether the parties have reached a binding settlement as illustrated in *Walker v Wilsher* (1889) 23 QBD 335.

The parties may agree that, for example, a 'without prejudice' communication can be disclosed to the court. In *Forster v Freidland*, the Court of Appeal stated that the privilege remains unless waived by each party. In *McTaggart v McTaggart* [1948] 2 All ER 754, a meeting between husband and wife was arranged by a probation officer in an attempt to achieve a reconciliation rather than have them resort to divorce proceedings, ie a 'without prejudice' situation. It was held, when the attempted reconciliation had proved unsuccessful and the divorce proceedings were in progress, that both husband and wife were entitled to object to the disclosure of the content of that 'without prejudice' conversation as the 'without prejudice' privilege vested in the parties who are in dispute and not in the intermediary or conciliator. If the spouses had agreed to disclose during the trial their attempts at reconciliation, the probation officer would not have been permitted to lodge an objection and the judge would have ruled the evidence admissible.

The 'without prejudice' negotiations will be disclosed where they have been used as a vehicle for fraudulent conduct. The decision in *Dubai Bank v Galadari* [1990] 1 Lloyd's Rep 120 suggests that where a party has attempted to negotiate a settlement by deception, the court is entitled to investigate the allegation to ensure that a fraud has not been committed behind the privilege afforded by 'without prejudice' negotiations.

Finally, it is worth noting that there are two major differences between 'without prejudice' communications and those which attract legal professional privilege. First, without prejudice communications cannot be adduced in evidence at trial unless both parties agree, whereas in the case of legal professional privilege, if the client waives the privilege, the lawyer is obliged to disclose the content of the communication. Secondly, a 'without prejudice' communication, unlike privileged material, cannot be proved by secondary evidence.

CONFIDENTIAL COMMUNICATIONS

As a matter of public policy the courts have refused to extend the principles of legal professional privilege to other 'professional' relationships, such as that between doctor and patient, where communications between the parties may have included confidential material. These cases include:

* between priest and penitent (*Attorney-General v Clough* [1963] 1 QB 773);
* between accountant and client (*Chantrey Martin & Co v Martin* [1953] 2 QB 286); and
* between doctor and patient (*R v McDonald* [1991] Crim LR 122).

The general position is that unless the communication is 'privileged' or is covered by public interest immunity, it cannot be protected from being disclosed and inspected by the other side as illustrated by the case of *Science Research Council v Nassé; Leyland Cars v Vyas* [1979] 3 All ER 673. Two employees claimed discrimination, one because she was a trade unionist, whilst the other claimed discrimination on the ground of his ethnic origin. As the cases were heard together, both employees sought the discovery of confidential reports on fellow employees who might have benefited from alleged discrimination. The Court of Appeal allowed the employer's claim to privilege, which was upheld by the House of Lords, although the House took the opportunity to reaffirm the principle that confidentiality alone was not a sufficient ground to protect documents from being disclosed.

In order to rebut the operation of the wide-ranging rules relating to disclosure, in a number of cases, it has been submitted to be in the higher public interest that certain communications should remain confidential and therefore should not be disclosed. Where the ground of confidentiality is raised, it has a public and a private dimension.

Protecting confidential communications in the public domain

In some situations, the courts have been asked to acknowledge that where a public body, such as a local authority, in discharging its statutory duties, has 'sensitive' or confidential material that is relevant to a fact in issue in the case, it may not be in the public interest for the material to be disclosed in the court proceedings. As an illustration of the approach taken by the courts in deciding whether evidence should remain confidential, consider the case of *Campbell* v *Tameside MBC*.

Campbell v Tameside MBC [1982] QB 1065

The prospective plaintiff, a schoolteacher employed by the defendant education authority, was violently assaulted by an eleven-year-old boy in her classroom, which caused her serious injuries. She alleged that the council had been negligent in allowing the child to attend the school with such behavioural problems and applied for pre-action discovery of all the documents in the defendant's possession relating to the boy including the reports of teachers, psychologists and psychiatrists. The defendant objected to allowing the documents to be inspected by the plaintiff on the basis that they were confidential documents of a class that was protected by public interest immunity. The judge ordered several of the documents to be disclosed, some of which indicated that the child was prone to violent behaviour. The defendant appealed and contended that the documents should remain confidential on the basis that if those who made the reports had known that they were to be used in legal proceedings they would have been inhibited from writing frankly about the pupil. In dismissing the appeal, the Court of Appeal held that the judge had rightly concluded that there was a real risk that the plaintiff would be denied justice if the documents were not disclosed.

In giving his judgment Lord Justice Ackner in the Court of Appeal made points of general importance. He stated that the exclusion of relevant evidence always calls for clear justification. All relevant documents, whether or not confidential, are subject to disclosure, unless on some recognised ground, including the public interest. Since it had been accepted by the court that the documents for which the plaintiff sought discovery were relevant to the contemplated litigation, there was a heavy burden on the education authority to justify withholding them from disclosure. The fact that information has been communicated by one person to another in confidence is not, of itself, a sufficient ground for protection from disclosure in a court of law of either the nature of the information or the identity of the informant if either of those matters would assist the court to ascertain facts which are relevant to an issue on which it is adjudicating. The private promise of confidentiality must yield to the general public interest, that in the administration of justice will out, unless by reason of the character of the information or the relationship of the recipient of the information, a more important public interest is served by protecting the information or the identity of the informant from disclosure in a court of law.

Private confidentiality

The law relating to the confidentiality of communications between parties acting in their private legal capacity, is to be found in a number of leading decisions. In the Court of Appeal case of *Wheeler* v *Le Marchant* (1881) 17 Ch D 675, Lord Jessel MR made the following observation:

> The principle protecting confidential communications is of very limited character. It does not protect all confidential communications which a man must necessarily make in order to obtain advice, even when needed for the protection of his life, or his honour or of his fortune ... The protection is of a very limited character and in this country is restricted to obtaining the assistance of lawyers.

In *Attorney-General* v *Mulholland* [1963] 1 All ER 767, Lord Denning stated:

> The only profession that I know which is given a privilege from disclosing information to a court of law is the legal profession, and then it is not the privilege of the lawyer but of

his client. Take the clergyman, the banker or the medical man. None of these is entitled to refuse to answer when directed to by a judge. Let me not be mistaken. The judge will respect the confidences which each member of these honourable professions received in the course of it, and will not direct him to answer unless not only is it relevant but also a proper, and indeed, necessary question in the course of justice to be put and answered.

In the vast majority of cases therefore, as the speech of Lord Wilberforce in *Science Research Council* v *Nassé* [1979] 3 All ER 673 confirms, there is no protection *per se* against a party from being compelled to disclose confidential information such as employment assessments, references and reports. In appropriate circumstances, however, this position may be partially tempered by a number of possibilities.

First, a witness may be able to rely on a recognised head of private privilege or, where the issue is in the 'public domain', to rely on the doctrine of public interest immunity. For example, a communication made in the course of seeking conciliation in matrimonial proceedings may attract both private and public privilege as explained in the speeches of Lords Hailsham and Simon in *D* v *NSPCC* [1978] AC 171. An interview with a child victim of a sexual offence may also be the subject of public interest immunity unless the disclosure of the information would tend to prove the accused's innocence, in which case there would be a strong argument for disclosure as stated in *R* v *K (TD) (Evidence)* (1993) 97 Cr App R 342. A similar immunity was claimed in respect of confidential documents relating to abortions carried out under the Abortion Act 1967 (*Morrow* v *DPP* [1994] Crim LR 58).

Secondly, the material may not be admitted in evidence under the residual discretion enjoyed by the judge to prevent the disclosure of confidential communications. In *British Steel Corporation* v *Granada Television Ltd* [1980] 3 WLR 774 Lord Wilberforce stated:

> As to information obtained in confidence, and the legal duty, which may arise, to disclose it to the court of justice, the position is clear. Courts have an inherent wish to respect this confidence, whether it arises between doctor and patient, priest and penitent, banker and customer, persons giving testimonials to employees, or in other relationships. A relationship of confidence between a journalist and his source is in no different category; nothing in this case involves or will involve any principle that such confidence is not something to be respected. But in all these cases, the court may have to decide, in the particular circumstances, that the interest in preserving this confidence is outweighed by other interests to which the law attaches importance.

JOURNALISTIC PRIVILEGE

Until 1981 the courts consistently ruled that there was no privilege that a journalist could invoke to protect the confidentiality of his or her sources of information. A distinction was drawn, as matter of public policy, between recognising the anonymity of informants used by the police whilst refusing to give a similar status to those people who gave confidential information to members of the media, even in cases where the media exposed issues of public interest.

British Steel Corporation *v* **Granada Television Ltd** [1980] 3 WLR 774

A confidential document belonging to the plaintiffs came into the hands of the defendant and was used as part of a television programme made by the defendant. The plaintiffs obtained a court order for the return of the documents but before returning the documents, the defendant mutilated them to conceal the identity of the person who had supplied the information. The plaintiffs then sought a court order to reveal the identity of the informer, even though the defendant had given an undertaking to the informer that his identity would not be revealed.

The House of Lords held that journalists did not enjoy the same privilege to protect their confidential sources of information as enjoyed by lawyers under the doctrine of legal professional privilege or by the police under public interest immunity and suggested that if the law recognised such confidences it would:

> place journalists in a favoured and unique position as compared with priest-confessors, doctors, bankers, and other recipients of confidential information and would assimilate them to the police in relation to informers.

The decision in *British Steel Corporation* v *Granada Television Ltd* caused considerable disquiet in media circles as imposing unnecessary restrictions on freedom of speech as well as limiting the media's ability to expose scandals in the public interest. As a result of this disquiet, the position of the media was partially changed by section 10 of the Contempt of Court Act 1981, which provides that:

> No court may require a person to disclose, nor is any person guilty of contempt of court for refusing to disclose, the source of information contained in a publication for which he is responsible, unless it be established to the satisfaction of the court that disclosure is necessary in the interests of justice or national security or for the prevention of disorder or crime.

The effect of section 10 is to introduce the test of 'necessity' in deciding whether it is the interests of justice or national security or the prevention of disorder or crime to require a journalist to disclose the identity of his confidential sources. In all other situations journalistic privilege will prevail to secure confidentiality of his sources of information. An illustration of the 'necessity' test is provided below.

Secretary of State for Defence *v* Guardian Newspapers [1984] 3 All ER 601

The *Guardian* newspaper had published details of the location of United States cruise missiles at the Greenham Common airbase. The Secretary of State for Defence sought to recover the documents and was anxious to know the source of the newspaper's information, as it had been contained in a classified memorandum that had a very limited circulation within the Cabinet. Counsel for the Secretary of State submitted that this was a matter of national security and that the person who had 'leaked' the information must be someone in a senior position in the government or the Civil Service. The *Guardian* relied on section 10 of the Contempt of Court Act 1981, but was compelled to reveal its source once the Secretary of State had discharged the legal burden of proving that the matter was one which could jeopardise national security, in view of the position that the 'mole' must hold to be in possession of such secret information. The name and position of the informer was given by the newspaper to the Ministry of Defence, otherwise its editor would have been in contempt of court. (The informer, Sarah Tisdale, was actually a grade III clerk in the Foreign Office, who had access to the copier on which the memorandum was duplicated prior to its limited promulgation within the Cabinet. She was later accused of breaching the Official Secrets Act 1911 and despite her guilty plea and unblemished record she was sentenced to six months' imprisonment.)

On the question of the wider application of section 10, the House of Lords held that it was a valid defence not only where a journalist was asked a direct question in court, but also in an action for the recovery of property where the property once recovered would help to reveal the newspaper's source. The House of Lords nevertheless held (with Lords Fraser and Scarman dissenting) that it was necessary to recover the documents and to identify the source of the leak in the interests of national security. This was an issue of grave importance for national security, as Britain's allies could not be expected to entrust the government with secret information if it was liable to unauthorised disclosure.

Guidance on the meaning of the 'necessity test' was given by Lord Griffiths in *Re: An Inquiry under the Company Securities (insider Dealing) Act 1985* [1988] AC 660 who stated:

> I doubt if it is possible to go further than to say that 'necessary' has a meaning that lies somewhere between 'indispensable' on the one hand, and 'useful' or 'expedient' on the other, and to leave it to the judge to decide towards which end of the scale of the meaning he will place it on the facts of any particular case. The nearest paraphrase I can suggest is 'really needed'.

The status of these early decisions on section 10 need to be reconsidered in the light of the Human Rights Act 1998. Article 10 of the European Convention of Human Rights guarantees the right to freedom of expression subject to a number of restrictions and exceptions that are prescribed by law and are necessary in a democratic society, including the recognised exceptions relating to national security and the prevention of crime. The leading Convention case is *Goodwin v United Kingdom* [1996] 22 EHHR 123, reported in its domestic context as *X Ltd v Morgan Grampian* [1991] 2 All ER 1. On the facts in this case, the European Court of Human Rights concluded the United Kingdom had acted in a disproportionate way in requiring the applicant journalist to disclose the identity of his informant. In the light of the Human Rights Act 1998, courts will be required to move away from the generalised principles expressed in earlier case law to a more specific case by case approach based on the individual facts in each case.

Further reading

Andrews, N.H., 'The Influence of Equity upon the Doctrine of Legal Professional Privilege' (1989) 105 LQR 608.

Heydon, J.H., 'Legal Professional Privilege and Third Parties' (1974) 37 MLR 601.

Tapper, C., 'Privilege and Confidence' (1972) 32 MLR 83.

Chapter 27

PREPARING FOR A CIVIL TRIAL

INTRODUCTION

Whilst most civil actions are concluded by a negotiated settlement, a party's lawyer should always conduct the proceedings on the assumption that the case may ultimately be decided at a trial. The theme of this chapter is to consider the steps that the lawyer takes in preparing the case for trial. Some of these preparatory steps will be imposed by the court as part of its case management powers under the Civil Procedure Rules, whilst other steps are part of good professional practice to ensure that, if required, the party can discharge its legal and evidential burdens of proof to the required standard and to be in a position to challenge the case put forward by the opposing side. This will include ensuring that all the party's witness statements comply with the formalities of the Civil Procedure Rules and, where the court has ordered the pre-trial exchange of witness statements, the statements have been properly served on the opposing party(ies). It is also important to ensure that those witnesses who are required to attend court to give oral evidence have been notified of the time and place of the trial and that the proper formalities have been complied with for those witnesses whose evidence will be given in their absence under the provisions of the Civil Evidence Act 1995. These procedural steps should be seen in the wider context of trial preparation and should be considered in conjunction with the other important pre-trial matters relating to the disclosure of documents discussed in Chapter 25, the procedure for admitting hearsay evidence considered in Chapter 29, as well as the evidential issues arising at the civil trial in Chapter 28. Before we consider these important practical steps it is necessary to identify the procedural and evidential context that governs a party's preparation for a civil trial.

THE COURT'S POWER TO CONTROL THE EVIDENCE

When preparing for a civil trial, a party's lawyer does not enjoy the same autonomy as his counterpart in a criminal case. The way in which a party will present its case to the court, including the evidence that it will be allowed to call at trial will be subject to the court's powers to control the evidence in the case under CPR rule 32.1. Under CPR rule 32.1(1) the court may give directions as to:

(a) the issues on which it requires evidence;
(b) the nature of the evidence which it requires to decide those issues; and
(c) the way in which the evidence is to be placed before the court.

These wide-ranging powers are further strengthened by CPR rule 32.1(2), which states:

> The court may use its power under this rule to exclude evidence that would otherwise be admissible.

The exercise of the powers under CPR rule 32.1(1) and (2) reflect the court's wider responsibility for managing the conduct of the case. The powers may be exercised at the pre-trial stage, at the beginning of the trial or at any time during the trial. For example, in many cases that reach trial the judge will use these powers at the beginning of the proceedings where he has the benefit of access to the party's full trial bundles in order to exclude evidence that is not directly relevant to proving a fact in issue.

The practical effects of CPR rule 32.1(1) and (2) are to:

- allow the court to override the wishes of the parties as to how they conduct their cases on all the issues including liability, quantum or the remedies sought;
- allow the court to impose its own wishes on the parties in relation to the evidence to be called at trial, including restricting the number of witnesses of fact and/or expert witnesses;
- decide which evidence is 'relevant' in the case;
- to restrict the parties as to how a fact in issue is to be proved at trial whether by oral evidence or by written evidence or by hearsay evidence; and
- to exclude evidence that 'would otherwise be admissible'.

WITNESS STATEMENTS TO BE USED AT TRIAL

An important aspect of the lawyer's preparation for trial is to ensure that all the witness statements that form part of his party's case comply with the requirements of the Civil Procedure Rules and that they contain all the factual and/or opinion evidence that will be heard by the court when the witness gives evidence.

Lord Woolf noted that under the 'old' system of civil litigation, witness statements had become increasingly lengthy documents and reflected too much influence of the parties' lawyers rather than being in the witness's own words. This resulted in many instances of witness statements being used as a vehicle for the lawyer's legal submissions. Consequently, under the reformed system of civil procedure, the rules relating to the format and content of witness statements are much more prescriptive and reflect the proactive powers of the court contained in CPR Part 32 to control the evidence to be heard in the case.

As we noted in Chapter 22, a party is required to identify as early as possible in the case the witnesses on whose evidence it intends to rely at trial and a statement or a proof of evidence will have been taken from each witness. The statement should contain everything that the witness might wish to say during his evidence-in-chief in the event of the case reaching trial. A party's lawyer should always be aware that in spite of many of the changes to the philosophy and practice of civil litigation introduced by the new Rules, CPR rule 32.2 maintains the traditional position that at trial any fact that needs proving by the evidence of the witness should be proved by the witness attending court and giving oral evidence, subject to the court's discretion.

Therefore, in maintaining the principle of orality in the English trial, in many cases on the fast track and on the multi-track, it will be necessary for a party's witnesses to attend court to give oral evidence. This will enable the judge to assess the demeanour and credibility of witnesses more effectively and to give their evidence the appropriate weight.

The form and content of witness statements

CPR Part 32 and the Practice Direction to Part 32 closely control the proper form and content of witness statements. CPR rule 32.4 defines a witness statement as:

> a written statement signed by a person which contains the evidence, and only that evidence, which that person would be allowed to give orally.

Paragraphs 17.1 to 22.2 of the Practice Direction to Part 32 set out in detail how witness statements should be laid out. Included in these provisions is the requirement that the witness statement should be headed with the title of the proceedings. The top right-hand corner of the first page of the statement should contain the following information:

- the party on whose behalf the statement is made;
- the initials and the surname of the witness;
- the number of the statement in relation to that witness;
- the identifying initials and number of each exhibit referred to; and
- the date the statement was made.

Paragraph 18.1 of the Practice Direction specifically addresses many of Lord Woolf's criticisms of the former regime as to witness statements, by providing that the statement must, if practicable, be in the witness's own words and should be written in the first person. The words 'if practicable' provide a useful qualification to this requirement, as it is common for the solicitor to edit the witness's words to exclude slang or to clarify certain words or phrases.

The statement should also contain:

- the full name of the witness;
- his place of residence, or, if he is making the statement in his professional, business or other occupational capacity, the address at which he works, the position he holds and the name of his firm or employer;
- his occupation, or if he has none, his description; and
- the fact that he is a party to the proceedings or is the employee of such a party if it be the case.

A number of other formalities must also be complied with including numbering each paragraph and each page. Any numbers referred to in the statement should be written in figures and not words.

Where the witness's statement refers to an exhibit such as a piece of real evidence, the exhibit must be verified and identified by the witness and remain separate from the statement. Exhibits should be numbered and, where the witness makes more than one statement in the same proceedings which refers to exhibits, the numbering of the exhibits should run consecutively throughout and not start again with each witness statement.

Under the court's proactive powers of case management, where the witness statement fails to comply with CPR Part 32 or with the Practice Direction, the court may refuse to accept the statement as evidence and impose any other penalty it thinks fit including refusing to award the costs incurred arising out of the statement's preparation.

Statement of truth

CPR rule 32.8 and the Practice Direction require that a witness statement must contain a statement of truth. This is a statement by the maker that he believes the facts in the statement to be true, which will usually be in the following form:

> I believe that the facts stated in this witness statement are true.

A failure to comply with these requirements may result in serious sanctions being taken against the party, including the court ruling that the evidence contained in the statement is inadmissible.

Where a statement is made falsely, CPR rule 32.14(1) provides that the witness may be prosecuted for contempt of court. The proceedings for contempt may be brought by the Attorney-General or by anyone else with the permission of the court under CPR rule 32.14(2).

Witness statements – serving on the other side

At the case management conference or at the directions stage when a case has been allocated to a management track, the court will order each party to exchange its witness statements with the other side. CPR rule 32.4 states that the court will order a party to serve on the other side the witness statements of the evidence that the party will rely on at trial. In many cases, the court will require that the witness statements will be exchanged at ten weeks after the directions hearing.

The court may also give further directions as to:

(a) the order in which the statements are to be served; and
(b) whether or not the witness statements are to be filed with the court.

The normal rule is that the court will order that the exchange of statements should be simultaneous, so as to avoid one party gaining an unfair advantage over its opponent by, for example, being able to assess the strength of the party's case before having to serve its own statements. If a party does not serve a witness statement within the required time limit, the witness cannot give oral evidence unless the court gives permission under CPR rule 32.10.

Witness summary

Under the 'old' system of civil litigation, a number of actions failed because a party's witness could not be traced or it was difficult to persuade a witness to attend court or in the case of an unco-operative witness, the lawyer could not be confident that what the witness would say in court would be favourable to his client's case. A failure to conclude the action satisfactorily for these reasons not only resulted in a waste of the court's valuable time but also imposed additional costs and stress on the parties and led to a feeling of injustice. To remedy this situation, Lord Woolf recommended the use of a witness summary.

A witness summary may be used if the lawyer wishes to keep open the possibility of calling a witness at trial and it has not been possible to obtain a signed statement from the witness before the time prescribed for the exchange of witness statements. The procedure will be appropriate where the witness cannot be traced or is proving to be unco-operative.

CPR rule 32.9 provides that a party can apply to the court without notice before the deadline for the exchange of witness statements for an order to serve a witness summary. The witness summary, which should accompany the application, will contain the following details:

- the evidence which would otherwise go in a witness statement; or
- if the party serving the summary does not know what evidence will be given, the matters about which the party proposes to question the witness; and
- the witness's name and address.

A good illustration of the use of a witness summary is provided by *Harrison and Harrison v Bloom Camillin (No 1) (1999) Independent*, 28 June. The claimant alleged that the defendants, who were a firm of solicitors, had been negligent in failing to serve proceedings within the limitation period against their former accountants. The defendants sought permission to serve witness summaries from various people, including the claimant's father and an employee of the accountants. In deciding the issue, Neuberger J stated that if there was a real sense of injustice or even a reasonably justified sense of injustice felt by the defendants if they were not allowed to call the witnesses in issue, they should be permitted to serve the witness summaries. The defendants were granted permission.

There is an important distinction between a witness statement and a witness summary. A witness statement will be a full proof of evidence, although at the court's instigation, a statement may be limited to certain issues. A witness summary only identifies the witness and indicates the matters, with which his evidence will deal and does not include a certificate by its maker as to its truth.

SECURING THE ATTENDANCE OF A WITNESS AT TRIAL

Where a witness is required to give oral evidence, an important matter that should be dealt with in preparing for trial is to secure the attendance of both lay and expert witnesses at the court on the appointed day and time. All witnesses who a party intends to call at trial should be kept fully informed of the expected trial date and, once the date has been fixed, the witnesses should be informed immediately. Details of the periods when a witness will be unavailable to give evidence will be given to the court in the listing questionnaire.

It is generally unwise to rely on lay witnesses attending trial voluntarily. Their attendance should be secured by requesting the court to serve a witness summons requiring the witness to attend court to give evidence or to produce a document(s) at the trial. The same comment can be made about the position of a police officer. It is good practice to serve a witness summons on a police officer, as the officer may not attend trial to give evidence for any party in a civil action unless a summons has been served.

It is a matter for the lawyer's judgment whether to serve a witness summons on an expert witness. The most appropriate course of action is to ask the witness whether he wishes to be put under an obligation to attend. If the witness is a busy person with other commitments, the witness will find it easier to be available for the trial if a summons has been served.

DEALING WITH WITNESSES WHO ARE 'ABSENT' AT THE TRIAL

In some cases, when preparing for trial, a party's lawyer may decide that it will not be necessary for a witness to attend the court. This decision most commonly arises where, for example, the witness gives uncontroversial evidence and the admission of his statement in evidence may be agreed with the other side without the witness having to attend the trial.

Alternatively, as noted in Chapter 24, a party may serve a notice to admit facts on the other side. Where the facts are admitted, it will not be necessary for the witness who would testify about those facts to attend the trial. The procedure is governed by CPR rule 32.18, which provides that one party may serve notice on another party requiring that party to admit the facts specified in the notice. Notice must be served no later than 21 days before trial.

If the party admits the facts, the admission may only be used in the proceedings in question and any admission made under the notice procedure may be amended by the court or withdrawn as the court thinks fit. Where the fact is admitted, it is no longer in dispute between the parties and evidence will not be required at trial to prove the fact. Not only will this expedite the proceedings but it will also save the party the cost of proving that fact at trial.

Where the party does not admit the fact and the fact is subsequently proved at trial, the costs of proving the fact shall be awarded to the party which served the notice, irrespective of the outcome of the trial.

More commonly a party's witness may be unavailable to attend trial. In this situation the witness's evidence may be give as a hearsay statement by the party serving a 'section 2' notice under the Civil Evidence Act 1995. Where the witness's evidence is given as hearsay, the judge will apply the provisions of section 4 of the 1995 Act to assess the weight to be accorded to the statement including the reason for the witness not appearing at trial. For a detailed examination of the law relating to the admission of hearsay evidence in civil proceedings, see Chapter 29.

Alternatively, where a party's witness is unavailable to attend trial, he may take advantage of CPR rule 32.3. In order to save time and to reflect the wider objectives of the Civil Procedure Rules, CPR rule 32.3 permits a witness to give evidence at trial and be cross-examined through a video link or by any other appropriate technology. Where a party intends to make use of this provision, it must apply to the court in advance of the trial. In deciding the issue, the other party's views will be taken into account.

WHERE 'NEW' EVIDENCE ARISES

Even in the most well-managed civil case, it is not always possible for the party's lawyer to anticipate all potential developments. Cases often have a momentum of their own and it is not unusual for new evidence to come to light after the exchange of witness statements and the disclosure of documents. Where it is intended to use such evidence at trial, it will be necessary for the party to apply for leave to the court at the earliest opportunity so as to minimise the potential prejudice to the other side by being confronted with evidence at trial of which it has not been notified.

PREPARING DOCUMENTS FOR USE AT TRIAL

As saw in Chapter 25, an important stage in preparing for trial is the requirement that each party should serve on the other a list of the documents in its possession which are relevant to the action. Under CPR rule 32.19(1), the party receiving the list is deemed to admit the authenticity of the documents unless he serves a notice that he wishes the document's authenticity to be formally proved at trial.

The procedure for serving a notice to admit or produce documents is that a party to whom any document is disclosed under CPR Part 31 is deemed to have admitted the document's authenticity unless he serves a notice requiring the authenticity of the document to be proved at trial (CPR rule 32.19(1)). There is no requirement for the disclosing party to seek an admission of authenticity.

CPR rule 32.19(2) provides that the notice requiring a disclosed document to be proved at trial must be served:

- by the latest date for serving witness statements; or
- within seven days of disclosure of the document.

Where a party inappropriately challenges the authenticity of a document there is likely to be a costs penalty under CPR rule 44.5.

It is important to note that admitting the authenticity of a document is not the same as the party admitting to the truthfulness of the document's contents. The appropriate time to challenge the truthfulness of the document will be at trial where the document is put in evidence.

EVIDENCE IN PROCEEDINGS OTHER THAN AT TRIAL

In preparing for trial, it may be necessary for the party's lawyer to attend a pre-trial hearing. The general position is that evidence at hearings other than at trial will be given by witness statement, unless otherwise directed by the court or a Practice Direction under CPR rule 32.6. This rule applies to interim applications, for example, an application for summary judgment or an interim payment. Normally, in such proceedings a party will rely on the matters set out in its statement of case or its application notice if verified by a statement of truth.

Exceptionally, where a party intends to call a witness to give evidence at a hearing other than at the trial, a separate application will have to be made to the court for permission. CPR rule 32.7(1) provides that, at a hearing other than the trial, a party may apply for the witness to attend the hearing and to be cross-examined, and if the court gives permission under paragraph (1) and the witness does not attend the hearing, that witness's evidence can only be heard by permission of the court (CPR rule 32.7(2)), although in view of the wider objectives of the Civil Procedure Rules, the court's discretion under CPR rule 32.7(1) is exercised sparingly.

EVIDENCE BY AFFIDAVIT

There is a further exception to CPR rule 32.7(1) that evidence must be provided by an affidavit rather than a witness statement in the following instances (Practice Direction to Part 32, paragraph 1.4):

(1) where sworn evidence is required by any enactment, Statutory Instrument, rule, order or Practice Direction;

(2) in any application for a search order, a freezing injunction, or an order requiring an occupier to permit another to enter his land; and

(3) in any application for an order against anyone for alleged contempt of court.

The court may give a direction under CPR rule 32.15 that evidence shall be given by affidavit instead of or in addition to a witness statement or statement of case, either on its own initiative or after any party has applied to the court for such a direction.

Further reading

Case Comment, 'Excluding Evidence as a Procedural Sanction' [2000] Civil Justice Quarterly 207.

Hogan, A., 'Running with the Fast Track' (1999) 1(2) Civil Litigation 6.

Lightman, D., 'Delay and the Civil Procedure Rules' (2001) 15 The Lawyer 29.

Chapter 28

THE EVIDENTIAL ISSUES AT A CIVIL TRIAL

INTRODUCTION

This chapter is concerned with the rules of evidence and procedure relating to the examination of witnesses at a civil trial. Traditionally, any law of evidence text has dealt in detail with the evidential issues arising out of witness testimony in recognition of the primacy of the trial under the adversarial system. However, this emphasis on the operation of the evidential rules at trial has always been more appropriate to criminal cases than to civil proceedings as many civil cases are concluded by negotiation between the parties before the court is required to decide the issues of liability and/or quantum. Following the implementation of the Civil Procedure Rules with the procedural requirements of the pre-action protocols, the emphasis on alternative dispute resolution and the court's wide powers of case management under CPR Part 32, the operation of the traditional evidential rules at a civil trial have been further modified. This comment especially applies to 'fast track' cases, where the trial is likely to be listed to last for no longer than five hours and to be held on one day or to be part-heard over several days. As a result, many of the traditional practices, for example, in relation to witness testimony and the reception of expert evidence will be curtailed, although the trial of actions on the multi-track dealing with high-value cases or complex issues of law, fact or evidence will generally continue to be conducted along more traditional lines.

It is against the background of the philosophy and procedural requirements of the Civil Procedure Rules that the evidential issues arising out of the examination of witnesses at a civil trial are considered in this chapter.

EVIDENCE AT TRIALS IN THE SMALL CLAIMS TRACK

At small claims hearings in the county court the strict rules of evidence do not apply and by paragraph 4.3 of the Practice Direction to CPR Part 27, the district judge can adopt any method that he feels is 'fair'. In practice this gives the district judge considerable discretion to decide how the hearing is conducted and the approach of one district judge may differ to another both in terms of the degree of informality adopted at the hearing and the approach taken by each party in presenting its evidence to the court.

At the beginning of most hearings on the small claims track the district judge will identify the issues in dispute between the parties and will outline the way in which he expects those issues to be dealt with and a proposed timetable for the hearing. He may indicate, for example, that the claimant will have 30 minutes to present his evidence by calling his witnesses or reading their statements to the court. The defendant will be similarly allocated 30 minutes for the presentation of evidence. On the rare occasions where the court has appointed a 'joint' expert, the expert's oral or written evidence (usually written evidence) will be allocated 15 minutes with 10 minutes being allocated to the district judge to give his reasons for the decision.

EVIDENCE AT TRIALS ON THE FAST TRACK AND MULTI-TRACK

In most cases heard on the fast track and the multi-track, a trial timetable will have been fixed after filing questionnaires. The timetable might indicate which party should call its witnesses first and prescribe a time limit for the cross-examination and re-examination of each witness. As most trials on the fast track will be held in a local county court and listed for only five hours, the time limits imposed by the trial timetable will be closely followed. In many cases this will inevitably limit the number of witnesses to be called by each side, the length of time each party has to put its evidence to the court and the time that has been allocated for each party to make a closing speech.

ORDER OF PROCEEDINGS AT TRIAL

As we noted in Chapter 27, in spite of these fundamental changes to trial practice and procedure under the Civil Procedure Rules, CPR rule 32.2 preserves a fundamental principle of the English common law tradition by establishing the general rule that any fact which needs to be proved by the evidence of witnesses is to be proved at trial by their oral evidence given in public.

In practice, for those cases reaching trial there remains some reliance on the traditional position that evidence should be given orally, as under the former procedural regime. Where oral evidence is to be heard, the normal order of proceedings will begin by the claimant's advocate opening the proceedings unless the legal burden of proof lies with the defence on all the issues and therefore the defence advocate will have the right to begin.

In most cases if it is permitted by the judge on the day of the trial and is provided for in the trial timetable, the claimant's advocate will make an opening speech setting out the background to the case and the facts that remain in dispute between the parties. Reference will usually only be made to the essential parts of the statement of case and to any agreed plans, photographs or exhibits. During the opening speech the advocate will refer to his case summary.

At the close of the claimant's opening speech the defence advocate may be given an opportunity to address the court, although it is more likely that the claimant's advocate will call his first witness. The first witness will usually be the claimant, although, as a general rule, the order in which a party's evidence is called rests with the party's advocate. This principle has been confirmed in a number of cases including *Barnes v BPC* [1976] 1 All ER 237, where Phillips J sitting in the Employment Appeal Tribunal stated:

> Plainly solicitors and counsel are entitled to conduct within the rules of court or of proce-
> dure the proceedings as they think fit and in particular to call witnesses in the order they
> think fit and in particular to call witnesses in the order they wish … The parties and their
> advisers must be left to conduct the case as they think fit.

Where a witness is called to give oral evidence, subject to the judge's powers to control the evidence in the case, the witness's oral testimony will follow the traditional
order of examination-in-chief, cross-examination and re-examination. The evidential issues arising out of each stage of the witness's testimony will now be
considered.

EXAMINATION-IN-CHIEF

Examination-in-chief is traditionally the stage in the proceedings where the witness
is questioned by the advocate for the party calling him. In a civil case as in a
criminal case, the purpose of examination-in-chief is to elicit evidence from the
witness that supports or is favourable to that party. Before the claimant's advocate
may start to question the witness the court must be satisfied that the witness is
competent to testify. A witness is competent where as a matter of law his evidence
will be received by the court. Where a witness is competent he is also compellable,
ie where he refuses to enter the witness box or, having been sworn refuses to speak
or to answer any questions properly put to him, the court may hold him to be in
contempt of court. This is not to say that a compellable witness should answer every
question put to him. He may properly decline to answer if, for example, the answer
would tend to incriminate him or his spouse in a criminal offence or the subject
matter of the question is covered by legal professional privilege. These matters are
dealt with in Chapter 26.

The general rule in civil proceedings is that all adult witnesses are competent and
compellable to give sworn oral evidence including the claimant and the defendant.
Where there is a doubt about the competence of an adult witness, the party's lawyers
should have anticipated and dealt with the problem at an early stage in the proceedings and a long time before the trial. Witnesses whose competency to give evidence at
the trial may be questioned are as follows:

* the spouse of a party to the action;
* the former spouse of the defendant;
* Sovereigns, Heads of State and diplomats;
* bankers;
* child witnesses; and
* mentally ill or handicapped witnesses.

Competency and compellability of witnesses

A party's spouse

Under section 1 of the Evidence Amendment Act 1853 a party's spouse is competent
and compellable to give evidence in civil proceedings.

A former spouse

The common law provided a number of exceptions to the general rule that all adult witnesses were competent and compellable to give evidence in civil proceedings. At various times convicts, non-Christians and atheists as well as those with a pecuniary interest in the outcome of the proceedings were regarded as incompetent. Whilst each of these historical relics have been swept away by judicial or legislative reform, one exception appears to remain. Following the termination of the marriage, a former spouse of one of the parties is incompetent to give evidence about matters that arose during the subsistence of the marriage. In *Monroe v Twistleton* (1802) Peake Add Cas 219, the court held that the plaintiff could not call the divorced wife of the defendant to prove a contract allegedly concluded during the subsistence of the marriage. The rule was subsequently followed in *O'Connor v Majoribanks* (1842) 4 Man & G 435. It remains uncertain whether the rule remains good law. One approach is to suggest that it was reformed by the Evidence Amendment Act 1853, by which the spouses of the parties are rendered competent and compellable witnesses. As a matter of statutory construction it might be possible to extend the meaning of the words 'husband' and 'wife' in the 1853 Act to include a former husband and wife, in which case the decision in *Monroe v Twistleton* no longer applies.

Sovereigns, Heads of State and diplomats

A witness who falls into one of these categories will be competent but not compellable to give evidence.

Bankers

A bank employee is a competent but not compellable witness to give evidence in a case where the bank is not a party to the proceedings. The immunity also prevents the witness from producing original bank books and records relating to the case. Under the Bankers' Books Evidence Act 1879 a copy of the bank's records will be admissible without the need to call bank personnel to verify the records.

Child witnesses

A 'child' is defined in civil proceedings as a person under the age of 18 by section 105 of the Children Act 1989. A child may give sworn or unsworn evidence, depending on his age, maturity and understanding. The test for determining whether the child is competent to give sworn evidence is borrowed from criminal proceedings and is based on the test laid down in *R v Hayes* [1977] 1 All ER 288:

> ... whether the child has sufficient appreciation of the solemnity of the occasion and the added responsibility to tell the truth, which is involved in taking an oath over and above the duty to tell the truth which is an ordinary duty of normal social conduct.

To determine the child's competency to give sworn evidence, the judge will ask the child a number of preliminary questions to form an opinion about his or her maturity and understanding. As the issue of the child's competence will be determined by a number of factors related to the child's personal circumstances and the facts of the particular case, the courts are reluctant to lay down 'hard' rules about the minimum age at which a child will be competent to give sworn evidence, although following the precedent in criminal cases, it will be unlikely that a child under 14 years of age will be capable of giving sworn evidence at a civil trial.

Where the child fails the *Hayes* test, the provisions of section 96 of the Children Act 1989 apply:

(1) Subsection (2) applies where a child who is called as a witness in any civil proceedings does not, in the opinion of the court, understand the nature of the oath.
(2) The child's evidence may be heard by the court if, in its opinion—
(a) he understands that it is his duty to speak the truth; and
(b) he has sufficient understanding to justify his evidence being heard.

A child witness may therefore give unsworn evidence if, in the opinion of the judge, the child is possessed of sufficient intelligence to justify the reception of the evidence and understands the duty of speaking the truth in the normal way of social conduct. As with the procedure to decide the test of sworn evidence, there is likely to be an initial inquiry by the judge to see how intelligent the child is by the judge asking him questions in the normal way. Once again, it is not possible to say what is the minimum age at which a child will be deemed to be competent to give unsworn evidence as the issue will be decided on the child's personal development, the nature of the case and the extent of the child's involvement in the events giving rise to the litigation. However, it is unlikely that a child less than five or six years old will be capable of giving coherent, unsworn evidence.

Mentally ill or handicapped witnesses

In former times the test to be applied to decide the competence of a mentally incapacitated witness was found in *R v Hill* (1851) 2 Den 254 where it was established that if, in the opinion of the judge, a witness called by one of the parties did not understand the nature and sanctity of the oath because of his mental impairment, he was incompetent to testify. Where it was decided that the witness was competent, it was up to the court to decide how much weight should be attached to his oral testimony. The court had discretion to disregard it altogether where the testimony was so tainted with insanity as to be incomprehensible.

The modern law takes a more pragmatic view in deciding whether a witness with a mental incapacity is capable of giving oral testimony, and as in the case of a child witness, the *Hayes* test is likely to form the basis of the judge's inquiry. The judge will approach the issue on the basis of whether the person is capable of understanding the solemnity of the occasion, the importance of telling the truth and of giving intelligible testimony. Where the witness is deemed competent he may give evidence on any issue.

Oath and affirmation

The general requirement in civil proceedings is that all witnesses should give sworn evidence and therefore, before the examination-in-chief of a competent witness, it will be necessary for him either to take the oath or to affirm. A judgment founded on a witness's unsworn evidence (other than that of a child) may be set aside as a nullity.

The general rule is subject to four exceptions where a witness may give evidence without having been sworn or affirmed:

1 hearings in the small claims track where it is not necessary for a witness to give sworn evidence (CPR rule 27.8(4));
2 the unsworn evidence of a child where he has failed the *Hayes* test as described above;
3 a witness called to produce a document may give unsworn evidence if the document's identity is either not in dispute or is to be proven by another witness (*Perry v Gibson* (1834) 1 Ad & El 48); and
4 a party's advocate may give unsworn evidence of the terms of a compromise reached by the parties (*Hickman v Berens* [1895] 2 Ch 638).

In all other situations before a witness begins to give sworn evidence he will be given the Bible and a card with the words of the oath printed as following:

> I swear by Almighty God that the evidence I shall give shall be the truth, the whole truth and nothing but the truth.

These words, which are to be found in section 1(1) of the Oaths Act 1978, govern the testimony of Christians and Jews. If the witness objects to this form of swearing an alternative oath affirmation will be offered to him. For those of other religious beliefs, section 1(3) of the 1978 Act provides that the oath shall be taken 'in any lawful manner'.

The 1978 Act goes on to recognise the secular nature of modern society by providing that where a witness gives sworn evidence, it is not the divine sanction for lying on oath which is considered to be important, but rather the legal sanction of a conviction for perjury. Therefore section 4(2) of the Oaths Act 1978 provides:

> Where an oath has been duly administered and taken, the fact that the person to whom it was administered had, at the time of taking it, no religious belief, shall not for any purpose affect the validity of the oath.

When a person is called as a witness and objects to being sworn, provision is made under the Act for an alternative method of binding the witness. Section 5 of the Oaths Act 1978 states:

> (1) Any person who objects to being sworn shall be permitted to make his solemn affirmation instead of taking the oath.
>
> . . .
>
> (4) A solemn affirmation shall be of the same force and effect as an oath.

The affirmation is:

> I, [*full name*] do solemnly, sincerely, and truly declare and affirm that the evidence I shall give shall be the truth, the whole truth and nothing but the truth.

A witness who affirms and then gives false evidence is committing perjury (1978 Act, section 5(4) above).

Witness testimony in examination-in-chief

The court, as part of its case management powers, is given wide powers to control the evidence in the case by giving directions as to the issues on which it requires evidence, the nature of the evidence which it requires to decide those issues and the way in which the evidence is to be placed before the court (CPR rule 32.1). This includes allowing a witness to give evidence through a video link or by other means, where the court considers it appropriate to do so (CPR rule 32.3). The court may further exclude evidence that is otherwise admissible and/or may limit cross-examination (*Grobbelaar* v *Sun Newspapers Ltd* (1999) *The Times*, 12 August). Therefore the traditional practice and procedure during examination-in-chief should be considered in conjunction with the court's case management powers in accordance with the overriding objective in CPR Part 1 and the court's powers to control the evidence in the case under CPR rule 32.1.

Where a witness is called to give evidence, his evidence-in-chief will begin with the witness telling the court his name, age and address. At this preliminary stage, leading questions may be asked as the matters are not in dispute between the parties. After the preliminary issues have been dealt with, the witness's written statement shall stand as his evidence-in-chief unless the court orders otherwise (CPR rule 32.5(2)). In exercising this power, in order to expedite the court proceedings, the judge may require the witness to swear as to the truth of his witness statement, which will have been exchanged with the other side before trial. After having sworn his statement as required, the witness will then be available for cross-examination. If the advocate requires the witness to add or to amplify on any issue arising out of his written statement the leave of the court must be obtained before the witness can add to his evidence or give evidence in relation to new matters which have arisen since the witness statement was served on the other parties.

In other cases it may be appropriate for the witness to give his examination-in-chief by oral evidence. This will give the judge the opportunity to consider the witness's demeanour, to form an impression about the accuracy and reliability of his factual evidence and to assess his credibility. Where the court permits the witness to give his evidence-in-chief orally or grants leave for the witness to be asked further questions, the following issues may arise during examination-in-chief.

EVIDENTIAL ISSUES ARISING OUT OF EXAMINATION-IN-CHIEF

Leading questions during examination-in-chief

The general rule is that during the examination-in-chief, the party's advocate cannot ask the witness leading questions. A leading question is either a question which assumes the existence of disputed facts that have yet to be established or asserted or is a question which suggests to the witness the answer to be given. The reason for not allowing leading questions is that the witness may be coached to give answers favourable to the side calling him or by answering leading questions by saying 'yes' or 'no', without the need for further elaboration in his own words. As an illustration of the rule, consider the following examples.

Examples

In an action for damages arising out of a road traffic accident, the advocate asks the witness: 'The defendant was driving his car too quickly wasn't he?'

In an action for assault and battery, the advocate asks the witness: 'On the night of the attack did the defendant hit the claimant around the face?'

In each of the above examples, the advocate is clearly leading the witness to give the answer the advocate requires. Where leading questions are asked, the judge will intervene and ask the advocate to put the questions again to the witness in an acceptable way.

There are a number of exceptions to this general rule where leading questions may be asked during examination-in-chief. These exceptions primarily relate to formal, introductory or collateral matters at the beginning of examination-in-chief as well as in relation to an issue not in dispute between the parties or on an issue that has been agreed between the parties. As we shall see later in this chapter, leading questions may also be asked where the party's witness has been ruled as 'hostile' by the judge to the party calling him.

Refreshing memory during examination-in-chief

In many civil cases there is a considerable delay between the events giving rise to the cause of action and the case coming to trial. As a result, many witnesses, including 'professional' witnesses such as police officers, are unlikely to have instant recall of significant parts of their evidence. As the purpose of a witness testifying in court is to test the accuracy and credibility of his knowledge of the facts in the case, a witness is permitted to refresh his memory at two stages – out of court before giving evidence and in court whilst giving evidence.

Out of court before giving evidence

It is common practice in civil proceedings for a witness to refresh his memory from his proof of evidence or from his personal notes before going into the witness box. There are no detailed rules regulating the use by a witness of a memory refreshing document before giving evidence as such rules would be unenforceable. However, where a witness has refreshed his memory out of court before giving evidence, the criminal case of *Owen v Edwards* (1983) 77 Cr App R 191 is authority for the point that the other party's advocate and the judge are entitled to inspect and cross-examine the witness on the memory refreshing document. This provision has become less important since the introduction of the compulsory pre-trial exchange of witness statements as in most cases the cross-examiner will have a copy of the witness's memory refreshing document in his trial bundle.

Where in cross-examination new issues are raised which were not referred to by the witness during examination-in-chief, the party calling the witness may put the memory refreshing document in evidence as part of its case under section 6(4) and (5) of the Civil Evidence Act 1995.

In court whilst giving evidence

A witness may refresh his memory during examination-in-chief from the witness box and also when testifying by a live television or video link. The law relating to the use of a memory refreshing document must now be considered from two perspectives depending on whether the document was made 'contemporaneously' to the events giving rise to the case or a 'non-contemporaneous' document.

A document created 'contemporaneously'

Traditionally, the law has recognised that a witness should be allowed to refresh his memory from a document that was created or verified by the witness when the events were fresh in his memory. In *Steinkellor v Newton* (1838) 9 C & P 313, the court stated that a witness may refresh his memory from a document written by the witness if it can be 'shown that the paper was written contemporaneously with the transaction it refers to'. Three conditions will have to be satisfied before a witness will be able refresh his memory from a contemporaneous document:

- the document was made or verified by the witness while the events were still fresh in the mind of the witness;
- the document must have been made by the witness himself, or supervised or verified by him immediately afterwards; and
- the document is produced in court for inspection by the other parties and the judge.

Where the original is not available, the witness may use a copy. This rule was recognised long before documents could be reproduced by photocopying or computers. In *Lord Talbot de Malahide v Cussack* (1864) 17 CLR 213, W1 made a memorandum of a transaction, which W2 copied. The original was lost and the court allowed W1 to refresh his memory from the copy on the basis that W1 had checked the copy to verify the accuracy of its contents. The question whether the document was made or verified whilst the matters were fresh in the witness's mind is determined on the facts of each case. When preparing the witness to refer to the document during examination-in-chief, the advocate should confirm with the witness that the document was made or verified whilst the events were still fresh in his mind. Whilst it is likely that a delay of a few hours will be acceptable, a much longer delay will not satisfy the requirement for contemporaneity, although the courts approach this issue with a degree of flexibility.

These observations must be read in conjunction with *Anderson v Whalley* (1852) 3 Car & Kir 54 and *Topham v McGregor* (1844) 1 Car & Kir 320. In *Anderson* entries made by a ship's log by the first mate and not verified by the captain until a week later could be used to refresh the captain's memory. In *Topham*, the author of an article written 14 years earlier was allowed to refresh his memory from a copy of the newspaper in which it had appeared as the article had been written whilst the events were still fresh in the writer's mind.

The memory refreshing document does not have to have been made by the witness. It is sufficient that its contents have been verified or confirmed by the witness. In *Burrough v Martin* (1809) 2 Camp 112, a captain who had inspected his ship's log throughout the voyage was allowed to refresh his memory from it although the entries had been made by another crew member. It is vital however that the witness should check the accuracy of the entries whilst the events were fresh in his mind and the criminal case of *R v Eleftheriou* [1993] Crim LR 947 is a salutary warning of the consequences when the witness does not verify the document. In *R v Eleftheriou*, Customs and Excise officers were observing premises and working in pairs. One of the officers would call out what he saw whilst the other officer wrote it down. At trial the officer who was calling out the information admitted that he looked up from time-to-time and saw his colleague recording large amounts of information. However, he did not verify what the writer had recorded and therefore the court ruled that the officer could not refresh his memory from the document. The officer who recorded the information could not give oral evidence on the matter as he did not have personal knowledge of the events recorded in the document and therefore his evidence would be hearsay.

If *R v Eleftheriou* had been a civil case, the document could have been admitted as hearsay evidence under section 1 of the Civil Evidence Act 1995, although the lack of verification by the observer of the document's contents would mean that the judge would give little weight to the evidence under section 4 of the 1995 Act.

A non-contemporaneous document

Where a witness has begun to give evidence he is also permitted to refresh his memory from a document that was made near in time to the events in question, even though the document does not come within the ordinary meaning of contemporaneous. This rule derives from the criminal case of *R v Da Silva* [1990] 1 WLR 31, where a prosecution witness had started to give evidence about an incident a year earlier but could not remember what had happened. The judge allowed the witness to withdraw from the witness box and refer to a document that had been made about a month after the incident. The Court of Appeal confirmed that the judge had discretion to allow a witness to refresh his memory from a non-contemporaneous document made nearer to the time of the incident. The witness could refer to the document whilst giving evidence provided the judge is satisfied:

- that the witness indicates that he cannot now recall the details of events because of the lapse of time since the events took place;
- that the statement was made much nearer to the time of the events and that the contents of the statement represented the witness's recollection at the time it was made;
- that the witness has not read the statement before coming into the witness box; and
- that the witness wishes to have an opportunity to read the statement before continuing to give evidence.

The main difference between a contemporaneous and a non-contemporaneous document is that a witness can refresh his memory from a contemporaneous document throughout the time that he is in the witness box. A non-contemporaneous document must be removed from the witness once he has started to give evidence again and no further reference may be made to it.

Cross-examination on the memory refreshing document

Where the other party's advocate merely inspects the document that has been used to refresh the witness's memory either outside court before giving evidence or whilst testifying, the document does not become part of the evidence in the case. The same principle applies where the advocate cross-examines the witness on those parts of the document that were raised in examination-in-chief. However, where the advocate goes on to cross-examine the witness on the other parts of the document, it becomes part of the evidence of the party calling the witness and the document can be put before the judge who may take a note of the whole of its contents even though it will contain hearsay evidence. The evidence will be admitted at trial under section 6(4) and (5) of the Civil Evidence Act 1995, which generally makes admissible any hearsay evidence contained in a document.

Section 6(4) and (5) provides:

> (4) Nothing in this Act affects any of the rules of law as to the circumstances in which, where a person called as a witness in civil proceedings is cross-examined on a document used by him to refresh his memory, that document may be made evidence in those proceedings.
>
> (5) Nothing in this section shall be construed as preventing a statement of any description referred to above from being admissible by virtue of section 1 as evidence of matters stated.

Where the memory refreshing document is admitted in evidence under section 6(4) and (5) it can be used to show the consistency of the witness's testimony as well as being evidence in its own right to prove the truth of the matters asserted as it is a hearsay statement for the purposes of the Civil Evidence Act 1995. In practice the importance of this provision should not be overestimated. It merely means that another piece of evidence will be heard from the witness to add to his oral testimony. It is matter for the judge to decide what, if any, weight, he gives to the witness's 'additional' evidence.

Unfavourable and hostile witnesses

At an early stage in the proceedings a party's solicitor will have taken a proof of evidence from each witness, which will contain the basis of the evidence that the witness will give to the court if the case proceeds to trial. In examination-in-chief where the witness's oral evidence in court largely reflects the content of his proof, the witness is regarded as 'coming up to proof'.

However, it is quite common for a witness during examination-in-chief not to give the answers expected of him by his examiner or to give evidence unfavourable to the party calling him. A witness who displays these tendencies is known as an 'unfavourable' witness. If the witness cannot recollect some fact, the advocate cannot assist him by putting leading questions, and will be frustrated that his witness's answers are unhelpful. It is not permitted for the witness's written statement to be put to him, nor can his examiner attack the credibility of his witness's evidence. At common law, all that can be done to retrieve the situation is to call other witnesses to give evidence on those matters that the unfavourable witness was expected to testify about. This principle is illustrated by *Ewer v Ambrose* (1825) 3 B & C 746, in which a witness called by the defendant to prove a certain partnership, gave evidence to the contrary. The judge ruled that all that the party could do was to call other witnesses to contradict the unfavourable witness's evidence.

Where a witness not only fails to come up to proof but gives evidence which is unfavourable to the side calling him, and shows, in the opinion of the judge, that he has no desire to tell the truth, he may be treated as a 'hostile' witness. His 'hostility' may be caused by some factor such as bribery, or merely by some animosity towards his examiner. Where the witness appears to be hostile, the examiner must apply to the judge for leave for the witness to be ruled as hostile. If necessary, the judge may be shown the witness's earlier statement to confirm his inconsistency. If the judge rules the witness as hostile and grants leave, the witness's credibility may be undermined in a number of ways.

First, at common law, the party calling the witness may ask the witness leading questions and cross-examine him by putting the client's version of events to the witness (*Rice v Howard* (1886) 16 QBD 681; *Price v Manning* (1889) 42 Ch D 372). Secondly, under section 3 of the Criminal Procedure Act 1865, which applies to both civil and criminal proceedings, the advocate can ask the witness whether or not he has made an earlier statement that is inconsistent with his present oral testimony. Where the witness agrees his earlier written statement or parts of it as the truth, then, in effect, he is adopting that version as being his evidence, subject to an assessment of his credibility by the court. The oral evidence he has given earlier has no evidential value.

If the witness denies making the earlier statement, the statement can be shown to him, and he can be asked to explain his inconsistency. The matter is then governed by section 6(3) of the Civil Evidence Act 1995, which states:

> Where in the case of civil proceedings section 3, 4, or 5 of the Criminal Procedure Act 1865 applies, which make provisions as to—
> (a) how far a witness may be discredited by the party producing him,
> (b) the proof of contradictory statements made by a witness, and
> (c) cross-examination as to previous statements in writing,
> this Act does not authorise the adducing of evidence of a previous inconsistent or contradictory statement otherwise than in accordance with those sections.

The effect of section 6(3) is that the judge can choose between the two versions of the witness's evidence, ie his out-of-court statement or his oral evidence and decide which version he believes. In exercising this choice, the judge will take into account a number of factors including the witness's demeanour, the reason for him denying making the previous statement, and the existence of any animosity between the witness and the party calling him. In many cases, the judge may disregard the witness's evidence entirely on the basis that by displaying hostility to the party calling him, he has destroyed his credibility in the eyes of the court.

Finally, it may not always be clear whether the witness is 'unfavourable' or 'hostile'. The courts handle the issue with caution. For example, in the criminal case of *R v Maw* [1994] Crim LR 841, the Court of Appeal said that in many cases where the witness has departed from his proof of evidence, it is undesirable for the court to proceed immediately to treat the witness as hostile. A better approach is to invite the witness to refresh his memory from the proof. If the witness does not allow his memory to be refreshed or does not give an explanation as to why his oral evidence is different from his proof, the court can then consider treating the witness as hostile.

As an illustration of the way in which the law relating to unfavourable and hostile witnesses operates, consider the following example.

Example

David is suing Brian for assault and battery. In her proof of evidence, Sandra, Brian's estranged wife, states that on the night of the assault she saw Brian go up to David and punch him three times in the stomach. At trial, in examination-in-chief, Sandra testifies that Brian did not hit David and after the attack the real assailant ran away into the night.

By taking the incremental approach adopted in R v Maw, the advocate may ask Sandra to refresh her memory from her proof of evidence. If the proof was made contemporaneously with the events, Sandra may continue to refer to the document whilst testifying. If the statement was not contemporaneous, it will be taken from Sandra after she has refreshed her memory.

The advocate may put the question again to Sandra. If Sandra continues to state that she did not see Brian assaulting David the advocate may conclude that she shows no desire to tell the truth. The advocate will apply to the judge to have Sandra ruled as hostile.

If the judge rules Sandra as hostile, the advocate may ask her leading questions and, under section 3 of the Criminal Procedure Act 1865, cross-examine Sandra as to whether she has made an earlier statement that is inconsistent with her present oral evidence. If Sandra adopts the earlier written statement (or parts of it) as her evidence, the oral evidence that she has given at trial has no probative value. Unlike in a criminal case, if Sandra adopts her written statement, it will be admissible as evidence of the truth of its contents as an exception to the hearsay rule as well as being relevant to the judge's assessment of her credibility.

If Sandra denies making the previous statement, the advocate may show Sandra her written statement and ask her to explain the inconsistency between her statement and her present oral evidence. The judge can then choose between the two versions of Sandra's evidence and decide which version he believes. In choosing which version, the judge may take into account a number of factors including Sandra's demeanour and the reason for her showing animosity to the party calling her. The judge may disregard Sandra's evidence altogether or give very little weight to it after assessing her credibility.

Making a submission of no case to answer

At the close of the claimant's case, the defence may make a submission of no case to answer where no case has been established in law by the claimant's evidence or where the claimant's evidence is so unreliable or unsatisfactory that the burden of proof has not been discharged (*Young* v *Rank* [1950] 2 KB 510). In practice, it is unusual for a civil trial to proceed to the point where it would be possible for a party to make a successful submission, as any potential weaknesses in the claimant's case should have been identified and dealt with at the pre-trial stage. However in those exceptional cases where a submission of no case to answer is made at a civil trial, *Mullan* v *Birmingham City Council* (1999) *The Times*, 29 July provides an illustration of the court's approach to such matters under the Civil Procedure Rules.

In *Mullan*, the claimant sued the defendant for personal injuries after having fallen on premises owned by the defendant. At the close of the claimant's case, the defendant invited the judge to consider the submission of no case to answer without requiring the defendant to decide whether or not to give evidence. Foskett J, sitting in the Divisional Court, held that the court had wide powers of case management under the Civil Procedure Rules at all stages of the proceedings to deal with the case expeditiously and fairly and to allot an appropriate share of the court's resources to it and to act in a way designed to reduce expense. CPR rule 3.1(2)(m) gave the court the power to take any step or make any order it thought fit for the purpose of managing the case and in pursuance of the overriding objective. First, in order to make a successful submission of no case to answer, it was necessary for the defendant to establish that the claimant had no reasonable chance of succeeding. There was no case to answer on the facts. By the close of the claimant's case the judge had formed the view that the claimant was not a reliable witness of fact. Secondly, the more flexible approach to case management under the Civil Procedure Rules enabled the court to decide that there was no case to answer without requiring the defendant council to give evidence, although it could have been required to do so if it had been in the 'best interests' of the case.

CROSS-EXAMINATION

Subject to the court's overriding powers to control the evidence in the case under CPR rule 32.1, each party has the right to cross-examine the other party's witnesses. CPR rule 32.11 allows a witness to be cross-examined on his witness statement whether or not the statement or any part of it was referred to during the witness's evidence-in-chief.

To remind you, the purpose of cross-examination is:

- to challenge the other party's witnesses on their factual evidence or on their opinion evidence; and
- to undermine the witness's credibility in the opinion of the fact finder.

Therefore questions in cross-examination may be directed to:

- a fact in issue in the case; or
- to undermine the witness's credibility in the opinion of the fact finder.

Cross-examining the witness on his factual evidence

Under the normal rules of witness testimony the advocate is under a duty to challenge in cross-examination those parts of the witness's factual evidence that contradict his party's case. A failure to cross-examine a witness on his factual evidence will be taken as an acceptance of the witness's evidence-in-chief on that particular issue and in his closing speech the advocate will not be allowed to attack the part of the witness's evidence that he did not attempt to contradict in cross-examination.

Where it is intended to contradict the witness on his factual evidence, the cross-examiner should put his party's version of the facts so as to give the witness an opportunity to explain the contradiction. In challenging the witness's answer in cross-examination about a fact in issue, it may be contradicted by the advocate questioning the witness or by calling further evidence.

Example

At the trial of an action for personal injuries arising out of an accident in the workplace, Frank, the defendant's safety manager, states in examination-in-chief that the company has safely used a specified system of work for the last five years, without any of its employees being injured. If it is part of the claimant's case that the system of work has not been safely implemented for the last five years, the claimant's advocate is under a duty in cross-examination to contradict Frank's evidence on this point by putting to him that the defendant company has not safely used this system of work as stated by Frank in his evidence-in-chief.

If the claimant's advocate fails to raise this issue in cross-examination, the claimant will be deemed to accept Frank's evidence on this point and it will not be possible for the advocate to contradict Frank's evidence in his closing speech.

Cross-examining witnesses on issues relating to their credibility

As well as attempting to undermine the factual evidence given by the witness during examination-in-chief, the cross-examiner may also seek to undermine the witness's personal credibility in order to persuade the fact finder that the witness ought not be believed on oath. This may be achieved by highlighting any inconsistencies between the witness's oral testimony at trial and a previous written or oral statement, or by raising general issues about the witness's credibility, or by cross-examining the witness on a range of collateral issues. Each of these provisions will now be considered.

Previous inconsistent statements

An effective way of undermining the witness's credibility presents itself when, at trial, the witness gives oral evidence that is inconsistent with his previous written or oral statement. The rule relating to the witness's previous inconsistent statement operates during cross-examination in the same way as the procedure to be adopted where a party's own witness is ruled hostile during examination-in-chief and gives the cross-examiner a number of options as to how to proceed. The first option is provided by section 4 of the Criminal Procedure Act 1865 and will apply where the advocate knows that the witness has made a previous oral or written statement that is inconsistent with his present oral testimony. Section 4 states:

> If a witness upon cross-examination as to a former statement made by him relative to the subject-matter of the indictment or proceeding and inconsistent with his present testimony, does not directly admit that he has made such a statement, proof may be given that he did in fact make it; but before such proof can be given the circumstances of the supposed statement, sufficient to designate the particular occasion, must be mentioned to the witness, and he must be asked whether or not he had made such a statement.

A literal interpretation of section 4 suggests that the section applies to the witness's previous oral or written statement as well as to a statement contained in an audiotape or videotape as the Act refers generally to the witness's 'former statement'. In most cases, section 4 will be used where the witness has made a previous oral statement as section 5 of the 1865 Act applies specifically where the witness's previous statement is in writing.

The effect of section 4 is that where the witness denies having previously made an oral statement which is inconsistent with his present oral testimony, the advocate must put to the witness the circumstances in which the alleged statement was made and then ask the witness whether he ever made such a statement. Where the witness denies that he has made an earlier statement inconsistent with his present testimony, the cross-examining party may prove that the previous statement was made, by calling a witness who heard the oral statement or by producing the written statement. It does not matter whether the previous inconsistent statement was made on oath or not. Where the previous inconsistent statement is admitted in evidence it will not only undermine the witness's credibility but, under section 6(5) of the Civil Evidence Act 1995, the statement may also be put in evidence as a true record of the events about which the witness is testifying.

An alternative procedure that can be adopted in cross-examination where the witness gives oral evidence inconsistent with his earlier written statement is provided by section 5 of the 1865 Act, which states:

> A witness may be cross-examined as to previous statements made by him in writing, or reduced in writing, relative to the subject-matter of the indictment or proceeding, without such writing being shown to him; but if it is intended to contradict such witness by the writing, his attention must, before such contradictory proof can be given, be called to those parts of the writing which are used for the purpose of so contradicting him: Provided always, that it shall be competent for the judge, at any time during the trial, to require the production of the writing for his inspection, and he may thereupon make such use of it for the purposes of the trial as he may think fit.

The section covers 'previous statements made ... in writing, or reduced in writing' to include not only the witness's written proof of evidence but also where the statement is contained, for example, in an accident report book or in the case of fatal accidents litigation, an inquest deposition. Section 5 gives the cross-examiner an element of surprise because the witness can be asked about those parts of his written statement that are inconsistent with his oral evidence without being shown his statement. If the witness continues to deny his previous statement and the advocate wishes to contradict the witness by using it, he must draw the witness's attention to those parts of his statement that are inconsistent with his oral testimony. This is usually done by the witness reading the relevant parts of the statement. The witness will then be asked which version of his evidence he wishes to be put before the court.

Where the witness decides to rely on what he said during examination-in-chief, the advocate has succeeded in showing the witness's inconsistency and therefore his credibility as a witness will invariably be diminished. Where the witness relies on his written statement contradicting his oral testimony, the previous statement may be admitted in evidence under section 6(5) of the Civil Evidence Act 1995. Under section 6(1) of the 1995 Act the statement becomes evidence of the facts in question and the judge is required to decide which version of events to believe or whether to disregard the witness's evidence altogether on the basis of his inherent unreliability.

Cross-examination on the witness's general credibility

The witness may be cross-examined to undermine his general credibility in the eyes of the judge, although the questions that may be asked are closely controlled by a number of factors. First, cross-examination on the witness's general credibility is subject to the court's power to control the evidence in the case as well as to the requirement that the trial should be conducted in compliance with the overriding objective of the Civil

Procedure Rules. Secondly, it should be remembered that the witness's credibility is a collateral issue in that it is only indirectly related to the main purpose of the trial which is to decide the issue of liability and/or quantum. The general rule at common law is that the answers a witness gives to a collateral issue should be final to prevent the cross-examining party from adducing evidence to contradict the answer the witness gives. This is referred to as the 'finality' rule. If the finality rule did not apply, a lot of valuable time would be taken up at the trial in considering issues that were not strictly relevant to deciding the case. Thirdly, the advocate is not permitted to go on a 'fishing expedition' where the sole purpose is to denigrate the witness's character gratuitously. Guidance as to how the courts must approach the issue can be found in Lord Justice Sankey's judgment in *Hobbs v Tinling* [1929] 2 KB 1.

> In allowing questions directed to undermining the witness's general credibility, the judge should have regard to the following considerations which are based on section 148 of the Indian Evidence Act 1872:
> (1) Such questions are proper if they are of such a nature that the truth of the imputation conveyed by them would seriously affect the opinion of the court as to the credibility of the witness on the matters to which he testifies. (2) Such questions are improper if the imputation which they convey relates to matters so remote in time, or of such a character, that the truth of the imputation would not affect, or would affect in a slight degree, the opinion of the court as to the credibility of the witness on the matters to which he testifies. (3) Such questions are improper if there is a great disproportion between the importance of the imputation made against the witness's character and the importance of his evidence.

Cross-examination on collateral matters – exceptions to the finality rule

As well as attempting to undermine the witness's credibility by raising the issue of his previous inconsistent statement and cross-examining him on his general credibility, there are a number of collateral issues, where, as exceptions to the general rule, the answer the witness gives during cross-examination may not be taken as final and where evidence contradicting the witness's reply may be admitted. The exceptions to the finality rule cover the following matters:

- where the witness has previous convictions;
- where the witness is biased;
- evidence of the physical or mental condition of the witness to show his unreliability; and
- where the witness has a reputation for untruthfulness.

Where the witness has previous convictions

The position in civil proceedings is governed by section 6 of the Criminal Procedure Act 1865 which provides that a witness may be questioned as to whether he has been convicted of any crime, and upon being questioned, if he either denies or does not admit the fact, or refuses to answer, it shall be lawful for the cross-examining party to prove such conviction.

A conviction for some offences will carry more weight in undermining the witness's credibility than other offences. Dishonesty offences under the Theft Acts 1968 and 1978 as well as perjury will be the most persuasive in undermining the witness's credibility as well as a conviction for a serious offence such as murder or rape. Cross-examination will not be allowed on a minor conviction where it comes within the restrictions imposed by section 4(1) of the Rehabilitation of Offenders Act 1974 preventing a witness from being asked a question about a 'spent' conviction.

Where the witness is biased

Whilst it is unlikely that few witnesses are truly independent because they know one of the parties or they support the case of the party calling them, this will not normally provoke the cross-examiner to accuse them of being biased. The exception to the finality rule will be invoked where a witness claims to be independent or impartial but where his conduct clearly shows that he is biased or in some way lacks impartiality. Where in cross-examination the witness denies that he is biased, evidence rebutting the witness's denial may be called by the cross-examiner. For example, in *Thomas v David* (1836) 7 Car & P 350, the witness denied being the plaintiff's mistress and rebutting evidence was allowed. In the criminal case of *R v Mendy* (1977) 64 Cr App R 4, the husband of the accused was waiting outside the courtroom until he was called to testify on her behalf. After he had been called and had given his evidence-in-chief, counsel for the prosecution asked him whether he had been told what other witnesses had said. The husband denied that before he entered the courtroom he had spoken to a man who had been seen in the public gallery taking notes of what earlier witnesses had said. Counsel was allowed to rebut this by calling a witness who had seen the man in conversation with the husband just before he entered the courtroom.

Evidence of the physical or mental condition of the witness to show his unreliability

If it is alleged that the witness suffers from a mental or physical infirmity that may affect the reliability of his evidence, he can be cross-examined on this matter to undermine his credibility. It is also open to a party to show through expert medical evidence that the witness is suffering from a mental or physical disability that undermines the reliability of his testimony.

Example

Where the witness testifies to hearing a conversation between the claimant and the defendant, the defence advocate can introduce expert medical evidence that the witness is partially deaf. The effect of such evidence will obviously undermine the witness's credibility.

The exception only operates in respect of a recognised mental or physical ailment or disability. Allegations that the witness is deluded or has a fertile imagination will not be admissible. Where a party wishes to undermine the witness's credibility in this way, it will be done through the normal stages of witness testimony and it will be up to the court to decide the issue on the evidence that is presented.

Reputation for untruthfulness

It is permitted in cross-examination to suggest to the witness that he has a reputation for untruthfulness. If the witness denies the suggestion, the cross-examiner may call a person who knows the witness to give evidence of witness's general reputation but not the reasons why the witness is regarded as untruthful.

RE-EXAMINATION

The third stage of witness testimony is re-examination, where the party calling the witness will be entitled to ask further questions. It will only be available where a witness has been examined-in-chief. Whether an advocate makes use of the opportunities provided by re-examination is a tactical consideration and should be considered where the evidence of the witness in examination-in-chief has been discredited in cross-examination or where it is apparent that some points need to be clarified. Re-examination is therefore available to repair the damage done to a witness's credibility during cross-examination and to explain or clarify any confusion or ambiguities in the witness's evidence. Leading questions are not permitted because, as in the examination-in-chief, the advocate is dealing with his own witness (see *Ireland* v *Taylor* [1949] 1 KB 300).

Rebutting an allegation of recent fabrication

An important issue that may arise during re-examination is where the opposing advocate, in cross-examination has suggested that the witness has recently made up or fabricated his evidence. Where the allegation has been made, re-examination provides an opportunity to repair any damage that may have been done to the witness's credibility by allowing evidence to be heard that will rebut the allegation. In effect, the rule allows the witness's previous consistent statement to be put before the court.

An illustration of the rule is found in the criminal case of *R* v *Oyesiku* (1972) 56 Cr App R 240. A police officer went to O's home to arrest him. The police officer testified that in the course of the arrest he was assaulted by O. O's wife had witnessed the incident, and before she had an opportunity to see or talk to her husband again, she told her solicitor that the police officer was the aggressor, and, that O, not knowing that the man in plain clothes, was a police officer, had merely tried to break free from his hold. When she gave evidence of her version of the incident, during cross-examination she was accused of recently fabricating her evidence to match that of O. The defence wished to call O's solicitor to give his account of what Mrs O had said and when she had said it. The judge refused leave and O was convicted. On appeal against conviction, the Court of Appeal ruled that the judge had been wrong to refuse leave to adduce evidence of Mrs O's previous statement and quashed O's conviction. This was a classic example of an assertion of recent fabrication, and the solicitor's evidence, not just as regards the account of what Mrs O had said to him, but also the time at which she had said it, would have completely refuted the assertion put to Mrs O in cross-examination.

In civil proceedings a witness's previous consistent statement may be admitted, with the leave of the court, both as to evidence of the facts contained in the statement and also as to evidence of the witness's consistency under section 6(2) of the Civil Evidence Act 1995:

> (2) A party who has called or intends to call a person as a witness in civil proceedings may not in those proceedings adduce evidence of a previous statement made by that person, except—
>
> (a) with the leave of the court, or
> (b) for the purpose of rebutting a suggestion that his evidence has been fabricated. This shall not be construed as preventing a witness statement (that is, a written statement of oral evidence which a party to the proceedings intends to lead) from being adopted by a witness in giving evidence or treated as his evidence.

RULES OF EVIDENCE AT A CIVIL TRIAL – MISCELLANEOUS ISSUES

Finally, before we leave the practice and procedure of witness testimony, some miscellaneous issues need to be considered that may arise during a civil trial.

Excluding otherwise admissible evidence under the Civil Procedure Rules

The Civil Procedure Rules give the court the power to exclude otherwise relevant and admissible evidence, where the admission of that evidence would be contrary to the interests of justice. In *Grobbelaar* v *Sun Newspapers Ltd* (1999) *The Times*, 12 August, the *Sun* newspaper was the defendant in a defamation action brought by the claimant. During the course of the trial, certain items of evidence were excluded by the judge under CPR rule 32.1 as an exercise of his power to control the evidence in the case. The defendant appealed against the trial judge's decision to exclude the evidence.

In allowing the appeal in part, the Court of Appeal reaffirmed the generally held view that CPR rule 32.1 gave the judge discretion to exclude admissible evidence. The Court of Appeal went on to state that prior to the implementation of the Civil Procedure Rules, a judge in a civil case had been unable to exclude evidence even where the prejudice resulting from its admission would outweigh its value in proving the party's case. The discretion under CPR rule 32.1 must be exercised fairly and in the pursuit of the 'interests of justice'. Although the rule does not allow the court to prevent a litigant advancing a vital point to his defence, the court has some control over the way in which the point is presented to the court where it is in the interest of saving costs.

This power should not be confused where the court of its own motion, or more likely at the submission of one of the parties, applies to have evidence excluded at trial on the basis that it has been obtained unfairly and/or illegally.

Improperly obtained evidence

Where evidence presented during examination-in-chief may have been obtained unlawfully or unfairly, the other party may apply to the judge to have the evidence excluded in the interests of a fair trial. However, the general position in civil proceedings is similar to the discretion exercised in criminal cases, in that where evidence is relevant to a fact in issue it will generally be admissible irrespective of whether it has been obtained illegally or unfairly.

Mood Music Publishing Co v De Wolfe Ltd [1976] Ch 119

The plaintiffs alleged that the defendants were in breach of their copyright in a piece of music by publishing a work under a different title which was very similar to their own. The defendants argued that the similarity was a matter of pure accident; to rebut this, the plaintiffs wanted to adduce evidence of other occasions when the defendants had produced very similar musical pieces to others in which the plaintiffs had the copyright. They also sought to adduce evidence of one occasion on which the plaintiffs had used entrapment, in that they had purposely allowed a piece of music to come into the hands of the defendants in the knowledge that they would plagiarise it with minor modifications.

  The Court of Appeal held that evidence of the other occasions, including that obtained by entrapment, was admissible. It was not oppressive or unfair to the defendants for it to be admitted in evidence; also, as it was a civil case, the defendants had fair notice of it from the pleadings.

Because of the nature of civil proceedings, for instance that it is very rare for a case to be decided by a jury and the liberty of the defendant is not at stake, the judge in a civil trial has no power to exclude improperly obtained evidence unless the impropriety is so grave that to condone it would amount to sanctioning an abuse of the proper administration of justice.

ITC Film Distributors v *Video Exchange Ltd* [1982] Ch 431 concerned an action for breach of copyright. During the trial, the defendants 'filched' some papers that the plaintiffs and their solicitors had brought into the courtroom for the presentation of their case. The defendants then tried to adduce them in evidence in that some of the content was helpful to their case! Whilst acknowledging that the judge in a civil trial has no inherent power to exclude evidence on the ground that it has been obtained by illegal or unfair means, Warner J held that as an exception to that general rule, the proper administration of justice demanded that the parties should feel safe to bring documents into the courtroom without having to guard them from the predatory actions of their opponents. Although the civil court seeks to hear all relevant evidence in order to reach the correct result, this was an example of an occasion where public interest dictated that relevant and technically admissible evidence should be excluded.

  Therefore, unless one of the parties obtains evidence in an unconscionable way as in the *ITC* case above, the position in civil cases is that relevant and probative evidence will be admissible even where the evidence has been obtained by illegal or unfair means. The general position was aptly stated by Lord Denning in *Helliwell* v *Piggott-Sims* [1980] FSR 582:

> so far as civil cases are concerned, it seems to me that the judge has no discretion. The evidence is relevant and admissible. The judge cannot refuse it on the ground that it may have been unlawfully obtained.

Civil trials and the European Convention on Human Rights

The general effect of the implementation of the Human Rights Act 1998 is dealt with in detail in Chapter 2. Although the incorporation of the European Convention on Human Rights into English law has greater significance for the rules of criminal evidence, Article 6(1), the right to a fair trial, covers the rules of evidence and procedure at a civil trial and specifically refers to the determination of a litigant's 'civil rights and obligations'. The conduct of a civil trial will be subject to two general principles under the European Convention – the right to a public hearing and the right to a reasoned decision.

Generally, the Civil Procedure Rules recognise and embody the right to a public hearing. The only aspect of trial procedure that might possibly be challenged as regards that right is a hearing in the small claims track, which in many cases will be held in the district judge's room. Although open to the public, many of these rooms do not have sufficient space to allow access to the general public. The Convention requirement for a reasoned decision will be satisfied by the judge's announcement of his decision at the conclusion of the case.

Further reading

Case Comment, 'Excluding Evidence as a Procedural Sanction' [2000] Civil Justice Quarterly 207.

Hogan, A., 'Running with the Fast Track' (1999) 1(2) Civil Litigation 6.

Lightman, D., 'Delay and the Civil Procedure Rules' (2001) 15 The Lawyer 29.

Chapter 29

THE ADMISSION OF HEARSAY EVIDENCE UNDER THE CIVIL EVIDENCE ACT 1995

INTRODUCTION

Many of the exclusionary rules of English evidence were developed as a response to the involvement of lay people in the fact-finding process. For example, the general rule excluding evidence of the accused's character and convictions in a criminal trial is largely based on the common law's scepticism of the ability of jurors and lay magistrates not to be unduly influenced by these factors when deciding the accused's guilt. The involvement of lay people was also one of the reasons for the common law's profound distrust of hearsay evidence as it was considered that jurors who sat in a civil trial would be too susceptible to the prejudices that lay people might suffer in the face of hearsay evidence. The admission of hearsay evidence also undermined some of the traditional principles of the adversarial process by exposing evidence to the possibility of concoction, distortion or unreliability where an oral or written statement was admitted in evidence that had been repeated by more than one witness or had been repeated on more than one occasion by the same witness. It also meant that effective cross-examination of hearsay evidence was not possible where the 'percipient' witness was not present in court.

As the involvement of lay people in the civil justice system declined following the abolition of juries, except in actions involving allegations of fraud, defamation, malicious prosecution and false imprisonment under section 69 of the Supreme Court Act 1981 and the County Courts Act 1984, and the conduct of trials by a judge sitting alone, a more relaxed approach was adopted to the admission of evidence in general in civil proceedings and hearsay evidence in particular.

The reforms began with the passing of the Evidence Act 1938, which made hearsay statements contained in documents admissible in civil proceedings under certain conditions. The Civil Evidence Act 1968 continued the process of reform by making admissible at trial first-hand oral hearsay statements and documentary hearsay evidence subject to the party's compliance with the Act's complex procedural provisions. The Civil Evidence Act 1972 extended the operation of the 1968 Act to statements of opinion by both a lay witness and an expert witness.

Whilst the introduction of the 1968 legislation was widely welcomed as a major improvement on the previous law and procedure, the Act proved difficult to apply and procedurally cumbersome. Some of the shortcomings of the complex procedural conditions were recognised by the Civil Justice Review (1988), which referred the matter of hearsay evidence in civil proceedings to the Law Commission.

Law Commission Report No 216, *The Hearsay Rule in Civil Proceedings*, recommended a simplification of the law and procedure relating to the admission of
hearsay evidence in civil proceedings so that as a general rule all relevant evidence,
including hearsay, should be admissible. The Law Commission specifically proposed that the hearsay rule in civil cases should be abolished. It recognised that the
major protection against the misuse of hearsay evidence should not be provided by
complex procedural safeguards – a key feature of the 1968 Act – but rather by the
court assessing the probative value of the evidence, the reasons for the evidence
being tendered in hearsay form and, on these and other relevant factors, giving
appropriate weight to the evidence admitted under the Act. Based on the Law
Commission's recommendations, the Civil Evidence Act 1995 was enacted and
came into force on 1 February 1997. The 1995 Act repealed Part I of the 1968 Act
(sections 1–10) dealing with the admission of hearsay evidence in civil proceedings.
(Part II of the 1968 Act remains in force and deals with the admission of evidence
of character and court judgments as evidence in civil cases. These issues are dealt
with in Chapter 31.)

The provisions of the Civil Evidence Act 1995 run in conjunction with CPR Part 33,
which deals with miscellaneous rules of evidence in civil proceedings and provides the
procedural framework for the admission of hearsay evidence at trial. Both sets of provisions are considered in detail below and at the end of this chapter there is a case
study (*Tom Thomas v Go-Fast Go-Karts (A Firm)*), which illustrates the admission of
hearsay evidence under the Civil Evidence Act 1995.

HEARSAY – THE AMBIT OF THE RULE

Even though the effect of section 1 of the Civil Evidence Act 1995 is to make virtually
all hearsay evidence admissible in civil proceedings, it is still important to have a clear
understanding of the essential characteristics of a hearsay statement. Section 1(2)(a) of
the 1995 Act defines hearsay as: 'a statement made otherwise than by a person while
giving oral evidence in the proceedings which is tendered as evidence of the matters
stated'.

The statutory definition, which is also adopted by CPR rule 33.1, incorporates the
characteristics of the common law definition of hearsay. The essential characteristics
of evidence that come within the ambit of the hearsay rule are as follows:

1 The evidence will be contained in a 'statement'. A statement is defined as 'any representation of fact or opinion however made' (1995 Act, section 13) and includes
   written statements, oral statements, gestures and a combination of each and, under
   the Civil Evidence Act 1972, a statement of opinion.
2 A statement will only fall within the ambit of the hearsay rule where the purpose
   of putting the statement in evidence is to prove the truth of its contents. The
   hearsay rule has no application where, for example, a witness's written statement
   is put in evidence for another purpose – to prove the words were spoken or to prove
   the speaker's state of mind.
3 If the statement is to come within the ambit of the rule it will have been made on
   'a prior occasion'. This means that the statement will have been made on an occa-

sion other than when the witness is giving evidence before the court in the present proceedings.

As an illustration of the hearsay rule, consider the following examples from a personal injury action arising out of a road traffic accident.

Examples

(a) *A written statement made by X at the scene of a road traffic accident which is read to the court in X's absence.*

(b) *X telling the court that after the accident he overheard Y saying to Z that 'he [Y] wasn't looking where he was going immediately before the collision'.*

(c) *The written entries in V's diary. V, whose flat overlooks the scene of the accident, wrote down in her diary the events she saw of the incident. V is too ill to come to court to give oral evidence.*

(d) *Y, a witness at the scene of the accident, whose statement is contained on an audiotape that is played to the court at trial.*

(e) *A video recording of the accident captured by a CCTV traffic control camera.*

The examples contained in (a)–(d) are *prima facie* admissible under the Civil Evidence Act 1995 as each one is a 'statement' within the meaning of the Act. Each 'statement' was made on a prior occasion other than whilst the witness was giving evidence in the present proceedings and the purpose of putting them in evidence is to prove the truth of the contents, ie proving the truth of what the witness had seen or heard at the scene of the accident.

Whilst the video recording of the incident in example (e) is a statement as defined by section 12 of the Civil Evidence Act 1995, it does not fall within the ambit of section 1 as it is neither a representation of fact or opinion and therefore is not admissible within the hearsay rule (*Taylor v Chief Constable of Cheshire* [1987] 1 All ER 225).

The general effect of the Civil Evidence Act 1995 has been to simplify the law and procedure relating to the admission of hearsay evidence in civil proceedings and to take forward many of the advances made by Part I of the Civil Evidence Act 1968. The practice and procedure for admitting hearsay evidence in civil proceedings under the Civil Evidence Act 1995 is dealt with below.

THE ABOLITION OF THE RULE AGAINST HEARSAY (CIVIL EVIDENCE ACT 1995, SECTION 1)

The following points should be noted about the general effect of section 1 and its associated provisions. First, section 1 abolishes the rule excluding evidence in civil proceedings on the basis that it is hearsay. Section 1(1) provides:

(1) In civil proceedings evidence shall not be excluded on the ground that it is hearsay.

The effect of section 1 is that virtually all hearsay evidence is admissible in civil proceedings, and, as a consequence, the court has no discretion to exclude evidence on the ground that it is hearsay. This principle extends to second-hand and multiple hearsay evidence as the 1995 Act specifically recognises that 'references to hearsay include hearsay of whatever degree' (section 1(2)(b)). Consider the following example on the application of the principles of multiple hearsay.

Example

A makes an oral statement to B. B repeats the statement to C and C repeats the statement to both D and E.

At trial, E may come to court to give oral evidence about what A is purported to have told B even though A's 'statement' has passed through a number of intermediaries. E's evidence is admissible as section 1 provides that evidence cannot be excluded on the ground that it is hearsay, including hearsay of whatever degree.

Whilst the evidence is admissible, it remains to be seen how much weight, if any, the court gives to E's evidence under section 4 of the 1995 Act. (See later in this chapter for an explanation of the operation of section 4.)

Under the 1995 Act, hearsay evidence will therefore be admissible in civil proceedings irrespective of how many intermediaries it has passed through, from the original maker of the statement to the person who gives evidence about it in court, or on how many occasions the statement has been repeated, as the judge has no discretion to exclude the evidence on the basis that it is hearsay.

Secondly, the Act applies to 'civil proceedings' as defined by section 11 of the Civil Evidence Act 1995. This includes proceedings in any of the ordinary courts of law, tribunals and arbitrations in which the strict rules of evidence are applied. The Act does not apply to proceedings in the wardship jurisdiction of the High Court as held in *Official Solicitor to the Supreme Court v K* [1965] AC 201 or to proceedings in the Court of Protection or in the Coroner's Court.

Thirdly, where a party in civil proceedings seeks to put evidence before the court which is admissible in its own right, the evidence will remain unaffected by the Civil Evidence Act 1995. Section 1(3) provides:

(3) Nothing in this Act affects the admissibility of evidence apart from this section.

We have already seen from the example above that a video recording produced by a CCTV camera is not a statement for the purposes of section 1 because it is not a representation of fact or opinion, therefore the 1995 Act has no application to its admissibility at trial. The same principle applies to a document having legal effect, such as a will in an action regarding a beneficiary's entitlement to a share in the deceased's estate. The admissibility of the will as documentary evidence does not come within the operation of the Civil Evidence Act 1995 as it is not a statement of fact or a statement of opinion.

Similarly, a statement admitted under the Criminal Procedure Act 1865, which is used to discredit a hostile witness (section 3) or which is used in cross-examination to prove that the witness made an oral or written statement that is inconsistent with his present oral testimony (sections 4 and 5) is also excluded from the 1995 Act's provisions as the purpose of putting these statements in evidence is not to prove the truth of their contents but rather to show the witness's inconsistency. It is therefore excluded from the operation of the hearsay rule, and most notably the notice provisions under section 2 of the 1995 Act.

Fourthly, the 1995 Act recognises that hearsay evidence in civil proceedings may also be admissible under other provisions. Section 1(4) states:

> (4) The provisions of sections 2 to 6 (safeguards and supplementary provisions relating to hearsay evidence) do not apply in relation to hearsay evidence admissible apart from this section, notwithstanding that it might be admissible by virtue of this section.

The effect of section 1(4) is that the procedural requirements for admitting hearsay evidence under the 1995 Act are specifically excluded from other provisions which admit hearsay evidence in civil cases. For example, section 34 of the Births and Deaths Registration Act 1953 allows for the admissibility of a certified copy of an entry in the register of births as evidence of the facts contained in it. Other provisions that have the same effect include section 65(3) of the Marriage Act 1949 and the Bankers' Books Evidence Act 1879. The admission of hearsay evidence under these provisions is prescribed by the substantive and procedural requirements in each of the specific provisions and are not subject to the provisions of the Civil Evidence Act 1995.

Finally, section 14(1) of the Civil Evidence Act 1995 provides that evidence will not be admitted under the Act where it is inadmissible under another rule of evidence. For example, it would not be possible for a witness's written statement to be put in evidence under the Act where that witness would not have been competent to give oral evidence at trial under section 5(1) of the 1995 Act. A witness would not be competent under the subsection where he was suffering from such mental or physical infirmity, or lack of understanding, as would render a person incompetent in civil proceedings.

PROCEDURAL SAFEGUARDS (CIVIL EVIDENCE ACT 1995, SECTION 2)

Where a party intends to present hearsay evidence at trial, section 2 of the 1995 Act and CPR rule 33.2(1) require that a notice informing the other party in the case about the intention to adduce hearsay evidence should be served. Section 2 provides:

> (1) A party proposing to adduce hearsay evidence in civil proceedings shall, subject to the following provisions of this section, give to the other party or parties to the proceedings—
> (a) such notice (if any) of that fact, and
> (b) on request, such particulars of or relating to the evidence,
> as is reasonable and practicable in the circumstances for the purpose of enabling him or them to deal with any matters arising from its being hearsay.
>
> ...
>
> (3) Subsection (1) may also be excluded by agreement of the parties; and compliance with the duty to give notice may in any case be waived by the person to whom notice is required to be given.

A major criticism about the operation of the Civil Evidence Act 1968 was the complexity of the notice provisions informing the other side of a party's intention to put a hearsay statement in evidence at the trial. As a consequence, the notice procedure under the 1995 Act is much simpler than its predecessor and are based on the recommendations in Law Commission Report No 216, at paragraphs 4.9 and 4.10.

Therefore, to prevent the other side from being surprised at trial and to allow the court at the pre-trial stage to deal with any issues arising out of the admission of the hearsay evidence, the hearsay notice must be served no later than the date for serving witness statements, and where the hearsay evidence is contained in a document, a copy of the document must be supplied to any party who requests a copy. A single hearsay notice may relate to more than one hearsay witness.

Whilst there is not a prescribed form for a section 2 notice, the notice will generally:

- indicate that the evidence is to be tendered as hearsay;
- identify the hearsay evidence;
- identify the person who made the hearsay statement to be given in evidence;
- state why the person who made the statement cannot be called to give evidence; and
- where appropriate, refer to which part of the witness statement the hearsay evidence is contained.

An illustration of a section 2 notice is to be found at the end of this chapter as part of the case study on *Tom Thomas* v *Go-Fast Go-Karts*.

Time limits for serving the notice

CPR rule 33.4 provides that where a party proposes to rely on hearsay evidence it must serve the notice no later than the latest date for serving witness statements or, where the hearsay evidence is contained in a document, a copy of the document should be given to any party who requests a copy.

Where a section 2 notice is not served

Where the notice requirement is not complied with, section 2(4) of the 1995 Act provides that a failure to serve a 'hearsay' notice does not affect the admissibility of the hearsay evidence at trial, but the court may penalise the offending party by imposing a costs penalty and/or the hearsay evidence may not be given the full weight it would have received under section 4 if the correct procedure had been complied with. Also, to ensure a fair trial, if hearsay evidence is introduced at trial where there has been no agreement or the other party has not been notified about it, the court may adjourn the proceedings to enable the other side to consider how it will deal with the evidence being tendered in this form.

The notice requirement – exceptions to the general rule

There are certain situations where hearsay evidence may be admitted without the need for the service of a section 2 notice. For example, a section 2 notice does not need to be served where the parties have agreed between themselves to waive the notice requirement under section 2(3). It is also not necessary to serve a notice where hearsay evidence is being adduced at an interim application or as a statement in a probate action that is alleged to have been made by the person whose estate is the subject of the proceedings. The requirement to serve a notice may also be excluded by a Practice Direction (CPR rule 33.3(c)).

Receiving a hearsay notice – the tactical considerations

When either the claimant or the defendant receives a hearsay notice, there are a number of actions that may be taken before trial and at the trial.

Before the trial

Making a request for further information

A party receiving a hearsay notice may accept that the evidence will be given as hearsay. This will happen in most cases where the reason given for the witness not attending trial to give oral evidence is that he has died or is physically or mentally unfit to give oral evidence. The party may request further information relating to the hearsay evidence. This may include seeking clarification of the circumstances in which the hearsay statement was made, or more details about the evidence to be introduced as hearsay or a confirmation of the present whereabouts of the witness. There is no prescribed time limit on a party requesting further information of the proposed hearsay evidence.

Power to call the 'hearsay' witness for cross-examination

In appropriate circumstances, where, for example, the witness's whereabouts is ascertained and he is available to give evidence, the party may also apply to the court for leave to serve a witness summons on that witness to attend the trial to be cross-examined. The power to call a witness for cross-examination is contained in section 3 of the Civil Evidence Act 1995 and CPR rule 33.4 which provide that where a party adduces hearsay evidence but does not call the maker of the statement, and the other party wishes to challenge the statement's maker, that party is allowed to call the maker in cross-examination to test the accuracy of the statement and the witness's credibility. The application should be made not more than 14 days after the day on which a notice of intention to rely on hearsay evidence was served on the applicant. Where the application is granted by the district judge, directions will be given as to how and where the witness will testify.

The policy behind section 3 of the 1995 Act is to prevent a party from failing to call a witness to give oral evidence by tendering his hearsay evidence in the witness's absence. Section 3 therefore preserves the long-cherished right in English evidence that, where possible, a party's witness should be cross-examined by his opponent.

At trial

Where hearsay evidence is presented at trial as part of either the claimant's or the defendant's case, section 5 of the 1995 Act and CPR rule 33.5 permit the other side to attack the credibility of the hearsay witness and the weight that should be given to his evidence.

Section 5(2) provides:

> (2) Where in civil proceedings hearsay evidence is adduced and the maker of the original statement, or of any statement relied upon to prove another statement, is not called as a witness—

(a) evidence which if he had been so called would be admissible for the purpose of attacking or supporting his credibility as a witness is admissible for that purpose in the proceedings; and

(b) evidence, tending to prove that, whether before or after he made the statement, he made any other statement inconsistent with it is admissible for the purpose of showing that he had contradicted himself.

(c) ....

Provided that evidence may not be given of any matter of which, if he had been called as a witness and had denied that matter in cross-examination, evidence could not have been adduced by the cross-examining party.

The purpose of section 5(2)(a) is to ensure that evidence relating to the credibility of a witness who is not called to give evidence is admissible as if the person had been called as a witness. As a result, evidence attacking the credibility of the absent hearsay witness will be allowed to suggest that the witness is biased in favour of the party calling him or has criminal convictions or is suffering from a mental incapacity. In effect, section 5(2)(a) prevents a party circumventing the issue of a witness's credibility by tendering his evidence as hearsay.

Section 5(2)(b) relates to where it is alleged that a 'hearsay' witness has made a prior inconsistent statement. Under paragraph (b), the witness's prior inconsistent statement can be introduced to undermine the witness's credibility.

Where it is intended to attack the credibility of the hearsay witness under section 5(2)(a) or (b), CPR rule 33.5 requires that notice must be given to the other side not more than 14 days after the day on which the section 2 notice was served.

Notice procedure for admitting plans, photographs and models

Where a party intends to put a plan or photograph or a model in evidence as part of its case, which is not contained in a witness statement or an expert's report, CPR rule 33.6 requires that notice should be given to the other party no later than the latest date for serving witness statements. After serving the notice, the party must allow any other party to inspect the plan or model etc with a view to agreeing the evidence.

WEIGHT TO BE ATTACHED TO THE HEARSAY STATEMENT (CIVIL EVIDENCE ACT 1995, SECTION 4)

An important development introduced by the Civil Evidence Act 1995 gives the courts the responsibility for ensuring that the more relaxed rules allowing for the admission of hearsay evidence are not abused. Whilst evidence can no longer be excluded at a civil trial on the sole ground that it is hearsay, the judge is still required to ensure that the evidence put before the court under the Act is reliable and that the parties do not take advantage of the more liberal evidential regime in admitting hearsay evidence. In fulfilling this 'policing' role, the courts are required to take into consideration the guidelines provided by section 4 in determining the weight to be accorded to the hearsay evidence.

Section 4 provides that:

(1) In estimating the weight (if any) to be given to hearsay evidence in civil proceedings the court shall have regard to any circumstances from which any inference can reasonably be drawn as to the reliability or otherwise of the evidence.

(2) Regard may be had, in particular, to the following—

(a) whether it would have been reasonable and practicable for the party by whom the evidence was adduced to have produced the maker of the original statement as a witness;

(b) whether the original statement was made contemporaneously with the occurrence or existence of the matters stated;

(c) whether the evidence involves multiple hearsay;

(d) whether any person involved had any motive to conceal or misrepresent matters;

(e) whether the original statement was an edited account, or was made in collaboration with another for a particular purpose;

(f) whether the circumstances in which the evidence is adduced as hearsay are such as to suggest an attempt to prevent proper evaluation of its weight.

The grounds identified in section 4(2)(a)–(f) are guidelines for the court to adapt to the specific facts and circumstances of each case and are not hard and fast rules which the courts are bound to follow.

Perhaps the most significant 'policing' provision is provided by section 4(2)(a). Where a party has unreasonably failed to produce the maker of the statement at the trial, the court may consider the witness to be inherently unreliable and as a result give the hearsay evidence little, if any, weight. Where the reason for the witness's absence is that he is ill or dead or unavailable by being overseas, the judge is likely to give 'full' weight to the evidence.

The significance of section 4(2)(b) is that the longer the lapse of time between the matters giving rise to the witness's testimony and when the witness's evidence is recorded (usually in written form), the presumption is raised that the witness's recollection and memory will be less reliable than where the statement is made when the events are fresh in his memory.

The dangers inherent in admitting multiple hearsay evidence are self-evident. Section 4(2)(c) recognises that the greater the number of times the statement is passed between the witnesses, the greater the potential for distortion or misinterpretation. Therefore in assessing the risk of distortion or misrepresentation, the judge will consider the identity of the intermediaries.

Where the evidence passes through several intermediaries, the judge is likely to give greater weight to the evidence if the intermediaries were acting in the course of their profession or occupation, especially if at some point in the chain one of the intermediaries is under a duty to check the accuracy of the information. Conversely, less weight is likely to be given to a statement that originates at a social occasion and is passed between the intermediaries as 'gossip' where there is no duty or opportunity to consider the accuracy of what each witness is saying.

Section 4(2)(d) acknowledges that the evidence may sometimes be tendered as hearsay to conceal or misrepresent a matter contained in the statement. As in most cases the witness will not be present in court, it is difficult to see how direct evidence could be established to prove this ground. However, collateral evidence may be adduced which would lead the judge to believe that the witness is not giving oral testimony due to his desire to conceal or misrepresent a matter contained in the statement. Such collateral evidence would be admissible under section 5(2)(a) of the 1995 Act.

Section 4(2)(e) covers occasions where a statement or document is an edited account of the evidence or is the result of collaboration between witnesses. Whilst such evidence is admissible under section 1 of the 1995 Act, the judge will inquire which matters have been omitted from the edited version or from the collaborative statement and, on the basis of this information, give the evidence its appropriate weight.

Section 4(2)(f) provides that the proper way to evaluate the weight and reliability of evidence is to cross-examine the maker of the original statement and re-emphasises that there is no tactical advantage to be gained in attempting to substitute oral testimony with written statements. Section 4(2)(f) is often applied in conjunction with section 4(2)(a), so that if a witness is available to give evidence, but there is no attempt to call the witness, this will have an adverse effect on the weight to be attached to the evidence.

USE OF PREVIOUS INCONSISTENT STATEMENTS (CIVIL EVIDENCE ACT 1995, SECTION 6)

As we saw in Chapter 26, the general rule in civil proceedings is that a party may not put in evidence a statement made by the witness on an occasion other than whilst giving evidence in the present proceedings. The reason for the rule, which also applies in criminal cases, is that what the witness may have said on a previous occasion other than whilst testifying in court has little probative value as it likely to be duplicating the witness's oral or written evidence heard by the court. As an exception to the general rule, a witness's previous consistent statement may be put to the court either with the court's leave or where it is suggested in cross-examination that the witness has recently fabricated or 'made up' his evidence. In re-examination, under section 6 of the 1995 Act, the witness's previous consistent statement may be put before the court to prove the consistency of the witness's oral testimony.

Section 6 provides:

(1) Subject as follows, the provisions of this Act as to hearsay evidence in civil proceedings apply equally (but without any necessary modifications) in relation to a previous consistent statement made by a person called as a witness in the proceedings.

(2) A party who has called or intends to call a person as a witness in civil proceedings may not in those proceedings adduce evidence of a previous statement made by that person, except—

(a) with the leave of the court, or

(b) for the purpose of rebutting a suggestion that his evidence has been fabricated. This shall not be construed as preventing a witness statement (that is, a written statement of oral evidence which a party to the proceedings intends to lead) from being adopted by a witness in giving evidence or treated as his evidence.

(3) Where in the case of civil proceedings section 3, 4 or 5 of the Criminal Procedure Act 1865 applies, which make provision as to—

(a) how far a witness may be discredited by the party producing him,

(b) the proof of contradictory statements made by a witness, and

(c) cross-examination as to previous statements in writing,

this Act does not authorise the adducing of evidence of a previous inconsistent or contradictory statement otherwise than in accordance with those sections.

This is without prejudice to any provision made by rules of court under section 3 above...

(4) Nothing in this Act affects any of the rules of law as to the circumstances in which, where a person called as a witness in civil proceedings is cross-examined on a document used by him to refresh his memory, that document may be made evidence in those proceedings.

(5) Nothing in this section shall be construed as preventing a statement of any description referred to above from being admissible by virtue of section 1 as evidence of matters stated.

The general rule established by section 6(1) is that where a party serves on the other side a notice of intention to tender hearsay evidence, but at trial calls the witness to give evidence in person, the witness's previous consistent statement will only be admissible with the leave of the court because evidence which merely replicates the witness's oral evidence has little probative value. Section 6 however also recognises a number of exceptions to this general rule. So, for example, section 6(2) will apply where it has been suggested in cross-examination that the witness has recently fabricated or made up his evidence and in re-examination the witness's previous consistent statement may be put before the court to rebut the allegation. In these circumstances, the witness's previous statement will show his consistency. Section 6(3) preserves the position regarding previous inconsistent statements made by the witness under section 3, 4, or 5 of the Criminal Procedure Act 1865. The effect of section 6(4) is to preserve the rules relating to the status of a memory refreshing document. A witness may refer to a memory refreshing document for that purpose, but the statement does not become part of the witness's evidence unless the advocate cross-examines the witness on a part of the document that the witness did not use to refresh his memory. In these circumstances, the statement becomes part of the evidence of the party which calls the witness (section 6(5)).

EVIDENCE FORMERLY ADMISSIBLE AT COMMON LAW (CIVIL EVIDENCE ACT 1995, SECTION 7)

Under section 9(3) and (4) of the Civil Evidence Act 1968 certain common law exceptions to the hearsay rule were expressly preserved and fell outside the ambit of the 1968 Act. As a consequence, if hearsay evidence that continued to be preserved at common law was to be tendered at trial, it was not necessary for the party to comply with the procedural requirements of the 1968 Act. These exceptions related to:

- informal admissions;
- hearsay evidence contained in published works and public documents; and
- evidence of a person's reputation.

The position under the 1995 Act has been slightly modified in the following ways.

Informal admissions

An informal admission is a statement made by the party or by a person having an identity with the party that is adverse to that party's interests (see Chapter 24). Whilst an informal admission can be made before trial or during the trial and in any medium of communication such as a written or oral statement or from the witness's conduct, demeanour or silence, the classic illustration of an informal admission is where, for example, after a workplace accident to one of his employees, the employer is overheard to say 'I knew we should have fixed that machinery' or where after a collision between two cars one of the drivers is overheard to say 'It was all my fault. I should have been looking where I was going'.

In each of the above examples the witness is making an informal statement that is adverse to the party's interests and in view of the fact that it would be unlikely that the witness would fabricate such an adverse admission, the common law allowed a witness who overheard the admission to come to court to testify about what he had heard.

The law relating to the admission of an informal admission in civil cases is now found in section 7(1) of the 1995 Act, the effect of which is to make the statement admissible under section 1(1) of the 1995 Act. This means that where a party wishes to put an informal admission in evidence at trial as hearsay evidence, a section 2 notice must be served and the evidence will be subject to the same procedural provisions as other hearsay evidence admitted under section 1.

Published works and public documents

Section 7(2) of the 1995 Act preserves the common law exception in making admissible in its own right, hearsay evidence contained in published works dealing with matters of a scientific nature or contained in a public document admissible in civil proceedings. The effect of section 7(2) is that such evidence may be tendered at trial without the need to serve a notice under section 2.

Evidence of reputation

Section 7(3) provides:

> (3) The common law rules effectively preserved by section 9(3) and (4) of the Civil Evidence Act 1968, that is, any rule of law whereby in civil proceedings—
>> (a) evidence of a person's reputation is admissible for the purpose of proving his good or bad character, or
>> (b) evidence of reputation or family tradition is admissible—
>>> (i) for the purpose of proving or disproving pedigree or the existence of a marriage, or
>>> (ii) for the purpose of proving or disproving the existence of any public or general right or of identifying any person or thing,
> shall continue to have effect in so far as they authorise the court to treat such evidence as proving or disproving that matter. ...

Under section 7(3), evidence of reputation or family tradition shall be admitted independently of the Act and there is no need to serve a hearsay notice on the other party.

PROOF OF STATEMENTS CONTAINED IN DOCUMENTS (CIVIL EVIDENCE ACT 1995, SECTION 8)

The effect of section 8 of the 1995 Act is that where a party needs to put a statement that is contained in a document before the court, it can be proved by using the original of the document or an authenticated copy. The effect of the section is to abolish the 'best' evidence rule in civil proceedings as it does not matter how many stages a copy is removed from the original. A 'document', under section 13, the Act's interpretation section, is widely defined to include maps, plans, graphs, drawings, photographs, discs and audiotapes. A 'statement' means any representation of fact or opinion, however made. A 'copy' is also widely interpreted to mean a transcript of an audio-visual tape as well as reproductions of images transposed from tapes and documents recorded in a computerised format. 'Production' in section 8(1)(a) means having a witness in court who can say what the document is and give other relevant details about it.

DOCUMENTS FORMING PART OF THE RECORDS OF A BUSINESS OR PUBLIC AUTHORITY (CIVIL EVIDENCE ACT 1995, SECTION 9)

In recommending the appropriate procedure for a party to put the records of a business or public authority before the court, the Law Commission in Report No 216 took account of the modern trend in business practice that record-keeping is often undertaken by a number of different personnel and is largely dependent on technology. It would therefore be inappropriate and impractical if a single witness was required to come to court to give evidence about a document created by a business or a public authority. As a consequence, section 9(1) of the 1995 Act permits the records of a business or public authority to be put in evidence as hearsay without the need for further proof provided the court is shown a signed certificate from an officer of the company or public authority that verifies its authenticity.

Section 9 provides:

(1) A document which is shown to form part of the records of a business or public authority may be received in evidence in civil proceedings without further proof.

(2) A document shall be taken to form part of the records of a business or public authority if there is produced to the court a certificate to that effect signed by an officer of the business or authority to which the records belong. ...

The word 'records' in the section is defined in section 9(4) as meaning 'records in whatever form', but is not explained further. In accordance with the purpose of the legislation and the safeguards provided, the words are to be given a broad interpretation to include manuscript entries in a ledger, the contents of computer databases or copies of accounts as well as other documents that will ordinarily be generated in the course of a business. A 'public authority' includes a local authority, government department, statutory undertaking and any person holding office under the authority of the Crown.

A 'business' is very widely defined to include 'any activity regularly carried on over a period of time, whether for profit or not, by anybody (whether corporate or not) or by an individual'. The wide ambit of a 'business' is likely to cover activities that would not normally be recognised as a 'business' including records kept by a person as part of his hobby.

Unless the court directs otherwise, CPR rule 33.6(2) and (3) requires that notice should be given to the other side of the intention to put the business document in evidence under the 1995 Act within the deadline for serving witness statements. Where a notice of intention has been given, the other side should be given the opportunity to inspect the document and to agree to its admission without further proof.

Finally, where the court believes that the record is not reliable, it may require an officer of the business or public authority to attend court to give oral evidence about the document's reliability (section 9(5)). Alternatively, the officer's evidence may be tendered as hearsay.

ADMISSIBILITY AND PROOF OF OGDEN TABLES

Ogden Tables are a set of tables produced by the Government Actuary's Department that give precise data about longevity, interest rates and work patterns. Section 10 of the 1995 Act provides for the admissibility of Ogden Tables as evidence without further proof to enable the court to use higher multipliers in personal injury cases or actions under the Fatal Accidents Act 1976 when computing losses for earnings and continuing care claims.

CASE STUDY UNDER THE CIVIL EVIDENCE ACT 1995

Tom Thomas	Claimant
AND	
Go-Fast Go-Karts (A Firm)	Defendant

Facts

You act for Tom Thomas who is suing Go-Fast Go-Karts in private nuisance arising out of the defendant's business activities situated next to your client's home. In his statement of case, Tom alleges that the noise and disruption from the business continues for up to 14 hours each day, seven days a week and this constitutes an unreasonable interference with the enjoyment of his land. As part of the evidence in the case you have diary entries written at the end of each day by Dora Thomas, Tom's mother, who has recently died, in which she records in detail how the defendant has made her life and her family's life a 'living hell' between 1 October 2000 and 25 July 2001. You wish to put the diary in evidence under the Civil Evidence Act 1995.

The diary comes within the meaning of a statement under section 1(2)(a) of the 1995 Act as a representation of fact or opinion under section 13. As Dora is not available to give oral testimony, her evidence will come within the hearsay rule as it is a statement made on a prior occasion other than whilst giving evidence in the present proceedings and the purpose of putting her statement before the court is to prove the truth of its contents. For Dora's diary to be put in evidence at trial as she is dead, it will be necessary to serve on the defendant the section 2 notice set out on the following page.

Section 2 notice

IN THE BARCHESTER   Case No. BB 0345
COUNTY COURT

Between

Claimant   Tom Thomas

                                               AND

Defendant   Go-Fast Go-Karts (a firm)

NOTICE OF DESIRE TO ADDUCE HEARSAY STATEMENT

Take Notice that at the trial of this action the Claimant desires to give in evidence
the statement made in the following document, namely the statement of Dora
Thomas contained in her diary entries consisting of 20 pages between 1 October
2000 and 25 July 2001, a copy of which is attached hereto.

And Further take notice that the particulars relating to the said statement are as follows:

  (a) It was made by the said Dora Thomas.
  (b) The said Dora Thomas may not be called to give evidence at trial as she is
      dead.

Dated 13 January 2002

Pitman and Co

Of Haven Square

Solicitors for the Claimant

To the Defendant

Notice of intention to attack absent witness's credibility

IN THE BARCHESTER   Case No. BB 0345
COUNTY COURT

Between

Tom Thomas   Claimant

AND

Go-Fast Go-Karts (A Firm)   Defendant

NOTICE OF INTENTION TO ATTACK CREDIBILITY OF ABSENT WITNESS

Take Notice that at the trial of this action the Defendant intends to attack the credibility of Dora Thomas, in respect of whom the Claimant has given notice of intention to adduce hearsay evidence in the following respect –

  (a) The defendant contends that Dora Thomas is the mother of Tom Thomas,
       the Claimant.
  (b) In October 1995, Dora Thomas was convicted of obtaining property by
       deception contrary to section 15 of the Theft Act 1968 by the Barchester
       Magistrates' Court. A certificate of conviction is hereto attached.

Dated 20 January 2002

Dodger and Co

Solicitors for the Defendant

To the Claimant

Receiving the hearsay notice – the tactical considerations

On receiving the notice, the defendant's lawyers may seek further and better information on the hearsay evidence, although on the facts this is unlikely. At trial, section 5(2)(a) of the Civil Evidence Act 1995 and CPR rule 33.5 allow the defendant to attack Dora's credibility. Evidence might be heard, for example, that Dora was short-sighted or deaf or was suffering from senile dementia when she compiled the diary entries. The defendant intends to put evidence before the court that Dora was convicted of obtaining property by deception in 1995. The defendant will be required to serve the notice on page 553.

If the judge is persuaded by the evidence attached to the notice, it will undermine the credibility and weight the judge will give to Dora's hearsay statement.

Giving weight to the hearsay evidence

When considering the probative value of Dora's evidence, as well as taking into account the attempts by the defendant to undermine the witness's credibility, the judge is required to consider the weight to give the statement under section 4. Clearly on the facts it would not have been reasonable under section 4(2)(a) to have produced Dora to give evidence! The judge is likely to take into account that the original statement was made contemporaneously with the events that are recorded in the statement (section 4(2)(b)). The evidence does not appear to involve multiple hearsay (section 4(2)(c)), although Dora may be considered to have a motive to misrepresent the matters referred to in her diary.

Admitting a document forming part of the records of a public authority

You intend to use the minutes of Barchester District Council's Environment Committee as part of the claimant's case. The minutes record that the business activities of Go-Fast Go-Karts represent an 'unacceptable intrusion on the lives of residents living near to the track'.

As the document forms part of the records of a public authority, it may be put in evidence under section 9(1) of the Civil Evidence Act 1995 without further proof, provided the minutes of the meeting are accompanied by a certificate signed by an authorised officer of the council acknowledging the authenticity of the document.

Unless the court directs otherwise, CPR rule 33.6(2) and (3) requires that you should serve a notice on the defendant's solicitors within the deadline for serving witness statements of your intention to put the business document in evidence under the 1995 Act. The defendant's solicitors should be given the opportunity to inspect the minutes and to agree to their admission without further proof.

If the court believes that the record is not reliable, which is unlikely here, it may, under section 9(5), require an officer of the local authority to attend court to give oral evidence or the officer's evidence may be tendered as hearsay.

Further reading

Ho, H.L., 'A Theory of Hearsay' [1999] Oxford Journal of Legal Studies 403.

Law Commission (1993) *The Hearsay Rule in Civil Proceedings*, Report No 216, Cm 2321, HMSO.

Salako, S.E., 'The Hearsay Rule and the Civil Evidence Act 1995: Where Are We Now?' [2000] Civil Justice Quarterly 371.

Chapter 30

OPINION EVIDENCE

INTRODUCTION

In civil proceedings, as in criminal cases, the general rule at common law was that a witness could only give evidence about the factual matters within his personal knowledge. He could not give his opinion on those matters or make inferences or assumptions from the facts in the case. The reason for the common law rule was that the responsibility for assessing the probative value of the evidence and thereby forming an opinion on the evidence lay with the judge or, where appropriate, with the jury. As an illustration of this general rule consider the following examples.

Examples

In an action for restraint of trade, affidavits sworn by traders expressing their opinions on the 'reasonableness' of a restraint of trade clause were held to be inadmissible.

At the hearing of a summons to interpret the terms of a charitable trust deed, the opinion of a barrister who had drafted a trust deed was held to be inadmissible.

In the first example, which was taken from *Haynes* v *Doman* [1899] 2 Ch 13, evidence of the traders' opinions on the reasonableness of the clauses was excluded because their evidence went beyond merely stating facts. The same reason was cited for excluding the barrister's opinion evidence in the second example, as his evidence also went beyond merely stating facts (see *Rabin* v *Gerson Berger Association* Ltd [1986] 1 WLR 526).

In modern civil proceedings the general rule excluding opinion evidence is subject to three exceptions:

1 opinion evidence relating to matters of public concern and family history;
2 non-expert opinion evidence on a matter within the competence and experience of a 'lay' witness; and
3 the opinion evidence of an expert witness.

These exceptions are recognised because they relate to matters of which the court has no direct experience or expertise, and, depending on the facts in issue in the case, an understanding of the matters about which the witness gives opinion evidence may be necessary if the fact finder is to decide the issue of liability and/or quantum. Each of the exceptions will now be considered.

OPINION EVIDENCE RELATING TO MATTERS OF PUBLIC CONCERN AND FAMILY HISTORY

At common law, opinion evidence was admissible to prove matters of public concern. This rule is now preserved by section 7(3) of the Civil Evidence Act 1995. Under section 7(3), a witness may be permitted to give his opinion to the court about a party's reputation, conduct or family tradition including the existence of a marriage. Evidence is admissible under section 7(3) in its own right and can be tendered at trial without invoking the hearsay notice provisions under section 2 of the Civil Evidence Act 1995.

Example

A witness would be permitted to state in evidence that 'he was sure that Albert and Polly were married in 1947' or that 'he is certain that generations of the Smith family have lived in the village since 1843'.

The witness is giving the court his personal opinion on matters of family history and tradition in both instances. Clearly, these are matters of which the court has no direct knowledge and, where the matters relate to a fact in issue in the case, the court may hear a witness's opinion. It is a matter for the court whether it believes the witness or the weight it gives to the witness's evidence.

NON-EXPERT OPINION EVIDENCE ON MATTERS WITHIN THE COMPETENCE AND EXPERIENCE OF A LAY WITNESS

A non-expert witness is allowed to give opinion evidence when it is derived from his personal knowledge on any matter in the case.

Examples

The witness states that at the time of the accident, in his opinion, 'Car A was travelling too quickly for the road conditions which were wet and where the visibility was poor.' The statement is admissible.

The witness said that when he went to speak to the driver of Car A, 'I smelled alcohol on the driver's breath and he appeared to be speaking in a slurred way'. This statement is admissible.

In each example, the witness is making a factual statement relating to matters within his personal knowledge that are relevant to the facts in issue in the case. The witness's opinion is admissible because he is in a better position than any other witness to tell the court about these matters. It may also be the only way in which this evidence will be heard as the matters may lie exclusively within the witness's knowledge and experience. In practice, the rule recognises that when testifying about some issues it may be impossible for a witness to distinguish between fact and opinion and therefore provides a convenient way for the court to hear evidence containing both fact and opinion.

The rule allowing a lay witness to give his opinion on a fact in issue has been given statutory effect by section 3(2) of the Civil Evidence Act 1972 which provides:

where a person is called as a witness in any civil proceedings, a statement of opinion by him on any relevant matter on which he is not qualified to give expert evidence, if made as a way of conveying relevant facts personally perceived by him, is admissible as evidence of what he perceived.

The matters covered by section 3(2) are generally considered to be within a lay witness's ordinary knowledge and, depending on a number of relevant factors, including the witness's age and experience in the matters relating to his testimony, the judge will give appropriate weight to his testimony.

The requirement of section 3(2) of the 1972 Act that the witness's opinion should be on a factual matter from within his ordinary knowledge is illustrated by the case of *Rasool* v *West Midlands Passenger Transport Executive* [1974] 3 All ER 638. In *Rasool*, the plaintiff was knocked down by the defendant's bus in Birmingham. The incident was witnessed by a Mrs Collum who made a signed statement but subsequently left the country to live in Jamaica. At trial, judicial attention was primarily concerned with the requirements for admitting the evidence as hearsay under the complex notice provisions of the Civil Evidence Act 1968. Mrs Collum's statement was admitted in evidence. It appeared to have escaped everyone's attention in the case that Mrs Collum in her statement had stated that 'The bus driver was in no way to blame for the accident'. This part of her statement was inadmissible as section 3(2) applies only to opinion evidence conveyed as facts perceived. On the facts of the case the witness's opinion in apportioning blame in the case went beyond the limits imposed by the section.

In *Sherrard* v *Jacob* [1965] NI 151, Lord MacDermott CJ indicated some of the issues on which non-expert opinion evidence might be permitted:

- the identification of handwriting, persons and things;
- a person's apparent age;
- the bodily plight or condition of a person, including death and illness;
- the emotional state of a person including whether she or he was distressed, angry or affectionate;
- the condition of things including whether it was worn or shabby, used or new;
- certain questions of value; and
- estimates of speed and distance.

In *Marcel Beller Ltd* v *Hayden* [1978] QB 694, the plaintiffs had taken out an insurance policy on the life of one of their employees. The employee was killed in a road accident after the car he was driving failed to negotiate a left-hand bend and careered through some railings situated on the right-hand side of the road. The defendant underwriter refused to pay out on the policy on the ground that the deceased had deliberately exposed himself to unnecessary risk by driving whilst intoxicated. At trial the plaintiffs called a Mr Braarup, who was a passenger in the car at the time of the accident. He was permitted to state in evidence his opinion on the following issues:

- the deceased appeared quite a sober man,
- the deceased could hold his drink,
- when setting out on his final journey the deceased appeared to be alright,
- the deceased did not appear the worse for drink and drove perfectly well,

- the car's speed at the bend was about 50 mph, which should have been a safe speed,
- the car's skid had been caused by ice or a wet road surface,
- the deceased had acted properly to correct the skid.

Another witness, Mr Van Boesschoten, who was driving in the opposite direction when the accident happened, was permitted to state that:

- when the deceased's car came round the bend, it was travelling very fast and the speed was between 60 and 70 mph.

Mr Van Boesschoten's passenger was also allowed to state:

- The car approached us very fast and I think its speed was between 60 and 70 mph.

Marcel Beller is a good illustration of the kinds of matters on which a witness will be permitted to give an opinion – as already noted, it is up to the judge to decide how much weight should be given to such evidence. On the facts, the trial judge chose to give little weight to Mr Braarup's evidence, whose testimony according to the judge 'was impaired both by drink he had taken and by the shock he had sustained'.

A good judicial explanation for admitting non-expert opinion evidence was given by Lord Justice McCowan in *Morales (An Infant)* v *Ecclestone* [1991] RTR 151. The plaintiff was an eleven-year-old boy who was injured by a car driven by the defendant. Two witnesses at the scene of the accident (Mr Bellchamber and Mr McKay) gave evidence at trial that in their opinion the driver had no chance at avoiding the collision. In confirming such observations were permitted as coming within the rule Lord Justice McCowan said that:

> They (the opinions) emanated from men at the scene watching the accident happen and basing their remarks on what they had observed of the speeds, the distances and the positions on the road of the parties involved. What they said could no more be objected to by the plaintiff's counsel than the defendant's counsel could have objected if Mr Bellchamber had said: 'He had plenty of time to observe the boy and to veer to his left and, if he had, he would not have hit the boy at all'. In neither case would the judge's function have been usurped. How much weight to attach to these remarks is another matter.

EXPERT EVIDENCE

Expert evidence is the major exception to the general rule that opinion evidence is inadmissible in civil proceedings. An expert may give his opinion on a matter that goes beyond the ordinary competence of the court where the expert's opinion is necessary to assist the court to reach a decision on the facts and other evidence in the case. In view of the highly complex nature of modern life, it has become increasingly common in recent years for the court to need the assistance of an expert. The list of the matters detailed below on which expert evidence may be required in civil proceedings is not exhaustive and continues to grow. The most common form of expert evidence is the professional opinion of a medical witness in a personal injury action. Other areas of expertise include:

- forensic accountancy;
- mechanical engineering;

- structural engineering;
- handwriting recognition;
- accident investigation;
- ballistics;
- blood tests;
- breath tests;
- blood-alcohol levels;
- facial mapping;
- facial identification;
- psychiatry;
- psychology;
- architectural matters;
- antiques;
- fine art;
- trichology;
- educational matters.

Under the Civil Procedure Rules, the admission of expert evidence is governed by Part 35 and the Practice Direction to Part 35, which adopt a new philosophical and procedural approach to the admission of expert evidence in civil proceedings.

The position before Woolf – trial by experts?

The rules relating to the admission of expert evidence under the 'old' system of civil litigation attracted much criticism from a number of influential sources. A common problem identified by Lord Woolf in the *Access to Justice* reports (see Chapter 23 of the *Interim Report* and Chapter 13 of the *Final Report*, Further reading below) was that whilst experts were required to take an independent objective approach to the issues in the case, it had become common practice for expert witnesses to adopt a partisan approach blindly supporting their instructing parties, who in most instances were also paying their fees. A second problem, recognised by Lord Woolf and echoed by the Law Society, the Bar Council and members of the judiciary, was that many civil trials had become 'trial by experts'. This unacceptable practice was highlighted in *Liddell* v *Middleton* [1995] RTR 36, in which the Court of Appeal voiced concern at the tendency to call numerous expert witnesses in personal injury cases, especially when many of them were usurping the function of the court by drawing conclusions in respect of findings of fact, which were strictly matters for the court to determine. The Court of Appeal went on to assert that there is no such concept as 'trial by experts' in English law and that the admission of expert evidence should be closely controlled as in many cases it contributed unnecessarily to the cost of litigation and the length of the trial. This theme was taken up by Lord Woolf at page 137 of the *Final Report*:

> A large litigation support industry, generating a multi-million-pound fee income, has grown up among professions such as accountants, architects and others, and new professions have developed such as accident reconstruction and care experts. This goes against all principles of proportionality and access to justice. In my view, its most damaging effect is that it has created an ethos of what is acceptable which has filtered down to smaller cases. Many

potential litigants do not even start litigation because of the advice they are given about cost, and in my view this is as great a social ill as the actual cost of pursuing litigation.

It was recognised that under the 'old' system of civil litigation the need for each party to instruct an expert was a common source of increased costs, complexity and delay.

In response to these criticisms, Lord Woolf, in his *Final Report*, recommended a radical change to the philosophy, practice and procedure of expert evidence in civil proceedings. The principal recommendation was that the admission of expert evidence should be under the complete control of the court through the exercise of the court's case management powers at the pre-trial directions stage. Therefore as part of its case management powers under the Civil Procedure Rules, the court has the power to control:

- the admission of expert evidence in terms of the issues on which expert evidence is required in the case;
- the nature of the expert evidence required to dispose of the case; and
- the way in which the expert evidence will be placed before the court.

As the strict rules of evidence do not apply to cases in the small claims track, CPR Part 35 primarily covers cases that have been allocated to the fast track and to the multi-track. Nevertheless, in cases allocated to the small claims track, the court is still under a duty to restrict the expert evidence in the case and the expert's overriding duty to the court remains. The court has complete control over the evidence and it can decide that no expert evidence is needed to resolve the case or that expert evidence should not be heard unless the court gives consent.

Who is an expert?

A witness is competent to give expert evidence, if, in the opinion of the judge, he is properly qualified in the subject calling for his expertise. The expertise may have been acquired through study, training or experience. The expert's role has long been recognised by the common law. In *Buckley* v *Rice-Thomas* (1554) 1 Plowd 118, Saunders J stated:

> If matters arise in our law which concern other science or faculties we commonly apply for the aid of that science or faculty which it concerns.

Later applications of the rule are provided by *Folkes* v *Chard* (1782) 3 Doug KB 157, where Lord Mansfield held that the opinion of scientific men upon proven facts may be given by men of science within their own science, and by *Beckwith* v *Sydebotham* (1807) 1 Camp 116, where shipwrights were allowed to testify about the seaworthiness of a ship!

In deciding whether a person has the necessary expertise, it is not necessary for the witness to hold any formal qualifications in his sphere of expertise, although most will be professionally qualified. For example, it is possible for the expertise to have been acquired through independent study as a hobby. In the criminal case of *R* v *Silverlock* [1894] 2 QB 766, a solicitor was permitted to give expert opinion evidence about the identity of handwriting. Whilst he held no formal qualification, he had studied the subject as a hobby for ten years, and satisfied the judge that he was competent to give his opinion as to whether disputed handwriting was that of the accused.

However, the reality of modern litigation and the technical complexity of many of the issues on which expert evidence will be heard, requires that most witnesses will be professionally qualified and/or employed in their area of expertise. The era of the 'enlightened amateur' is over.

Irrespective of the witness's background, it is the responsibility of the party calling the witness to prove to the court that the witness is appropriately qualified to give expert evidence. This is usually done by putting evidence to the court that the person is a member of a recognised professional body such as a practitioner of medicine along with details of his qualifications and other notable professional achievements.

The witness must be available to answer questions put to him by the judge. Where, as a matter of law, the witness satisfies the judge as to his suitability to be an expert, the witness will be considered competent to testify. The witness's competence remains an issue for the judge and in *Stevens* v *Gullis* [2000] 1 All ER 527, the Court of Appeal confirmed that this wide discretion available to the judge could not be overridden. In *Stevens*, the Court of Appeal refused to interfere with the trial judge's decision that it was not appropriate for a particular witness to give evidence as an expert.

The ambit of expert evidence

The expert must confine his evidence to matters that are within his expertise. In modern law, the ambit of expert evidence and the matters on which the witness will be allowed to testify are governed by section 3(1) of the Civil Evidence Act 1972, which provides:

> Subject to any rules of the court…where a person is called as a witness in civil proceedings, his opinion on any relevant matter on which he is qualified to give expert evidence, shall be admissible…
>
> (3) In this section 'relevant matter' includes an issue in the proceedings in question.

As an illustration of section 3(1), consider the following examples.

Examples

Jo, who is the proprietor of 'Deep-Freeze Ices', is suing in negligence and for breach of contract arising out of the purchase of a new refrigeration system, which Jo alleges in her statement of case is not fit for the purpose intended. At the trial of the action, a refrigeration engineer instructed by Jo is permitted to state that in his opinion the design and manufacture of the refrigeration system was not appropriate for the purpose it was intended.

In an action for personal injuries arising out of the defendant's vehicle 'running down' the claimant, an expert vehicle examiner is allowed to state that the poor condition of the brakes on the defendant's car was the cause or one of the main causes of the defendant's vehicle colliding with the claimant.

As section 3(1) requires, the expert has to confine his evidence to his area of expertise and he will not be permitted to give his opinion on the legal or technical merits of the case (*Crosfield* v *Techno-Chemical Laboratories* (1913) 30 RPC 297). For the same reason the expert is not allowed to give his opinion on the merits of the parties' case or the party's conduct during the action, as illustrated by Anthony Lincoln J's comments in *Re LP (Minors: Care and Control)* [1990] FCR 147, where he criticised the attitude adopted by the psychiatrist expert witness:

> His report, whatever his intention, is a sustained criticism, couched in strong language of the local authority's conduct. It would have been more helpful if he had set out the pros and cons of each household in a balanced manner ... The greater part of his report is devoted to an analysis of the affidavits in the case. I approach his recommendations with caution.

In *British Celanese Ltd* v *Courtaulds Ltd* (1935) 152 LT 537, the House of Lords confirmed that the expert's function was to explain words, or terms of science or art appearing on documents which have to be construed by the court, to give expert assistance to the court or to inform the court as to the state of public knowledge with regard to the matters before it. In *United States Shipping Board* v *St Albans* [1931] AC 632, the Privy Council suggested that the role of the expert required him to give:

> [T]he opinion of scientific men upon proven facts may be given by men of science within their own science.

An illustration to the modern approach in admitting expert evidence is provided by *Barings Plc (In Liquidation)* v *Coopers & Lybrand (No 2)* (2001) *The Times*, 7 March. The case concerned allegations of negligence by the claimant against the defendants as its auditors. The defendants submitted that the claimant had been contributorily negligent in failing to spot the potentially damaging actions of L, one of the claimant's employees. The claimant applied to strike out three expert evidence reports filed by the defendants relating to banking management issues by submitting that the reports were inadmissible as they dealt with issues that were not within the realm of expert evidence.

In dismissing the application, the judge held that where an acknowledged expertise existed that was governed by established principles and rules of conduct and such expertise was likely to assist the court's determination of the issues before it, the reports would be admissible as expert evidence if the witness whom a party sought to call could show that he held such expertise which would provide useful evidence. It was apparent in this case that there existed a body of expertise in the field of investment bank management which was relevant to the issues to be decided by the court.

Admission of expert evidence under the Civil Procedure Rules

CPR Part 35 and its Practice Direction provide a detailed procedural framework for the admission of expert evidence in civil proceedings. Importantly, under CPR rule 35.1, the court has the power to restrict the admission of expert evidence:

> Expert evidence should be restricted to that which is reasonably required to resolve the proceedings.

In deciding whether expert evidence is 'reasonably required' to resolve the proceedings, the courts will take into account the facts and circumstances of the case and must also have regard to the Rules' overriding objective of enabling the court to deal with the case 'justly', which includes ensuring that the parties are on an equal footing, saving expense and dealing with the case in ways which are proportionate to the case (CPR rule 1.1(1) and (2)). The court's control over the admission of expert evidence is part of its general power to control all the evidence in the case under CPR rule 32.1.

The decision whether to seek the assistance of an expert will be made either at the case management conference or on the application of one of the parties. It is important to note that expert evidence may only be called with the court's permission under CPR rule 35.4(1), and where the court decides that expert evidence is 'reasonably required' to resolve the proceedings, the parties are required to assist the court to identify an expert who is appropriately qualified in his sphere of expertise and with the overriding objective of the Civil Procedure Rules in mind to assist the court in disposing of the case justly and swiftly. The court may also:

* limit the number of expert witnesses each party may call, either generally or relating to a specific issue;
* direct that evidence is to be given by one or more of the experts chosen by agreement between the parties; or
* where the parties cannot agree, direct that an expert be nominated by the court.

Where an expert is appointed, CPR rule 35.4(4) provides that, when giving directions on expert evidence, the court may limit the amount of the expert's fees and expenses that can be recovered from any other party. This discretion is exercised with the conduct of the parties in mind. This power is in addition to the court's discretion to restrict an expert witness's fees on a with notice basis at the time of the detailed assessment of costs under CPR Part 44, or in respect of cases allocated to the fast track, in accordance with the court's powers under CPR Part 45.

It should not be forgotten that expert evidence will not be required in every case. By considering the particular facts and circumstances of the case and by applying the court's powers to control the evidence and with due regard to the overriding objective of the Rules, the court may direct that expert evidence is not required at all or that expert evidence should not be heard on a particular issue.

A good illustration of the application of the Civil Procedure Rules' overriding objective as regards the admission of expert evidence is provided by *D* v *Walker* below.

D (A Child) *v* Walker [2000] 1 WLR 1382

W, the defendant in an action for personal injuries, had agreed with the claimant, D, that an expert's report should be jointly prepared for both parties by an occupational therapist. The manner in which the expert was instructed was not satisfactory in that the defendant's solicitors were unhappy with the letter of instruction that had been prepared by the claimant's solicitor.

On receiving the expert's report the defendant's solicitors raised concerns as to its conclusions, which detailed the extent of lifelong care that the claimant would require as a result of his injuries and for which the defendant would be liable to pay. The defendant made an application to the court seeking permission to instruct his own expert witness to assess the claimant's need for lifelong care. The application was refused and the defendant appealed to the Court of Appeal on the ground that the overriding objective of the Civil Procedure Rules was to deal with cases justly and that it was unjust in refusing his application to instruct another expert.

The Court of Appeal held, in allowing the appeal, that in a substantial case such as this the correct approach was to appoint a jointly instructed expert as the first step towards obtaining expert evidence in the case. However, if after having obtained a joint expert's report, a party, for reasons which were not fanciful, wishes to obtain further information before making a decision as to whether or not there is a particular part of the expert's report that it may wish to challenge, then it should, subject to the court's discretion, be allowed to obtain that report.

In giving the judgment of the Court of Appeal in *D v Walker*, Lord Woolf MR explained that whilst it was not possible to make generalisations, in making the decision about expert evidence, the overriding objective required the court to deal with the case justly and in a way that was proportionate to the value of the claim and the complexity of the issues. If the damages claimed were modest, to ensure proportionality, the court might refuse a party to instruct a second expert and merely permit the dissatisfied party to put further questions to the joint expert. In *D v Walker*, as a substantial amount of money depended on whether the claimant required full or part-time care, it was appropriate for further expert evidence to be heard.

The expert's overriding duty

One of the principal criticisms of the former regime was that too many experts had become partisan advocates for the party calling them and did not fulfil the essential requirement of impartial objectivity in assisting the court (*Interim Report*, page 182; *Final Report*, page 243). The requirement that the expert should be impartial is not a recent innovation. The authoritative statement on the duties of expert witnesses before the introduction of the Civil Procedure Rules is found in Cresswell J's judgment in *National Justice Compania Naviera SA v Prudential Assurance Co Ltd (The Ikarian Reefer)* [1993] 2 Lloyd's Rep 68:

1. Expert evidence presented to the Court should be, and seen to be, the independent product of the expert uninfluenced as to the form or content by the exigencies of litigation, see *Whitehouse v Jordan* [1981] 1 WLR 246, *per* Lord Wilberforce.
2. An expert witness should provide independent assistance to the court by way of an objective unbiased opinion in relation to matters within his expertise, see *Polivitte Ltd v Commercial Union Assurance Co. Plc* [1987] 1 Lloyd's Rep. 379, *per* Garland J; and *Re J* [1990] FCR 193, *per* Cazalet J. An expert witness in the High Court should never assume the role of an advocate.
3. An expert witness should state the facts or assumption on which his opinion is based. He should not omit to consider material facts which could detract from his concluded opinion (*J (A Minor) (Child Abuse: Expert Evidence), Re* [1991] FCR 193).
4. An expert witness should make it clear when a particular question or issue falls outside his expertise.
5. If an expert's opinion is not properly researched because he considers that insufficient data are available then this must be stated with an indication that the opinion is no more than a provisional one (*J (A Minor) (Child Abuse: Expert Evidence), Re* [1991] FCR 193). In cases where an expert witness has prepared a report that could not assert that the report contained the truth, the whole truth and nothing but the truth without qualification, that qualification should be stated in the report, (*Derby and Co. Ltd. v Weldon (No 9), The Times,* 9 November, *per* Staughton LJ).
6. If, after exchange of reports, an expert witness changes his view on the material having read the other side's expert's report or for any other reason, such change of view should be communicated (through legal representative) to the other side without delay and when appropriate, to the court.

7. Where expert evidence refers to photographs, plans, calculations, analyses, measurements, survey reports or other similar documents, these must be provided to the opposite party at the same time as the exchange of reports.

Many of the principles found in *National Justice Compania Naviera SA* are enshrined in the Civil Procedure Rules. Although an expert may be called at the instigation of one of the parties, the witness's overriding duty lies with the court (CPR rule 35.3(1)) and not to the instructing party or the party paying the expert's fees (CPR rule 35.3(2)). An expert, whether jointly instructed by all the parties or instructed by one of the parties, should be objective and unbiased in the way in which he prepares his report and gives his opinion for the benefit of the court. Where the judge believes that the witness is incapable of fulfilling this duty, it will be considered inappropriate for the witness to testify as an expert (*Stevens v Gullis and Pile* [2000] 1 All ER 527 and *Liverpool Roman Catholic Archdiocesan Trust v Goldberg (No 3)* (2001) 98(32) LSG 37).

The case of *Liverpool Roman Catholic Archdiocesan Trust v Goldberg* above concerned allegations of professional negligence brought by L against G, a barrister, arising from tax advice given by G. An issue arose at trial about the admissibility of an expert's reports on which G intended to rely. The report had been prepared by F, who was a friend and colleague of G. F had commented in his report that whilst he believed that his relationship with G would not affect his evidence, his personal sympathies were engaged to a greater degree than would probably be normal with an expert witness. The judge ruled that G's evidence was inadmissible. Whilst it was not expressly excluded by section 3 of the Civil Evidence Act 1972 or by case law, that a relationship could not exist between the expert and the party calling him, justice had be seen to be done, and F's admission that he would be more than usually sympathetic towards G meant that his impartiality might be called into question.

The form of expert evidence

When giving directions about expert evidence, the court will also indicate whether it is necessary for the expert to give oral evidence at trial. CPR rule 35.5(1) presumes that expert evidence will be given in a written report unless the court directs otherwise. Where the case has been allocated to the fast track, the court will not direct the expert to attend the hearing unless it is in the 'interests of justice' for him to give oral evidence. The presumption that expert evidence is to be given in writing reflects aspects of the overriding objective of the Civil Procedure Rules – saving time and expense.

The Practice Direction to Part 35 deals with the form and contents of the expert's report. In keeping with the general philosophy of expert evidence, the report should be addressed to the court and not to the instructing party. Paragraph 1.2 of the Practice Direction prescribes that the expert's report should:

1   give details of the expert's qualifications;
2   give details of the literature or other material which the expert has relied on in making the report;
3   say who carries out any test or experiment which the expert has used for the report and whether or not the test or experiment has been carried out under the reporting expert's supervision;

4   give the qualifications of the person who carried out any such test or experiment;
5   where there is a range of opinion on the matters dealt with in the report:
     (a) summarise the range of opinion, and
     (b) give reasons for the reporting expert's own opinion;
6   contain a summary of the conclusions reached;
7   contain a statement that the expert understands his duty to the court and has com-
     plied with that duty; and
8   contain a written statement setting out the substance of all material instructions
     (whether written or oral) on the basis of which the report was written. (CPR rule
     35.10(3) requires that the statement should summarise the facts and instructions
     given to the expert which are material to the opinions expressed in the report or
     upon these opinions are based.)

Finally, the expert's report should be verified by a statement of truth in which he states:

> I believe that the facts I have stated in this report are true and that the opinions I have
> expressed are correct.

Where an expert's report is submitted in a form that does not comply with the requirements of the Practice Direction, the court may debar the expert's evidence from being
tendered in the case.

Expert evidence and the 'ultimate' issue

It was a well-established principle at common law that a witness was not allowed to
express an opinion on the ultimate issue in the case. The 'ultimate' issue is the question of liability between the parties, which, according to the common law, should
always exclusively be a matter for the fact finder to decide. In civil cases, the ultimate
issue rule was abolished by section 3 of the Civil Evidence Act 1972, which provides:

> (1) Subject to any rules of court made in pursuance ... of this Act, where a person is
> called as a witness in any civil proceedings, his opinion on any relevant matter on which he
> is qualified to give expert evidence shall be admissible in evidence.
> ...
> (3) In this section 'relevant matter' includes an issue in the proceedings in question.

It is of course a matter of discretion how much weight the judge will give to the expert
witness's evidence on the ultimate issue as he is not under any obligation to accept the
expert's opinion.

Expert evidence and legal professional privilege

In general an expert's report will attract legal professional privilege and will therefore
not have to be disclosed provided the document was commissioned by the party's
solicitor and compiled by a third party (the expert) for the purpose of contemplated or
pending litigation. However, whilst this statement may succinctly explain the general
position, in practice, the position is not so clear-cut.

Letter of instruction to an expert witness

It would be reasonable to expect that a letter of instruction from a solicitor to an expert would be privileged from inspection by the other side. However, in order to promote openness and transparency in civil proceedings, the instructions form part of the expert's report and are not privileged from disclosure. To mitigate any unfairness from the operation of the rule, the court will not permit a specific document to be disclosed or for a witness to be questioned in court other than by the instructing party unless CPR rule 35.10(4) applies:

> (4) The instructions referred to in paragraph (3) [the letter of instructions to the expert] shall not be privileged against disclosure, but the court will not, in relation to those instructions—
>> (a) order disclosure of any specific document; or
>> (b) permit any questioning in court, other than by the party who instructed the expert,
> unless it is satisfied that there are reasonable grounds to consider the statement of instructions give under paragraph (3) to be inaccurate or incomplete.

Therefore, where the court considers the letter of instruction to the expert is inaccurate or incomplete, the court may allow the expert to be cross-examined on the contents of his instructions where it is in the 'interests of justice' to do so.

The expert's report

Where each party instructs its own expert, the expert's report will attract legal professional privilege provided the report falls within the definition of a privileged document, ie that it was created for the purpose of contemplated or pending litigation. The privilege will continue to apply until the commissioning party intends to rely on the expert's report at trial. In these circumstances it is likely that the court will order the report to be disclosed under the standard disclosure procedure and the privilege will be waived. The position is governed by CPR rule 35.11, which states:

> Where a party has disclosed an expert's report, any party may use that expert's report as evidence at the trial.

Where an expert's report has not been disclosed, CPR rule 35.13 states that the party will not be able to use the report at trial unless the court gives permission. In view of the overriding objective and the philosophy of the Civil Procedure Rules, it is unlikely that the court's permission will very often be given.

Where the party commissions a second report, which it does not intend to use at trial, because, for example, the first report was not favourable to the party's case, legal professional privilege may still be claimed and the first report does not have to be disclosed.

Example

C is suing D for breach of contract and misrepresentation over the costs of the purchase of an industrial boiler to heat C's business premises. C alleges that the boiler does not work properly. C's solicitor instructs E1, an expert heating engineer to give his opinion on the cause of the boiler's malfunctioning. In his report E1 attributes the boiler's malfunctioning to poor maintenance carried out by C. E1 further states that there appears to be no evidence that the boiler was poorly manu-

factured. C's solicitors also obtain a report from E2, who in her report identifies a clear link between the boiler's poor quality of manufacture and the machine's poor performance.

If C's solicitor does not use E1's report at trial because of its unfavourable conclusion to his case, the report continues to attract legal professional privilege and does not have to be disclosed. If E2's report is relied on at trial, it is likely that its disclosure will be ordered under the standard disclosure procedure and that the legal professional privilege in the report will be waived.

The operation of legal professional privilege attaching to experts' reports is shown in the case example below.

Carlson v Townsend [2001] 3 All ER 663

The claimant, C, brought a personal injury claim in respect of a back injury he suffered while employed by the defendant. C's solicitors informed the defendant's insurers that they intended to instruct one of three consultant orthopaedic surgeons, T, R and O'D, to prepare a report. This information was given in accordance with paragraph 3.14 of the Pre-Action Protocol for Personal Injury Claims, which provided that before any party instructed an expert, it should give to the other party a list of names of one or more experts with expertise in the field. Under the protocol, the other side can object to the nominated experts and the first party should then instruct a mutually acceptable expert. The defendant's insurers objected only to O'D, and in the event T was instructed and he duly reported to the claimant's solicitors.

On the day before T's report was to be received, the defendant's insurers had written to the claimant's solicitors saying that they assumed that the instructions to the medical expert had been on a joint basis between the parties. C's solicitors immediately challenged this contention and subsequently refused to disclose T's report. Instead they sent a medical report by S, who was not one of the original list of nominated experts.

The defendant applied to the court for an order requiring that T's report should be disclosed. At the first hearing the district judge ordered the disclosure of T's report. C appealed against this decision, and the appeal was upheld on the basis that since T had been solely instructed by C there had been no implied or express waiver of legal professional privilege in the report. The defendant appealed against the decision.

In dismissing the appeal, the Court of Appeal held that the defendant's failure not to object specifically to T as an expert witness did not transform T into a single nominated witness and therefore there was no waiver by the claimant of the legal professional privilege that attached to T's report. Whilst the Pre-action Personal Injury Protocol encouraged voluntary disclosure of experts' reports, it was not a mandatory requirement and the court would not override the claimant's privilege in T's report.

The expert's report and the hearsay rule

As a matter of public policy, the rules relating to the admission of hearsay evidence are relaxed in connection with an expert's report. An expert does not need to have personal knowledge of all the relevant matters within his field of expertise and may, in preparing his report and testifying in court, refer to any relevant books, articles and research data. A strict interpretation of the hearsay rule would preclude these materials from being adduced as part of the expert's evidence, which, in practical terms, would make it impossible for the expert to assist the court. See *H* v *Schering Chemicals Ltd* [1983] 1 WLR 143, where in an action for damages against a drugs company, it was held that the expert could refer to reputable research sources from within his sphere of expertise on which he based his opinion evidence.

Further reading

Baskind, E., 'The Expert Witness in England and Wales: The End of the "Hired" Gun? An English Perspective' (2001) International Review of Law, Computer and Technology 229.

Fetto, N., 'Keeping the Woolf Away from your Expert' (2001) 151 NLJ 766.

Whitfield, A., 'Status of the Expert in Giving Evidence and Preparing a Report for the Court' (2001) Clinical Risk 60.

Woolf MR, Lord (1995) *Access to Justice, Interim Report*, Lord Chancellor's Department.

Woolf MR, Lord (1996) *Access to Justice, Final Report*, HMSO.

Chapter 31

EVIDENCE OF A PARTY'S CHARACTER AND CONVICTIONS

INTRODUCTION

The general rule in both civil and criminal proceedings is that evidence of the claimant or the defendant's character including his criminal convictions is not, as a matter of law, permitted to be put before the court. The reason for this general rule is that the court may be unduly prejudiced by hearing evidence of past conduct that may not be relevant to the issues in the present case. So, for example, in *Narracott v Narracott and Hesketh* (1864) 3 SW & Tr 408, a husband was not permitted to adduce evidence of his general humanity to disprove his wife's allegation of cruelty as it was held not to be relevant to an issue before the court.

Whilst, in criminal proceedings the disclosure of evidence of the accused's character is closely controlled to ensure that the defendant receives a fair trial, the position in a civil case is rather different for a number of reasons. First, the social stigma attached to a criminal conviction is much greater than where a party loses a civil case. Also, a major reason for many of the exclusionary rules of criminal evidence is to redress the imbalance in resources between the State as a prosecutor and a private individual as the defendant. In civil proceedings there is a much greater 'equality of arms' between the parties, which is reflected in CPR rule 1.1.(2)(a), which requires the courts to ensure, that as far as possible, the parties are on an equal footing. Also, as noted previously in respect of a number of other rules of civil evidence, the absence of lay people in the decision-making process in civil cases more readily allows the admission of relevant but potentially prejudicial evidence such as character evidence as the judge trying the case will not be unduly prejudiced by hearing evidence of the party's character and give appropriate weight to that evidence.

The purpose of this chapter is to consider the operation of the rules that allow evidence of a party's character and convictions to be heard by the court in civil proceedings both at common law and under statute. The statutory exceptions to the rules are found at sections 11–13 of the Civil Evidence Act 1968. The exceptions are often referred to as 'judgments as evidence of the facts upon which they were based', but as sections 11–13 regulate the admission of aspects of a party's character in civil proceedings, this is an appropriate place to consider them. We begin, however, by considering the meaning of 'character' in civil cases. (Note that the law relating to the admission of the character evidence of witnesses other than the parties as a collateral issue is considered in Chapter 26.)

THE MEANING OF 'CHARACTER'

It is often assumed that evidence of character relates only to past convictions and other aspects of 'bad' character. In practice, this meaning is not entirely accurate, as the word 'character' in civil proceedings has three distinct strands. These are:

1   a person's general reputation in the community;
2   a person's propensity to act in a certain way; and
3   previous specific acts that usually refers to previous convictions.

The admissibility of character evidence in civil proceedings is determined by whether the evidence is relevant to a fact in issue in the case or whether it is relevant in assessing the credibility of the claimant or the defendant. The evidential effect of each provision is considered below.

Good character

We have seen that it is always possible for the defence to put forward evidence of the accused's good character in criminal proceedings (Chapter 21). Where the accused is of good character he will be entitled to a *Vye* direction (see *R v Vye*; *R v Wise*; *R v Stephenson* [1993] 3 All ER 241). It is unclear to what extent evidence of good character and disposition is admissible in civil proceedings. Whilst there appears to be no specific authority on the point, the admission of evidence of a party's good character would be based on the common principle of the relevance of the evidence to a fact in issue or to an associated collateral issue. A case in which the relevance of good character was an issue was *Cornwell v Myskow* [1987] 2 All ER 504. The plaintiff, who was an actress, complained of a defamatory newspaper article written by the defendant. At the trial, evidence was admitted of reviews of plays that the actress had appeared in long after publication of the alleged defamatory article and oral evidence was heard to the same effect. The jury found for the plaintiff but the defendant appealed. In allowing the appeal, the Court of Appeal held that although evidence as to reputation at the time of publication and reviews published fairly shortly afterwards were admissible, evidence of reputation at the time of the trial was not. In effect therefore, it was open to the plaintiff to put forward evidence of her good character at the time the defamatory statement was published – but not at the time of the trial as this is not strictly relevant to a fact in issue.

A party's character as a fact in issue

Evidence of a party's character may be put before the court where it is relevant to proving a fact in issue in those proceedings. An obvious example is an action for defamation where evidence of the party's character may be relevant to establishing both liability and assessing the award of damages. In respect to liability, if the defamatory statement suggested that the claimant was dishonest and the defendant pleaded justification, ie that the statement was true, then evidence of the claimant's conviction for theft would be relevant to the issue of character. In respect to the assessment of damages, if the claimant proves that the defendant has defamed him, ie he has published an untrue statement that has damaged his reputation, in order to assess the amount of damages, evidence of the claimant's general reputation is relevant. In *Scott v Sampson* (1881–2) LR 8 QBD 491, an action for defamation in which justification was pleaded, it was held that to enable the jury to assess the amount of damages recoverable for loss of reputation, evidence of the plaintiff's general reputation was relevant and admissible.

An action for defamation is the most obvious example where evidence of a party's character is relevant to a fact in issue in civil proceedings. The same principle would apply however, in an action for personal injuries arising out of a road traffic accident. Evidence that the defendant was convicted of driving without due care and attention in criminal proceedings arising out the same matter would be admissible for the claimant to plead under section 11 of the Civil Evidence Act 1968. Where section 11 applies, it gives rise to a presumption of negligence against the defendant in the civil proceedings, which may only be rebutted on proof of certain facts. See below for an explanation of section 11.

SIMILAR FACT EVIDENCE IN CIVIL PROCEEDINGS

Exceptionally in criminal proceedings, evidence of the accused's specific acts and propensity to behave in a certain way may be admissible to show his guilt for the offence with which he is presently charged. This evidence would be heard by the court under the similar fact evidence rule. In deciding whether to admit evidence under the rule, the judge in a criminal case must carefully balance the probative value of the similar fact evidence against its great prejudicial effect to the accused (*DPP v P* [1991] 2 AC 447).

In a civil case, similar fact evidence or the evidence of the defendant's propensity to act in a specific way may also be admissible where it is relevant to proving a fact in issue in the case. The essential element in determining the admissibility of similar fact evidence in civil proceedings is not so much on the basis of the prejudicial effect as against probative value, but the relevance of the similar fact evidence to the facts in issue. For this reason, in civil cases, similar fact evidence is more readily admitted than in criminal cases. Consider the following examples of the application of similar fact evidence in civil proceedings.

Hales *v* Kerr [1908] 2 KB 601

In an action in negligence in which the plaintiff alleged that he had contracted ringworm from a dirty razor used by the defendant hairdresser, evidence was admitted that two other of the defendant's customers had contracted ringworm.

Joy *v* Phillips Mills & Co Ltd [1916] 1 KB 849

This was a claim for workman's compensation by the father of a stable boy who had been kicked to death by a horse. The boy had been found near the horse, holding a halter. Evidence was admitted that the boy had previously teased the horse with a halter in order to rebut the plaintiff's allegation that the accident had occurred in the course of the boy's employment.

Sattin *v* National Union Bank (1978) 122 SJ 367

The plaintiff sued the defendant bank in respect of the loss of a diamond deposited with the bank as security for an overdraft. The defence of the bank was that it had used reasonable safeguards in securing the property deposited at the bank by its customers. The Court of Appeal held that the claimant was entitled to adduce evidence of another occasion when jewellery deposited with the bank had gone missing, because it was relevant to rebut the defence put forward.

A useful guide to the grounds for admitting similar fact evidence in civil proceedings was provided by Lord Denning in *Mood Music Publishing Co Ltd v De Wolfe Ltd* [1976] Ch 119 where he stated:

> In civil cases the courts will admit evidence of similar facts if it is logically probative, that is, if it is logically relevant in determining the matter which is in issue: provided that it is not oppressive or unfair to the other side; and also that the other side has fair notice and is able to deal with it.

Designers Guild Ltd v Russell Williams (Textiles) Ltd (t/a Washington DC) [1998] FSR 275 is also worth noting in this context. It was a case involving alleged infringements of the copyright relating to fashion designs. The claimant design company sought the leave of the court to cross-examine the defendant about the fact that the defendant had previously given an undertaking and paid a small sum to a designer, O, in respect of another of the defendant's designs, which O had alleged were an infringement of O's copyright. In his submission to the court the claimant argued that such cross-examination was admissible as similar fact evidence.

In allowing the defendant to be cross-examined in respect of the allegations of breach of copyright of O's designs by the defendant, the court held that as a general rule, in admitting similar fact evidence, it would be guided by the following factors:

- the relevance of the evidence to the facts in issue;
- whether any of the similarities between the defendant's past behaviour and his behaviour in the present case could be explained as a coincidence;
- whether the matters raised in cross-examination were logically probative, ie were they relevant to proving a fact in issue;
- whether the questions asked in cross-examination were oppressive or unfair; and
- whether the other party has had fair notice of the questions that were to be put to him.

On the facts, the allegation that the defendant was in the habit of infringing copyright was capable of being relevant in deciding whether the similarities were coincidental or not.

EVIDENCE OF THE PARTY'S CHARACTER RELEVANT TO CREDIT

In civil proceedings, any witness who gives evidence, including the claimant and defendant, is liable to be cross-examined as to his credibility as a witness. This is known as a collateral issue. Where the witness's character is a collateral issue, ie it is not probative of a fact in issue before the court, the general rule in respect to collateral issues is that evidence is not allowed to be introduced which contradicts the witness's answer – the 'finality' rule. An important exception to the finality rule is provided by section 6 of the Criminal Procedure Act 1865:

> A witness may be questioned as to whether he has been convicted of any felony or misdemeanour, and upon being so questioned, if he either denies or does not admit the fact, or refuses to answer, it shall be lawful for the cross-examining party to prove such conviction.

The effect of section 6 is that where in cross-examination the claimant or the defendant is asked whether he has any convictions, and denies the convictions, evidence proving the fact of the conviction(s) may be put before the court that contradicts the answer of the claimant or defendant.

Whilst section 6 permits the cross-examiner to adduce evidence that rebuts the party's assertion of good character, it is a matter of judicial discretion how far the advocate is allowed to go in cross-examination to undermine the witness's credibility in the eyes of the court. The section is clearly subject to the common law discretion to restrain unnecessary or unduly oppressive questions. It should also be remembered that the purpose of the questions is to undermine the party's credibility as a witness and that evidence may be excluded where its prejudicial value is weighed against its probative effect. For guidance on the proper approach when asking questions in cross-examination as to credit, see *Hobbs* v *Tinling* [1929] 2 KB 1, *per* Lord Justice Sankey.

The operation of section 6 as an exception to the finality rule with respect to a witness other than the claimant or the defendant was considered in Chapter 28.

ADMISSIBILITY OF A PARTY'S PREVIOUS CONVICTIONS (CIVIL EVIDENCE ACT 1968, SECTION 11)

Before the implementation of the Civil Evidence Act 1968 it was not possible in a civil trial to put before the court the verdict in a criminal case or the judgment in another civil case as evidence of the facts on which the court's decision was based. The rule was commonly known as 'the rule in *Hollington* v *Hewthorn*'. In *Hollington* v *F Hewthorn & Co Ltd* [1943] KB 587 the plaintiff, Hollington, brought an action against an employee of the defendant company and against the company itself, alleging that the employee's negligent driving had caused his injuries. The plaintiff was refused leave to adduce in evidence of the fact that, arising from the same incident, the defendant employee had been convicted in criminal proceedings of driving without due care and attention. Three grounds were given by the Court of Appeal for its refusal to admit the evidence. First, the opinion of the magistrates who convicted the driver was irrelevant in the civil trial. Secondly, the findings of fact by the magistrates especially following a guilty plea would be qualitatively different from the findings of fact employed by the judges in the High Court and, thirdly, it would be extremely difficult, or impossible, to identify the facts upon which the conviction was founded as neither magistrates nor juries were required to give any reasons for their decisions.

However logical the reservations expressed by the Court of Appeal in *Hollington* v *Hewthorn*, the decision meant that in many civil cases a lot of time was wasted in civil proceedings in proving a relevant fact in issue to the lesser standard of 'on the balance of probabilities' that had already been proven 'beyond reasonable doubt' in a criminal trial. In response to this unsatisfactory position, the decision in *Hollington* v *Hewthorn* was reversed by Parliament in passing section 11 of the Civil Evidence Act 1968, which provides:

> (1) In any civil proceedings the fact that a person has been convicted of an offence by or before any court in the United Kingdom or by a court-martial shall (subject to subsection (3) below) be admissible in evidence for the purpose of proving, where to do so is relevant to any issue in those proceedings, that he committed that offence, whether he was so

convicted upon a plea of guilty or otherwise and whether or not he is a party or not to the civil proceedings; but no conviction other than a subsisting one shall be admissible in evidence by virtue of this section.

(2) In any civil proceedings in which by virtue of this section a person is proved to have been convicted of an offence by or before any court in the United Kingdom or by a court-martial there or elsewhere—

    (a) he shall be taken to have committed that offence unless the contrary is proved; and

    (b) without prejudice to the reception of any other admissible evidence for the purpose of identifying the facts on which the conviction was based, the contents of any document which is admissible as evidence of the conviction, and the contents of the information, complaint, indictment or charge-sheet on which the person in question was convicted, shall be admissible in evidence for that purpose.

(3) Nothing in this section shall prejudice the operation of section 13 of this Act or any other enactment whereby a conviction or any other finding of fact in any criminal proceedings is for the purpose of any other proceedings made conclusive evidence of that fact.

(4) Where in any civil proceedings the contents of any document are admissible in evidence by virtue of subsection (2) above, a copy of that document, or of the material part thereof, purporting to be certified or otherwise authenticated by or on behalf of the court or authority having custody of that document shall be admissible in evidence and shall be taken to be a true copy of that document or part unless the contrary is shown.

Section 18 of the 1968 Act has the effect that 'civil proceedings' include:

... in addition to civil proceedings in any of the ordinary courts of law—

    (a) civil proceedings before any other tribunal, being proceedings in relation to which the strict rules of evidence apply; and

    (b) an arbitration or reference, whether under an enactment or not, but does not include civil proceedings in which the strict rules of evidence do not apply.

Whilst section 11(1) refers to a 'subsisting' conviction, where the conviction is subject to an appeal, the civil proceedings will most likely be adjourned, until the appeal has been heard as in *Re Raphael, Raphael v D'Antin* [1973] 1 WLR 998, but section 11 has no application to a conviction that has been quashed or to a conviction in a foreign court.

The effect of section 11

The effect of section 11 is to make admissible a subsisting conviction from a United Kingdom criminal court or court-martial where that conviction is 'relevant' to an issue in the civil proceedings. Whilst in most cases evidence of a conviction usually relates to one of the parties (more often than not, the defendant) provided the conviction is 'relevant' to the proceedings, it will be admissible where it has been made against any person who is associated with the civil case.

There has been some conflicting judicial opinion about the precise probative effect of the application of section 11. One approach suggests that the section merely creates a statutory presumption that the defendant committed the criminal offence and the words in section 11(2)(a) 'unless the contrary is proved' places a legal burden on the defendant to rebut the presumption. A second approach suggests that the section not only shifts the legal burden to the defendant but has considerable weight in proving the claimant's allegations against the defendant. Each approach was adopted by a different judge in the

Court of Appeal in *Stupple* v *Royal Insurance Co Ltd* [1971] 1 QB 50. Stupple, who had been convicted of a robbery from a bank which had been indemnified by the defendant company, brought a claim for the recovery of money that had been discovered by the police as proceeds of the robbery under the Police (Property) Act 1897. In dismissing the plaintiff's appeal, the Court of Appeal stated that Stupple's conviction, and the fact that it was upheld on appeal, was in effect conclusive evidence, but the Court of Appeal could not agree on the question of its weight in the civil proceedings. Lord Denning considered that the evidence of the conviction did more than just shift the burden of proof onto Stupple, and was 'a weighty piece of evidence in itself'. But Lord Justice Buckley stated that proof of a conviction under section 11 raises a legal, or persuasive, presumption:

> ... which, like any other presumption, will give way to evidence establishing the contrary on a balance of probability, without itself affording any evidential weight to be taken into account in determining whether that onus has been discharged.

The correct approach is probably to suggest that the weight of the conviction depends on the circumstances in which it was obtained. A conviction following a contested jury trial is likely to have more weight in any civil proceedings than where the defendant pleaded guilty in the magistrates' court.

Rebutting the conviction

Section 11(2)(a) of the Civil Evidence Act 1968 states that the person is taken to have committed the offence 'unless the contrary is proved'. A key question is how does the defendant discharge the legal burden in rebutting the presumption? This may be done in a number of ways. The defendant can:

- deny the conviction by submitting that he was not the person convicted;
- allege that the conviction was erroneous by submitting that he mistakenly pleaded guilty to the charge when he had in fact a good defence to it, or was otherwise wrongly convicted; or
- deny that the conviction is relevant to any fact in issue in the civil proceedings, for example, that his conviction for a strict liability offence is not relevant to the other party's allegation of negligence.

To succeed in rebutting the presumption created by section 11, the party must satisfy the court to the ordinary civil standard of on the balance of probabilities (*Wauchope* v *Mordecai* [1970] 1 WLR 317). However, whilst Parliament clearly intended that section 11 should not establish absolute liability by identifying the grounds by which the presumption can be rebutted, the House of Lords in *Hunter* v *Chief Constable of the Lancashire Police Force*, sub nom *McIlkenny* v *Chief Constable of the West Midlands* [1980] 2 All ER 227, suggested that the defendant would have an uphill task to prove that the conviction was wrong considering that it had convicted him after finding him guilty beyond reasonable doubt.

Example

Barsetshire County Council, as the statutory highway authority, sues Joanne in negligence for the costs of repairs to its traffic lights arising out of a road traffic accident during which the defendant's car left the carriageway and collided with the claimant's property. Arising out of the incident, Joanne is convicted on 3 December 2001 of careless driving by Barchester Magistrates' Court.

In the civil action, the claimant will plead the fact of Joanne's conviction, the effect of which is to reverse the legal burden of proof. The claimant will no longer have to prove that Joanne drove negligently under the normal 'he who asserts must prove' principle. The criminal conviction for careless driving is 'relevant' in the civil proceedings as it is based on the same facts and is relevant to proving a fact in issue in the civil case – the defendant was driving her car in a negligent way at the time of the accident.

Where Joanne has been convicted of careless driving, to rebut the presumption of negligence created by the claimant pleading the conviction, Joanne has the legal burden of proving that either her conviction is not relevant to the proceedings or that on the balance of probabilities her conviction was wrong, ie that she did not drive carelessly at the time of the accident or that the conviction is not relevant to a fact in the civil case.

The probative effect of section 11 is most clearly illustrated where the criminal offence and the civil action are based on the same facts, or very similar facts. In some situations however, where the facts of the criminal case of which the defendant was convicted are not precisely the same as the facts in the civil action, a conviction pleaded under section 11 has little probative value.

Example

Barchester County Council, as the statutory highway authority, sues Joanne in negligence for the costs of repairs to its traffic lights arising out of a road traffic accident during which the defendant's car left the carriageway and collided with the claimant's property. Arising out of the incident Joanne has been found guilty of driving with defective brakes, which is a criminal offence of strict liability.

As the concept of strict liability will not be recognised in the civil action, the conviction has little probative fact as the conviction and the civil action are based on different facts.

To succeed at the civil trial in negligence, Barchester County Council has to prove that Joanne owed them a duty of care, that Joanne breached the duty and as a result of the breach, the claimant suffered damage to its traffic lights.

The procedural safeguards

Where a party intends to rely at trial on a conviction under section 11 of the 1968 Act, the party's solicitor will obtain a certificate of conviction from the criminal court that convicted the defendant. The Practice Direction to Part 16, 'Statements of Case', requires that the conviction should be referred to in the party's particulars of claim and should also include the following details:

- the type of conviction, finding or adjudication and its date;
- the court or court-martial which made the conviction, finding or adjudication; and
- the issue in the claim to which it relates.

The claimant must then specifically set out those matters in his particulars of claim where he wishes to rely on them in support of his claim including:

- any allegation of fraud;
- the fact of any illegality;

- details of any misrepresentation;
- any facts relating to mitigation of loss or damage.

Therefore in compliance with requirements of the Practice Direction, in its statement of case, Barchester County Council will plead Joanne's conviction in the following way:

> The claimant intends to rely on evidence of the defendant's conviction for careless driving contrary to section 3 of the Road Traffic Act 1988 on 3 December 2001 at Barchester Magistrates' Court. This conviction relates to the issue of the defendant's negligence.

When the defendant receives a statement of case that relies on a conviction, under the normal rules of pleading, where the defence denies all or some of the allegations contained in the claimant's statement of case, the defendant should deal with these issues in its defence. As we noted in the example above, this will require the defendant to plead that the conviction is not relevant to the proceedings or that on the balance of probabilities the conviction was wrong or that the conviction is not relevant to the facts in the civil case.

FINDINGS OF ADULTERY AND PATERNITY (CIVIL EVIDENCE ACT 1968, SECTION 12)

Section 12 of the Civil Evidence Act 1968 reverses the decision in *Hollington* v *Hewthorn* above as far as the common law applied to the findings of a court in respect of adultery and paternity. The effect of section 12 is to create two persuasive presumptions that the person found guilty of adultery shall be taken to have committed adultery and that the person found by a court to have been the father of a child shall be taken to be or has been the child's father.

Section 12 provides:

(1) In any civil proceedings—
  (a) the fact that a person has been found guilty of adultery in any matrimonial proceedings; and
  (b) the fact that a person has been found to be the father of a child in relevant proceedings before any court in England and Wales or adjudged to be the father of a child in affiliation proceedings before any court in the United Kingdom,

shall (subject to subsection 3 below) be admissible in evidence for the purpose of proving, where to do so is relevant to any issue in those civil proceedings, that he committed the adultery to which the finding relates or, as the case may be, is (or was) the father of that child, whether he not he offered any defence to the allegation of adultery or paternity and whether or not he is a party to the civil proceedings; but no finding or adjudication other than a subsisting one shall be admissible in evidence by virtue of this section.

(2) In any civil proceedings in which by virtue of this section a person is proved to have been found guilty of adultery as mentioned in subsection (1)(a) above or to have been found or adjudged to be the father of a child as mentioned in subsection (1)(b) above—
  (a) he shall be taken to have committed the adultery to which the finding relates or, as the case may be, to be (or have been) the father of the child unless the contrary is proved; and

(b) without prejudice to the reception of any other admissible evidence for the purpose of identifying the facts on which the finding or the adjudication was based,
the contents of any document which was before the court, or which contains any
pronouncement of the court, in the other proceedings in question shall be admissible in evidence for that purpose.

(3) Nothing in this section shall prejudice the operation of any enactment whereby a
finding of fact in any matrimonial or affiliation proceedings is for the purposes of any other
proceedings made conclusive evidence of any fact.

In practice, section 12 has a similar legal effect to section 11, by stipulating that a finding of adultery in matrimonial proceedings or a finding that a person is the father of a
child in relevant proceedings shall be admissible in evidence in any subsequent civil
proceedings where it is required to prove adultery or the paternity of a child. It further
provides that, in any later civil proceedings, that person shall be taken to have committed that adultery, or be the father of that child, unless the contrary is proved.
Section 12(2) creates a statutory persuasive presumption that the court's finding is
correct unless the contrary is shown. The Practice Direction to Part 16 (Amendments
to Statements of Case) also requires that where the court has made a finding under
section 12, it should be pleaded.

In *Sutton* v *Sutton* [1970] 1 WLR 183, Mrs Sutton's divorce petition alleged adultery
between H, her husband, and a Mrs G from February 1963 onwards and relied on section 12 of the Civil Evidence Act 1968 with respect to a finding by a judge in the divorce
suit between Mr and Mrs G that adultery was proved between H and Mrs G in the
period from October 1963 to February 1964. Both H and Mrs G denied the allegations
of adultery. The Court of Appeal held that the effect of section 12 was to reverse the
incidence of the legal burden of proof, and therefore required the party seeking to disprove the adultery as found under section 12 to the civil standard, ie on the balance of
probabilities. On the facts, the legal burden rested with H and Mrs G to disprove on
the balance of probabilities the adultery found in the previous divorce proceedings but
that on any other allegation of adultery, the legal and evidential burdens of proof lay
with Mrs Sutton as there had not been a finding of the court on these issues.

Finally, unlike section 11, there is no problem as to the weight to be attached to the earlier decision of the court, as the earlier case and the current proceedings are both civil cases.

DEFAMATION PROCEEDINGS AND CONVICTIONS (CIVIL EVIDENCE ACT 1968, SECTION 13)

Section 13 of the Civil Evidence Act 1968 reverses the decision in *Hollington* v
Hewthorn above as applied to defamation proceedings by providing that:

(1) In an action for libel or slander in which the question whether the plaintiff did or did
not commit a criminal offence is relevant to an issue arising in the action, proof that at the
time when the issue falls to be determined, he stands convicted of that offence shall be
conclusive evidence that he committed that offence; and his conviction thereof shall be
admissible accordingly.

Section 13 creates a persuasive presumption that the person convicted shall conclu-
sively be taken to have committed the offence in question. Therefore a defamation

action based on the defendant's allegation that the claimant committed the offence in respect of which he has been convicted will be struck out as an abuse of the process of the court unless the statement contains some other defamatory material. In *Levene* v *Roxhan* [1970] 1 WLR 1322, L was convicted of five offences and on 9 July 1963, of three others. On 23 July 1963, a newspaper article was published which referred to the convictions and to other matters, some of which were connected and others were independent. On 10 June 1969, L issued a writ for libel against the author, the editor and the publisher, alleging that parts of the article were defamatory of him. The defendants applied to strike out the statement of claim as an abuse of the court process, relying on section 13 of the 1968 Act. The application was refused and the defendants appealed to the Court of Appeal. In dismissing the appeal, the Court of Appeal held that if the article had only referred to the previous convictions, it would have been proper to strike out the statement of claim, but that since there were other allegations which were not covered by section 13, the judge was correct not to have struck the proceedings out.

The operation of section 13 differs greatly from section 11 in that the conviction is conclusive evidence of the commission of that offence. The section employs almost a strict liability approach to prevent the convicted party from re-opening the issue of his conviction(s) at the civil trial. Section 12 of the Defamation Act 1996 amended section 13 of the 1968 Act and limits the admission of a conviction to that of the claimant.

Further reading

Case Comment, *Al Hawaz v Thomas Cook Group Ltd* (unreported, October 2000) (2000) 144(47) Solicitors Journal 1150.

Glanville, S., 'Litigation and Evidence: The Rule in *Hollington v Hewthorn & Co Ltd*' (1996) 14(11) ILT 263.

Manchester, C., 'The Admissibility of "Spent" Convictions in Civil Cases' (1997) 1(3) E & P 152.

INDEX